The Politics of the Presidency

REVISED 9th EDITION

To Mary, Anna, and Christine

The Politics of the Presidency

Revised 9th Edition

Joseph A. Pika, *University of Delaware (Emeritus)*

John Anthony Maltese, *University of Georgia*

Andrew Rudalevige, *Bowdoin College*

FOR INFORMATION:

CQ Press
An Imprint of SAGE Publications, Inc.
2455 Teller Road
Thousand Oaks, California 91320
E-mail: order@sagepub.com

SAGE Publications Ltd.
1 Oliver's Yard
55 City Road
London, EC1Y 1SP
United Kingdom

SAGE Publications India Pvt. Ltd.
B 1/I 1 Mohan Cooperative Industrial Area
Mathura Road, New Delhi 110 044
India

SAGE Publications Asia-Pacific Pte. Ltd.
3 Church Street
#10-04 Samsung Hub
Singapore 049483

Executive Publisher: Monica Eckman
Editorial Assistant: Zachary Hoskins
Copy Editors: Amy Marks, Lynn Weber
Typesetter: Hurix Systems Pvt. Ltd.
Proofreaders: Lawrence Baker, Caryne Brown, Rae-Ann Goodwin, Alison Syring
Cover Designer: Candice Harman
Marketing Manager: Amy Whitaker

Printed in the United States of America

Library of Congress Cataloging-in-Publication Data

Names: Pika, Joseph August, 1947– author. | Maltese, John Anthony, author. | Rudalevige, Andrew, 1968– author.

Title: The politics of the presidency / Joseph A. Pika, University of Delaware, John Anthony Maltese, University of Georgia, Andrew C. Rudalevige, Bowdoin College.

Description: Revised Ninth Edition. | Washington, DC : CQ Press, an Imprint of SAGE Publications, Inc., [2018] | Includes bibliographical references and index.

Identifiers: LCCN 2017027445 | ISBN 9781506367798 (Paperback : acid-free paper)

Subjects: LCSH: Presidents—United States—Textbooks.

Classification: LCC JK516 .P53 2018 | DDC 352.230973—dc23 LC record available at https://lccn.loc.gov/2017027445

This book is printed on acid-free paper.

17 18 19 20 21 10 9 8 7 6 5 4 3 2

Contents

III. THE PRESIDENT AND PUBLIC POLICY

Tables and Figures

TABLES

FIGURES

Preface

Few presidents have entered office in such tumultuous times as Barack Obama in 2009 and Donald Trump in 2017. Supporters of each had unrealistically high expectations of what the new president could achieve, and each had a hard core of opponents who could not be convinced that either was a legitimate president. As the nation's first president of color, Obama broke a barrier that had stood for more than two centuries and confronted a remarkably challenging list of public problems. At the top of the list was the worst economic recession in more than half a century, followed in quick succession by two wars, a dysfunctional health care system, a rapidly warming planet, widespread public distrust of politics, and a Washington riven by partisan discord. Trump, the first president with no prior government experience, surprised the nation by first winning the Republican nomination and then vanquishing Hillary Clinton. He promised to upend the Obama legacy and return the nation to its past greatness, but faced a bitterly polarized country. Would Trump meet with greater success than Obama had?

After more than two centuries of change and development, the presidency stands not only as the nation's preeminent public office but also as its most problematic. Because presidents today are far more important for peace and prosperity than were their nineteenth-century counterparts, ensuring the selection of qualified candidates and enhancing the winner's effectiveness in office are major concerns of specialists and citizens alike. In the post–World War II period, however, few presidents have left office with a record of unqualified success. In fact, academic and media observers have labeled most presidents since Lyndon B. Johnson as "failures," although reputations sometimes improve with the passage of time.

Johnson enjoyed unparalleled success in getting his Great Society legislative program through Congress, but he could not extricate himself or the country from the Vietnam War. Richard Nixon managed to end the war and initiate new relationships with the Soviet Union and China, but Watergate cost him the confidence of the country. Gerald R. Ford and Jimmy Carter failed to convince voters that they could exercise effective leadership. Like Johnson, Ronald Reagan persuaded Congress to approve his program of economic reforms, but the budgetary consequences of those policies and his mishandling of the Iran-contra affair tarnished his reputation—a reputation that is improving as time goes by. George H. W. Bush and Bill Clinton were threatened by the same difficulties that beset Ford and Carter—a perception of inconsistency and even ineffectiveness. Clinton also is viewed as possessing a severely flawed character, committing errors in his personal life that prompted an unsuccessful effort to remove him from office. During his two terms, George W. Bush's public approval ratings went from the highest ever recorded to among the lowest, dragged down by the war in Iraq, the Hurricane Katrina disaster, and a meltdown of the nation's financial system that dominated his last months in office. Lost along the way was Bush's ambitious second-term agenda, which included Social Security reform, immigration reform, and rewriting the tax code, as well as his party's control of Congress. The election of 2012 told us the public regarded Obama's performance as good enough to warrant four more years in office. Although he wound down U.S. involvement in Iraq and Afghanistan, new terrorist threats in the Middle East and a much-criticized agreement with Iran placed Obama's legacy into question; Republicans pledged to repeal and replace his signature accomplishment—health care reform; and while the U.S. economy had pulled out of recession, the initial pace of growth was slow and the recovery naggingly uneven.

Given the inflated expectations of performance held by the public and political elites, it is reasonable to wonder if any modern president can be considered a success. It should be noted, however, that most failed chief executives contributed to the public's negative perception through their actions.

Our focus in *The Politics of the Presidency* is on how presidents govern—the country and in Washington. The book views the presidency as essentially a political office—that is, the chief executive must govern more through skilled political leadership than through the assertion of constitutional prerogatives, though the latter are gaining in significance as politics in Washington become more intractable. We examine how effectiveness in office varies with the character, personality, and political style of the incumbent while recognizing that there are important continuities from one administration to the next. Major developments in society, the U.S. political system, and the international arena also affect how well or how poorly a president performs in office. By examining this full range of influences, *The Politics of the Presidency* provides a comprehensive treatment of the nation's most important political office.

We begin Part I with an analysis of the origins and development of the presidency and an examination of the changing conceptions of the office. We then explore the president's relations with the public in electoral politics and in the process of governing. Next, we look at the kinds of people who have become president and how they interact with the office itself. In Part II, we analyze the president's relations with other government elites—members of Congress, the bureaucracy, and the judiciary. In Part III, we focus on how presidents formulate and implement domestic, economic, and national security policies. We conclude with a look at the challenges and opportunities a new president will confront.

In the past, post-election editions of this text have summarized the early days of a new administration in a new concluding chapter. But given the frenetic pace and important impact of the Trump administration, we have revised the present edition more extensively than any in the past. The final chapter still addresses the transition, inauguration, and "first 100 days" of the new presidency. But every chapter has been updated to incorporate the changes introduced or represented by President Trump. This should significantly extend the life of this edition in ways that meet the needs of students as well as instructors. We include discussions of the 2016 presidential election and the initial months of the Trump administration's relations with Congress and the judiciary, as well as the efforts to build a new administrative team. Chapters now provide coverage of the Republicans' continued wrestling with Obama's policy legacy and their struggles to work as a governing party, the most recent Supreme Court appointments made by both Obama and Trump, and the continued response to the economic recession that began in 2007. From the second Electoral College misfire in twenty years, to the terrorist attacks of 9/11 and the ensuing wars in Afghanistan and Iraq (not to mention the rise of ISIS), the increasingly polarized nature of politics, and Trump's electrifying victory, we cover the twists and turns of the past decade while incorporating findings from a wide range of scholarship. At the same time, we have sought to retain a strong appreciation for historical development, starting with an exploration of the constitutional foundations of the presidency. We conclude with a review of Obama and Trump's performance amidst continued partisan conflict and an estimate of how the new administration is likely to fare.

We continue to thank Philip Mundo and Thomas Langston as well as the reviewers—Dana Harsell, University of North Dakota; Samuel Hoff, Delaware State University; Michael Julius, University of Minnesota, Twin Cities; Laura Olson, LeHigh University; Matthew Schousen, Franklin & Marshall College; Andrew Sidman, John Jay College of Criminal Justice; Michael Siegel, Federal Judicial Center; Barry Tadlock, Ohio University; Raymond Tatalovich, Loyola University Chicago; and B. Dan Wood, Texas A&M—for their helpful comments on the ninth edition. Their reflections helped our thinking, even if we did not always follow their advice.

We are grateful to Charisse Kiino, Nancy Matuszak, and Zachary Hoskins of CQ Press for their encouragement and contributions to this edition, and to Amy Marks for her thorough and judicious copy editing. We also appreciate the research assistance provided over the years by Amanda Rosenburg, Brian Beedenbender, Elizabeth Coggins, Josh Templet, Julia Kohen, Mark Cutrona, Mitchell Freddura, and Rebecca Riley as well as the clipping services contributed by Frank Langr. We are thrilled to welcome Andrew Rudalevige to the author team for the 9th edition. John Maltese accepts primary responsibility for chapters 1, 3, and 7 and Joseph Pika for chapters 2 and 4. Pika and Rudalevige shared responsibilities for 5, 6, 8, 9 and 10, and Maltese and Rudalevige for 11.

About the Authors

Joseph A. Pika is the James R. Soles professor emeritus of political science and international relations at the University of Delaware. He holds a Ph.D. from the University of Wisconsin and taught previously at SUNY at Buffalo. He is coauthor with Jason D. Mycoff of *Conflict & Compromise: Presidential and Congressional Leadership, 2001–2006* and coauthor with John Anthony Maltese and H. Phillips Shively of *Government Matters: American Democracy in Context.* He served for seven years on the Delaware State Board of Education, four years as president.

John Anthony Maltese is the Albert B. Saye professor and associate dean of the University of Georgia's School of Public and International Affairs. He holds a Ph.D. from Johns Hopkins University. He is the author of *The Selling of Supreme Court Nominees* and *Spin Control: The White House Office of Communications and the Management of Presidential News,* and coauthor with Joseph A. Pika and H. Phillips Shively of *Government Matters: American Democracy in Context.* He is a Josiah Meigs Distinguished Teaching Professor and was named the Georgia Professor of the Year by the Carnegie Foundation and the Council for Advancement and Support of Education (CASE). Professor Maltese also writes extensively about classical music, for which he won a Grammy Award from the National Academy of Recording Arts and Sciences.

Andrew Rudalevige is the Thomas Brackett Reed professor of government at Bowdoin College and chair of the American Political Science Association's Presidents and Executive Politics section. He holds a Ph.D. from Harvard University and taught previously at Dickinson College and the University of East Anglia. His books include *Managing the President's Program, The New Imperial Presidency: Renewing Presidential Power after Watergate,* and, as co-editor, *The George W. Bush Legacy* and *The Obama Presidency: Appraisals and Prospects.* Prior to his academic career, he worked in state and local politics in Massachusetts.

CHAPTER 1

The Changing Presidency

Mark Skrobola (MCS@flickr)

The White House—nerve center of the executive branch and home of its chief.

For most Americans, the president is the focal point of public life. Almost every day, we see the president on media platforms old and new, meeting with foreign dignitaries, proposing policies, or grappling with national problems. This person appears to be in charge, and such recurrent images of an engaged leader are reassuring. But the reality of the presidency rests on a very different truth: Presidents are seldom in command and usually must negotiate with others to achieve their goals. It is only by exercising adroit political skill in winning public and elite support and knowing how to use it that a president can succeed in office. This lesson has come to dominate scholarly accounts of the presidency, but it has not always been fully appreciated by either the public or the presidents themselves.

The Scope of Presidential Power

In some respects, modern presidents are stronger than ever before. At the beginning of the twentieth century, presidents embraced new, expansive views of presidential power that by midcentury were accepted as normal. They used the power of the "bully pulpit" to shape public opinion. With the advent of radio and television, they became the leading voice in government. Congress added to the power of presidents by requiring them to submit annual federal budgets for congressional approval—an action that made presidents policy leaders in a way they had never been before. Staff support for presidents multiplied. And by leading the United States to victory in two world wars and playing for high stakes in the Cold War, presidents took center stage on the world scene.

Yet after World War II, there were a string of "failed" or otherwise abbreviated presidencies. Of the ten presidents serving from 1945 through the end of the twentieth century, only three—Dwight D. Eisenhower, Ronald Reagan, and Bill Clinton—served out two full terms of office. Despite strong public support when they were thrust into the presidency, Harry S. Truman and Lyndon B. Johnson left office repudiated by their party after they involved the country in controversial military conflicts abroad. Both were eligible to run for another term, but neither chose to do so. John F. Kennedy was assassinated before completing his first term. Richard Nixon resigned in disgrace two years after his landslide reelection. Nixon's vice president, Gerald R. Ford, failed to win the presidency in his own right after completing Nixon's term. Jimmy Carter lost his reelection bid after his public approval ratings plummeted to a record low of 21 percent because of the Iranian hostage crisis and runaway inflation. George H. W. Bush, whose approval rating skyrocketed to 89 percent during the Persian Gulf War, confronted an economic recession and criticism of his domestic agenda and was not reelected. Even Reagan and Clinton were distracted by scandal in their second terms. Reagan faced congressional investigations and an independent counsel probe into the Iran-contra affair. Clinton was subjected to an independent counsel probe and became the first president since Andrew Johnson in 1868 to be impeached by the House of Representatives. Like Johnson, Clinton was acquitted by the Senate. Moreover, both Reagan and Clinton were constrained in their second terms by a Congress controlled by the opposition party, as was George W. Bush after the turn of the century.

Barack Obama was similarly constrained after the 2014 midterm elections, when Republicans took control of both houses of Congress. And even though Donald J. Trump took office in 2017 with fellow Republicans solidly in control of Congress, the president's low public approval ratings, divisions among Republicans, united opposition from Democrats, and an inexperienced White House stymied even the initial effort to repeal and replace the "Obamacare" health law. These experiences

Courtesy of the Library of Congress, Prints and Photographs Division

This is James Hoban's original architectural drawing of the White House from 1792. Like the building itself, the office of the presidency has changed over time.

remind us that presidential power is not a fixed commodity. Formal powers mean little if presidents cannot convince others to follow their lead. As Richard Neustadt so succinctly put it, "Presidential power is the power to persuade."[1]

Dramatic changes in presidential fortunes are not new to American politics, nor are failed presidencies. Only about 20 percent of all U.S. presidents have served two full terms. Through both success and failure, however, one might think that constitutional provisions would serve as a steady source of presidential power. But as the following sections demonstrate, those provisions were not only the subject of great debate at the Constitutional Convention but also have been interpreted differently by presidents and others ever since. Quite simply, the scope of presidential power and the conceptions of the office have changed dramatically over the years.

Inventing the Presidency

Those who invented the presidency in 1787 did not expect the office to become the nation's central political institution. In fact, Article 2 of the Constitution, which deals with the executive branch, is known for its brevity and lack of clarity, particularly in comparison with the carefully detailed description of the legislative branch in Article 1. But within the presidency's vague constitutional description lay the seeds of a far more powerful position, one that has grown through elaboration of its explicit, **enumerated powers** as well as interpretation of its implied and **inherent powers**. Moreover, through the years, Congress and the public have caused the range of responsibilities associated with the presidency to expand, particularly in response to changes in society and America's position in the world. What has developed since 1789 is the office that now stands at the center of American government and American politics. As Stephen Skowronek puts it, the president has become "the lightning rod of national politics."[2]

The office of the presidency gained stature and a set of precedents from its initial occupant, George Washington. During the nineteenth century, however, the office languished, so much so that Lord Bryce, the British chronicler of American government, felt compelled to explain in 1890 that because of the institution's weaknesses, great men do not become president. Government during this period centered on Congress and political parties, an American invention the founders did not anticipate. A few presidents—most notably Thomas Jefferson, Andrew Jackson, and Abraham Lincoln—seemed to foreshadow strong presidents of the future, but most receded quickly from history. How, then, did the presidency come to assume its exalted position? The answer is complex and involves a variety of factors. At one level, the original design of the office—its structure, mode of selection, and powers—continues to exercise important influence on its operation today. But the office has changed over time in response to the influence of its occupants, changing expectations in Congress and by the public, and the internal dynamics of institutional development.

Constitutional Design

The events leading to the American Revolution led the colonists to disparage anything resembling a monarch. Thomas Paine's enormously influential pamphlet, *Common Sense,* published in January 1776, sharply dismissed the institution of monarchy, calling it "the most prosperous invention the Devil ever set on foot for the promotion of idolatry."[3] Paine called for a new government that had no executive. Some 120,000 copies of *Common Sense* were sold in just the three months following its publication.[4] The pamphlet's rallying cry against monarchy and executive power had hit a nerve.

In the weeks leading to the Declaration of Independence, the Continental Congress urged the colonies to adopt new constitutions in anticipation of statehood. The resulting state constitutions drafted in 1776 and 1777 "systematically emasculated the power of the governors."[5] Pennsylvania's constitution, drafted by Benjamin Franklin, provided for a unicameral legislature but no chief executive at all. Those states that did create chief executives made them subordinate to the legislature. Most governors served one-year terms, were elected by the legislature, and had little or no appointment or veto powers.[6] Even where governors were not chosen by the legislature (such as in Massachusetts), their powers were checked by a privy council.[7] New York stood out as the exception to this practice of weak governors and strong legislatures.[8]

As a result, most state legislatures became all powerful, which led to something of a backlash against strong legislatures by other participants and observers of the political process. For example, after serving as governor of Virginia for two years, Thomas Jefferson strongly criticized the concentration of power in the Virginia legislature. The Virginia Constitution explicitly called for the separation of the three branches, but the executive and judicial branches were so dependent upon the legislative branch that their powers had been eviscerated. Although mindful of the fear of executive power, Jefferson wrote that his experience with the Virginia legislature had convinced him that "173 despots would surely be as oppressive as one."[9] If an unchecked executive could lead to tyranny, so too could an unchecked legislature. These experiences would inform the delegates to the Constitutional Convention in 1787 and make them more willing to accept a strong executive than they would have been immediately after the Revolution.

Experience with the Articles of Confederation would also inform the delegates. The articles were a compact among the thirteen states that the Continental Congress had endorsed in 1777 and the states had ratified by 1781. The articles not only avoided the creation of anything resembling a president but also failed even to create an independent executive branch. Over time, this omission proved problematic. Attempts to administer laws through ad hoc committees, councils, or conventions proved unsuccessful, and Congress found it necessary to create several permanent departments in 1781 (including treasury, foreign affairs, and war). Although Congress appointed eminent men such as Robert Livingston, John Jay, and Robert Morris to head them, the departments remained mere appendages of the legislature.[10] Because the articles also failed to create a federal judiciary, the resulting government revolved around a single legislative body. In their zeal to ward off monarchy, the writers of the articles ignored the principle of separation of powers. And because the states had not delegated much power to the national government under the new scheme, the Confederation Congress remained impotent. Indeed, the national government had so little power to control the states that the confederation seemed to be but a "cobweb."[11] Congress did not even have the authority to regulate commerce among the states. This flaw led to a dire situation in which states fought with each other for economic advantage. Protective tariffs and trade barriers became routine weapons used by one state against another. Trade was complicated further by the states' different currencies. Some states went so far as to pass legislation canceling their debts. With no federal judiciary to turn to, those affected by such legislation sometimes had no legal recourse. The resulting chaos became a driving force for the Constitutional Convention.

Riots and mob actions in various states, culminating in Shays's Rebellion in Massachusetts, also signaled the need for change. Shays's Rebellion—an uprising in 1786–1787 by more than two thousand farmers who faced foreclosures because of high property taxes and economic depression—underscored the chaos. Massachusetts had to rely on a volunteer army to stop the rebellion because Congress was powerless to act. This failure of Congress highlighted the need for a national government capable of maintaining public order and prompted several states to vote to send delegates to the proposed Constitutional Convention. Even more significant, it helped to legitimize the idea of a strong *executive.* As Forrest McDonald has written, "Shays' Rebellion stimulated many Americans, especially in New England, to talk openly of monarchy as a safer guardian of liberty and property than republican institutions could be, particularly in a country as large as the United States."[12]

The delegates to the Constitutional Convention came to Philadelphia with these problems in mind. They agreed that the power of the national government had to be increased, although they disagreed over *how* to increase it and how *much* to increase it. Virtually all agreed that the new constitution should impose some form of separation of powers with a distinct executive branch at the national level. But delegates disagreed fundamentally about what that executive branch should look like and just how strong it should be. Despite that disagreement, it is striking that just eleven years after the Declaration of Independence, support had grown for an executive (and even support for a *strong* executive) because of events at the state and the national levels. In short, the delegates brought to the task of designing an executive office two conflicting attitudes: a healthy skepticism for executive power and a new appreciation of its necessity.

Initial Convention Debates. James Madison, the thirty-six-year-old Virginian commonly credited as the chief architect of the Constitution, was the first delegate to arrive in Philadelphia. He was convinced that the national government had to be refashioned, especially to increase its power over the states, but he had given little thought to executive power. In a letter to George Washington two weeks earlier, Madison admitted, "A national Executive must . . . be provided," but confessed, "I have scarcely ventured as yet to form my own opinion either of the manner in which it ought to be constituted or of the authorities with which it ought to be cloathed."[13]

The Virginia Plan—written mostly by Madison but introduced on the first working day of the convention by fellow Virginian Edmund Randolph—reflected this uncertainty. The plan called for an executive of unspecified size and tenure, selected by the legislature, and with unclear powers.[14] Indeed, the executive did not appear to be a matter of high importance to Randolph. His opening speech on May 29, 1787, included a lengthy analysis of the defects of the Articles of Confederation, but did not include the lack of an executive as one of them.[15]

When the convention began its executive branch deliberations on June 1, Randolph revealed his preference for a weak executive by arguing for a plural executive. More than a quarter of the delegates agreed.[16] Although we now take a single president for granted, the delegates debated whether there should be a singular or plural executive—one president or multiple presidents. Benjamin Franklin, for one, had long argued for a plural executive.[17] When his fellow delegate from Pennsylvania, James Wilson, moved that the executive should be singular, a "lengthy embarrassed silence ensued."[18] Franklin broke the silence by encouraging the delegates to express their views on the matter. The debate that followed was the first of many between those advocating a strong executive and those advocating a weak one.

Roger Sherman, a delegate from Connecticut, took the most extreme position on a weak executive. He saw no need to give the executive an explicit grant of power in the Constitution. Sherman believed the executive should be completely subservient to the legislature: "Nothing more than an institution for carrying the will of the Legislature into effect" and "appointed by and accountable to the Legislature only."[19] In addition, he argued that Congress should be able to change the size of the office at will. Wilson's motion for a singular executive—a first step toward creating a strong one—eventually won on June 4. But Sherman's suggestion for legislative appointment, something that Wilson and other proponents of a strong executive vigorously opposed, had won on June 2. On yet another issue, presidential veto power, the delegates steered a middle course. After voting for a single executive, the delegates gave the executive a qualified veto power, subject to an override by a two-thirds vote of the legislature.

These decisions, however, proved to be just the beginning of the debate over the position. On June 15 William Paterson introduced the New Jersey Plan, which proposed simply amending the existing Articles of Confederation rather than replacing them with a new constitution. The plan reintroduced the idea of a plural executive and said the executive should be elected by Congress for a single term.[20] Although the primary motivation of the New Jersey Plan was to protect the power of small states (the Virginia Plan apportioned representation in the national legislature according to population; the New Jersey Plan called for equal representation regardless of size), it is clear that those favoring the New Jersey Plan preferred a weak executive.

Since the first debates on executive power in early June, Gouverneur Morris, a delegate from Pennsylvania, joined the convention. Morris, who had spent most of his life in New York, became, along with James Wilson, one of the most influential proponents of a strong executive. He stood out because of his appearance—he had a wooden leg as a result of a carriage accident and a crippled arm as a result of a scalding as a child—but as Richard J. Ellis writes, "It was his rapier wit, infectious humor, and brilliant mind that set him apart and drew others."[21] On July 17 he began his offensive. Attempting to free the executive from its dependence on the legislature, Morris called for popular election by freeholders. Sherman vigorously objected, and Morris's motion was quickly defeated by a resounding margin. But the battle lines were drawn, and the debate over presidential selection was far from over.

Heated arguments over presidential selection continued for the next week, but when the delegates finished talking on July 26, the plan for an executive that had been agreed on in early June remained unchanged: legislative appointment of a single executive for one unrenewable seven-year term. Thereupon the delegates turned their resolutions over to a five-member Committee of Detail chaired by Wilson. Its task was to take the resolutions passed by the Committee of the Whole and turn them into a draft of the Constitution.

Committee Work and Final Action. One of the notable contributions of the Committee of Detail was its decision to use the word *president* to identify what the delegates had simply referred to as "the executive." The committee rejected the word *governor,* suggested by John Rutledge of South Carolina, because of the negative connotations associated with the royal governors who had ruled the colonies. The committee chose *president* because it was an innocuous term. Derived from the Latin word *praesidere* ("to sit in front of or at the head of" and "to defend"), *president* had historically been used to denote passive guardianship rather than strong executive power. The presiding officer of Congress under the Articles of Confederation was called its president. George Washington, who performed a mostly ceremonial function at the Constitutional Convention, served as its president.[22] Arguably, this choice of a term helped to sugarcoat executive power and make it more palatable.

In its draft of the Constitution, the Committee of Detail followed the convention's wishes and gave the president relatively little power. That it gave the president

Courtesy of the Library of Congress, Prints and Photographs Division

George Washington presides over the signing of the Constitution by members of the Constitutional Convention in Philadelphia on September 17, 1787. This depiction of the event was painted by Howard Chandler Christy and hangs in the U.S. Capitol.

a specific constitutional grant of power at all was, however, significant. The alternative would have been to follow Sherman's suggestion and allow Congress to dictate presidential powers. The Committee of Detail followed the convention's recommendation for a single executive elected by Congress to one seven-year unrenewable term, subject to impeachment, and with a qualified veto power. The draft also gave the president the power to appoint executive officers, to grant pardons, and to receive ambassadors. But many powers traditionally associated with the prerogative of the executive—such as raising armies, making war, making treaties, appointing ambassadors, and coining money—were all withheld from the president and given to the legislative branch.[23]

Convention debate resumed on August 6. When the delegates took up the article dealing with the president, it was obvious that they remained dissatisfied. But they could not agree on how to improve things, and debate ended on August 31, with the powers of the president largely unchanged. At that point, the convention sent unresolved issues to the Committee on Postponed Matters. The committee, chaired by David Brearly of New Jersey, consisted of one member from each state (including Gouverneur Morris). It was in that committee that the final constitutional vision of the presidency took shape.

One of the committee's most significant accomplishments was its cobbling together of a compromise plan for presidential selection. Various proposals had been introduced either for popular election of the president or selection by an electoral body, but the delegates had always reverted back to selection by Congress. The Committee on Postponed Matters revisited this issue and offered a novel twist on James Wilson's suggestion. The committee proposed that a president—and a vice president (the first time this position had been recommended)—be chosen by an Electoral College, consisting of electors from each of the states. Each state would be free to choose its electors (equaling that state's combined number of senators and representatives in the U.S. Congress) as its state legislature saw fit. Electors would meet and vote in their respective states. Each elector would have two votes, only one of which could be cast for a candidate from that elector's state. When the votes from all states' electors were counted, the candidate with the most votes would be elected president and the runner-up would be elected vice president. If no candidate received a majority in the Electoral College, the Senate would choose from among the five candidates who had received the most electoral votes. (The convention later changed this provision so that the House of Representatives, with each state delegation having an equal vote, would decide the outcome in such cases.)

The committee's proposed Electoral College seemed to resolve the problems that had stymied the convention. First, it placated both large and small states. Basing the number of electors on the combined number of a state's senators and representatives served as a compromise between equal and proportional allocation of electors. Large states could support the plan with the hope that they would dominate the Electoral College. At the same time, small states were pleased that each elector could cast only one vote for a home-state candidate. Small states were further assured that if the election were thrown to Congress, each state would have an equal vote. Second, the compromise plan satisfied proponents of an independent president and proponents of congressional selection of the president. Proponents of congressional selection argued that a presidential candidate would seldom get a majority of votes from the Electoral College. They believed that Congress would choose the president most of the time anyway, with the Electoral College acting simply as a nominating convention. Advocates of an independent president, on the other hand, saw the Electoral College as an explicit rejection of congressional selection and believed the electors would select the president.[24] Even on those occasions when a candidate did not get a majority, Congress was limited in its choice to the five candidates who had received the most votes in the Electoral College.[25] This provision clearly limited Congress more than the original plan, in which congressional choice was unrestricted. Finally, the proposal for both a president and a vice president resolved concerns about succession if presidents did not complete their terms. In short, as Georgia delegate Abraham Baldwin noted at the time, the Electoral College was "not so objectionable when well considered, as at first view."[26]

Besides its plan for an Electoral College, the Committee on Postponed Matters made a few other significant decisions. It shortened the president's term from seven to four years and made the president eligible for reelection to an unlimited number of terms. And—of great importance to advocates of a strong executive—it gave the president a number of executive powers that the delegates had previously given to the Senate, including expanded appointment power and the power to make treaties. The resulting language was again a compromise. The president could nominate ambassadors and other public ministers, Supreme Court justices, and all other officers whose appointments were not otherwise provided for. Actual appointment would come only with the "advice and consent" of the Senate. And although the president could make treaties, they could be ratified only by a two-thirds vote of the Senate.[27]

The convention as a whole spent several days in early September scrutinizing the proposals of the Committee on Postponed Matters. The only major change came on September 6, when the convention gave the House of Representatives the power to choose the president if no candidate received a majority in the Electoral College. The change was the result of fear among the delegates that the Senate was becoming too powerful. When voting for president, each state delegation in the House would have one vote. This guaranteed that each state would have an equal vote (a counterbalance to the Electoral College itself, which gives large states an advantage).

On September 8 the delegates created a five-member Committee of Style, chaired by Morris, to write a final draft of the Constitution. This committee was responsible for the opening words of Article 2: "The executive Power shall be vested in a President of the United States of America." As we shall see, the ambiguity of this sentence continues to be the subject of debate, and it stood in marked contrast to the opening words of Article 1, which seemed to explicitly limit Congress's powers to those listed in the Constitution: "All legislative powers herein granted shall be vested in a Congress of the United States." Ironically, the **vesting clause** of Article 2 was accepted by the whole of the Constitutional Convention without any discussion of its specific language.[28] The constitutional language regarding the presidency resulted from compromise, but it was a compromise that ultimately favored the strong executive model more than the weak one. It gave the president powers independent of Congress, although it imposed certain checks on that power. For example, it gave the president the power to appoint subject to the advice and consent of the Senate; the power to negotiate treaties subject to Senate ratification; and the power to veto subject to supermajority congressional override. Still, the outcome of the compromises generally gave the president the important ability to move first and set the agenda; it favored the strong executive model on each element of the executive summarized in Table 1-1. Credit usually goes to a small group of delegates, especially Wilson and Morris, who used their strategic positions within the convention's working committees to further their goal of a strong executive.

Interpreting Constitutional Language

The ambivalence over executive power exhibited by the convention became a permanent feature of American political culture. Like the delegates in 1787, Americans have had to confront the trade-off between tyranny and effectiveness—the one to be feared and the other to be prized. The anti-Federalists, who opposed ratification of the Constitution, frequently pointed to the risks inherent in a national executive, which some considered even more threatening than its British counterpart. As George Mason, a delegate from Virginia who ultimately refused to sign the Constitution, had argued, "We are not indeed constituting a British monarchy, but a more dangerous monarchy, an elective one."[29] But others—Alexander Hamilton, for example—saw the newly created presidency as essential to effective government, the source of energy, dispatch, and responsibility in the conduct of domestic and foreign affairs.[30]

This ambivalence has been reflected over the years in differing interpretations of constitutional language concerning presidential power. The vesting clause drafted by Morris and the Committee of Style—"The executive Power shall be vested in a President of the United States of America"—has proven to be, as presidential scholar Charles C. Thach Jr. put it in the 1920s, the "joker" in the game of presidential power.[31] Constitutional language limits both legislative and judicial power. Article 1 limits legislative powers to those "herein granted." Article 3 uses the phrase "the judicial power shall extend to," followed by an enumeration of those powers, which suggests the same sort of limitation of power as in Article 1. But Article 2 contains no such limit. Whether the omission was

TABLE 1-1 Models of Executive Considered by the Constitutional Convention

Elements of Executive	*Weak-Executive Model*	*Strong-Executive Model*	*Decision by Convention*
Relation to Congress	To put into effect will of Congress	Powers independent of Congress	Powers independent of Congress but with checks and balances
Number of Executives	Plural or single individual checked by council chosen by Congress or specified in Constitution	Single individual with no council or only advisory one chosen by means other than congressional selection	Single individual with Senate advisory on some matters
Method of Choosing Tenure	By Congress Limited term; no chance for reelection	Not specified No limitation on terms	By Electoral College No limitation on terms
Method of Removal	By Congress during term of office	Only for definite, enumerated reasons after impeachment and conviction by judicial body or Congress	For treason, bribery, high crimes, and misdemeanors, by impeachment by majority of House and conviction by two-thirds of Senate
Scope and Source of Powers	Limited powers delegated by Congress	Broad powers from Constitution, not subject to congressional interference	Broad powers delegated by Constitution with congressional checks
Appointment and Foreign Policy and Warmaking Powers	None—province of Congress	Would appoint judicial and diplomatic officials and participate in foreign policy and warmaking powers, including making of treaties	Appoints executive and judicial officials with consent of Senate; shares foreign policy and warmaking powers with Congress; Senate must approve treaties negotiated by president
Veto	None	Veto over legislation passed by Congress, exercised alone or with judiciary	Qualified veto, may be overridden by two-thirds vote of House and Senate

SOURCE: Joseph E. Kallenbach, *The American Chief Executive: The Presidency and the Governorship* (New York: Harper and Row, 1966), chap. 2.

intentional is unclear because the full convention never debated the language. Thach, however, points to letters that Morris wrote in which he admitted how much impact small, seemingly inconsequential changes of phraseology could have on the meaning of constitutional clauses. Although Morris did not refer explicitly to presidential power in these letters, his advocacy of a strong executive is well known, and Thach suspects that Morris embraced the language of Article 2 with "full realization of its possibilities."[32] Certainly Alexander Hamilton seized on the distinction between the Article 1 and 2 vesting clauses as early as 1793, as a way to justify President Washington's power to issue a neutrality proclamation in the wars between France and England.[33]

In any case, by failing to limit executive power to those "herein granted," Article 2 suggests that the scope of presidential power is not confined to the powers enumerated in the Constitution. Carried to its extreme, this view gives the president unlimited executive power. The ambiguity of the first sentence of Article 2 has led to three widely divergent theories of presidential power: the constitutional theory, the stewardship theory, and the prerogative theory.

Proponents of the **constitutional theory**, such as William Howard Taft, argue that presidential power is strictly limited. According to the constitutional theory, presidents have only those powers that are either enumerated in the Constitution or granted by Congress under its constitutional powers. Taft put it this way in his book *Our Chief Magistrate and His Powers:*

> The true view of the Executive function is, as I conceive it, that the President can exercise no power which cannot fairly and reasonably be traced to some specific grant of power or justly implied and included within such grant as proper and necessary to its exercise. Such specific grant must be either in the Federal Constitution or in an act of Congress passed in pursuance thereof. There is no undefined residuum of power that he can exercise because it seems to him to be in the public interest. . . . [Presidential power] must be justified and vindicated by affirmative constitutional or statutory provision, or it does not exist.[34]

In contrast, the **stewardship theory** holds that the president can do anything not explicitly *forbidden* by the Constitution or by laws passed by Congress under its constitutional powers. Theodore Roosevelt embraced this view as president and explained it in his *Autobiography:*

> My view was that every Executive officer and above all every Executive officer in high position was a steward of the people bound actively and affirmatively to do all he could for the people. . . . I declined to adopt [the] view that what was imperatively necessary for the Nation could not be done by the President, unless he could find some specific authorization to do it. My belief was that it was not only his right but his duty to do anything that the needs of the Nation demanded unless such action was forbidden by the Constitution or by the laws. Under this interpretation of executive power I did and caused to be done many things not previously done by the President and the heads of the departments. I did not usurp power but I did greatly broaden the use of executive power.

In other words, I acted for the common well being of all our people whenever and in whatever measure was necessary, unless prevented by direct constitutional or legislative prohibition.[35]

Taft, who had served as Roosevelt's secretary of war but later ran against him for president, took direct issue with the stewardship theory in his book:

My judgment is that the [stewardship theory], ascribing an undefined residuum of power to the President, is an unsafe doctrine and that it might lead under emergencies to results of an arbitrary character, doing irremediable injustice to private right. The mainspring of such a view is that the Executive is charged with responsibility for the welfare of all the people in a general way, that he is to play the part of a Universal Providence and set all things right, and that anything that in his judgment will help the people he ought to do, unless he is expressly forbidden not to do it. The wide field of action that this would give the Executive one can hardly limit.[36]

The **prerogative theory** is the most expansive of these three theories of presidential power. John Locke defined the concept of prerogative power in his *Second Treatise of Government* as the power "to act according to discretion for the public good, without the prescription of the law, *and sometimes even against it.*"[37] The prerogative theory not only allows presidents to do anything that is *not* forbidden but allows them to do things that *are* explicitly forbidden when in the national interest. Lincoln exercised such prerogative power at the outset of the Civil War. From the outbreak of hostilities at Fort Sumter, South Carolina, on April 12, 1861, to the convening of Congress in a special session on July 4, Lincoln stretched the executive's emergency powers further than ever before. This period has been described as a time of "constitutional dictatorship."[38] Lincoln unilaterally authorized a number of drastic actions. He called up the militia and volunteers, blockaded Southern ports, expanded the army and navy beyond the limits set by statute, pledged the credit of the United States without congressional authority to do so, closed the mails to "treasonous" correspondence, arrested persons suspected of disloyalty, and suspended the writ of *habeas corpus* in areas around the nation's capital. Admitting that most of these matters lay within the jurisdiction of Congress rather than the president, Lincoln asserted that they were done because of popular demand and public necessity and with the trust "that Congress would readily ratify them." But he deliberately chose not to call the national legislature in to special session until he was ready to do so, and then he presented it with *faits accomplis.*

Although Lincoln's use of executive power was most freewheeling in the early days of hostilities, he continued to exercise firm control over the war until it ended. He controlled the mail and newspapers, confiscated property of people suspected of impeding the conduct of the war, and even tried civilians in military courts in areas where civilian courts were operating. To justify such actions, he appealed to military necessity, asserting that the Constitution's commander in chief clause (requiring command of the armed forces) and its take care clause (that the laws be faithfully executed) combined to create a "war power" for the president that was virtually unlimited. Lincoln's success in defending that position is demonstrated by the fact that neither Congress nor the courts placed any significant limits on his actions during the war.

A century later, Richard Nixon pointed to Lincoln's actions in an attempt to justify illegal covert actions he had authorized as president. In fact, Nixon went so far as to claim that if a president chooses to do something illegal because he believes it to be in the national interest, it is—by definition—no longer illegal. He explained this in a televised interview with David Frost in 1977:

> When the President does it, that means that it is not illegal. . . . If the President, for example, approves something because of the national security, or in this case because of a threat to internal peace and order of significant magnitude, then the President's decision in that instance is one that enables those who carry it out, to carry it out without violating the law. Otherwise they're in an impossible position.[39]

Following the 9/11 terrorist attacks, President George W. Bush also exercised prerogative powers. As part of the "war on terror" he authorized the detention of "enemy combatants" at Guantánamo Bay, Cuba. He argued that detainees could be held there indefinitely without charge, without access to a lawyer, and without regard to the laws of armed conflict, which many argued violated the Geneva Conventions and basic due process rights.[40] He also authorized the CIA to establish secret prisons in several countries to detain and interrogate al-Qaida suspects, a possible violation of international law.[41] The president eventually admitted that "an alternative set of procedures" was used as part of the interrogation process at those prisons, but insisted that the procedures, though "tough," were lawful and did not constitute torture.[42] But behind the scenes, two deputy attorneys general in the Office of Legal Counsel had written memos that justified the use of torture against terror suspects and argued that international law should not interfere with the president's prerogative war power to use torture if necessary.[43]

Bush also used his war power domestically. Critics claimed that he violated the Foreign Intelligence Surveillance Act of 1978 when he authorized the use of domestic wiretaps without warrants. The nonpartisan Congressional Research Service found the wiretaps to be "inconsistent with the law."[44] The Bush administration, however, pointed to the use of emergency war power by Lincoln and other presidents as justification for the wiretaps and noted that the Authorization for Use of Military Force passed by Congress on September 14, 2001, implicitly gave approval for the president to take broad measures in response to the war on terror.[45] Despite an initial promise to close the military facility at Guantánamo Bay, President Obama approved in March 2011 the resumption of military trials there for terror suspects after a two-year suspension.[46] Obama's critics claimed that his use of prerogative power was at least as expansive as Bush's. For example, Obama waged a seven-month air war in Libya in 2011 relying only on his power as commander in chief. On the domestic front, he made aggressive use of executive orders and prosecutorial discretion regarding such issues as immigration, deportation, and the environment, many of which President Trump rescinded with executive orders of his own.

All of this serves as a reminder that the ambiguity of the opening sentence of Article 2, section 1, has allowed individual presidents to expand significantly the power of the office. As constitutional scholar Edward S. Corwin wrote in 1957, "Taken by and large, the history of the presidency is a history of aggrandizement."[47] By the 1970s, Arthur Schlesinger Jr. coined the phrase, "the imperial presidency" to describe the office.[48]

Presidents have also relied on ambiguities in their specifically enumerated powers, in sections 2 and 3 of Article 2, to further that aggrandizement. Together, the enumerated powers have created at least five presidential roles that have evolved and expanded over time.

Chief Administrator. This role for the president is more implicit than explicit as set forth in the Constitution. It rests on the executive power clause (Article 2, section 1, paragraph 1) as well as passages dealing with the right to require opinions from the heads of government departments (Article 2, section 2, paragraph 1) and the power to make personnel appointments subject to whatever approval Congress may require (Article II, section 2, paragraph 2). George W. Bush took the role of chief administrator very seriously. He actively embraced the concept of the **unitary executive**—a concept not widely discussed outside the conservative Federalist Society before Bush took office.[49] Supporters of the unitary executive argue that because the president alone possesses the executive power, the president must have absolute control over the executive branch and its administration, including the ability to control all subordinates and to veto or nullify their exercise of discretionary executive power. Moreover, the president must be able to fire any executive branch officials at will.[50] This view of the presidency holds that attempts by Congress to limit the president's removal power, even in the case of independent agencies, are improper, as are other oversight measures that interfere with executive branch functions.

If fully implemented, these ideas would be a major shift in the balance of power because traditionally Congress has jealously guarded its oversight powers, thereby denying the president anything approximating a monopoly of administrative power. Moreover, in 1935, the Supreme Court unanimously recognized Congress's power to limit the president's ability to fire officers who perform quasi-legislative or quasi-judicial functions in independent agencies within the executive branch.[51] In 1926, the Court had ruled that only purely executive officials performing purely executive functions can be fired by the president at will.[52] Given the large number of independent federal agencies, the Court's ruling places a significant limitation on the president's removal power.

Commander in Chief. This role is specifically enumerated in Article 2, section 2, paragraph 1: "The President shall be Commander in Chief of the Army and Navy of the United States, and of the Militia of the several States, when called into the actual Service of the United States." But did this language merely confer a title on the president or imply wide-ranging powers in times of emergency? Lincoln believed the latter. From this germ of constitutional power has grown the enormous control that modern presidents exercise over a permanent military establishment and its deployment. The Constitution stipulates that the legislative and executive branches share the war power, but the pressure of events and the presidency's institutional advantages in taking decisive action have led Congress to give greater discretion to the executive. Nor was this delegation of power completely unexpected. Recognizing the need to repel attacks when Congress was not in session, the Constitutional Convention altered language describing the role of Congress in armed hostilities from "make" war to "declare" war (Article 1, section 8, paragraph 11), thereby expanding the president's realm of discretionary action.[53] Over time, presidents have invoked the commander in chief clause to justify military expenditures without congressional authorization, emergency powers to suppress rebellion, the internment of American citizens of Japanese descent during World War II, the seizure of domestic steel mills during the undeclared armed conflict in Korea in the 1950s, and the use of warrantless wiretapping as part of the war on terror.[54]

The 1973 War Powers Resolution says that presidents may not commit troops for more than sixty days without Congress authorizing the use of military force or formally declaring war. In fact, both before and after passage of the resolution, presidents have initiated the use of force far more frequently than they have awaited congressional authorization. Most significantly, they have continued to wage war—sometimes for years—without a congressional declaration of war. They do so, as political scientist Richard Pious points out, by relying on "congressional resolutions of support, UN resolutions, NATO resolutions, congressional authorizations, and what they consider to be self-executing treaty provisions, relying on whatever is at hand."[55] A recent example of the use of unilateral military force came in April 2017 when President Trump authorized U.S. military strikes in Syria without specific congressional approval. He did so in response to that government's use of chemical weapons against its own people. President Obama chose not to launch an attack on Syria in 2013 after a similar use of chemical weapons. He sought but failed to win congressional authorization for a strike (which, at the time, Trump strongly opposed).

John C. Yoo, a strong proponent of the unitary executive who served as deputy attorney general in George W. Bush's Office of Legal Counsel from 2001 to 2003, took a particularly expansive view of the president's Commander in Chief power in a memo dated September 25, 2001: "The Constitution vests the President with the plenary authority, as Commander in Chief and the sole organ of the Nation in its foreign relations, to use military force abroad—especially in response to grave national emergencies created by sudden unforeseen attacks on the people and territory of the United States." Yoo, therefore, concluded that military actions in the wake of the 9/11 attacks "need not be limited to those individuals, groups, or states that participated in the attacks on the World Trade Center and the Pentagon." He argued that Congress could not "place any limits on the President's determinations as to any terrorist threat, the amount of military force to be used in response, or the method, timing, and nature of the response. These decisions, under our Constitution, are for the President alone to make."[56] Pious has noted that some of the framers, such as Madison, came to an opposite conclusion. Madison "claimed that the Constitution assigned all war and foreign affairs powers to the legislature, with only such exceptions as were explicitly assigned by the Constitution to the executive."[57]

Chief Diplomat. When combined with the president's expanded war power, constitutional primacy in the conduct of foreign affairs establishes the office's claim to being the government's principal agent in the world, if not its "sole organ." Presidents are not only authorized to make treaties "by and with the

Advice and Consent of the Senate" but also empowered to nominate ambassadors, subject to Senate approval (Article 2, section 2, paragraph 2) and to receive diplomatic emissaries from abroad (Article 2, section 3). Presidents have varied in how closely they collaborate with the Senate in making treaties, most waiting until after negotiations have been concluded before allowing any Senate participation. More significant, the conduct of foreign affairs has come to rely on **executive agreements** between heads of state in place of treaties. These agreements do not require Senate ratification, as treaties do, although many are given legislative approval by statute (as was NAFTA, the North American Free Trade Agreement, under President Clinton) or a joint resolution of Congress (as was SALT I, the first strategic arms limitation talks with the Soviet Union, under President Nixon). Statutes and joint resolutions require only a simple majority, rather than the two-thirds approval necessary for Senate ratification of a treaty.[58] When given such legislative approval, they are referred to as "congressional-executive agreements."[59] The scope of President Obama's power to negotiate and implement a nuclear agreement with Iran without congressional approval became a contentious issue in 2015 (see chapter 10).

Chief Legislator. This feature of the job did not fully develop until the twentieth century. Before then, the president's role in legislation was essentially negative: the ability to veto. Today, however, the president's power to provide leadership for Congress rests primarily on the ability to shape the legislative agenda through active leadership. Congress fostered this development in 1921, when it passed legislation requiring the president to submit a budget for the whole of government. Constitutional language in Article 2, section 3, merely obliged the president to give "the Congress Information of the State of the Union" and to recommend such other measures for its consideration as deemed "necessary and expedient." Legislative leadership is now considered a task for all presidents to fulfill, and they routinely develop detailed legislative agendas and present them to Congress and the nation.

Chief Magistrate. This area of presidential activity is perhaps the least clearly recognized, but it is one that George W. Bush expanded as part of his embrace of the unitary executive. It is based on the oath clause of Article 2, section 1, paragraph 8, of the Constitution, directing the president to "preserve, protect and defend the Constitution of the United States," and the general charge in Article 2, section 3, directing the president to "take Care that the Laws be faithfully executed." Proponents of a unitary executive argue that these clauses require coordinate construction. In other words, the president, along with the courts and Congress, has the power and the duty to interpret the Constitution to make sure that it is preserved and faithfully executed. President Bush's interpretation led to his controversial use of presidential signing statements when signing a bill into law. Presidents since James Monroe have issued them, but usually they were ceremonial in nature—designed to state why the president signed a law or to celebrate its passage. Occasionally, however, a president would use them to point out portions of a bill he thought were unconstitutional. In some rare instances, the president would say that he would not execute that provision. Other presidents, Clinton, for example, noted constitutional problems in their signing statements, but made it clear that they would enforce the provision until a court struck it down.[60] Starting with Reagan, signing statements were used more systematically—often to clarify how the president believed executive branch agencies should interpret ambiguous sections of the law. In 1986, the Justice Department added signing statements to the legislative history section of the U.S. Code.[61]

Bush, however, used signing statements routinely to state his intent *not* to enforce specific provisions of legislation. The American Bar Association (ABA) Task Force on Presidential Signing Statements reported in August 2006 that Bush had challenged more than 800 specific provisions of legislation he signed. In a single signing statement accompanying the Consolidated Appropriations Act of 2005, Bush issued 116 specific objections relating to almost every part of the bill.[62] Bush's signing statements rejected encroachments on the unitary executive. For example, he rejected congressional oversight of Patriot Act authority to search homes secretly and to seize private papers. Although he signed the McCain amendment banning the use of torture by U.S. officials, Bush quietly indicated that he could disregard the law and use torture under his commander in chief powers when he deemed it necessary.[63] In short, Bush claimed the right to disobey laws that he had signed whenever he felt those laws conflicted with his interpretation of the Constitution without waiting for action by a court. His conception of the power of the chief magistrate went far beyond the normal executive branch role, but until 2006, most people—including members of Congress—were largely unaware of Bush's extensive use of signing statements.[64] On March 9, 2009, President Obama instructed executive officials not to enforce any of President Bush's signing statements without first consulting with the attorney general, but he indicated that he would use signing statements under some circumstances.[65] In fact, he issued a signing statement just two days later, in which he reserved the right to bypass dozens of provisions in the $410 billion spending bill that he was signing into law.[66] During his presidency, Obama issued forty-one signing statements.[67]

George W. Bush interpreted all five presidential roles broadly. Law professor Jeffrey Rosen called it "the largest expansion of executive power since FDR."[68] Because the constitutional job description for presidents is permissive rather than confining, it aids such aggrandizement of presidential power. And once expanded, executive power seldom contracts to its previous level—a phenomenon that has been apparent during the Obama administration across all five arenas of presidential power, and will likely continue under Trump.

Expansion of the Presidency

Students of the presidency commonly divide the office's development into two major periods: traditional and modern. In the traditional era, presidential power was relatively limited, and Congress was the primary policymaker. The modern era is typified by presidential dominance in the policymaking process and a significant expansion of the president's powers and resources. The presidency of Franklin D. Roosevelt was the turning point into the modern era. Political scientist Fred Greenstein argues that the modern presidency is distinguished by four features: (1) The president is expected to develop a legislative program and to persuade Congress to enact it, (2) presidents regularly engage in direct policymaking through actions not requiring congressional approval, (3) the presidential office has become an extensive bureaucracy designed to enable presidents to undertake the first two points, and (4) presidents have come to symbolize the nation and to personify its government to such an extent that the public holds them primarily responsible for its condition and closely monitors their performance through intensive media coverage.[69]

A number of factors contributed to the expansion of the American presidency. These include actions by individual presidents, statutes enacted by Congress, the emergence of customs, and institutional development. We examine each of these factors in turn.

Expansion by Individual Presidents

Several early presidents, including George Washington, Thomas Jefferson, Andrew Jackson, and Abraham Lincoln, are often credited with providing their successors with an institutional legacy that left the office more powerful than before.[70] This assertion is true to a certain extent, but it was three twentieth-century presidents, Theodore Roosevelt, Woodrow Wilson, and FDR, who were largely responsible for expanding presidential power and creating the modern presidency.

Theodore Roosevelt (1901–1909). As president, Theodore Roosevelt helped the United States become a world power. Concerned over the rise of Japan as a threat to American interests in the Pacific, Roosevelt sought and obtained a major role in negotiating the Portsmouth treaty, which terminated the Russo-Japanese War of 1905. Closer to home, he intervened in the affairs of neighbors to the south when he considered it vital to U.S. national interests, sending troops to the Dominican Republic and Cuba. Even more blatant was Roosevelt's part in fomenting the rebellion of Panama against Colombia so that the United States could acquire rights to build a canal. An avowed nationalist with the desire to expand U.S. influence in international affairs, Roosevelt ordered the navy to sail around the world as a symbolic demonstration of American military might. The image of U.S. naval ships sailing off the shores of other countries would serve as a potent reminder to those nations that the United States was now a major world power. When Congress balked at the expense, Roosevelt countered that he had sufficient funds to get the navy there; if the lawmakers wanted the fleet back home, they would have to provide the money for the return trip.

Roosevelt also responded vigorously to the rapid industrialization of American life and its attendant evils. He had charges pressed against corporations that violated antitrust laws, and he pushed legislation through Congress that gave the Interstate Commerce Commission power to reduce railroad rates. When coal mine operators in Colorado refused to agree to arbitration of a dispute with their workers, Roosevelt threatened to have troops seize the mines and administer them as a receiver for the government. He was the first American chief executive to intervene in a labor dispute who did *not* take management's side. Roosevelt also championed major reclamation and conservation projects as well as meat inspection and pure food and drug laws. Indeed, Roosevelt issued nearly as many executive orders as all of his predecessors combined, dwarfing their use of administrative authority.

Perhaps most important, Roosevelt did much to popularize the presidency after three decades of lackluster leaders. (Of the eight men who served between Lincoln and Roosevelt, only Grover Cleveland is considered at all significant.) A dynamic personality, an attractive family, and love of the public spotlight enabled Roosevelt "to put the presidency on the front page of every newspaper in America."[71] Considering himself the "steward of the people" and seeing the office as a "bully pulpit" from which the incumbent should set the tone of American life, Roosevelt was the first president to provide meeting rooms for members of the press and to hold informal news conferences to link the presidency with the people. His style of leadership depended on extensive use of popular speech, a distinctive reinterpretation of statesmanship that ushered in the era of the "rhetorical presidency."[72] In keeping with his stewardship theory of presidential power, Roosevelt was also the first president to rely on broad discretionary authority in peacetime as well as in crisis.[73]

Woodrow Wilson (1913–1921). Although Theodore Roosevelt laid the groundwork for use of popular appeals during his presidency, it was his successor, Wilson, who linked inspirational rhetoric to a broad program of action in an effort to address domestic and foreign affairs. Jeffrey Tulis has argued that this effort rested on a systematic, ambitious reinterpretation of the president's role in the constitutional order.[74] A skilled public speaker, Wilson was the first president since John Adams to go before Congress in person to give his State of the Union message, a practice we now take for granted.[75] Like Jefferson, he was a powerful party chief who worked through congressional leaders and the Democratic caucus to influence legislation. He also did not hesitate to take his case to the people, casting himself as the interpreter as well as the representative of their interests.

During his first term in office, Wilson pushed through a vast program of economic reform that lowered tariffs, raised taxes on the wealthy, created a central banking system, regulated unfair trade practices, provided low-interest loans to farmers, and established an eight-hour day for railroad employees. When the United States became involved in World War I during his second term, Wilson went to Congress and obtained authority to control the economic as well as the military aspects of the war, rather than prosecuting it through unilateral executive action. This grant gave him the power to allocate food and fuel, license trade with the enemy, censor the mail, regulate the foreign language press of the country, and operate railroads, water transportation systems, and telegraph and telephone facilities. At the end of the war, he made a triumphant trip to Europe, where he assumed the leading role in writing the Versailles peace treaty.

Wilson also provided a lesson in how *not* to work with Congress: His adamant refusal to accept any reservations proposed by the Senate for the League of Nations Covenant of the Treaty of Versailles ensured that the United States would not participate. Wilson's archenemy, Sen. Henry Cabot Lodge, R-MA, calculated that the president's intransigence and personal hatred of him was so intense that the president would reject all compromises proposed to the treaty. Lodge was right: Wilson said it is "better a thousand times to go down fighting than to dip your colors to dishonorable compromise."[76] A trip to win popular support for the League ended in failure and a physical breakdown when Wilson suffered a stroke. As a result, the country whose leader proposed the League of Nations ended up not belonging to the organization at all.

Franklin D. Roosevelt (1933–1945). Confronted by enormous domestic and international crises, FDR began a program of action and innovation unmatched by any chief executive in U.S. history. In most respects, his service is now used as a yardstick against which the performance of his successors is measured.[77] When Roosevelt came into office in March 1933, business failures were legion, 12 million people were unemployed, banks all over the country were closed or doing business under restrictions, and Americans had lost confidence in their leaders and themselves. Counseling the nation in his inaugural address—the first of four—that "the only thing we have to fear is fear itself," the new chief executive swung into action: A four-day bank holiday was declared, and an emergency banking bill was prepared within a day's time. During Roosevelt's first one hundred days in office, the nation witnessed a social and economic revolution in the form of his New Deal. Congress adopted a series of far-reaching government programs insuring bank deposits, providing crop payments for farmers, establishing codes of fair competition for industry, granting labor the right to organize, providing relief and jobs for the unemployed, and creating the Tennessee Valley Authority, a government corporation, to develop that region. With these measures and others, such as Social Security, public housing, and unemployment compensation, Roosevelt established the concept of the "positive state" in America—a government that has the obligation to take the lead in providing for the welfare of all the people.

Internationally, Roosevelt extended diplomatic recognition to the Soviet Union, embarked on the Good Neighbor policy toward South America, and pushed through the Reciprocal Trade Program, which lowered tariffs with other nations. In his second term, FDR began the slow and difficult task of preparing the nation for its eventual entry into World War II. He funneled aid to the allies; traded fifty overage destroyers to Britain for naval and air bases in the British West Indies, Newfoundland, and Bermuda; and obtained passage of the nation's first peacetime draft. After Pearl Harbor, in his words, "Dr. New Deal" became "Dr. Win-the-War." He took over economic control of the war effort granted to him by Congress, and established the victorious strategy of concentrating on defeating Germany before Japan. While hostilities were still going on, he took the lead in setting up the United Nations, but he died before he could see the organization established in 1945.

Roosevelt was an innovator whose actions reshaped the presidential office. He was not only an effective legislative leader but also a skilled administrator responsible for a thorough reorganization of the executive branch, including the creation of the Executive Office of the President (EOP) (see chapter 6). Even more important, FDR was probably the most effective molder of public opinion the nation has ever known. He pioneered the use of "fireside chats" over radio to explain his actions to the people. In addition, he raised the presidential press conference to new heights as a tool of public persuasion. As a man who could take idealistic goals, reduce them to manageable and practical programs, and then sell them to Congress and the American people, Roosevelt has no peer.

Expansion through Statute

Congress is another major source of change in the presidency. Legislators have mandated activities that earlier presidents exercised on a discretionary basis or have formally delegated responsibility for activities that traditionally resided with Congress. One of the contemporary presidency's major responsibilities—serving as the nation's economic manager—is nowhere suggested in the Constitution.[78] Congress foisted this power on the president. In 1921, Congress passed the Budget and Accounting Act as part of an effort to increase the fiscal responsibility and efficiency of government. The act created the Bureau of the Budget (BOB) in the Treasury Department and required the president to use the expert advice of the bureau to propose annual fiscal policy to the government. Quite simply, the legislation compelled the president to take an active role in domestic policy formulation. James Sundquist said the following:

> Before 1921, a president did not have to have a program for the whole of the government, and none did; after that date he was compelled by the Budget and Accounting Act to present a program for every department and every bureau, and to do it annually. Before 1921, a president did not have to propose a fiscal policy for the government, and many did not; after 1921, every chief executive had to have a fiscal policy, every year. That made the president a leader, a policy and program initiator, and a manager, whether he wished to be or not.[79]

Naturally, strong presidents exerted policy leadership before 1921, but nothing had compelled them to act. Likewise, it is wrong to assume that the Budget and

Accounting Act automatically produced strong presidents. The first three affected by the act, Warren Harding, Calvin Coolidge, and Herbert Hoover, dutifully submitted proposals to Congress but seldom exerted strong leadership to secure enactment.[80] That pattern changed under FDR, who used the crisis of the Depression as a rallying cry for policy enactment.

Over time, Congress further expanded presidential power. It created the EOP in 1939, as a source of expert advice to help presidents formulate policy. Congress also added to the president's economic responsibilities by passing the Employment Act of 1946. As Sundquist explains, the act "compels the president to maintain a continuous surveillance of the nation's economy, to report on the state of its health at least annually, and if there are signs of pathology—inflation, recession, stagnation—to recommend corrective action."[81] Despite giving the president new tasks, Congress did not surrender its traditional right to alter presidential proposals, thereby ensuring that tax rates and spending proposals would continue to be a mainstay of partisan politics as well as legislative-executive relations. (See chapter 9 for the politics of economic policymaking.)

Congress has taken comparable action in other areas as well. In 1947, Congress charged the president with coordinating national security policy—foreign policy, intelligence collection and evaluation, and defense policy—through the creation of the National Security Council (NSC). President Truman resisted the newly created NSC as an intrusion on his powers and was slow to use it. In fact, no president can be *required* to use such a structure, but during the Cold War one president after another established administrative machinery designed to achieve the same goal of coordinating American foreign policy (see chapter 10).

During George W. Bush's administration, the Republican-controlled Congress sanctioned many of the actions Bush had already taken unilaterally under his war power. Prior to the Democrats' regaining control in the 2006 midterm elections, Congress passed the Military Commissions Act of 2006. As Richard Pious wrote, the act

> authorized the military commissions initially promulgated by Bush's military order to try noncitizen detainees in the War on Terror; granted vast delegation of power to the president to determine their rules of procedure; delegated to the president the power to determine by executive order what interrogation techniques would be used on detainees (with the exception of a set of limited techniques defined to constitute torture that would be prohibited, such as sleep deprivation and waterboarding); allowed the president to "interpret the meaning and application" of international conventions involving treatment of prisoners; permitted information acquired through harsh interrogations (prior to passage of the Detainee Treatment Act of 2005) [which contains the McCain amendment] to

be used in trials if the commission found the statements reliable and in the "interests of justice"; and stripped federal courts of pending habeas corpus petitions filed by detainees (as of October 2006 numbering 196).[82]

In 2008, the Supreme Court ruled that the Military Commissions Act unconstitutionally suspended the right of *habeas corpus*.[83] Congress passed a revised Military Commissions Act of 2009 in response to that decision that accorded more protections to defendants.

Upon entering office, President Obama sought and received statutory authority for a different type of executive power. Faced with an economic emergency unparalleled since the Great Depression, Obama asked Congress for legislation authorizing the executive branch to seize troubled financial institutions deemed by the Treasury secretary to be too important to fail.[84] The resulting financial reform bill reminds us that Congress can authorize presidents to act in areas wholly absent from the original constitutional design or encourage executives to devise new ways to exercise their traditional responsibilities.

Expansion through Custom and Practice

Across a wide range of presidential activities, "action based on usage may acquire legitimacy."[85] This may link back to the presidential-congressional relations just discussed. In a 1915 case, for instance, the Supreme Court upheld presidents' ability to withdraw lands from public use, since Congress had never objected to their doing so over the years. "Unauthorized acts would not have been allowed to be so often repeated as to crystalize into a regular practice," the Court determined. After all, "government is a practical affair, intended for practical men."[86]

Likewise, nowhere in the Constitution does it say that presidents would serve as leaders of their party, but that task has been associated with the office since Thomas Jefferson first established his dominance of the Democratic-Republicans' congressional caucus. Enormous variation may be found in how presidents pursued such activities and in how successful they were. Some, like Jefferson, had a close relationship with their party, while other executives were virtually abandoned by their partisan allies (Rutherford B. Hayes). At other times, presidents sought, and seemed to derive, greater influence by appearing to serve "above" party (Eisenhower). If the political parties continue to weaken or have difficulty reasserting themselves as structures vital to democracy, this informal part of the president's job description could disappear.

A third example of precedent and custom can be found in Theodore Roosevelt's attempt to mediate a labor-management dispute. Earlier presidents had intervened on the side of company owners, but Roosevelt put his prestige on the line when he sought to resolve the anthracite coal strike of 1902, a struggle that had paralyzed a vital industry. Other presidents followed suit: Wilson intervened in eight major disputes, Harding in two, FDR in eleven, and Truman in three.[87] The response of one president to emergency conditions became an accepted precedent for his successors, if they wished to pursue it.

Institutional Sources of Change

The modern presidency cannot be considered a one-person job, a reality that has had significant consequences for the evolution of the office. To dispatch the many responsibilities placed at the president's door, the presidency has become a working collectivity. During FDR's first term, the average number of full-time White House staffers was forty-seven. By Nixon's second term, that number had grown to well over five hundred. The shift toward what has been called the "institutional presidency" is partly a result of changing customs and practice, but it is also something that was furthered by statute.

Congress spurred the increase in staff by creating the EOP in 1939 and then passing subsequent legislation to create additional staff units, such as the Council of Economic Advisers (CEA) and the NSC, within that structure. At the same time, presidents unilaterally created their own specialized staff units. These include the Congressional Liaison Office (to help secure congressional passage of presidential initiatives), the Office of Communications (to help communicate the president's agenda to the public and to coordinate the flow of information from the many departments and agencies within the executive branch), and the Office of Public Liaison (to maintain support from interest groups). By some counts, the president's full-time executive staff under Nixon, including presidential advisers in the EOP, grew to more than five thousand. During FDR's first term, comparable executive staff (including groundskeepers and the White House police force) numbered only 103.[88]

Presidential Culture

Understanding the presidency's institutional development provides an important perspective on the functions of the office, but we also need to address a less concrete question: What does the presidency *mean* to Americans? The final section of this chapter focuses on the development of the office's emotional and psychological significance.

Despite the framers' ambivalence toward executive power, the office of president quickly acquired mythic dimensions when it was filled by the country's first true hero. George Washington, argues Seymour Martin Lipset, supplied the virtues of a charismatic leader who serves as "symbol of the new nation, its hero who embodies in his person its values and aspirations. But more than merely symbolizing the new nation, he legitimizes the state, the new secular government, by endowing it with his 'gift of grace,'" the near magical qualities such leaders supposedly possess.[89] A cult of personality grew up around Washington so that well into the nineteenth century citizens displayed his likeness in their homes, named their children after him, and paid him endless tributes.

In the process of contributing stability and identity to the new nation, Washington also endowed the presidential office with a special meaning that has become part of our collective heritage. Bruce Buchanan refers to this as **presidential culture**, "widely held meanings of the presidency, derived from selected episodes in the history of the institution and transmitted from one generation to the next by political socialization." Buchanan explains that families, teachers, and the media sustain this view of the presidency as an office with the ability to deliver the nation from danger as a result of its occupants' greatness. Somehow, it is widely believed, the institution "has the potential to make extraordinary events happen" and the incumbent "should be able to realize that potential."[90] Occupants of the position, then, are expected to live up to these levels of performance and are roundly criticized when they fall short.

Why have such unrealistic expectations taken hold? One reason is that we have glorified the memories of past presidents. The "great" presidents, particularly those who took decisive action and bold initiatives, and even some of the "not so great," are treated as folk heroes and enshrined in a national mythology—figures whose birthdays we celebrate, whose virtues we are urged to emulate, and whose achievements we memorialize. Schoolchildren throughout America are regaled with stories of Washington and Lincoln every February. Every summer, thousands of vacationers make the pilgrimage to visit shrines located along the Potomac in Washington, D.C., or scattered throughout the nation in presidential libraries and museums. Historical and popular glorification, however, does not constitute the full story. The presidency has always been important in American civic life, but it may have assumed even greater proportions in the modern era, assisted by new technologies and resting on new conceptions of the office.

A number of political scientists have pointed to the importance of the presidency in meeting the emotional and psychological needs of the populace. In particular, it is argued that citizens have expressive needs for confidence, security, reassurance, and pride in citizenship.[91] In the view of Murray Edelman, citizens suffer from a "general sense of anxiety about the comprehensive function played in human affairs by chance, ignorance, and inability to comprehend, plan, and take responsibility for remote and complicated contingencies." The natural response is to seek emotional comfort through attachment to reassuring symbols, "and what symbol can be more reassuring than the incumbent of a high position who knows what to do and is willing to act, especially when others are bewildered and alone?"[92] We know that American children develop a highly idealized image of presidents that emphasizes both their power and their benevolence, a source of reassurance that may be transferred from childhood to adulthood.

Fred Greenstein suggests additional psychological needs that are met through the presidency. Citizens seeking to sort through the complexity of political life turn to presidents for cognitive assistance. Presidents personify the government and make it possible to become engaged by what would otherwise be an impersonal abstraction. By following the president's activities, citizens may also experience a sort of vicarious participation in public affairs, giving them a sense of power and control that ordinarily would be unavailable. As a symbol of stability, predictability, and national unity, the president soothes fears and enables us to proceed with our daily lives.[93]

This aspect of the presidential office has become particularly "potent as a symbol of the public welfare, built-in benevolence, and competence to lead."[94] Barbara Hinckley points out that "symbols evoke ideas the society wants to believe are true. . . . [They] can substitute for something that does not exist otherwise." In fact, Hinckley argues that because the Constitution failed to clarify the presidency's nature and responsibilities, symbols have become enormously significant: "The office is undefined; thus presidents become what people want them to be."[95] And the people want them to be many things. The list of desirable personal attributes is impressive, as Ray Price, an aide to Richard Nixon during the 1968 presidential campaign, pointed out in a memo to the staff:

> People identify with a President in a way they do with no other public figure. Potential presidents are measured against an ideal that's a combination of leading man, God, father, hero, pope, king, with maybe just a touch of the avenging Furies thrown in. They want him to be larger than life, a living legend, and yet quintessentially human; someone to be held up to their children as a model; someone to be cherished by themselves as a revered member of the family, in somewhat the same way in which peasant families pray to the icon in the corner. Reverence goes where power is.[96]

The problem for candidates (and incumbents) is how to project an image that matches these public expectations. Theodore Lowi has argued that "the expectations of the masses have grown faster than the capacity of presidential government to meet them."[97] According to Lowi, modern presidents resort to illusions to cover failures and seek quick fixes for their flagging public support in foreign adventures. As we discuss in chapter 3, advances in the means of communication have increased the ability of presidents to do this. Such behavior—portrayed by Lowi as rooted in the presidential institution, not in individual presidents' personalities—is ultimately self-defeating because it inflates expectations and ensures public disappointment, which may help to explain the string of failed presidencies described at the beginning of this chapter.

Conclusion: The Changeable, Political Presidency

There can be little doubt that today's presidency is a far cry from the office designed by the Constitutional Convention. Responsibilities have grown enormously as have means to fulfill them. So have the mythic dimensions of the office. Unlike the office that was launched in 1789, today's presidency is firmly rooted in the national consciousness as the consequence of childhood socialization and a secular mythology whose idealized images are magnified with the passage of time. There is no way to determine whether the office of president means more to Americans today than it did two centuries ago in the emotional and psychological needs it meets, but certainly, it occupies a more central—some observers would argue excessive—place in the public consciousness.

The contemporary presidency is not a static construct, however. As this overview of institutional development demonstrates, Americans' perceptions of the office and what they want from it can and does change over time. All too often, observers of the presidency treat temporary conditions as if they were permanent—mistaking a snapshot for a portrait.

To summarize, the presidency is variable for several reasons. First, in no other public office do the personality, character, and political style of the incumbent make as much difference as they do in the presidency. As an institution, the presidency exhibits important continuities across administrations, but the entry of each new occupant has an undeniably pervasive effect on the position's operation. The presidency is also heavily influenced by changes outside the office and throughout the U.S. political system—whether in the formal political structure (Congress, the executive branch, the courts), in the informal political institutions (political parties and interest groups), in society at large, in the mass media, or in conditions surrounding substantive issues, particularly national security and the economy. Because of their extensive responsibilities, presidents must contend with all of these influences. Furthermore, although the Constitution and historic precedents give structure to the office, the powers of the presidency are so vague that incumbents have tremendous latitude to shape the office to their particular desires.

The presidency is not only highly *changeable* but also essentially *political.* On occasion, especially in times of crisis, presidents rule by asserting their constitutional prerogatives, but usually they are forced to govern by political maneuvering—by trying to persuade the many participants in the political process. This is a very complex task. Not only must they perform on the public stage of mass politics, but also they must master the intricacies of elite politics, a game played among skilled insiders. In the following chapters, we first examine "public politics" (chapters 2, 3, and 4) and then turn to the skills that presidents bring to relations with other public elites (chapters 5, 6, and 7). These separate dimensions are linked in discussions of major policy areas (chapters 8, 9, and 10).

Suggested Readings

Corwin, Edward S. *The President: Office and Powers, 1789–1984,* 5th ed. New York: New York University Press, 1984.

Ellis, Richard J., ed. *Founding the American Presidency.* Lanham, MD: Rowman and Littlefield, 1999.

Farrand, Max, ed. *The Records of the Federal Convention of 1787.* New Haven, CT: Yale University Press, 1911.

Lowi, Theodore J. *The Personal President: Power Invested, Promise Unfulfilled.* Ithaca, NY: Cornell University Press, 1985.

McDonald, Forrest. *The American Presidency: An Intellectual History.* Lawrence: University Press of Kansas, 1994.

Milkis, Sidney M., & Michael Nelson. *The American Presidency: Origins and Development, 1776–2007,* 5th ed. Washington, DC: CQ Press, 2007.

Nelson, Michael, ed. *The Presidency and the Political System,* 9th ed. Washington, DC: CQ Press, 2010.

Neustadt, Richard E. *Presidential Power: The Politics of Leadership.* New York: Wiley, 1960.

Rudalevige, Andrew. *The New Imperial Presidency: Renewing Presidential Power after Watergate.* Ann Arbor: University of Michigan Press, 2006.

Skowronek, Stephen. *The Politics Presidents Make: Leadership from John Adams to Bill Clinton,* rev ed. Cambridge, MA: Harvard University Press, 1997.

Yoo, John. *The Powers of War and Peace: The Constitution and Foreign Affairs after 9/11.* Chicago: University of Chicago Press, 2006.

Resources on the Web

For extensive information about the Constitutional Convention of 1787, see teaching http://americanhistory.org/convention/introduction/.

For an up-to-date list of presidential signing statements, see www.presidency.ucsb.edu/signingstatements.php.

Notes

1. Richard E. Neustadt, *Presidential Power: The Politics of Leadership* (New York: Wiley, 1960), 26.

2. Stephen Skowronek, *The Politics Presidents Make: Leadership from John Adams to George Bush* (Cambridge, MA: Harvard University Press, 1993), 20.

3. Quoted in Forrest McDonald, *The American Presidency: An Intellectual History* (Lawrence: University Press of Kansas, 1994), 127.

4. McDonald, *The American Presidency,* 126.

5. Richard J. Ellis, ed., *Founding the American Presidency* (Lanham, MD: Rowman and Littlefield, 1999), 1.

6. McDonald, *The American Presidency,* 132–133.

7. Richard M. Pious, *The American Presidency* (New York: Basic Books, 1979), 23.

8. Sidney M. Milkis and Michael Nelson, *The American Presidency: Origins and Development, 1776–1993,* 2nd ed. (Washington, DC: CQ Press, 1994), 5. One of the drafters of the New York Constitution, Gouverneur Morris, later influenced the creation of presidential power at the 1787 Constitutional Convention.

9. Thomas Jefferson, *Notes on the State of Virginia,* quoted in Ellis, *Founding the American Presidency,* 4.

10. Charles C. Thach Jr., *The Creation of the Presidency, 1775–1789: A Study in Constitutional History* (Baltimore, MD: Johns Hopkins University Press, 1923), chap. 3.

11. Pious, *The American Presidency,* 22.

12. McDonald, *The American Presidency,* 151.

13. Quoted in Ellis, *Founding the American Presidency,* 6.

14. Milkis and Nelson, *The American Presidency,* 13–14.

15. McDonald, *The American Presidency,* 163.

16. Ibid., 164.

17. Ellis, *Founding the American Presidency,* 31–32.

18. McDonald, *The American Presidency,* 164; see also Max Farrand, ed., *The Records of the Federal Convention of 1787* (New Haven, CT: Yale University Press, 1911), 1:65.

19. Farrand, *Records,* 1:65.

20. Ibid., 1:244.

21. Ellis, *Founding the American Presidency,* 13.

22. This paragraph is based on McDonald, *The American Presidency,* 157.

23. Ibid., 171.

24. Ellis, *Founding the American Presidency,* 112–113.

25. We use the term *Congress* loosely here. As we have pointed out, the original recommendation of the Committee on Postponed Matters called for the *Senate* alone to choose from among the top five presidential candidates. As finally ratified, the Constitution called for the *House* alone to choose from the top five candidates. After the ratification of the Twelfth Amendment in 1804, the Constitution called for the House to choose from among the top *three* presidential candidates.

26. Quoted in Andrew Rudalevige, *The New Imperial Presidency* (Ann Arbor: The University of Michigan Press, 2006), 22.

27. This account of the Committee on Postponed Matters is drawn largely from McDonald, *The American Presidency,* 176–178; see also Milkis and Nelson, *The American Presidency,* 21–22.

28. Edward S. Corwin, *The President: Office and Powers,* 4th ed. (New York: New York University Press, 1957), 12.

29. Quoted in Michael Nelson, ed., *Guide to the Presidency,* 2nd ed. (Washington, DC: CQ Press, 1996), 30. Although this sort of hostility toward a strong executive was common among anti-Federalists, Herbert J. Storing has pointed out that there are greater differences of opinion among them than one might expect. Some anti-Federalists continued to argue for a plural executive or an executive council, but others agreed that a unitary executive was necessary. Storing points out that among anti-Federalists there was even "a fair amount of sympathy for a strong (even, under some circumstances, a hereditary) executive to resist the aristocratic tendencies of the legislature; and some of the Anti-Federalists objected that the President would be too weak to stand up to the Senate and would become a mere tool of aristocratic domination." Herbert J. Storing, ed., *The Complete Anti-Federalist* (Chicago: University of Chicago Press, 1981), 1:49.

30. Alexander Hamilton, *Federalist* No. 70.

31. Thach, *The Creation of the Presidency,* 138.

32. Ibid., 139.

33. Alexander Hamilton, "Pacificus, #1," June 29, 1793, http://press-pubs.uchicago.edu/founders/documents/a2_2_2–3s14.html.

34. William Howard Taft, *Our Chief Magistrate and His Powers* (New York: Columbia University Press, 1916), 139–140.

35. Theodore Roosevelt, *Autobiography* (New York: Macmillan, 1913), 388–389.

36. Taft, *Our Chief Magistrate,* 144–145.

37. Quoted in Corwin, *The President,* 8 (emphasis added).

38. Clinton Rossiter, *Constitutional Dictatorship* (Princeton, NJ: Princeton University Press, 1948).

39. Interview with Richard Nixon by David Frost, televised May 19, 1977; quoted in Craig Ducat, *Constitutional Interpretation,* 7th ed. (Belmont, CA: West, 2000), 206.

40. Charles Babington, "Critics of Guantánamo Urge Hill to Intervene," *Washington Post,* June 16, 2005, A2.

41. Dana Priest, "CIA Holds Terror Suspects in Secret Prisons; Debate Is Growing within Agency about Legality and Morality of Overseas System Set Up after 9/11," *Washington Post,* November 2, 2005, A1.

42. "Bush: CIA Holds Terror Suspects in Secret Prisons," CNN.com, September 7, 2006.

43. Christopher S. Kelley, "Rethinking Presidential Power: The Unitary Executive and the George W. Bush Presidency" (paper presented at the annual meeting of the Midwest Political Science Association, Chicago, April 7–10, 2005), 25. The two memos are Jay S. Bybee, "Memorandum for Alberto Gonzales, Re: Standards of Conduct for Interrogation under 18 U.S.C. Sections 2340–2340A," Office of Legal Counsel, August 1, 2002 (full text at www.washingtonpost.com/wp-srv/nation/documents/dojinterrogation memo20020801.pdf); and John Yoo, "Memorandum to The Honorable Alberto R. Gonzales," Office of Legal Counsel, August 1, 2001.

44. Scott Shane, "Report Questions Legality of Briefings on Surveillance," *New York Times,* January 19, 2006, A19. The *New York Times* first reported the administration's use of domestic wiretaps in December 2005: James Risen and Eric Lichtblau, "Bush Lets U.S. Spy on Callers without Courts," *New York Times,* December 15, 2005, A1.

45. Edward Epstein, "Wiretap Defense Invokes Lincoln, Roosevelt; Attorney General Says They Didn't Get Warrants, Either," *San Francisco Chronicle*, January 25, 2006, A3.

46. Scott Shane and Mark Landler, "Obama Clears Way for Guantánamo Bay Trials," *New York Times*, March 7, 2011, www.nytimes.com/2011/03/08/world/americas/08guantanamo.html.

47. Corwin, *The President*, 30.

48. Arthur M. Schlesinger Jr., *The Imperial Presidency*, 2nd ed. (Boston: Houghton Mifflin, 1989).

49. Kelley, "Rethinking Presidential Power."

50. Christopher S. Yoo, Steven G. Calabresi, and Anthony J. Colangelo, "The Unitary Executive in the Modern Era," *Iowa Law Review* 90 (January 2005): 606.

51. *Humphrey's Executor v. United States*, 295 U.S. 602 (1935).

52. *Myers v. United States*, 272 U.S. 52 (1926). In 1988, the Court ruled in *Morrison v. Olson*, 487 U.S. 654, that Congress could limit the power to remove an independent counsel, even though an independent counsel is a purely executive official performing a purely executive function. The lone dissenter was Justice Antonin Scalia.

53. McDonald, *The American Presidency*, 173–174.

54. Louis Fisher, *Constitutional Conflicts between Congress and the President*, 5th ed. (Lawrence: University Press of Kansas, 2007), chap. 9.

55. Richard M. Pious, "Inherent War and Executive Powers and Prerogative Politics," *Presidential Studies Quarterly* 37 (March 2007): 77.

56. John C. Yoo, "Memorandum Opinion for the Deputy Counsel to the President: The President's Constitutional Authority to Conduct Military Operations against Terrorists and Nations Supporting Them," September 25, 2001. The full text of the memorandum is posted at the U.S. Department of Justice website at www.justice.gov/sites/default/files/olc/opinions/2001/09/31/op-olc-v025-p0188_0.pdf. Yoo's book, *The Powers of War and Peace: The Constitution and Foreign Affairs after 9/11* (Chicago: University of Chicago Press, 2005), explicates this theory.

57. Pious, "Inherent War and Executive Powers," 70.

58. Fisher, *Constitutional Conflicts*, chap. 8.

59. For a defense of congressional-executive agreements, see John C. Yoo, "Laws as Treaties? The Constitutionality of Congressional-Executive Agreements," *Michigan Law Review* 99 (February 2001): 757. For a critique of congressional-executive agreements, including the argument that NAFTA is unconstitutional, see Laurence H. Tribe, "Taking Text and Structure Seriously: Reflections on Free-form Method in Constitutional Interpretation," *Harvard Law Review* 108 (April 1995): 1221.

60. American Bar Association Task Force on Presidential Signing Statements, "Report," August 2006, 7–14. The full text of the report is available at www.abanet.org/media/docs/signstatereport.pdf.

61. Kelley, "Rethinking Presidential Power," 27.

62. American Bar Association Task Force on Presidential Signing Statements, "Report," 14; Kelley, "Rethinking Presidential Power," 32. A single signing statement may contain multiple challenges. These figures relate to the number of specific challenges within signing statements rather than the total number of signing statements themselves.

63. American Bar Association Task Force on Presidential Signing Statements, "Report," 16.

64. Charlie Savage, "Bush Challenges Hundreds of Laws, President Cites Powers of His Office," *Boston Globe*, April 30, 2006, A1. Although this article is what brought public attention to Bush's use of signing statements, political scientist Christopher S. Kelley had already written a doctoral dissertation on the topic: Christopher S. Kelley, "The Unitary Executive and the Presidential Signing Statement" (PhD diss., Miami University, 2003).

65. Charlie Savage, "Obama Looks to Limit Impact of Tactic Bush Used to Sidestep New Laws," *New York Times,* March 10, 2009, A12.

66. Charlie Savage, "Obama Says He Can Ignore Some Parts of Spending Bill," *New York Times,* March 12, 2009, A18.

67. For a list of the signing statements and more background about signing statements, see *The American Presidency Project,* a website maintained at the University of California at Santa Barbara: www.presidency.ucsb.edu/signingstatements.php?year=2013&Submit=DISPLAY.

68. Jeffrey Rosen, "Bush's Leviathan State: Power of One," *New Republic,* July 24, 2006.

69. Fred Greenstein, "Change and Continuity in the Modern Presidency," in *The New American Political System,* ed. Anthony King (Washington, DC: American Enterprise Institute, 1978), 45–46.

70. See, for example, Corwin, *The President,* chap. 1.

71. Clinton Rossiter, *The American Presidency,* rev. ed. (New York: Harcourt, Brace, 1960), 102.

72. Jeffrey K. Tulis, *The Rhetorical Presidency* (Princeton, NJ: Princeton University Press, 1987), chap. 4.

73. Milkis and Nelson, *The American Presidency,* 208.

74. Tulis, *The Rhetorical Presidency,* chap. 5. Also see Jeffrey K. Tulis, "The Two Constitutional Presidencies," in *The Presidency and the Political System,* 6th ed., ed. Michael Nelson (Washington, DC: CQ Press, 2000).

75. Thomas Jefferson had discontinued the practice as an undesirable indication of monarchist tendencies.

76. William E. Leuchtenburg, *The Perils of Prosperity, 1914–1932,* 2nd ed. (Chicago: University of Chicago Press, 1993), 59.

77. William E. Leuchtenberg, *In the Shadow of FDR: From Harry Truman to Ronald Reagan,* rev. ed. (Ithaca, NY: Cornell University Press, 1985).

78. James L. Sundquist uses the term *economic stabilizer,* and earlier Clinton Rossiter had used the term *Manager of Prosperity.* See Sundquist, *The Decline and Resurgence of Congress* (Washington, DC: Brookings, 1981), chap. 4.

79. Ibid., 39.

80. Ibid., 33.

81. Ibid., 66–67.

82. Pious, "Inherent War and Executive Powers," 78. Legal challenges to the act were filed almost immediately, and in *Boumediene v. Bush,* 553 U.S. (2008) the U.S. Supreme Court ruled that detainees have the right to file habeas corpus petitions.

83. *Boumediene v. Bush,* 553 U.S. 723 (2008).

84. Edmund L. Andrews and Eric Dash, "U.S. Seeks Expanded Power in Seizing Firms," *New York Times,* March 24, 2009, online edition, www.nytimes.com/2009/03/25/business/economy/25webbailout.html; Hillary Stemple, "Obama Signs Financial Reform Legislation," *Jurist,* July 21, 2010, jurist.org/paperchase/2010/07/obama-signs-financial-reform-legislation.php.

85. Fisher, *Constitutional Conflicts,* 24.

86. *United States v. Midwest Oil Co., 236 U.S. 459 (1915)*

87. Corwin, *The President,* 175–177.

88. Gary King and Lyn Ragsdale, eds., *The Elusive Executive: Discovering Statistical Patterns in the Presidency* (Washington, DC: CQ Press, 1988), Table 4-1, 205. The precise size of presidential staff, however, is hard to calculate. For a discussion of this and an overview of the debates over how to count presidential staff, see John Hart, *The Presidential Branch: From Washington to Clinton,* 2nd ed. (Chatham, NJ: Chatham House, 1995), 43–45, 112–125.

89. Seymour Martin Lipset, *The First New Nation: The United States in Historical and Comparative Perspective* (New York: Norton, 1979), 18.

90. Bruce Buchanan, *The Citizen's Presidency: Standards of Choice and Judgment* (Washington, DC: CQ Press, 1987), 25, 28.

91. See especially Murray Edelman, *The Symbolic Uses of Politics* (Urbana: University of Illinois Press, 1964); and Fred I. Greenstein, "What the President Means to Americans: Presidential 'Choice' between Elections," in *Choosing the President*, ed. James David Barber (Englewood Cliffs, NJ: Prentice Hall, 1974).

92. Edelman, *The Symbolic Uses of Politics*, 76–77.

93. Greenstein, "What the President Means to Americans," 142–147. It should be noted that in this essay Greenstein deemphasized the likelihood that children socialized to a positive feeling about the president as an authority figure would extend this reliance on an "unconscious symbolic surrogate of childhood authority figures" into adulthood.

94. Murray Edelman, "The Politics of Persuasion," in Barber, *Choosing the President*, 172.

95. Barbara Hinckley, *The Symbolic Presidency: How Presidents Portray Themselves* (New York: Routledge, 1990), 5, 8.

96. As cited in Michael Novak, *Choosing Our King: Powerful Symbols in Presidential Politics* (New York: Macmillan, 1974), 44.

97. Theodore J. Lowi, *The Personal President: Power Invested, Promise Unfulfilled* (Ithaca, NY: Cornell University Press, 1985), xii.

CHAPTER 2

Election Politics

AP Photo

Before widespread air travel, candidates relied on whistle-stop tours conducted from a campaign train. Here, Harry S. Truman and his wife speak to a crowd in Philadelphia before his come-from-behind victory in the 1948 presidential election.

Just as the president is the focal point of public life for most Americans, it follows that the presidential election is the country's pivotal political event. More citizens participate in this process than in any other aspect of civic life—nearly 139 million in 2016—and their choices have enormous significance for the nation and, indeed, for the world. Historians break history into four-year blocks of time coinciding with presidential terms, and U.S. policymaking follows the same rhythm. The election is usually a unifying event, a collective celebration of democracy coming at the conclusion of an elaborate pageant replete with familiar rituals, colorful characters, and plot lines that capture attention despite being familiar.

Today's selection process bears little resemblance to what the founders outlined in the Constitution. Most of the changes have been extraconstitutional—that is, they have resulted from the evolution of political parties, media practices, and citizen expectations rather than constitutional amendments. There has been almost constant tinkering with the rules governing presidential elections, with most changes producing greater democratization. Remnants of **indirect democracy** persist, including the means used to select delegates to the party nominating conventions and voters in the Electoral College. The 2000 and 2016 elections, when George W. Bush and Donald J. Trump won in the Electoral College but lost the popular vote, renewed the debate about election rules. Bush's victory rested on winning all of Florida's electoral votes by a mere 537 votes out of nearly 6 million ballots. It took thirty-six days to settle the contest while Americans relearned the arcane workings of the Electoral College and discovered the fallibility of voting methods and counting rules. In contrast, Bush's reelection victory in 2004 was clear-cut, as were Barack Obama's in 2008 and 2012. Trump's win in 2016 once again triggered questions about the method Americans use to select their national executive.

At the conclusion of this chapter, we review recommendations for reform intended to improve system performance and provide for a greater degree of direct democracy. We first examine the major transformations in the nomination and general election phases of the process.

Evolution of the Selection Process

In 1789 and 1792, electing a president was simple. Each member of the Electoral College cast two votes, one of which had to be for a person outside the elector's state. Both times George Washington was elected by unanimous votes.[1] And both times John Adams received the second highest number of votes to become the vice president. In 1789, the process took three months: No one campaigned, electors were chosen on the first Wednesday of January, they met in their respective states to vote on the first Wednesday in February, and the votes were counted on April 6. In 1792, the procedure took even less time. The contrast with today's process could not be sharper: Candidates now launch nomination campaigns two years or more before the general election, collectively spending a billion dollars or more in pursuit of the office, and everyone expects to know the winner on election night.

Consensus support for Washington ensured smooth operation of the selection procedure during the first two elections: There was widespread confidence that the nation's wartime hero would govern in the interest of all the people. When political consensus eroded, elites developed a separate nomination procedure. Policy differences in Congress created the basis for an important institution not mentioned in the Constitution—the political party. By the early 1790s, the Federalist Party had formed around the economic policies of Secretary of the Treasury Alexander Hamilton, and his supporters in Congress backed his programs.[2] Resigning as secretary of state in 1793, Thomas Jefferson joined James Madison, then serving in the House of Representatives, as a critic of Hamilton's policies, and they formed the rival Republican Party, which came to be known as the Democratic-Republican Party.[3] By the mid-1790s, cohesive pro- and anti-administration blocs had formed in Congress, and congressional candidates were labeled either Democratic-Republicans or Federalists.[4]

Political parties had an almost immediate impact on the Electoral College. Electors became party loyalists, whose discipline was apparent in 1800, when Jefferson, the Democratic-Republicans' candidate for president, and Aaron Burr, the party's candidate for vice president, tied in the Electoral College vote. Loyal to their party, the electors had cast their ballots for both candidates, but the Constitution had no provision for counting the ballots separately for president and vice president. Jefferson and Burr each received seventy-three votes to President Adams's sixty-five. The House of Representatives decided the election, where Jefferson won after thirty-six ballots. Hamilton broke the tie by throwing his support behind Jefferson, his longtime rival. Party loyalty, with infrequent exceptions, has prevailed in Electoral College balloting ever since. (The Twelfth Amendment to the Constitution, ratified in 1804, provided for separate presidential and vice presidential balloting.[5])

The rise of parties also altered presidential selection by creating a separate nomination stage: The parties had to devise a method for choosing their nominees. Influence over presidential selection shifted from the local notables who had served as electors to party elites. In 1796, the Federalists' leaders chose their candidate, John Adams, and the Democratic-Republicans relied on their party members in Congress, the **congressional caucus,** to nominate Jefferson. Four years later, the congressional caucus became the nominating mechanism for both parties, a practice that continued until 1824, when the system broke down.

The caucus system meant that a party's members of Congress, already assembled in the nation's capital and facing minimal transportation problems, selected a nominee. Because legislators were familiar with potential presidential candidates from all parts of the new country, they were the logical agents for choosing candidates for an office with a nationwide constituency. Caucuses provided peer review of candidates' credentials: Essentially, a group of politicians assessed a fellow politician's skills, abilities, and political appeal. But the congressional caucus violated the constitutional principle of separation of powers by giving members of the legislative body a routine role in choosing the president rather than an emergency role, assumed only in the event of an Electoral College deadlock. The caucus also could not represent areas in which the party had lost the previous congressional election, a problem quickly encountered by the Federalists, whose support was largely limited to New England. Moreover, interested and informed citizens who participated in grassroots party activities, especially campaigns, had no means to participate in congressional caucus deliberations.

The 1824 election brought an end to nomination by congressional caucus. First, the Democratic-Republicans in Congress insisted on nominating Secretary of the Treasury William Crawford, who had recently suffered a debilitating stroke. Then, in the general election, Andrew Jackson, nominated by the Tennessee legislature, won more popular votes and more electoral votes than any other candidate but failed to achieve a majority in the Electoral College. The election again was decided by the House, where John Quincy Adams emerged victorious after he agreed to make Henry Clay, another of the five contestants, secretary of state in return for his support. These shenanigans permanently discredited *King Caucus,* as its critics called it. Favorite sons nominated by state legislatures and state conventions dominated the 1828 campaign, but this method proved too decentralized to select a national official. A device was needed that would represent party elements throughout the country, tap the new participatory fervor, and facilitate the nomination of a candidate.

National Party Conventions

What developed was the **party nominating convention**, an assembly made truly national by including delegates from all the states. Rail transportation made such meetings feasible, and the expanding citizen participation in presidential elections made the change necessary. Influence over selection of the party nominee, therefore, shifted to state and local party leaders, particularly those able to commit large blocs of delegate votes to a candidate.

Two minor parties with no appreciable representation in Congress, the Anti-Masons and the National Republicans, led the way with conventions in 1831.[6] To rally support in 1832, the Democrats, under President Andrew Jackson (elected in 1828), also held a convention. Major political parties have nominated their presidential and vice presidential candidates by holding national conventions ever since. National committees composed of state party leaders call the presidential nominating conventions into session to choose nominees and to adopt a platform of common policy positions.[7] Delegates are selected by states and allocated primarily on the basis of population.

Although today's conventions in some ways resemble those of the past, the nomination process has undergone drastic revision, especially after 1968, when Democrats introduced reforms that diminished the conventions' importance. Just as influence over selection of the party nominee shifted from Congress to party leaders, it has moved within the party from a small group of organization professionals to a broad base of activists and voters. The origins of this shift can be traced to the development of presidential primary elections that began early in the twentieth century. (Florida passed the first primary election law in 1901.)

Under the system that operated from roughly 1850 to 1950, party leaders from the largest states could bargain over presidential nominations. Most influential were those who controlled large blocs of delegates and would throw their support behind a candidate for the right price. These power brokers—hence the term **brokered conventions**—might seek a program commitment in the platform, a position in the president's cabinet, or other forms of federal patronage in return for support. To be successful, candidates had to curry favor with party and elected officials before and during the national convention. An effective campaign manager might tour the country selling the candidate's virtues and securing delegate commitments prior to the convention, but about half the conventions began with no sense of the likely outcome. Protracted bargaining and negotiation among powerful state and local party leaders were often the result. In 1924, the Democrats were badly divided over the role of the Ku Klux Klan and needed 103 ballots cast over seventeen days to nominate John W. Davis, an effort that must have seemed pointless later when he attracted only 29 percent of the popular vote. Nevertheless, the convention was a deliberative body that reached decisions on common policy positions as well as on nominees. Providing a way to accommodate the demands of major elements within the party established the base for a nationwide campaign.

In this respect, modern conventions are quite different. Not since 1952, when the Democrats needed three ballots to nominate Governor Adlai Stevenson of Illinois for president, has it taken more than one ballot to determine either party's nominee.[8] Even predictions that Trump's 2016 opponents would use multiple ballots to block his nomination did not come to pass. Raucous floor battles over procedures and delegate credentials have given way to a stream of symbols and speakers whose appearances are carefully choreographed to appeal to a prime-time television audience. Conventions now serve as ratifying assemblies for a popular choice made during the preceding primary elections rather than deliberative bodies, and candidates with popular appeal have the advantage over those whose appeal is primarily with party leaders.

Although much of the convention's business is still conducted in backroom meetings, the most important business—choosing the presidential nominee—already has been decided through the grueling process used to select convention delegates. Compared with their forerunners, modern conventions conduct their business in a routine fashion, adhere to enforceable national party standards for delegate selection and demographic representation, and are more heavily influenced by rank-and-file party supporters than by party leaders.[9] These changes appeared gradually through a process often fraught with conflict that centered on the rules governing delegate selection.

Reform of the Selection Process

The pace of change accelerated when the Democratic Party adopted internal reforms after it lost the presidency in 1968. In addition to the actions already noted, rules adopted by a variety of actors—one hundred state political parties and fifty legislatures, the national political parties, and Congress—reformed the process, and they continue to modify it. Sometimes individuals turned to the courts to interpret provisions of these regulations and reconcile conflicts. In addition, the rules were adjusted so drastically and so often that, particularly in the Democratic Party, candidates and their supporters found it difficult to keep up.

Reform has been especially pervasive in the nomination process. Following their tumultuous convention in 1968, when Vietnam War protesters clashed with police in the streets of Chicago, the Democrats adopted a set of guidelines that reduced the influence of party leaders, encouraged participation by rank-and-file Democrats, and expanded convention representation of previously underrepresented groups, particularly youth, women, and African Americans. The result was a pronounced shift of influence within the party from *party professionals* toward *amateurs,* a term encompassing citizens who become engaged in the presidential contest because of a short-term concern, such as an attractive candidate (candidate enthusiasts) or an especially important issue (issue enthusiasts).

States, seeking to conform to the party's new guidelines on participation, adopted the **primary** as the preferred means of selecting convention delegates. Primaries allow a party's registered voters—and, in some states, Independents—to express a presidential preference that is translated into convention delegates. The **party caucus** is another way to select delegates. The caucus is a local meeting of registered party voters that often involves speeches and discussion about the candidates' merits. A caucus is more social, public, and time-consuming (often requiring two hours to complete) than a primary, in which voters make choices in the privacy of the voting booth. The caucus method is also multistage: Delegates from the local caucuses go to a county convention that selects delegates to a state convention that selects the national delegates. In 1968, only seventeen states chose delegates through primaries, the remainder using caucuses dominated by party leaders. In 2016, of the fifty-one contests (including D.C.) thirty-six states held primaries in both parties, twelve states used caucuses in both parties, and three states held a primary in one party and a caucus in the other.[10] Because of these changes, nominations are more apt to reflect the voters' immediate concerns, nominees are unofficially chosen well before the convention, and the influence of party leaders is reduced. The cost of these changes is the loss of peer review—politicians evaluating the capability of fellow politicians. Moreover, the changes have enhanced the importance of the media. By operating as the principal source of information about the candidates and by emphasizing the "horse race"—who is ahead—the media have become enormously influential during the delegate selection process. Not everyone was satisfied with the general movement toward a more democratized selection process, as evidenced by several counter reforms that appeared during the 1980s.

The Contemporary Selection Process

Despite the seemingly perpetual flux that characterizes presidential elections, it is possible to identify four broad stages in the process: (1) defining the pool of eligible candidates; (2) nominating the parties' candidates at the national conventions following delegate selection in the primaries and caucuses; (3) waging the general election campaign, culminating in election day; and (4) validating results through the Electoral College.

No two presidential election cycles are identical, but the customary timeline is relatively predictable (see Figure 2-1). Potential candidates actively maneuver for position during the one or two years preceding the election. Selection of convention delegates begins in January and February of the election year, with conventions typically scheduled first for the **out party**, the one seeking the White House.[11] Traditionally, the general election campaign begins on Labor Day and runs until election day, the first Tuesday after the first Monday in November, but modern campaigns really begin once the major parties' nominees become clear. When the nomination contest is heated, we may not know the nominees until June, as happened in 2008 when Senator Obama and Sen. Hillary Rodham Clinton fought to the end. In 2016, the parties' nominating conventions were held in late July, so the general election

FIGURE 2-1 The 2016 Presidential Contest Timeline

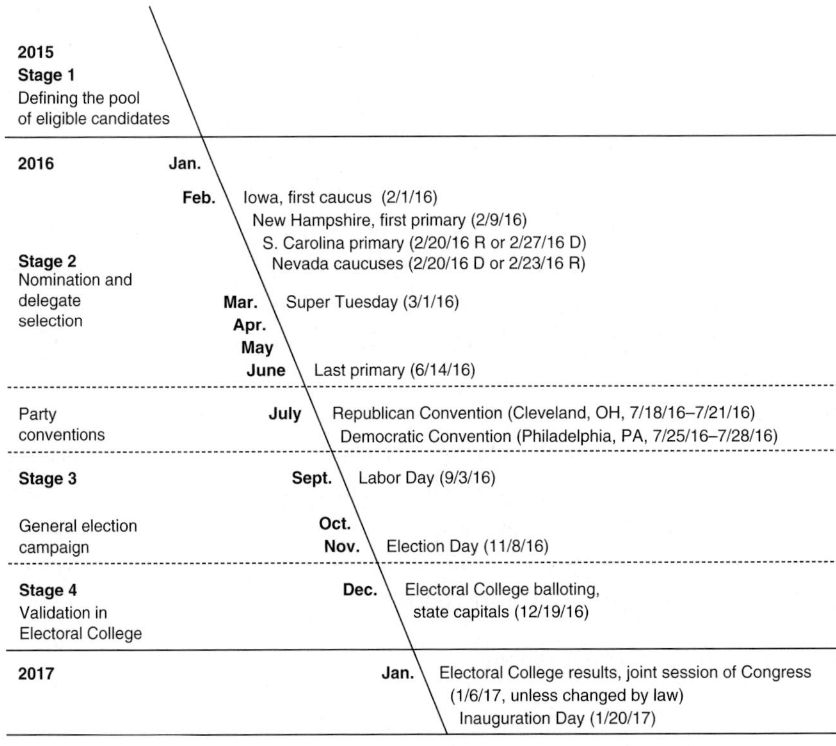

campaign began a full month earlier. Unlike in 2000, voters usually know the general election winner on election night, and the mid-December balloting by electors in their state capitals is usually automatic. Finally, the electors' ballots are officially tabulated the first week in January during a joint session of the U.S. Congress, presided over by the incumbent vice president. The duly elected president is inaugurated on January 20, a date set in the Twentieth Amendment. (A separate, public swearing-in took place on January 21, 2013, for Obama, because the 20th fell on a Sunday.)

Defining the Pool of Eligibles

Who is eligible to serve as president? The formal rules relating to qualifications are minimal and have been remarkably stable over time. Individuals need to meet only three requirements set forth in Article 2, section 1 of the Constitution. One must be a natural-born citizen, at least thirty-five years of age, and a resident of the

United States for fourteen years or longer. In 2016, more than 135 million Americans met these constitutional requirements, but the pool of plausible candidates was far smaller.[12]

From time to time, a candidate whose citizenship is questioned seeks the presidency. Large numbers of Americans erroneously believed that Obama was born in Kenya, not Hawaii as his birth certificate makes clear. Both George Romney (candidate in 1968) and John McCain (nominee in 2008) were born to American parents outside U.S. territory (in Mexico and the Panama Canal Zone, respectively). Barry Goldwater (nominee in 1964) was born in Arizona before it was a state. The Supreme Court has never ruled on the meaning of the Constitution's "natural born" requirement, but the Congressional Research Service, which is charged with advising Congress on a host of legal issues concluded in 2011 that "the weight of legal and historical authority indicates that the term 'natural born' citizen would mean a person who is entitled to U.S. citizenship 'by birth' or 'at birth,' either by being born 'in' the United States and under its jurisdiction, even those born to alien parents" or "by being born abroad to U.S. citizen-parents."[13] In 2016, Republican candidate Sen. Ted Cruz was born to a U.S. citizen mother and a Cuban father in Canada. Anticipating questions, two former solicitors general of the United States wrote in the *Harvard Law Review* that both British common law and actions of the first Congress defined "natural born" as someone who does not have to go through the naturalization process to become a citizen.[14] Cruz met that criterion and finished second in the Republican balloting.

The informal requirements for the presidency are less easily satisfied. People who entertain presidential ambitions must have **political availability**, the political experiences and personal characteristics that make them attractive to political activists and to the general voting public. Potential candidates accumulate these credentials through personal and career decisions made long before the election year, but there is no explicit checklist of informal qualifications for the presidency. One method to determine what particular political experiences and personal characteristics put an individual in line for a nomination is to look at past candidates, but the attitudes of political leaders and the public change over time, as was evident in 2016.

Political Experience of Candidates

Who is nominated to run for president? Until 2016, the answer had been people with experience in one of a few civilian, elective, political offices or the military. Nominees' backgrounds had changed very little since the second half of the nineteenth century.[15] Since 1932, with only two exceptions, major-party nominees had been drawn from one of four positions: (1) the presidency, (2) the vice presidency, (3) a state governorship, or (4) a U.S. Senate seat. (See Appendix B.) Candidates with other backgrounds were unsuccessful. In 2000, five aspirants who lacked experience in elected office unsuccessfully sought the Republican nomination. In 1992, H. Ross Perot, a billionaire businessman, sought election without a party nomination and did so again in 1996, as nominee of the Reform Party. Republicans considered Herman Cain, a businessman, in 2012, but non-politicians Donald Trump, Carly Fiorina and Ben Carson ran in 2016 with Trump the surprise nominee. Trump is the first major party nominee in history to have no record of public service—elected, appointed, or military—before entering the presidency.

Presidents and Vice Presidents. Since 1932, the party controlling the presidency has turned to the presidency or vice presidency for candidates, and the out party has turned primarily to governors and secondarily to senators. In only three of the twenty-two elections from 1932 to 2016 was the name of an incumbent president or vice president not on the ballot. Fifteen times, the incumbent president was renominated, and in four of the seven instances when the incumbent president was either prohibited by the Twenty-Second Amendment from running again (Dwight D. Eisenhower in 1960, Ronald Reagan in 1988, Bill Clinton in 2000, George W. Bush in 2008, Barack Obama in 2016) or declined to do so (Harry S. Truman in 1952 and Lyndon B. Johnson in 1968), the incumbent vice president won his party's nomination. The exceptions occurred in 1952, 2008, and 2016. When Truman halted his reelection effort in 1952, Adlai Stevenson became the nominee rather than the vice president, seventy-five-year-old Alben Barkley. In 2008 and 2016, the incumbent party had an open competition for the presidential nomination because Vice Presidents Dick Cheney and Joe Biden chose not to pursue the office.

There are no guarantees that an incumbent president will be renominated, but it is enormously difficult for the party in power to remove these leaders from the national ticket. Party leaders are reluctant to admit they made a mistake four years earlier, incumbents can direct federal programs toward politically important areas or make politically useful executive branch appointments, and presidents enjoy far greater name recognition and media exposure than others seeking the nomination. Even unpopular presidents are renominated. The Republicans chose Gerald R. Ford despite an energy crisis and slow economy. Democrats renominated Jimmy Carter when both inflation and unemployment were high, Americans were being held hostage in Iran, and Soviet troops occupied Afghanistan.

Incumbent vice presidents who choose to run are more likely to win their party's nomination today than in the past.[16] Recent presidential candidates have chosen running mates who are arguably more capable than their predecessors, which makes these individuals more viable prospects for the presidency. Moreover, presidents now assign their vice presidents meaningful responsibilities, including political party activities (especially campaigning in off-year elections), liaison assignments with social groups, and diplomatic missions abroad. As the position's visibility and significance have increased, so have the political chances of its occupants improved.[17]

If it is an asset in securing the party's nomination, the vice presidency once seemed a liability in winning the general election. George H. W. Bush's victory in 1988 broke a 152-year-old record of losing campaigns. Richard Nixon, Hubert Humphrey, and Al Gore lost as incumbent vice presidents in 1960, 1968, and 2000.

Senators and Governors. From 1932 through 2016, the party out of power nominated eleven governors, six senators, two former vice presidents, one general (Eisenhower), and two businessmen (Wendell Willkie and Trump). (See Table 2-1.) Both major parties have looked to governors as promising candidates, except for the period from 1960 to 1972, when Sen. John F. Kennedy (D-1960), Sen. Barry Goldwater (R-1964), Sen. George McGovern (D-1972), and former vice president Nixon (R-1968) won the nomination. Governorships later regained prominence with the nomination of former governors Carter (D-1976), Reagan (R-1980), and Mitt Romney (R-2012); and sitting governors Michael Dukakis (D-1988), Bill Clinton (D-1992), and George W. Bush (R-2000). In the other five elections since 1960 the party out of power turned to a former vice president (Walter Mondale, the Democratic nominee in 1984), to senators (Robert Dole in 1996, John Kerry in 2004, and Obama in 2008), and of course to businessman/TV personality Trump in 2016.

These patterns may understate the importance of the Senate as a recruiting ground for president. Many senators have sought their parties' presidential nomination since the early 1950s. Senators share the political and media spotlight focused on the capital, enjoy the opportunity to address major public problems and develop a record in foreign affairs, and they usually can pursue the presidency without leaving the Senate. Nevertheless, only three times in American history have senators been elected directly to the White House (Warren Harding in 1920, Kennedy in 1960, and Obama in 2008).[18]

Instead of a stepping-stone to the presidency, the Senate has been a path to the vice presidency, which then gave its occupants the inside track either to assume the

TABLE 2-1 Principal Experience of In- and Out-Party Candidates before Gaining Nomination, 1932–2016

Election Year	*In Party*	*Out Party*
1932	President (R)	Governor (D)
1936	President (D)	Governor (R)
1940	President (D)	Businessman (R)
1944	President (D)	Governor (R)
1948	President (D)	Governor (R)
1952	Governor (D)	General/educator (R)
1956	President (R)	Governor (former) (D)
1960	Vice president (R)	Senator (D)
1964	President (D)	Senator (R)
1968	Vice president (D)	Vice president (former) (R)
1972	President (R)	Senator (D)
1976	President (R)	Governor (former) (D)
1980	President (D)	Governor (former) (R)
1984	President (R)	Vice president (former) (D)
1988	Vice president (R)	Governor (D)
1992	President (R)	Governor (D)
1996	President (D)	Senator (R)
2000	Vice president (D)	Governor (R)
2004	President (R)	Senator (D)
2008	Senator (R)	Senator (D)
2012	President (D)	Governor (former) (R)
2016	Former senator, former secretary of state (D)	Businessman/ TV personality (R)

presidency through succession or to win nomination on their own. Vice Presidents Truman, Nixon, Johnson, Humphrey, Mondale, Quayle, Gore, and Biden served as senators immediately before assuming their executive posts. (Ford, who succeeded to the presidency when Nixon resigned in 1974, had moved into the vice presidency from the House of Representatives. Dick Cheney, elected vice president in 2000 and 2004, had served in the House before becoming secretary of defense and was then a businessman.) Service in the Senate, therefore, has been an important source of experience for presidents since 1932, but almost all have gained seasoning in the vice presidency.

Until 2008, governors seemed to have a competitive advantage over senators. Bill Clinton and George W. Bush moved directly into the Oval Office from a governor's mansion. Two others—Carter and Reagan—were former governors who were free to devote themselves full time to the demanding task of winning the nomination, an opportunity not available to the senators who sought the presidency in those years. Governors can claim valuable executive experience in managing large-scale public enterprises and thousands of state government employees, in contrast to a senator's legislative duties and direction of a small personal staff. Moreover, the public's concern with foreign affairs declined after 1976 and was replaced by anxiety over the domestic economy, taxes, the budget, education, and health care. This shift in public attitudes was especially evident in 1992 and 2000, when Clinton and Bush benefited from the Cold War's reduced prominence during their successful election campaigns.

With the terrorist attacks of 9/11, public concerns once again shifted to national security, which may have boosted senators over governors in the nomination contest. At the outset of 2008, it seemed the war in Iraq would be the dominant issue, again giving senators prominence, but public attention shifted during the year to domestic issues, led by the economy. The Democratic candidates included four sitting senators (Biden, Clinton, Dodd, and Obama), two former senators (Edwards, Gravel), one House member (Kucinich), one sitting governor (Richardson), and one former governor (Vilsack). Among Republican contestants were two sitting senators (Brownback, McCain), one former senator (F. Thompson), four former governors (Gilmore, Huckabee, Romney, and T. Thompson), three sitting members of the House (Hunter, Paul, and Tancredo), and one former mayor (Giuliani). In 2012, Republicans examined the credentials of one sitting governor (Perry), three former governors (Huntsman, Pawlenty, and Romney), two House members (Bachmann, Paul), one former House Speaker (Gingrich), one former senator (Santorum), and a businessman (Cain).

In 2016, Republicans needed a spreadsheet to keep track of their seventeen candidates, while Democrats faced a less complex contest. Republican candidates included four current senators, Ted Cruz (Texas), Rand Paul (Kentucky), Marco Rubio (Florida), and Lindsey Graham (South Carolina); one former senator, Rick Santorum (Pennsylvania); four sitting governors, Chris Christie (New Jersey), Bobby Jindal (Louisiana), John Kasich (Ohio), and Scott Walker (Wisconsin); five former governors, Jeb Bush (Florida), Jim Gilmore (Virginia), Mike Huckabee (Arkansas), George Pataki (New York), and Rick Perry (Texas); a former pediatric neurosurgeon, Ben Carson; and a former Hewlett-Packard CEO, Carly Fiorina.[19] In late summer, the field was joined by billionaire businessman and television personality Donald Trump. Such widespread interest reflected Republican confidence that the White House would change hands in 2016, a belief that almost any reasonable candidate could raise enough money to launch a campaign, and a wide-open contest where there was no clear front-runner.

In sharp contrast, Hillary Clinton was the clear front-runner among Democrats pursuing the nomination and only four others joined the contest: former senator Jim Webb (Virginia), sitting senator Bernie Sanders (Vermont), former governor Martin O'Malley (Maryland), and former senator and former governor Lincoln Chafee (Rhode Island).[20]

Personal Characteristics of Candidates

Although millions meet the formal requirements for president, far fewer meet the informal criteria that have guided past choices. Most constraining have been the limits imposed by social conventions on gender and race, constraints that the Democrats challenged in 2008 and 2016. Until Obama's victory over Clinton for the nomination in 2008, only males of European heritage had been nominated for president by either of the two major parties, although several women and African Americans had waged national campaigns since 1972. Former representative Geraldine Ferraro of New York was the Democrats' 1984 nominee for vice president and Sarah Palin, governor of Alaska, was the Republicans' vice presidential nominee in 2008. In 2008, Bill Richardson became the first Latino to seek a major party's presidential nomination; two candidates of Cuban heritage were in the Republican field in 2016, Cruz and Rubio.

Presidential aspirants also have had to pass other "tests" based on personal characteristics, although these informal requirements have changed in the past five decades.[21] Until 1960, candidates had to meet unspoken demographic and religious requirements: that they hail from English ethnic stock and practice a Protestant religion. The successful candidacy of Kennedy, a Roman Catholic, challenged the traditional preference for Protestants. The Democrats nominated Alfred Smith, a Catholic, in 1928, but he lost the general election. Kerry's Catholicism was not an issue in 2004. The Republican senator Barry Goldwater was the first nominee from a partly Jewish background, and Sen. Joseph Lieberman, an Orthodox Jew, joined the Democratic ticket in 2000. Religion as an issue resurfaced in 2008 when critics incorrectly alleged that Obama was a Muslim and again in 2012, when Republican Mitt Romney became the first Mormon to win the nomination. Recent candidates have come from Irish, Norwegian, Greek, and Kenyan heritage, suggesting that the traditional preference for English stock has weakened. Clinton's heritage is English/Welsh and Trump's ethnic background is also traditional, German (father) and Scottish (mother).

Representing an idealized version of home and family life also seemed essential to winning nomination. Nelson Rockefeller's divorce in 1963 from his wife of more than thirty years and his rapid remarriage virtually ensured the failure of his campaign for the Republican nomination in 1964 and 1968. In 1980, Reagan became the first divorced and remarried president. Trump, now in his third marriage, is the second. Public attitudes about other moral and ethical questions may become deciding factors. Gary Hart's widely reported extramarital affair ended his presidential hopes for 1988, even though he began the campaign as the clear Democratic front-runner. Bill Clinton's alleged extramarital relationships and marijuana use became issues in 1992, but an admission of past alcohol abuse did not damage George W. Bush in 2000, nor did a youthful use of recreational drugs affect Barack Obama's prospects in 2008.

It appears, therefore, that several of the informal qualifications applied to the presidency have altered with the passage of time, probably because of changes in the nomination process itself as well as broader currents in U.S. society. One observer suggests that the proliferation of presidential primaries "provides a forum in which prejudices can be addressed openly,"[22] and the public is possibly becoming more tolerant. As demonstrated in 2008 and 2016 as African Americans, women, and descendants of immigrants from Asia, Latin America, and eastern and southern Europe occupy governorships and seats in the U.S. Senate, they enhance their chances of becoming serious candidates for the presidency.

AP Photo/Andrew Harnik

Fox News sponsored the first 2015–2016 presidential debate among ten Republican candidates. Sparks flew between candidates as well as between candidates and the debate moderators.

Competing for the Nomination

Once the pool of eligible candidates is established, the selection process begins. This phase has two major components: (1) choosing delegates to the two parties' national conventions and (2) selecting the nominees at the conventions. By far the more complicated of these steps, the selection of delegates, became the principal focus of party reform efforts after 1968 and continues to undergo change. Prior to the conventions, candidates crisscross the country to win delegates, who then attend the convention to select the party's nominee.

The first primary of 2016 was held in New Hampshire following the Iowa caucuses. Delegate selection concluded in June, when a handful of states held primaries. Through this complex process, the Republicans selected 2,472 convention delegates, and the Democrats 4,763. Consistent with post-1968 reforms, most delegates were chosen through primaries. Participation has been growing; in 2016 an estimated 57.68 million citizens voted in primaries, up sharply from 2000 and 2004 but down slightly from 2008.[23]

For 2016, Iowa, New Hampshire, Nevada, and South Carolina were again positioned to be the first four states selecting delegates. The calendar had Iowa conducting the first caucuses on February 1 and New Hampshire the first primary on February 9, 2016. Republican officials successfully prevented a repeat of 2012 when other states moved their events forward in the schedule; for 2016, states would have received severe delegate reductions for jumping the line and new rules rewarded states that delayed their events until after mid-March. The final primary was held in the District of Columbia on June 14, although several state conventions were slated to run through the remainder of the month.[24]

In truth, the nomination contest begins much earlier than January of the election year. By starting their campaigns early, candidates seek to amass the financial backing, attract the media attention, and generate the popular support necessary to ensure eventual victory. In contrast to 2007, when all the Democratic candidates had either announced their candidacy or launched exploratory committees by the end of January, most Republicans got off to a slow start in 2016. Ben Carson was first to announce in November 2014 and Ted Cruz followed in March 2015, but Donald Trump did not declare until June 2015 and several candidates were even later.

The Nomination Campaign

The nomination campaign is a winnowing process in which each of the two major parties eliminates from the pool of potential candidates all but the one who will represent the party in the general election. As political scientist Austin Ranney argued in 1974, the nomination phase of the campaign is more important than the election stage because "the parties' nominating processes eliminate far more presidential possibilities than do the voters' electing processes."[25] In the 1970s, aspirants typically did not know how many opponents they would face or who they would be. The competition took place in weekly stages, with candidates hopscotching the nation in pursuit of votes and contributions. First-time candidates had to organize a nationwide political effort, a chore that dwarfs the campaign required to win a Senate seat or governorship in even the largest states.

This competitive situation has changed. As more states moved their primaries to earlier spots in the schedule—a pattern called **front-loading**—the critical events take place during a very brief window near the beginning of the six-month process. Instead of having the opportunity to adjust strategy along the way, candidates need to establish campaign organizations in many states and to raise enormous sums of money early in the process. Many of the traditional uncertainties—for example, new candidates entering the competition—have become less likely, as early contests quickly trigger the departure of weaker candidates instead of creating opportunities for new entries.[26] In 2008, both parties chose 50 percent of their convention delegates by the end of the day on February 5, and more than three-quarters of all delegates by the first Tuesday in March.[27] But predictions for early nominations were proved wrong when the Democrats' contest extended into June. In 2012, both Republicans and Democrats tried unsuccessfully to slow down the process and lengthen it. Republicans desperately hoped that their rules changes would produce a more compressed process in 2016, producing early unity around a nominee. But as Trump's nomination began to appear inevitable, many establishment Republicans (members of the "Never Trump" group) regretted the changes they had introduced.

Presidential hopefuls spend considerable time before January of the election year laying the campaign's groundwork. Decades ago, journalist Arthur Hadley called this period the "invisible primary," a testing ground for the would-be president to determine whether his or her candidacy is viable.[28] Candidates must assemble a staff to help raise money, develop campaign strategy, hone a message, and identify a larger group of people willing to do the advance work necessary to organize states for the primaries and caucuses. Candidates visit party organizations throughout the country, especially in the two traditional early states, Iowa and New Hampshire, to curry favor with activists and solicit endorsements.[29] Democrats authorized two states—Nevada and South Carolina—to join the early group of contests in 2008, but Florida and Michigan then demanded to be added as well. The resulting legal and political challenges complicated candidates' strategies. A similar scramble occurred in 2012, again caused by Florida and Michigan as well as Nevada, which defied Republican efforts to start the process later. No such challenges to the calendar emerged in 2016.

Because media coverage provides name recognition and potentially positive publicity, developing a favorable relationship with reporters and commentators is crucial. Those hopefuls the media ignore because they do not regard them as serious contenders find it almost impossible to become viable candidates. Even the suggestion that some candidates are "top tier" and others "second tier," the terms widely used in 2008, 2012, and 2016 to sort the large fields, could adversely affect a candidacy. As Ranney suggested, most candidates' campaigns are scuttled, if not officially canceled, during the "invisible primary" stage.

Financing Nomination Campaigns

Candidates for the nomination must raise funds early to prepare for the competition. Dramatic changes occurred between 1976 and 2016 in how those funds are gathered. Federal funds became available for the first time in the 1976 election: Candidates could qualify to receive federal funds that matched individual contributions of $250 or less if they could raise $100,000 in individual contributions, with at least $5,000 collected in twenty different states. The intent was to shift funding away from a few wealthy "fat cats" to a broader base of contributors,[30] to help underdog candidates contest the nomination, and to enable candidates to remain in the race despite poor showings in early contests. A key goal was disclosure of contributions, a reform put into place following revelations of how President Nixon's campaign had used cash contributions to fund a variety of dirty tricks during the 1972 election.

By checking a box on their federal income tax forms, taxpayers authorized the government to set aside $3.00 of their tax payments for public financing of campaigns. The Federal Election Commission (FEC), a bipartisan body of six members nominated by the president and confirmed by the Senate, oversaw the administration of the public financing provisions. The changes were initially popular, but participation in the system dropped from 28.7 percent of all tax returns in 1980 to 6 percent in 2013.[31] Candidates also became less supportive; those who accept public financing must abide by limitations on total expenditures and a cap on spending in individual states that is based on population. As the competitive landscape shifted, most candidates preferred to avoid these limits. The 2004 election was the first in which both parties' nominees had declined federal matching funds.

In 2008, 2012, and 2016, the leading candidates also declined these funds, making the system's future bleak. Neither Obama nor Clinton used matching funds in 2008, and each raised totals that dwarfed those of previous candidates. Neither Trump nor Clinton used matching funds in 2016.[32] Today, only weak candidates rely on matching funds. In 2008, six candidates qualified for $21.73 million in matching funds, down from $62.26 million in 2000 and $28.4 million in 2004.[33] In 2012, no major-party candidate received matching funds—only three third-party candidates did so. Martin O'Malley was the only major party candidate to do so in 2016.

Between 1976 and 2012, candidates' personal wealth played a role in the prenomination stage and ultimately triggered the shift away from public funds. In 1996, Steve Forbes loaned his campaign $37.5 million. He was ultimately unsuccessful, but Forbes dramatically influenced the Republican nomination process by outspending his rivals in Iowa, New Hampshire, and several other early contests. Even Bob Dole, who led all candidates in fund-raising that year, could not match such expenditures because he had to observe the federal limits.[34] This experience shaped Bush's strategy in 2000. Anticipating that Forbes would pursue a similar tactic the second time around, Bush raised a record $94 million in private funds, double that of Forbes and McCain, his closest competitors; he, therefore, avoided the spending limits associated with public funding and the problems Dole had encountered.[35] When the emphasis was on small contributions, candidates solicited funds from large numbers of individuals through direct mail and later the web.[36] Although public funds reduced financial disparities among candidates, their financial resources were still highly unequal, and in most election years, the field's leading fund-raiser won the nomination.[37] As we saw in 2008 and 2012, there are no incentives for candidates to take public funds. The new system favors very wealthy candidates or those who—like Bush in 2000 and 2004, Clinton and Obama in 2008, and Romney in 2012—can tap or establish networks of donors during the invisible primary before the Iowa and New Hampshire contests, raising enough money early to turn down public funding and sail through to the end. Usually, the calendar of contests and funding system rules will also favor front-runners, making it hard for primary voters to give other candidates a second look.[38]

For 2016, observers anticipated that wealthy donors would be more important than ever. This expectation followed the Supreme Court's decision in 2010 in the case of *Citizens United v. Federal Election Commission,* which opened the doors to oceans of political cash. The decision allowed unions, corporations, and associations to spend unlimited amounts in elections and "paved the way for . . . the creation of super-PACs [political action committees], which can accept unlimited contributions from corporations, unions and individuals for the purpose of making independent expenditures," spending intended to influence the outcome of elections but not coordinated with a candidate's campaign.[39] Super-PACs must disclose their donors, giving them a bit of transparency, but they are often headed by candidates' political allies, making non-coordination highly questionable. Associates of both Romney and Obama operated super-PACs during the 2012 general election, claiming not to coordinate their activities with their preferred candidate.

Did super-PACs influence the 2012 Republican nomination race? Both Newt Gingrich ($17 million) and Rick Santorum ($7.6 million) benefited from super-PAC spending that helped to prolong their challenges to the front-runner and eventual nominee, Mitt Romney, who had money spent in his behalf, as well ($16.7 million). But super-PACs also spent large sums on ads *against* the candidates: $24.5 million against Santorum, more than $20 million against Gingrich, and $12.2 million against Romney.[40] Negative spending was especially strategic, intended to reduce damage to Romney from his opponents' successes in key states. Overall, there is no definitive evidence that Romney's campaign coordinated expenditures with the super-PACs that helped him, but it is clear that super-PACs complicate both the strategic calculations of candidates and the public's ability to follow the campaign's dynamics.

As always, politicians learn from the last contest, and new efforts emerged in 2016 to stretch loopholes in campaign finance laws. Before officially declaring his candidacy, Jeb Bush attended events to help raise money in support of a super-PAC pledged to support him, and it was expected that after disassociating himself from the group the PAC would assume responsibility for some of the activities traditionally associated with a campaign, such as television advertising and direct mail.[41] This would be a departure from 2012. Fearing that she would lose ground to her potential general election opponent, Hillary Clinton also began to work cooperatively with a Democratic super-PAC, attending fund-raising events though not asking for contributions herself.[42] Another super-PAC, Correct the Record, was created to monitor media coverage and campaign criticisms directed at Clinton; it would coordinate with her campaign but not be controlled by it, another nuance.[43]

For reformers concerned with the influence of money in politics, there was an even worse development in 2016: the rise of **nonprofit social welfare groups**. Like a super-PAC, donations to nonprofits are unlimited, but unlike their cousins, the donors need not be disclosed, creating what reformers call **dark money**. This money ostensibly must be spent on projects advancing the public good, in this case, financing ads that support the same issues advanced by a candidate. Money can be used to underwrite a potential candidate's travel, to conduct polling, and to build volunteer lists. Fears grew that "for the first time in a generation, there will be a clear avenue for America's richest to secretly spend an unchecked sum to choose their party's nominee for the White House."[44] By early 2015, four Republican candidates—Rick Perry, Rick Santorum, Bobby Jindal, and John Kasich—had such nonprofits helping them run for president using anonymous donations.

Despite all the concern about money flooding the system, two other stories dominated the 2016 nomination stage. Donald J. Trump emerged victorious after loudly proclaiming that he was the only "self-funded" candidate, thereby turning personal wealth into an asset because it made him beholden to no one. Trump loaned funds to his campaign as needed throughout the primary/caucus stage though he also raised substantial funds. By the end of June, 2016, Trump had spent $71 million, second to Ted Cruz's $86 million total. Trump had loaned his campaign nearly $50 million at this point and had raised another $37 million.[45] Among Democrats, Bernie Sanders had raised and spent nearly as much money as the successful nominee, Hillary Clinton, but his contributions came largely in small donations. By the end of June 2016, Sanders had spent only $3 million less than Clinton and had less money on hand. For Jeb Bush, the $34 million he raised and the $121.7 million raised by his super-PAC went for naught.[46]

Dynamics of the Contest

Before front-loading became so pronounced, candidates competed in as many locations as funds allowed. This was especially true for Democrats, whose rules call for proportional allocation of delegates: As long as candidates achieve at least 15 percent of the vote, they are awarded a share of delegates proportional to the vote share.[47] Republican candidates also faced proportional rules in 2012 and 2016, when fewer states awarded all delegates to the first-place finisher in a primary. The earliest contests, the Iowa caucuses and New Hampshire primary, attract most of the major contenders because they are the first tests of rank-and-file voter sentiment. Iowa returned to prominence in 2008 after being overshadowed for many years by New Hampshire, where the delegate total is small but the winner receives immediate national attention. The small New Hampshire electorate enables candidates with more modest financial resources to conduct labor-intensive campaigns, as was the case for McCain.

A new twist in the 1988 campaign was the large number of primaries held on Tuesday, March 8, a day subsequently known as Super Tuesday. Twenty states selected delegates, sixteen through primaries and four through caucuses. In 1992, only eleven states participated in Super Tuesday, but the Democratic designers accomplished their goal of boosting the chances of a moderate candidate when Clinton won all six of the southern primaries and two caucuses, while Paul Tsongas, his principal rival, claimed victories in just two primaries and one caucus. The media renamed Super Tuesday to "Titanic Tuesday" and "Mega Tuesday" in 2000 because the delegate total rose dramatically when New York and California joined the list of states holding primaries that day. In 2008, the list grew to twenty-two contests to choose delegates on February 5. Although Hillary Clinton had hoped to score a knockout that day, when nearly 40 percent of all convention delegates were selected, she split the results with Obama. McCain, on the other hand, pulled away from Romney, his closest competitor. In 2012, both California and New York moved their contests to later dates and Super Tuesday shrank in significance when only ten states chose delegates. Twelve states held events on the first Tuesday in March 2016.

Holding primaries early in the nomination process is a reversal from the past, when late primaries could be decisive. Until 1996, California scheduled its primary on the final day of delegate selection, giving Golden State voters the chance to determine a party's nominee, as with Goldwater in 1964 and McGovern in 1972. After their loss in 1996, Republicans adopted rules that encouraged states to schedule their primaries later in 2000 by providing them with bonus delegates.[48] But the schedule was only slightly less front-loaded in 2000, and the contests were concluded earlier than ever before—March 9, when both McCain and former senator Bill Bradley, the number-two candidate in each party, discontinued their campaigns.

The two parties set a "window" for delegate selection, providing special exceptions for Iowa and New Hampshire, and extended to South Carolina and Nevada in 2008, 2012, and 2016. In these relatively small states, candidates engage in **retail politics**, meeting with voters on a more personal basis than is possible in larger states, where candidates must rely on media advertising in practicing **wholesale politics**. The Democrats overcame a congested field in 2004 to unofficially select their nominee before the middle of March. Observers expected the same thing to happen in 2008, but Clinton and Obama were so evenly matched that the states scheduled later in the process—Pennsylvania, for one—played an unexpectedly important role. For a while, Democrats wondered whether the nomination campaign would continue until the convention decided on a nominee, a scenario that has not occurred since 1952. But **superdelegates**, elected and party officials who attend the convention by virtue of their leadership positions, sided with Obama, whose delegate total exceeded Clinton's after all primaries and caucuses had been concluded. In 2016, superdelegates heavily favored Clinton over Sanders.

Republicans, even less accustomed to crowded candidate fields, experienced an "open convention" in 1976, when Ford's victory over Reagan was not sealed until just before the delegates convened. With a very crowded field in 2016, Republicans enacted rules that concentrated the delegate selection process into three months. Nearly two-thirds of Republican delegates had been selected by April 1, 2016. As more and more Republican candidates dropped out of the competition, pressure grew on the remaining candidates, Cruz and Kasich, to coordinate their efforts in order to deny Trump a first-ballot nomination at the convention, but the effort failed.

State caucuses operate in the shadow of the primaries, although they remain important for candidates able to mobilize an intensely motivated group of supporters who can exert greater influence than in a primary. Until 2008, the Iowa caucuses, long the first-in-the-nation delegate selection contest, had diminished in importance as a launching pad for presidential contenders. McCain sidestepped Iowa altogether in 2000 to focus on New Hampshire, but Dean's 2004 defeat in Iowa signaled the decline of his candidacy. Obama's 2008 victory in Iowa triggered a surge of favorable media coverage, and his campaign targeted other caucus contests, allowing him to keep pace with Clinton's emphasis on primaries. In 2012, Santorum's singular focus on Iowa paid off with a thirty-four-vote win over Romney, though the final result was delayed for two weeks, denying Santorum a media "bounce." Although the number of states holding caucuses can vary, the overall role of caucuses has been declining steadily.

Media Influence and Campaign Consultants

"For most of us, the combination of media coverage and media advertising is the campaign; few voters see the candidates in person or involve themselves directly in campaign events," wrote Marjorie Randon Hershey after the 2000 election.[49] Little has changed. As the nomination process has grown in complexity, the influence of the media also has grown. Candidates who must campaign in a score of states within two weeks, as they have done since 1992, necessarily rely on the media to communicate with large numbers of potential voters. Televised ads, network- and station-sponsored debates, prime-time news coverage, the Internet and now Twitter are critical to candidates' efforts. Even talk show appearances have gained in importance.

The media tend to focus on the game aspects of the pre-election-year maneuvering and the early contests. As candidates begin to emerge, journalists concentrate on the competition for financial contributions, the reputations of professionals enlisted to work on a campaign, and speculations about the candidates' relative chances of success based on polls and nonbinding straw votes in various states. Once the delegate selection contests begin, the media focus on political tactics, strategy, and competitive position more than on the candidates' messages and issue stands, particularly in covering Iowa, New Hampshire, and the other early contests. In general the media use a winner-take-all principle that, regardless of how narrow the victory or the popular-vote margin, gives virtually all the publicity to the victorious candidate. In the 1976 Iowa caucuses, for example, Carter was declared the "clear winner" and described as leading the pack of contenders even though he received only about 14,000 votes, 28 percent of the 50,000 cast; he actually trailed the "uncommitted" group.[50] Gore defeated Bradley in the 2000 New Hampshire primary by a mere 49.7 percent to 45.6 percent, but Bradley's narrow loss was a less important story than Gore's victory.[51] Kerry salvaged his campaign with a first-place finish in Iowa in 2004, even though he led John Edwards by only a modest number of votes. Sometimes, a surprise showing by a runner-up may garner the most attention: After winning just 16 percent of the votes to finish an unexpected second in the Iowa caucuses in 1984, Gary Hart got as much publicity as Walter Mondale, who captured three times as many votes.[52]

As the fate of presidential candidates has passed from a small group of party professionals to rank-and-file voters, media coverage and public opinion polls have grown in importance. The media help determine who the viable candidates are and label them first as likely or unlikely and later as winners or losers. The media also sponsor a series of public candidate debates; after Republican hopefuls participated in twenty debates in 2012, party leaders in 2016 were intent on reducing that total in order to minimize the impact of ultimately unsuccessful candidates. With so many candidates, the first prime-time debate sponsored by Fox News in Cleveland, Ohio, was limited to the top ten hopefuls as measured in the national polls. The other seven candidates (dubbed the "undercard," or the "kids' table") appeared in an earlier contest on the same day, August 6, 2015. In these ways, the media influence the results of future contests as voters and contributors gravitate to the perceived winners and desert the apparent losers. Polls reflecting voters' presidential preferences are a fixture of media coverage. Favorable polls impress media representatives as well as political activists and many rank-and-file voters, leading to more victories for the poll leaders in both nonprimary and primary contests. The result of this reinforcement process is that, by the time the delegates gather for their party's national convention, one candidate usually has enough delegates to receive the nomination.[53]

The National Convention

No part of the selection process has undergone more dramatic change than the nominating conventions. Long the province of party leaders, today's conventions are largely media extravaganzas choreographed to project images designed to reawaken party loyalty, appeal to contemporary public concerns, and project the most desirable aspects of the newly anointed presidential ticket. In short, the convention is important for two reasons. First, whatever may have happened during the long search for delegates, the actual nomination occurs at the convention. Second, a well-run convention can boost a candidate's chances in the general election, whereas a convention in disarray or one that distracts voters' attention from the candidate can be damaging.

Between 1976 and 2012, the FEC provided funding to the Democratic and Republican Parties to finance their nominating conventions, but that public subsidy ($18.24 million each in 2012) was repealed by Congress in 2014 putting the parties on their own. In 2012, Congress appropriated another $50 million each for security costs, and the same funding was provided to state and local law enforcement to help with security in 2016. Both parties spent much more for their conventions, an additional $60 million each in 2008 and an estimated $100 million in 2012.[54] Facing the need to raise even more money in 2016, the major political parties expected to raise significant funds from corporations and received permission from the FEC to set up separate political committees for convention fund-raising, and the limits on individual contributions were increased substantially to $133,600 for the 2015–2016 election cycle.[55]

Nominating the Ticket

Since the early 1950s, conventions have offered little drama about the choice of the presidential nominee. In the thirty-six conventions held by the two major parties from 1948 through 2016, only two nominees—Thomas Dewey in 1948 and Adlai Stevenson in 1952—failed to win a majority of the convention votes on the first ballot. In all other cases, victory has gone to the candidate who arrived at the convention with the largest number of pledged delegates. Nevertheless, the state-by-state balloting remains a traditional feature of the process.

Selecting the vice presidential nominee is the convention's final chore and the only chance to create any suspense. Although, in theory, the delegates make the choice, it has been a matter of political custom since 1940 to allow presidential nominees to pick their running mates after conferring with leaders whose judgment they trust. Parties traditionally attempt to balance the ticket—that is, broaden its appeal by selecting a person who differs in helpful ways from the presidential nominee. In 1980, George H. W. Bush's links to the eastern establishment and moderate wing of the Republican Party complemented the conservative, western Reagan. Ferraro balanced the 1984 Democratic ticket geographically and in other ways: The first woman to serve as a major-party candidate in a presidential contest, she was also the first Italian American.

In 1988, Dan Quayle brought generational balance to the ticket, and the party's conservatives enthusiastically supported him despite media questions about Quayle's National Guard service during the Vietnam War, his modest academic performance, and his ability to perform as president should the need arise. Clinton violated political tradition by selecting Al Gore, a fellow southerner and baby boomer, but the choice was well received by the party faithful and probably helped Clinton erode Republican support in the South. For the 1996 election, Dole chose Jack Kemp, a one-time presidential candidate who was highly popular with Republican activists. In 2000, George W. Bush asked a fellow western conservative, Dick Cheney, to join the ticket as a way to offset his own lack of Washington and White House experience. In what the media described as a "bold" move, Gore added Lieberman to the 2000 ticket, breaking a long-existent barrier to having a practicing Jew on a national ticket. Kerry's choice of Edwards, a southerner, brought regional balance to the 2004 ticket. Obama turned to Sen. Joseph Biden in 2008, an eastern liberal with extensive Washington experience and ties to Pennsylvania, a hotly contested state. McCain chose Gov. Sarah Palin of Alaska in an effort to shake up the election, but she proved to be a liability in nationally broadcast interviews. Romney chose a rising star in the party—Wisconsin Rep. Paul Ryan—in 2012 as a way to tap the enthusiasm of the Tea Party movement and highlight the nation's budget problems. Clinton's choice in 2016, Tim Kaine, senator from Virginia, shored up her support in a key state. Trump chose Mike Pence, governor of Indiana and a former member of Congress, as a way to strengthen ties with conservative Republicans and provide government as well as Washington experience to the ticket.

The final night of the convention is devoted to acceptance speeches. The presidential nominee tries to make peace with former competitors and to reunite party factions that have confronted one another during the long campaign and the hectic days of the convention. Major party figures usually come to the stage and pledge their support.

Conducting Party Business

Parties continue to write and adopt convention platforms, although participants acknowledge that winning presidential candidates may disavow planks with which they disagree. Because delegates, party leaders, and major groups affiliated with the party have strong feelings about some issues, the platform provides an opportunity to resolve differences and find a politically palatable position.[56] Civil rights and the Vietnam War once prompted major disagreements within the Democratic Party; civil rights, foreign policy, and abortion have been important bones of contention among Republicans.

Despite intraparty differences, conventions provide strong incentives for compromise, to bring back to the fold a disgruntled segment of the party that might otherwise offer only lukewarm support during the fall election or launch a third-party effort. To avoid such damage, almost every presidential candidate decides to provide major rivals and their supporters with concessions in the platform and a prime-time speaking opportunity during the convention. Occasionally, this tactic can backfire. At the Republican convention in 1992, Pat Buchanan was given an opportunity to address a national audience, but his comments proved so controversial that he was not invited to speak four years later.

National nominating conventions have become so predictable that network television coverage has been reduced dramatically since 1996. To obtain the traditional "gavel to gavel" coverage that ushered in the television age, viewers must follow proceedings on cable news networks, such as CNN and Fox News, or on the Internet. Parties have become so adept at scripting these quadrennial gatherings that their very existence is jeopardized, though surprises still occur such as Clint Eastwood's rambling prime-time monologue at the 2012 Republican convention and Ted Cruz's refusal to endorse Trump in his 2016 speech.[57]

The General Election

With nominees unofficially selected by March (in most cases) and officially nominated in late summer, the nation moves into the general election period. Candidates must develop new political appeals for this stage, primarily a contest between the nominees of the two major parties and, occasionally, a major Independent candidate. The campaign's audience increases greatly: More than twice as many people vote in the general election as participate in the nomination process. Candidates and staff must decide how they can win the support of these voters, appeal to people who identify with the other party, and woo partisans who backed losing candidates for the nomination. Time is a further complication because the nationwide phase of the presidential contest when most citizens become attentive is compressed into ten weeks, traditionally running from Labor Day to election day. Since 1996, however, the two eventual party nominees have begun campaigning as soon as the opponent is known, thereby extending the campaign into a longer competition.

The general election phase differs from the nomination phase for two reasons: (1) the way the Electoral College works and (2) the distinctive provisions of the campaign finance laws. Compared with changes effected in the nomination stage, the constitutional requirements surrounding the president's election have been remarkably stable over time, while campaign finance laws have undergone significant change since 1972.

The Electoral College

Presidential candidates plan and carry out their general election strategies with one ultimate goal: winning a majority of the Electoral College votes cast by state electors. At first, electoral votes were determined by congressional districts. The winner of a popular-vote plurality in each district would receive the associated electoral vote, with the statewide winner of the popular vote getting the two electoral votes representing senators. But legislatures soon began to adopt the **unit** or **general-ticket rule**, whereby all the state's electoral votes went to the candidate who received the plurality of the statewide popular vote. This rule benefited the state's largest party and maximized the state's influence in the election by permitting it to throw all its electoral votes to one candidate. By 1836, the unit system had replaced the district plan. Since then, two states have returned to the old plan: Maine in 1969 and Nebraska in 1992. In the aftermath of the 2012 election, Republicans considered supporting this plan broadly.

The final product is a strange method for choosing a chief executive. Although most Americans view the system as a popular election, it is not. When voters mark their ballots, the vote actually determines which slate of electors pledged to support the party's presidential candidate will vote. The electors are party loyalists, chosen variously in primaries, at party conventions, or by state party committees. In mid-December, the electors pledged to the winning candidate meet in their state capitals to cast ballots. (Twenty-seven states and the District of Columbia attempt by law to bind the electors to vote for the winner of the popular vote, but some observers question whether such laws are constitutional.[58]) The electoral votes are transmitted to Washington, D.C., and counted in early January. Next, the presiding officer of the Senate—the incumbent vice president—announces the outcome before a joint session of Congress. If, as usually happens, one candidate receives an absolute majority of the electoral votes, currently 270, the vice president officially declares that candidate president. Because the winner of the popular vote usually wins in the

Electoral College as well, we call this final stage of the selection process the *validation* of the popular-vote outcome. For candidates who win without a popular-vote plurality, as George W. Bush did in 2000 and Donald Trump in 2016, the Electoral College may validate a victory but not necessarily provide legitimacy.

Financing the General Election

Mounting a nationwide campaign requires greater financial resources than winning the nomination. For the general election, public financing is available to nominees of the major parties, and any party that won 25 percent or more of the popular vote in the last presidential election is considered a major party. However, only one of the last six major party candidates has chosen to tap this source of funding.

In the 2004 presidential election, the federal government gave each major-party candidate \$74.62 million, up from \$67.56 million in 2000.[59] McCain received \$84.1 million in 2008, but Obama declined public funding. Neither Romney nor Obama sought such funding in 2012, nor did Trump or Clinton in 2016. Candidates of minor parties, those who won between 5 percent and 25 percent of the vote in the previous election, receive partial public financing, and they can raise private funds up to the major-party limit. Candidates whose parties are just getting started or did not win at least 5 percent of the vote in the previous election receive no help, a major disadvantage. Perot spent an estimated \$63 million of his own money to mount his 1992 campaign, but in 1996 he accepted \$29 million in federal funds and was limited to using only \$50,000 of his own money in the general election. The official Reform Party nominee in 2000, Pat Buchanan, received \$12.6 million as a result of Perot's 8.4 percent share of the vote in 1996. But the party was ineligible for public funding in 2004 after Buchanan's poor showing of 0.43 percent of the popular vote. Candidates of parties that won less than 5 percent of the vote in the previous election can be partially reimbursed after the current election if they receive at least 5 percent of that vote.

Campaign expenditures other than those from public funding may be paid by two sources. Until 2002, there had been no limit on **independent campaign expenditures**, which are made by individuals or political committees that advocate the defeat or election of a presidential candidate but are not made in conjunction with a candidate's campaign. The new law, the Bipartisan Campaign Reform Act or BCRA, applied to the 2004 campaign and prohibited corporations and labor unions from spending their treasury funds on television ads broadly construed as for or against candidates thirty days before a primary and sixty days before a general election.[60] In June 2007, however, the U.S. Supreme Court in *Federal Election Commission v. Wisconsin Right to Life* weakened these provisions. More significantly, another Supreme Court decision discussed earlier, *Citizens United v. Federal Election Commission* (2010), allows corporations, unions, and nonprofit organizations to spend as much as they want in support of or in opposition to candidates. Independent expenditures in the presidential campaign rose to an estimated $560 million with a four-to-one advantage for Romney in 2012. (The total in 2008 had been $150 million.)[61] Total independent expenditures rose again in 2016 but less dramatically than many observers had predicted given the proliferation of super-PACS and nonprofit public welfare groups.

In addition, the BCRA placed new limits on fund-raising and spending by state and local party organizations. Until 1996, party organizations raised funds, commonly called **soft money**, that had largely been used for grassroots activities such as distributing campaign buttons, stickers, and yard signs; registering voters; and transporting voters to the polls. Total spending from these sources remained steady in 1988 and 1992 at $42.5 million and grew to $65 million in 1996 when each launched **issue advocacy** campaigns, media advertisements that do not expressly support or oppose a candidate but ostensibly educate the public about an issue or a candidate's position on an issue.[62] The Democratic National Committee (DNC) ads helped Bill Clinton well before the nomination contests began. When Dole ran short of money in late spring 1996, the Republican National Committee (RNC) stepped in with a similar campaign. In 2000, these activities grew even larger: The national parties spent more for television advertising in the presidential election than did the candidates, especially in the **battleground states**, those most hotly contested by the major candidates.[63] In Florida, the key to Bush's victory, pro-Bush expenditures exceeded those for Gore by about $4 million.[64]

The BCRA "prohibits federal candidates and officeholders, and groups they control, from raising, directing or spending soft money" and sought to halt the activities triggered by Clinton's aggressive fund-raising in 1995 and 1996.[65] In the place of soft money, however, independent expenditures rose dramatically, from $14.7 million in 2000 to $192.4 million in 2004 and dropped slightly to about $170 million in 2008. Both parties were big spenders: The DNC spent $120 million in 2004 (much less in 2008) and the RNC $59 million in 2008.[66] The growth trajectory resumed in 2012; the RNC spent $386 million for Romney and the DNC spent $292 million for Obama. Both parties spent less in the 2016 presidential election, further evidence of how the landscape has changed. According to the authoritative Center for Responsive Politics, the DNC supported Clinton with less than $7 million and spent another $7 million against Trump. The RNC spent almost $8 million helping Trump and only $346,000 against Clinton.

Until 2008, the system of public financing introduced in the 1976 election was viewed as a success: Major party candidates no longer depended on wealthy contributors and other private sources to finance their campaigns; expenditures of the two major-party candidates were limited and equalized, an advantage for Democrats who were historically outspent by their opponents.[67] Each presidential election sets new records: 2008 was the first billion-dollar presidential election; spending in 2012 and 2016 exceeded a billion.[68] Obama's advantage in 2008 was striking. By refusing public funds, he was able to spend as much as he wanted during the general election stage and continued raising money through the election. Once McCain accepted public funding, his campaign was limited to $84.1 million for the general election. Obama spent nearly four times as much.[69] In 2012, Romney's campaign spent $433.3 million, but additional spending by outside groups and the Republican Party brought the total to $1.24 billion. On the Democratic side, Obama's campaign spent $683.5 million, but the total was $1.1 billion after adding expenditures by the party and outside groups.[70] For 2016, the Center for Responsive Politics put the combined resources of Clinton's campaign and supportive outside groups at nearly $770 million. Trump and his allies had combined resources of $408 million. Self-funding was also a factor. Trump ended up spending more than $66 million of his own funds, and Hillary Clinton spent a little less than $1.5 million of hers.

With such high spending levels, today's candidates rely heavily on donors giving the maximum legal contribution to the candidates ($2,700 in 2016), but the era of "fat cats" is also back. Billionaire casino-owner Sheldon Adelson and his wife contributed an estimated $92.8 million to multiple groups supporting Romney and other Republican candidates in 2012 and another $82.5 million in 2016, including $20.4 million to pro-Trump groups.[71]

Targeting the Campaign

As in the nomination process, candidates must decide which states will be the focus of their efforts in the fall campaign. The most important consideration is the Electoral College: A candidate must win a majority—270—of the 538 electoral votes.[72] This fact places a premium on carrying the states with the most electoral votes (see Figure 2-2). From 2004 through 2016, the candidate winning the eleven largest states—California, Florida, Georgia, Illinois, Michigan, New Jersey, New York, North Carolina, Ohio, Pennsylvania, and Texas—could win the presidency while losing the thirty-nine other states and the District of Columbia. Understandably, candidates from both major parties concentrate their personal visits and spending on states with the most electoral votes.

Another element affecting candidates' decisions on where to campaign is competitiveness, the chance of winning a particular state. Are the party's candidates generally successful there, or do the results swing back and forth from one election to the next? Distinctly one-party states are likely to be slighted by the major-party candidates as a waste of time and money, while swing states with large populations draw a good deal of attention.

In formulating campaign strategy, therefore, candidates and their advisers start with the electoral map as modified by calculations of probable success. The Electoral College creates fifty-one separate presidential contests—fifty states plus the District of Columbia—primarily following the winner-take-all principle; the goal is a popular-vote victory, no matter how small the margin. The winner in a large state benefits from the unit rule by getting all the state's electoral votes. In 2000, Bush won Florida by a margin of 537 votes of the 5.963 million legitimate ballots cast.[73] But he won all twenty-five of the state's electoral votes, which gave him 271 votes in the Electoral College.[74] Bush's victory in Florida was not final until a controversial 5–4 U.S. Supreme Court decision in *Bush v. Gore* (2000). This decision reversed the Florida Supreme Court's order for a statewide recount, which led to Gore's final concession on December 13. Seven justices agreed that Florida did not have a clear, consistent standard to govern manual recounts, but only five—all Republican appointees—believed that a deadline established in an obscure 1887 law that precluded recounts within six days of Electoral College balloting applied in this instance. Despite deep disagreement on the Court, the Florida recount was halted, and Bush emerged the victor.

Electoral votes were reapportioned for the 2004 and 2012 presidential elections, reflecting the results of the 2000 and 2010 censuses and the subsequent reallocation of seats in the House of Representatives. States in the North, East, and Midwest lost seats, while those in the South and West gained.[75] Following the 2010 census, Texas gained four votes and Florida two, with six other states gaining one each: Arizona, Nevada, Georgia, South Carolina, Utah, and Washington. The big losers were New York (lost two) and Ohio (lost two), while Michigan, Illinois, Missouri, Iowa, Louisiana, Massachusetts, New Jersey, and Pennsylvania lost one vote each.

Democratic candidates have confronted a difficult strategic problem arising from the historic realignment of the South in presidential politics. Southern voters solidly supported Democrats for many decades following the Civil War. Until 1992, no Democrat had ever won the White House without carrying a majority of southern states. Southern support evaporated even for Jimmy Carter in 1980, when only Georgia supported its favorite son. No southern state voted for the Democratic ticket in 1984 or 1988. The Solid South was a Republican stronghold until Clinton won Arkansas, Georgia, Louisiana, and Tennessee in 1992.[76]

George W. Bush won the entire South in 2000, including Gore's home state of Tennessee. Eleven states switched columns from 1996, including Florida, New Hampshire, and West Virginia, a traditional Democratic stronghold. Gore could have won the election with either New Hampshire's four votes or Florida's twenty-five; many Gore voters believed that liberal Democrats supporting Ralph Nader in both states prevented that. Buchanan may also have denied Bush victories in New Mexico and Wisconsin and their sixteen electoral votes.[77]

For all the money spent in the 2004 campaign, the outcome changed from 2000 in only three states: Iowa and New Mexico moved to Bush and New Hampshire to Kerry. Once again, no southern state voted for the Democratic candidate, which meant the Kerry campaign had virtually no room for error in reaching 270. The election came down to Ohio's twenty electoral votes, and the nation waited anxiously to see if there would be a repeat of 2000, but in the end, Kerry lost Ohio by 118,599 votes out of 5,627,903 cast.

With his solid financial advantage, Obama pursued a fifty-state strategy in 2008 while concentrating resources on the crucial target states. As a result, nine states shifted party columns from how they voted in 2004, including three in the South—Florida, North Carolina, and Virginia. In the West, Colorado, Nevada, and New Mexico shifted to the Democrats; and in the Midwest, Indiana, Iowa, and Ohio went Democratic. One electoral vote also shifted in Nebraska, the result of a congressional district supporting Obama while the rest of the state supported McCain. With broad popular support, Obama won in the Electoral College, 365 to 173, the largest margin of victory since Clinton in 1996. For 2012, states that Obama won in 2008 lost a net of six votes in the Electoral College following the census. In two other states (North Carolina and Indiana), the popular-vote plurality shifted from Democrat to Republican, and Obama lost the one district vote he had received in Nebraska. In the end, Obama won thirty-three fewer electoral votes. His popular-vote total was also down by 4.5 million votes.

The key to Trump's success in 2016 were victories in three states the Democrats believed were secure. Clinton lost Michigan by a paltry 10,704 votes; Pennsylvania by 44,292 votes; and Wisconsin by 22,748. Combined, they had 46 electoral votes. Had Clinton been able to halve the margin in each of those states (fewer than 39,000 total votes), she would have won. In addition, votes for the left-leaning Green candidate exceeded Trump's margin of victory in each state. Florida, Iowa, Ohio and one congressional district in Maine also switched columns. Clinton lost 100 electoral votes from Obama's total in 2012 (in addition to five faithless electors). Trump won thirty states and Clinton twenty plus D.C., producing a 304–227 victory. Clinton's total popular vote was down slightly from Obama's in 2012, but Trump's was up by nearly two million over Romney's. Nevertheless, Clinton won nearly 2.9 million more popular votes than Trump.

Appealing for Public Support

Presidential campaigns spend millions of dollars and untold hours pursuing two goals: motivating people to cast a ballot and winning their support for a particular candidate. Several factors other than campaign appeals determine who votes and how they vote. Voters' choices depend on their long-term political predispositions, such as party loyalties and social group affiliations, and their reactions to short-term forces, such as the particular candidates and issues involved in specific elections. Candidates and their campaign professionals try to design appeals that activate these influences, attract support, and counter perceived weaknesses.

FIGURE 2-2 State Size by Number of Electoral Votes, 2016

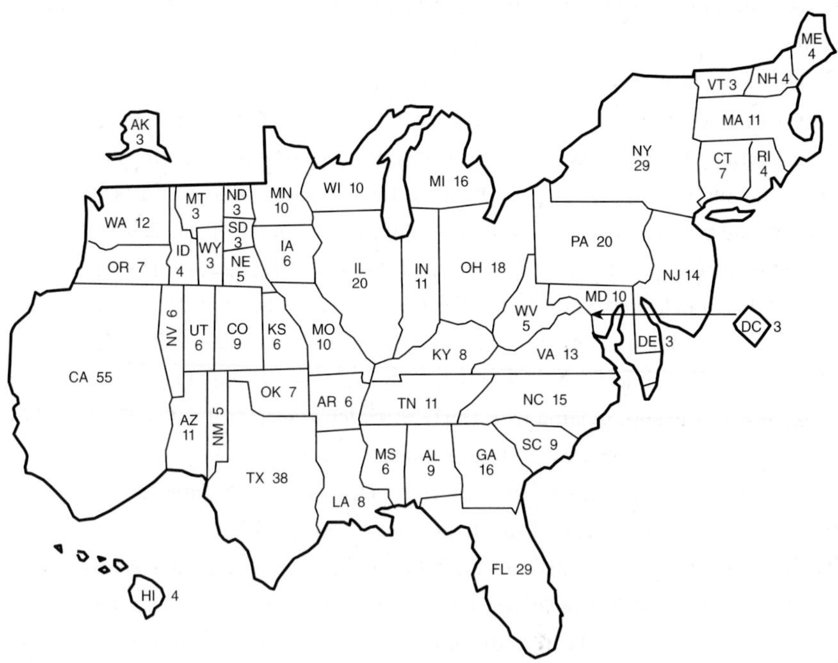

SOURCE: For more information on shifting state electoral vote totals over time see http://uselectionatlas.org/INFORMATION/index.php and www.presidency.ucsb.edu/elections.php.

Because the audience is larger and the time is shorter during the general election period than during the nomination period, candidates use their resources primarily for mass-media appeals. Advertising expenditures have risen accordingly, with campaigns spending half their public funding on radio and television messages. Since 1952, television has been the chief source of campaign information for most Americans and is still used more than the internet, newspapers, or radio. Rather than being national in scope, however, advertising is targeted to selected markets in crucial Electoral College states, a pattern especially apparent since 2000 when both campaigns have focused on a defined list of battleground states. Obama's money advantage allowed him to challenge in many more states in 2008, even those considered long shots, such as McCain's home state of Arizona. In 2016, the campaigns focused on a dozen states with most attention on Florida, North Carolina, Pennsylvania, and Ohio.

Students of elections have categorized influences on voter decisions as either long term or short term. Long-term influences include partisanship and group membership, whereas candidate image, issues, and campaign incidents are short term.

Long-Term Influences. Partisan loyalty, although still important for a large part of the public, has become less significant as a determinant of election outcomes. Conditions have changed considerably since researchers studying presidential elections in the 1950s concluded that the single most important determinant of voting was the voter's **party identification**.[78] This general psychological attachment, shaped by family and social groups, tended to intensify with age. For the average person looking for guidance on how to vote amid the complexities of personalities, issues, and events of the 1950s, the party label of the candidates was the most important reference point. Partisanship was also fairly constant: About 45 percent of Americans in 1952 and 1956 said they thought of themselves as Democrats, and about 28 percent viewed themselves as Republicans, for a combined total of nearly three-fourths of the electorate. When asked to classify themselves further as "strong" or "weak" partisans, Republicans and Democrats both tended to divide equally between those two categories. Independents in 1952 and 1956 averaged about 23 percent of the electorate.

In the mid- to late 1960s, however, partisan affiliation in the United States began to change (see Table 2-2). Beginning with the 1968 election, the number of Independents started to rise, primarily at the expense of the Democrats; by 1972, Independents constituted one-third of the electorate. Even voters who stayed with the Democrats were more inclined than formerly to say they were weak, rather than strong, party members. By 1988, some polls found that Independents outnumbered Democrats. Voters who entered the electorate in 1964 or later are much more likely to be political Independents than were voters of earlier political generations, a development that has been linked to the influence of Vietnam and Watergate and later to declining confidence in government.

Total partisanship—the combined percentage of citizens declaring themselves Democrats or Republicans—fell to its lowest level between 1972 and 1976, rebounded slightly in the 1980s, and sank again in the 1990s. The percentage of Independents has remained strong since the 1970s. By the 2004 election, the electorate's composition was 33 percent Democrats, 28 percent Republicans, and 39 percent Independents. Another 17 percent of Independents "leaned" Democratic, and 12 percent "leaned" Republican.[79] In 2008, Independents outnumbered Democrats 40 percent to 34 percent with Republicans a distant third at 26 percent. Independents reversed places with Democrats in 2012 and Republicans lost slightly (see Table 2-2). The Pew Research Center found 2012 to have been more like 2008; about one-third of the voters were Democrats, one-quarter Republican, and the remainder Independent, with 10 percent more voters "leaning" Democratic. In the lead up to the 2016 election, both Pew and Gallup found that Independents approached forty percent and consistently outnumbered both Democrats and Republicans.[80] Campaigns seek support by activating traditional party loyalties, yet they also attempt to lure identifiers of the other party by blurring traditional themes, a tightrope act that can confuse the general public.

Social group membership is another potentially important influence on voting that candidates try to tap. Patterns of group support established during the New Deal persisted during succeeding decades, although with decreasing vibrancy. In the 1940s, Democrats' support came from southerners, union members, Catholics, and people with limited education, lower incomes, and a working-class background. Northerners, whites, Protestants, and people with more education, higher incomes, and a professional or business background supported Republican candidates. Table 2-3, which is based on Gallup polls, shows the support of various groups on the eve of presidential elections from 1952 through 2012. The support of many groups for their traditional party's candidates varied over that period. Democrats lost the southern white vote: In 1988, only one in three white votes went to Dukakis, and only 26 percent of white males supported him.[81] On the other hand, support of nonwhites for Democrats strengthened after 1964 and reached near-historic levels in 2008.[82]

Obama's victorious coalition in 2008 rested on strong support among women (56 percent), African Americans (95 percent), Hispanics (67 percent), and young voters. Exit polls showed Obama winning 69 percent of support from first-time voters and a similar percentage among the eighteen- to twenty-nine-year-old voters (66 percent).[83] Obama lost among white voters (55 percent to 43 percent), those sixty and older (51 percent to 47 percent), Protestants (54 percent to 45 percent), and rural voters (53 percent to 45 percent). He garnered the votes of just 31 percent of southern whites, but his advantage in other categories was so great that the popular-vote outcome—53 percent to 46 percent in his favor—was not in question.

In 2016, Clinton hoped to reassemble the Obama coalition and Trump worked to erode it. The first woman to head a major party ticket won less of the women's vote than the campaign had expected (54 percent to 42 percent), a smaller margin than Obama enjoyed in 2008. Trump carried men 53 percent to 41 percent. Black voters again voted overwhelmingly for the Democrat (88 percent to 8 percent) and Whites for the Republican (58 percent to 37 percent). Younger voters went for Clinton (55 percent of 18- to 29-year olds), but down 11 percent from Obama; older voters supported Trump. Clinton's support rose with education and Trump led among Whites without a college degree, 67 percent to 28 percent. Trump's decisive advantage among rural voters (62 percent to 34 percent) helped explain his victories in Michigan, Ohio, Pennsylvania, and Wisconsin where he won rural counties by large margins, offsetting Clinton's advantage in urban areas. After raucous and fragmenting nomination campaigns in both parties, partisans went back home: Republicans supported Trump 90 percent to 7 percent, and Democrats voted for Clinton 89 percent to 9 percent. Independents chose Trump 48 percent to 42 percent.[84]

The weakening of party loyalties means candidates must target many groups. Organized labor, far from a monolithic entity, has been seriously divided in many elections, and both camps have openly courted ethnic groups. Moreover, new groups emerged over the past half-century as critical factors: Women, fundamentalist Christians, young voters, and Hispanics have attracted particular attention. But because many American voters have lost their partisan anchor, short-term influences—candidates, issues, and events—and presidential performance are now more important to them.

Short-Term Influences. During presidential campaigns, the public focuses a great deal of attention on the candidates' personality and character traits. Each campaign organization strives to create a composite image of its candidate's most attractive features. To do this sometimes means transforming liabilities into assets: Age becomes mature judgment (Eisenhower); youth and inexperience become vigor (Kennedy). Alternatively, a candidate can direct attention to the opponent's

TABLE 2-2 Party Identification, 1952–2012 (Percentage)

Party	*1952*	*1956*	*1960*	*1964*	*1968*	*1972*	*1976*	*1980*	*1984*	*1988*	*1992*	*1994*	*1996*	*1998*	*2000*	*2002*	*2004*	*2008*	*2012*
Strong Democratic	22	21	20	27	20	15	15	18	17	17	18	15	18	19	19	17	17	19	25
Weak Democratic	25	23	25	25	25	26	25	23	20	18	18	19	19	18	15	17	16	15	15
Total	47	44	45	52	45	41	40	41	37	35	36	34	37	37	34	34	33	34	40
Strong Republican	14	15	16	11	10	10	9	9	12	14	11	16	12	10	12	14	16	13	13
Weak Republican	14	14	14	14	15	13	14	14	15	14	14	15	15	16	12	16	12	13	11
Total	28	29	30	25	25	23	23	23	27	28	25	31	27	26	24	30	28	26	24
Independent	23	23	23	23	30	34	37	34	34	36	38	35	35	36	40	36	39	40	37

SOURCE: Data drawn from the American National Election Studies (ANES), Center for Political Studies at the University of Michigan's Institute for Social Research; and the *ANES Guide to Public Opinion and Electoral Behavior,* Table 2A.1, www.electionstudies.org/nesguide/toptable/tab2a_1.htm. Data for 2012 found at http://sda.berkeley.edu/sdaweb/analysis/?dataset=nes2012.

NOTE: Responses to this question: "Generally speaking, do you usually think of yourself as a Republican, a Democrat, an Independent, or what?" Independents include voters labeled as "Independent Democrats" and "Independent Republicans," sometimes referred to as "leaners."

personal liabilities, a risky move because some voters see such an effort as dirty campaigning.

The 1988 and 2012 campaigns provide good examples of how candidates try to shape each other's image. George H. W. Bush succeeded in creating a negative portrait of Michael Dukakis in 1988, whose favorable image was based on very little information. Interviews conducted with small groups of Democrats who had supported Reagan in 1980 and 1984 shaped the Bush campaign's charges that the Democratic nominee was sympathetic to criminals, weak on defense, opposed to saying the pledge of allegiance in school, and a liberal who favored high taxes and big government.[85] In 2012, the Obama campaign defined Romney as a wealthy, hard-hearted businessman responsible for U.S. workers losing their jobs. Unfortunately for Romney, a secret video tape of a fund-raising dinner where he had denounced forty-seven percent of the people as seeking government handouts seemed to confirm much of the stereotype.

In 2016, the Clinton campaign and supportive outside groups focused their advertising efforts on Donald Trump's personality and why it made him unfit for the presidency. Trump aired far fewer ads than Clinton and they had more policy content, providing more comparisons of himself with Clinton. But ads sponsored by pro-Trump outside groups were quite negative. Trump pursued the unconventional strategy of relying heavily on social media (his supporters loved his Twitter messages) and large rallies where he made controversial statements that attracted blanket media coverage. Many comments focused on crimes allegedly committed by Clinton that triggered chants by his supporters of "Lock her up." A comprehensive study of the election's political advertising concluded that 2016 was the "second most negative in the last decade and a half."[86]

Voters look for many qualities in a president. Honesty, trustworthiness, the ability to bring about change, care about people like themselves, and having a vision for the future are often mentioned. In 1992, change favored Clinton, and in 1996 it was having a vision for the future that distinguished him from Dole.[87] In 2000, honesty was the trait mentioned most by voters (24 percent), and 80 percent of those who mentioned it voted for George W. Bush, also perceived as the stronger leader and more likeable despite Gore's greater experience and greater care about people.[88] In 2004, Bush was regarded as more honest and trustworthy (47 percent to 40 percent), the stronger leader (56 percent to 36 percent), and clearer on the issues (57 percent to 34 percent), while Kerry was slightly more likely to understand the problems of "people like you" (46 percent to 44 percent).[89]

In 2008, candidates for the nomination focused on experience versus change: Which candidate would bring the necessary experience to the job and be able to hit the ground running on "day one," as Hillary Clinton put it, as opposed to which would be an agent for change? Change emerged as a more powerful appeal than experience. Both Clinton (eight years in the White House as first lady and eight years in the Senate) and John McCain, (four years in the U.S. House and twenty-two in the Senate) modified their campaigns to highlight their capacity to serve as change agents, an indication of the power of Obama's appeal for "change you can believe in." By election day, exit polls showed that 59 percent of voters thought McCain had the right experience to be president vs. 51 percent for Obama.[90] Voters preferred Obama's judgment over McCain's (57 percent to 49 percent), and more people thought Obama was in touch with people like themselves (57 percent to 39 percent). Obama's empathy advantage was again strong in 2012 and there were strongly unfavorable perceptions of Romney. Leadership and empathy were especially important to Independent voters, a group hotly pursued by both campaigns.

Although the public knew both 2016 candidates quite well, neither was viewed favorably. In fact, polls showed that Trump and Clinton had the lowest favorability ratings of any candidates since the question became a polling standard in 1980. Trump's unfavorable ratings exceeded his favorable ratings by an average of -24 percent during the campaign's final three months and Clinton's averaged -16 percent. The difference was that among voters who disliked *both* candidates, Trump led by 22 percent of the vote. Exit polls showed that Clinton had an enormous advantage among voters in experience (90 percent to 8 percent) and judgment (66 percent to 26 percent) but Trump was viewed as far more likely to bring about change (83 percent to 14 percent). Twenty percent of Trump voters did not believe he had the temperament to be effective in office, just as twenty percent of Clinton's voters doubted she was honest and trustworthy, probably the lingering doubts about her missing e-mails and Trump's repeated attacks on "Crooked Hillary."[91]

Issues are another major short-term influence on voting behavior. University of Michigan researchers in the 1950s suggested that issues influence a voter's choice only if three conditions are present: (1) the voter is aware that an issue or a number of issues exist, (2) issues are of some personal concern to the voter, and (3) the voter perceives that one party represents his or her position better than the other party does.[92] When the three conditions were applied to U.S. voters in the 1952 and 1956 presidential elections, researchers found that these criteria existed for relatively few voters—at most one-quarter to one-third. Another one-third of the respondents were unaware of *any* of the sixteen principal issues about which they were questioned. Even the two-thirds who were aware of one or more issues frequently had no personal concern about them. Finally, many of those who were aware and concerned about issues were unable to perceive differences between the two parties' positions. The analysts concluded that issues *potentially* determined the choice of, at most, only one-third of the electorate. (The proportion who *actually* voted as they did because of issues could have been, and probably was, even less.)

Studies of political attitudes in the 1960s and 1970s found that the number and types of issues of which voters were aware had increased.[93] Voters during the Eisenhower years exhibited some interest in traditional domestic matters, such as welfare and labor-management relationships, and in a few foreign policy issues, such as the threat of communism and the danger of the atomic bomb. Beginning with the 1964 election, however, voters' interests broadened to include concerns such as civil rights and the Vietnam War. The war in particular remained an important consideration in the 1968 and 1972 contests and was joined by new matters—crime, disorder, and juvenile delinquency, which, along with race problems, were known as social issues. Salient issues vary from election to election. Greater issue clarity existed between the candidates in the elections of 1984, 1992, 1996, and 2004.[94] Exit polls in 2004 revealed that Bush voters identified moral values and terrorism as their most important issues, while the economy and jobs, Iraq, and health care mattered most to Kerry voters.[95] Many pundits concluded quickly that abortion, gay marriage, and related issues important to the religious right had determined the outcome, but other surveys, posing different questions, suggested that the emphasis was on public safety issues—terrorism, Islamic extremism, and homeland security; foreign policy was second in importance, and the economy was third.[96]

The economy dominated voter concerns in 2008 and 2012; 63 percent of voters in 2008 and 59 percent in 2012 cited it as their most important concern. Of those who were very worried about the economy in 2008, 59 percent favored Obama; voters in 2012 split evenly on whether Obama or Romney could do a better job on the economy, but a plurality saw things as getting better and a majority (53 percent to 38 percent) blamed Bush for the nation's economic problems rather than Obama.[97] Voters' feelings about George W. Bush had weighed heavily against McCain in 2008. Seventy-one percent of the voters disapproved of the way Bush was performing as president, and 48 percent said McCain would continue Bush's policies.[98]

Immigration dominated the 2016 campaign from the moment Donald Trump declared his candidacy in June 2015, but on election day voters ranked the economy as most important: 52 percent ranked the economy number one followed by 18 percent terrorism and 13 percent immigration. Clinton held a 52–41 advantage among those listing the economy most important but trailed Trump 40–57 on terrorism and 33–64 on immigration.

Campaign events loomed large in 2016. The FBI played a prominent role, first declaring in June 2016 that Clinton would not be prosecuted for using a private email server while Secretary of State that potentially made classified documents vulnerable. But a mere nine days before the election, Director James Comey announced that the FBI was examining another group of emails found on the computer of a close Clinton aide. Even though Comey announced three days before the election that the new emails would not result in charges against Clinton, the candidate believed that the sudden doubt injected into voters' minds cost her the election. Clinton was also filmed stumbling during a bout with pneumonia, and WikiLeaks released a barrage of embarrassing emails hacked from the DNC by agents of the Russian government. Following the election, investigations by the FBI, U.S, intelligence agencies, and congressional committees focused on whether the Russian actions were undertaken in collusion with Trump campaign officials. Trump was embarrassed by the release of an *Access Hollywood* audio and videotape shortly before the second debate in which he described grabbing attractive women by their genitals.[99] Eventually, a dozen women came forward to denounce his unwanted advances over the years.

In 2004, Martin Wattenberg observed that today's presidential elections are heavily candidate centered, but not in the way we typically think of them. Voters are casting ballots less on the basis of candidates' personal qualities than on candidate-centered issues, those that the nominee has chosen to stress during the campaign. Beginning in 1976, the percentage of positive comments made about the candidates (even the winners) has declined sharply from the 1952 to 1972 period, prompting Wattenberg to conclude that "the more people come to know about the candidates, the less they like them."[100] And in some instances—Reagan in 1980, George W. Bush in 2000, and research will probably show, Trump in 2016—the public made more unfavorable than favorable comments about the winner.

Incumbency. Incumbency may be viewed as a candidate characteristic that also involves issues. Service in the job provides experience no one else can claim. Incumbency provides concrete advantages: An incumbent already has national campaign experience (true for all incumbents except Ford, who had been appointed to the vice presidency), can obtain media coverage more easily, and has considerable discretion in allocating federal benefits.

Four of the seven incumbent presidents who ran for reelection between 1976 and 2012 won (Reagan, Clinton, George W. Bush, and Obama), while only one of the past four incumbent vice presidents who sought the presidency was successful (George H. W. Bush). The failure of Ford, Carter, and G. H. W. Bush to gain a second term demonstrates the *disadvantages* of incumbency, particularly if service in the presidency coincides with negative economic conditions, such as a recession and high inflation or an unresolved foreign crisis for which a president is blamed, even if erroneously. Experience in the job, then, is not a political plus if a sitting president's record is considered weak or national conditions seem to have deteriorated under the incumbent's stewardship. The president may be held accountable by voters who cast their ballots *retrospectively* rather than *prospectively;* in other words, these voters evaluate an administration's past performance rather than try to predict future performance.

Retrospective voting perhaps explains Carter's defeat in 1980 and Bush's in 1992. Many voters perceived Carter's failure to resolve the hostage crisis in Iran as a demonstration of national weakness; in contrast, when Reagan ran for reelection in 1984, restoring pride in America was a major campaign theme. Both elections found citizens voting retrospectively, first providing a negative and then a positive verdict. In 1996, Clinton benefited from the peace and prosperity of his first term, but this record was not transferred to his chosen successor. Gore, perhaps unwisely, tried to distance himself from Clinton to avoid association with the president's objectionable personal conduct. In doing so, he also distanced himself from the administration's achievements.[101] In 2004, "Bush generally won approval for his handling of the war on terrorism but was, on average, negatively evaluated for his handling of Iraq and foreign relations, generally."[102] Personal incumbency was not a factor in 2008 and 2016, but party incumbency was. For the first and second times since 1952, neither party's nominee was an incumbent president or vice president. Democrats actively linked Bush's record to the Republican nominee in 2008 even though the president made no campaign appearances with McCain. In stark contrast, Clinton featured Barack and Michelle Obama during rally after rally, particularly during the final month of the 2016 campaign. The Obamas' message was clear: "Our legacy is on the line. Vote for Hillary." But, as we have seen, the Obama coalition did not reassemble for Clinton or at least not with the same enthusiasm. More generally, extending partisan control of the presidency past two terms requires overcoming voters' instinct that it is "time for a change."[103]

Presidential Debates. Voters have the opportunity to assess the issue positions and personal characteristics of presidential and vice presidential contenders during nationally televised debates. Debates, first staged in 1960 and held each election year since 1976, are the most widely watched campaign events. Candidates seek to avoid making a mistake on live television, a particular danger for incumbents. Ford

TABLE 2-3 Group Voting Patterns in Presidential Elections, Selected Years (Percentage)

Year (Party)	*1952 (R)*		*1960 (D)*		*1964 (D)*		*1968 (R)*			*1976 (D)*		*1980 (R)*			*1988 (R)*		*1992 (D)*			*2000 (R)*			*2004 (R)*		*2012 (D)*	
Nominees Group	*Stevenson*	*Eisenhower*	*Kennedy*	*Nixon*	*Johnson*	*Goldwater*	*Humphrey*	*Nixon*	*Wallace*	*Carter*	*Ford*	*Carter*	*Reagan*	*Anderson*	*Dukakis*	*Bush G. H. W.*	*Bush G. H. W.*	*Clinton*	*Perot*	*Gore*	*Bush G. W.*	*Nader.*	*Bush G. W.*	*Kerry*	*Obama*	*Romney*
Sex																										
Male	47	53	52	48	60	40	41	43	16	37	63	38	53	7	44	56	37	39	19	38	53	5	50	50	43	53
Female	42	58	49	51	62	38	45	43	12	38	62	44	49	6	48	52	36	48	10	48	43	4	57	43	52	44
Race																										
White	43	57	49	51	59	41	38	47	15	32	68	36	56	7	41	59	40	40	15	39	52	4	45	55	39	57
Nonwhite	79	21	68	32	94	6	85	12	3	87	13	86	10	2	82	18	12	76	4	78	12	4	90	10	92	6
Education																										
College	34	66	39	61	52	48	37	54	9	37	63	35	53	10	42	58	39	43	14	42	49	5	55	45	43	55
High school	45	55	52	48	62	38	42	43	15	34	66	43	51	5	46	54	37	45	12	46	44	4	57	53	48	47
Grade school	52	48	55	45	66	34	52	33	15	49	51	54	42	3	55	45	35	43	15	NA	NA	NA	67	33	NA	NA
Occupation																										
Business	36	64	42	58	54	46	34	56	10	31	69	33	55	10	NA	NA	NA	NA	NA	NA	NA	NA	NA	NA	NA	NA
White collar	40	60	48	52	57	43	41	47	12	36	64	40	51	9	NA	NA	NA	NA	NA	NA	NA	NA	NA	NA	NA	NA
Manual	55	45	60	40	71	29	50	35	15	43	57	48	46	5	NA	NA	NA	NA	NA	NA	NA	NA	NA	NA	NA	NA
Age																										
Under 30	51	49	54	45	64	36	47	38	15	48	5	47	41	11	37	63	44	38	14	43	45	9	61	39	57	38
30–49	47	53	54	46	63	37	44	41	15	33	67	38	52	8	45	55	35	43	17	41	50	5	53	47	49	48
50 and older	39	61	46	54	59	41	41	47	12	36	64	41	54	4	49	51	37	46	11	46	46	3	51	49	46	50
Religion																										
Protestant	37	63	38	62	55	45	35	49	16	30	70	39	54	6	42	58	NA	NA	NA	NA	NA	NA	47	53	41	56
Catholic	56	44	78	22	76	24	59	33	8	48	52	46	47	6	51	49	NA	NA	NA	45	45	5	53	47	52	45
Region																										
East	45	55	53	47	68	32	50	43	7	42	58	43	47	9	51	49	33	47	15	52	38	6	57	43	58	38
Midwest	42	58	48	52	61	39	44	47	9	40	60	41	51	7	47	53	35	45	13	43	47	4	53	47	47	51
South	51	49	51	49	52	48	31	36	33	29	71	44	52	3	40	60	42	40	13	36	56	3	50	50	42	52
West	42	58	49	51	60	40	44	49	7	41	59	35	54	9	46	54	36	43	15	43	47	6	55	45	46	52
Members of Labor Union																										
Families	61	39	65	35	73	27	56	29	15	46	54	50	43	5	63	37	NA	NA	NA	NA	NA	NA	64	36	NA	NA
National	45	55	50	50	61	39	43	43	14	38	62	41	51	7	46	54	37	44	14	43	47	5	46	49	48	49

SOURCE: Excerpted from Gallup Report, November 1988, 6, 7; the Gallup Poll Monthly, November 1992, 9; 1996 data provided by Gallup Organization from poll conducted November 3 to November 4, 1996; and 2000 data released November 6, 2000, and posted on www.gallup.com. The 2004 data appear in the Gallup Poll Tuesday Briefing, November 5, 2004, 42–44. Data for 2008 from www.gallup.com/poll/112132/Election-Polls-Vote-Groups-2008.aspx. Data for 2012 from www.gallup.com/poll/158519/romney-obama-gallup-final-election-survey.aspx.

NOTE: NA = not available.

misspoke in 1976 by saying that the countries of Eastern Europe were not under Soviet domination; Reagan appeared to be confused and out of touch during his first debate with Mondale in 1984 but rallied in the second encounter. Challengers try to demonstrate their knowledge of issues and their presidential bearing to a nationwide audience. Kennedy in 1960, Reagan in 1980, and George W. Bush in 2000 benefited from debating a more experienced opponent because they exceeded performance expectations and dispelled negative impressions. Candidates usually prepare carefully prior to the meeting and follow a conservative game plan of repeating themes already prominent in the campaign. As a result, the exchanges often seem wooden rather than spontaneous, although there can be moments of drama. Trailing candidates see the debates as a way to reverse the trend. Kerry was the consensus victor in all three debates with George W. Bush but could not turn the race around. McCain lost all three presidential debates in 2008, though he was more effective in the final debate. Obama appeared passive in the first 2012 debate under Romney's pressure, but the president rallied in the final two debates, reassuring his supporters.

Donald Trump pointedly approached the debates in a confident, relaxed manner, refusing to sequester himself for days of preparation as most candidates have done. Post-debate polls showed that he lost all three encounters, the first of which was the most watched presidential debate in history with 84 million television viewers. Trump's unrehearsed style contrasted with Clinton's careful, lawyer-like approach.[104] The second debate, coming on the heels of the *Access Hollywood* tape, was probably most dramatic. After several days of controversy and pressure for him to withdraw from the race, Trump instead held a pre-debate press conference featuring several of the women who had charged Bill Clinton with unwanted sexual advances and then gave them prime seats in the debate audience. In the third debate, Clinton and Trump traded insults. Her opponent was "unfit, and he proves it every time he talks," Clinton charged; "Such a nasty woman," Trump snarled back.

The vice presidential debate that drew the largest audience was held in 2008. An estimated 69.9 million viewers tuned in to see the encounter between longtime senator Joe Biden and national neophyte Sarah Palin. Governor Palin's poor performance in several televised interviews had aroused speculation whether she would self-destruct during this high-stakes encounter, but she held her own for most of the debate, using a folksy style that contrasted sharply with Biden's occasional lapse into Washington speak.

Vice presidential candidates have debated since 1976 without much impact on the outcomes. Dan Quayle's performance was the focus of two vice presidential debates. Much younger than Lloyd Bentsen, his 1988 opponent, Quayle was asked repeatedly what he would do if forced to assume the duties of president. When Quayle compared himself to former president John F. Kennedy, Bentsen pounced with withering directness: "Senator, I served with Jack Kennedy. I knew Jack Kennedy. Jack Kennedy was a friend of mine. Senator, you're no Jack Kennedy." Quayle never recovered.[105] Tim Kaine's encounter with Mike Pence in the sole 2016 VP debate was memorable only for the number of times Kaine interrupted Pence and Pence's repeated denial of Trump's past comments.

Televised debates enable even the least engaged citizen to develop an impression of the major-party contenders. Candidates, however, have become quite adept at stagecraft, and the public may now expect more than just a polite exchange of policy challenges as candidates try to display assertiveness, empathy, humor, or character.

Election Day

One of the ironies of presidential elections since 1960 is that although more citizens have acquired the right to vote, until 2004, a smaller proportion had exercised that right. As Table 2-4 indicates, the estimated number of people of voting age has more than doubled since 1932. After reaching a peak in 1960, however, the

AP Photo, File

The debates between Democratic Senator John F. Kennedy and Republican Vice President Richard Nixon in 1960 were the first to be televised. Kennedy benefited from his strong performance in the debates against his more politically experienced opponent. Today, candidates use this forum to challenge opponents' ideas and portray themselves as presidential and likeable.

percentage of people who voted declined in the next five presidential elections. Despite a modest increase in 1984, only 50.1 percent went to the polls in 1988. This pattern was unexpectedly reversed in 1992, when 55.2 percent voted.[106] The resurgence proved short-lived, however. Only 49.1 percent showed up in 1996, the lowest turnout since 1924. There was a modest uptick in 2000 to 51.2 percent, and a startling increase in 2004, variously set at 55.3 percent based on the *voting-age population* (all those eighteen and older) or 60.7 percent using the more accurate measure of the *voting-eligible population,* which excludes noncitizens and felons. In 2008, turnout rose to 56.9 percent for the voting-age population (including noneligible residents, immigrants, and prison inmates) and to 63 percent of the voting-eligible population. These levels declined in 2012 to 53.6 percent (voting age) and 58.7 (voting eligible) but rose again in 2016 to 54.7 percent (voting age) and 60.2 percent (voting eligible). Turnout has declined in four of the most recent campaigns that had an incumbent on the ticket, probably reflecting the difference in excitement between changing leaders and continuing leaders, helping to explain the resurgence in 2016.[107] Optimists believe that the long-term decline in voter participation has been halted. Indeed, the trend ran counter to most theories of why people do not vote. Most states had eased laws pertaining to registration and voting, said to prevent citizens from going to the polls. Federal laws made it far easier for a person to register and to vote for president in 1996, the low point in the trend, than in 1960. A person's lack of education is often put forward as a reason for not voting, but the level of education of U.S. citizens rose as participation declined. Lack of political information is yet another frequently cited explanation, but more Americans than ever are aware of the candidates and their views on public issues, thanks to media coverage and the debates. Finally, close political races are supposed to stimulate people to get out and vote because they think their ballot will make a difference in the outcome. But the recent increases could also be temporary.

Why did voting decline after 1960, surge in 1992, decline again in 1996, recover in 2000, and jump in 2004 and 2008? Abramson, Aldrich, and Rohde link the long-term decline to the erosion in political party identification and to lower **political efficacy**—the belief that citizens can influence what government does.[108] But these authors note that neither party identification nor political efficacy changed significantly in 1992 and 1996 to explain the numbers. Evidence suggests that Perot's presence contributed to the 1992 turnout increase; 14 percent of Perot voters (which translates into nearly three million voters, a substantial portion of the larger turnout) indicated in exit polls that without Perot on the ballot, they would not have voted. By 1996, when turnout again declined, the "motor voter" bill, which

TABLE 2-4 Participation of General Public in Presidential Elections, 1932–2016

Year	*Estimated Population of Voting Age (in millions)*	*Number of Votes Cast (in millions)*	*Number of Votes as Percentage of Population of Voting Age*
1932	75.8	39.7	52.4
1936	80.2	45.6	56.0
1940	84.7	49.9	58.9
1944	85.7	48.0	56.0
1948	95.6	48.8	51.1
1952	99.9	61.6	61.6
1956	104.5	62.0	59.3
1960	109.7	68.8	62.8
1964	114.1	70.6	61.9
1968	120.3	73.2	60.9
1972[a]	140.8	77.6	55.1
1976	152.3	81.6	53.6
1980	164.6	86.5	52.6
1984	174.5	92.7	53.1
1988	182.8	91.6	50.1
1992	189.0	104.4	55.2
1996	196.5	96.5	49.1
2000	205.8	105.4	51.2
2004	221.3	122.3	55.3
2008	230.8	131.3	56.9
2012	240.9	130.3	53.6
2016	250.1	136.7	54.7

SOURCES: U.S. Bureau of the Census, *Current Population Reports,* Series P–25, No. 1085 (Washington, DC: U.S. Government Printing Office, 1994); 1996, 2000, and 2004 data from Federal Election Commission (FEC) website, www.fec.gov; and U.S. Census Bureau website, www.census.gov. Data for 2008, 2012, and 2016 from United States Elections Project, www.electproject.org/2008g, www.electproject.org/2012g, and www.electproject.org/2016g, respectively.

[a] beginning in 1972, persons eighteen to twenty years old were eligible to vote in all states.

requires states to provide voter registration opportunities through driver's license agencies, among other public offices, had increased registration, and Democrats made a concerted effort to register newly naturalized citizens. In 2004, a high percentage of voters expected the election to be close, and both parties tried hard to get their voters to the polls. These factors may help account for the jump in turnout, but voting in the United States remains low among the disadvantaged and when compared to other industrialized nations. Therefore, we cannot be certain what caused the changes between 1992 and 1996 or 2000 and 2008. Today, more states are adopting restrictive requirements designed to combat purported voter fraud even though the number of documented voter fraud cases remains quite low.

Validation

Translating the popular vote into the official outcome is the final stage of the selection process, in which the Electoral College produces the true winner. Until 2000, it had been more than a century since the constitutionally prescribed process failed to do so or produced a winner who was not also the "people's choice," although we had been dangerously close to such an Electoral College *misfire* on a number of occasions.

Despite the separation of the presidential and the vice presidential balloting in 1804, there remain three possible ways for a misfire to occur. First, the Electoral College does not ensure that the candidate who receives the most popular votes wins the presidency: John Quincy Adams in 1824, Rutherford B. Hayes in 1876, and Benjamin Harrison in 1888 became president even though they finished second in total popular vote to their respective political opponents. The same thing happened in 2000, when Gore won a national plurality of 543,895 votes but lost in the Electoral College. In 2016, Clinton won nearly 2.9 million more popular votes than Trump but finished second in the Electoral College.[109] Second, candidates may fail to win an Electoral College majority, thereby throwing selection into the House of Representatives. This situation occurred in 1800, 1824, and 1876.

The 2016 election illustrates well a third danger of the Electoral College system: An elector need not cast his or her ballot for the candidate who wins the plurality of votes in the elector's state. This problem of the **faithless elector** occurred eight times in the twentieth century, and in 2004 a Minnesota elector apparently mismarked his ballot and cast votes for John Edwards both as president and vice president. It is not particularly dangerous when isolated electors make an error or refuse to follow the result of their states' popular votes, but widespread desertion would be another matter. A record number of electors ignored their state results in 2016, four in Washington state, two in Texas, and one in Hawaii, with others thwarted while attempting to do so in Maine, Minnesota, and Colorado. This was the highest number of faithless electors in history, surpassing the six in 1808. Several voiced support for the defeated Bernie Sanders but others were trying to block the election of Trump.[110]

The Electoral College as it operates today violates some major tenets of political equality that are central to our contemporary understanding of democracy. Each person's vote does not count equally: One's influence on the outcome depends on the situation in one's state. For the many Americans who support a losing candidate, it is as though they had not voted at all because under the general-ticket system all the electoral votes of a state go to the candidate with a plurality of its popular votes. Perot received 19,741,048 votes, 18.9 percent of the total cast nationally in 1992, but he won no electoral votes because he did not finish first in any state or in any of the House districts in Maine and Nebraska. Citizens who live in populous, politically competitive states have a premium placed on their votes because they are in a position to affect how large blocs of electoral votes are cast. Similarly, permitting the House, voting by states, to select the president is not consistent with the "one person, one vote" principle that has become a central tenet of American democracy.[111]

Proposals to reform the Electoral College system attempt to remove the possibility of system failures and uphold a more modern understanding of democracy. They range from the rather modest suggestion of prohibiting faithless electors—votes would be cast automatically—to scrapping the present system and moving to a direct popular election. Intermediate suggestions would nationalize the congressional district plan used in Maine and Nebraska, divide electoral votes proportionally between (or among) the contenders, or provide the popular-vote winner with a hundred bonus votes, enough to ensure his or her victory in the Electoral College. No proposal is foolproof, and most must develop safeguards against new problems.

Is the Electoral College a constitutional anachronism that should no longer be preserved? In the aftermath of the 2000 election, attention once again focused on this eighteenth-century process, with many people stressing its inadequacies and others praising its genius. The constitutional amendments proposed then were just the latest in a long line; in fact "there have been more proposals for Constitutional amendments on changing the Electoral College than on any other subject," more than 700 throughout U.S. history.[112] The passage of a constitutional amendment is problematic because national legislators will calculate how the new system will affect their states' influence on the outcome (or their chances to pursue the office) and vote accordingly. A new reform proposal seeks to sidestep the difficulty of passing a constitutional amendment.

The National Popular Vote reform proposal asks states to adopt legislation that awards all of the state's electoral votes to the winner of the *national* popular vote, even if that person did not finish first in the state's balloting. Maryland was the first state to adopt such legislation in 2007, although the change will not go into effect until enough other states have adopted similar legislation to total 270 electoral votes.[113] By 2017, ten states (Maryland, Hawaii, Illinois, New Jersey, Vermont, Washington, Massachusetts, California, Rhode Island, and New York) and the District of Columbia, totaling 165 electoral votes, had adopted the reform legislation, and twelve other states passed the bill in one house of the legislature. Among other advantages, advocates point out that the 2012 general election focused candidates' attention on a handful of battleground states, especially Ohio, Florida, Virginia, and Iowa. In fact, the postconvention travel of the two parties' presidential and vice presidential candidates was limited to twelve states, barely one-fourth of the fifty-one contests nationally.[114] And 99 percent of television advertising, the principal method of modern campaigning, was concentrated in ten states. To avoid having most of the nation relegated to being spectators, supporters argue, adopting their reform would force candidates to wage a truly national contest.[115]

Defenders of the current system note that the most serious misfires occurred during periods of intense political divisiveness (for example, 1824 and 1876), when alternative selection systems would have been just as severely tested. Several of the close calls in the twentieth century, such as those in 1948 and 1968, occurred when political parties were suffering serious internal divisions. An examination of the historical conditions surrounding the misfires shows that only 1888, 2000, and 2016 offer clear examples of a popular-vote winner who lost the general election.[116] If popular-vote rules had been in place in 2000, the chaos would have been even more widespread because the results would have been challenged in many states with close outcomes, not just in Florida. A national recount would have been far more complex than state-by-state challenges. Democrats sought reform after 2000. In the wake of 2012, Republicans in key battleground states that went to Obama (Pennsylvania, Florida, Ohio, Michigan, Wisconsin, and Virginia) considered adopting either proportional or district-based systems of allocating electoral votes, hoping to provide support for the Republican presidential candidate in 2016. Changing the rules *can* change the outcome, but in 2016, Trump won five of those six battleground states under the unaltered rules. Only Virginia remained in the Democrats' column.[117]

Defenders also argue that the present system has been remarkably successful in producing peaceful resolutions even in tumultuous years. Its virtues include the requirement that candidates not only receive significant popular support but also have support sufficiently distributed geographically to enable the winner to govern. George W. Bush, for example, won thirty states in 2000, including eleven that had voted for Clinton in 1996. A report in the *Washington Times* notes that, even more significant, because of Bush's strength in the South and the West, "Had the

2000 presidential election been conducted using the new numbers [from the 2000 census] rather than the numbers based on the 1990 census Texas governor George W. Bush would have defeated Vice President Al Gore by a more comfortable 278 to 260 margin," a result closer to the 2004 outcome.[118] Ethnic minority groups, it is argued, receive special leverage under the present system because they are concentrated in states with large electoral vote totals and receive attention because their support might make the difference between winning all the electoral votes or none. Finally, some observers express concern that a system of direct election would encourage the development of minor parties based on regional or ideological interests that might organize in hopes of denying any candidate a majority or winning plurality and, thereby, force a runoff. Two-party stability, it is suggested, would be threatened. Following the 2016 election, Gallup found that public support for the Electoral College system had risen, especially among Republicans who showed a sharp drop in support for a popular majority system.[119]

Analysts differ over the wisdom of retaining the present electoral system, and even the brush with electoral crisis in 2000 did not produce a uniform response. Maintaining government legitimacy is a shared concern. Historically, successful candidates unable to secure a popular-vote majority gained legitimacy through an Electoral College majority. This happened twice to Bill Clinton and once to George W. Bush, although Clinton at least won the popular-vote plurality. Defenders of the Electoral College believe legitimacy is achieved through continuity with the past, but reformers believe it is achieved through enhancing popular control and avoiding controversy like that surrounding Bush's 2000 victory and Trump's in 2016.

Conclusion: Transitions to Governing

The presidential selection process has been altered many times throughout American history. Some of the informal changes resulting from new practices pursued by the political parties and candidates have been just as important as those resulting from constitutional amendments and statutes. The current system—largely a product of modifications introduced after 1968—stresses the preferences of voters expressed through presidential primaries over those of party professionals, enhances the role of the mass media, and centers on the candidates' ability to raise campaign funds. Front-loading the delegate selection schedule has transformed the dynamics of the early stages of the contest and substantially lengthened the overall process. Despite all this, the general election winner is still chosen by balloting in the Electoral College, not the national popular vote.

For the individual and election team that prevail in this long, grueling process, victory requires a sudden change in focus. The successful candidate realizes that winning is the means to an end, not an end in itself. Making that transition is sometimes difficult. Putting together a team of political executives to staff the new administration and establishing a list of program and policy priorities is accomplished during the transition, the period between election and inauguration. In the modern presidency, governing involves some of the same activities as getting elected, but the two are far from identical. Trump faced unusual problems in 2017 after using the election to wage war against the Republican, Democratic, and Washington establishments. We review the record of Trump's initial 100 days and his struggles in making this transition in the book's final chapter.

The burning question for everyone is how effective will the president be in leading the nation. Presidents vary along a wide range of dimensions—abilities, interests, personality—even as the office exhibits certain commonalities over time. In chapter 4, we turn to the problem of understanding how a president's personal characteristics influence performance in office, and subsequent chapters focus on presidents' political success. First, however, we examine their relationship with the public between elections, a relationship that has increased in importance in modern times.

Suggested Readings

Abramson, Paul R., John H. Aldrich, and David W. Rohde. *Change and Continuity in the 1980 Elections.* Washington, DC: CQ Press, 1982.

———. *Change and Continuity in the 1984 Elections.* Washington, DC: CQ Press, 1986.

———. *Change and Continuity in the 1988 Elections.* Washington, DC: CQ Press, 1990.

———. *Change and Continuity in the 1992 Elections.* Washington, DC: CQ Press, 1994.

———. *Change and Continuity in the 1992 Elections,* rev. ed. Washington, DC: CQ Press, 1995.

———. *Change and Continuity in the 1996 Elections.* Washington, DC: CQ Press, 1998.

———. *Change and Continuity in the 1996 and 1998 Elections.* Washington, DC: CQ Press, 1999.

———. *Change and Continuity in the 2000 and 2002 Elections.* Washington, DC: CQ Press, 2003.

———. *Change and Continuity in the 2004 and 2006 Elections.* Washington, DC: CQ Press, 2007.

———. *Change and Continuity in the 2008 and 2010 Elections.* Washington, DC: CQ Press, 2012.

Abramson, Paul R., John H. Aldrich, Brad T. Gomez, and David W. Rohde. *Change and Continuity in the 2012 and 2014 Elections.* Washington, DC: CQ Press, 2015.

Bartels, Larry M. *Presidential Primaries and the Dynamics of Public Choice.* Princeton, NJ: Princeton University Press, 1988.

Campbell, Angus, Philip Converse, Warren Miller, and Donald Stokes. *The American Voter,* abbr. ed. New York: Wiley, 1964.

Ceaser, James W., and Andrew E. Busch. *Red over Blue: The 2004 Elections and American Politics.* Lanham, MD: Rowman and Littlefield, 2005.

Ceaser, James W., Andrew E. Busch, and John J. Pitney Jr. *Epic Journey: The 2008 Elections and American Politics.* Lanham, MD: Rowman and Littlefield, 2009.

Mayer, William G., ed. *In Pursuit of the White House: How We Choose Our Presidential Nominees.* Chatham, NJ: Chatham House, 1996.

———. *In Pursuit of the White House, 2000: How We Choose Our Presidential Nominees.* Chatham, NJ: Chatham House, 1999.

———. *The Making of the Presidential Candidates,* 2008. Lanham, MD: Rowman and Littlefield, 2007.

Nelson, Michael, ed. *The Elections of 1996.* Washington, DC: CQ Press, 1997.

———. *The Elections of 2000.* Washington, DC: CQ Press, 2001.

———. *The Elections of 2004.* Washington, DC: CQ Press, 2005.

———. *The Elections of 2008.* Washington, DC: CQ Press, 2009.

Pomper, Gerald M., ed. *The Election of 1996: Reports and Interpretations.* Chatham, NJ: Chatham House, 1997.

———. *The Election of 2000: Reports and Interpretations.* Chatham, NJ: Chatham House, 2001.

Wayne, Stephen J. *The Road to the White House 2008.* New York: Wadsworth, 2007.

Resources on the Web

On the arcane workings of the Electoral College, see www.archives.gov/federal-register/electoral-college/index.html.

For an extensive collection of data on the presidency, including information about recent elections, see the American Presidency Project, www.presidency.ucsb.edu/.

For thorough analysis of voter turnout, see the United States Elections Project, www.electproject.org/home/voter-turnout/voter-turnout-data. Also see America Goes to the Polls 2006, 2008, 2010, 2012, 2014, 2016 a joint project of NonprofitVOTE and the US Elections Project, www.nonprofitvote.org/america-goes-to-the-polls-2016/execsummary/.

National Popular Vote reform effort, www.nationalpopularvote.com/index.php.

For a rich collection of presidential election maps, see www.uselectionatlas.org/.

Notes

1. Besides George Washington, James Monroe is the only candidate to approach this distinction; he won all but one Electoral College vote in 1820. Michael Nelson, ed., *Guide to the Presidency,* 4th ed. (Washington, DC: CQ Press, 2007), 2:1819.

2. William Chambers, *Political Parties in a New Nation: The American Experience,* 1776–1809 (New York: Oxford University Press, 1963), chap. 2.

3. Jefferson's Republican Party served as the basis for the Democratic Party. The Democratic-Republican Party was officially designated the Democratic Party in 1840. Paul David, Ralph Goldman, and Richard Bain, *The Politics of National Party Conventions* (New York: Vintage, 1964), chap. 3.

4. Joseph Charles, *The Origins of the American Party System* (New York: Harper Torch, 1956), 83–94.

5. Other constitutional amendments dealing with presidential selection have expanded participation (Amendments 15, 19, 24, 26), set the term of office (20, 22), and sought to cope with death or disability (20, 25).

6. David, Goldman, and Bain, *The Politics of National Party Conventions,* 50. The National Republican Party was soon to give way to the Whigs, with many Whig supporters joining the Republican Party when it was formed in the 1850s (57–59).

7. Ibid., 61.

8. First-ballot convention decisions have been surprisingly prevalent. Through 2012, the two major parties selected their candidates on the first ballot at sixty-one of eighty-seven conventions. Many of the multiballot conventions were held from 1840 to 1888, when sixteen of the twenty-two went past the first ballot. What distinguishes the post-1952 era is that *none* of the twenty-eight conventions went past one ballot.

9. Richard C. Bain and Judith H. Parris, *Convention Decisions and Voting Records,* 2nd ed. (Washington, DC: Brookings, 1973), 1–6.

10. "2016 Presidential Primaries, Caucuses, and Conventions Alphabetically by State," www.thegreenpapers.com/P16/events.phtml.

11. "Because 1956 was the first time that the Republicans were both the incumbent party and the one that met second, it is when the tradition of the Democrats having the later nomination was fully replaced with one of giving that privilege to the incumbents." Bruce E. Altschuler, "Scheduling the Party Conventions," *Presidential Studies Quarterly* 36 (December 2006): 662.

12. U.S. Census Bureau, "Characteristics of the Foreign Born Population by Nativity and U.S. Citizenship Status: 2009," Table 1.1, www.census.gov/population/www/socdemo/foreign/cps2009.html.

13. Jack Maskell, "Qualifications for President and the 'Natural Born' Citizenship Eligibility Requirement," *CRS Report* R42097 (November 14, 2011), 2; www.fas.org/sgp/crs/misc/R42097.pdf.

14. Neal Katyal and Paul Clement, "On the Meaning of 'Natural Born Citizen,'" *Harvard Law Review* 128:5 (March 2015), http://harvardlawreview.org/2015/03/on-the-meaning-of-natural-born-citizen/. See PolitiFact.com for March 26, 2015, www.politifact.com/truth-o-meter/article/2015/mar/26/ted-cruz-born-canada-eligible-run-president-update/.

15. John Aldrich, "Methods and Actors: The Relationship of Processes to Candidates," in *Presidential Selection,* ed. Alexander Heard and Michael Nelson (Durham, NC: Duke University Press, 1987).

16. Before Richard Nixon's selection in 1960, the last incumbent vice president to be nominated was Martin Van Buren in 1836.

17. Joseph A. Pika, "Bush, Quayle, and the New Vice Presidency," in *The Presidency and the Political System,* 3rd ed., ed. Michael Nelson (Washington, DC: CQ Press, 1990). Also see Joseph A. Pika, "The Vice Presidency: New Opportunities, Old Constraints," in *The Presidency and the Political System,* 6th ed., ed. Michael Nelson (Washington, DC: CQ Press, 2000); and Joseph A. Pika, "Dick Cheney, Joe Biden, and the New Vice Presidency," *The Presidency and the Political System,* 8th ed., ed. Michael Nelson (Washington, DC: CQ Press, 2009).

18. Ronald D. Elving, "The Senators' Lane to the Presidency," *Congressional Quarterly Weekly Report,* May 20, 1989, 1218.

19. Charlie Cook, "Nineteen's a Crowd: Why Are So Many Republicans Running for President?" *National Journal,* May 2, 2015, http://ujreview.com/2015/05/02/charlie-cook-nineteens-a-crowd-why-are-so-many-republicans-running-for-president/. See the regularly updated list maintained by Larry Sabato of the Center for Politics at *Sabato's Crystal Ball,* University of Virginia, www.centerforpolitics.org/crystalball/2016-president/.

20. For example, many of his colleagues suggested that Senator Paul's presidential hopes lay behind his late-May 2015 use of a dramatic filibuster and other delaying tactics to prevent renewal of government authority to fight terrorism by collecting citizens' phone data. Paul added to this impression by tweeting

supporters in real time about the success of his strategy. Dustin Volz, Brendan Sasso, Sarah Nimms, and Rachel Roubein, "How the Senate Fell Apart and Failed to Deal with the Patriot Act," *National Journal*, May 22, 2015, www.nationaljournal.com/tech/NSA-Patriot-Act-Rand-Paul-20150522.

21. For a statement of informal expectations from 1959, see Sidney Hyman, "Nine Tests for the Presidential Hopeful," *New York Times*, January 4, 1959, sec. 5, 1–11.

22. Michael Nelson, "Who Vies for President?" in Heard and Nelson, *Presidential Selection*, 144.

23. See Nonprofit Voter Engagement Network, *America Goes to the Polls: A Report on Voter Turnout in the 2008 Presidential Elections*, www.nonprofitvote.org/documents/2010/10/america-goes-to-the-polls-2008-pdf.pdf. With fewer primaries and a contest in only one party, the total in 2012 was 50 percent lower, estimated at 27.7 million, http://www.electproject.org/2012p. For 2016 see Drew DeSilver, "Turnout was high in the 2016 primary season, but just short of the 2008 record," Pew Research FactTank (June 10, 2016), www.pewresearch.org/fact-tank/2016/06/10/turnout-was-high-in-the-2016-primary-season-but-just-short-of-2008-record/.

24. "2012 Presidential Primaries, Caucuses, and Conventions Alphabetically by State," www.thegreenpapers.com/P12/events.phtml.

25. Austin Ranney, "Changing the Rules of the Nominating Game," in *Choosing the President*, ed. James David Barber (Englewood Cliffs, NJ: Prentice Hall, 1974), 71.

26. Barbara Norrander, "The End Game in Post-Reform Presidential Nominations," *The Journal of Politics* 62 (November 2000): 999–1013.

27. See the useful table "Chronological Cumulative Allocation of Delegates," www.thegreenpapers.com/P08/ccad.phtml.

28. Arthur Hadley, *The Invisible Primary* (Englewood Cliffs, NJ: Prentice Hall, 1976). For valuable updates, see Emmett H. Buell Jr., "The Invisible Primary," in *In Pursuit of the White House*, ed. William G. Mayer (Chatham, NJ: Chatham House, 1996), and Barbara Norrander, *The Imperfect Primary* (New York: Routledge, 2010), 35–45.

29. One study argues that party endorsements have become even more important than candidates' positions in the polls in determining the nominee. Marty Cohen, David Karol, Hans Noel, and John Zaller, *The Party Decides: Presidential Nominations Before and After Reform* (Chicago: University of Chicago Press, 2008). Also see the same authors' chapter, "The Invisible Primary in Presidential Nominations, 1980–2004," in William G. Mayer, ed., *The Making of the Presidential Candidates*, 2008 (Lanham, MD: Rowman and Littlefield, 2007), chap. 1.

30. In 2012, individuals were limited to contributions of $2,500 to a presidential candidate for each election, up from the previous $1,000 limit (the nomination and general election are considered separate contests), $5,000 per year to a political action committee (a group that contributes to more than one candidate), $30,800 to the national committee of a political party, and a total contribution of no more than $117,000 over two years. Presidential candidates are free to spend an unlimited amount of their and their immediate family's money on their campaigns, but if they accept public financing, their contributions to their campaigns are limited to $50,000 per election. These limits were raised for the 2015–2016 cycle to $2,700 for contributions to candidate campaigns, $33,400 to a national party, and a total of $100,200 per year. See the Federal Election Commission brochure on "Contributions" for the limits set for 2011–2012, www.fec.gov/pages/brochures/contrib.shtml#electionlimits.

31. Peter Overby, "Presidential Candidates Move Away From Public Financing," NPR, April 14, 2015, www.npr.org/2015/04/14/399641392/presidential-candidates-move-away-from-public-financing. Also see David D. Kirkpatrick, "Death Knell May Be Near for Public Election Funds," *New York Times*, January 23, 2007.

32. In prior election cycles, John Connally, Steve Forbes, Maurice Taylor, Orrin Hatch, and George W. Bush—all Republicans—refused prenomination public funding. On 2008, see Kirkpatrick, "Death Knell."

33. The lower totals, the lowest since creation of the system in 1976, reflected the absence of Bush and Kerry in 2004 and Clinton and Obama in 2008. All could have easily qualified for the funding. See press releases from the Federal Election Commission, February 3, 2005, and July 16, 2008, https://beta.fec.gov/updates/2004-presidential-campaign-finance-activity-summarized/ and http://classic.fec.gov/press/press2008/20080714matching.shtml, respectively.

34. Anthony Corrado, "Financing the 1996 Elections," in *The Election of 1996,* ed. Gerald M. Pomper (Chatham, NJ: Chatham House, 1997).

35. Anthony Corrado, "Financing the 2000 Elections," in *The Election of 2000,* ed. Gerald M. Pomper (Chatham, NJ: Chatham House, 2001), 98.

36. Not all individual contributions are small, and it is legal for political action committees to help finance nomination campaigns, but their contributions are not matched by federal funds as in the case of individuals.

37. This did not happen in 2004 when Howard Dean led the field in fund-raising or in 2008 when McCain was not the leader. Overall, it is not clear whether the additional financial resources produce victory or whether contributors simply choose to give their money to the leading candidate.

38. From the text of July 18, 2002, press release announcing creation of the Task Force on Financing Presidential Nominations, www.cfinst.org/pr/prRelease.aspx?ReleaseID=23.

39. Andrew Mayersohn, "Four Years after Citizens United: The Fallout," *Open Secrets,* Center for Responsive Politics, January 21, 2014, www.opensecrets.org/news/2014/01/four-years-after-citizens-united-the-fallout.

40. Dino P. Christenson and Corwin D. Smidt, "Following the Money: Super PACs and the 2012 Presidential Nomination," *Presidential Studies Quarterly* 44:3 (September 2014): 410–430.

41. The Editorial Board, "How Super PACS Can Run Campaigns," *New York Times,* April 27, 2015, www.nytimes.com/2015/04/27/opinion/how-super-pacs-can-run-campaigns.html?_r=2.

42. Maggie Haberman and Nicholas Confessore, "Hillary Clinton Embraces a 'Super PAC,' Trying to Erode a Republican Edge," *New York Times,* May 6, 2015, www.nytimes.com/2015/05/07/us/politics/hillary-clinton-to-court-donors-for-super-pac.html?_r=1.

43. Nicholas Confessore and Eric Lichtblau, "'Campaigns' Aren't Necessarily Campaigns in the Age of 'Super PACs,'" *New York Times,* May 17, 2015, www.nytimes.com/2015/05/18/us/politics/super-pacs-are-remaking-16-campaigns-official-or-not.html?nlid=69310600.

44. Shane Goldmacher, "Buying a Nominee," *National Journal,* January 24, 2015, www.nationaljournal.com/magazine/the-secret-fundraising-scheme-that-will-make-super-pacs-look-quaint-in-2016-20150123.

45. FEC, "Presidential Pre-nomination Campaign Receipts through June 30, 2016," Presidential Table 1; "Presidential Pre-nomination Campaign Disbursements through June 30, 2016," Presidential Table 2, www.fec.gov/press/summaries/2016/tables/presidential/PresCand2_2016_18m.pdf.

46. See fund-raising data for individual candidates on the website of the Center for Responsive Politics, https://www.opensecrets.org/pres16/candidate?id=N00037006.

47. In 1984, the minimum was 20 percent, a rule that favored the front-runner, Walter Mondale. Complaints from defeated candidates Jesse Jackson and Gary Hart resulted in lowering the qualifying level to 15 percent for the 1988 contest, and that rule has continued. Most Republican contests have been conducted under winner-take-all rules, although some states use proportional rules for both parties.

48. Alan Greenblatt and Rhodes Cook, "Nominating Process Rules Change," *Congressional Quarterly Weekly Report,* August 17, 1996, 2299. For the 2000 election, see Andrew E. Busch, "New Features of the 2000 Presidential Nominating Process: Republican Reforms, Front-Loading's Second Wind, and Early Voting," in *In Pursuit of the White House 2000,* ed. William G. Mayer (New York: Chatham House, 2001).

49. Marjorie Randon Hershey, "The Campaign and the Media," in Pomper, *The Election of 2000,* 47.

50. C. Anthony Broh, *A Horse of a Different Color: Television's Treatment of Jesse Jackson's 1984 Presidential Campaign* (Washington, DC: Joint Center for Political Studies, 1987), 4.

51. For discussion of the primary contests in 2000 and election results, see William G. Mayer, "The Presidential Nominations," in Pomper, *The Election of 2000.*

52. Broh, *A Horse of a Different Color,* 44.

53. Exceptions to this pattern can be found when two candidates end the preconvention period fairly even. This was the case with McGovern and Humphrey in 1972, Ford and Reagan in 1976, Mondale and Hart in 1984, and Clinton and Obama in 2008; in each case, however, the preconvention leader took the nomination.

54. The difference in convention costs is made up by contributions from individuals and organizations to the convention organizing committees in each city. See www.opensecrets.org/pres08/convcmtes.php?cycle=2008.

55. R. Sam Garrett and Shawn Reese, "Funding of Presidential Nominating Conventions: An Overview," *Congressional Research Service* CRS Report R43976, April 9, 2015, www.fas.org/sgp/crs/misc/R43976.pdf.

56. Judith Parris, *The Convention Problem: Issues in Reform of Presidential Nominating Procedures* (Washington, DC: Brookings, 1972), 110; and Terri Susan Fine, "Presidential Nominating Conventions in a Democracy," *Perspectives on Political Science* (Winter 2003): 32–40.

57. Edwin Diamond, Gregg Geller, and Chris Whitley, "Air Wars: Conventions Go Cable," *National Journal,* August 31, 1996, 1859. In 2004, the major networks carried only three hours of prime-time convention coverage, less than one hour a night and a far cry from the once-continuous coverage typical of the 1950s and 1960s.

58. "No elector has ever been prosecuted for failing to vote as pledged." From U.S. Electoral College FAQ, www.archives.gov/federal-register/electoral-college/faq.html#popular. However, in 2016 three electors were not allowed to cast their vote as they wished. Electors in Maine and Minnesota wanted to support Bernie Sanders but were told such a vote would violate state law. An elector in Colorado was replaced when he tried to vote for Kasich. Kyle Cheney, "Electoral College sees record-breaking defections," *Politico* (December 19, 2016) http://www.politico.com/story/2016/12/electoral-college-electors-232836. For a list of the state laws, see U.S. National Archives and Records Administration, www.archives.gov/federal-register/electoral-college/electors.html.

59. Federal Election Commission press release, "2004 Presidential Campaign Financial Activity Summarized," February 3, 2005, http://classic.fec.gov/press/press2005/20050203pressum/20050203pressum.html. Nominees receiving full funding may accept other direct contributions only to meet legal and accounting fees, so George W. Bush's enormous fund-raising advantage during the prenomination phase in 1999–2000 could not be repeated for the general election phase.

60. See Fred Wertheimer, president of Democracy 21, "Opening Remarks," conference on the Bipartisan Campaign Reform Act, June 23, 2003; found on the organization website under "BCRA and Other Campaign Finance Laws," www.democracy21.org/.

61. Center for Responsive Politics, www.opensecrets.org/outsidespending/index.php and www.opensecrets.org/pres12/index.php#out.

62. Herbert Alexander and Monica Bauer, *Financing the 1988 Election* (Boulder, CO: Westview, 1991), Table 2.1; Herbert Alexander and Anthony Corrado, *Financing the 1992 Election* (Boulder, CO: Westview, 1995), chap. 5, Table 5.1; and Federal Election Commission, *The Presidential Public Funding Program* (Washington, DC: Author, 1993), 31.

63. Corrado, "Financing the 2000 Elections," 107.

64. Ibid., 109. In 2000, independent expenditures by political groups favored Gore by a margin of seven to one, with Planned Parenthood leading the way.

65. Wertheimer, “Opening Remarks.”

66. Federal Election Commission press release, “Public Funds” (2004). Also see the records reported by the Center for Responsive Politics at www.opensecrets.org/pres08/indexp.php.

67. Although presidential candidates are free to refuse public funds, no major-party nominee had done so in the general election through 2004, perhaps because the maximum contribution limitations made raising money from individuals and groups more difficult. Candidates may also have thought the public favors the use of public, rather than private, funds. This changed dramatically in 2008 when Obama reversed his previous public position and refused public funding.

68. Center for Responsive Politics, “2008 Presidential Election,” www.opensecrets.org/pres08/. For 2016, the Center estimates that candidates raised $1.5 billion and super PACs another $615 million. https://www.opensecrets.org/pres16.

69. Michael J. Malbin, “Small Donors, Large Donors and the Internet: the Case for Public Financing after Obama,” in *Presidential Public Financing* (Washington, DC: Campaign Finance Institute, 2009).

70. Amy Parnes and Kevin Cirilli, “The $5 Billion Presidential Campaign?” *The Hill*, January 21, 2015, http://thehill.com/blogs/ballot-box/presidential-races/230318-the-5-billion-campaign.

71. Center for Responsive Politics, “2014 Top Donors to Outside Spending Groups,” www.opensecrets.org/outsidespending/summ.php?disp=D; “Top Individual Contributors: All Federal Contributions,” 2016, https://www.opensecrets.org/overview/topindivs.php?cycle=2016.

72. The Twenty-Third Amendment, ratified in 1961, gave the District of Columbia the right to participate in presidential elections. Previously, District residents were excluded. Their inclusion accounts for there being three more electoral votes (538) than the total number of senators and representatives (535). Citizens living in U.S. territories and the commonwealth of Puerto Rico do not have a vote in the general election.

73. For election results and a brief account of the events surrounding the Florida outcome, see Gerald M. Pomper, “The Presidential Election,” in Pomper, *The Election of 2000*, 125–135. For an in-depth journalistic account of the Florida situation, see *Deadlock: The Inside Story of America's Closest Election*, comp. Political Staff of the *Washington Post* (New York: Public Affairs, 2001).

74. Gore received 266 votes. One elector from the District of Columbia, Barbara Lett-Simmons, who should have cast her ballot for Gore and Lieberman, instead cast a blank ballot as a means of protesting the lack of D.C. statehood and a vote in Congress. Therefore, the two-party total is not 538. A copy of the ballot can be viewed at the Electoral College website of the National Archives, www.archives.gov/federal_register/electoral_college/2000_certificates/vote_dc.html.

75. New York and Pennsylvania each lost two House seats. Connecticut, Illinois, Indiana, Michigan, Mississippi, Ohio, Oklahoma, and Wisconsin each lost one. Arizona, Florida, Georgia, and Texas each gained two seats; and California, Colorado, Nevada, and North Carolina each gained one. Because of widespread criticism following the 1990 census, the Census Bureau agreed to conduct a postcensus survey to determine the extent to which some population groups had been undercounted. The results of that study should have led to adjustments in congressional representation, but the secretary of commerce recommended following the initial census findings. A similar debate followed the 2000 census. Utah filed suit to have its residents serving as missionaries abroad included in the count, which would give it the additional seat awarded to North Carolina. In *Utah v. Evans* (2002), the Supreme Court decided in favor of North Carolina.

76. In 1992, Clinton amassed 370 electoral votes by winning thirty-two states, each state that had voted for Dukakis in 1988 and all but one of the twelve where the previous Democratic nominee had won at least 45 percent of the vote. Clinton totaled 379 electoral votes in 1996, winning twenty-nine of the same states and adding two longtime Republican strongholds—Arizona and Florida.

77. Gore lost New Hampshire by 7,300 votes; Nader garnered 22,198 there. Nader also received 97,488 votes in Florida, thousands more than Gore needed for victory. Bush lost New Mexico by

366 votes; Buchanan received 1,392 there. In Wisconsin, Bush lost by 5,708, while Buchanan secured 11,471. See official 2000 election results at www.fec.gov/pubrec/2000presgeresults.htm.

78. Angus Campbell et al., *The American Voter,* abbr. ed. (New York: Wiley, 1964).

79. For similar figures for the 2000 election, see Paul R. Abramson, John H. Aldrich, and David W. Rohde, *Change and Continuity in the 2000 and 2002 Elections* (Washington, DC: CQ Press, 2003), 171. The Harris Poll, using a different question and methodology, set identification in early 2004 at 33 percent Democrat, 28 percent Republican, and 24 percent Independent. The Harris Poll 15, "Democrats Still Hold a Small Lead in Party Identification," February 7, 2004, www.prnewswire.com/news-releases/democrats-still-hold-a-small-lead-in-party-identification-according-to-national-harris-interactive-survey-71866417.html.

80. Pew Research Center for the People & the Press, "Partisan Polarization Surges in Bush, Obama Years," June 4, 2012, www.people-press.org/2012/06/04/section-9-trends-in-party-affiliation/. On 2016 see Pew findings, www.pewresearch.org/data-trend/political-attitudes/party-identification/, and Gallup findings, www.gallup.com/poll/15370/Party-Affiliation.aspx.

81. Gerald M. Pomper, "The Presidential Election," in *The Election of 1988: Reports and Interpretations,* ed. Gerald M. Pomper (Chatham, NJ: Chatham House, 1989), 136.

82. Offsetting gains in nonwhite voting, white fundamentalist Christians have gained significance in national politics. This group has become solidly Republican and in 1988 was nearly as large a proportion of the voting population as blacks (9 percent versus 10 percent). See poll results reported in Gerald M. Pomper, "The Presidential Election," in Pomper, *The Election of 1996,* 134.

83. "Election Results 2008," *New York Times,* November 5, 2008, http://elections.nytimes.com/2008/results/president/exit-polls.html.

84. Jon Huang, Samuel Jacoby, Michael Strickland, and K. K. Rebecca Lai, "Election 2016: Exit Polls," *New York Times,* November 8, 2016, https://www.nytimes.com/interactive/2016/11/08/us/politics/election-exit-polls.html. Exit polling conducted in 2016 by Edison Research for the National Election Pool, a consortium of ABC News, The Associated Press, CBSNews, CNN, Fox News, and NBC News. The voter survey was based on questionnaires completed by 24,537 voters leaving 350 voting places throughout the United States on Election Day including 4,398 telephone interviews with early and absentee voters.

85. Marjorie Randon Hershey, "The Campaign and the Media," in Pomper, *The Election of 1988,* 78, 80–83. and Paul J. Quirk, "The Election," in Pomper, *The Election of 1988,* 76.

86. Erika Franklin Fowler, Travis N. Ridout, and Michael M. Franz, "Political Advsertising in 2016: The Presidential Election as Outlier?" *The Forum* 2016; 14(4): 445–469, p. 457.

87. Exit poll conducted by Voter News Service and reported in Nelson, "The Election: Turbulence and Tranquility," in Nelson, *The Elections of 1996,* 57.

88. Pomper, "The Presidential Election," in Pomper, *The Election of 2000,* 146.

89. ABC News Survey, conducted October 9 through November 4, 2004, archived on *National Journal.*

90. David B. Holian and Charles Prysby, "Candidate Character Traits in the 2012 Election," *Presidential Studies Quarterly* 44:3 (September 2014): 484–505.

91. Harry Enten, "Trump Won Despite Being Unpopular, So Can He Govern That Way," FiveThirtyEight, November 22, 2016, https://fivethirtyeight.com/features/trump-won-despite-being-unpopular-so-can-he-govern-that-way/.

92. Campbell et al., *The American Voter,* chap. 7.

93. For 1960s data, see Gerald M. Pomper, *Voters' Choice: Varieties of American Electoral Behavior* (New York: Dodd, Mead, 1975), chap. 8. For 1970s data, see Norman Nie, Sidney Verba, and John Petrocik, *The Changing American Voter* (Cambridge, MA: Harvard University Press, 1979), chap. 7.

94. Paul R. Abramson, John H. Aldrich, and David W. Rohde, *Change and Continuity in the 2004 Elections* (Washington, DC: CQ Press, 2006), 149.

95. Katherine Q. Seelye, "Moral Values Cited as a Defining Issue of the Election," *New York Times,* November 4, 2004, www.nytimes.com/2004/11/04/politics/campaign/04poll.html?ei=5070&en=19005b.

96. Abramson, Aldrich, and Rohde, *Change and Continuity in the 2004 Elections,* 142, 158–159.

97. Pew Research Center for the People & the Press, "Changing Face of America Helps Assure Obama Victory," November 7, 2012, www.people-press.org/2012/11/07/changing-face-of-america-helps-assure-obama-victory/. Also see Justine D'Elia and Helmut Norporth, "Winning with a Bad Economy," *Presidential Studies Quarterly* 44:3 (September 2014): 467–483.

98. Pew Research Center for the People & the Press, "Inside Obama's Sweeping Victory," November 5, 2008, http://pewresearch.org/pubs/1023/exit-poll-analysis-2008.

99. Paige Lavender, "These Might Be Donald Trump's Most Disgusting Comments Yet about Women," *Huffington Post,* October 7, 2016, www.huffingtonpost.com/entry/donald-trump-women-comments_us_57f8016de4b0e655eab4148d.

100. Martin Wattenberg, "Personal Popularity in U.S. Presidential Elections," *Presidential Studies Quarterly* 34 (March 2004): 146.

101. Pomper, "The Presidential Election," in Pomper, *The Election of 2000,* 142.

102. Abramson, Aldrich, and Rohde, *Change and Continuity in the 2004 Elections,* 176.

103. See Alan I. Abramowitz, "Will Time for Change Mean Time for Trump?" *PS* (October 2016): 659–660.

104. Nielsen, "First Presidential Debate of 2016 Draws 84 Million Viewers," *Nielsen Insights,* www.nielsen.com/us/en/insights/news/2016/first-presidential-debate-of-2016-draws-84-million-viewers.html.

105. See the transcript of this debate and others at www.debates.org/index.php?page=october-5-1988-debate-transcripts.

106. The 1992 turnout represented an increase of about 13 million voters over the 1988 total. Twenty-three candidates shared the votes, although only four—Bush, Clinton, Perot, and the Libertarian Party candidate, Andre Marrou—were on ballots in all fifty states. Federal Election Commission press release, January 14, 1993.

107. Michael P. McDonald, "Turnout in the 2012 Presidential Election," *Huffington Post,* February 11, 2013, www.huffingtonpost.com/michael-p-mcdonald/turnout-in-the-2012-presi_b_2663122.html; Michael P. McDonald, United States Elections Project, "2016 General Election Turnout Rates," www.electproject.org/2016g; and George Pillsbury and Julian Johannesen, *America Goes to the Polls 2016,* Nonprofit Vote and U.S. Elections Project, www.nonprofitvote.org/documents/2017/03/america-goes-polls-2016.pdf.

108. Abramson, Aldrich, and Rohde, *Change and Continuity in the 2004 Elections,* chap. 4.

109. Official results can be found at www.fec.gov/pubrec/2000presgeresults.htm and www.fec.gov/pubrec/fe2016/2016presgeresults.pdf.

110. In 1960, 1968, 1972, 1976, and 1988, single electors in Oklahoma, North Carolina, Virginia, Washington, and West Virginia, respectively, failed to cast their ballots for the candidate receiving the popular-vote plurality in their states. For complete results of Electoral College voting, see Nelson, *Guide to the Presidency,* 2, 1820–1844; see 1819 for a list of faithless electors. Also see the list maintained by Fair Vote: The Center for Voting and Democracy, www.fairvote.org/faithless-electors/. On results in 2016 see Kyle Cheney, "Electoral College Sees Record-Breaking Defections," *Politico,* December 19, 2016, www.politico.com/story/2016/12/electoral-college-electors-232836.

111. Numerous efforts emerged in the wake of the 2000 election to shed light on the unfairness of the current system. To explore the over- and underrepresentation of citizens depending on state of residence, see "Federal Representation 2002–2010," www.thegreenpapers.com/Census00/FedRep.phtml?sort=Elec#Elec.

112. See "U.S. Electoral College: Frequently Asked Questions," www.archives.gov/federal_register/electoral_college/faq.html#tie.

113. John R. Koza et al., *Every Vote Equal: A State-Based Plan for Electing the President by National Popular Vote* (Los Altos, CA: National Popular Vote Press, 2006). The campaign's progress can be tracked at www.nationalpopularvote.com/index.php.

114. "Four out of Five Americans Were Ignored in 2012 Presidential Election," http://archive.nationalpopularvote.com/pages/misc/4-of-5-ignored-in-2012.php.

115. Robert Richie and Andrea Levien, "The Contemporary Presidency: How the 2012 Presidential Election Has Strengthened the Movement for the National Popular Vote Plan," *Presidential Studies Quarterly* 43:2 (June 2013): 353–376.

116. William C. Kimberling, "Electing the President: The Genius of the Electoral College," *FEC Journal* (Fall 1988): 16.

117. Rob Richie, "Electoral College Chaos: How Republicans Can Put a Lock on the Presidency," www.fairvote.org/electoral-college-chaos-how-republicans-could-put-a-lock-on-the-presidency.

118. Sean Scully, *Washington Times,* December 29, 2000, A12. Gore carried all but two of the states that lost House seats, and Bush won all of the states that stood to gain seats except California.

119. Ibid., 19–20. Gallup "Americans' Support for Electoral College Rises Sharply," December 2, 2016, www.gallup.com/poll/198917/americans-support-electoral-college-rises-sharply.aspx?g_source=electoral&g_medium=search&g_campaign=tiles.

CHAPTER 3

Public Politics

Courtesy of the Library of Congress, Prints and Photographs Division

Woodrow Wilson throws out the first ball on opening day of the baseball season in 1916. Wilson helped to usher in the modern public presidency.

For more than a century, students of the presidency have argued that the chief executive's continuing relationship with the American public is a major factor in governing the nation. Writing in 1900, Henry Jones Ford concluded that only presidents can "define issues in such a way that public opinion can pass upon them decisively."[1] Woodrow Wilson, anticipating his own approach to the office, echoed that sentiment: "His [the president's] is the only national voice in affairs. Let him once win the admiration and confidence of the country and no other single force can withstand him; no combination of forces will easily overpower him."[2]

As discussed in chapter 1, this preeminent position was strengthened during the second half of the twentieth century. In 1960, Richard Neustadt explained how the presidents' "public prestige," their "standing with the public outside Washington," influences the decisions of other government officials and nongovernmental elites, including members of Congress and the bureaucracy, state governors, military commanders, party politicians, journalists, and foreign diplomats.[3] By the mid-1980s Samuel Kernell was arguing that "**going public**"—issuing campaign-like appeals for citizen support rather than the traditional strategy of bargaining with other elites—had become the key to presidential success in the modern era.[4] Broadcast television was once seen as the most powerful tool for going public, but by 1999 Kernell and Matthew A. Baum suggested that the rise of cable television had made traditional network appeals more difficult. Hundreds of channels of alternate programming meant that presidents were losing the captive audiences they used to command when all three major networks preempted their regular schedules to carry presidential appearances.[5] Since then, social media and the Internet have continued to fragment those audiences even as they became effective ways to target presidential communication to specific constituencies. No matter the means or the difficulty involved, presidents cannot afford to stop courting voters after the returns are in on election day; modern chief executives must woo the American public between elections just as they do during election seasons.

Despite a president's best efforts, maintaining public support is often difficult. Approval ratings can change quickly and can be influenced by the state of the economy and crises abroad—events that are sometimes unrelated to specific presidential action. In the week after the terrorist attacks on the World Trade Center and the Pentagon, George W. Bush's Gallup approval rating shot up thirty-five points, reaching a high of 90 percent in September 2001, but plummeted to a low of 25 percent the month before Barack Obama's November 2008 win as president. By the time Bush left office in January 2009, his approval rating had rebounded slightly to 34 percent.[6] Bush's father, George H. W. Bush, suffered a similar fate. He enjoyed an 89 percent approval rating during the Persian Gulf War only to have it dwindle to 32 percent—largely because of a faltering economy. After defeating the incumbent in 1992, Bill Clinton failed to generate high levels of public support during his first three years as chief executive but left office in 2001 with the highest approval rating of any departing president since the advent of public opinion polls.[7] Even after he was impeached, Clinton maintained high job approval ratings—a factor that some observers attributed to the strong economy, which may have aided his acquittal in the Senate.[8] Obama entered office with a 68 percent Gallup approval rating, but it dipped to a low of 38 percent during his first term. By the time he left office, however, it had rebounded to a very strong 59 percent. In contrast, Donald J. Trump's initial Gallup approval rating stood at only 45 percent and quickly slid—hitting an early low of 35 percent in March when efforts to repeal and replace the Affordable Care Act stalled. Gallup also reported that the percentage of respondents who believed that Trump "keeps his promises" dropped precipitously from 62 percent in January 2017 to 45 percent in April 2017.[9] For his part, Trump tweeted on February 6, "Any negative polls are fake news, just like the CNN, ABC, NBC polls in the election."[10]

This chapter begins with an analysis of enduring public attitudes toward the presidency and then considers the ways chief executives try to hold the support of the American people. These include the use of public appeals, targeted communications to interest groups and party activists, and efforts to use the media to the president's advantage. We conclude the chapter by arguing that these tactics have helped to create a "permanent campaign" that presidents wage between elections.

Public Attitudes toward the Presidency

Citizens relate to the presidency on many levels. At the conscious level, people develop attitudes toward three major components of a political system: (1) the political community of which they are a part; (2) the regime, or formal and informal "rules of the game" followed in the constitutional system; and (3) the authorities, the public officials who hold positions in the government structure.[11] If these attitudes are sufficiently strong and positive, the public may follow its leaders even if it does not like a particular incumbent or the policies that leader advocates.

The president, it can be argued, is the focus of public attitudes in each of these three areas. Like the British monarch, the U.S. chief executive is the symbol of the nation, a personification of government capable of inspiring feelings of loyalty and patriotism, particularly in times of crisis when the leader becomes the rallying point for national efforts. Franklin D. Roosevelt's political friends and foes alike turned to him for leadership when the Japanese attacked Pearl Harbor in December 1941. George W. Bush enjoyed a similar rallying effect after the September 11, 2001, terrorist attacks. Calls to support the president quickly drown out critical voices—at least in the short run.

Because presidents are central figures in the constitutional system, they can benefit from upholding the accepted rules of the game or suffer from violating them. Many Americans felt that Richard Nixon violated his constitutional obligations as well as basic democratic values by placing himself above the law during the Watergate scandal; evidence indicated that he participated in a cover-up designed to hide the truth about an illegal break-in directed by White House aides. The Monica Lewinsky scandal, however, showed that many Americans seemed to make a distinction between the types of abuses of power that Nixon engaged in and Clinton's efforts to cover up a sexual affair with Lewinsky. Most viewed Clinton's affair as a private matter that had nothing to do with his job as president.[12]

Finally, presidents are major actors in the policymaking process. The positions they adopt elicit support or opposition, and their overall performance in office becomes the object of citizens' evaluations. Again, Clinton showed that Americans could make a distinction between job performance and personal approval. As he was leaving office in January 2001, a Gallup poll showed a 65 percent job approval rating but only a 41 percent personal approval rating. An April 2000 Gallup poll was even more striking: 59 percent job approval but only 29 percent personal approval.

Fred Greenstein has suggested that presidents meet a variety of psychological needs of the citizenry. As a cognitive aid, the president can make government and politics comprehensible. By focusing on the president's activities, citizens simplify a distant and complex world. The president also provides an outlet for feelings experienced by supporters and opponents, giving citizens the opportunity to develop and express emotions about politics. On the subconscious level, some citizens may seek vicarious participation, a desire to identify with a powerful political figure much as people do with fictional figures and entertainment personalities. Presidents, at least historically, symbolized national unity as well as stability and predictability, providing citizens with psychologically satisfying feelings that may meet fundamental needs for membership and reassurance. Finally, presidents serve as lightning rods within the political system—figures to blame for bad times and to credit for good times.[13] Because presidents play a central role in the nightly dramas communicated on every news platform—television, Internet, social media of all stripes, and around-the-clock cable outlets such as CNN, Fox News, and MSNBC—their importance as objects of psychological feelings may be greater today than ever before. Now they are not just on our television screens but also on the smartphone screens in our pockets.

Beyond basic beliefs and psychological needs, the public also has views about the day-to-day operation of the political system—in particular, the major issues of the day and the policies the government should follow in dealing with them. These views, generally assumed to be less stable and enduring than beliefs about the political culture, are often described as matters of "public opinion." A citizen's attitudes on policy issues and presidential performance depend on his or her identity with a particular group, such as a political party, and his or her social, economic, and geographic background. As the nation's leading political figure, the president is expected to develop and help put into effect policies—perhaps controversial policies—that are binding on the entire populace. People respond favorably or unfavorably to each chief executive's particular personality and political style and to the events that occur while a president is in office. People also assess presidents by the way they relate to particular groups—political parties as well as social (religious, ethnic, racial), economic (business, labor), and geographic divisions of the population.

Clearly, many diverse factors affect public opinion of the president. At times people see the chief executive as the embodiment of the nation; on other occasions people link the president with a particular issue or policy they favor or oppose. We turn next to the symbolic dimensions of the presidency and how people develop their attitudes toward the office and its occupant. We then look more closely at public opinion polls.

Symbolic Dimensions of the Presidency

Ceremony and pomp surround the presidency. A presidential inauguration resembles the coronation of a monarch, complete with the taking of an oath in the presence of notables and "the hailing by the multitudes."[14] Public appearances are accompanied by a display of the special presidential seal and the playing of "Hail to the Chief" as the president arrives. News conferences are conducted under a set of rules designed to communicate deference and respect as much as elicit hard news.

Particular occasions have been elevated to ritualistic status. The State of the Union address, for example, allows the president to outline an agenda for Congress and the nation. Woodrow Wilson resurrected this ceremony after more than a century of disuse, and today it is an annual occasion for high drama and solemn pronouncements aimed as much at the prime-time television audience as the political elites in attendance. Members of Congress, Supreme Court justices, the cabinet, and the diplomatic corps as well as distinguished visitors gather in the House chamber and chatter expectantly until the sergeant-at-arms solemnly announces the president's arrival, at which point the audience respectfully rises to its feet and applauds. Following a formal introduction from the Speaker of the House, there is another standing ovation. After the speech, a phalanx of congressional leaders accompanies the president as he leaves the hall, and members reach out along the way to shake hands or just to touch the president.

These outward manifestations of respect, made part of recurrent governing rituals, indicate the near reverence accorded the position of president. Respect for the *presidency* as distinct from the *president,* the current officeholder, is deeply ingrained in American political culture. George Washington and his advisers gave the office dignity by enhancing its ceremonial functions and designing a set of "republican rituals," for which no direct precedents existed, based on their exclusive experience with monarchy.[15] But Washington's major contribution to the presidency was to imbue the office with nearly mythical stature. At one time Washington's likeness was displayed so widely that it became a virtual icon, the picture of a venerated saint displayed by fervent believers in hopes of deriving blessings.[16] The hero worship lavished on Washington during his lifetime and the subsequent cult that developed in commemorating his service to the nation ensured that the presidency will always be associated with the nation's own sense of moral virtue and collective destiny.[17]

In the late nineteenth century, Washington's birthday became a day of national celebration second only to the Fourth of July. In many states, Abraham Lincoln's birthday, too, came to be celebrated as a holiday. Eventually, the two were combined into Presidents' Day. Every February, elementary school teachers regale their classes with stories about these presidents, whose youthful endeavors illustrate the fundamental virtues of truthfulness ("Father, I cannot tell a lie"), honesty (walking miles to return change), and hard work (as wilderness surveyor and rail-splitter). In like ways, we celebrate the lives of Washington's successors, and we also expect them to live up to the heroic qualities of their predecessors.

Consistent with this symbolic role, the nation routinely turns to the president to perform a variety of ceremonial chores, many of them minor, such as lighting the national Christmas tree and issuing proclamations on the observance of special days. But Americans also call upon presidents to perform more important symbolic tasks, such as helping citizens deal with their collective grief when disaster strikes. President Obama expressed the feelings of millions when he publicly mourned the mass shooting deaths of nine people attending a prayer service at Emanuel African Methodist Episcopal Church in Charleston, South Carolina, in June 2015. It was at least the fifteenth eulogy he had delivered as president, leading the *Washington Post* to dub the president "the eulogizer-in-chief."[18] Some of those eulogies had been for victims of other shooting sprees, such as the twenty school children and six adult staff members who were killed by a gunman at Sandy Hook Elementary School in Newtown, Connecticut, in December 2012. And before that he sought to comfort the nation when a gunman killed six people and wounded thirteen others, including Rep. Gabrielle Giffords, D-AZ, in Tucson, Arizona, in January 2011.

The presidency, more than any other aspect of political life, links Americans with both the past and the future. In focusing on the current White House occupant, citizens simultaneously derive a sense of fulfillment from past accomplishments and reassurance about the future. Presidents often help to evoke such

AP Photo/Carolyn Kaster

President Obama comforted family members and delivered a powerful eulogy in June 2015 at the funeral service of Pastor and State Senator Clementa Pinckney in Charleston, S.C. after nine worshipers were killed in a black church by a white gunman. Perhaps the most moving moment was the president quietly beginning to sing "Amazing Grace."

feelings of continuity through symbolism. When Clinton gave his farewell address on January 18, 2001, he was flanked by busts of Lincoln and FDR. When Bush took the oath of office two days later, he used the same 1767 Bible used in the inauguration ceremonies of George Washington, Warren Harding, Dwight D. Eisenhower, Jimmy Carter, and his father, George H. W. Bush. As Bush took the oath of office, former presidents Carter, Bush, and Clinton sat behind him. Obama evoked the memory of Lincoln throughout the 2008 presidential campaign. He announced his candidacy in front of the Old State Capitol in Springfield, Illinois, where Lincoln had announced his candidacy in 1858. He retraced part of Lincoln's train trip from Philadelphia to Washington, D.C., for the inauguration, spoke in front of the Lincoln Memorial on the Saturday before being sworn in on the same Bible Lincoln used at his first inaugural, and chose Lincoln's luncheon menu and replicas of his White House china for the post-inaugural meal in the Capitol rotunda.[19] Donald Trump followed Obama's example and also used Lincoln's Bible when he was sworn in.[20]

Barbara Hinckley once argued that presidents and their speechwriters are highly attuned to the public's expectations of a chief executive. In turn, the White House projects "a symbolic presentation of the presidential office" expressed through the chief executive's public actions and statements.[21] Her study traced the Truman through Reagan administrations and showed that, with remarkable consistency, the picture portrayed to the public emphasized several common themes: The president, the American people, and the nation were presented as indistinguishable from each other and as together carrying out most of the work of "government"; Congress, when mentioned, was usually dismissed rather than recognized as an equal branch of government; identifiable population groups were pictured as sharing in the larger purposes that unite the nation; political and electoral activity was far less prominent in presidential discourse than references to religious objects such as God and the Bible; and presidents were presented as being without peers and enjoying a unique relationship with the public.[22]

As Hinckley suggested, there is always the possibility that the public might be able to reshape the presidency and its position in the constitutional order by altering expectations of the office and its occupants. After the Democrats' humiliating defeat in the 1994 midterm elections, for example, it looked as if Congress might be able to assert itself as a prime force through the Republicans' "Contract with America." Although House Speaker Newt Gingrich (R-GA)—the chief architect of the contract and the leader of the "Republican revolution"—dominated the headlines during his first 100 days as Speaker, he quickly lost his momentum.[23] Then, in the famous 1995–1996 budget battle, President Clinton reasserted himself. Republicans called for sharp budget cuts that would have affected major entitlement programs such as Medicaid, Medicare, and Social Security. Clinton called the cuts irresponsible and rallied the opposition to the Republican plan. Deadlock over the budget led to government shutdowns in November and December 1995 and in January 1996. By a margin of two to one, the public blamed the Republicans for the shutdowns, and Clinton emerged victorious from the budget battle. One poll showed that Gingrich's approval rating had plummeted to 25 percent, while Clinton's had risen to 52 percent. Had Congress won instead, the stage might have been set for a long-term shift in the balance of power between Congress and the president—one that might have undermined the president's symbolic position as the nation's leader.

Such a scenario is unlikely. Even if Congress had won, it is hard to imagine the presidency being displaced from its preeminent position—at least for long. Individual presidents may face periods of weakness and defeat, but the power of the presidency itself endures. As we have seen, enormous pressures for continuity have developed around the presidential office. Expectation of heroic performance and belief in the identity between presidents and the nation are attitudes deeply embedded in the political culture. Collectively, these beliefs about the presidency provide the incumbent with a remarkably durable base of popular support.

It is not surprising, then, that the president is the public official most likely to be correctly identified in surveys. Traditionally, presidents have also enjoyed general respect and admiration. In Gallup polls asking Americans to name the man, living anywhere in the world, whom they most admire, the president of the United States has almost always been the first choice.[24] Despite George W. Bush's declining job approval ratings, respondents chose him every year of his presidency until 2008 when president-elect Barack Obama won the distinction by a substantial margin—a position he has held each year since then.[25] Even when confronting the Whitewater scandal, the Lewinsky affair, and impeachment, Clinton remained the most admired man in the world in every Gallup poll from 1993 through 2000 (he tied with Pope John Paul II in 2000, a year when there was relatively little consensus among Americans about what man they most admired). For many years, first ladies topped the list of most admired women, but since 2002 former first lady Hillary Rodham Clinton has edged out sitting first ladies Laura Bush and Michelle Obama for that distinction—doing so again after her defeat in 2016.[26]

The initial basis for admiration of the president is formed in childhood through a process social scientists call "**political socialization**." Early work on the development of childhood attitudes toward the president showed that children viewed the president as both powerful and benevolent—a "good" person who cares about people, wants to help them, and wants to "get things done." Moreover, the president personified government for children. Until they were teenagers, most children were not even aware that the president shared the running of government with Congress and the federal judiciary.[27] A survey of children between the ages of 6 and 12 conducted during the 2016 election found that nearly two-thirds expressed no interest in becoming president. The trait they most looked for in a president is honesty (44 percent), followed by kindness (19 percent) and "smarts" (18 percent).[28]

Tracking Public Opinion

Since 1938, the Gallup organization periodically has polled a cross section of Americans on whether they approve or disapprove of the way the president is handling the job. The emphasis of the question—worded consistently across that long time series—is on performance in office rather than personal qualities, a sort of continuing referendum on how the president is handling the job.[29] These polls can be accessed online at www.gallup.com. Many other organizations also conduct polls, including some that measure presidential approval ratings. In addition to independent pollsters keeping a finger on the pulse of public opinion, every president since Nixon has retained his own paid polling consultants.[30] Earlier presidents—FDR, for example—secretly sought polling data from unpaid, unofficial advisers.[31] White House pollsters go far beyond simple tracking of presidential approval. As political scientist Diane Heith has written, presidential pollsters "helped their administrations isolate constituencies by focusing on what linked individuals to the president and the administration's policies."[32] The White House can gather highly specific polling data on everyone from homeowners to born-again Christians. At the height of the energy crisis in the 1970s, Carter's pollsters even created polling categories based on the type of home heating the respondent used.[33] By focusing on specific demographic groups and identifying issues that resonate with them, presidents are able to engage in highly targeted public appeals.

Presidents also use polling and focus groups to test language that they plan to use in speeches.[34] Ronald Reagan's administration used focus groups in 1987 and 1988 to help plan the president's State of the Union address, his speech to Congress about the summit meeting with Soviet leader Mikhail Gorbachev, and his response to the Iran-contra affair. Using such focus groups helped the White House to fashion messages that were both appealing and believable.[35] Bill Clinton made extensive use of polls and focus groups in formulating his agenda. Some observers describe the Clinton White House as driven by polls.[36] Molly Andolina and Clyde Wilcox have noted that Clinton often frustrated opponents by his "ability to cut right or left, depending on prevailing sentiments." They pointed out that in his second term he adeptly embraced issues that enjoyed popular support so that even in the face of a Senate impeachment trial in February 1999, 69 percent of the respondents of a Pew Research Center survey liked Clinton's policies.[37]

George W. Bush was known for publicly scoffing at those who tailor policy to fit the latest poll results. He praised people "who are willing to stand on principle; people not driven by polls or focus groups; people who stand for what they believe no matter what the critics may say."[38] As political scientist Kathryn Dunn Tenpas noted, Bush pledged throughout his 2000 presidential campaign not to govern by public opinion polls. "Shackled by that promise," she wrote, "President Bush and his staff have shrouded his polling apparatus, minimizing the relevance of polls and denying their impact." Yet Tenpas noted that public records and interviews with major players in the Bush administration called into question the administration's "purportedly 'anti-polling' ethos" and showed "an administration closely in keeping with historical precedent."[39] The Obama White House used polling and focus groups more openly to help sell the administration's economic policies and gauge public reaction to issues such as the government bailout of financial institutions.[40]

Job approval ratings of presidents almost always decline as their administration progresses, as illustrated in Figure 3-1. Paul Brace and Barbara Hinckley have called this depletion of public support a **decay curve.**[41] Since polling began, Clinton is the only president whose average Gallup job approval rating was higher for his last year in office (60 percent) than for his first (48.8 percent), although both Reagan and Obama left office with a significant uptick in their ratings (see Figure 3-1). The decay that most presidents experience in their approval ratings can be attributed to the deflation of unrealistically high expectations of performance, and by the simple fact that presidential decisions in different policy areas naturally displease different groups of constituents over time. The curve typically bottoms out near the thirtieth month of an initial term. Brace and Hinckley suggested that this decay normally occurs "irrespective of the economy, the president, or outside events." If a president is fortunate enough to be reelected, an uncertain prospect at best, the second-term decline usually begins earlier and follows a steeper path.

Beyond this cycle, however, Brace and Hinckley recognized that events capturing the public's attention may increase or diminish presidential support. In general, events that "dramatize conflict in the nation," even if the president has taken no action to trigger them, are likely to reduce support. Events that "unify the nation around its symbols" are likely to increase support. Bush's approval ratings soared after 9/11 and spiked upward when the United States invaded Iraq in March 2003. Still, the decay curve was evident. Bush's Gallup approval rating dropped consistently from a high of 90 percent in September 2001 to 57 percent in the March 3–5, 2003, poll—a steady decay of about six points every three months.[42] It then jumped to 69 percent in a March 24–25, 2003, Gallup poll taken just after the start of the war in Iraq but fell back to 50 percent within six months, staying in that range through his reelection in 2004. It then dropped steeply to 25 percent by October 2008 before rebounding slightly. Obama's Gallup approval ratings also decayed steadily. They dropped below 60 percent for the first time in July 2009, below 50 percent for the first time in November 2009, and below 40 percent for the first time in August 2011 before rebounding to 50 percent and above in the fall of 2012, and declining somewhat after his reelection.[43] Through 2015 it hovered in the mid to upper 40s, and then rose in 2016 to a high of 59 percent when he left office. In contrast, Trump entered office with historically low ratings. Sometimes domestic or international events beyond the control of presidents may conspire to increase or decrease their

FIGURE 3-1 Presidential Approval, 1961–May 2017

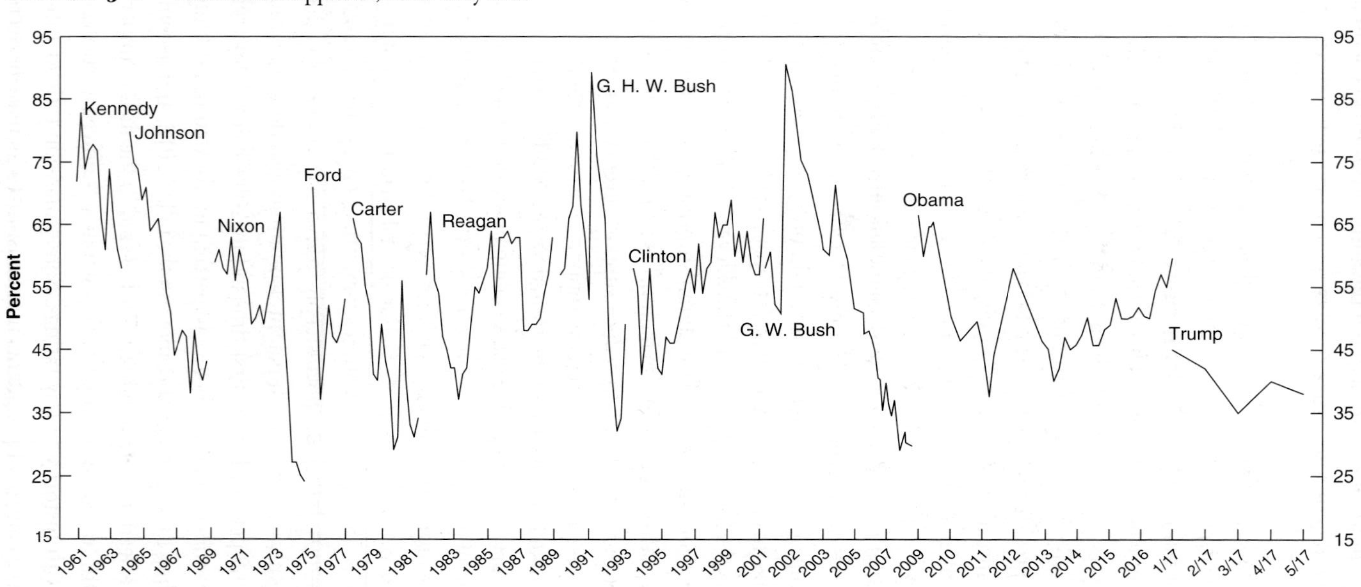

SOURCE: Based on data from the Gallup Poll (www.gallup.com).

NOTE: Question: "Do you approve or disapprove of the way _____ (last name of president) is handling his job as president?" Shown is the percentage who "approved," averaged by quarter. Individual survey results were graphed in previous editions of *Vital Statistics on American Politics*.

public support, but sometimes presidents are responsible for their own good or bad fortune by taking actions that trigger positive or negative public responses.[44]

To the extent that presidents rely on public support for policy success, the decay curve suggests that they are well advised to "hit the ground running" and accomplish as much as they can as early as they can in their administrations.[45] Along with public support, other pieces of political "capital," such as a mandate from a strong electoral margin and congressional support, are also likely to be strongest at the start of a president's term.[46] David Gergen, an adviser to presidents Nixon, Ford, Reagan, and Clinton, recognized this phenomenon early on. As a member of Reagan's transition team in 1980, he wrote a detailed memorandum comparing the first 100 days of every administration since FDR's. Gergen showed that the successful presidents were those who immediately established a clear and simple agenda and used their capital to achieve it.[47] Reagan followed Gergen's advice and framed his entire legislative agenda around just four major issues that the administration carefully promoted and implemented. In contrast, both Carter and Clinton—despite a Congress controlled by their own party—largely squandered their first months in office.

Like Reagan, George W. Bush charted a clear-cut legislative agenda for his first 100 days in office. For Bush, those days were especially important. He came to office without a clear electoral mandate (indeed, he lost the 2000 popular vote to Al Gore), without strong support in Congress (he had a small Republican majority in the House, but the Senate was evenly divided between Republicans and Democrats), and his initial Gallup job *dis*approval ratings were at 25 percent, then the highest of any new president since polling began. His approval ratings were also bifurcated by a distinct partisan wedge, which political scientist Gary Jacobson identified as the largest for any newly elected president in polling history. Jacobson's analysis of the twenty-eight Gallup and CBS News/*New York Times* presidential approval polls of Bush taken before 9/11 showed the following:

> Bush's approval ratings averaged 88 percent among self-identified Republicans but only 31 percent among Democrats. This 57-point difference marked Bush as an even more polarizing figure than the former record holder, Bill Clinton (with an average partisan difference in approval of 52 points for the comparable period of his administration).[48]

The 9/11 terrorist attacks reduced the gap to an average of forty-five points.

In contrast, Obama came to office in 2009 with the highest approval ratings of any new president in thirty years, but soon—with a sixty-five-point gap—became the most polarizing first-year president since Gallup began tracking such figures: 88 percent of Democrats approved of his job performance, compared with only

23 percent of Republicans.[49] He also faced the greatest economic crisis since the Great Depression of the 1930s and wars abroad in Iraq and Afghanistan. His first major legislative success was a $787 billion economic recovery bill that he signed into law on February 17. Even though the economy initially dominated the president's agenda, some observers expressed concern that Obama was tackling too many issues. As *New York Times* columnist David Brooks wrote on March 19, the president wanted to solve not only the economic crisis but, simultaneously, "the four most complicated problems facing the nation: health care, energy, immigration and education."[50] After a bruising fight, Obama secured congressional passage of health care reform a year later, but when Republicans took control of the House of Representatives in the 2010 midterm elections and then both houses of Congress in the 2014 midterm elections, his ability to secure major legislative victories diminished. Trump entered office with only 45 percent approval ratings, and those quickly fell. As early as January 26, 2017, a majority of Americans disapproved of his job as president. With no signature legislative accomplishments other than the successful confirmation of his Supreme Court nominee in his first three months in office, his approval ratings fell.

Figure 3-1 shows results of the Gallup poll on presidential performance from Kennedy through the first four months of Trump. An examination of the figure shows evidence of the decay curve for every president except Clinton. Starting in the mid-1960s, it became common for presidential approval ratings to fall below 50 percent, and even incoming presidents confronted lower initial ratings. Eisenhower and Johnson had approval ratings of 78 percent when Gallup first gathered information about them as president, and Kennedy had an approval rating of 72 percent—even though he received only 49.7 percent of the popular vote in the 1960 election.[51] Obama was the first president since Carter to have an initial job approval rating of more than 60 percent; in comparison, Reagan's was only 51 percent, and Trump never commanded support of even 50 percent during his first 100 days in office. Until George W. Bush, whose first-year average of 66.4 percent approval was skewed upward by the events of 9/11, there had been a similar decline in average first-year ratings from 70.1 percent for Kennedy's first year to 48.8 percent for Clinton's. Some of this decline may be attributable to cynicism borne of Vietnam, Watergate, Iran-Contra, and Whitewater, and the ability of television to demystify the presidency. The decline may also reflect a persistent trend toward tighter presidential elections, often coupled with a lack of enthusiasm for either candidate and "divided government," in which one party controls the White House and another controls Congress. Neither Clinton in 1992 or 1996 nor

Bush in 2000 received 50 percent of the popular vote (indeed, Al Gore won the popular vote in 2000, as did Hillary Clinton in 2016). Even Reagan's "landslide" in 1980—with 90.9 percent of the electoral vote—was based on only 50.7 percent of the popular vote, nearly identical to Bush's tally in 2004. For whatever reason, Americans seemed warier of new presidents than in times past—less willing to give them the benefit of the doubt or a "honeymoon" period and more apt to withhold support until they prove themselves. Obama initially seemed to be an exception to that rule, but his popularity soon waned—at least until the end of his presidency.

Rallying Public Support

Presidents are not passive objects of public attitudes; instead, presidents and their aides take the initiative in shaping public perceptions. Over time, the White House has developed several specialized staff units devoted to maintaining favorable public relations and for promoting its agenda on Capitol Hill, with interest groups, and with members of the president's own party.[52] In performing these tasks, aides take actions and fashion appeals designed to win the support of different kinds of audiences, including other elites, the public at large, and specific constituencies.

The Rise of the Public Presidency

We now take public appeals by the president for granted, but as noted in chapter 1, scholars such as Jeffrey Tulis contend that the rise of the "rhetorical" presidency is really a twentieth-century phenomenon.[53] Arguably, the now-commonplace practice of presidents going public to build public support for specific legislative initiatives is one of the most significant changes of the modern presidency.[54] As presidents have embraced public appeals, the source of presidential power has expanded from narrowly defined constitutional underpinnings to a broader plebiscitary base.[55]

Tulis argues that presidents avoided the widespread use of public appeals in the nineteenth century because they adhered to a fundamentally different understanding of our political order from the one commonly held today. Their avoidance of public appeals reflected the founders' distrust of "pure" or "direct" democracy. Although the founders believed that public *consent* was a requirement of republican government, they also believed that the processes of government should be insulated from the whims of public *opinion*. They attempted to instill "deliberation" in government through indirect elections, separation of powers, and an independent executive. In such a system, public appeals by the president were proscribed because they were thought to "manifest demagoguery, impede deliberation, and subvert the routines of republican government."[56] Policy rhetoric by presidents—to the extent that it existed—was primarily written and principally addressed to Congress, as opposed to modern-day policy rhetoric, which is primarily spoken and principally addressed to the people. It was "*public* (available to all) but not thereby *popular* (fashioned for all)."[57]

Presidents avoided going public, which is specifically designed to whip up public opinion, because it went against the existing interpretation of the constitutional order. That is not to say that other sorts of popular appeals were never made. Government-sponsored partisan newspapers flourished in the early part of our history and were clearly a means of generating public support—often by ridiculing the opposition with highly inflammatory articles.[58] *The Federalist Papers,* published in the New York press and widely distributed in bound volumes, are early examples of public appeals. Indeed, Federalists made a point of befriending influential printers, thereby forming a network for the distribution of information favorable to the Federalist cause.[59] Once in power, Federalists were accused of thwarting the circulation of opposition papers through control of the post office.[60] Arguably, however, the authors of these early examples designed them primarily to build public consent for broadly based structures—partisan newspapers for emerging political parties and *The Federalist Papers* for a new form of government—rather than as more direct tools for mobilizing public opinion for congressional passage of specific policy initiatives.[61] Securing legislation remained an elite process of bargaining.

Nineteenth-century presidents did not maintain total public silence. They made occasional speeches to the people and even made some tours around the country (called "swings around the circle"). But public speeches were not as important as public appearances on those tours. President Washington, for example, initiated a "grand tour" of two months' duration by visiting the South in 1791, a region where suspicions of central authority had run strong during the constitutional ratification campaign. Washington himself emphasized the importance of "seeing and being seen" on the tour. Although he gave public remarks, Tulis emphasizes that they contained only "general articulations of republican sentiment, not even a clear enunciation of principle."[62]

Indeed, eighteenth- and nineteenth-century presidential speeches had an overall character very different from presidential speeches given today: They were largely ceremonial and usually devoid of policy content. They were also much less frequent. Tulis calculated that, from George Washington through William McKinley, presidents averaged thirteen public speeches a year—80 percent or more of them very brief "thank you" remarks. The first eleven presidents averaged three public speeches a year.[63] In comparison, Clinton averaged one public speech almost every other day during his first three years in office.[64] To underscore the very different nature of rhetorical "common law" that existed in the nineteenth century, Tulis points out that Andrew Johnson was the first president to engage in a full-scale popular appeal over the heads of Congress for the passage of legislation and that he had an article of impeachment brought against him for doing so.[65]

Tulis identifies Theodore Roosevelt and Woodrow Wilson as catalysts for the new rhetorical presidency. He cites Roosevelt's public campaign to win passage of the Hepburn Act, which gave the Interstate Commerce Commission authority to regulate railroad shipping rates, as the first example of a president's securing legislation with the help of going public.[66] Use of the "**bully pulpit**" dovetailed neatly with Roosevelt's broad "stewardship theory" of presidential power (see chapter 1). Like Roosevelt, Wilson believed that presidents had powers beyond those specifically enumerated in the Constitution, and he saw public opinion as an important source of that additional power.[67] He expanded the use of rhetoric and used it in new ways. He was the first elected president to have engaged in a full-scale speaking tour as part of the general election campaign.[68] Once in office, Wilson changed the norms of presidential rhetoric. He was largely responsible for the shift to policy rhetoric primarily spoken and principally addressed to the people. When Wilson delivered his State of the Union report orally—the first president to do so since John Adams—he had clearly fashioned his message for the people even though he presented it to Congress. One of Wilson's most dramatic appeals for public support—his whistle-stop train tour to promote the League of Nations—was cut short in Colorado when he suffered a stroke on September 26, 1919.

Presidential Appeals

Appeals for public support are now a routine part of presidential governance. Presidents use that support as a bargaining chip with Congress—a way to persuade (or coerce) it to follow their leads. Barack Obama embraced that strategy as soon as he entered the White House. He quickly took to the road to campaign for his policy agenda. Many of the stops were in the so-called swing states of Arizona, Colorado, Florida, Illinois, and Indiana in just two weeks in February. George W. Bush had done the same thing in the early days of his administration. After using his first address to a joint session of Congress on February 27, 2001, to mobilize national support for his agenda, Bush took off on speaking tours to promote its centerpiece, a $1.6 trillion tax cut, to specific audiences. In the two days following his address to Congress, Bush gave speeches touting his tax cut in Arkansas, Georgia, Iowa, Nebraska, and Pennsylvania—states with wavering senators he thought could be convinced to vote for his plan. The explicit purpose of these speeches was to urge the American people to put pressure on Congress to pass the president's initiatives. In contrast, Donald Trump pointedly avoided such tours during his early days in office.[69]

Unlike major addresses, such as the annual State of the Union and other prime-time television speeches, minor addresses such as those given on the road allow the president to target appeals to specific constituencies and generate local media coverage. As can be seen in Figure 3-2, the number of minor addresses increased dramatically starting in the Reagan years. Kernell has noted that both Clinton and George W. Bush averaged a minor address almost every other day.[70]

Corresponding with the increase in going public is the growth in presidential travel, which also began under Reagan (see Figure 3-3). It reflects the presidents' permanent campaign for public support.[71] Even Clinton's inability to run for a third term did not deter him from campaign mode. George W. Bush followed suit. He crisscrossed the country to stump for his tax-cut proposals in 2001 and 2003 and barnstormed for fellow Republicans before the 2002 midterm elections, visiting fifteen states in just the last five days before the election.[72] Media observers noted that Bush preferred these public appeals to wooing individual legislators as Lyndon Johnson famously did.[73] By May 21, 2014, Obama had already taken one thousand flights on *Air Force One*—still 675 behind the total number that George W. Bush took during his eight years in office.[74] Such appeals do not always work. Bush hit the road to win support for Social Security reform in 2005, and Obama hit the road to win support for gun control in 2013, but neither proposal went anywhere, despite the speeches and White House efforts to market them.[75]

Unlike his predecessors, Obama made innovative uses of new technology to further his agenda.[76] First he revolutionized the use of digital media during his 2008 bid for the White House, using Facebook, YouTube, and online appeals for donations in ways that are now commonplace, but were then cutting edge.[77] Then he brought those tactics to his administration. He even created a new White House post, director of new media.[78] In particular, the Obama White House used online social networking to instigate offline community organizing. It took Obama's campaign e-mail list, renamed it "Organizing for America," and used it to ask 13 million supporters to go door-to-door with petitions in support of administration policy, a process that generated still more e-mail addresses. Organizing for America asked e-mail recipients to host house parties to inform neighbors of administration policies, such as the economic stimulus package.[79] When Congress voted on important issues like Obama's proposed budget, Organizing for America sent e-mails urging recipients to contact their members of Congress to support the legislation.[80] In his first year in office, Bush had done this the old-fashioned way: through speeches. In Fargo, North Dakota, Bush had urged a cheering, flag-waving crowd to put pressure on their senators: "If you like what you hear today, maybe e-mail some of the good folks from the United States Senate from your state," Bush said. "If you like what you hear, why don't you just give 'em a call and write 'em a letter."[81]

In addition to mobilizing grassroots support through e-mail appeals, Obama has also used innovative ways to target other messages to specific constituencies. He delivered his weekly radio address on YouTube and became the first sitting president to appear on late night talk shows. By March 12, 2015, he had appeared on *The Tonight Show with Jay Leno* three times, *The Late Show with David Letterman* twice, and *Late Night with Jimmy Fallon* and *Jimmy Kimmel Live!* once. By then he had also appeared three times on *The Daily Show with Jon Stewart,* three times on *Oprah,* twice on *The View* and once on *The Colbert Report.*[82] He also chalked up other firsts: appearing on ESPN to fill his brackets for the NCAA Men's Basketball Championship; delivering a speech to a music awards show on Spanish-language Univision; using the Internet-only show *Between Two Ferns* to urge young people to sign up for health care insurance under the Affordable Care Act; and becoming the first president to participate in a Twitter town hall meeting. Shortly after taking office, Obama also held a "virtual" town hall meeting where visitors to the White House website were asked to vote on which questions they wanted the president to answer. To submit a question or to vote, people had to register at the White House website—thereby providing still more names and e-mail addresses to add to the Organizing for America mailing list. Voting on the questions also provided feedback to the White House on which issues were most salient to the public. Hundreds of thousands of people submitted questions for the town hall, and some 3.6 million cast votes.[83]

Obama also traveled to nine nations during his first one hundred days in office, and after ten months in office he had set a record for foreign travel by a first-year president: seven trips to sixteen countries, three of which he visited twice. By May 2015, he had taken forty trips to fifty different countries.[84] Such travel reflects another change associated with modern presidents: They travel outside the United States, and they do so with increasing frequency (although Trump, in comparison, got off to a slow start—not leaving the country until May 2017). No

FIGURE 3-2 Presidential Addresses, 1933–2011 (Yearly Averages for First Three Years of First Term)

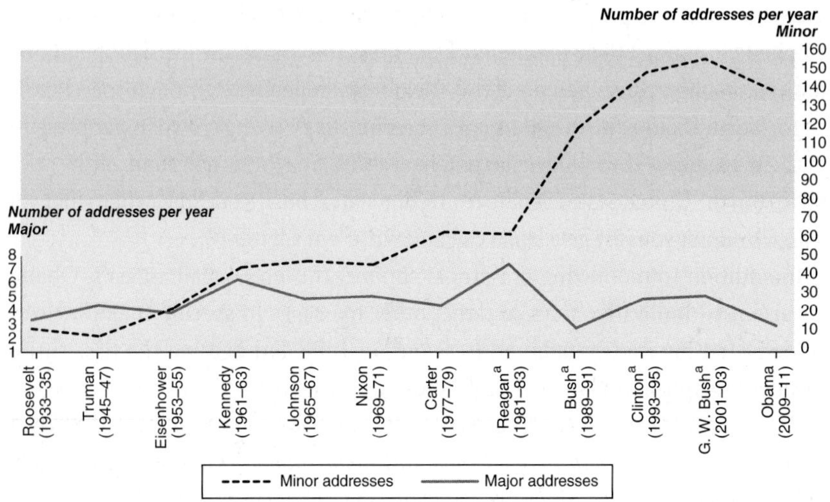

SOURCES: Data for Roosevelt, Truman, Eisenhower, Nixon, and Carter are from William W. Lammers, "Presidential Attention-Focusing Activities," in *The President and the American Public*, ed. Doris A. Graber (Philadelphia: Institute for the Study of Human Issues, 1982), Table 6-1, 152. Data for Kennedy, Johnson, Reagan, G. H. W. Bush, Clinton, and G. W. Bush are from the Public Papers of the Presidents series. See also Samuel Kernell, "The Presidency and the People: The Modern Paradox," in *The Presidency and the Political System*, ed. Michael Nelson (Washington, DC: CQ Press, 1984), 242.

NOTE: To eliminate public activities inspired by concerns of reelection rather than governing, only the first three years have been tabulated. For this reason, Gerald R. Ford's record of public activities during his two-and-one-half years of office has been omitted.

[a]Includes television addresses only.

sitting president left the United States until Theodore Roosevelt went to Panama in 1906 to inspect construction of the Panama Canal.[85] Now this phenomenon of "going international," as political scientist Richard Rose has dubbed it, is commonplace. As Rose puts it, presidents can no longer do their jobs simply by staying in the United States.

Whereas Herbert Hoover spent only three days abroad in his term of office and Franklin Roosevelt spent only nine days abroad in his first term, Richard Nixon spent fifty-nine days abroad in his first four years in office, and Jimmy Carter fifty-six days.[86]

According to Mark Knoller, a CBS News reporter who gathers statistics on presidential travel, George W. Bush surpassed those numbers in his first two-and-a-half years in office with sixty-five days of foreign travel to thirty-two nations by August

FIGURE 3-3 Days of Political Travel by Presidents, 1933–2011 (Yearly Averages for First Three Years of First Term)

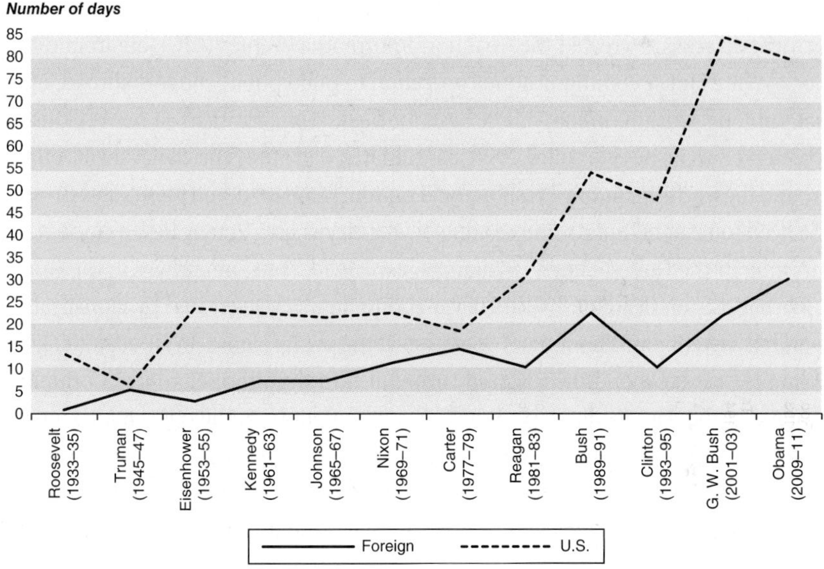

SOURCE: Samuel Kernell and Gary C. Jacobson, *The Logic of American Politics* (Washington, DC: CQ Press, 2014), 335.

NOTE: To eliminate public activities inspired by concerns of reelection rather than governing, only the first three years have been tabulated. For this reason, Gerald R. Ford's record of public activities during his two-and-one-half years of office has been omitted.

2003.[87] By the time he left office, Bush had visited seventy-five nations, several more than once.[88] Foreign trips highlight the president's role as head of state and can paint a picture of the president as diplomat and peacemaker. Nixon's dramatic trips to China and the Soviet Union in 1972 (an election year) were beamed back live to American television with newly developed satellite technology.[89] Reagan's trips abroad provided many memorable television moments, including his emotional visit to the Normandy beaches of France, which became the backdrop for dramatic reelection ads in 1984.

Aside from foreign travel, "going international" has also come to include efforts by presidents to monitor and build public opinion abroad. Reagan was the first to do this in a systematic way.[90] The Reagan administration made a concerted effort to reach an international audience in 1981 and 1982 to deflect criticism of the president's decision to deploy nuclear weapons in Europe. This extensive public relations campaign in Western Europe included a speech by Reagan transmitted live by satellite and timed to air in prime time on European television.[91] Obama held a televised town hall meeting in Strasbourg, France, before attending an April 2009 NATO summit.

George W. Bush arguably took going international to new heights. After the 9/11 terrorist attacks, he created the Coalition Information Center (CIC), an around-the-clock White House communications operation to build public support abroad, especially among Muslims in the Middle East, for the war on terrorism. James Wilkinson, who served as its director until 2003, coordinated daily press briefings at CIC offices around the world, including Washington, London, Islamabad, and Kabul, and stressed the need to respond rapidly to breaking news everywhere. "It may be 3 o'clock in the morning in the United States," Wilkinson explained, "but somewhere in the world, a journalist is on deadline."[92] The never-ending news cycle created by globalization required a twenty-four-hour news operation at the White House. In January 2003, the White House expanded the CIC and turned it into the Office of Global Communications. In the days leading up to the U.S. invasion of Iraq, the office issued a daily bulletin called "The Global Messenger" to counter Iraqi "propaganda" with "truthful, accurate and effective messages."[93] The White House disbanded the office in 2005 and transferred its functions to the under secretary of state for public diplomacy.

Lloyd Bishop/NBC/NBCU Photo Bank via Getty Images

President Obama was the first sitting president to appear on late night talk shows, and his appearances soon became commonplace. Here is one such appearance on Late Night with Jimmy Fallon *in which the president participated in a skit as well as an interview.*

Appeals by Surrogates

Presidential surrogates, ranging from the vice president and members of the cabinet to party officials and political consultants, also promote the president's agenda through speaking tours, satellite interviews with local media outlets, and nationwide television appearances on the Sunday morning talk shows and cable outlets such as CNN, MSNBC, and Fox News. Nixon was one of the first presidents to aggressively choreograph the use of these surrogates as part of a broader strategy of going public. He sought to build, as his chief of staff, H. R. Haldeman, put it, "a stable of television personalities from within the Administration."[94]

Nixon was also one of the first presidents to use late night talk shows and other entertainment outlets to promote himself and his agenda. Before becoming president, he appeared on *The Jack Paar Program* in 1963 to chat, play the piano, and help rebuild his image after his stinging loss to Pat Brown in the 1962 California gubernatorial race. He made a one-line ("sock it to me") cameo appearance on *Rowan & Martin's Laugh-In* during the 1968 presidential campaign. Once in the White House, Nixon hired a full-time staffer named Al Snyder, a former television executive from New York, to book television appearances for administration officials, but until Obama no sitting president actually appeared on a late night talk show. Snyder placed Vice President Spiro Agnew on *The Tonight Show with Johnny Carson* and Attorney General John Mitchell on *The Dick Cavett Show* and even arranged for the White House communications director, Herb Klein, to cohost the Cavett show. Snyder also booked more traditional appearances on programs such as *Meet the Press* and arranged local media appearances by administration officials along with advising them where and how to get the best media exposure when they traveled around the country.[95] Another Nixon staffer, Virginia Savell, coordinated speaking tours by administration surrogates. In Nixon's first year in office, she arranged for surrogate speakers to crisscross the country promoting everything from Nixon's proposed family assistance plan to postal reform.[96]

Surrogates—whether traveling around the country on speaking tours or appearing on television—follow a carefully scripted "line of the day" that is part of the broader message the administration is trying to convey at that point in time. When George W. Bush focused on education reform during his first week in office, his surrogates followed suit. Education secretary Roderick Paige made the rounds on the morning shows and cable news outlets, as did Vice President Dick Cheney and White House chief of staff Andrew Card. Republican members of Congress joined in, as did other proponents of education reform. In everything from public speeches to background interviews with reporters, administration surrogates stressed education reform. At the same time, the White House arranged for photo opportunities, such as that of the president reading to children at a local school.

The point of such activities is to convey a carefully orchestrated message that is reinforced by different people in a variety of contexts. Such coordination was clearly on display on December 19, 1998, the day the House of Representatives voted to impeach President Clinton. In a morning statement to reporters, White House press secretary Joe Lockhart three times decried "the politics of personal destruction." House minority leader Richard Gephardt repeated the line that morning in a speech on the floor of the House. So, too, did the president say it in his Rose Garden speech after the impeachment vote.

One advantage of surrogates is that they can be used to target very specific constituencies. Another way of targeting specific constituencies is through links with interest groups, as we discuss in the next section.

Targeted Communications: Presidents and Interest Groups

Presidents have come to recognize the value of targeting appeals to organized interests and mobilizing interest groups to support presidential policy. Liaison with such groups is now an important part of governance. As Mark A. Peterson has written, "Working with (as well as working against) interest groups to piece together support among the public and in Congress played a large role in the [Clinton] administration's political and policy strategies."[97] People who organize to advocate a particular interest are highly attentive to public issues affecting their members. These groups also have ongoing links with Congress and the bureaucracy that provide them with policymaking influence. It is not surprising, therefore, that they are a prime target of presidential communication. For example, presidents give major public addresses on business to conventions of the National Association of Manufacturers or the Chamber of Commerce of the United States and on labor relations to meetings of the American Federation of Labor and Congress of Industrial Organizations (AFL–CIO). Chief executives also dispatch surrogates to meet with these groups and to promote the administration's programs. White House aides serve as a channel for private communications with group representatives and will sometimes arrange meetings with the president.

Interest groups want to hear about current matters of public policy, but they also want to be reassured that the president is sympathetic to the problems group members face. Not surprisingly, chief executives pay particular attention to the groups that helped them get elected. They hope to convert their electoral coalition into one that helps them govern as well. Democratic presidents typically have focused on labor unions and civil rights organizations; Republicans have concentrated on business and professional organizations. Presidents also know that as the leader of the nation they are supposed to represent *all* the people—not just those who supported their election. Chief executives cannot afford to ignore prominent interest groups, even those politically opposed to them.

Presidents have established channels for routine communication with particular groups through systematic White House liaison. Truman used David Niles, formerly on FDR's staff, as a liaison with blacks and Jews.[98] Eisenhower, who cultivated an image of being above politics, deemphasized, but did not completely ignore, group relations, and the Kennedy and Johnson administrations designated White House staff members to work with Jews, Catholics, and other groups. Gradually, however, the range of group ties became more predictable. Presidents since Nixon have assigned aides to work with eight population groups: business, labor, Jews, consumers, blacks, women, Hispanics, and the elderly.[99] Most of these ties were pursued through the Office of Public Liaison, a White House staff unit first conceived and implemented in the Nixon administration (under the direction of Charles Colson) and officially consolidated and named an independent staff unit under Gerald R. Ford.[100] George W. Bush also made a concerted effort to cultivate ties with conservative Christians.[101] The Obama administration changed the name of the Office of Public Liaison to the Office of Public Engagement, calling the renamed and enlarged office "the front door to the White House through which ordinary Americans can participate and inform the work of the president." In keeping with its innovative use of new technology, the Obama administration used the White House website to invite direct citizen communication. The office also engaged groups as well as individual citizens through meetings and conversations held across the country.[102] Donald Trump disbanded the new Office of Public Engagement, reviving the Office of Public Liaison instead.

Targeted Communications: Presidents and Political Parties

Outreach to political parties is also an important part of the modern public presidency. Presidents since Truman have assigned staff to serve as liaisons with their political parties.[103] As early as the Nixon administration, this staff was referred to as the Office of Political Affairs, although it did not become a freestanding entity listed in the U.S. *Government Organization Manual* until the Reagan administration.[104] By 2008, the office had become controversial. John McCain, the 2008 Republican presidential nominee, pledged to abolish the office if elected; Henry A. Waxman

(D-CA), the Democratic chair of the House Oversight and Government Reform Committee, issued a report in October 2008 that recommended its elimination. Obama initially chose to retain the office, appointing Patrick Gaspard, the national political director of his 2008 presidential campaign, to direct it.[105] Then, in January 2011, a report by the Office of Special Counsel concluded that the George W. Bush administration had used the office to support House Republican candidates in violation of federal law.[106] Soon thereafter, the Obama administration decided to disband the office.[107] Its absence proved to be short lived. In anticipation of the 2014 midterm elections, the Obama administration revived the office, but under a new name: the Office of Political Strategy and Outreach.[108] Under Trump, the name reverted to the Office of Political Affairs. The White House website said that the office "develops, supports, and advances partnerships in support of the President and his policy agenda."[109]

As political scientist Kathryn Dunn Tenpas has noted, the Office of Political Affairs changed a good deal from president to president, but all shared at least three core functions. First, the office served as a formal liaison to national, state, and local party organizations as well as to congressional campaign committees. Such a liaison was a two-way street. On the one hand, it allowed the White House to monitor the actions of relevant political actors and receive input from them. On the other hand, it provided an opportunity for the White House to mobilize political support from these actors. In 1969, Harry S. Dent—head of Nixon's Office of Political Affairs—mobilized state Republican chairs to lobby U.S. senators from their states to vote for Clement Haynsworth, one of Nixon's Supreme Court nominees, and to orchestrate a grassroots letter-writing campaign in behalf of the nomination.[110] The office made similar efforts in behalf of George H. W. Bush's Supreme Court nominees, David Souter and Clarence Thomas, in 1990 and 1991. The office also used such ties to promote the president's legislative agenda, building *support* for presidential initiatives and mobilizing *opposition* to programs the president did not support. For example, the office used pressure from party activists to help gain votes for Senate cloture and helped guard against veto overrides, and it also applied grassroots pressure on members of Congress to vote against legislation. Creating a groundswell of grassroots opposition sometimes made it easier for the president to oppose certain policies. For example, George H. W. Bush used the Office of Political Affairs very effectively to help stop campaign finance reform.[111] It also appeared that the office may have tried to politicize the hiring and firing of U.S. attorneys under George W. Bush. When Sara M. Taylor, who had served as Bush's political affairs director from 2003 to 2007, was subpoenaed to answer questions about the allegations before the Senate Judiciary Committee after she left her post, President Bush invoked executive privilege, and Taylor refused to answer most questions.[112]

Second, the office served as liaison with major supporters of the president, including private citizens who had donated money to support the president's political activities. If such a supporter requested a signed photo from the president or a White House tour, the Office of Political Affairs arranged it. Some critics alleged that the Clinton administration went beyond this simple sort of constituent service and improperly used the office to raise funds and reward donors. A 1998 report by the House Committee on Government Reform and Oversight, chaired by Rep. Dan Burton (R-IN), pointed to efforts by members of Clinton's Office of Political Affairs to create a computerized White House database to identify potential donors and share the information with the Democratic National Committee. "This is the President's idea and it's a good one," Marsha Scott, a member of the office, wrote in a draft memorandum to White House chief of staff Mack McLarty in 1994. She wrote that the database would be used to "identify and contact key supporters in all fifty states" and would allow the White House to identify, by early 1995, "key financial and political folks in each state who can work with us."[113] Another memo, dated October 25, 1994, noted that the president wanted the database to correlate contributions from individuals and their invitations to, and attendance at, White House events.[114] In other words, the Office of Political Affairs used the list to reward donors with invitations to meet the president, attend White House functions, or spend the night in the Lincoln Bedroom.

Finally, the office engaged in what Tenpas calls "electioneering." This function included planning early reelection strategies for presidents in their first terms. Tim Kraft engaged in such planning in the Carter administration before becoming Carter's campaign manager for the 1980 election, just as Ed Rollins and Lee Atwater worked in the office during the first Reagan administration before moving over to the 1984 Reagan-Bush campaign headquarters.[115] Ken Mehlman served as the director of George W. Bush's political affairs office before managing Bush's 2004 reelection campaign.[116] Often the office looked for ways to expand the president's electoral base in anticipation of a reelection bid. It was especially important for Clinton to expand his electoral base because he won the White House in 1992 with just 43 percent of the popular vote in a three-way race. George W. Bush—winning the White House with roughly 48 percent of the popular vote—was in a similar situation when he first took office in 2001. In addition to engineering reelection strategies, the office used presidential resources to help elect members of Congress from the same political party as the president. During the 2002 midterm elections, Bush's eleven-person office scheduled campaign appearances by leading Republican celebrities, such as former New York mayor Rudolph Giuliani, to help regional candidates raise money and win votes.[117] Typically, the office arranged presidential appearances in the candidate's home state or congressional district, coordinated photo opportunities for the candidate at the White House, and maintained liaison with House and Senate campaign committees.

Presidents try to influence the outcome of midterm congressional elections, but they are limited in terms of what they can do—particularly regarding elections for the House of Representatives. First, they are confronted with a daunting historical trend: The president's party almost always loses seats in midterm House elections (see Table 3-1). In the thirty-nine midterm elections since 1862, the president's party lost House seats in all but three of them: 1934, 1998, and 2002 (at first glance, it looks like the president's party also picked up seats in 1902, but it did not if you factor in the new seats created that year by redistricting). Second, the sheer number of House elections (currently 435) precludes the president from participating in many of them. Bush's efforts in the 2002 midterm elections were called "unprecedented," with a record ninety campaign appearances; yet he still made personal campaign appearances for only twenty-three congressional candidates.[118] Third, members of the House who run for reelection almost always win. Incumbents benefit from previous campaign experience, close relationships with voters, greater knowledge of issues, and superior financial resources, all of which give them an advantage over their opponents.[119]

Partisan redistricting has also made House seats safer. Based on the reelection rates of incumbents running for reelection in the general election, the House elections of 2002 (when 96 percent of incumbents won) and 2004 (when 98 percent of incumbents won) were the least competitive since World War II.[120] The 2014 elections followed that trend, with 95 percent of incumbents winning in the general election.[121] Thus, presidents who attempt to campaign against sitting members of Congress during the general election face very difficult odds. However, these reelection rates do not take into account strategic retirements by incumbents, nor incumbents who were defeated in primary elections. A more nuanced analysis of incumbency advantage by political scientist Gary Jacobson suggests that the electoral advantages that naturally accrue to incumbents are not what they once were. He concludes that the actual electoral advantage of sitting House members has fallen to its lowest levels since the 1950s, even though House incumbents continue to win reelection at high rates.[122] Incumbents fared particularly poorly in 2010 when fifty-four incumbent House members lost in the general election (four other incumbents lost primary elections). Still, 85 percent of House incumbents won reelection. Only fourteen incumbents lost in 2014, but twelve of them were Democrats.

Senatorial midterm elections usually offer a somewhat better opportunity for presidents to influence results. A third of the Senate's one hundred seats are at stake every two years, so the chief executive can concentrate on these contests in a way not possible for House races. Bush made campaign appearances for sixteen Republican Senate candidates in 2002, and the Republican Senatorial Campaign Committee launched an aggressive series of television ads attacking Democratic incumbents for failing to support homeland security.[123] That combination—together with high turnout among Republican voters—led to the Republicans' picking up two Senate seats in 2002 (enough to shift control in the Senate to Republicans), but they lost six seats in 2006. Although sitting senators are in the same position as House members in being able to bring their names to the attention of constituents, incumbency is not as advantageous for a senator as it is for a House member. Senators represent an entire state rather than a small homogenous district, and the prestige associated with being a senator means races will be hard fought. Challengers are much more visible to the electorate than are those who run against House incumbents. Popular presidents, therefore, are better able to help candidates who challenge incumbent senators of the opposite party by increasing the challengers' visibility through public association. The ability of presidents to help their party in sixth-year midterm elections (such as 2014) is more limited, in part because presidents tend to have less popular standing themselves by that point in their term. On average, the president's party has lost six Senate seats in those elections since World War II.[124] Democrats in 2014 lost nine. As a point of comparison, Republicans under Reagan lost eight in 1986. Democrats under Clinton bucked the trend in 1998 and lost no seats (see Table 3-1).

Midterm election outcomes generally depend on the condition of the national economy and the president's standing in public opinion polls at the time of the elections.[125] Voting in these contests tends to be *negative;* that is, those who disapprove of the president's performance in office are more likely to vote in such elections than those who approve.[126] Obama's Gallup approval rating stood at 44 percent on election day in 2010, and Democrats lost six Senate seats. Gary Jacobson contends that the president's role in congressional elections is essentially indirect: The state of the economy and the president's ratings in the public opinion polls influence the caliber of candidates who run in congressional elections. If, for example, these are not favorable, the opposition party will be able to field an unusually large proportion of formidable challengers with well-financed campaigns, and the president's

TABLE 3-1 Losses by President's Party in Midterm Elections, 1862–2014

Year	*Party Holding Presidency*	*President's Party: Gain/ Loss of Seats in House*	*President's Party: Gain/ Loss of Seats in Senate*
1862	R	−3	8
1866	R	−2	0
1870	R	−31	−4
1874	R	−96	−8
1878	R	−9	−6
1882	R	−33	3
1886	D	−12	3
1890	R	−85	0
1894	D	−116	−5
1898	R	−21	7
1902	R	9[a]	2
1906	R	−28	3
1910	R	−57	−10
1914	D	−59	5
1918	D	−19	−6
1922	R	−75	−8
1926	R	−10	−6
1930	R	−49	−8
1934	D	9	10
1938	D	−71	−6
1942	D	−55	−9
1946	D	−55	−12
1950	D	−29	−6
1954	R	−18	−1
1958	R	−47	−13
1962	D	−5	3
1966	D	−47	−4
1970	R	−12	2
1974	R	−48	−5
1978	D	−15	−3
1982	R	−26	1
1986	R	−5	−8
1990	R	−10	−1
1994	D	−55	−9
1998	D	4	0
2002	R	8	1
2006	R	−30	−6
2010	D	−63	−6
2014	D	−13	−9

SOURCE: Harold W. Stanley and Richard G. Niemi, *Vital Statistics on American Politics, 2015–2016* (Washington, DC: CQ Press, 2016).

NOTE: Entry is the difference between the number of seats won by the president's party in that midterm election and the number of seats won by that party in the preceding general election. Because of changes in the overall number of seats in the Senate and House, in the number of seats won by third parties, and in the number of vacancies, a Republican loss is not always matched precisely by a Democratic gain, or vice versa.

[a] Although the Republicans gained nine seats in the 1902 elections, they lost ground to the Democrats, who gained twenty-five seats after the increase in the overall number of representatives after the 1900 census.

party in Congress may lose a considerable number of seats.[127] Democrats fared miserably in the 1994 midterm elections when Bill Clinton's Gallup approval ratings came near their lowest point—fluctuating between 39 percent on September 6 and 48 percent on October 22. On the other hand, the Democrats' strong showing in the 1998 midterm elections reflected Clinton's consistently high approval ratings, which hovered near 66 percent despite (or perhaps because of) the looming threat of impeachment, which voters saw as congressional overreach. Bush's approval rating just before the 2002 elections was (at 63 percent) not quite as high as Clinton's in 1998, but it still tied with Reagan's 1986 rating "for second highest in any postwar midterm election."[128] In comparison, Bush's approval ratings hovered around 37 percent in the days leading up to the 2006 midterm elections, and Obama's were around 45 percent in 2010 and 49 percent in 2012.

The President and the Media

Historically, the most important link between the president and the American public has been the press. In the early years of the Republic, the press was as partisan as it is in many European countries today. The partisan press reached its peak during the presidency of Andrew Jackson, when federal officeholders were expected to subscribe to the administration organ, the *Washington Globe,* which was financed primarily by revenues derived from the printing of official government notices.[129]

The partisan press began to decline during the presidency of Abraham Lincoln. The establishment of the Government Printing Office in 1860 destroyed the printing-contract patronage that had supported former administration organs.[130] The invention of the telegraph led to the formation of wire services, which provided standardized and politically neutral information to avoid antagonizing the diverse readerships of the various subscribing newspapers. Advertising provided newspapers with a secure financial base independent of the support of presidential administrations. By the end of the nineteenth century, "news about the White House was transmitted to the public by independent, nonpartisan news organizations," a factor that continues to affect relationships between the president and the press today.[131]

Not until 1896, though, did the White House become a regular beat for reporters. Given their role in establishing the public presidency, it is not surprising that both Woodrow Wilson and Theodore Roosevelt formalized innovative ties with those reporters in the early part of the twentieth century. Roosevelt began the practice of meeting with them (often during his late afternoon shave). In 1902, he had a pressroom built in the new West Wing of the White House and began having an aide, William Loeb, give daily press briefings. Wilson continued the practice of daily press briefings (conducted by Joseph Tumulty) and became the first president to hold regularly scheduled press conferences. He held his first in the East Room of the White House on March 15, 1913—just eleven days after his inauguration—for 125 reporters.[132]

In the twentieth century, several media took their place beside newspapers as important channels between the president and the people. Radio became a dominant force in communications in the 1920s, as did television in the 1950s. By the end of the century, cable and satellite technology had dramatically increased the number of potential sources of news and commentary, and the Internet had revolutionized the way people communicate and gather information. The emergence of broadcast technology, coupled with the array of new media (cable, satellite technology, and the Internet) by now, allow presidents to communicate messages directly to the people rather than having their messages relayed (and interpreted) by journalists. President Trump's early reliance on Twitter, though seemingly not always coordinated with broader White House communications, is one such method of direct communication.

Presidential Media

Today, an enormous variety of media cover the words and actions of the U.S. president. These media differ in the ways they deal with executive branch developments and in their target audiences. They also vary in importance to chief executives and their programs. Over the past sixty years, the way Americans get information has undergone a fundamental change. Only 9 percent of U.S. households had television sets in 1950, a figure that grew to 87 percent by 1960 and 98 percent by 1980.[133] Not surprisingly, the White House began to focus more attention on using television to promote its policies. By 1959, 57 percent of the public claimed to get most of its news from newspapers and 51 percent from television (more than one response was allowed in the survey); only 19 percent claimed to get their news from television alone. By 1997 only 37 percent cited newspapers as a principal source, and 69 percent cited television; 47 percent claimed to get their news only from television.[134] By 2013, only 6 percent claimed that newspapers were their primary source of news.[135] Not surprisingly, different age groups tend to rely on different news outlets. A 2016 Pew Research Center study found that while only 5 percent of those in the 18–29 age group often get their news from print newspapers, 48 percent of those 65 and over do.[136] In addition, the White House must be attentive to the most influential media figures—a select group of columnists, elite reporters, anchors of the broadcast news, and executives of the media organizations. Indeed, there is substantial evidence that the stated views of news commentators and experts have a greater impact on citizens' policy preferences than the president's own comments.[137]

Syndicated columnists earn White House attention because they reach powerful audiences outside government, including business and labor leaders, lobbyists, and academics, as well as top officials in government—members of Congress, members of the bureaucracy, judges, governors, and mayors. These columnists influence views on the political feasibility of a president's proposed programs. They deal in matters of opinion rather than just factual developments affecting the presidency. As political scientists Michael Grossman and Martha Kumar have noted, "They are guaranteed space, they have no assigned topics, they are freed from the pressure of breaking news stories at deadline, and they have the opportunity to introduce their own perspectives into their stories."[138]

Television anchors such as David Muir and Lester Holt are important to the president because of the respect they command and the size of the audiences they reach (even now, about 22 million people each weekday night).[139] However, their influence has been undercut by the rise of twenty-four-hour cable news networks, the Internet, and social media. According to Gallup, the percentage of Americans who say they watch cable news networks daily rose from 23 percent in 1995 to 40 percent in 2008, and the percentage who say they watch network news daily fell from 62 percent in 1995 to 34 percent in 2008. Most significant is the dramatic rise in the Internet as a source of news. In 1995 only 3 percent said that they used the Internet daily as a source of news. By 2011, a Pew survey found that 41 percent of Americans got most of their news from the Internet.[140] That, too, varies by age group. The above-mentioned 2016 Pew study found that only 27 percent of the 18–29 group often get their news from television, as opposed to 85 percent for those over 65, with 50 percent of the 18–29 group often getting news online, as opposed to only 20 percent of those 65 and over.[141] Likewise, mainstream media are no longer the sole, or even primary, source of news, especially among younger people. Smartphones and tablets have made the news more mobile, and YouTube, Facebook, Twitter, and blogs have allowed anyone with access to the Internet to post anything they want.

Because far more people watch television than read newspapers, the information the ordinary citizen receives about the presidency depends on what is included in the evening news and covered on cable outlets such as CNN, Fox News, and MSNBC, and the Internet. At the same time, television coverage of the presidency has serious limitations: Newscasts devote very little time to the most important stories (about seventy-five seconds on average); emphasis is placed on events that are visually exciting; a focus on the president personalizes complex developments; and broadcasts usually lack in-depth reporting and analysis.[142] Sound bites of the president speaking on the evening network newscasts shrank from an average of forty-two seconds in 1968 to less than seven seconds in 1996.[143]

Cable provides additional television outlets for presidents. C-SPAN carries many presidential speeches in their entirety, as well as White House press briefings. Cable news channels also offer a degree of expanded coverage, but the actual news stories are similar in length to those on the evening newscasts. Most significant, cable has given presidential surrogates many more venues to state their cases. When Fox News and MSNBC joined the cable news lineup in 1996, they relied heavily on talk shows to fill their airtime. Such shows are cheap to produce and require limited resources. They are also popular with viewers—so much so that CNN followed suit and expanded the number of its talk shows in 2001.

Helping to shape both print and broadcast coverage are the bureau chiefs and other media executives who determine which stories are covered, how they are handled, which reporters will cover the White House, and who should be represented in "pools" that travel with the president to cover significant events. The White House press corps is also an important determinant of what will be reported and how it will be reported. These are the reporters assigned to the White House itself. They attend the daily press briefings, travel with the president, and have as their primary responsibilities the task of reporting what the president is doing. Some members of the press corps are especially influential. Reporters for the *New York Times* and the *Washington Post* are examples because of the readership of their papers; in addition to public officials and important people in the private sector, their readers are the other Washington reporters.[144] The *Times,* in particular, is known to influence network news decisions about which stories to cover.[145] Also significant are the reporters for the wire services—Associated Press (AP) and United Press International (UPI)—because they provide coverage of the president for newspapers across the country. Collectively, the press corps frames most of what we read and see about the president.

Cable, satellite technology, the Internet, and social media also provide unparalleled opportunities for direct communication with the American people. In the 1992 presidential campaign, Bill Clinton very effectively followed a strategy of "narrowcasting"—using media outlets such as MTV, *The Arsenio Hall Show, The Phil Donahue Show,* and Don Imus's radio talk show to transmit direct, targeted messages to particular constituencies—tactics he and his successors brought to the White House. More recently, Obama made unprecedented use of social media and other forms of digital engagement to target his messages.[146] He even bypassed the White House press corps altogether in December 2014 when he announced his decision to ban oil and gas leasing in Bristol Bay, Alaska, via a video on his Facebook page instead of through a daily briefing with reporters.[147] As important as these new avenues of communication are, presidents still need to cultivate ties with established White House reporters, although a 2015 study by the *Columbia Journalism Review* suggested that the Obama administration had not succeeded at doing that.[148]

Presidents and reporters alike now face new competition from ordinary citizens. The Internet has democratized the process through the extensive use of online blogs and innovations such as YouTube and Facebook. Meanwhile, cell phone technology allows instant text messaging. The Obama administration attempted to use these new channels of communication to its advantage, but they can also be used by administration detractors, just as more traditional venues such as *Saturday Night Live* are.

We turn next to the two White House staff units that deal most directly with the press and communications planning: (1) the Press Office and (2) the Office of Communications.

The White House Press Office

Franklin Roosevelt officially created the **White House Press Office** in 1933. As we have seen, a routinized White House relationship with the press had been in place since Theodore Roosevelt directed William Loeb to provide daily briefings for reporters. Every president after Theodore Roosevelt assigned a member of his staff to deal with the press, with Herbert Hoover being the first to hire an aide, George Akerson, for whom the press was the *sole* responsibility. Akerson served from 1929 to 1931 and was the equivalent of a modern-day **press secretary**, although that post was not formally created until FDR's creation of the Press Office in 1933.

The Press Office is in the West Wing and maintains day-to-day contact with the reporters assigned to cover the White House. The Briefing Room and space for reporters are located downstairs in an area that used to house a swimming pool. Junior staff has space next to the Briefing Room in what is called the Lower Press Office. Senior staff members, including the press secretary, have their offices upstairs. Altogether the Press Office consists of about twenty people, some of whom specialize in a certain issue area such as foreign affairs. These include several deputy press secretaries as well as the junior staffers who write press releases and do other sorts of research. The most visible (and most senior) member of the Press Office is the press secretary.

The press secretary is the most important person in the executive branch for day-to-day contact with the presidential media. Typically holding two daily briefings, the press secretary provides routine information on executive branch appointments and resignations, on presidential actions and policies, and on the president's schedule—visits, meetings, and travel plans. By the end of an administration there may have been more than two thousand such briefings. In addition, the press secretary holds private meetings with select reporters to provide background information to explain the president's actions on a particular problem or program.

Press secretaries try to balance serving the interests of three constituencies: (1) the president, (2) members of the White House staff, and (3) members of the media.[149] The secretary can perform well only if granted continuous access to, and the confidence of, the president so that journalists may assume that the news comes from the chief executive. If presidents try to be their own press secretaries, as may have been true of Lyndon Johnson, even a capable and influential person such as Bill Moyers will not succeed in managing the message.[150] When secretaries are excluded from White House decisions, as appeared to be the case with Clinton's first press secretary, Dee Dee Myers, their credibility suffers. Trump's press secretary, Sean Spicer, faced credibility issues from his first days in office when he claimed, despite evidence to the contrary, that Trump had drawn the "largest audience ever to witness an Inauguration, period."[151] His performance in subsequent briefings also became fodder for satirical sketches on *Saturday Night Live,* with comedian Melissa McCarthy offering pointed parodies of Spicer's interaction with the press.

The modern era's press secretaries varied in effectiveness. Among those considered successful are Stephen Early (FDR), James Hagerty (Eisenhower), Jody Powell (Carter), and Mike McCurry (Clinton). Some, such as Hagerty and Powell, were effective because their presidents kept them informed on virtually everything going on in the White House. But sometimes even well-informed press secretaries do not want to know everything. After leaving office, Mike McCurry admitted that he purposely stayed out of the loop so that he could truthfully respond that he did not know all the answers concerning the Monica Lewinsky affair.[152] On the other hand, Nixon's press secretary, Ron Ziegler, was so out of the loop that he, like Myers, lost credibility with reporters. This was true even before the Watergate affair when, after months of denying any White House involvement, Ziegler was forced to declare those denials "inoperative." Indeed, Nixon purposely diminished the importance of the press secretary when he became president. White House reporters considered Nixon's choice of Ziegler—who was only twenty-nine years old and had no background in journalism—a slap in the face.[153] Another secretary who did not have a particularly good relationship with reporters was Larry Speakes, who became Reagan's press spokesman when James Brady was shot and incapacitated in the assassination attempt on the president. After leaving office, Speakes provoked cries of outrage when he admitted in his memoirs that he had manufactured presidential quotes during Reagan's Iceland summit meeting with Soviet leader Mikhail Gorbachev in November 1985. Fearing that Reagan was being upstaged, Speakes created a public relations solution to the problem, and the fabricated quotes were given prominent attention back home.[154]

The White House Office of Communications

Richard Nixon created the **White House Office of Communications** in 1969.[155] Its functions are quite different from those of the Press Office. As originally conceived, the Office of Communications had four primary goals: (1) long-range communications planning, (2) the coordination of news from all the many departments and agencies of the executive branch, (3) outreach to local media, and (4) oversight of presidential surrogates. The Press Office is largely *reactive;* it responds to the questions and needs of the White House press corps. The Office of Communications, on the other hand, is primarily *proactive;* it is responsible for setting the public agenda and making sure that all the players on the presidential team are adhering to that agenda. This includes setting the "line of the day" and choreographing presidential photo opportunities.

The precise jurisdiction of the Office of Communications has varied somewhat from administration to administration. Outreach to local media has at times been subsumed by a subunit of the Press Office. In fact, the Press Office itself has at times been a subunit of the Office of Communications (and vice versa). For at least part of the administrations of former presidents Reagan, Bush, and Clinton, the Office of Communications became an umbrella term for a variety of offices supervised by the communications director. At various times, this body included the Press Office as well as the Offices of Planning, Speechwriting, Scheduling and Advance, Public Liaison (outreach to interest groups), Media Affairs (outreach to local media), Political Affairs (outreach to members of the president's political party), and Public Affairs (liaison with public information officers throughout the executive branch).

For Nixon, a primary motivation in creating the office was to install a mechanism for bypassing the critical filter of the White House press corps. Outreach to local media, the coordination of surrogate speakers, and the use of venues such as television, radio, and mass mailings to communicate directly with the people were all a part of that effort. For presidents since Reagan, the emphasis has been on long-range communications planning, and tactics of circumvention are often part of that plan. As previously mentioned, George W. Bush's administration not only maintained the Office of Communications but also, for a time, a new Office of Global Communications designed to reach a worldwide audience. Vice President Cheney, who had considerable experience with communications planning as White House chief of staff for President Ford, maintained that it is essential for the White House to manage presidential news. Cheney admitted the following:

> That means that about half the time the White House press corps is going to be pissed off, and that's all right. You're not there to please them. You're there to run an effective presidency. And to do that, you have to be disciplined in what you convey to the country. The most powerful tool you have is the ability to use the symbolic aspects of the presidency to promote your goals and objectives.

That means the White House has to control the agenda. "You don't let the press set the agenda," Cheney emphasized. "They like to decide what's important and what isn't important. But if you let them do that, they're going to trash your presidency."[156] Responsibility for controlling the communications agenda rests with the Office of Communications and a variety of other communications advisers—some of whom are not officially members of the White House staff.

Such sharing of communications responsibilities is not unusual. In his first term, President Reagan benefited greatly not only from the skill and experience of communications director David Gergen, who had also served in the Nixon and Ford administrations, but also from the talents of James A. Baker III and Michael Deaver, other members of the White House staff who carefully managed the president's media and public image. This team was especially adept at selecting the "line of the day," often as part of a broader "theme of the week," and creating "photo opportunities" featuring the president to highlight it. Baker was a master tactical leaker and Deaver set the stage. Donald Regan later wrote the following:

> [Deaver] saw—designed—each presidential action as a one-minute or two-minute spot on the evening network news, or picture on page one of the *Washington Post* or the *New York Times,* and conceived every presidential appearance in terms of camera angles. . . . Every moment of every appearance was scheduled, every word was scripted, every place where Reagan was expected to stand was chalked with toe marks.[157]

Reagan, the former Hollywood actor, followed the script masterfully. The administration of George W. Bush also proved to be adept at staging photo opportunities, including his May 2003 "tail-hook" landing in an S-3B Viking Navy jet on the USS *Abraham Lincoln*. President Bush told reporters that he had flown the jet himself en route to the ship. Initially, the White House said that the president had to take the jet because the ship was out of helicopter range. It turned out, however, that the ship was in easy helicopter range—only thirty miles off the coast of California, with cameras carefully positioned so as not to see the coastline.[158] Nevertheless, photographs of Bush in his "top gun" gear conveyed the image of a strong, courageous leader in control. In the long term, however, the photo op, which included a huge "Mission Accomplished" sign, backfired when the war in Iraq dragged on for years. Some attempts at image making do not work—just ask 1988 Democratic presidential nominee Michael Dukakis, who looked ridiculous when his aides arranged a photo op of him driving a tank, or John Kerry, whose windsurfing excursion was morphed into an effective negative ad by the Bush campaign in 2004.

Presidential Press Conferences

Presidents cultivate their own ties with reporters—often through off-the-record sessions when traveling on *Air Force One* and during other informal gatherings—but the presidential press conference is the best-known avenue for interaction between presidents and reporters. FDR perfected the art of the press conference. He held a total of 998 while president—an average of almost seven a month. His gatherings were informal—usually held in his office—but there was strict control over how reporters could use material from the press conferences, as there had been since President Wilson first began the practice of regular press conferences in 1913. Despite the control, FDR's system—as Kernell has pointed out—was one of "hard news, openly conveyed."[159]

The emergence of broadcast media and their desire to cover press conferences eroded the intimacy of these interactions between presidents and reporters. It also reduced the White House's dependence on reporters to communicate the president's views to the public. Radio and television became ways to reach the masses directly. Indeed, press conferences came to be used more to meet the people than to meet the press when President Kennedy began the practice of televising them live in 1961. (Eisenhower had allowed filming, but the White House controlled which clips could be broadcast.) As President Nixon's chief of staff put it bluntly in a 1970 White House memo, "The President wants you to realize and emphasize to all appropriate members of your staff that a press conference is a TV operation and that the TV impression is really all that matters."[160] Nixon also began the practice of prime-time televised news conferences. Kennedy's were almost always held at either 11:00 A.M. or 4:00 P.M. Lyndon Johnson never held one after 4:50 P.M. Nixon changed that. He preferred 9:00 P.M. Back in the age when the networks preempted regularly scheduled programs to cover such conferences, that time guaranteed a large audience. It was also just late enough that it was difficult for the morning newspapers to dissect the president's performance. By the next evening's network news programs, it was already "old" news.

George H. W. Bush and Bill Clinton both held most of their press conferences during midday rather than prime-time evening hours. Although their sessions were less widely viewed—CNN was the principal source of coverage—these two presidents held press conferences quite frequently and therefore earned points with reporters for their accessibility. George W. Bush held only seventeen formal solo full-length press conferences during his first term, the lowest number for any president in the television age. Obama held only twenty-one during his first term.[161] In comparison, George H. W. Bush held eighty-four during the same period of time.[162] By the time George W. Bush left office, he had given a total of fifty solo press conferences.[163] Presidents supplement press conferences with more informal exchanges with reporters. These informal exchanges give presidents greater control because they can stop the questioning at any point. In addition, Presidents George W. Bush and Barack Obama held many joint press conferences with foreign leaders, both in the United States and abroad, but these events also give more control to the president than solo press conferences. Questions are more apt to focus on the subjects being discussed by the leaders, and half the questions are addressed to the other participant.

Without the strict ground rules that gave earlier presidents control over what information reporters could use from press conferences, presidents facing live television coverage of their press conferences have sought other ways to minimize risks. Members of the president's staff draw up a list of questions reporters are likely to ask, together with suggested answers and supporting information. Some presidents hold full-scale mock news conferences for practice. Reagan, for example, liked two-hour practices, dividing the time between foreign policy and domestic policy. Staff would point out errors and critique the president's performance. On the day of the news conference, photos of the reporters expected to attend were fixed to their likely places on a seating chart, and difficult questions were reviewed.[164] The emphasis, in short, shifted to performance.

Nixon liked to emphasize the appearance of risk he was taking in such performances. He likened himself to "the man in the arena" facing hostile adversaries when he confronted the press. To symbolize his lack of fear of these adversaries, he sometimes held press conferences with no podium to shield him from reporters. In a particularly tense press conference on October 26, 1973, that took place just after the so-called "Saturday Night Massacre" when Nixon fired Watergate special prosecutor Archibald Cox and both the attorney general and deputy attorney general resigned in protest, Nixon accused the press of "outrageous, vicious, distorted" reporting. He then added with a smile, "Don't get the impression that you arouse my anger. You see one can only be angry with those he respects."[165] Overall, presidents control the interchange at these conferences. At times, the White House limits questions to domestic policy or foreign policy, and presidents can always refuse to answer certain questions on the grounds that the subject matter is too sensitive for public discussion, a frequent response to foreign and military questions.

The success of a press conference depends on the skills of the president. Eisenhower came across badly in them. He appeared to have trouble expressing himself clearly and grammatically and displayed meager knowledge about many vital issues of the day. Revisionist accounts have suggested that he may have used this as a tactic to avoid sensitive issues.[166] President Johnson also came across poorly in formal televised press conferences. By contrast, FDR and Kennedy were masters of the press conference. Roosevelt had a keen sense of what was newsworthy and even suggested reporters' lead stories to them. He also prepared members of the press for actions he took on controversial problems by educating them initially with confidential background information; consequently, reporters tended to support his decisions because they understood his reasoning. Kennedy, who had served a brief stint as a newspaperman and enjoyed the company of reporters, used his press conferences to great advantage; his ability to field difficult questions with flashes of humor impressed not only the members of the press but also the public. Clinton did not have the close relationship with reporters that Roosevelt and Kennedy enjoyed, but he also performed well in press conferences, as did Obama. Most people who have studied or been involved in modern-day press conferences have concluded that they serve primarily the president rather than the media. As George Reedy, Johnson's press secretary, pointed out, a president rarely receives an unexpected question on an important issue in a conference, and should that happen, the president could respond with a witty or a noncommittal remark.[167] Michael Grossman and Martha Kumar have summarized the president's advantage as follows: "The President decides when to hold a conference, how much notice reporters will be given, who will ask the questions, and what the answers will be."[168]

In managing their relationships with the media, presidents must take into account their particular strengths and weaknesses. Nicknamed the Great Communicator, Reagan benefited enormously from his previous professional experience in radio, films, and television. To take advantage of those skills, the president frequently addressed the nation on prime-time television and used a series of Saturday radio broadcasts to explain and justify his administration's policies. The administration also avoided or restricted the use of other media formats that Reagan did not handle as well as prepared speeches, specifically those that required him to give spontaneous answers to questions. He did not participate in call-in shows and seldom invited reporters to the White House for informal, on-the-record question-and-answer sessions. Reagan seldom would answer impromptu questions from reporters at photo sessions, and he held fewer press conferences in eight years than Carter did in four. Nationally televised speeches were Reagan's best vehicle for communicating his views to the American people.

Relations between the President and the Media: Conflict or Collusion?

It is common for presidents to view the press unfavorably. George Washington, whom journalists treated rather well, was inclined not to run for a second term because of what he considered a critical press.[169] Since then, virtually all presidents have expressed outrage, indignation, resentment, or consternation over their treatment in the media, although Trump's condemnations were particularly immediate and harsh. The day after his inauguration, he called reporters "among the most dishonest human being beings on earth."[170] He later dismissed CNN, the *New York Times,* and the three major networks, accusing them of peddling "fake news," and adding that those organizations were "the enemy of the American people."[171]

Over the years, members of the press have also criticized the way presidents handle media relations. Typically, chief executives are accused of "managing" the news and, as their terms in office progress, of isolating themselves from the media and the public. Some, such as Johnson, Nixon, and Trump were also charged with deliberately lying to the media and the public, as was Clinton, when questioned about his relationship with Monica Lewinsky. George W. Bush was accused of misleading the public when he included an unsubstantiated charge in his 2003 State of the Union address that "Saddam Hussein recently sought significant quantities of uranium from Africa." Critics suggest that Trump is even more cavalier with the facts, routinely spreading false stories and conspiracy theories.[172]

There is little question that a built-in conflict exists between the president and the media. Chief executives want to suppress information they feel will endanger the nation's security or put their administrations in a bad light. George W. Bush was livid when newspapers published details of his secret wiretap program designed to combat terrorism. On the other hand, members of the media are eager for news, however sensitive it may be. And as a president's approval ratings fall—as Bush's did in his second term—press coverage becomes harsher. A president's lame-duck status also leads to more dismissive coverage.[173] Another source of tension between presidents and the press is the latter's post-Watergate penchant for what might be called "attack journalism": stories focused on scandal.[174] President Trump's defenders, such as Kellyanne Conway, accused the media—both during the campaign and transition, and then during his presidency—of unleashing an "unprecedented deluge of negative criticism and coverage" of Trump.[175] They also tout his use of Twitter as a way for Trump to connect directly with his 28 million followers (as of April 2017) without being subjected to the filter of a "hostile" media. Despite the potential for conflict, there is a basis for cooperation between presidents and the press that ultimately produces a collusive relationship.[176] Quite simply, the two are mutually dependent: Neither presidents nor the press can perform their jobs without the assistance of the other, and cooperation is, therefore, beneficial to both. The president must be able to communicate with the public through the media, and the media must have the administration's cooperation if they are to cover the most important official in the national government and give the public an accurate assessment of presidential activities. Moreover, the White House offers a range of media services designed to seduce reporters into favorable coverage. The product is an exchange relationship, a set of negotiated terms for the interaction between the media and the president that favors the White House and disadvantages the public.[177] As David Broder has argued, "We have been drawn into a circle of working relationships and even friendships with the people we are supposed to cover. The distinction between press and government has tended to become erased."[178]

Grossman and Kumar have argued that the general relationship between the president and the media goes through certain predictable phases.[179] During the initial period of "alliance," both parties agree that the focus should be on the new administration's appointees and its proposed goals and policies—the presidency is "open"; reporters are likely "to have their phone calls answered, to be granted interviews, and to get information that has not been specifically restricted."[180] During the second phase, "competition," the president wants to concentrate on portraying members of his administration as part of a happy team, committed to common goals and policies, while the media focus on conflicts among personalities in the administration and controversies over policies.[181] Presidents restrict access to themselves and others in the administration and may even go on the attack against especially critical reporters or organizations. The final phase of presidential-media relationships is "detachment." Surrogates manage the news, and presidents appear only in favorable settings scheduled to coincide with major events. The media, in turn, engage in more investigative reporting and seek information from sources other than the White House.

The Clinton administration's relationship with the press did not seem to follow the typical phases identified by Grossman and Kumar. The period of alliance was unusually brief, and relations became obviously strained within a matter of months. Clinton also got off to a rocky start with the White House press corps by pointedly circumventing them and restricting their access. The period of "competition" set in early, and Clinton exacerbated it by offering outspoken criticism of the press on several occasions, including a bitter public exchange with Brit Hume of ABC News on June 12, 1993, and a first-year-ending interview with *Rolling Stone* magazine in which he blamed the media for giving a false impression of his administration.[182] One study found that television news coverage provided more negative than positive comments for all but one of Clinton's first sixteen months in office. In fact, nearly three-quarters of all network reporters' assessments of Clinton during that period were judged negative.[183] The early months of the Trump administration followed a similar path. Many people in the executive branch help presidents deal with the media, but the media also have their share of resources. A large number of reporters cover the White House, many of whom have expertise in substantive areas such as law, science, welfare, and defense policy.[184] Nevertheless, members of the media may not use their skills to full advantage. Journalists covering the presidency generally lack confidence in dealing with the substance of policies and consequently focus their coverage on four areas in which they feel most comfortable: (1) administration scandals, (2) internal dissension, (3) a public gaffe or tactical blunder, and (4) the ebb and flow of electoral contests and public opinion polls.[185] The result is unintended collusion between the presidency and the media that keeps the public less—rather than more—informed about American government. This line of criticism, focused on journalistic norms and practices, goes beyond those who believe that particular presidents received less vigorous scrutiny than they deserved. For example, some observers have suggested that poor journalism led to Reagan's vaunted "Teflon coating," a term commonly used during his presidency to suggest that negative stories did not seem to stick to Reagan.[186]

The ever-increasing speed with which news is reported—and the emergence of a never-ending news cycle—has arguably made the media less careful in what they convey about the president and other political figures. In their haste to keep up with the opposition, news organizations often pick up and report breaking news stories without independent corroboration. Bill Kovach and Tom Rosenstiel have written that

> [i]nformation is moving so fast, news outlets are caught between trying to gather new information and playing catch-up with what others have delivered ahead of them. The result for any news organization is a set of flexible standards that are often bent beyond recognition as the organization relies on another's reportage.[187]

The Internet and more recent developments such as the rise of social media have fundamentally altered the way news is reported. The traditional old media had served as a gatekeeper of what news was reported. Today, however, virtually anyone can post a story.

Conclusion: The Permanent Campaign

The rise of the public presidency corresponds with the development of the **permanent campaign**. Sidney Blumenthal popularized that phrase in a 1982 book of the same name, but the phrase had been used before—notably in a transition memo from adviser Pat Caddell to president-elect Jimmy Carter in 1976.[188] Blumenthal noted that the traditional distinction between *campaigning* and *governing* had broken down and that the resulting permanent campaign had remade government "into an instrument designed to sustain an elected official's popularity."[189] More recently, Hugh Heclo described the permanent campaign this way:

> Permanent campaign is shorthand for an emergent pattern of political management that the body politic did not plan, debate, or formally adopt. It is a work of inadvertence, something developed higgledy-piggledy since the middle of the twentieth-century. The permanent campaign comprises a complex mixture of politically sophisticated people, communication techniques, and organizations—profit and nonprofit alike. What ties the pieces together is the continuous and voracious quest for public approval.[190]

The Clinton presidency was a quintessential example of the permanent campaign in action.[191] Charles O. Jones noted that Clinton remained in full campaign mode even in his final year in office. "Here was a prime example of the campaigning style of governing, practiced by a virtuoso," Jones wrote.[192] George W. Bush and Barack Obama both followed suit; Trump likewise began to hold campaign-style rallies packed with his supporters less than a month after taking office.

The White House staff units discussed in this chapter are important tools for waging that campaign. The problem with such tactics is that campaigning—by its very nature—is *adversarial*; while governing is—or at least should be—largely collaborative. As Heclo put it, "Campaigning is self-centered, and governing is group-centered."[193] When the permanent campaign becomes the predominant governing style, however, collaboration becomes difficult. Bush's embrace of the unitary executive, discussed in chapter 1, also served to undercut collaboration, as did Trump's penchant for chaos and unpredictability.[194]

Kernell has noted that the elite bargaining community that used to collaborate to produce policy is neither as isolated from public pressure nor as tightly bound together by established norms of behavior as it used to be.[195] He contends that presidents once promoted their programs primarily by negotiating with other political elites in Congress and the executive branch, but today they more often choose to "go public" by circumventing those elites and appealing directly to the American people for support.[196] Presidents make these appeals through the means we have discussed in this chapter: public speeches, public appearances, and political travel, coupled with targeted outreach using White House staff units such as the Office of Communications and the Office of Public Liaison. The new media are now an important component of such appeals.

Suggested Readings

Brace, Paul, and Barbara Hinckley. *Follow the Leader: Opinion Polls and Modern Presidents.* New York: Basic Books, 1992.

Cohen, Jeffrey E. *The Presidency in the Era of 24-Hour News.* Princeton, NJ: Princeton University Press, 2008.

Cornwell, Elmer E. *Presidential Leadership of Public Opinion.* Bloomington: Indiana University Press, 1965.

Doherty, Brendan. *The Rise of the President's Permanent Campaign.* Lawrence: University Press of Kansas, 2012.

Edwards, George C., III. *The Public Presidency: The Pursuit of Popular Support.* New York: St. Martin's Press, 1983.

———. *The Strategic President: Persuasion and Opportunity in Presidential Leadership.* Princeton, NJ: Princeton University Press, 2009.

Eisinger, Robert M. *The Evolution of Presidential Polling.* New York: Cambridge University Press, 2003.

Grossman, Michael Baruch, and Martha Joynt Kumar. *Portraying the President: The White House and the News Media.* Baltimore, MD: Johns Hopkins University Press, 1981.

Hinckley, Barbara. *The Symbolic Presidency: How Presidents Portray Themselves.* New York: Routledge, 1990.

Katz, James E., Michael Barris, and Anshul Jain. *The Social Media President: Barack Obama and the Politics of Digital Engagement.* New York: Palmgrave Macmillan, 2013.

Kernell, Samuel. *Going Public: New Strategies of Presidential Leadership,* 4th ed. Washington, DC: CQ Press, 2006.

Kumar, Martha Joynt. *Managing the President's Message: The White House Communications Operation.* Baltimore, MD: Johns Hopkins University Press, 2007.

Maltese, John Anthony. *Spin Control: The White House Office of Communications and the Management of Presidential News,* rev. 2nd ed. Chapel Hill: University of North Carolina Press, 1994.

Ornstein, Norman J., and Thomas E. Mann, eds. *The Permanent Campaign and Its Future.* Washington, DC: American Enterprise Institute, 2000.

Patterson, Bradley H., Jr. *The White House Staff: Inside the West Wing and Beyond.* Washington, DC: Brookings Institution Press, 2000.

Shapiro, Robert Y., Martha Joynt Kumar, and Lawrence R. Jacobs, eds. *Presidential Power: Forging the Presidency for the Twenty-First Century.* New York: Columbia University Press, 2000.

Tulis, Jeffrey K. *The Rhetorical Presidency.* Princeton, NJ: Princeton University Press, 1987.

Notes

1. Henry Jones Ford, *The Rise and Growth of American Politics: A Sketch of Constitutional Development* (New York: Macmillan, 1900), 283.

2. Woodrow Wilson, *Constitutional Government in the United States* (1908; repr., New York: Columbia University Press, 1961), 68.

3. Richard E. Neustadt, *Presidential Power: The Politics of Leadership* (New York: Wiley, 1960), 86–107.

4. Samuel Kernell, *Going Public: New Strategies of Presidential Leadership,* 4th ed. (Washington, DC: CQ Press, 2006).

5. Matthew A. Baum and Samuel Kernell, "Has Cable Ended the Golden Age of Presidential Television?" *American Political Science Review* 93 (March 1999): 99–114.

6. For a complete summary of Bush's approval ratings by Gallup and other organizations, see www.pollingreport.com.

7. The numbers in this paragraph are based on Gallup polls. The latest Gallup polls can be found on the web at www.gallup.com. Summaries of polls from a variety of polling organizations can be found at www.pollingreport.com. President Clinton's final Gallup job approval rating, based on nationwide surveys taken from January 5 to 7, 2001—before Clinton pardoned fugitive financier Marc Rich—was 65 percent. Other polls showed similar results: CNN/*Time* (64 percent), CBS (68 percent), and NBC/*Wall Street Journal* (66 percent). Ronald Reagan came closest with his final Gallup job approval rating of 63 percent. For an account of Clinton's early low poll ratings, see George C. Edwards III, "Frustration and Folly: Bill Clinton and the Public Presidency," in *The Clinton Presidency: First Appraisals,* ed. Colin Campbell and Bert A. Rockman (Chatham, NJ: Chatham House, 1996).

8. Molly W. Andolina and Clyde Wilcox, "Public Opinion: The Paradoxes of Clinton's Popularity," in *The Clinton Scandal and the Future of American Government,* ed. Mark J. Rozell and Clyde Wilcox (Washington, DC: Georgetown University Press, 2000), 171–194.

9. Jim Norman, "Majority in US No Longer Thinks Trump Keeps His Promises," Gallup, April 17, 2017, www.gallup.com/poll/208640/majority-no-longer-thinks-trump-keeps-promises.aspx.

10. Philip Bump, "Equating Bad Polls with Fake News, Trump Further Inflates His Surrealistic Bubble," *Washington Post,* February 6, 2017, www.washingtonpost.com/news/politics/wp/2017/02/06/equating-bad-polls-with-fake-news-trump-further-inflates-his-surreality-bubble/.

11. David Easton, *A Systems Analysis of Political Life* (New York: Wiley, 1965), chaps. 10–13.

12. Andolina and Wilcox, "Public Opinion," 189. For example, a CBS/*New York Times* poll conducted from September 22 to 23, 1998, showed that 65 percent of those surveyed felt the affair was a private matter (83 percent of Democrats thought it was a private matter, as opposed to 67 percent of Independents and 40 percent of Republicans). See also Robert J. Spitzer, "The Presidency: The Clinton Crisis and Its Consequences," in Rozell and Wilcox, *The Clinton Scandal and the Future of American Government,* 3–4.

13. Fred I. Greenstein, "What the President Means to Americans: Presidential 'Choice' between Elections," in *Choosing the President,* ed. James David Barber (Englewood Cliffs, NJ: Prentice Hall, 1974), 144–146.

14. Joseph E. Kallenbach, *The American Chief Executive: The Presidency and the Governorship* (New York: Harper and Row, 1966), 275.

15. Barry Schwartz, *George Washington: The Making of an American Symbol* (Ithaca, NY: Cornell University Press, 1987), 58–63.

16. Schwartz's discussion of the various public portrayals of Washington and their iconography is especially valuable.

17. Schwartz, *George Washington,* especially part 2.

18. Steven Mufson, "The More Eulogies Obama Gives, the Harder It Is to Be Optimistic," *Washington Post,* June 25, 2015, www.washingtonpost.com/politics/whitehouse/as-eulogizer-in-chief-obama-invokes-the-nations-common-creed/2015/06/25/3c5548ca-1b3b-11e5-ab92-c75ae6ab94b5_story.html.

19. ABC News, "Obama Will Eat Like Lincoln on Inauguration Day," January 10, 2009, http://blogs.abcnews.com/politicalpunch/2009/01/obama-will-eat.html.

20. Erin McCann, "The Two Bibles Donald Trump Used at the Inauguration," *New York Times,* January 18, 2017, www.nytimes.com/2017/01/18/us/politics/lincoln-bible-trump-oath.html?_r=0.

21. Barbara Hinckley, *The Symbolic Presidency: How Presidents Portray Themselves* (New York: Routledge, 1990), 130.

22. Ibid., 131–133.

23. Colin Campbell, "Demotion? Has Clinton Turned the Bully Pulpit into a Lectern?" in *The Clinton Legacy,* ed. Colin Campbell and Bert A. Rockman (New York: Chatham House, 2000), 56.

24. Findings of the Survey Research Center at the University of Michigan in the mid-1960s indicated that of all the occupations in the United States, including "famous doctor," "president of a large corporation like General Motors," "bishop or other church official," "Supreme Court justice," and "senator," more than half the adults named the president as the most respected. See also Jeffrey M. Jones, "Obama Bests Trump as Most Admired Man in 2016," Gallup, December 28, 2016, www.gallup.com/poll/200771/obama-bests-trump-admired-man-2016.aspx.

25. Gallup Poll, "Most Admired Man and Woman," www.gallup.com/poll/1678/most-admired-man-woman.aspx.

26. Results by year for both most admired man and most admired woman can be found at www.pollingreport.com.

27. Fred I. Greenstein, *Children and Politics* (New Haven, CT: Yale University Press, 1965); Robert Hess and Judith Torney, *The Development of Political Attitudes in Children* (Chicago: Aldine, 1967); and David Easton and Jack Dennis, *Children in the Political System: Origins of Political Legitimacy* (New York: McGraw-Hill, 1969).

28. Colby Itkowitz, "Here's How America's Kids View the Presidency in an Age of Donald Trump," *Washington Post,* October 4, 2016, www.washingtonpost.com/news/inspired-life/wp/2016/10/04/this-is-how-kids-view-the-presidency-in-the-age-of-donald-trump/.

29. Paul Brace and Barbara Hinckley, *Follow the Leader: Opinion Polls and Modern Presidents* (New York: Basic Books, 1992), 19.

30. Diane J. Heith, "Presidential Polling and the Potential for Leadership," in *Presidential Power: Forging the Presidency for the Twenty-First Century,* ed. Robert Y. Shapiro, Martha Joynt Kumar, and Lawrence R. Jacobs (New York: Columbia University Press, 2000), 382.

31. Robert M. Eisinger, *The Evolution of Presidential Polling* (New York: Cambridge University Press, 2003), 3.

32. Heith, "Presidential Polling," 384.

33. Ibid., 387.

34. Ibid., 392.

35. John Anthony Maltese, *Spin Control: The White House Office of Communications and the Management of Presidential News,* 2nd rev. ed. (Chapel Hill: University of North Carolina Press, 1994), 213–214.

36. Carl M. Cannon, "Hooked on Polls," *National Journal,* October 17, 1998, 2438 ff.

37. Andolina and Wilcox, "Public Opinion," 183.

38. "Remarks by President George W. Bush at the National Republican Congressional Committee Dinner," March 15, 2007, www.presidentialrhetoric.com/speeches/03.15.07.html.

39. Kathryn Dunn Tenpas, "Words vs. Deeds: President George W. Bush and Polling," *The Brookings Review* 21 (Summer 2003): 32–35, www.brook.edu/press/review/summer2003/tenpas.htm.

40. Jeff Zeleny, "Obama's Political Protector, Ever Close at Hand," *New York Times,* March 9, 2009, A1.

41. Paul Brace and Barbara Hinckley, "Public Opinion Polls: The New Referendum," in *Understanding the Presidency,* ed. James P. Pfiffner and Roger H. Davidson (New York: Longman, 1997), 125. See also Brace and Hinckley, *Follow the Leader.* An earlier study that made a similar finding about the decay of presidential support was John Mueller, *War, Presidents, and Public Opinion* (New York: Wiley, 1973).

42. Jeffrey M. Jones, "Bush Approval Ratings One Year after the Peak," Gallup Tuesday Briefing, October 1, 2002, www.gallup.com; supplemented by approval ratings posted at www.gallup.com.

43. See www.pollingreport.com.

44. Brace and Hinckley, *Follow the Leader,* 23–24, 32.

45. James P. Pfiffner, *The Strategic Presidency: Hitting the Ground Running,* 2nd rev. ed. (Lawrence: University Press of Kansas, 1996).

46. Paul C. Light, *The President's Agenda: Domestic Policy Choice from Kennedy to Clinton,* 3rd ed. (Baltimore, MD: Johns Hopkins University Press, 1999).

47. Maltese, *Spin Control,* 180.

48. Gary C. Jacobson, "The Bush Presidency and the American Electorate," in *The Presidency of George W. Bush: An Early Assessment,* ed. Fred I. Greenstein (Baltimore, MD: Johns Hopkins University Press, 2003), 199.

49. Jeffrey M. Jones, "Obama's Approval Most Polarized for First-Year President," January 25, 2010, www.gallup.com/poll/125345/obama-approval-polarized-first-year-president.aspx.

50. David Brooks, "Perverse Cosmic Myopia," *New York Times,* March 20, 2009, A27.

51. Johnson's first approval ratings came just after President Kennedy was assassinated in 1963. On taking office in January 1965, after being elected in his own right, Johnson's approval rating was 71 percent.

52. Bradley H. Patterson Jr., *The White House Staff: Inside the West Wing and Beyond* (Washington, DC: Brookings Institution Press, 2000). See also Charles E. Walcott and Karen M. Hult, *Governing the White House: From Hoover through LBJ* (Lawrence: University Press of Kansas, 1995), chaps. 3, 10.

53. Jeffrey K. Tulis, *The Rhetorical Presidency* (Princeton, NJ: Princeton University Press, 1987).

54. Kernell, *Going Public,* chap. 2.

55. Jeffrey K. Tulis, "The Two Constitutional Presidencies," in *The Presidency and the Political System,* 6th ed., ed. Michael Nelson (Washington, DC: CQ Press, 2000), 115–116. For an alternate view, see Mel Laracey, *Presidents and the People: The Partisan Story of Going Public* (College Station: Texas A&M University Press, 2002).

56. Tulis, *The Rhetorical Presidency,* 95.

57. Ibid., 46; see, generally, chaps. 1, 2.

58. See, for example, Richard L. Rubin, *Press, Party, and Presidency* (New York: Norton, 1981); and Culver H. Smith, *The Press, Politics, and Patronage* (Athens: University of Georgia Press, 1977).

59. Robert A. Rutland, *The Newsmongers* (New York: Dial Press, 1973), 58.

60. Frank Luther Mott, *American Journalism* (New York: Macmillan, 1941), 119–120.

61. Laracey, however, contends that every president from 1800 to 1860 "supported a newspaper that was regarded as at least the semiofficial voice of his administration" and that those newspapers are "the forgotten way of going public" for many nineteenth-century presidents—especially those from Andrew Jackson through Abraham Lincoln (1829–1865). Nevertheless, Laracey admits that, from Ulysses S. Grant through the second administration of Grover Cleveland (1869–1897), presidents did not engage in the tactic of going public. See Laracey, *Presidents and the People,* 8, 146.

62. Tulis, *The Rhetorical Presidency,* 69.

63. Based on Table 3-1 in Tulis, *The Rhetorical Presidency,* 64.

64. Samuel Kernell and Gary C. Jacobson, *The Logic of American Politics,* 4th ed. (Washington, DC: CQ Press, 2008), 347.

65. Tulis, *The Rhetorical Presidency,* 91–93.

66. Ibid., 106.

67. James W. Caesar, *Presidential Selection: Theory and Development* (Princeton, NJ: Princeton University Press, 1979), 181–184.

68. Tulis, *The Rhetorical Presidency,* 182.

69. Julie Hirschfeld Davis, "A Homebody President Sits Out His Honeymoon Period," *New York Times,* April 16, 2017, www.nytimes.com/2017/04/16/us/politics/travel-trump-obama-bush.html?hp&action=click&pgtype=Homepage&clickSource=story-heading&module=first-column-region®ion=top-news&WT.nav=top-news.

70. Kernell, *Going Public,* 4th ed., 12–23.

71. For a discussion of the permanent campaign and its impact on presidential governance, see Norman J. Ornstein and Thomas E. Mann, eds., *The Permanent Campaign and Its Future* (Washington, DC: American Enterprise Institute, 2000); see also Brendan J. Doherty, *The Rise of the President's Permanent Campaign* (Lawrence: University Press of Kansas, 2012).

72. John C. Fortier and Norman J. Ornstein, "President Bush: Legislative Strategist," in *The George W. Bush Presidency,* ed., Fred Greenstein (Baltimore, MD: Johns Hopkins University Press), 166.

73. Elizabeth Wilner, "This President Hits the Road, Not the Phones," *Washington Post,* May 29, 2005, B1.

74. David Jackson, "Obama Takes 1,000th Flight Aboard Air Force One," *USA Today,* May 14, 2014, www.usatoday.com/story/theoval/2014/05/14/obama-air-force-one-new-york-city-mark-knoller/9086325/.

75. Ibid.

76. For a recent book-length discussion of this, see James E. Katz, Michael Barris, and Anshul Jain, *The Social Media President: Barack Obama and the Politics of Digital Engagement* (New York: Palmgrave Macmillan, 2013).

77. Tim Murphy, "Meet Obama's Digital Gurus," *Mother Jones,* September/October 2012, www.motherjones.com/politics/2012/10/obama-campaign-tech-staff.

78. Eric Benderoff, "Macon Phillips: The Man behind WhiteHouse.gov," *Chicago Tribune,* February 24, 2009, http://articles.chicagotribune.com/2009-02-24/news/0902240054_1_media-tools-social-media-white-house. One minute after Obama was sworn in as president, Macon Phillips, the director of new media, began a blog on the newly designed White House website. See www.whitehouse.gov/blog/change_has_come_to_whitehouse-gov/.

79. "Obama E-mails Push Stimulus; Democratic Strategists Fire Up Post-Election Grassroots Effort," *Grand Rapids Press,* January 31, 2009, A2.

80. Jon Ward, "Obama Ramps Up High-Tech Pitch for Budget," *Washington Times,* March 26, 2009, A6.

81. "Bush Tax Cuts Clear First Hurdle," *World News Tonight,* March 8, 2001.

82. Mark Knoller, "Knoller's Numbers: President Obama's Late-Night TV Appearances," CBS News, March 12, 2015, www.cbsnews.com/news/knollers-numbers-president-obamas-late-night-tv-appearances/. See also Linda Feldman, "President Obama Takes Over for Stephen Colbert," *The Christian Science Monitor,* December 9, 2014, www.csmonitor.com/USA/Elections/Vox-News/2014/1209/President-Obama-takes-over-for-Stephen-Colbert.-How-did-Obama-do-video; Ted Johnson, "President Obama Reads Mean Tweets on 'Jimmy Kimmel,'" *Variety,* March 12, 2015, http://variety.com/2015/tv/news/president-obama-reads-mean-tweets-on-jimmy-kimmel-1201451964/.

83. James Oliphant and Frank James, "Obama Hosts 'Virtual' Town Hall," *Baltimore Sun,* March 27, 2009, 19A.

84. Wikipedia maintains a list: http://en.wikipedia.org/wiki/List_of_presidential_trips_made_by_Barack_Obama.

85. Mark Knoller, "Obama Heads to Asia, Breaks Foreign Travel Record," CBS News, November 11, 2009, www.cbsnews.com/8301-503544_162-5618462-503544.html.

86. Richard Rose, *The Postmodern President,* 2nd ed. (Chatham, NJ: Chatham House, 1991), 38.

87. E-mail from Mark Knoller to John Anthony Maltese, September 13, 2003.

88. E-mail from Mark Knoller to John Anthony Maltese, October 11, 2008.

89. For an account of the public relations aspects of Nixon's trip, see Margaret Macmillan, *Nixon and Mao: The Week That Changed the World* (New York: Random House, 2007), especially chap. 17.

90. Maltese, *Spin Control,* 195.

91. Mark Hertsgaard, *On Bended Knee: The Press and the Reagan Presidency* (New York: Farrar Straus, 1988), 273.

92. Quoted in Johanna Neuman, "Response to Terror: Public Diplomacy Is Shaped in President's Ornate War Room," *Los Angeles Times,* December 22, 2001, A3. See also John Anthony Maltese, "The Presidency and the News Media," in *Media Power, Media Politics,* ed. Mark J. Rozell (Lanham, MD: Rowman and Littlefield, 2003), 4–5.

93. Elaine Monaghan, "U.S. Set to Bombard Globe with Words," *The Times* (London), March 20, 2003, 4.

94. Memo, H. R. Haldeman to Herb Klein, March 20, 1969, in "Memos/Herb Klein (March 1969)," Box 49, H. R. Haldeman Files, Nixon Presidential Materials Project. For a thorough discussion of the use of presidential surrogates from Nixon through Clinton, see Maltese, *Spin Control.*

95. Maltese, *Spin Control,* 34, 222.

96. Ibid., 35.

97. Mark A. Peterson, "Clinton and Organized Interests: Splitting Friends, Unifying Enemies," in Campbell and Rockman, *The Clinton Legacy,* 147.

98. Joseph A. Pika, "Interest Groups and the White House under Roosevelt and Truman," *Political Science Quarterly* (Winter 1987–1988): 647–668.

99. Joseph A. Pika, "Interest Groups and the Executive: Presidential Intervention," in *Interest Group Politics,* ed. Allan J. Cigler and Burdett A. Loomis (Washington, DC: CQ Press, 1983), 318. Also see Mark A. Peterson, "The Presidency and Organized Interests: White House Patterns of Interest Group Liaison," *American Political Science Review* (September 1992): 612–625; Joseph A. Pika, "Opening Doors for Kindred Souls: The White House Office of Public Liaison," in *Interest Group Politics,* 3rd ed., ed. Allan J. Cigler and Burdett A. Loomis (Washington, DC: CQ Press, 1991); Martha Joynt Kumar and Michael Baruch Grossman, "Political Communications from the White House: The Interest Group Connection," *Presidential Studies Quarterly* (Winter 1986): 92–101; Walcott and Hult, *Governing the White House,* chap. 6; and Bradley H. Patterson Jr., *The Ring of Power: The White House Staff and Its Expanding Role in Government* (New York: Basic Books, 1988), chap. 14.

100. For a discussion of Colson and his tactics as Nixon's liaison with interest groups, see Maltese, *Spin Control,* 38, 82–84.

101. James Harding, "Preaching to the Converted," *Washington Post,* January 4, 2003, A1; and Jim VandeHei, "Pipeline to the President for GOP Conservatives; Give and Take Flows through Public Liaison Aide," *Washington Post,* December 24, 2004, A15.

102. White House, "President Obama Launches Office of Public Engagement," May 11, 2009, https://obamawhitehouse.archives.gov/the-press-office/president-obama-launches-office-public-engagement.

103. Patterson, *The Ring of Power,* 230.

104. Kathryn Dunn Tenpas, "Institutionalized Politics: The White House Office of Political Affairs," *Presidential Studies Quarterly* (Spring 1996): 511.

105. Carol E. Lee, "White House Political Office Will Remain," *Politico,* November 21, 2008, www.politico.com/news/stories/1108/15880.html.

106. "Bush Political Office Overstepped Limits, Investigators Say," CNN, January 25, 2011, www.cnn.com/2011/POLITICS/01/25/bush.political.office/.

107. Press Briefing by Press Secretary Jay Carney, June 30, 2011, www.whitehouse.gov/the-press-office/2011/06/30/press-briefing-press-secretary-jay-carney.

108. Zeke J. Miller, "Obama Reopens Political Affairs Office," *Time,* January 24, 2014, http://swampland.time.com/2014/01/24/obama-reopens-political-affairs-office/.

109. See www.whitehouse.gov/participate/internships/departments#PA.

110. John Anthony Maltese, *The Selling of Supreme Court Nominees* (Baltimore, MD: Johns Hopkins University Press, 1995), 77.

111. Tenpas, "Institutionalized Politics," 514.

112. Jon Ward, "Bush Limits Access to Ex-aides; Asserts Executive Privilege Again in Probe of U.S. Attorney Firings," *Washington Times,* July 10, 2007, A1.

113. House Committee on Government Reform and Oversight, Investigation of the Conversion of the $1.7 Million Centralized White House Computer System, Known as the White House Database, and Related Matters, 105th Cong., 2nd sess., 1998, H. Rept. 105 828, 43–44, www.mega.nu:8080/ampp/whodb.pdf.

114. Ibid., 44.

115. Tenpas, "Institutionalized Politics," 512.

116. Elisabeth Bumiller, "Preparing to Raise the Curtain on 2004," *New York Times,* June 23, 2003, A17.

117. Cynthia Kopkowski, "Politicians Hitch Bandwagon to Stars," *Atlanta Journal-Constitution,* July 20, 2002, 1A.

118. John C. Fortier and Norman J. Ornstein, "Congress and the Bush Presidency" (paper delivered at the conference on "The Bush Presidency: An Early Assessment," Woodrow Wilson School, Princeton University, NJ, April 25–26, 2003, www.princeton.edu/csdp/events/Bush2003/fortierpaper.pdf, 39).

119. David Leuthold, *Electioneering in a Democracy: Campaigns for Congress* (New York: Wiley, 1968).

120. Alan I. Abramowitz, Brad Alexander, and Matthew Gunning, "Incumbency, Redistricting, and the Decline of Competition in U.S. House Elections," *Journal of Politics* 68 (February 2006): 75.

121. See "Reelection Rates over the Years," www.opensecrets.org/bigpicture/reelect.php.

122. Gary C. Jacobson, "It's Nothing Personal: The Decline of the Incumbency Advantage in US House Elections," *Journal of Politics* (July 2015).

123. Fortier and Ornstein, "Congress and the Bush Presidency," 39–40.

124. James Hohmann, "The 2014 Senate Elections—and Beyond," in *The Surge: 2014's Big GOP Win and What It Means for the Next Presidential Election,* ed. Larry J. Sabato (Lanham, MD: Rowman and Littlefield, 2015), 60.

125. Edward Tufte, "Determinants of the Outcomes of Midterm Congressional Elections," *American Political Science Review* (September 1975): 812–826.

126. Samuel Kernell, "Presidential Popularity and Negative Voting: An Alternative Explanation of the Midterm Decline of the Presidential Party," *American Political Science Review* (March 1977): 44–66.

127. Gary Jacobson, *The Politics of Congressional Elections* (Boston: Little, Brown, 1983), 138 ff. Jacobson argues that the 2002 midterm election results were "entirely consistent" with such a model. He further adds, "Contrary to a great deal of postelection commentary, the results of the 2002 midterm congressional elections were neither surprising nor historically anomalous" (Gary C. Jacobson, "Terror, Terrain, and Turnout," *Political Science Quarterly* 118, no. 1 (2003): 1).

128. Jacobson, "Terror, Terrain, and Turnout," 3.

129. James Pollard, *The Presidents and the Press* (New York: Macmillan, 1947), chap. 1.

130. William Rivers, *The Opinion-Makers* (Boston: Beacon Press, 1967), 7.

131. Michael Baruch Grossman and Martha Joynt Kumar, *Portraying the President: The White House and the News Media* (Baltimore: Johns Hopkins University Press, 1981), 19.

132. Elmer E. Cornwell, *Presidential Leadership of Public Opinion* (Bloomington: Indiana University Press, 1965), 17; and Stephen Hess, "Press Relations," in *Encyclopedia of the American Presidency,* ed. Leonard W. Levy and Louis Fisher (New York: Simon and Schuster, 1994), 1230.

133. Harold W. Stanley and Richard G. Niemi, *Vital Statistics on American Politics,* 5th ed. (Washington, DC: CQ Press, 1995), Table 2-1, 47.

134. *TV Dimensions 2000* (New York: Media Dynamics, 2000), 245.

135. Lydia Saad, "TV Is Americans' Main Source of News," Gallup.com, July 8, 2013, www.gallup.com/poll/163412/americans-main-source-news.aspx.

136. Amy Mitchell, Jeffrey Gottfried, Michael Barthel, and Elisa Shearer, "The Modern News Consumer," Pew Research Center, July 7, 2016, www.journalism.org/2016/07/07/pathways-to-news/.

137. Benjamin I. Page, Robert Y. Shapiro, and Glenn R. Dempsey, "What Moves Public Opinion?" *American Political Science Review* (March 1987): 23–43; and Donald L. Jordan, "Newspaper Effects on Policy Preferences," *Public Opinion Quarterly* (Summer 1993): 191–204. Page, Shapiro, and Dempsey examined the impact of television reports, whereas Jordan concentrated on the effects of newspapers.

138. Grossman and Kumar, *Portraying the President,* 209–210.

139. Chris Ariens, "Evening News Ratings: Week of April 3," *Adweek,* April 11, 2017, www.adweek.com/tvnewser/evening-news-ratings-week-of-april-3–2/326231.

140. Pew Research Center for the People and the Press, "Internet Gains on Television as Public's Main Source of News," Janury 4, 2011, www.people-press.org/2011/01/04/internet-gains-on-television-as-publics-main-news-source/.

141. Mitchell et al., "The Modern News Consumer."

142. There are some notable exceptions to this rule. The *PBS NewsHour,* broadcast nightly, takes an hour to examine two or three topics in depth; ABC's *Nightline* looks at one topic for twenty-five minutes. PBS's *Washington Week* invites major political reporters to analyze the significant news developments of the previous week.

143. Baum and Kernell, "Has Cable Ended the Golden Age?" 99.

144. Stephen Hess, *The Washington Reporters* (Washington, DC: Brookings, 1981), chap. 2; Leon Segal, *Reporters and Officials* (Lexington, MA: D. C. Heath, 1973), chap. 1.

145. Hess, *The Washington Reporters,* 31.

146. Katz, Barris, and Jain, *The Social Media President: Barack Obama and the Politics of Digital Engagement.*

147. Susan Milligan, "The President and the Press," *Columbia Journalism Review* (March/April 2015), www.cjr.org/analysis/the_president_and_the_press.php?utm_content=bufferea272&utm_medium=social&utm_source=twitter.com&utm_campaign=buffer.

148. Jackson Connor, "Obama Administration's Relationship with Press among the Worst Ever, Report Shows," *Huffington Post,* March 4, 2015, www.huffingtonpost.com/2015/03/04/obama-press-worst-ever-administrations-relationship_n_6794920.html. See also Diane Heith, "Obama and the Public Presidency," in Bert Rockman et al., eds., *The Obama Presidency: Appraisals and Prospects* (Washington, DC: CQ Press, 2013).

149. Grossman and Kumar, *Portraying the President,* chap. 5.

150. M. L. Stein, *When Presidents Meet the Press* (New York: Messner, 1969), 166.

151. Matt Ford, "Trump's Press Secretary Falsely Claims: 'Largest Audience Ever to Witness an Inauguration, Period,'" *The Atlantic,* January 21, 2017, www.theatlantic.com/politics/archive/2017/01/inauguration-crowd-size/514058/.

152. John F. Kennedy Jr., "Mike McCurry's About-Face," *George,* March 1999, 78.

153. Maltese, *Spin Control,* 24, 29.

154. Larry Speakes, *Speaking Out: Inside the Reagan White House* (New York: Scribner's, 1988), 136, 153.

155. For a full account of the office and its precursors, see Maltese, *Spin Control.*

156. Interview with John Anthony Maltese, March 10, 1989, Washington, DC, quoted in Maltese, *Spin Control,* 2.

157. Donald T. Regan, *For the Record* (New York: Harcourt Brace Jovanovich, 1988), 248.

158. William Douglas, "Bush's 'Great Image,'" *Newsday,* May 2, 2003, A06; Dana Milbank, "Explanation for Bush's Carrier Landing Altered," *Washington Post,* May 7, 2003, A20; and Elisabeth Bumiller, "Keepers of Bush Image Lift Stagecraft to New Heights," *New York Times,* May 16, 2003, 1.

159. Kernell, *Going Public,* 63.

160. Quoted in Maltese, *Spin Control,* 44.

161. Mark Knoller, "Obama's First Term: By the Numbers," CBS News, January 19, 2013, www.cbsnews.com/news/obamas-first-term-by-the-numbers/.

162. Project for Excellence in Journalism, "All the President's Pressers," October 16, 2006, www.journalism.org/node/2409.

163. Christina Bellantoni, "Obama Sets Record in News Conferences," *Washington Times,* November 27, 2008, A8. In addition to the forty-nine solo press conferences referenced in this article, President Bush gave a final solo press conference on January 12, 2009.

164. Patterson, *The Ring of Power,* 174.

165. To view the exchange on YouTube, go to www.youtube.com/watch?v=iucE78-C2Po.

166. Fred I. Greenstein, *The Hidden-Hand Presidency: Eisenhower as Leader* (New York: Basic Books, 1982), 66–70.

167. George Reedy, *The Twilight of the Presidency* (New York: New American Library, 1970), 164.

168. Grossman and Kumar, *Portraying the President,* 244.

169. Pollard, *The Presidents and the Press,* 14.

170. Julie Hirschfeld Davis and Matthew Rosenberg, "With False Claims, Trump Attacks Media on Turnout and Intelligence Rift," *New York Times,* January 21, 2017, www.nytimes.com/2017/01/21/us/politics/trump-white-house-briefing-inauguration-crowd-size.html.

171. Michael M. Grynbaum, "Trump Calls the News Media the 'Enemy of the American People,'" *New York Times,* February 17, 2017, www.nytimes.com/2017/02/17/business/trump-calls-the-news-media-the-enemy-of-the-people.html.

172. For example: David Leonhardt, "All the President's Lies," *New York Times,* March 20, 2017, www.nytimes.com/2017/03/20/opinion/all-the-presidents-lies.html.

173. Howard Kurtz, "The Press, Turning Up Its Nose at Lame Duck," *Washington Post,* February 5, 2007, C1.

174. Larry J. Sabato, *Feeding Frenzy: Attack Journalism and American Politics* (Baltimore, MD: Lanahan, 2000).

175. Rebecca Savranky, "Conway: 'Unprecedented' Negative Coverage of Trump 'Unfair to Our Democracy,'" *The Hill,* January 22, 2017, http://thehill.com/homenews/administration/315518-conway-unprecedented-negative-coverage-of-trump-unfair-to-our.

176. Grossman and Kumar, *Portraying the President,* chap. 1.

177. Michael Grossman and Francis Rourke, "The Media and the Presidency: An Exchange Analysis," *Political Science Quarterly* (Fall 1976): 455–470. Also see Timothy E. Cook and Lyn Ragsdale, "The President and the Press: Negotiating Newsworthiness at the White House," *The Presidency and the Political System,* ed. Michael Nelson (Washington, DC: CQ Press, various editions).

178. Quoted by Patterson in *The Ring of Power,* 170.

179. Grossman and Kumar, *Portraying the President,* chap. 11.

180. Ibid., 178.

181. This tendency first became apparent during the second year of the Reagan administration, when reporters began to ask him more embarrassing questions, such as why he did not set an example by making more generous donations to private charities. They also appeared not to take seriously the president's statement that members of his administration were one big happy family.

182. Martha Joynt Kumar, "President Clinton Meets the Media: Communications Shaped by Predictable Patterns," in *The Clinton Presidency: Campaigning, Governing, and the Psychology of Leadership,* ed. Stanley A. Renshon (Boulder, CO: Westview, 1995), 167–171.

183. Study conducted by Robert Lichter of the Center for Media and Public Affairs as reported in Howard Kurtz, "The Bad News about Clinton," *Washington Post,* September 1, 1994, D1.

184. Stephen Hess showed that in 1978, 73 percent were college graduates and 33 percent had graduate degrees (*The Washington Reporters,* 83); Leo Rosten reported that in 1936, 51 percent were college graduates and 6 percent had an advanced academic degree; and see *The Washington Correspondents* (New York: Harcourt, Brace, 1937), 159–160.

185. James Fallows, "The Presidency and the Press," in *The Presidency and the Political System,* 3rd ed., ed. Michael Nelson (Washington, DC: CQ Press, 1990).

186. Hertsgaard, *On Bended Knee,* 203.

187. Bill Kovach and Tom Rosenstiel, *Warp Speed: America in the Age of Mixed Media* (New York: Century Foundation Press, 1999), 51.

188. Sidney Blumenthal, *The Permanent Campaign* (New York: Simon and Schuster, 1982); see also Ornstein and Mann, *The Permanent Campaign and Its Future,* vii.

189. Blumenthal, *The Permanent Campaign,* 7.

190. Hugh Heclo, “Campaigning and Governing: A Conspectus,” in Ornstein and Mann, *The Permanent Campaign and Its Future,* 15. See Doherty, *The Rise of the President’s Permanent Campaign,* for efforts to track presidential efforts along these lines more systematically.

191. George C. Edwards III, “Campaigning Is Not Governing: Bill Clinton’s Rhetorical Presidency,” in Campbell and Rockman, *The Clinton Legacy,* 33.

192. Jones, “Preparing to Govern in 2001,” in Ornstein and Mann, *The Permanent Campaign and Its Future,* 185.

193. Heclo, “Campaigning and Governing,” 11.

194. Chris Zillizaa, “Chaos Worked for Trump as a Candidate. As President? Not So Much.” CNN .com, April 3, 2017, www.cnn.com/2017/04/03/politics/trump-chaos-cillizza/.

195. Kernell, *Going Public,* 23.

196. Ibid., 2.

CHAPTER 4

Presidential Character and Performance

REUTERS/Win McNamee

In a dramatic moment intended to halt media reports and rumors, on January 26, 1998, President Clinton denies having had a sexual relationship with "that woman," Monica Lewinsky. He was later forced to publicly apologize for lying about the relationship and to defend himself against impeachment charges.

President Barack H. Obama left office at noon on January 20, 2017. As they always do at the end of a term, the media and learned academics devoted considerable time to reviewing the president's performance and assessing his legacy. They also posed another question: What kind of president was Donald J. Trump likely to be? As Trump first vanquished sixteen opponents to win the nomination and then defied almost all predictions to win the general election, journalists culled through Trump's past for clues.[1] Although Trump was the rare billionaire who sought out rather than shunned publicity and had collaborated on several books with ghost authors about himself, there was no way to predict how someone without a political past would approach the office of president. In fact, the public shares a fascination with all presidents. We dwell on their accomplishments, deconstruct their decisions, and speculate on their place in history, making it all seem very personal, a reflection of the president's strengths, weaknesses, emotional needs, and attitudes. The reality is more complex than that, but the design of American government enhances the importance of a president's individual qualities.

Observers make a connection between the personal qualities of presidents and their performance in office, but the link is not always clear. When Bill Clinton left office at the completion of a controversial eight-year roller-coaster ride on the national scene, he left behind many lingering questions centered on his personal character and judgment, especially concerning his sexual relationship with former White House intern Monica Lewinsky, which became the focus of a special prosecutor's investigation. Different questions surrounded Bush. What shaped his performance as a wartime president? As Fred Greenstein has suggested, Al Gore, had he won the 2000 election, would probably have reacted to the 9/11 terrorist attacks much the same way as Bush, but it is less clear that a President Gore would have launched a preemptive invasion of Iraq.[2] Even after Republicans suffered defeat in the 2006 midterm elections, Bush continued on a path in Iraq that was widely rejected. Did his persistence reflect a personality-based inability to admit mistakes—a pattern comparable to that found for Woodrow Wilson, Herbert Hoover, and Lyndon B. Johnson—or did it simply arise from a different view of the consequences for America's international interests?

And what of Obama? Was his biracial identity the key to understanding his commitment to build consensus on so many issues during his two terms in office? What about that cool persona captured in the description of his campaign style—"no drama Obama"? Insider accounts suggest that this was the real Obama, not a contrived image. And how do we explain Obama's shift in strategy following the 2014 midterm election to challenge the Republican-controlled congressional opposition rather than seek compromise? Did this reflect his personality, political calculation in light of disappointing election results, or an effort to secure his legacy? In sharp contrast to "no drama" Obama, Trump thrived on drama during the 2016 campaign and his first months as president. After burying his Republican competitors under a heap of insults, candidate Trump used mass rallies to denounce Hillary Clinton's dishonesty, challenge the NATO alliance, praise Vladimir Putin, and incite anti-immigrant and anti-Muslim hatred. The more outrageous the statements the larger the headlines. Once elected, he picked fights by phone with staunch international allies (Australia, Germany, United Kingdom, Mexico) and issued a string of tweets that attacked the media, shamed individual corporations, denounced fellow Republicans who had voted against his health care proposal, and claimed that Obama had wire-tapped Trump Tower in NYC during the campaign. What explained such petulant, politically damaging behavior, and would it change as Trump settled into the job? What would happen if a crisis broke out?

The presidency invites such speculation because its occupants wield enormous power in a one-person office rather than as part of a collective institution. Many analysts attributed the conduct of the Vietnam War (1964–1973) and the Watergate scandal (1972–1974), in which White House aides covered up illegal activities committed to help reelect the president, to the unique emotional needs of Presidents Lyndon Johnson and Richard Nixon.[3] As the nation approached the 2016 election, people speculated on what Jeb Bush, Ted Cruz, Scott Walker, or Hillary Clinton would be like as president. Could Trump overcome his capricious Twitter outbursts to exercise balanced judgment from the Oval Office?

In this chapter, we look more closely at what kinds of people have served as president and how their personal qualities may have shaped their conduct. We are especially concerned with presidents' backgrounds, skills, psychological traits, and management styles and how these factors influence their performances in office. We therefore examine the abilities and attitudes that presidents develop before entering office, ways in which their personalities affect how they do the job, and their habitual modes of working. We also look at how presidents interact with their staffs, those assistants whose positions were created to extend presidents' personal capabilities. To conclude, we take a closer look at the factors that shaped Barack Obama's performance in office, and we offer a preliminary assessment of Donald Trump.

Determinants and Evaluations of Performance

For generations, historians and political scientists have argued about how important a leader's characteristics are for understanding and explaining events. Does one, for example, place great significance on the intelligence, stature, and wisdom of Abraham Lincoln in explaining the Union's ultimate victory? Or was victory the product of forces beyond Lincoln's control, such as the changing nature of modern warfare in an industrial age, which favored the North? Did the United States and the Soviet Union avert nuclear war during the Cuban missile crisis of 1962 because of the decision style adopted by John F. Kennedy? Or was the outcome the result of organizational routines for crisis management and other random occurrences perhaps not intended by either side during the confrontation? The larger questions are, therefore, just how much importance should one ascribe to the president's personal characteristics, and whether these elements are powerful predictors of performance in office.

Specialists have not reached agreement on the importance of these factors, although there is widespread belief that it does indeed matter—and probably a great deal—who is president. Fred Greenstein argues, "If some higher power had set out to design a democracy in which the individual on top mattered, the result might well resemble the American political system."[4] Every four years the nation devotes enormous effort and resources to selecting a leader, and this confidence in the difference an individual can make is revealed when citizens insist they "voted for the person, not the party." Public attention focuses on the presidency, with the mass media personalizing the solution to public problems and portraying presidents as the embodiment of the larger political process. Moreover, presidents and their media advisers encourage personalization when they highlight traits the public regards as desirable.

Not everyone agrees that presidents' individual characteristics are critical to understanding their accomplishments. The alternative is to stress the environment within which presidents operate as the truly significant determinant of outcomes. The most influential interpretation in this tradition is the work of Stephen Skowronek, whose analysis rests on comparison of presidents facing similar challenges in different time frames. Thus Thomas Jefferson, Andrew Jackson, Abraham Lincoln, Franklin D. Roosevelt, and Ronald Reagan shared common "leadership tasks" associated with the decline and reconstruction of the links among societal interests and the political parties essential to a political order. Trump may be playing a similar role today. Similarly, James Monroe, James K. Polk, Theodore Roosevelt, and Lyndon Johnson had more in common with each other—the position they inherited in relation to the dominant political order—than with their immediate predecessors and successors. Although the title of Skowronek's principal work—*The Politics Presidents Make*—emphasizes the role of leadership, the unfolding evolution of larger forces in American social and political life defines the tasks presidents confront and severely limits the possibilities they enjoy at the beginning of their terms. In some ways, his book might be more accurately titled *The Presidents Politics Make.*[5]

Nevertheless, there is broad consensus among students of the presidency that each chief executive brings to the job a combination of attitudes, skills, strengths, and shortcomings that will influence the performance in office and may at times have an enduring effect on the nation's history. Disagreement still exists on the relative significance of these causal factors and exactly how they are related to job performance and policy outcomes. A number of analysts have suggested ways to conceptualize these issues; a modified, considerably simplified diagram based on two of the most prominent treatments is presented in Figure 4-1.

All presidents bring to the job enduring personality traits as well as attitudes and beliefs toward a wide range of political structures, institutions, and relationships. These personal characteristics and attitudes take shape within a distinctive

FIGURE 4-1 Relationship of Background to Performance

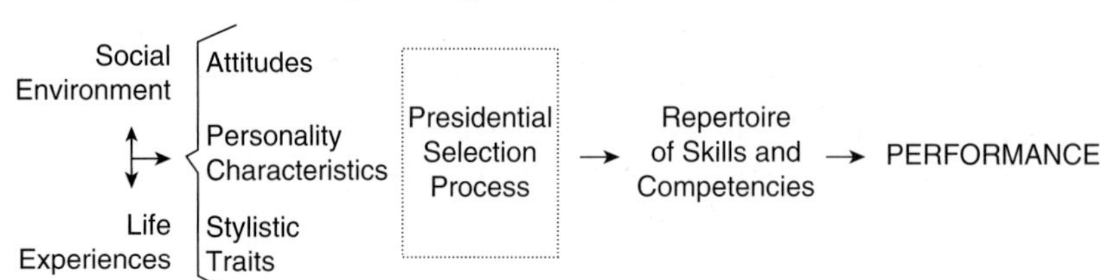

SOURCES: Bert A. Rockman, *The Leadership Question* (New York: Praeger, 1984), 189; Fred I. Greenstein, *Personality and Politics* (New York: Norton, 1975), 27.

social context—family situation, place in the community, educational experience, and so on. In addition, their adult professional experiences prior to entering office, particularly as they relate to role demands of the presidency, produce a personal style that may be more or less congruent with the demands of serving as chief executive. The presidential selection process filters out personal styles, skills, and competencies that are not role appropriate. Ultimately, presidents may be more or less likely to produce successful outcomes as these individual traits interact with the situations the presidents confront. In concentrating on the importance of leaders' individual characteristics, one recognizes that presidents are in the position to have potentially decisive impacts on political events. Even if the environment—forces beyond the control of the individual leader—has a determinative effect on events, "environments are always mediated by the individuals on whom they act."[6]

Just as analysts disagree over the determinants of presidential behavior, so too do they disagree over how to evaluate a president's performance, although the general public and professional presidency watchers engage in evaluations all the time. Polls provide current, short-term assessments of public approval (discussed in chapter 3), and journalists constantly assess the administration's record in dealing with Congress or in addressing particular policy areas (chapters 5–10). Certain evaluation points have become institutionalized: For example, the end of an administration's first one hundred days in office (a carryover from FDR's first term) always produces a spate of articles. Other evaluation points are at midterm and on departure from office.[7] In other words, the public, journalists, and academics are constantly engaged in *contemporary evaluation* of presidential performance.

Scholars and others use a variety of criteria to evaluate presidential performance. Bruce Buchanan has drawn broad distinctions between subjective and objective criteria. Judgments based on subjective grounds emphasize the "appearance and demeanor" of leadership, including success in projecting the image of integrity and charisma, the "moral desirability of a president's means or ends," and the pragmatic test of self-interest—the extent to which the president contributed to a citizen's well-being. Objective criteria, on which professionals are more likely to make their evaluations, focus on presidential skill in making things happen, especially short-term successes, or on the lasting results produced for the nation.[8] Recent ranking exercises stress a number of criteria, from legislative skill to integrity to the degree to which a president polarized the polity.[9] But instant ratings run the danger of missing the long view of a given president's legacy. As Bert Rockman put it, politicians can "leave greater or lesser footprints. Assessing the depth and durability of those marks is hazardous while the administration under evaluation is still in power. The real answers will come later—much later."[10]

Bill Clinton's conduct reawakened concern with **presidential character**, a term with many contradictory meanings. James Pfiffner helps address this murky area: How should Americans assess the personal failures of presidents when they lie about trivial or important matters, violate marriage vows, or intentionally seek to deceive the public?[11] Pfiffner reviews numerous instances of presidential untruths in terms of the teller's intent and the seriousness of the lie, a recognition that evaluation of this conduct depends heavily on context. Although the public widely regards telling the truth as a moral obligation, Pfiffner accepts the possibility of a "justified lie."[12] Therefore, lies to protect the national security, concerning trivial matters (for example, describing one's personal history or illustrating a point), or to prevent embarrassment and preserve political viability are less serious than those used to cover up important facts or deceive the public on policy matters. Trump's first months in office triggered new debates about presidential lying, "fake news," and "alternative facts." Pfiffner's discussion of Clinton's marital infidelity is placed in the context of other presidents known to have committed similar acts or suspected of doing so: Franklin Roosevelt, Dwight D. Eisenhower, John Kennedy, and Lyndon Johnson.[13]

Efforts to evaluate presidential performance and conduct are not new. Since 1948, scholars—primarily historians—have been asked periodically to "rate" American presidents. In essence they were to assess the "depth and durability" of presidential footprints and provide a *historical evaluation.* Table 4-1 shows the results of seven of these efforts. Each poll was structured a bit differently and surveyed a different panel of "experts."[14] Yet one finds considerable consensus among participants on the top ten and the bottom ten, with the exception of Nixon and Grant, whose reputations have undergone a marked resurgence. Because of the similar results across polls, Robert Murray and Tim Blessing concluded that historians "had in mind more than vague and uncritical generalities when they evaluated presidential performances."[15] Assessments of the more recent presidents are particularly susceptible to change with the passage of time. Note how Eisenhower moved from twentieth place in 1962 to ninth in the Lindgren-Calabresi poll in 2000, eighth in the 2009 C-SPAN poll, and fifth in the 2017 version. Harry S. Truman's standing among professionals was already strong by 1962 and has remained so. Reagan's evaluation by historians has improved from below average to borderline great.[16] As he left office, Clinton finished in the middle of the pack at number twenty-four, a couple positions behind George H. W. Bush, but moved to fifteenth in the 2009 and 2017 C-SPAN rankings. With vivid recollections of wars in Iraq and Afghanistan, George W. Bush placed seventh from the bottom, in thirty-sixth place, in the same rankings and now to thirty-third.[17] Even before he finished his service, speculation was rampant about how Barack Obama would be regarded. *New York Magazine* asked fifty-three historians to evaluate how Obama would be remembered in twenty years and published the results on the eve of his penultimate State of the Union address.[18] Nate Silver, a well-known expert on election statistics, hazarded an early evaluation, placing Obama at seventeenth (borderline between average and good) based on Obama's reelection results compared to those of other presidents who had sought two terms in office.[19] C-SPAN (2017) placed him at twelfth.

In addition to analyzing 846 completed surveys, Murray and Blessing conducted sixty in-depth interviews with historians to determine their evaluative criteria. The most important personal trait contributing to presidential achievement, in the view of the participating historians, was decisiveness; intelligence, particularly the capacity for growth, and integrity were close behind.[20] Greatness, many seemed to feel, is achieved by those leaders able to exercise moral, inspirational leadership, who have "a capacity for creative innovation and an imagination that was fired by a clear vision of the future."[21] James MacGregor Burns's discussion of leadership emphasizes similar abilities as the source of "transformational" leadership, by which presidents appeal to the higher goals and motives of followers to achieve true change.[22] Greenstein suggests that a president's job performance is shaped by six qualities: (1) proficiency as a *public communicator*; (2) *organizational capacity* to rally colleagues and (3) structure activities; (4) *political skill* insofar as it is linked to a *vision* of public policy;

TABLE 4-1 Selected Ratings of U.S. Presidents

Schlesinger Poll (1948)	*Schlesinger Poll (1962)*	*Murray-Blessing Poll (1982)*	*Lindgren-Calabresi Poll (2000)*	*C-SPAN Poll (2009)*	*Nate Silver Meta—Analysis (2008–2011)*	*C-SPAN Poll (2017)*
Great	Great	Great	Great			
1. Lincoln	1. Lincoln	1. Lincoln	1. Washington	1. Lincoln	1. Lincoln	1. Lincoln
2. Washington	2. Washington	2. F. Roosevelt	2. Lincoln	2. Washington	2. F. Roosevelt	2. Washington
3. F. Roosevelt	3. F. Roosevelt	3. Washington	3. F. Roosevelt	3. F. Roosevelt	3. Washington	3. F. Roosevelt
4. Wilson	4. Wilson	4. Jefferson	Near great	4. T. Roosevelt	4. T. Roosevelt	4. T. Roosevelt
5. Jefferson	5. Jefferson	Near great	4. Jefferson	5. Truman	5. Jefferson	5. Eisenhower
6. Jackson	Near great	5. T. Roosevelt	5. T. Roosevelt	6. Kennedy	6. Truman	6. Truman
Near great	6. Jackson	6. Wilson	6. Jackson	7. Jefferson	7. Wilson	7. Jefferson
7. T. Roosevelt	7. T. Roosevelt	7. Jackson	7. Truman	8. Eisenhower	8. Eisenhower	8. Kennedy
8. Cleveland	8. Polk/Truman (tie)	8. Truman	8. Reagan	9. Wilson	9. Kennedy	9. Reagan
9. J. Adams	9. J. Adams	Above average	9. Eisenhower	10. Reagan	10. Reagan	10. L. Johnson
10. Polk	10. Cleveland	9. J. Adams	10. Polk	11. L. Johnson	11. Polk	11. Wilson
Average	Average	10. L. Johnson	11. Wilson	12. Polk	12. L. Johnson	12. Obama
11. J. Q. Adams	11. Madison	11. Eisenhower	Above average	13. Jackson	13. Jackson	13. Monroe
12. Monroe	12. J. Q. Adams	12. Polk	12. Cleveland	14. Monroe	14. Monroe	14. Polk
13. Hayes	13. Hayes	13. Kennedy	13. J. Adams	15. Clinton	15. Madison	15. Clinton
14. Madison	14. McKinley	14. Madison	14. McKinley	16. McKinley	16. J. Adams	16. McKinley
15. Van Buren	15. Taft	15. Monroe	15. Madison	17. J. Adams	17. Obama (based on 2012 election)	17. Madison
16. Taft	16. Van Buren	16. J. Q. Adams	16. Monroe	18. G. H. W. Bush	18. Clinton	18. Jackson
17. Arthur	17. Monroe	17. Cleveland	17. L. Johnson	19. J. Q. Adams	19. McKinley	19. J. Adams
18. McKinley	18. Hoover	Average	18. Kennedy	20. Madison	20. J. Q. Adams	20. G.H.W. Bush
19. A. Johnson	19. B. Harrison	18. McKinley	Average	21. Cleveland	21. Cleveland	21. J.Q. Adams
20. Hoover	20. Arthur/ Eisenhower (tie)	19. Taft	20. J. Q. Adams	22. Ford	22. G. H. W. Bush	22. Grant

21. B. Harrison	21. A. Johnson	20. Van Buren	21. G. H. W. Bush	23. Grant	23. Grant	23 Cleveland
Below average	Below average	21. Hoover	22. Hayes	24. Taft	24. Ford	24. Taft
22. Tyler	22. Taylor	22. Hayes	23. Van Buren	25. Carter	25. Taft	25. Ford
23. Coolidge	23. Tyler	23. Arthur	24. Clinton	26. Coolidge	26. Carter	26. Carter
24. Fillmore	24. Fillmore	24. Ford	25. Coolidge	27. Nixon	27. Coolidge	27. Coolidge
25. Taylor	25. Coolidge	25. Carter	26. Arthur	28. Garfield	28. Arthur	28. Nixon
26. Buchanan	26. Pierce	26. B. Harrison	Below average	29. Taylor	29. Nixon	29. Garfield
27. Pierce	27. Buchanan	Below average	27. Harrison	30. B. Harrison	30. Garfield	30. B. Harrison
Failure	Failure	27. Taylor	28. Ford	31. Van Buren	31. Van Buren	31. Taylor
28. Grant	28. Grant	28. Tyler	29. Hoover	32. Arthur	32. Hayes	32. Hayes
29. Harding	29. Harding	29. Fillmore	30. Carter	33. Hayes	33. Taylor	33. G.W. Bush
		30. Coolidge	31. Taylor	34. Hoover	34. B. Harrison	34. Van Buren
		31. Pierce	32. Grant	35. Tyler	35. Hoover	35. Arthur
		Failure	33. Nixon	36. G. W. Bush	36. Tyler	36. Hoover
		32. A. Johnson	34. Tyler	37. Fillmore	37. Fillmore	37. Fillmore
		33. Buchanan	35. Fillmore	38. Harding	38. G. W. Bush	38. W. H. Harrison
		34. Nixon	Failure	39. W. H. Harrison	39. A. Johnson	39. Tyler
		35. Grant	36. A. Johnson	40. Pierce	40. W. H. Harrison	40. Harding
		36. Harding	37. Pierce	41. A. Johnson	41. Harding	41. Pierce
			38. Harding	42. Buchanan	42. Pierce	42. A. Johnson
			39. Buchanan		43. Buchanan	43. Buchanan

SOURCES: Harold W. Stanley and Richard G. Niemi, *Vital Statistics on American Politics, 1999–2000* (Washington, DC: CQ Press, 2000), Table 6-2, 244–245; and James Lindgren and Steven Calabresi, "Rating the Presidents of the United States, 1789–2000: A Survey of Scholars in Political Science, History and Law," *Constitutional Commentary* 18 (Winter 2001): 583–605 (Sponsored by Federalist Society and *Wall Street Journal*); C-SPAN 2009 Historians Leadership Survey, https://static.c-span.org/assets/documents/presidentSurvey/2009%20C-SPAN%20Presidential%20Survey%20Scores%20and%20Ranks%20FINAL.PDF; Nate Silver, "Contemplating Obama's Place in History, Statistically," *New York Times* FiveThirtyEight Blog, January 23, 2013, http://fivethirtyeight.blogs.nytimes.com/2013/01/23/contemplating-obamas-place-in-history-statistically/?_r=0. C-SPAN 2017 Presidential Historians Survey, https://www.c-span.org/presidentsurvey2017/?page=overall.

NOTE: These ratings result from surveys of between 49 and 846 scholars. The initial rating of Reagan was obtained in a separate poll conducted in 1989. The Silver rating of Obama factors in election results.

(5) *cognitive style* in processing advice and information; and (6) *emotional intelligence,* by which he means the ability to manage one's own emotions for constructive purposes.[23]

As Greenstein makes clear, it is now necessary to factor an additional consideration into assessing performance: Modern presidents no longer govern alone. Since the 1930s, they have been assisted by a large number of aides appointed to serve in the **Executive Office of the President (EOP).** Aides have the capacity to amplify a president's personal capabilities; mobilizing such efforts is a new dimension of the job just as public communications have taken on a much greater significance than they had prior to the twentieth century.

To examine the importance of individual characteristics, we turn first to a discussion of the backgrounds from which presidents have been drawn. As depicted in Figure 4-1, a president's life and occupational experiences are distant from the actual service in office and should therefore have only limited power to explain performance. Nevertheless, the patterns uncovered tell us something about leadership in America.

What Manner of Person?

Each president brings to the office a cumulation of life experiences derived from a position in American society and previous professional experience. The selection process described in chapter 2, rather than producing a random sampling of Americans, typically favors some backgrounds over others. After reviewing the historical pattern for social background and education, scholars have found, not surprisingly, that presidents have disproportionately been drawn from traditionally dominant groups in American society. It is less clear, however, just what this has meant for performance in office.

Social Background

Although there is no single indicator of social status on which all Americans would agree, occupation is probably the most important criterion for social ranking in the United States.[24] Moreover, the occupation of an individual's father provides a reasonably accurate picture of his or her class origins. By analyzing such origins, one can determine the extent to which presidents have achieved their positions of power as a result of their own abilities or the advantages of family background.[25] The presidency has long been cited as an example of how ability can enable individuals to overcome disadvantages and rise to power.

But the reality of presidents' personal histories, argues Edward Pessen, contradicts "the log cabin myth" and demonstrates that "the political race here as elsewhere has usually been won by those who had the advantage of starting from a favorable position."[26] Pessen characterized the family background of each president through Reagan in terms of six basic groupings: (1) upper-upper and (2) lower-upper, (3) upper-middle and (4) lower-middle, and (5) upper-lower and (6) lower-lower.[27] In making his evaluations, Pessen compared the presidents' family backgrounds with the economic and social conditions that existed at the time rather than using a permanent yardstick.

Five distinguished American families have produced ten presidents, more than one-fifth of the total. Included were John Adams and his son John Quincy Adams; James Madison and Zachary Taylor, who had grandparents in common; William Henry Harrison and his grandson Benjamin Harrison; cousins Theodore and Franklin Roosevelt; and George H. W. Bush and his son George W. Bush. All five families meet Pessen's criteria for upper-class status. It is also not uncommon for presidents to come from politically prominent families, also more often than not upper-class. John Tyler was the son of a Virginia governor; William Howard Taft's father served as secretary of war, attorney general, and ambassador to Austria and Russia; and John Kennedy's father was the chairman of the Securities and Exchange Commission and ambassador to Great Britain. Franklin Pierce's father was governor of New Hampshire (though Pessen locates the family between the lower-upper and upper-middle classes). George H. W. Bush's father accumulated a fortune working on Wall Street before being elected to the Senate from Connecticut. (See Table 4-2 for presidents' social class distribution.)

Other chief executives from upper-class origins but whose fathers did not hold high political office include George Washington, Thomas Jefferson, James Monroe, James K. Polk, and Woodrow Wilson. Pessen ranks Chester Arthur as upper-middle class. A number of presidents, including Pierce, Rutherford B. Hayes, Grover Cleveland, Warren G. Harding, Calvin Coolidge, and Truman, fall into a special bridge category between upper-class and middle-class origins. Altogether, Pessen considers sixteen presidents to be drawn from upper-class roots (the Bushes would make eighteen) and six more as bordering on this exclusive group—a total of twenty-four, more than half of all those who have served in the White House. Personal wealth would certainly make Donald Trump the twenty-fifth member of this group.[28] Trump's father became a millionaire as a result of his post–World War II building projects, but the homes and apartment buildings he constructed, often with federal grants, were for the poor and middle classes, not the wealthy.

TABLE 4-2 Pessen's Analysis of Presidential Social Class

Social Class	*President*
Upper-Upper	G. Washington, T. Jefferson, J. Madison, J. Q. Adams, W. H. Harrison, J. Tyler, Z. Taylor, B. Harrison, T. Roosevelt, W. H. Taft, F. D. Roosevelt, George H. W. Bush,* George W. Bush*
Middle-Upper	J. Polk, J. Kennedy, D. Trump*
Lower-Upper	J. Adams, J. Monroe, F. Pierce, R. Hayes, G. Cleveland, W. Harding, W. Wilson, C. Coolidge, H. Truman,
Upper-Middle	A. Jackson, M. Van Buren, J. Buchanan, U.S. Grant, C. Arthur, W. McKinley, H. Hoover, L. Johnson, G. Ford, J. Carter
Middle	A. Lincoln, D. Eisenhower, R. Reagan, W. Clinton,* B. Obama*
Lower-Middle	M. Fillmore, J. Garfield, R. Nixon
Upper-Lower	A. Johnson
Lower-Lower	None

SOURCE: Adapted from Edward Pessen, *The Log Cabin Myth: The Social Backgrounds of the Presidents* (New Haven, CT: Yale University Press, 1984), 68.

*Presidents rated by authors, not by Pessen. Table updated by the authors.

Ten presidents are in Pessen's upper-middle category, leaving only seven who can be regarded as drawn from middle- or lower-class roots; Bill Clinton and Barack Obama would make nine. The presidents most socially disadvantaged include Andrew Johnson, whose father held a variety of jobs, including janitor and porter at an inn; Millard Fillmore, probably the only president truly born in a log cabin as the son of a dirt farmer; and James Garfield, whose father pulled the family into prosperity through manual labor as a canal worker in the Midwest. Despite the stories about Lincoln's modest background, his father owned more property and livestock at the time of Abraham's birth than did the majority of his neighbors, and his prominence continued to grow.

Although presidents have come from diverse backgrounds, and Pessen's categories should not be taken as definitive, he is right to note that those with upper-class origins have been the most prevalent, and most others were drawn from prosperous and socially respected backgrounds. Even so, the trend over time has been toward more modest origins. The first six chief executives came from socially, and in many cases politically, prominent families. Not wholly by coincidence, they served during the period when presidential candidates were nominated by congressional caucus. After both political parties adopted the national nominating convention in the early 1830s, candidates from less privileged backgrounds also began to make it to the White House. Fillmore, Lincoln, Andrew Johnson, and Garfield—four presidents with humble origins—are concentrated in the period of 1850 to 1880. Since then, presidents have come from both upper-class (the two Roosevelts, Taft, Wilson, Kennedy, and the Bushes) and modest family circumstances (Truman, Eisenhower, Nixon, Reagan, Clinton, and Obama).

Three twentieth-century presidents—Eisenhower, Nixon, and Reagan—were the sons of poor men who tried numerous jobs without much success. Eisenhower's father was a mechanic in a creamery for a time after an investment failed; Nixon's father was a streetcar conductor in Columbus, Ohio, before trying his luck as a painter, carpenter, glass worker, and sheep rancher; and Reagan's father worked on and off as an itinerant shoe salesman. Clinton's father, a traveling salesman, died before his son was born, and Clinton's mother became a nurse anesthetist. His grandfather, with whom he lived until age four, was first the town iceman and later a neighborhood grocer, and his stepfather was a car salesman. Obama's father was a graduate student who abandoned his family and returned home to Kenya. After four years in Indonesia, Obama lived with his grandparents in Hawaii, a sales manager and bank employee. The fathers of Lyndon Johnson, Gerald R. Ford, and Jimmy Carter met mixed success in business: Johnson's father traded in commodities and livestock; Ford's stepfather (the president was born Leslie King and adopted as Gerald R. Ford Jr.) operated a paint and lumber business; and Carter's father founded a successful peanut warehouse.

Education

Education is often closely correlated with social class. Most U.S. presidents have been well educated. Only nine of the forty-four individuals (Cleveland served two nonconsecutive terms) had no formal instruction at a college or university. Moreover, the trend has been toward chief executives with greater college training. Of the eighteen who occupied the presidency in the twentieth century, only Truman did not attend an institution of higher learning.[29] The schools presidents attended are among the most highly regarded in the nation. Harvard University leads the list with seven chief executives as alumni—the two Adamses, the two Roosevelts, Kennedy, George W. Bush (from the business school), and Obama (a Harvard law degree). Alma maters of other presidents include major private universities such as Princeton (Madison and Wilson), Yale (Taft and the two Bushes; Ford and Clinton also have Yale law degrees), Stanford (Herbert Hoover), Georgetown (Clinton), Columbia (Obama), Penn (Trump) and a number of prestigious smaller private colleges, such as Allegheny (William McKinley), Amherst (Coolidge), Bowdoin (Pierce), Dickinson (James Buchanan), Hampden-Sidney (William Henry

Harrison), Kenyon (Hayes), Union (Arthur), and Williams (Garfield). Well-known public universities also figure among presidents' alma maters: Miami University of Ohio (Benjamin Harrison); the University of Michigan (Ford); the University of North Carolina (Polk); William & Mary (Jefferson, Monroe, and Tyler); and the two service academies, Annapolis (Carter) and West Point (Ulysses S. Grant and Eisenhower). Twentieth-century presidents hailing from families with more modest social standing sometimes attended less prestigious institutions: Johnson attended Southwest Texas State Teachers College (now Texas State University–San Marcos), Nixon graduated from Whittier College in California before attending Duke University Law School, and Reagan majored in economics and sociology at Eureka College in Illinois.

That so many presidents attended prestigious institutions of higher learning probably has less to do with innate abilities or career aspirations than with family status or a desire to improve their economic and social positions. An example is James Garfield, the son of a canal construction worker, who died when Garfield was two. Garfield managed, after a long struggle for education, to graduate from Williams College and become the principal of a church school before being admitted to the bar and eventually going into politics. More presidents attended private than public schools because private schools were established earlier, particularly in the northeastern states, such as New York and Massachusetts, which have produced ten presidents, and the midwestern states, such as Ohio, which has produced six. Although most citizens today would probably agree that a college education is essential if presidents are to understand the complex problems confronting the nation, no direct correlation exists between quality of institution or years of training and performance.

Career Experience

Although the family occupational backgrounds of the presidents are fairly broad, their own careers prior to and outside politics have been much less diverse. Twenty-six of the forty-four chief executives practiced law at some time. Other occupations include the military (William Henry Harrison, Taylor, Grant, and Eisenhower), education (Wilson and Lyndon Johnson), journalism (Harding and Kennedy), engineering (Hoover), real estate development (Trump), and entertainment (Reagan, Trump). Washington and Madison were gentleman farmers. Carter combined farming with his family peanut business after giving up his career as a navy engineer to return to Georgia when his father died. George W. Bush was an oilman and managing general partner of a baseball team.

Two presidents who pursued less prestigious careers before entering public life were Truman, who, in addition to trying his hand at farming, was a haberdasher and a railroad timekeeper, and Andrew Johnson, who was a tailor. It is not surprising that so many presidents were lawyers, because that profession is closely linked with political careers. Law is a prestigious occupation; it rewards skill in interpersonal negotiation and conciliation as well as verbal and argumentative facility, and enables its practitioners to return to private life more readily than is true of medicine or engineering, for example.[30] Since World War II, however, fewer chief executives have come from the law; of the fourteen presidents since 1945, only four—Nixon, Ford, Clinton, and Obama—were lawyers. As increasing numbers of people from nonlegal backgrounds—business and teaching, in particular—become senators and governors (the positions from which today's presidents often are recruited), still more presidents without legal training may occupy the White House.

Until 2017, only three presidents—career military officers—had not held public office before becoming president. Taylor, Grant, and Eisenhower were thrust into the vortex of presidential politics because of heroic exploits in the Mexican War, the Civil War, and World War II, respectively. As professional military men, they had not even been involved in partisan activities. Taylor, elected as the Whig candidate in 1848, had never voted before in a presidential election and had no party affiliation.[31] Grant, the Republican Party candidate elected in 1868, had voted for Buchanan, the Democratic standard-bearer in 1856, and had political views that have been described as "obscure."[32] Even more perplexing for party leaders was Eisenhower, the Republican Party candidate in 1952 and 1956, whom a number of liberal Democratic leaders had tried to draft for their party's nomination in 1948.[33] Trump, unlike all his predecessors, held no public office, either elected or appointed, or military position before becoming president.

For most U.S. chief executives, the road to the presidency involved a long apprenticeship in public office with careers usually begun at lower levels of the political system when they were in their twenties or thirties. Andrew Johnson and Coolidge began their public careers as city aldermen or councilmen. Others were first elected to county offices: John Adams was a highway surveyor; Truman was a member of the county court—an administrative, not a judicial, position. Some presidents, including Jackson, Buchanan, Cleveland, McKinley, and Taft, entered public service as prosecuting or district attorneys; others, such as Hayes and Benjamin Harrison, served as city solicitors or attorneys. Clinton began his career in 1976 as Arkansas's attorney general. Several chief executives—Jefferson,

Lincoln, the two Roosevelts, and Obama among them—began their public careers as state legislators.

The typical career pattern for these presidents was to move up the political ladder by winning offices representing progressively larger constituencies. Approximately two-thirds of the presidents served in either the House of Representatives or the Senate or both. Exceptions include Wilson, who spent most of his adult life as a professor of government and then as president of Princeton University; in 1910, at age fifty-four, he was elected governor of New Jersey just two years before winning the presidency. Reagan was primarily a radio, movie, and television performer until his fifties, when he became active in national politics in Barry Goldwater's 1964 presidential campaign. In 1966, he was elected to the first of two terms as governor of California; in 1980, he was elected president. George W. Bush became governor of Texas in 1994 at age forty-seven and was reelected in 1998. Neither Taft nor Hoover held any elective office before being chosen president. Taft served as a judge at the county, state, and federal levels and later became governor general of the Philippines and secretary of war. Hoover chaired the Commission for Relief in Belgium after World War I; oversaw prices, production, and distribution of food during World War I as U.S. food administrator; and served as secretary of commerce under Harding and Coolidge.

Most presidents come to the White House from another high public office (see chapter 2). Typical positions include the vice presidency, state governorships, the U.S. Senate, and appointive executive office. From one era to the next, these offices have varied in the extent to which their occupants have been favored or disfavored in their pursuit of the presidency.

How is experience related to performance? Most observers assume experience can make a president more or less familiar with the problems confronting the nation as well as with the institutions and people who must collectively address these problems. Moreover, an earlier career in elective office may enable individuals to develop the skills necessary for exercising leadership—bargaining skills, facility in public speaking, and the ability to persuade or inspire others. Candidates, therefore, usually argue that their particular blend of experience—whether in state, national, or nonpublic sectors—has made them best qualified for the position.

Background-Performance Links

How have scholars linked these biographical characteristics to presidential performance? Have they discovered systematic patterns that would enable the public to predict which candidates will enjoy greatest success in office? Unfortunately, there are no simple answers.

Our review shows that most presidents achieved political success with a substantial boost from their family circumstances, advantages that included political and social standing as well as educational and professional opportunities unavailable to most of their fellow citizens. "The common characteristic [of presidents] . . . for all their dissimilarities in other respects, has been the essential conservatism of their social, economic, and political beliefs. . . . All of them were champions of the prevailing order," according to Pessen.[34] Because the selection process is not neutral toward social class, it seems likely that most presidential aspirants will sustain the status quo.

Sociologists E. Digby Baltzell and Howard G. Schneiderman have more specifically sought to link class origin with performance in office. They correlate Pessen's analysis of class origins with a ranking of presidential performance based on the Murray-Blessing survey of American historians described earlier.[35] Their conclusion challenges some of the myths surrounding the presidency.

> There has been . . . not only a high correlation between high social origins and getting to the presidency, as Pessen clearly has shown, [but] once elected to office, men of privileged origins have performed far better than those of lower social status.[36]

Of the eight presidents consistently ranked by historians as great or near great, five were from upper-class families (Washington, Jefferson, T. Roosevelt, Wilson, and FDR), two from the upper-middle class (Jackson and Truman), and only one from the middle and lower classes (Lincoln, who is generally ranked number one). Originally, no presidents drawn from the upper class were found among those regarded by historians as failures (Andrew Johnson, Buchanan, Grant, Harding) but more critical views of Pierce and W. H. Harrison have changed that. Overall, Baltzell and Schneiderman find that eleven of the fifteen upper-class presidents included in their study (73 percent) were judged to have performed above average in office, while only six of the twenty-one presidents drawn from below the upper class (29 percent) were comparably rated.[37] Although it does not provide a clear explanation for how background is translated into success, the Baltzell-Schneiderman analysis suggests that an upper-class background does make a difference: "Our best aristocratic traditions have stressed *doing* a better job rather than the prevalent, middle-class ideology which has always stressed *getting* a better job."[38]

Richard Neustadt was a forceful advocate of electing an experienced politician to the presidency. As he argued beginning in 1960, when the first edition of his influential book *Presidential Power and the Modern Presidents* appeared, "The Presidency is no place for amateurs."[39] Neustadt's observation seemed to capture the difficulties Eisenhower experienced in office, although evaluations of Ike's performance have risen over time. As articulated in some of Neustadt's later editions, experience enhances presidents' self-confidence, which in turn makes it easier for them to make the choices about power that are critical to success. Yet "the quality of experience" may count "more than the quantity," an admission Neustadt made after two highly experienced presidents, Lyndon Johnson and Richard Nixon, seemed to flounder if not fail in office. Neustadt ultimately concluded that "the variety of experience is such that none of it can be applied predictively with confidence."[40] Bert Rockman reached a similar conclusion after looking at the length and types of government experience in relation to performance. In comparing the government experience of the top ten and bottom ten presidents as ranked by an expert panel, the bottom ten actually had modestly *greater* government experience than the top ten (16.9 mean years versus 15.1) and more than twice as many years of congressional experience (7.6 mean years versus 3.7).[41] Experience, it appears, offers no guarantee of success, something that supporters of Trump must have been counting on.

We are left with fundamental uncertainties about how life experience may have a bearing on performance. In addition to social class and career experience, there has also been considerable interest in the psychological traits presidents bring to the office, the subject of the next section.

Psychological Characteristics of U.S. Presidents

In October 1972, just before voters were to choose between Richard Nixon and George McGovern, political scientist James David Barber drew attention to the inherent shortcomings of evaluating a candidate's life experience when deciding how to vote. Barber made a prediction. The person who would win had grown up as part of a Republican family in a small town. He had excelled in school, studied piano, had a younger brother rowdier than himself, and had been elected president of his college class. Following military service during World War II, he had attended graduate school and followed an uncertain career path until gaining election to Congress in a contest marked by anticommunist appeals. After two terms in the House and service in the Senate, he was considered a member of his party's liberal wing and respected for hard work and independent thinking. The description fit both Nixon and McGovern. Despite the similarities in life experiences, few doubted that the two would make very different presidents.[42]

The similarity between the major-party candidates in 1972 was uncanny even in light of the broadly similar backgrounds from which presidents are drawn. Yet no two people, regardless of how similar their life circumstances, will bring identical personalities to the office. They bring a set of distinctive psychological characteristics, features that may loom large under the intense pressures focused on the presidency. Psychological traits are more proximate to presidential behavior than life experiences, but that does not make them easier to study or evaluate. Fred Greenstein points out that psychologists view personality as a complex phenomenon, involving diverse factors such as how people adapt to the world by screening reality (cognition), how they express feelings (affect), and how they relate to others (identification).[43] These structures are likely to be deeply rooted, making it even more necessary to infer their existence rather than to observe them directly. Analysts, in short, introduce personality as a construct to account for the regularities in a person's behavior. For these reasons, examinations of psychological characteristics are more uncertain and subjective than examinations of professional experience and social backgrounds.

Despite these problems, political scientists and historians have used psychological concepts to help explain why political figures behave as they do, a field of study known as **psychobiography**. Several presidents, including Wilson, Lyndon Johnson, Nixon, Carter, and Clinton, have been the subjects of such biographies.[44] These studies tend to concentrate on childhood experiences, particularly relationships with parents, and how such experiences shaped the presidents' self-perceptions, degree of self-confidence, and psychological needs.

Even with the upsurge in interest, analysts remain divided on how to conduct these studies and the theoretical framework within which they should be conducted. Two broad approaches can be adopted: (1) single-subject case studies and (2) multisubject case studies. The former seek to develop a comprehensive analysis of the full array of behaviors manifested by one person, with particular attention paid to explaining the origins of recurrent patterns. The latter also rely on close examination of biographical materials but seek to draw conclusions from similarities found among several actors' behavior.[45] An example of a single-subject case study is Alexander George and Juliette George's comprehensive work on Woodrow Wilson, which attempts to explain his strikingly complex and contradictory behavior. Barber's study, *The Presidential Character,* has identified similarities between Wilson's conduct and that of three other presidents—Hoover,

Lyndon Johnson, and Nixon—so they may be treated as examples of a similar personality type.

Practitioners of these two styles of inquiry disagree on how analysis should proceed.[46] There are multiple, competing theories of personality and a lack of established rules on how such research should be conducted. Particularly bothersome to many is the extent to which researchers may inject subjective evaluations into the collection and interpretation of case study materials. Although the research remains controversial, it would be unrealistic to overlook the importance of personality in trying to understand the presidency, because this office imposes fewer constraints on the occupant's behavior than does any other in American government.[47] In other words, presidents have great opportunities to be themselves in performing their day-to-day responsibilities.[48] Their emotional fitness for the job is therefore enormously important.

Barber's Approach to Studying Personality

In 1972, Barber made another forecast, more famous than his election prediction—one that brought considerable attention to him and the study of presidential personality. He predicted Nixon would be susceptible to the same "danger" Wilson, Hoover, and Johnson had been—namely, "adhering rigidly to a line of policy long after it had proved itself a failure."[49] Given the right set of circumstances, Nixon was likely to pursue a self-defeating plan of action even in the face of mounting evidence of its likely failure. The causes were rooted in his personality—his emotional needs, no less than they had been for the other three men. Nixon's conduct during Watergate, the extended investigations conducted by Congress during 1973 and 1974 into questionable campaign practices of the 1972 election, seemed to validate the prediction and the method on which it was based.

Was Barber's prediction lucky, or had he uncovered the secret of how to predict presidential performance based on systematic personality analysis? If so, the next step would be to make such insights available to voters before an election to produce more informed decisions.

Barber's work attempts to identify broad character patterns that predict general patterns of presidential conduct in office. Central to his analysis are three personal characteristics—(1) *character*, (2) *worldview*, and (3) *style*—and two environmental conditions—(1) *power situation* and (2) *climate of expectations*. Together these elements determine the likelihood of presidential success. Character, the most important of Barber's analytic constructs, develops during childhood and is expressed in two analytic dimensions: (1) energy and (2) affect. Presidents may be active or passive in terms of the effort invested in their jobs; they also may be positive or negative about their positions. Both dimensions influence performance.

The resulting four-cell typology is presented in Figure 4-2, with the principal personality trait Barber identifies for each type. **Active-positives** exhibit personal growth and adaptability; they enjoy their work and find it a challenge to use power productively as a means to pursue goals beneficial to others. Their success rests on a fundamental sense of self-confidence expressed in goal-oriented behavior. Yet they are flexible in their pursuit of goals and willing to change or abandon them rather than suffer a costly political defeat. In short, they are pragmatic politicians. Barber's active-positives include FDR, Truman, Kennedy, Ford, Carter, George H. W. Bush, and Clinton.[50]

Active-negative presidents also invest a great deal of energy in being president, but unlike their active-positive counterparts, they do not appear to derive enjoyment from serving in the office. Rather than exercising political power for the benefit of the citizenry, active-negative chief executives seem to seek power for its own sake, exhibiting compulsiveness as if they are driven to pursue a political career instead of doing it for pleasure. This behavior arises from a poor self-image and lack of self-confidence, traits caused by painful childhood experiences; they seek power and domination over others as compensation for their own lack of self-esteem. In this pursuit, active-negatives may come to believe that the policies they favor are morally right, vital to the nation's interest, and impossible to compromise. They may pursue a course of action even if it obviously is not working, exhibiting a pattern of "rigidification" that can ultimately cause their own political failure. Thus, they constitute a great danger to the nation. Barber classifies four twentieth-century presidents as active-negatives: Wilson, Hoover, Johnson, and Nixon.

FIGURE 4-2 Barber's Typology of Character

		Affect	
		Positive	Negative
Activity Level	Active	**Adaptive:** self-confident; power used as means to achieve beneficial results	**Compulsive:** power as a means to self-realization; "driven"; problem managing aggression
	Passive	**Compliant:** seek to be loved; easily manipulated; low self-esteem	**Withdrawn:** respond to sense of duty; avoid power; low self-esteem

SOURCE: James David Barber, *The Presidential Character: Predicting Performance in the White House,* 4th ed. (Englewood Cliffs, NJ: Prentice Hall, 1992).

Passive-positive presidents are not in politics to seek power either for the betterment of the American people or to compensate for their own sense of inadequacy. Rather, they choose politics because they are, in Barber's terms, "political lovers." They genuinely enjoy people and want to help them by doing small favors; in return, they feel wanted and loved. Barber suggests that passive-positive presidents have low self-esteem combined with a superficial optimism about life; they tend to let others set goals for them and find it difficult to make decisions. The danger they pose is one of drift, leaving the affairs of state undirected. Barber identifies three passive-positive chief executives: Taft, Harding, and Reagan.

Passive-negative presidents combine two characteristics one would *not* expect to find in the person who attains the nation's highest office: an unwillingness to invest much energy in that office and a lack of pleasure in serving. Such persons pursue public service because they believe it is something they *ought* to do. They have a fundamental sense of uselessness and compensate for it by dutifully agreeing to work on behalf of their fellow citizens. Exemplifying passive-negative chief executives are Coolidge and Eisenhower.

Barber examines two other personal factors that influence presidential behavior but play a smaller role in his analysis than character. **Worldview** consists of a president's "politically relevant beliefs, particularly his conceptions of social causality, human nature, and the central moral conflicts of the time."[51] Rather than dealing with specific policy issues, these attitudes are general in nature and therefore more likely to have wide applicability. Barber sees them as developed primarily during adolescence.

Style is the president's "habitual way of performing three political roles: rhetoric, personal relations, and homework."[52] Style focuses on how presidents typically work with words, people, and substantive problems. These patterns are developed largely during early adulthood, particularly in conjunction with the president's "first independent political success," which usually occurs in college or in a first elective or appointive office. **Character** colors both worldview and style but does not determine them in any direct way.

Barber analyzed the life histories of presidents from Taft through George H. W. Bush. These analyses are summarized in Figure 4-3. Some of his classifications have been highly controversial, but after 1972, journalists sought out his views of each candidate during presidential elections, and he offered inauguration-eve predictions of how the new president would perform.

Barber also made a tentative analysis of Clinton as an active-positive.[53] Another analyst, Stanley A. Renshon, offered a "preliminary assessment" of Clinton based

FIGURE 4-3 Barber's Characterization of Modern Presidents

Activity Level	Affect: Positive	Affect: Negative
Active	Franklin Roosevelt Harry Truman John F. Kennedy Gerald R. Ford Jimmy Carter George H. W. Bush William J. Clinton Barack Obama*	Woodrow Wilson Herbert Hoover Lyndon Johnson Richard Nixon
Passive	William H. Taft Warren Harding Ronald Reagan George W. Bush*	Calvin Coolidge Dwight Eisenhower

SOURCE: Adapted from James David Barber, *The Presidential Character: Predicting Performance in the White House*, 4th ed. (Englewood Cliffs, NJ: Prentice Hall, 1992). For Barber's views on Clinton, see the *News & Observer* (Raleigh, NC), January 17, 1993.

*Possible characterization (not evaluated by Barber).

on events of the presidential campaign and Clinton's first year in office, and those arguments have been expanded subsequently.[54] Renshon concluded that Clinton could be a hybrid type within Barber's framework, a borderline active-negative with a "strong need to be validated." Clinton, argued Renshon, had developed an idealized view of himself—his skills, his accomplishments, and his motives. Renshon continued,

> Most people wish to think well of themselves but Bill Clinton appears to have come to believe the *best* of himself and to have discounted evidence from his own behavior that all is not as he believes it to be.

"Unlike active-negatives who use power to overcome low estimates of themselves," Renshon suggests, "it is also possible that political leaders might well use power to validate high estimates of themselves"—something Barber had not anticipated and Clinton might embody.[55] Fred Greenstein, writing toward the end of Clinton's presidency, agreed: "The ever-smiling, hyperactive Clinton has all of the outward signs of an active-positive character. Yet his actions, particularly his astonishing recklessness in the Monica Lewinsky affair, reveal him to be as emotionally deficient as any classically active-negative president."[56] As these analyses suggest, Barber's categories are not as rigid as they sometimes appear.

Trump's character and temperament received enormous comment during the campaign, most of it colored by considerable partisanship. For many observers,

Trump is simply a classic example of a narcissistic personality—someone with "an inflated sense of their own importance, a deep need for admiration and a lack of empathy for others."[57] In truth, what politician does not match this description to some degree? But narcissists exhibit "excessive self-love and the attendant qualities of grandiosity. . . . Highly narcissistic people are always trying to draw attention to themselves. Repeated and inordinate self-reference is a distinguishing feature of their personality."[58] Trump's life has been full of self-referential behavior, from naming buildings, golf courses and products after himself to ostentatious displays of his wealth to confirming his own sex appeal. But Stanley Renshon argues that terming Trump a narcissist is too simplistic. Renshon agrees that Trump craves recognition for his accomplishments, as a way to validate himself, and Renshon also sees a pronounced need to be liked and noticed. Think of Trump's "bromance" with Russian president Vladimir Putin during the 2016 campaign. Trump seemed enormously pleased that Putin (reputedly the wealthiest person in the world) had said nice things about him. Similarly, Trump would stress during the campaign when Republican opponents or Hillary Clinton had treated him nicely or badly. "He wants to be liked, and it comes with a threat" that unfriendly behavior will be met with hostile retaliation, a pattern we repeatedly saw played out in the election.[59] In terms of Barber's typology, Trump appears to combine the need to be loved characteristic of a passive-positive, the anger of an active-negative, with the drive to serve the nation's interests found in an active-positive.

Reactions to Barber

Because Barber's work was widely popularized in the press, it is important to assess its analytic quality. Academics have been especially critical, suggesting it suffers from the fundamental problem common to all studies in the field—reductionism, paying "insufficient attention to the full range of possible psychological and nonpsychological determinants of behavior."[60] Insufficient attention is given to the impact of the environment on presidents, including the nature of the problems they confront, the political support they enjoy, and the constraints within which they operate.

Barber's classification of presidents also has been questioned. The behavior patterns associated with his character types fit some presidents grouped into the same cell better than others. For example, evidence on Eisenhower published after Barber completed his analysis suggests Ike was a more active president than was generally recognized when he was in office.[61] Hoover's reluctance to use extensive federal aid to restore the economy might better be understood as arising from his worldview rather than unresolved emotional needs.[62] Another study, using markedly different methods, finds Reagan's personality to be most similar to those of Franklin Roosevelt and Kennedy, although Barber considered Reagan a passive-positive and the other two active-positives.[63] Trump, as just noted, does not seem to fit well into any one category. Barber acknowledged that no president fits any type perfectly—that each is a mixture of all four types.[64] Nevertheless, he argued that a dominant pattern can be identified.

Was Barber guilty of positing an ideal personality type that may also conceal a partisan bias? When Barber's study first appeared, all the active-positives were liberal Democrats. Republicans Ford and George H. W. Bush were subsequently added to that group. What the approach may favor, however, is the heroic model of presidential leadership, which assigns principal responsibility for solving national problems to the White House. Barber recognized that not all active-positives will be successful in office and may pose risks for the political system; their "hunger for and attention to results" may lead them to challenge structures and norms the public believes are better preserved than overturned.[65] FDR's effort in 1937 to alter the structure of the Supreme Court by increasing its membership to as many as fifteen posed a challenge to the tradition of checks and balances and illustrates this possible danger.[66]

Can types other than active-positives achieve substantial success? Jeffrey Tulis argues that in Barber's terms Lincoln should be considered an active-negative, but few would argue that his stewardship of the nation during the Civil War was unsuccessful.[67]

In sum, Barber's work does not represent a panacea to a nation searching for effective leaders. Like most social science, Barber's work is best thought of in terms of probabilities, not certainties. He aspired to present voters with the kind of information on candidate backgrounds and records that would improve the likelihood of informed electoral choices, but the kind of research necessary for personality analysis is difficult to undertake at any time and perhaps most difficult in the heat of an electoral contest. Journalists may be able to improve their coverage of candidates' records and identify behavioral patterns of concern, but the chance of conducting a complete study of candidates' personalities in the midst of a campaign is negligible. Nor is it clear who in our society should be given such inordinate influence as to declare some personalities "fit" and others "unfit" for office. Further, it is not clear how voters should be guided when opposing candidates for president reside in the same category—Ford and Carter in 1976 were both termed active-positive, for instance. Therefore, the practical value of Barber's work remains an open question.[68]

Despite these criticisms of Barber, continuing to study the personalities of presidents and their emotional fitness for the position is of critical importance. Perhaps the most compelling justification comes from those who have experienced the power of presidential personalities firsthand. Clark Clifford, a longtime Washington power broker who served in the Truman and Johnson administrations, voiced the prevailing wisdom among government veterans: "The executive branch of our government is like a chameleon. To a startling degree it reflects the character and personality of the president."[69]

Management Styles of Modern Presidents

Presidents do not govern alone. Those serving before Franklin Roosevelt drew heavily on the assistance of cabinet secretaries and the bureaucracies they headed. Since Roosevelt, another source of advice and assistance—political and policy specialists—has emerged to supplement the traditional sources. To what extent do presidents use these various sources of assistance? How do they structure their advisory systems and make decisions? Should we, in fact, think of the presidency as an individual-dominated office where personality reigns supreme or as a collective that might actually control and constrain the impact of a president's ambitions and goals?[70] This section provides a brief discussion of the development of presidential staffing and the management styles presidents use with these assistants.

Just as important as attitudes drawn from life experiences and skills developed in previous careers is a president's aptitude for management. Aides have the potential to magnify presidents' skills, compensate for their shortcomings, and reduce the impact of dangerous personality traits.

The Development of Presidential Staffing

The presidential staff has grown substantially since Congress authorized its modern structure in 1939. Today the EOP houses a wide range of expert staff units, including the well-known Office of Management and Budget (OMB), Council of Economic Advisers (CEA), and National Security Council (NSC) (all discussed more fully in later chapters), as well as the lesser-known Office of U.S. Trade Representative, Office of Science and Technology Policy, and others. Perhaps best known, and certainly most notorious in Washington circles, is the White House

Office, a unit that has traditionally emphasized the president's personal and political concerns.

Like his predecessors, FDR had a limited number of aides, many in clerical positions who were borrowed from other parts of the federal bureaucracy. Sensing he needed to expand these resources, in 1936 he appointed a blue-ribbon group of public administration professors, headed by Louis Brownlow, to study the modern president's management needs. The resulting structure, based on recommendations from that group but reorganized many times since, has always been viewed as a response to the Brownlow Commission's defining sentence: "The President needs help." As Roosevelt and others recognized, the president required additional "eyes and ears" as well as brains to help discharge the ever-growing list of responsibilities placed at the White House door. Presidential staffing is an attempt to help presidents avoid "overload," the possibility that job demands will exceed the capacity of any individual, whose time and ability are finite. The staff can *amplify* the capabilities one person brings to the presidency, but it also can *buffer* the direct impact of a president's personality on performance. Presidents have been given great latitude in their use of staff resources, a flexibility that ensures responsiveness to new problems and perceived needs.

Staff size, although a recurrent political issue, is difficult to monitor with precision. Best estimates place the size of today's Executive Office at approximately 1,800 employees.[71] Moreover, the percentage of positions at higher levels of policymaking responsibility appears to have increased substantially over the years.[72] Staff growth has been accompanied by a shift in influence, with one analyst going so far as to suggest that the new structure constitutes a "presidential branch" of government distinct from the larger executive branch.[73] Clearly, presidents can draw on a wide range of assistance outside and within the presidency.

Presidential Management Styles

Style is no doubt an overused term in describing characteristic patterns of presidential behavior, but a number of analysts have focused on how presidents structure and use their advisory systems in making decisions. We term these behavior patterns a president's **management style**. Alexander George identified three personality factors that determine management style: (1) the executive's habitual ways of dealing with information (acquiring, storing, retrieving, evaluating, and using it); (2) the president's sense of competence in dealing personally with problems, which in turn determines the tasks delegated to others; and (3) the president's orientation toward conflict, particularly the tolerance for competition and dissent among advisers.[74]

Because it reflects personality characteristics and distinctive traits, each president's management style is by definition unique. Until the 1970s, presidents chose to operate within one of three broad advisory structures, with multiple variations reflecting their management styles.[75] Richard Johnson's three models (formalistic, competitive, and collegial) are a starting point for describing how the staff systems work. Presidents between Reagan and Obama (and arguably since Nixon) have adopted a "standard model" of staff structure centered on established routines for reporting information, coordinating policy decisions, and staffing implementation.[76] The **formalistic** pattern emphasizes clear division of labor among staff assistants, well-defined procedures, and a carefully controlled flow of information to the president, usually through a chief of staff, who tries to deflect problems not worthy of presidential attention. Truman, Eisenhower, and Nixon constructed and operated such systems, although differences in operation reflected the unique combination of needs and contributions each brought to the presidency. Ford and Carter initially tried to work without a chief of staff, but internal disorder eventually forced them to reverse that course. Every president since has appointed a chief of staff, and the hierarchical model became the standard for modern presidents. The **competitive** pattern, typified by FDR, encouraged conflict among advisers and thrived on diversity of opinion, with the president reserving ultimate judgment to himself. Conflict is endemic to decision making within the American government, but Roosevelt encouraged even more of it. Early indications are that Trump prefers such a system. Under a **collegial** system, emphasis is on group problem solving, teamwork, and shared responsibility for outcomes, with the president participating in the process and choosing among identified options. Kennedy, particularly the idealized version of what transpired during the Cuban missile crisis of October 1962, typified this style, and elements can be found in later administrations. Recent scholarship has raised some questions about standard accounts of how Kennedy and his closest advisers (known collectively as the ExComm) crafted policy in the face of Soviet missiles being discovered in Cuba. A secret White House taping system captured all but one of the ExComm's high-stakes deliberations, and it is clear that Kennedy, far from being influenced by his advisers, held out against their early unanimous pressure for more aggressive responses to Soviet moves. Nonetheless, in repeatedly defending his position, Kennedy benefited from the assertive questioning of his advisers and their collective struggle to confront the unthinkable—nuclear war.[77]

Presidents might follow more than one pattern or construct hybrid combinations. Ford followed a collegial pattern in domestic policy but was more formalistic in foreign policy.[78] Carter's system was described as a mixture of collegial and formalistic.[79] Reagan constructed a variant of the formalistic and collegial models during his first term when he relied heavily on three senior aides (the "troika"), a system that drew considerable praise from many observers, particularly when its successor in the second term became less collegial and notably less successful.[80] Clinton's style evolved from a highly undisciplined, sometimes collegial style to a somewhat more disciplined collegial pattern. George W. Bush adopted a formal style with himself at the "hub of a quadrangle" of senior aides who had ready access to him; others list six aides with direct access.[81] Bush employed systematic delegation from the outset but abandoned it on occasion.[82] President Obama initially named an assertive chief of staff, Rahm Emanuel, who needed to coordinate a large number of other prominent advisers, including a group of so-called policy "czars" who oversaw major problem areas including climate policy, health reform, and the auto industry restructuring, as discussed in chapter 6.[83] Even though Obama changed chiefs of staff, his management style was stable, emphasizing a steadiness that earned him the sobriquet "no drama Obama." Although Donald Trump initially named Reince Preibus his chief of staff, early journalistic reports suggested two other influential poles in the White House staff centered on Stephen K. Bannon, his campaign strategist, and Jared Kushner, his son-in-law.[84] It is important to note that the size of government, as well as the number and complexity of issues that confront modern presidencies, have forced "every modern president to rely at least to some extent on formalistic procedures,"[85] although Trump's improvisational style could challenge that pattern.

In general, formalistic structures place more modest demands on presidential time and knowledge. Delegating a larger range of tasks conserves time and may increase the probability that experts will deal with the problem. Because much of the work is processed in written form, the formal system is less appropriate for presidents who prefer to rely on group interaction, discussion, and even argument as part of the decision-making process. Competitive and collegial structures place heavier demands on the president, who not only must rely largely on his own substantive knowledge in making choices among competing alternatives but also must be able to monitor a policymaking process inherently political in nature. Advisers and the areas they represent push hard for the president to adopt their solutions and maneuver to gain an advantage. Winning such battles may reduce the quality of decisions.

Democratic presidents, using FDR as a model, tend to adopt a more interactive advisory system, sometimes described as a "spokes-in-a-wheel" system, with the president at the center of several principal aides in and out of the White House. Such a system encourages dispute and argumentation. Republican presidents, following Eisenhower's lead, have operated within a more structured system, in which the chief executive relies on a single chief of staff or a limited number of advisers and on systematic review processes. This approach is thought less susceptible to political maneuvering—though more likely to buffer the president from information he might need. Over time, partisan staffing differences have diminished as consensus developed on what the White House needs. But informal structures also shape how the White House operates,[86] and staffs may be more or less faithful to the formal models they create. Ultimately, if the advisory system reflects the kind of personality variables identified by Alexander George, the system will be modified to meet the incumbent's particular needs.

Multiple Advocacy: Learning a Decision Process

The best-known effort to prescribe a specific decision process for presidents to follow is George's system of **multiple advocacy**.[87] In essence, he suggested that presidents should be able to learn a set of techniques to follow in managing advisers and making decisions. Although recognizing that a given president may find this style "uncongenial to his cognitive style and work habits," George believed the advantages would make it worthwhile for a president to consider. For example, Nixon found it painful to be the object of direct, face-to-face argument among his advisers, but he might have modified the system advocated by George to derive its benefits.[88]

George defined multiple advocacy as a *mixed* system—benefiting from both centralized and decentralized features—that tries to ensure that the president benefits from a wide review of policy options and hears a variety of viewpoints before making a final decision. It tries to build on the inevitable conflict among individual advisers and bureaucratic agencies by channeling that conflict in productive ways. The overall process must be structured so that every relevant viewpoint receives a fair hearing. One of the major tasks, then, in operating such a system is monitoring the breadth of options being considered and the opportunities that advocates of such views have to be heard. To operate in this system, the president requires a full-time assistant, a "custodian-manager" who acts as an "honest broker" among the advisers pushing their positions on the president and ensures that several crucial tasks be performed, namely to "collect and analyze information, formulate policy problems, identify and appraise alternative options," and coordinate efforts across government departments.[89]

George hoped that systematic review of options, one of the claimed benefits of a formalistic system, could be achieved under multiple advocacy, with the added benefit of the open debate and discussion encouraged by competitive and collegial systems.[90] The president should act as a magistrate—"one who listens to the arguments made, evaluates them, poses issues and asks questions, and finally judges which action to take either from among those articulated by advocates or as formulated independently by himself after hearing them."[91] Consistent with this role, presidents need to suppress the urge to announce their own preferences early in the process and ensure that they remain faithful to the premise on which the system rests, the guarantee of giving an equal hearing to all views.

Such a process can be time-consuming, and George recognized that presidents would have to decide when it should be used. There may be times when they already know the policy they wish to pursue, and because constitutional responsibility in the American executive is unitary rather than collective, presidents can always exercise individual discretion. Paul Kowert raised another issue: "While some leaders thrive on diversity of opinion, others are immobilized by it," so "leaders must guard not only against too little advice, but also against too much."[92] If overwhelmed by information, a leader might withdraw from contentious issues and allow policy to drift into "deadlock," a plausible interpretation of Reagan's inaction in the face of growing budget deficits (see chapter 9) and the exchanges of arms for hostages that lay at the heart of the Iran-contra incident (see chapter 10).[93]

Even George did not believe that use of a multiple advocacy system and the magistrate presidential style that accompanies it can ensure good decisions. Rather, he urged its adoption as a way to improve the quality of information made available to presidents and to prevent the bad decisions that result from faulty procedures.[94]

Understanding Presidents: Barack Obama and Donald J. Trump

Explaining presidential behavior and linking its determinants to performance is like putting together the pieces of a puzzle—but a puzzle whose final shape is uncertain. One way to illustrate how background, experience, personality, and management style shape behavior and performance is to take an in-depth look at individual cases.

It is too soon to provide a final evaluation of Barack Obama's effectiveness in office, and even earlier for judgments about Trump, but we can trace major features of their lives and explore ways in which they potentially affected performance. Obama and Trump offer strikingly contrasting personal portraits. Obama articulated his ambition to be president shortly after graduating from law school, even before he had held any elected public office.[95] Just as the Illinois state Senate was a stop on the way to a federal office, so too he began to plan a presidential bid well before completing his first year in the U.S. Senate. Trump's career path stands alone among presidents: real estate developer, casino owner, reality show star, and brand merchandiser. He reportedly flirted with the idea of running for president in 1987, but his seriousness rose by 2000 when he created a committee to explore his candidacy only to pull the plug. Soon after the 2012 election, he patented the slogan "Make America Great Again."[96] Obama was in many ways an unknown—catapulting to national prominence through his keynote address to the Democratic National Convention in 2004 even before he had won election to the U.S. Senate. He emerged as a "progressive pragmatist," endorsing many of the traditional positions typical of liberal Democrats but with a consensus-seeking style that invited ideological opponents to find common ground. Trump was known for his flamboyant life style and public romances. His pronouncements on public issues shifted so much he seemed to be a "political chameleon." Trump changed his party registration seven times between 1999 and 2012.[97] Republican opponents in the 2016 primaries quoted his earlier liberal-leaning policy positions as a way to question his commitment to conservative values. Obama was elected to office as an agent of change, promising to transform the way politics were conducted as well as citizens' lives, but he soon learned that in order to succeed he had to play the game as usual. Styling himself as the agent of a populist movement in 2016, Trump confidently pledged to fix the many ills Americans faced at home and abroad while ruthlessly draining the swamp of Washington. His opening battles with the swamp creatures left it unclear whether Trump would tame Washington or Washington would tame him. A man without clear roots who grew up in exotic Indonesia and Hawaii, Obama appealed to Americans' pride in the multiracial, multiethnic community that they had created. Even as his business interests became global, Trump's life remained parochial compared to Obama: childhood in Queens, real estate career in Manhattan, casino owner in Atlantic City, and vacations in Florida. Although occasionally outspoken about his immigrant mother's Scottish heritage, Trump became linked in the public mind to crackdowns on illegal immigrants, retreats from global agreements, and turning away from the world as he worked to put America first. The following are snapshots of their lives.

Barack H. Obama's Life

On the day he was sworn into office, Barack Obama registered many firsts, summarized by David Maraniss:

> The first president to enter the White House with a literate and introspective memoir behind him, Obama is his own book of firsts. He is the first president with a foreign father. He is the first president to grow up in Hawaii, the 50th state. He is the first president whose parents earned doctoral degrees. He is the first president who once could speak the Indonesian language. He is the first president who was president of the *Harvard Law Review.* He is the first president who was a hapa, as they are called in Hawaii, with parents of different races. He is the first president who has a sister from Asia and a sister from Africa and a wife from the black working-class South Side of Chicago. And he is the first African American president, yet one with no slaves but a few slaveholders in his ancestry.[98]

Obama's early years provided far greater exposure to multicultural influences than most Americans experience, including four years of immersion in a non-Western culture followed by eight more in ethnically diverse Hawaii. A month's visit to Kenya just before he entered law school sought to resolve a lifelong confusion about his heritage, but it was not until he became firmly entrenched in Chicago that his identity as a black man became clearer. As David Maraniss argues, "Hawaii and Chicago are the two main threads weaving through the cloth of Barack Obama's life. Each involves more than geography."[99] Hawaii shaped the boy; Chicago was the proving ground for his political skills. Barack Obama's father—or more precisely his absence—stands at the center of the president's childhood; as a result, the president has been shaped by a series of strong women—his mother, his grandmother, and now his wife, Michelle. Restlessness characterizes his own life as well as those of his closest relatives—father, mother, grandparents—who were remarkably mobile.

The president's father, also named Barack Hussein Obama, arrived in the United States from Kenya as a student at the University of Hawaii in 1959, the first African student admitted to the school. A self-confident intellectual with an impressively deep speaking voice and political ambitions in Kenya, he married Stanley Ann Dunham, an unconventional first-year student originally from Kansas, whom he met in a Russian language class. The new family soon added a son, known during childhood as Barry. When Barry was two, his father left the family behind to pursue a graduate degree at Harvard University, much as he had left behind a child

Polaris

Audacity, included in the title of his second book, is a fitting word for Barack Obama's meteoric rise to the presidency—bold, intrepid, and a touch arrogant in ignoring normal constraints.[100] In fact, Obama's story is anything but normal, a striking contrast to the story of inheritance surrounding George W. Bush. Obama's path to the presidency was unlike that of any other chief executive, traditional or modern. This point is inevitably true for the son of a black man and a white woman, making him the first black president in American history.

and pregnant wife when he moved from Kenya. Divorce followed within a year, and Barry saw his father only once more during a month-long visit to Hawaii when he was ten. The need to understand his heritage led Obama on a pilgrimage to Kenya where he learned more about his now-deceased father's frustrations and a life that fell short of the idealized image of greatness that Barack had carried throughout childhood.

After Ann Dunham remarried, this time to an Indonesian graduate student, the family left the United States, and Barry attended school from ages six to ten in Jakarta, Indonesia, a period little described in his speeches or writings.[101] It was during this time that his mother would wake Obama early in the morning to instruct him in a variety of subjects as a way to compensate for limitations in his Indonesian education. Barry returned to Hawaii in 1971 to live with his maternal grandparents and attend the Punahou School, a private college prep school, where he was one of very few black students. His grandparents had moved frequently during their marriage, living in California, Texas, Oklahoma, and Washington state. His grandfather, a salesman, initially managed a furniture store and later sold insurance. His grandmother met with greater success, rising through the administrative ranks to become a vice president in a local bank. When Ann Dunham Soetoro returned from Indonesia with Barry's half-sister, Maya Soetoro, the family was reunited while his mother completed her education. She later returned to Indonesia to conduct field research and begin her work with local artisans. Barack chose to remain behind, but mother and son worked at maintaining contact.[102] Soetoro later worked for the U.S. Agency for International Development and the Ford Foundation as a specialist in providing financial support for local artisans in Pakistan, India, and New York City, completing her Ph.D. in anthropology along the way.

Barry stayed behind to complete high school and play basketball, his true love, giving no indication of his future in politics. Unlike Clinton, there were no leadership roles or efforts to build networks that would later help him secure power. Nor was he a distinguished student—he got Bs—enough to remain eligible to play basketball. He has acknowledged in his memoir, *Dreams from My Father,* that there was lots of partying, which included the use of illegal drugs.[103] Unlike Bill Clinton who coyly admitted using marijuana but claimed he did not inhale, Obama has acknowledged, "When I was a kid, I inhaled. . . . That was the point."[104] Unlike most politicians, in fact, Obama's early life is an open book. Only 20,000 copies of his autobiography were published in 1996. By 2007, it had sold 800,000 copies and his admissions in the book as well as the details of his life were far better known than those of other politicians whose autobiographies are usually scrubbed clean of damaging details.[105] Despite this apparent openness, however, Stanley Renshon notes it is difficult to determine just what makes Obama tick. Renshon emphasizes the role of **redemption** in Obama's personal and public life—the search for "standing and legitimacy" for himself and the fulfillment of its full potential for his nation. The personal search arises from ambivalent feelings about his childhood: "Out of a quickly failed biracial union, Obama was left with an absent father, a peripatetic mother [whom he idealized] and an uncertain personal and racial identity."[106] As a leader, he seeks to transform the nation so that it redeems "its promises of justice and fairness at home and abroad," thereby carrying on "both his father's and his mother's life's work."[107]

Obama attended Occidental College for two years and completed his undergraduate degree at Columbia University. By the time he arrived in New York

City, he had shifted from using Barry to Barack.[108] He also developed greater self-discipline in his studies, his personal life, and his physical conditioning.[109] Arguably, his first independent political success came at Occidental, when he delivered a speech during a rally supporting divestment from South Africa, a moment he reports in his autobiography. After a few brief postgraduation jobs in business, he became a community organizer in Harlem before moving to Chicago to do much of the same for three years. There, he learned firsthand about the power of black ministers, came to better understand his place in black America, and developed skills at grassroots coalition building as he carried the message of self-help to groups that had been ignored by the political power structure.[110] But he came to realize that his impact was limited, something he sought to change. His big leap was to Harvard Law School, where he was elected to serve as president of the *Harvard Law Review*, the first black student to serve in that capacity. One key to his success was the ability to speak with members of several competing camps among students, ranging from conservative ideologues to black radicals. Laurence Tribe, the nationally known faculty member explained of Obama, who worked for him as a research assistant, "He just seems to have the surest way of calmly reaching across what are impenetrable barriers to many people."[111] Following graduation, he moved to Chicago to practice civil rights law and teach at the University of Chicago Law School.

He met his future wife, also a Harvard Law graduate, during a summer internship with an influential Chicago law firm. His persistence paid off when she overcame her initial reluctance and agreed to date him. Michelle Robinson was firmly rooted in Chicago's working-class black community, and she provided a foundation and steadiness that had been missing throughout most of Barack's life. They married in 1990 and settled in a mixed-race, mixed-income neighborhood not far from the University of Chicago.[112]

Obama's Prepresidential Career

Chicago became the foundation for Obama's political career when at age thirty-five he won a seat in the Illinois Senate in 1996 after navigating difficult political waters. He served in the Illinois legislature for eight years, widened his network of contacts, and established a respectable record of accomplishments while displaying considerable political ambition. In 2000 he lost a primary campaign in an effort to unseat a black Democratic incumbent in the U.S. House of Representatives. In 2001, he considered running for attorney general but withdrew from the campaign. In 2002, he began planning his campaign to wrest the U.S. Senate seat from the Republicans and secured the nomination against six opponents; he won the Illinois Senate seat in a race against Alan Keyes after the campaign of a wealthier Republican opponent collapsed in scandal. Obama waltzed to victory in 2004, a success that was capped by his first appearance on the national stage, his keynote address to the Democratic National Convention that electrified delegates in Boston and party loyalists around the country. "There is not a liberal America and a conservative America—there is the United States of America," he memorably declared. Two years after entering the Senate, he declared himself a candidate for president, the final leg of a long journey, both geographically and personally.

Obama's prepresidential political experience was quite slim. Two of his four years in the Senate were spent on the presidential campaign trail, and although he had star power in Washington, D.C., his role in Congress was modest, befitting a freshman. On the campaign trail, however, his short service in the Senate was portrayed as an asset—he had not yet succumbed to the allures of the nation's capital but had been there long enough to understand the many ways it needed to be changed. Moreover, Obama's personal gifts—confidence and intelligence, commanding and inspiring rhetoric, an unflappable manner, and a straightforward approach to solving problems—quickly laid to rest doubts about inexperience. His personal story—the focus of his speech to Democrats in 2004—reveals admirable persistence, enormous self-assurance, and a generous dollop of good luck, something one can neither inherit nor consciously develop as a skill. He proved remarkably successful in luring high-powered politicians from governors' mansions and the U.S. Senate into his cabinet, a sign that he inspires those with whom he works.

Obama as President

Upon entering the presidency, Obama was untested as a manager. Senators seldom move directly from Capitol Hill to the White House (Obama is only the third in U.S. history), and managing a Senate staff pales in comparison to managing the EOP—let alone the entire executive branch. Some observers expressed concern about the large number of prominent advisers that he assembled and whether the resulting clash of egos might prove difficult to tame. The early months of most administrations are the most difficult, beset with the pains of getting acclimated to new challenges, new team members, and new pressures. Presidency watchers observed closely to see how decisions were made and which aides and appointees emerged as the most powerful figures in the Obama administration.

In contrast to George W. Bush, Obama proved to be a hands-on executive, becoming deeply engaged in policy discussions as he sought to build consensus behind administration decisions. This was seen most clearly in the deliberations on Afghanistan policy during the fall of 2009, which required ten meetings of the NSC over three months. Obama had to contend with a request from the military for higher troop levels than he wanted to commit and with others, led by Vice President Biden, who wanted dramatic reductions in troop levels and the shift to a counterinsurgency strategy. As Robert Gates recounts the experience from his position as secretary of defense, the vice president and other White House advisers suspected that the Pentagon was trying to "bully" a new and inexperienced president into making large and politically unpopular troop commitments before an overall administration strategy had been set.[113] The president met with his senior advisers in a series of two- to three-hour meetings to hear all sides of the debate. Leaks to the press made the president's political advisers highly suspicious of his military advisers and injected conflict into the discussions. In the end, Obama managed to strike a balance—a temporary increase in troop levels and a date certain to begin the drawdown of U.S. forces.

Former secretary Gates believed that Obama repeated two patterns found in earlier administrations: centralizing foreign policy decision making and believing that the White House can micromanage the military from afar.[114] Gates remembers complaining to White House advisers trying to control the U.S.-enforced no-fly zone established in Libya to help forces opposed to dictator Muammar Gaddafi, "You can't use a screwdriver reaching from D.C. to Libya on our military operations."[115] Gates saw the same temptation during relief efforts launched by the military in Haiti following the catastrophic 2010 earthquake and in Afghanistan operations.

Obama's decision-making style can best be thought of as following the *collegial* model, a style that poses heavy demands on the president's time and personal resources. He makes it a point of pride to review all options and assess their prospects. During the prolonged period needed to recast Afghan policy, his most severe critics complained that he was "dithering,"[116] but a thorough policy review is necessarily time consuming. In the words of Fred Greenstein, Obama demonstrated a cognitive style "marked by analytic detachment and a capacity for complex thinking," skills that are especially well suited for the collegial model.[117] Gates's criticism is more telling: He argues that the decision process around the Afghan troop surge was far more contentious and less collegial than it should have been. Contending teams presented unnecessarily black and white alternatives that left a residual distrust and bitterness that lingered throughout the administration's remaining time in office.[118] Obama's careful, deliberative style also suggested that he was risk averse, but we know that was not always the case. When Obama ordered the team of Navy SEALs to attack the compound that intelligence officials thought might house Osama bin Laden, there was only a 50 to 80 percent probability that the target was there. Rather than launching a massive bombing attack, Obama chose the option that had proven most difficult to undertake in the past—a helicopter raid.[119] (See chapter 10.) Interestingly, Gates tells us that support for the bin Laden raid was not unanimous; several of Obama's senior advisers either opposed the raid (such as the vice president) or preferred a less risky option (including the secretary of defense and vice chairman of the Joint Chiefs of Staff).[120]

Most of the time, Obama exudes cool detachment, which can be a problem when it pervades his public communications. The president's appearances in public were especially numerous during his first two years in office, even before the onset of a reelection campaign. As Steven Wayne details, during his first year Obama "gave two major addresses before joint sessions of Congress; held six press conferences; gave 152 one-on-one interviews; made 554 public remarks, statements, and comments to assembled individuals and groups inside and outside the White House,"[121] all while visiting the most countries ever by a president during his first year in office. The second year was little different with 428 speeches and remarks, 245 statements, five news conferences, five interviews with foreign journalists, and weekly radio/web addresses. Jonathan Alter dubbed him the "Professor-in-Chief" for his many efforts to explain policy and the professorial air of his comments.[122] In fact, Obama has relied heavily on his communication skills throughout his life and career, from his initial political success at Occidental College through the electrifying convention speech in 2004, through his acceptance of the Democratic nomination in front of 70,000 screaming partisans, and on into the administration. Detractors say there is too much exposure and the tone is too pedantic, but clearly his staff believes that Obama is the administration's greatest asset, encouraging them to put him in these settings.

Although personally comfortable with international issues and well liked at the outset overseas, not until the second term was Obama severely tested in high-pressure international situations. Some analysts thought his experience as a community organizer and a participant in Chicago's bare-knuckle politics would prove transferable to these challenges. Critical tests came in 2014–2015 over Ukraine and Iran. When Ukrainians resisted Russian president Vladimir Putin's plan to draw Ukraine away from Europe and into a closer alliance with its neighbor to the east, Putin seized Crimea, Ukrainian territory, and encouraged separatists in eastern

Ukraine to launch an armed struggle for independence. Obama sought to rally reluctant European allies to oppose these territorial aggressions and to support the shaky Ukraine government without risking another military commitment of U.S. forces. Obama's relationship with Israel's prime minister was strained from the outset over the president's persistent pressure on Netanyahu to reach an agreement with the Palestinians, but communication neared a complete breakdown when Netanyahu visited Washington in March 2015 to denounce a pending agreement with Iran over development of nuclear weapons.

Obama's patience and negotiating skills were also needed at home. His negotiations with assertive congressional Republicans—particularly House Speaker John Boehner—produced mixed success. Some observers believed that the Republicans came out best in three showdowns: (1) in winter 2010, during the lame-duck congressional session when Obama made concessions by continuing the Bush tax cuts; (2) in spring 2011, when spending cuts were the price for avoiding a shutdown of the federal government; and (3) in summer 2011, when Republicans demanded additional spending cuts to raise the debt ceiling. Obama's most fervent progressive supporters felt that he had conceded too much to his bargaining opponents. At various times in his career, Obama has shown the capacity to be a tough competitor: when he challenged the legal standing of signatures on nominating petitions in Chicago and won his Illinois state Senate seat and also when he did an about-face on accepting public financing in 2008 because it would help his campaign. He has been quoted as saying, "'If you can win, you should win, and get to work doing the people's business.'"[123] More than halfway through his term, supporters were waiting to see that same steely determination displayed in Washington's policy battles. That finally appeared in late 2012 during additional budget negotiations when Obama's tough stand won Republican concessions and following his party's midterm defeats of 2014 when he aggressively used unilateral executive action to circumvent congressional opponents. The latter strategy triggered lawsuits and even charges that he was acting unconstitutionally.

Was Obama's temperament right for the job? Is it good for presidents to sometimes lose their tempers or show strong emotion? There was no concern that Obama might be volatile, but was he stable to a fault? During the BP oil spill, for example, a gap seemed to open between the public's collective anger at corporate incompetence and the president's measured problem solving. When the president tried to generate anger during an interview, it rang untrue.[124] And as partisan tensions grew in Washington, the concern arose whether "his temperament is *so* even that he sometimes fails to convey the passion needed to rally support for his policies."[125] There were occasional flashes of anger triggered by the budget battles of 2011. During a spring 2011 speech at George Washington University, Obama harshly denounced the Republican budget plan devised by Rep. Paul Ryan, R-WI, who occupied a front-row seat.[126] And in behind-the-scenes negotiations with Republican leaders in the summer of 2011, he expressed frustration with his Republican counterparts, for both their stubborn unwillingness to compromise and their bargaining tactics.[127] But the question posed by Renshon during the 2008 campaign remained unanswered for many citizens: "What does he feel passionately about?"[128]

From all accounts, Obama was a fast learner on policy matters. It is less clear whether he learned as quickly the organizational lessons about how to run the government, which requires presidents to rely on aides around him. There was considerable flux in the White House with several high-profile assistants leaving within two years, including White House chief of staff Rahm Emanuel; Larry Summers, chief architect of the administration's economic policy; and retired general James L. Jones, the initial national security adviser. No doubt, there were personal considerations surrounding each of those departures, but constant turnover at the center can disrupt an administration. Six years into the administration, there had been four White House chiefs of staff. Initial allegiance to relying on a "team of rivals" ran up against the managerial costs of such an approach.[129]

The domestic challenges that Obama confronted as he entered office were enormous, as were those on the international front, including one war winding down (Iraq), another heating up (Afghanistan), nuclear threats rising in Iran and North Korea, pressures to redesign the international financial system, and a transformation of politics in the Middle East. No president has entered office with a more challenging agenda, and international challenges were not even his worst problems. Devising solutions to these problems was made more difficult by the highly charged, partisan atmosphere. The nation's hopes continued to rest heavily on this one man, and the nation's collective judgment was that he had done well enough to warrant four more years. But second terms are notoriously difficult (see chapter 11).

Donald J. Trump's Life

As a self-proclaimed "winner," Donald John Trump overcame enormous odds to become the forty-fifth President of the United States. A first-time politician triumphed over a field of sixteen other Republican candidates, including leading members of the party's establishment. Then, in Hillary Clinton, he faced a Democrat who had been a national presence for decades as first lady, senator from New York, and secretary of state. Clinton raised more money, ran more television ads, received more newspaper editorial endorsements, and was the choice of the national foreign policy establishment. As election day approached, Trump trailed in the national polls by three to four percent of the popular vote. Nor did victory in the Electoral College seem likely since he would need to capture a group of states widely described as a "Democratic firewall," so solidly pro-Clinton that they could not be pried away. The candidate, himself, may have harbored doubts as relatively little planning had been completed for assuming control of the executive branch, explained by his advisers as a reflection of Trump's concern lest he jinx the outcome. Trump's victory was improbable, but so was his successful business and entertainment career, which experienced significant setbacks that belie the image of "winner," including five bankruptcies and a failed venture in professional football.

Donald was the fourth of five children born to Fred Trump and the former Mary Anne MacLeod. Fred was the first-generation son of a German immigrant, and Mary had immigrated from Scotland in 1930 to escape the economically depressed Outer Hebrides. By the time they married, Fred was already a successful real estate developer in Queens, a borough of New York City. His investments enabled him to weather the 1930s, despite the Depression, and business prospered during the housing boom that followed World War II when returning servicemen started families after the long delay caused by the war. Mid-priced homes and low-priced apartments were Trump's niche in the market. His workaholic habits and compulsive cost-cutting helped him become a millionaire.

Donald spent most of his childhood in a grand, twenty-three room house on a large lot located in a solidly middle- to upper-income neighbourhood. The family had "a chauffeur, a cook, an intercom system, a color television, and a sprawling electric train set,"[130] none of which was commonly available. He attended a private school through seventh grade where his behavior was a consistent problem, including fights, classroom mischief, and unruly behavior, a record which contributed to his being sent to a strict military boarding academy for high school. Donald thrived in the competitive environment where cleanliness and neatness earned rewards and excelling on the athletic field gained recognition from peers. During the summers, he worked on his father's building projects.

Although Trump the candidate stressed his Ivy League credentials, he started his college career at Fordham University and transferred to the University of

Pennsylvania's Wharton School after his sophomore year where he majored in (surprise, surprise) real estate. (Three of Trump's four older children also attended Penn with Ivanka following her father's example and transferring there as a junior from Georgetown.[131]) He was not an especially noteworthy student either in his academic or extracurricular record. Throughout his time in college, he went home to New York on weekends to work in the family business.

There is no evidence that Trump was engaged by the burning public issues of his time in college—the Vietnam War and civil rights. Unlike Bill Clinton and other future politicians of his era, Trump did not go through elaborate stratagems to avoid being drafted into the military. After college graduation, his physical rated him I-Y (medically disqualified to serve except in national emergency) because of bone spurs in his heels. His birthday also gave him a high number in the draft lottery held in 1969.[132] Nor is there evidence that he was drawn to campus politics, whetting his taste for higher office and honing skills that would later prove useful. Lyndon Johnson, for example, developed many of the nuanced interpersonal skills he later needed in Congress and the White House as a student when he became the "big man on campus." Ronald Reagan made a stirring speech at a critical point during a campus rally. Bill Clinton campaigned successfully for president of his class, learning how to win support from a cross-section of students. But nothing comparable emerges from Trump's record at either Fordham or Penn.

Trump's Prepresidential Career

For most presidents, analysts look at the series of public responsibilities they have held prior to entering the White House to understand how the president's beliefs evolved and skills developed. In the case of Donald Trump, however, we have little to work with. The principal question about Trump is "How transferable are the skills he developed in business to his new role in the White House?"

Donald moved directly into his father's business and became president of Trump Management at age 25, overseeing his father's rental properties. But Donald's aspirations were greater; he wanted to become a player in Manhattan real estate, a goal he acknowledged in the semiautobiographical *Art of the Deal,* published in 1987.[133] Perhaps this desire can be traced to the fascination of a young adolescent with the glitz and excitement of a nonsuburban world (as the *Washington Post* team suggests[134]), or perhaps his competitive nature simply drove him to go where he could make the most money in real estate. Whatever his motivation, we know that after helping to manage his father's properties for several years, Donald moved into a Manhattan apartment and, against his father's advice, worked to carve out a niche in a new market. He did not do so alone. One early mentor was lawyer Roy Cohn, famous for his role in the Communist witch hunt launched in the early 1950s by Senator Joseph R. McCarthy (R-WI). Cohn advised the Trumps as they fought against the U.S. Justice Department's 1973 charge of racial discrimination in renting their apartments. Cohn served as Trump's lawyer until his death in the mid-1980s and fashioned a key feature of Trump's style: "when attacked, counter-attack with overwhelming force."[135]

James David Barber looked closely at other presidents' *first independent political success* as the determinant of their lifelong characteristic style. In Trump's case, we can identify his *first independent professional success* as modernizing the Commodore Hotel, a rundown eyesore in central Manhattan, and transforming it into the glittering Grand Hyatt Hotel. To accomplish this goal, Trump had to convince New York City politicians, the owners of the property, and the Hyatt hotel chain that he could come up with the financial backing needed for the project. He used political connections to secure favorable tax exempt status (a first for a commercial project) from New York's Urban Development Corporation.[136] The project did not go as smoothly as Trump had hoped, but over the period 1976–1980 he managed to solve one crisis after another and brought it to a successful conclusion. To succeed, he had played one interest off against another, alternatively used bluster and blandishments to win support, and overcame all obstacles through long hours of hard work and abundant self-confidence.

Donald quickly turned to his next project, building his future home at one of New York's most prestigious locations, Trump Tower on Fifth Ave. The skyscraper opened in 1983, populated by posh shops and luxury condos, including Trump's office on the twenty-sixth floor and the three-story, gold-plated penthouse that housed his family. "Trump tower permanently ingrained Trump, his name, and his celebrity into the firmament of Manhattan, just as he had dreamed about as a young boy looking over the bridge from Queens."[137] Other high-profile projects followed, but nothing so grand as his 58-story home.

The next stage in Trump's career took him to Atlantic City where he opened his first casino in 1984 and then invested heavily—too heavily, in fact—in two more casinos. To purchase and build his casino empire, Trump borrowed several billion dollars at high interest rates and ultimately ran into a cash flow problem: His three casinos were not generating sufficient revenue to cover his payment obligations. He owed more than three billion dollars. He was at risk of not only losing the Atlantic City properties but of also losing virtually all his other holdings, parts of which he was forced to sell, including his plane, yacht, and airline. Though his father provided him with emergency financial help, Trump defaulted on his bond payments. All three casinos, as well as New York's Plaza Hotel, went into bankruptcy. Through some fancy legal footwork with his creditors, Trump remained nominally in control of the casinos and then began the climb back from near catastrophe by shifting his personal debts onto investors. These maneuvers enabled him to return to billionaire status by 2004.[138]

At that point, Hollywood beckoned in the form of a reality TV show, *The Apprentice.* Trump had originally agreed to host for one year, but the show's success extended his run to fourteen seasons, concluding in 2015, at least partly due to his controversial campaign comments about Mexican immigrants. He demonstrated the ability to improvise most of his lines following the rough outline of a script. "You're fired!," the show's famous punchline delivered after he evaluated the contestants' performance, was his own creation. Actor Trump devoured television ratings numbers the same way that candidate Trump followed the polls during the 2016 campaign. Even more important, the character that Trump created over that fourteen-year period—an all-powerful, supremely self-confident, occasionally humble, truth-teller who got results—became the foundation for the persona he projected throughout the presidential campaign.[139] Candidate Trump conducted his campaign rallies off-script just as actor Trump had performed on *The Apprentice.*

Building on his growing celebrity, Trump moved into branding his name at home and around the world. Businesses signed licensing agreements to put Trump's name on a long line of housing projects, golf courses, and products (water, wine, steaks, clothing, fragrances, eyewear, leather accessories, a real estate training program billed as a "university," etc). All of these generated revenue. Globally, Trump sought local partners to help build hotels and Trump Tower wannabes under the Trump name and, in some cases, to manage them. Projects are located in Turkey, Panama, Philippines, South Korea, Ireland, Scotland, Canada, India, and others were attempted in Russia, Georgia, Azerbaijan, and Kazakhstan.[140] By the time he ran for president, the Trump brand had become global in scope.

Trump as President

After months of hearing Republican and Democratic opponents as well as the mainstream media deride Trump's qualifications for president, it is challenging to arrive at a balanced assessment. President Obama, for example, used especially strong language to denounce Trump on the campaign trail as "uniquely unqualified" to serve as president, echoing the language used by the *Washington Post's* editorial board in its endorsement of Hillary Clinton.[141]

Foremost among Trump's shortcomings are mastery of *policy substance* and *policy process.* Presidents make choices among options—about *what* to do and *how* to do it—and without a long history of immersion in the details of health policy, environmental policy, social security, the Middle East, nuclear policy, North Korea, etc. the concern is that the president will improvise rather than make well-grounded choices, or he will simply listen to the advice of the last person to talk with him before a decision is made. As Congress prepared to take action on the first item of Trump's legislative agenda, repeal and replacement of the Affordable Care Act ("Obamacare"), the president confirmed concerns about his shallow grasp of substance when he stated, "Nobody knew health care could be so complicated."[142] In fact, anyone who had followed the debate since Bill Clinton's unsuccessful effort to reform health care in 1993–1994, knew precisely how complex the topic was. And after China's leader Xi Jinping explained the limits of his ability to control North Korea's nuclear program, Trump acknowledged following a summit meeting, "After listening for 10 minutes, I realized it's not so easy . . . It's not what you would think,"[143] a reversal of the position candidate Trump had taken on the campaign trail. Those suspicious of Trump's thin knowledge feared that these instances were just the tip of the iceberg of what the new president did not know.

Process knowledge is also important. Presidents make choices among tactical and strategic options about how to accomplish their goals on the national and international stage. Trump's career certainly provided him with experience in the nuances of the real estate, gambling, entertainment, and endorsement industries. But how would he fare in settings where the stakes were so much higher—life and death, poverty or wealth—for millions of citizens, not just success or failure for his own fortunes? Critics wondered how long it would take him to realize that the negotiating and bargaining skills from business would not automatically transfer to national and international politics. And to whom would he turn to learn about the finer points of the political world, the intricacies of Congress, the limits on presidential power imposed by the judiciary, the delicate dance steps required in diplomacy? Again, early missteps—problems in drafting a travel ban on some Muslim countries that could survive judicial review; the failure to secure congressional passage of the repeal/replace health plan; strained interactions with the leaders of traditional allies Australia and Germany as well as a major opponent, China—suggested the steep learning curve Trump faced in his new job.

Finally, it is unclear what Trump believes when it comes to politics. What are the values that will guide his actions? Over his lifetime, Trump's pronouncements on political issues have reflected both the blue of liberalism and the red of conservatism, the colors used on today's political maps. And his political compass seems to spin at random, providing one heading one day and reversing polarity the next. Consistency is not his forte, but Trump's reversals did not seem to worry the public in 2016. Voters had punished earlier candidates for apparent reversals (think of the widespread criticism levelled at John Kerry in the 2004 election for alleged "flip-flops," or at Hillary Clinton for voting for the war in Iraq but later opposing it), but Trump seemed to get away with it. Before he had to make meaningful decisions on a wide range of issues, there was little reason for Trump to worry about consistency. But "Make America Great Again" is not a governing philosophy; it is a campaign slogan. Now in a position where his every word matters, even those contained in early morning Tweets, Trump's inconsistent and ill-formed opinions are likely to make a major difference. You cannot declare NATO obsolete and not expect your European allies and potential adversaries like Russia to draw conclusions. Nor can you loudly and repeatedly denounce China a currency manipulator without expecting results. In both cases, Trump reversed field within the first 100 days of the administration.

By contrast, only a few authorities argued that Trump might bring personal strengths to the job. Stanley Renshon, as we noted earlier, made the case that pundits were dismissing Trump too quickly as a narcissist. Instead, he argued, Trump would bring several valuable presidential qualities to the job, including "Ambition, risk-taking, resilience, and the capacity to fight back."[144] But few academics ventured such favourable assessments.

Along this line, we find that Trump brings a mix of personal strengths and weaknesses to his new position. We gleaned a number of these from *The Washington Post's* collective biography. Trump has shown the capacity to handle high-stress situations, and he works hard at his job, usually sleeping only four hours a day. Trump has shown the capacity to deal with stress on numerous occasions, never more than when he faced down the pressure from scores of bankers who were about to destroy the personal fortune he had so carefully assembled. The combination of stress plus being a borderline workaholic like his father could be deadly, and one of the things Trump will need to be conscious of is finding ways and opportunities to relax. Trump projects immense self-confidence, potentially to a fault. He is confident that he can learn the intricacies of complex problems and fix them—that was his daily role as a builder/developer. On the campaign trail, he portrayed himself as the Mr. Fix-It of American politics, the guy who would make right all the wrongs that national elites had screwed up for so long. But unlike physical systems, political problems seldom have clear-cut solutions. Politics consists of shades of gray, not the black and white of physical systems.

Trump's bargaining style relies on the alternating use of carrots and sticks, something he demonstrated throughout this career. Aggressive demands are replaced with more reasonable proposals, a way to keep competitors and potential partners off balance. A related pattern is to create chaos and then become the voice that reveals order. His unpredictability is calculated—he can combine tactical flexibility with strategic constancy. But political bargaining partners, allies and opponents alike, value predictability. Without it, alliances may be put under unnecessary strain and tensions can become dangerously unstable (think NATO, and China, respectively). And unlike most previous presidents entering office, Trump appears to feel unconstrained by past commitments, a freedom that gives him enormous room to maneuver in pursuit of deals but makes other international actors very nervous.

Trump's career has enabled him to become a skilful manipulator of the media; it remains unclear just how effective he will be as a communicator in the long run, though his novel tactics were certainly successful in the 2016 election. For much of his professional life, Trump was the consummate self-promoter, finding ways to hype his projects, his products, and himself. His love life was fodder for the New York tabloids during the prolonged divorce proceedings with Ivana and Marla, his first two wives, and his very public affairs with Marla and Melania. He has never hesitated to oversell his accomplishments. Everything warrants being described as "huge" or by some other superlative. Trump's own term for the pattern is "truthful hyperbole" or "an innocent form of exaggeration,"[145] but the truthfulness is often lost. As Barbara Res, a longtime Trump employee pointed out in an interview with the *Washington Post,* he is a master at dealing in the "big lie," repeating something so many times that it begins to become the truth.[146] And he has the capacity to reach beyond the media; some twenty-eight million followers receive Trump's tweets, and during the campaign, he repeatedly attacked the mainstream media while championing working class jobs and values as a "blue-collar billionaire."

Like playing fast and loose with the truth, there are other personal qualities that are of questionable desirability. Trump's reluctance to delegate could be dangerous. As the head of a family-run business, Trump has relied throughout his career on a small circle of highly loyal advisers that has evolved to include his adult children (Don Jr., Eric, and Ivanka) as they have entered the business. His organization, though wide in scope, has always been very tightly run. The result is that Trump delegates reluctantly and only to those in whom he has total trust. For example, the slow selection of officials for senior Trump administration positions has been partly traced to the president's demand that he review every case. Even at its grandest, Trump's business empire never had the breadth and depth of responsibilities of the federal government. We see this tendency in the president's growing reliance on Ivanka and her husband, Jared Kushner, who fill prominent roles on the White House staff, the first time a president has leaned so heavily on family members since creation of the Executive Office of the President in 1939. Presidents need to learn how to rely on the government machinery around them, not retreat to the narrow range of opinions that might be most comfortable.

Trump takes pride in being an instinctual decision maker, someone who makes judgments from the "gut." Early reports are that Trump is, in addition, a reluctant reader, not especially curious about policy. Trump prefers to receive information in manageable, efficient memos or in oral briefings. Other presidents have had similar preferences. George W. Bush sought to be efficient in using his time, and Gerald Ford preferred oral briefings. Not every president needs mounds of night time reading material (Obama) or solitude to design grand strategies (Nixon). Of these presidents, only Bush was known for making decisions according to gut instincts. The concern of Trump observers is that uninformed or partially informed decisions could be the result. An early example seemed to be the informal way in which Trump decided a week after taking office to launch the administration's first counterterrorism operation conducted by a Navy SEALs team in Yemen. The president approved the request from Secretary of Defense James Mattis during a dinner meeting that included some other members of the administration's national security team. The informality of the "deliberation" that included 25–40 minutes of discussion of the raid contrasted sharply with the elaborate process that the Obama administration had followed for similar issues.[147] Informal process paired with instinctual decision making could be a lethal combination.

President Trump provides a fascinating portrait of a successful businessman promising to apply the same skills that made him wealthy in behalf of the nation. It is too early to know how well those skills will transfer to the enormous enterprise that is the federal government.

Conclusion: Seeking Presidential Success

Paul Quirk has posed a deceptively simple question: What does a president need to know? Quirk identifies a list of presidential competencies that could serve as the basis for making decisions about how best to allocate the president's time, energy, and talent as well as that of the White House staff and the innermost group of presidential advisers.[148] In Quirk's view, presidents require a minimal level of *substantive familiarity* so that they can make intelligent choices among policy options. Moreover, presidents need a degree of *process sensibility* that reflects familiarity with how government decisions are made and carried out, as well as with how such systems might best be designed. Finally, presidents need the capacity for *policy promotion,* the means to achieve their goals through bargains with other Washington elites and through appeals for broad public support. Every president brings a different mix of personal competencies to the job and needs to compensate for personal weaknesses or to complement strengths with the help of others. In Quirk's view, it is critical that each president have a well-designed strategy for how to succeed, what Quirk terms *strategic competence.* This strategy involves decisions on how to allocate time, energy, and talent in relation to mastering substantive issues, delegating tasks, and establishing the prerequisites for successful delegation—for example, selecting personnel.[149]

How are these competencies developed? Implicitly, Quirk seems to suggest that experience in government at the federal level is a critical qualification for presidents. Without it, they have difficulty developing adequate levels of process sensibility and substantive familiarity. But Quirk's advice is directed more to presidents than to voters. Above all else, Quirk urges presidents to approach the office self-consciously, with an eye to developing a management strategy—know yourself and take the steps necessary for effectiveness. Only in this way can a president hope to achieve a measure of success. It is not clear how readily presidents will accept such advice. Are they likely to recognize their own shortcomings? One might expect that any newly elected president, imbued with ambition and flush with success, will proceed to the task of governing filled with self-confidence. Moreover, one might expect those presidents whose personalities drive them to pursue achievement will be least likely to undertake self-analysis.

In many respects, this chapter has explored a question similar to the one posed by Quirk: What personal qualities make a successful president? As we have seen, there are no simple answers. Competencies may be part of the solution, but so are temperament and attitudes. As this chapter demonstrates, we can only speculate on how the qualities necessary for success are derived from family background, career experience, personality, and beliefs. This is true in no small measure because success is the product of these personal qualities interacting with the constraints and opportunities of situations. Despite this fundamental uncertainty, there remains a pervasive confidence that the president's personal qualities have the utmost effect on performance in office, and, therefore, the American people are likely to continue their search for men and women with heroic qualities.

Suggested Readings

Barber, James David. *The Presidential Character,* 4th ed. Englewood Cliffs, NJ: Prentice Hall, 1992.

George, Alexander L., and Juliette George. *Woodrow Wilson and Colonel House: A Personality Study.* New York: John Day, 1956.

———. *Presidential Personality and Performance.* Boulder, CO: Westview, 1998.

Greenstein, Fred I. *Personality and Politics: Problems of Evidence, Inference, and Conceptualization.* New York: Norton, 1975.

———. *The Presidential Difference: Leadership Style from FDR to Clinton.* New York: Free Press, 2000.

Hargrove, Erwin. *Jimmy Carter as President: Leadership and the Politics of the Public Good.* Baton Rouge: Louisiana State University Press, 1988.

Kearns, Doris. *Lyndon Johnson and the American Dream.* New York: Harper and Row, 1976.

Kranish, Michael and Marc Fisher. *Trump Revealed: The Definitive Biography of the 45th President.* New York: Simon & Schuster, 2016

Maraniss, David. *First in His Class: The Biography of Bill Clinton.* New York: Simon and Schuster, 1995.

———. *Barack Obama: The Story.* New York: Simon and Schuster, 2012.

Mazlish, Bruce. *In Search of Nixon: A Psychohistorical Inquiry.* Baltimore, MD: Pelican, 1973.

Pfiffner, James P. *The Character Factor: How We Judge America's Presidents.* College Station: Texas A&M University Press, 2004.

Remnick, David. *The Bridge: The Life and Rise of Barack Obama.* New York: Knopf, 2010.

Renshon, Stanley A. *High Hopes: The Clinton Presidency and the Politics of Ambition.* New York: New York University Press, 1996.

———. *In His Father's Shadow: The Transformations of George W. Bush.* New York: Palgrave Macmillan, 2004.

———. *Barack Obama and the Politics of Redemption.* New York: Routledge, 2011.

Rockman, Bert A. *The Leadership Question: The Presidency and the American System.* New York: Praeger, 1984.

Schultz, William Todd. *Handbook of Psychobiography.* New York: Oxford University Press, 2005.

Resources on the Web

C-SPAN, "American Presidents: Life Portraits," www.americanpresidents.org.

Miller Center of Public Affairs, "American President: An Online Reference Resource," millercenter.org/president.

Washington Post, *Trump Revealed:* The Reporting Archive, 407 documents collected for the book https://www.washingtonpost.com/graphics/politics/trump-revealed-book-reporting-archive/.

White House site on American presidents, www.whitehouse.gov/1600/presidents.

Notes

1. For an especially comprehensive effort, see Michael Kranish and Marc Fisher, *Trump Revealed: The Definitive Biography of the 45th President* (New York: Simon & Schuster, 2016). See especially the online archive of documents used in writing the book at https://www.washingtonpost.com/graphics/politics/trump-revealed-book-reporting-archive/.

2. Fred I. Greenstein, review of Stanley A. Renshon, *In His Father's Shadow: The Transformations of George W. Bush,* in *Presidential Studies Quarterly* 35 (September 2005): 623.

3. The most influential of these interpretations was offered by James David Barber, *The Presidential Character: Predicting Performance in the White House,* 4th ed. (Englewood Cliffs, NJ: Prentice Hall, 1992).

4. Fred I. Greenstein, *The Presidential Difference: Leadership Style from FDR to Clinton* (New York: Free Press, 2000), 3. The most recent (third) edition is *The Presidential Difference: Leadership Style from FDR to Obama* (Princeton, NJ: Princeton University Press, 2009).

5. Stephen Skowronek, *The Politics Presidents Make: Leadership from John Adams to George Bush* (Cambridge, MA: Harvard University Press, 1993). For another work that deals with the importance of a president's environment, defined in a different way, see Bert A. Rockman, *The Leadership Question: The Presidency and the American System* (New York: Praeger, 1984).

6. Fred I. Greenstein, "Can Personality and Politics Be Studied Systematically?" *Political Psychology* 13:1 (1992): 109. For a general discussion of studying personality and politics with special attention to the presidency, see Fred I. Greenstein, *Personality and Politics: Problems of Evidence, Inference, and Conceptualization,* 2nd ed. (New York: Norton, 1975); and Rockman, *The Leadership Question.*

7. See, for example, Colin Campbell, Bert A. Rockman, and Andrew Rudalevige, eds., *The George W. Bush Legacy* (Washington, DC: CQ Press, 2007).

8. Bruce Buchanan, *The Citizen's Presidency* (Washington, DC: CQ Press, 1987), 102–104. Buchanan proposes a set of "competent process standards" that are more susceptible to empirical verification (108–134).

9. See, for example, Justin Vaughn and Brandon Rottinghaus, "New Ranking of U.S. Presidents," *Washington Post* online (February 16, 2015), www.washingtonpost.com/blogs/monkey-cage/wp/2015/02/16/new-ranking-of-u-s-presidents-puts-lincoln-1-obama-18-kennedy-judged-most-over-rated/.

10. Bert A. Rockman, "Conclusions: An Imprint but Not a Revolution," in *The Reagan Revolution?* ed. B. B. Kymlicka and Jean V. Matthews (Chicago: Dorsey, 1988), 205. Other works in this vein, important because of the significance attributed to the Reagan experience, include the following: Larry Berman, ed., *Looking Back on the Reagan Presidency* (Baltimore, MD: Johns Hopkins University Press, 1990); Sidney Blumenthal and Thomas Byrne Edsall, eds., *The Reagan Legacy* (New York: Pantheon Books, 1988); Charles O. Jones, ed., *The Reagan Legacy: Promise and Performance* (Chatham, NJ: Chatham House, 1988); and John L. Palmer, ed., *Perspectives on the Reagan Years* (Washington, DC: Urban Institute, 1986).

11. James P. Pfiffner, *The Character Factor: How We Judge America's Presidents* (College Station: Texas A&M University Press, 2004).

12. Ibid., 19. See the table on page 21.

13. Ibid., 82–90. Pfiffner concludes that Clinton was reckless and irresponsible in his behavior and that he extended the effect of his lies by telling them to cabinet members and White House staff aides he

knew would repeat the untruths. But the lies "did not constitute the same level of institutional threat to the polity that Watergate and Iran-Contra did." Ibid., 139. Eisenhower's affair occurred during World War II, not his presidency.

14. Arthur Schlesinger's initial effort polled 55 scholars, and his second included 75, with historians constituting the greater part of each group. The Murray-Blessing poll was based on 846 responses to a nineteen-page, 180-question survey sent to 1,997 Ph.D.-holding American historians with assistant professor rank (an additional 107 responses were returned late). The Lindgren-Calabresi survey included 78 presidential scholars from history, political science, and law with an explicit attempt to balance the sample based on ideology. In 2009, C-SPAN asked sixty-five historians and presidential specialists to evaluate all presidents on ten dimensions with a cumulative score and one for each dimension. C-SPAN used the same dimensions in 2017, with ninety-one historians and presidency specialists participating. For information on poll samples, see Henry J. Abraham, *Justices and Presidents* (New York: Oxford University Press, 1985), appendix B. For discussion of these efforts as well as their own, see Robert K. Murray and Tim H. Blessing, *Greatness in the White House: Rating the Presidents, Washington through Ronald Reagan,* 2nd updated ed. (University Park: Pennsylvania State University Press, 1994), chaps. 1, 2. The ranking of Ronald Reagan was completed in 1988–1990 and is reported in this updated edition.

15. Murray and Blessing, *Greatness in the White House,* 24.

16. Tim H. Blessing and Anne A. Skleder, "Top Down: A General Overview of Present Research on Ronald Reagan's Doctrinal Presidency," in *Reassessing the Reagan Presidency,* ed. Richard S. Conley (Lanham, MD: University Press of America, 2003), 30. The authors report the results of an unpublished poll about Reagan similar to the poll conducted in 1990.

17. C-SPAN 2009 Historians Leadership Survey, legacy.c-span.org/PresidentialSurvey/presidential-leadership-survey.aspx.

18. "53 Historians Weigh-In on Barack Obama's Legacy," *New York* (January 11, 2015), nymag.com/daily/intelligencer/2015/01/53-historians-on-obamas-legacy.html.

19. Nate Silver, "Contemplating Obama's Place in History, Statistically," *New York Times* FiveThirtyEight Blog (January 23, 2013), fivethirtyeight.blogs.nytimes.com/2013/01/23/contemplating-obamas-place-in-history-statistically/?_r=0.

20. Murray and Blessing, *Greatness in the White House,* 41–43, and appendix 8, 139. The personal traits conducive to success also were examined in terms of how they changed for different times. For the modern era, 1945 to the present, respondents ranked intelligence first and integrity second, with other qualities in declining order: sensitivity to popular demands, charisma, previous political experience, pleasing physical appearance, intense patriotism, and an aristocratic bearing.

21. Ibid., 63.

22. James MacGregor Burns, *Leadership* (New York: Harper and Row, 1977).

23. Greenstein, *The Presidential Difference,* 5–6.

24. Donald Matthews, *The Social Background of Political Decision Makers* (New York: Random House, 1954), 23.

25. Edward Pessen, *The Log Cabin Myth: The Social Backgrounds of the Presidents* (New Haven, CT: Yale University Press, 1984), 56–57.

26. Ibid., 171.

27. Ibid., 56–63. Pessen views a family's class as a combination of wealth and possessions, income and occupational prestige, lifestyle, status, influence, and power. He recognizes, moreover, that analysts' characterizations are subjective. For an interesting sidelight, see the response of Pessen to the scathing book review written by Fred Greenstein for the *Journal of Interdisciplinary History* 16:2 (Autumn 1985): 351–352. Pessen's letter to the editors, "Comment and Controversy," *Journal of Interdisciplinary History* 17:2 (Autumn 1986): 504–507.

28. Kranish and Fisher, *Trump Revealed,* 32.

29. Truman attended night classes at the Kansas City Law School, but it was a proprietary institution not then affiliated with a university. It is now part of the Law School of the University of Missouri–Kansas City.

30. Max Weber, "Politics as a Vocation," in *Max Weber: Essays in Sociology,* ed. H. H. Gerth and C. W. Mills (New York: Oxford University Press, 1946), 85.

31. Hugh Montgomery-Massingberd, ed., *Burke's Presidential Families of the U.S.A.* (London: Burke's Peerage, 1975), 250.

32. Ibid., 320.

33. Robert Donovan, *Conflict and Crisis: The Presidency of Harry S Truman, 1945–48* (New York: Praeger, 1977), chap. 40. It should also be noted that military officers have demonstrated leadership skills and may be called on to develop substantial political skill while building careers or in dealing with foreign leaders. Eisenhower, for example, did both.

34. Pessen, *The Log Cabin Myth,* 171.

35. E. Digby Baltzell and Howard G. Schneiderman, "Social Class in the Oval Office," *Society* 26 (September/October 1988): 42–49. The ranking of presidential performance used in this study was conducted by Robert K. Murray and Tim H. Blessing and was first published in the *Journal of American History* 70 (December 1983): 535–555.

36. Baltzell and Schneiderman, "Social Class in the Oval Office," 47.

37. William Henry Harrison and Garfield were not rated because of the brief time they served in office.

38. Baltzell and Schneiderman, "Social Class in the Oval Office," 49.

39. Richard E. Neustadt, *Presidential Power and the Modern Presidents* (New York: Free Press, 1991), 151.

40. Ibid., 205.

41. Rockman, *The Leadership Question,* 212. Rockman uses a performance ranking compiled by the *Chicago Tribune* in 1982.

42. We are indebted to Leonard P. Stark, now a federal district judge, for this account and continuing stimulation on the subject of presidential personality. See his senior honors thesis, "Personality and Presidential Selection: Evaluating Character and Experience in the 1988 Election" (University of Delaware, 1991), 47–48. Barber's article was "The Question of Presidential Character," *Saturday Review,* September 23, 1972, 62–66.

43. Greenstein, *Personality and Politics,* 3.

44. Alexander L. George and Juliette George, *Woodrow Wilson and Colonel House: A Personality Study* (New York: John Day, 1956); Doris Kearns Goodwin, *Lyndon Johnson and the American Dream* (New York: Harper and Row, 1976); Bruce Mazlish, *In Search of Nixon: A Psychohistorical Inquiry* (Baltimore, MD: Pelican, 1973); Betty Glad, *Jimmy Carter: In Search of the Great White House* (New York: Norton, 1980); and Stanley A. Renshon, *High Hopes: The Clinton Presidency and the Politics of Ambition* (New York: New York University Press, 1996). For an excellent biography of Clinton that provides psychological insights but is not informed by psychological theory, see David Maraniss, *First in His Class: A Biography of Bill Clinton* (New York: Simon and Schuster, 1995).

45. For an extended discussion, see Greenstein's treatment of these issues in *Personality and Politics,* chaps. 3 and 4, as well as the introduction.

46. See, for example, Alexander L. George's discussion of Barber's book *The Presidential Character* in George, "Assessing Presidential Character," *World Politics* 26 (January 1974): 234–282. This essay is reprinted with several related essays in Alexander L. George and Juliette George, *Presidential Personality and Performance* (Boulder, CO: Westview, 1998), 145–197.

47. For later efforts to rebut critics, see Betty Glad, "Political Leadership: Some Methodological Considerations," in *Political Leadership for the New Century: Personality and Behavior among American Leaders,* ed. Linda O. Valenty and Ofer Feldman (Westport, CT: Praeger, 2002), 9–23; and Paul A. Kowert, "Where 'Does' the Buck Stop? Assessing the Impact of Presidential Personality," *Political Psychology* 17 (September 1996): 421–452.

48. Although the call of conservatives during the Reagan years was "let Reagan be Reagan," Clinton's aides had begun the practice during his gubernatorial years of "protect[ing] Clinton from Clinton." See Maraniss, *The Clinton Enigma* (New York: Simon and Schuster, 1998), 60.

49. Barber, *The Presidential Character,* 34.

50. James David Barber, "Predicting Hope with Clinton at Helm," *News & Observer* (Raleigh, NC), January 17, 1993. Barber did not offer a preliminary evaluation of George H. W. Bush.

51. Barber, *The Presidential Character,* 5.

52. Ibid.

53. Barber, "Predicting Hope."

54. Stanley A. Renshon, "A Preliminary Assessment of the Clinton Presidency: Character, Leadership, and Performance," *Political Psychology* 15:2 (1994): 375–394. Also see a slightly revised version of the paper in *The Clinton Presidency: Campaigning, Governing, and the Psychology of Leadership,* ed. Stanley A. Renshon (Boulder, CO: Westview, 1995), 57–87. Also see Renshon, *High Hopes.*

55. Renshon, "Preliminary Assessment," 381, 380, 382.

56. Greenstein, *The Presidential Difference,* 255.

57. Stanley Renshon, "You Don't Know Trump As Well As You Think," *USA Today* (March 25, 2016), http://www.usatoday.com/story/opinion/2016/03/25/donald-trump-narcissist-business-leadership-respect-column/82209524/.

58. Don P. McAdams, "The Mind of Donald Trump," *The Atlantic* (June 2016), https://www.theatlantic.com/magazine/archive/2016/06/the-mind-of-donald-trump/480771/.

59. Renshon as quoted in Ben Smith, "I Asked a Psychoanalyst to Explain Donald Trump," *BuzzFeed* (December 3, 2015), https://www.buzzfeed.com/bensmith/trump-on-the-couch?utm_term=.rxryvmmENO#.sh8g4jjJlR.

60. Greenstein, *Personality and Politics,* 19.

61. Fred I. Greenstein, *The Hidden-Hand Presidency* (New York: Basic Books, 1982). Barber, however, responded that the new evidence confirms his original analysis even more fully. See Barber, *The Presidential Character,* 522–525.

62. See George, "Assessing Presidential Character"; and Michael Nelson, "The Psychological Presidency," in *The Presidency and the Political System,* 4th ed., ed. Michael Nelson (Washington, DC: CQ Press, 1995).

63. Dean Keith Simonton, *Why Presidents Succeed: A Political Psychology of Leadership* (New Haven, CT: Yale University Press, 1987), 151–152.

64. Barber, *The Presidential Character,* 487.

65. Ibid., 298.

66. Ibid., 296–299.

67. Jeffrey Tulis, "On Presidential Character," in *The Presidency in the Constitutional Order,* ed. Jeffrey Tulis and Joseph M. Bessette (Baton Rouge: Louisiana State University Press, 1981), 283–313.

68. For another effort at guiding electoral choice, see Stanley A. Renshon, *The Psychological Assessment of Presidential Candidates* (New York: New York University Press, 1996).

69. Clark Clifford, "The Presidency as I Have Seen It," in *The Living Presidency,* ed. Emmet John Hughes (New York: Coward, McCann, and Geoghegan, 1973), 315, cited by Greenstein in *The Presidential Difference,* 189.

70. This dichotomy is captured by Peri E. Arnold, "The Presidency as Individual and Collective," *Review of Politics* 49 (Summer 1987): 432–434, a review of Colin Campbell, *Managing the Presidency: Carter, Reagan and the Search for Executive Harmony.*

71. U.S. Office of Personnel Management, "Comparison of Total Civilian Employment of the Federal Government by Branch, Agency, and Area as of June 2013 and September 2013," Table 2, www.opm.gov/policy-data-oversight/data-analysis-documentation/federal-employment-reports/employment-trends-data/2012/september/table-2/.

72. Joseph A. Pika, "Management Style and the Organizational Matrix: Studying White House Operations," *Administration and Society* 20:1 (May 1988): 11.

73. John Hart, *The Presidential Branch: From Washington to Clinton* (Chatham, NJ: Chatham House, 1995).

74. Alexander L. George, *Presidential Decisionmaking in Foreign Policy* (Boulder, CO: Westview, 1980), 139–168.

75. See Richard Tanner Johnson, *Managing the White House* (New York: Harper and Row, 1974). Also see Johnson, "Presidential Style," in *Perspectives on the Presidency,* ed. Aaron Wildavsky (Boston: Little, Brown, 1975).

76. Charles E. Walcott and Karen M. Hult, "White House Structure and Decision Making: Elaborating the Standard Model," *Presidential Studies Quarterly* 35 (June 2005): 303–318.

77. We now know that Robert F. Kennedy's account of those deliberations, which influenced so much early scholarship, idealized his own performance. See Robert F. Kennedy, *Thirteen Days: A Memoir of the Cuban Missile Crisis* (New York: Norton, 1969) and especially Sheldon M. Stern, *The Cuban Missile Crisis in American Memory: Myths Versus Reality* (Stanford, CA: Stanford University Press, 2012). Also see Aleksandr Fursenko and Timothy Naftali, *"One Hell of a Gamble": Khrushchev, Castro, and Kennedy 1958–1964* (New York: Norton, 1997).

78. Roger Porter, "A Healing Presidency," in *Leadership in the Modern Presidency,* ed. Fred I. Greenstein (Cambridge, MA: Harvard University Press, 1988), 218.

79. George, *Presidential Decisionmaking,* 159.

80. Colin Campbell, *Managing the Presidency: Carter, Reagan, and the Search for Executive Harmony* (Pittsburgh, PA: University of Pittsburgh Press, 1986), 93–111; James Pfiffner, *The Strategic Presidency: Hitting the Ground Running* (Chicago: Dorsey, 1988), 30–37; and Buchanan, *The Citizen's Presidency,* 124–133.

81. Stanley A. Renshon, *In His Father's Shadow: The Transformations of George W. Bush* (New York: Palgrave Macmillan, 2004), 126–127, 256. Others have suggested that Bush recreated a "troika" with aides Andrew Card, Karen Hughes, and Karl Rove or that there were six aides with direct access to him: those three plus Vice President Cheney, Condoleezza Rice, and Alberto Gonzales. See Andrew Rudalevige, "'The Decider': Issue Management and the Bush White House," in *The George W. Bush Legacy,* ed. Colin Campbell, Bert A. Rockman, and Andrew Rudalevige (Washington, DC: CQ Press, 2007), 135–163.

82. See especially the dramatic case of Bush's decision, at Cheney's urging, to deny foreign terrorism suspects access to U.S. courts, as described in Barton Gellman and Jo Becker, "'A Different Understanding with the President,'" *Washington Post,* June 24, 2007, A1.

83. Karl Rove, "The Obama White House May Be a Crowded Mess," *Wall Street Journal,* January 29, 2009, online.wsj.com/article/SB123318823268126605.html; and Stephen J. Wayne, *Personality and Politics: Obama For and Against Himself* (Washington, DC: CQ Press, 2012), chap. 4.

84. Maggie Haberman, Jeremy W. Peters, Peter Bakeapril, "In Battle for Trump's Heart and Mind It's Bannon vs. Kushner," *New York Times* (April 6, 2017), https://www.nytimes.com/2017/04/06/us/politics/stephen-bannon-white-house.html?emc=edit_cn_20170407&nl=first-draft&nlid=69310600&te=1 See also Jeremy W. Peters and Maggie Haberman, "Trump Undercuts Bannon, Whose Job May Be in

Danger," *New York Times* (April 13, 2017), https://www.nytimes.com/2017/04/12/us/politics/steve-bannon-white-house-trump.html?emc=edit_cn_20170413&nl=first-draft&nlid=69310600&te=1

85. Alexander L. George and Eric Stern, "Presidential Management Styles and Models," in George and George, *Presidential Personality and Performance,* 263.

86. Walcott and Hult, "White House Structure and Decision Making," 313.

87. Alexander L. George, "The Case for Multiple Advocacy in Making Foreign Policy," *American Political Science Review* 66 (September 1972): 751–785. Also see George, *Presidential Decisionmaking,* chap. 11.

88. George, *Presidential Decisionmaking,* 203, 203–204.

89. Alexander L. George and Eric K. Stern, "Harnessing Conflict in Foreign Policy Making: From Devil's Advocate to Multiple Advocacy," *Presidential Studies Quarterly* 32 (September 2002): 490.

90. Discussions of the standard model (hierarchical) frequently link its purported benefits to systematic review of options by diverse advisers, a vital element of multiple advocacy. Walcott and Hult, "White House Structure and Decision Making," 314–316.

91. Ibid., 201.

92. Paul A. Kowert, *Groupthink or Deadlock: When Do Leaders Learn from Their Advisers?* (Albany: State University of New York Press, 2002), 4, 23.

93. Ibid., chap. 6.

94. George, *Presidential Decisionmaking,* 204.

95. Renshon quotes a recollection from Obama's brother-in-law in roughly 1989 that the presidency was a possibility. Renshon, "Psychological Reflections on Barack Obama and John McCain," 401.

96. Kranish and Fisher, Trump Revealed, 275–292.

97. Ibid., 271, 290.

98. David Maraniss, "Restless Searcher on an Improbable Path," *Washington Post,* January 20, 2009, A4.

99. David Maraniss, "Though Obama Had to Leave to Find Himself, It Was Hawaii That Made His Rise Possible," *Washington Post,* August 24, 2008, 22. On Obama's childhood, also see Jennifer Steinhauer, "Charisma and a Search for Self in Obama's Hawaii Childhood," *New York Times,* March 17, 2007, www.nytimes.com/2007/03/17/us/politics/17hawaii.html?_r=1. More broadly, see Maraniss, *Barack Obama: The Story* (New York: Simon and Schuster, 2012); and David Remnick, *The Bridge: The Life and Rise of Barack Obama* (New York: Knopf, 2010).

100. Barack Obama, *The Audacity of Hope* (New York: Random House, 2006).

101. For a fascinating look at which parts of Obama's life have been explored by himself and the media, see Slate.com's interactive timeline constructed by Christopher Beam and Chris Wilson at www.slate.com/id/2196908.

102. Janny Scott, "A Free-Spirited Wanderer Who Set Obama's Path," *New York Times,* March 14, 2008, www.nytimes.com/2008/03/14/us/politics/14obama.html?pagewanted=1.

103. B. J. Reyes, "Punahou Left Lasting Impression on Obama," *Honolulu Star Bulletin,* February 8, 2007.

104. Katharine Q. Seelye, "Obama Offers More Variations from the Norm," *New York Times,* October 24, 2006.

105. Lois Romano, "Effect of Obama's Candor Remains to Be Seen," *Washington Post,* January 3, 2007.

106. Stanley A. Renshon, "Redemption, Fairness, and the Politics of Transformation in the Obama Administration," *Political Psychology* 32:6 (December 2011): 1038.

107. Ibid., 1039.

108. Richard Wolffe, Jessica Ramirez, and Jeffrey Bartholet, "When Barry Became Barack," *Newsweek,* March 31, 2008, www.newsweek.com/id/128633/page/1.

109. Janny Scott, "Obama's Account of New York Years Often Differs from What Others Say," *New York Times,* October 30, 2007, www.nytimes.com/2007/10/30/us/politics/30obama.html.

110. Serge Kovaleski, "Obama's Organizing Years, Guiding Others and Finding Himself," *New York Times,* July 7, 2008, www.nytimes.com/2008/07/07/us/politics/07community.html.

111. As quoted in Amanda Ripley, "Obama's Ascent," *Time,* November 3, 2004, www.time.com/time/magazine/article/0,9171,750742–2,00.html.

112. Kenneth T. Walsh, "Obama's Years in Chicago Politics Shaped His Presidential Candidacy," *U.S. News and World Report,* April 11, 2008, www.usnews.com/articles/news/campaign-2008/04/11/obamas-years-in-chicago-politics-shaped-his-presidential-candidacy.html?PageNr=1.

113. Robert M. Gates, *Duty: Memoirs of a Secretary of War* (New York: Knopf, 2014), chap. 10.

114. Ibid., 584–588.

115. Ibid., 522.

116. This was the adjective used by former vice president Dick Cheney.

117. Fred I. Greenstein, "Barack Obama: The Man and His Presidency at the Midterm," *PS* (January 2011): 7–11. This analysis later appeared in the newest edition of Greenstein's book, *The Presidential Difference: Leadership Style from FDR to Barack Obama,* 3rd ed. (Princeton, NJ: Princeton University Press, 2009).

118. Gates, op. cit. 385 and 474ff.

119. For a riveting account of the raid see Nicholas Schmidle, "Getting Bin Laden," *The New Yorker,* August 8, 2011.

120. Gates, op. cit. 543.

121. Wayne, *Personality and Politics,* op. cit., 112–113.

122. Jonathan Alter, *The Promise: President Obama, Year One* (New York: Simon and Schuster, 2010), 267.

123. Quoted in Renshon, "Psychological Reflections on Barack Obama and John McCain," 404.

124. Wayne, *Personality and Politics,* 79.

125. Greenstein, "Barack Obama: The Man and His Presidency at the Midterm," 11.

126. Lloyd Grove, "Democrats' Negotiator in Chief," *The Daily Beast,* May 19, 2011, www.thedailybeast.com/articles/2011/05/19/debt-ceiling-drama-white-house-point-man-gene-sperlings-bid-for-republican-votes.html.

127. See the account of Obama's frustration with Rep. Eric Cantor and Rep. John Boehner in Peter Wallsten, "Obama's role in debt talks scrutinized," *Washington Post,* August 5, 2011.

128. Renshon, "Psychological Reflections on Barack Obama and John McCain," 405.

129. Andrew Rudalevige, "Rivals, or a Team? Staffing and Issue Management in the Obama Administration," in *The Obama Presidency: Appraisals and Prospects,* ed. Bert Rockman et al. (Washington, DC: CQ Press, 2012).

130. Kranish and Fisher, *Trump Revealed,* 32.

131. Ibid., 47–50.

132. Ibid., 48. For more detail see Craig Whitlock, "Questions Linger about Trump's Draft Deferments during the Vietnam War," *Washington Post* (July 21, 2015), https://www.washingtonpost.com/world/national-security/questions-linger-about-trumps-draft-deferments-during-vietnam-war/2015/07/21/257677bc-2fdd-11e5-8353-1215475949f4_story.html?utm_term=.77c6ebd11976.

133. Donald J. Trump and Tony Schwartz, *Trump: The Art of the Deal* (New York: Random House, 1987), 78 as cited in *Trump Revealed,* 58.

134. Kranish and Fisher, *Trump Revealed,* 31.

135. Ibid., 64.

136. Ibid. 75ff.

137. Ibid., 96.

138. Ibid. Chapter 11, 188–209. Also see Russ Buettner and Charles V. Bagli, "How Donald Trump Bankrupted His Atlantic City Casinos, but Still Earned Millions," *New York Times* (June 11, 2016), https://www.nytimes.com/2016/06/12/nyregion/donald-trump-atlantic-city.html.

139. Ibid., Chapter 12, 210–220.

140. For a list of existing projects and products see the website of The Trump Organization, http://www.trump.com/merchandise/signature-collection/.

141. Washington Post Editorial Board, "The Washington Post Editorial Board Endorses Hillary Clinton for President," *Washington Post*, (October 12, 2016), https://www.washingtonpost.com/video/editorial/the-washington-post-editorial-board-endorses-hillary-clinton-for-president/2016/10/13/02cbb490-9097-11e6-bc00-1a9756d4111b_video.html.

142. Kevin Liptak,"Nobody Knew Health Care Could Be So Complicated," CNN (February 28, 2017), http://www.cnn.com/2017/02/27/politics/trump-health-care-complicated/index.html.

143. David Sanger and William J. Broad, "A 'Cuban Missile Crisis in Slow Motion' in North Korea," *New York Times* (April 16, 2017), https://www.nytimes.com/2017/04/16/us/politics/north-korea-missile-crisis-slow-motion.html?emc=edit_cn_20170417&nl=first-draft&nlid=69310600&te=1.

144. Stanley Renshon, "You Don't Know Trump As Well As You Think," *USA Today* (March 25, 2016), http://www.usatoday.com/story/opinion/2016/03/25/donald-trump-narcissist-business-leadership-respect-column/82209524/).

145. Kranish and Fisher, op. cit., 105 as cited from Trump and Schwartz, op. cit., 56–58.

146. Kranish and Fisher, op. cit., 109.

147. Missy Ryan and Thomas Gibbons-Neff, "A Raid in Remote Yemen and a SEAL's Death Still Reverberate for Trump," *Washington Post* (March 1, 2017), https://www.washingtonpost.com/world/national-security/a-raid-in-remote-yemen-and-a-seals-death-still-reverberate-for-trump/2017/03/01/0adc7b32-fd08-11e6-8ebe-6e0dbe4f2bca_story.html?utm_term=.cdb8cc5e4ade.

148. Paul Quirk, "Presidential Competence," in *The Presidency and the Political System*, 7th ed., ed. Michael Nelson (Washington, DC: CQ Press, 2003), 158–189; and Paul Quirk, "What Must a President Know?" *Transactional Society* 23 (January/February 1983).

149. Quirk, "Presidential Competence."

CHAPTER 5

Legislative Politics

Win McNamee/Getty Images

During his first address to Congress in February 2017, President Donald Trump called for bipartisan support for his sweeping agenda. He pledged that "a new chapter of American greatness is now beginning" and promised that "everything that is broken in our country can be fixed. Every problem can be solved."

Presidents cannot govern alone, but their necessary partnership with Congress is often uneasy, providing the nation with high political drama. These two branches must cooperate to pass laws, adopt budgets, enter into international treaties, declare wars, and appoint officials to the executive branch. In most cases, the institutions must find a compromise position but sometimes engage in painful confrontations. Before reviewing the full context of legislative-executive relations, we briefly review three particularly contentious cases drawn from the past three presidencies.

Three Confrontations in Interbranch Relations

After Republicans lost control of Congress in the midterm elections of 2006, George W. Bush confronted an effort led by Democrats to force changes in U.S.

policy toward Iraq. In 2011, Barack Obama struggled to reach a compromise agreement with congressional Republicans that would allow the country to raise its borrowing limit—the debt ceiling. Finally, in 2017, Donald Trump's promise to "repeal and replace" the Affordable Care Act threatened to founder on deep divisions among majority Republicans as well as shifting public opinion.

Democrats Oppose Bush's Iraq War

In 2006, the Democrats took back control in the House and the Senate. Fresh from their election victories, members of the new majorities were determined to change policy in Iraq by shifting the combat role from U.S. forces to the Iraqis and bringing U.S. forces home. Shortly after the 110th Congress was sworn in, President Bush announced on January 10, 2007, in a prime-time speech to the nation, a new strategy of his own—"the surge." The plan would commit 28,500 additional U.S. combat troops who would aim to reduce sectarian violence and build confidence in the new Iraqi government. Democrats were unconvinced that the strategy would work and instead described it as an "escalation" reminiscent of the Vietnam era. Some critics feared that the new policy would widen the war and lead to conflict with Syria and Iran. Strong voices in the antiwar movement urged the Democrats to force the president to cancel the surge and withdraw all American forces from Iraq. Pledging to remain true to the public's verdict in the previous election, Democrats faced a range of possibilities:

> Should Congress deny Bush the funds he would need to increase the U.S. forces in Iraq? Should it give him the money, but with a slew of conditions and strings attached? Should it limit the number of troops? Cut off the funding for the war completely? Or simply issue a politically devastating vote of no confidence, with lawmakers from both parties joining in, and hope that's enough to get Bush to back down?[1]

At the heart of this confrontation was the president's constitutional authority to exercise his powers as commander in chief versus Congress's constitutional authority to shape policy.

Democrats proved to be divided and failed to come to a common position on the questions above. On February 16, House Democrats, joined by a limited number of Republicans, voted 246–182 in favor of a nonbinding resolution that opposed the troop increase. Senate Republicans used procedural tactics to block a similar effort. Liberal Democrats urged their colleagues to cut off funding for the war, impose mandatory deadlines for withdrawal, or require another congressional vote to reauthorize the use of force rather than rely on the approval granted back in October 2002. Moderate colleagues were less willing to force the president's hand and were fearful of endangering the troops already in place. Even Republicans critical of the president's policies were unwilling to adopt language that allowed Congress to "micromanage" the war and reduce the president's control.

Funding bills served as the main battlefield in this political conflict. Bush needed additional money to continue the war, and Democrats kept adding provisions that were unacceptable to the president, resulting in a May 1 veto, only his second to that point. Neither the House nor the Senate could muster the two-thirds vote required for an override. After extensive negotiations with the White House, Congress met the president's demand to remove timelines for withdrawing troops from Iraq and established instead eighteen benchmarks for the Iraqi government to meet. The bill required the president to provide Congress with periodic reports on Iraqi performance in meeting these benchmarks.

Democrats continued their efforts to force a change in policy, this time using the Defense Department's authorization and appropriations bills for fiscal year 2008 as the vehicle for pressuring the White House.[2] But so long as Senate Republicans remained united, Democrats could not win the votes they needed to cut off debate on key issues. Senate majority leader Harry Reid, D-NV, was accordingly reduced to grumbling about Bush "pulling the strings on the 49 puppets he has here in the Senate."[3]

Republicans Balk at Raising the Debt Ceiling for Obama

For months the nation seemed to be teetering on the brink of financial catastrophe, and the deadline was fast approaching—August 2, 2011. That was the day on which the Obama administration announced it would run short of money to pay the U.S. government's obligations, including veterans benefits, contractor invoices, and Social Security. Current bills for August would total $307 billion, while projected revenues were $172 billion. Normally, the Treasury would borrow the difference by selling bonds, mainly to individuals, but Congress has to authorize those sales, and the limit had been reached.

Republicans insisted that increasing the debt ceiling yet again was tantamount to throwing gasoline on a fire—it would sustain the bad habits of spending more than the government was taking in. Thus, they insisted on accompanying spending cuts. Three times over the summer, Republicans had walked away from the debt ceiling negotiations when Democrats insisted that a solution to the nation's budget problems had to include tax increases as well as spending cuts. And in the end no one was happy with the final deal, which managed to "kick the can down the road" for another round of future battles. The policy options and battle lines were complicated. Most independent observers agreed that solving the structural deficit problem facing the United States in the coming decades would require some combination of (1) discretionary spending cuts, (2) reduction of future entitlement payments under Social Security and Medicare, and (3) additional tax revenues. But the details here were particularly devilish. Democrats generally opposed (2), Republicans disliked (3), and no one embraced (1) once discussion moved from slogans to specifics. Newly elected freshmen, many of whom were linked to the Tea Party movement within the Republican Party, were determined to change government priorities, starting with dramatic reductions in government spending, and they were opposed to compromise. Their constant pressure on Speaker John Boehner, R-OH—reflecting their sixty to eighty votes—forced him to walk away from two draft agreements with President Obama, the most promising of which involved $3 trillion in spending cuts and $1 billion in revenue increases.[4] Boehner, however, could not even count on support within the House leadership, where the number-two Republican, Eric Cantor, was reportedly angling for Tea Party support in a future challenge for the number-one position. Players unfamiliar with the art of compromise were driving the process.

Round-the-clock negotiations produced an eleventh-hour agreement: a two-step increase in the debt ceiling of $2.4 trillion in exchange for spending reductions of $917 billion followed by additional reductions of at least $1.5 trillion identified by a "super committee" of six Republicans and six Democrats drawn equally from the House and the Senate. If the committee failed to come up with at least $1.2 trillion in additional savings by December 23, 2011, through spending cuts and revenue increases, then Congress would adopt automatic spending cuts known as **sequesters** divided equally between defense and nondefense programs. Cuts would not go into effect until 2013, after the next round of elections was concluded. Similarly, the debt ceiling would not need to be increased until after the elections. The deal passed comfortably in both the House (269–161) and the Senate (74–26). House Democrats split 95–95, many unhappy that tax increases were not part of the agreement. Pro-defense Republicans were upset at the prospect of future cuts, and other "no" voters wanted larger spending cuts immediately.[5]

Numerous commentators noted that this performance showed American government was dysfunctional. Approval ratings for both the president and Congress declined as voters expressed disappointment with each, though the president fared slightly better. And more problems lay ahead—the fiscal year budget required approval by October 1, 2011; the federal gas tax was up for renewal; President Bush's 2001 tax cuts were scheduled to end; and unemployment insurance benefits would decline by the end of the year. If anything, dysfunction could get worse, as pointed out by the highly respected British journal *The Economist,* which also summarized the dilemma:

> American politics has always been fractious; that is part of its strength. Checks and balances prevent abuse of power and compel compromise. But checks and balances combined with polarisation allow a small number of legislators to bring government to a halt.[6]

"Obamacare" after the 2016 Election

Since the passage of the Affordable Care Act in 2010, House Republicans had voted more than 60 times to repeal it, in part or in whole.[7] A Democratic Senate and, after 2015, the presidential veto pen, had kept "Obamacare" in place; the law had even survived two Supreme Court decisions and a botched rollout marked by crashing websites and statutory deadlines delayed by presidential directives. But in early 2017 Republicans controlled both the House and Senate, and new president Donald J. Trump had repeatedly called for the repeal of the health care law he termed a "disaster." Indeed, he said, "Everything is broken about it. Everything."[8] Obamacare seemed doomed.

Still, while the law generally was not widely loved—even its advocates argued for revisions—it had many specific provisions that had proved very popular, such as the requirement that insurers cover individuals even if they had preexisting medical conditions. On the campaign trail, Trump said he would replace Obamacare with "something terrific"; indeed, he told the *Washington Post* the week before his inauguration that "we're going to have insurance for everybody. There was a philosophy in some circles that if you can't pay for it, you don't get it. That's not going to happen with us." He added that the new plan would provide "great health care. . . . Much less expensive and much better."[9]

Those promises were not accompanied by a specific legislative proposal. Even so they ran headlong into deep divisions within the Republican caucus about how to proceed in overturning the law. While many (including Trump) argued that Obamacare had to be repealed *and replaced,* others thought repeal sufficient. The conservative House "Freedom Caucus" wanted to deregulate the insurance marketplace and slash federal spending on health care; moderates preferred providing tax credits to offset insurance costs and worried about rolling back coverage, including the expansion of Medicaid that Obamacare had funded, money on which more than 30 states now depended.

To avoid having to win over Democratic votes, the Republicans sought to use a process called "reconciliation"—which prevented legislation from being filibustered in the Senate but could only be used to change provisions that had a monetary impact. (This meant most regulatory change could not be passed in this manner.) However, getting to even 51 senators was a hard sell given a narrow Senate majority that ranged from Ted Cruz of Texas on the far right to the more purple Susan Collins of Maine.

On March 6, Speaker Ryan unveiled the American Health Care Act, a bill crafted by the Republican leadership and quickly shepherded through committee, even before the Congressional Budget Office (CBO) had analyzed its costs. The bill eliminated the Obamacare individual mandate and the law's taxes on high earners, established tax credits to replace the law's premium subsidies, and cut $880 billion from projected Medicaid spending over ten years. When the CBO did report, it projected that federal spending under the bill would decline $337 billion over the next decade—but also that 24 million fewer people would have insurance coverage after that time, and that many, especially those over 50 in rural areas, would see huge and immediate increases in their out-of-pocket health costs. Democrats pounced, and Republicans split: some were nervous about cuts to coverage, while others were angry that the bill maintained health care entitlements at all.

Though many of the bill's provisions seemed to contradict his past promises, President Trump fully endorsed the measure and held a series of White House meetings with legislators. Vice President Mike Pence and budget director Mick Mulvaney—former House members themselves—were dispatched to Capitol Hill. But these efforts failed to persuade House members under immense pressure from constituents. Moves to the right alienated Republican moderates; moves to shore up subsidies caused the Freedom Caucus to scoff at "Obamacare Lite." Public support surged for the existing law as fears of losing even imperfect health coverage rose.

Unable to construct a House majority—and with a Senate majority even more elusive—Ryan pulled the AHCA from the floor on March 24. "We're going to be living with Obamacare for the foreseeable future," he concluded.[10] However, eager for a win on this signature issue, negotiations with Freedom Caucus members continued. A second version of the AHCA fell short in April. But in early May, amendments pushing both to the right (allowing states to waive key insurance requirements) and the center (placing $8 billion in a fund subsidizing "high-risk pools" for those expensive to insure)—combined with immense pressure from the White House and the House leadership—managed to convince 217 Republicans (and zero Democrats) to approve the bill. Many "yes" voters confessed they were in the dark regarding the impact of the measure but wanted "a win" that would show that the GOP majority could hold together on major legislation.[11]

The Senate, for its part, indicated it would begin from scratch in drafting its own version. There was no guarantee it could bridge its own internal divides.

In October 2016, then-candidate Trump had promised that fixing the health care system was "going to be so easy." But as President Trump collided with the realities of legislative policymaking, he changed his mind: "Nobody knew that health care could be so complicated."[12]

What do these three cases demonstrate? Finding solutions to major national problems requires Congress to act in concert with the president, but Congress is seldom a fully cooperative partner in shaping solutions, which sets the stage for the kind of dramatic confrontations detailed here. In recent years, the struggles have seemed never-ending. President Obama and congressional Republicans once again went to war over the budget in 2013, leading to a sixteen-day government shutdown that furloughed 800,000 federal employees. A range of confrontations continued throughout the remainder of Obama's term: over the Affordable Care Act; immigration policy; the Keystone XL oil pipeline and the broader question of environmental regulation; and a range of foreign policy crises in Europe (Ukraine), Asia, and the Middle East. As President Trump took office in 2017 after a divisive presidential campaign, Congress was immediately confronted with investigations over Russian involvement in the presidential campaign, as well as more standard but still contentious questions over Trump's Cabinet nominations, proposed budget, and wider legislative plans.

These confrontations require a larger context, and in this chapter we trace the development of the chief executive's legislative role in the twentieth century and analyze the constitutional relationship between the president and Congress. We then discuss the president's formal legislative powers and describe presidential strategies to influence legislation. Finally, we analyze what factors contribute to the success and failure of presidents in reaching their legislative goals.

Development of the President's Legislative Role

The Constitution, in Article 1, section 8, grants Congress seventeen powers that cover a wide range of subjects—for example, levying and collecting taxes, borrowing money, and regulating foreign and interstate commerce—as well as the power to choose the means to execute the enumerated powers. Clearly, the framers expected Congress, not the president, to have primary responsibility for formulating national policy and the president's legislative role to be secondary. Until the twentieth century, most presidents limited their involvement in the congressional process. Even Thomas Jefferson and Abraham Lincoln, the two most inclined to lead Congress, encountered strong opposition, and their activism did not alter the pattern of congressional supremacy.[13]

Theodore Roosevelt and Woodrow Wilson greatly expanded the presidency's legislative role early in the twentieth century as the national government responded to rapid industrialization and urbanization. Roosevelt worked closely with congressional leaders and sent several messages to Congress that outlined a legislative program. He saw it as the duty of the president to "take a very active interest in getting the right kind of legislation."[14] Wilson, who as a political science professor had argued that strong presidential leadership of Congress was needed for the nation to cope with its growing problems, took the lead in defining his program's goals, helped formulate bills, reinstated the practice abandoned by Jefferson of personally delivering the State of the Union message to Congress, used cabinet members to build congressional support for bills, and personally lobbied for some of his most important measures, such as the Federal Reserve Act and the Clayton Antitrust Act.[15] (See chapter 1.)

Franklin D. Roosevelt undertook the next major expansion of the president's legislative role. Taking office in 1933, with the economy mired in the Great Depression, FDR called Congress into a special session; during a one-hundred-day period the president proposed and Congress passed legislation to meet the economic crisis. Together they overhauled the banking system, authorized a program of industrial self-government under the National Recovery Administration, buttressed farm income with the Agricultural Adjustment Act, regulated financial markets under the Truth in Securities Act, and created the Tennessee Valley Authority, a program of comprehensive economic development for one of the nation's most depressed areas. This period of unprecedented activity established the media's practice of assessing a new president's first one hundred days.

During the remainder of his first term, FDR continued to develop measures to promote soil conservation and restrict excess agricultural production; guarantee labor the right to organize and bargain collectively; and establish a system of social insurance to protect people against the loss of work due to economic slowdowns, physical disability, or old age. FDR established the expectation that the president would be actively involved at all stages of the legislative process by submitting a program to Congress, working for its passage, and coordinating its implementation.

Today's presidents do just that: They send Congress messages that analyze problems and outline proposed solutions, assign aides to monitor the bills and lobby for passage, and ensure adherence to a common legislative program for the executive branch enforced through a central clearance process monitored by the Office of Management and Budget (OMB).[16] They threaten to veto legislation that fails to meet presidential demands or that they regard as unwise or contrary to their purposes. Harry S. Truman and Dwight D. Eisenhower institutionalized the president's legislative role by creating structures and processes to assist in carrying it out on a systematic basis with help from OMB's predecessor agency, the Bureau of the Budget (BOB), and the White House staff.[17]

By the mid-1960s, it appeared to some observers that the presidency dominated the legislative process. In 1965, Samuel P. Huntington wrote, "The congressional role in legislation has largely been reduced to delay and amendment." Tasks such as taking the initiative in formulating legislation, assigning legislative priorities, generating support for legislation, and determining final content had "shifted to the executive branch," which, in Huntington's view, had gained "at the expense of Congress."[18] Others argued that Congress remained vitally important to the process by constantly modifying and altering policy through appropriations, amendments, and renewals of statutory authorizations.[19]

But Congress and the president are not engaged in a zero-sum game in which the power of one decreases as the power of the other increases. Since 1933, Congress has increased its power by vastly expanding the subjects on which it legislates. During this same time, presidents also assumed greater responsibility as innovators of policy. In three brief periods of intense legislative activity—1933–1937, 1964–1966, and 1981—activist presidents (FDR, Lyndon Johnson, and Ronald Reagan) led responsive Congresses in the adoption of major changes in domestic policy. In foreign policy, Congress responded to presidential leadership in establishing the role of the United States in world affairs during and immediately after World War II.

At times Congress has reacted to what was viewed as excessive presidential power. During the 1970s, for example, Congress expanded its control over the executive branch through increased use of the legislative veto (see chapter 6), sought to curb presidential use of military force abroad with the War Powers Resolution (see chapter 10) and the Intelligence Oversight Act, and strengthened its ability to determine federal spending by redesigning the congressional budget process (see chapter 9).

All presidents since FDR, with the possible exception of Eisenhower, have aspired to lead Congress as a way to lead the nation. Some have succeeded temporarily; others have been totally unsuccessful. For example, in 1981, Reagan took command of bipartisan conservative congressional majorities, which passed his taxing and spending proposals and sharply altered the course of domestic social and economic policy the nation had followed since the 1930s.[20] But his period of dominance was short-lived; congressional critics of his policies regrouped in 1982, support among Senate Republicans sagged, and legislative concerns shifted as budget deficits soared to unprecedented levels. Reagan discovered, as had Roosevelt in 1937 and Johnson in 1967, that congressional approval of a president's program is not automatic. Congressional support must be cultivated and maintained and can disappear rapidly when conditions change. Reagan's immediate successor, George H. W. Bush, offered mostly modest initiatives, but he, too, could not develop sustained congressional support from a Democratic-controlled Congress. By contrast, congressional Democrats initially enacted much of Clinton's initial legislative agenda with only limited Republican help.[21] When Republicans won control of Congress in 1994, Clinton's agenda and strategies changed drastically.

Despite his much-publicized calls to reduce partisan conflict, George W. Bush on most fronts advanced a markedly conservative legislative agenda, reflecting Republican control of Congress. When Sen. Jim Jeffords of Vermont left the Republican Party, handing the Senate to the Democrats, the administration was forced to reexamine its tactics for winning congressional support. Bush's initial tax plan and education reform proposal scored early wins; after the 9/11 terrorist attacks strengthened the president's hand, Bush scored additional domestic successes. He successfully made the creation of a new Department of Homeland Security an issue in the 2002 midterm campaigns. But his legislative program scored fewer victories thereafter. Bush's top priority after being reelected in 2004 was to reform Social Security, an initiative that found no traction on Capitol Hill. After the Democrats' election victories during the midterm elections of 2006, Iraq moved to center stage and became the focus of congressional challenges to the president's authority as commander in chief.[22] House Republicans abandoned the president in the fall of 2008, when the administration proposed a $700 billion rescue package (termed a "bailout" by its critics) for the banking system. Congress reluctantly approved a hastily revised plan, but Bush was clearly devoid of political capital even in the face of the nation's most serious economic crisis since the Great Depression.

President Obama also found Congress skeptical of his economic plans. He secured passage of a massive economic stimulus bill in February 2009 without a single Republican vote in the House; three Republicans in the Senate—secured important concessions from the Democrats and helped the majority party fend off a threatened Republican filibuster. Obama was able to secure passage of his landmark health care reforms in 2010, but with nary a Republican vote. Efforts to strengthen environmental protection laws failed, however, and showdown votes over the fiscal year 2010 and 2011 budgets revealed just how divided Congress was over where to move next in the effort to bring the economy back to health. Obama sought to exert leadership, but Congress refused to be a passive partner.

Once Obama's Democrats lost control of the House in 2010, Republicans were able to thwart most of the administration's legislative program. On several must-pass measures, Speaker Boehner turned to Democrats' votes to offset opposition within his own party. As one observer noted, "evidence suggests that Obama was more effective when he was less visibly involved in negotiating and lobbying for legislation. Most Republicans in Congress reflexively opposed whatever Obama proposed."[23] In the face of that phenomenon, legislative leadership lay outside the Obama White House, primarily with Senate majority leader Harry Reid. Reid also effectively frustrated the Republican House's attempts at legislative activism, such as the repeal of Obamacare. But Reid lost both roles when Republicans regained control of the Senate after the November 2014 midterm elections. In the end the last *six* years of the Obama administration saw fewer laws passed than in the *two* years attacked by Harry Truman in 1948 as the "do-nothing Congress." In 2016 even a vacancy on the Supreme Court went unfilled, as the Republican majority rolled the dice on tying that obstruction to the outcome of that fall's election.

It was a successful gamble, and allowed Donald Trump's nomination of Neal Gorsuch to serve as his first clear legislative success (see Chapter 7). Trump also signed a number of congressionally generated resolutions rolling back regulations issued in the last year of the Obama administration. But on other fronts, as the brief account of the health care debate suggests, Trump and the congressional leadership found rougher going. Trump's first supplemental budget, which included funding to build the border wall he had promised during the campaign, conflicted with that promise's corollary: that Mexico would pay for it. Ultimately no money was provided for the wall in fiscal 2017.

Fiscal conservatives likewise balked at expensive infrastructure proposals and asked why the administration's first budget did not include cuts to entitlement programs like Medicare. Other legislators opposed the sharp cuts to local domestic programs that were included. A vague pledge to cut tax rates seemed to have a brighter future, but well into the spring no specific tax reform proposal had been drafted.

The Presidential-Congressional Relationship

Institutional competition between Congress and the presidency arises from the Constitution's separation of powers, but the Constitution also mandates a sharing of powers: Joint action is required to authorize programs, appropriate money to pay for them, and levy taxes to provide the funds. Neither branch can achieve its goals or operate the government without the other. Since the early 1970s, however, presidential-congressional relations have been highly competitive because of heightened distrust between the branches and intensified party differences between presidents and members of Congress. Charles O. Jones describes the relationship as one in which "these separated institutions often *compete* for shared powers."[24]

Competition by Design: The Separation of Powers

James Madison's *Federalist* No. 51 makes it clear that the framers had intended presidential-congressional conflict:

> To what expedient . . . shall we finally resort, for maintaining in practice the necessary partition of power among the several departments, as laid down in the constitution? The only answer that can be given is . . . by so contriving the interior structure of the government as its several constituent parts may, by their mutual relations, be the means of keeping each other in their proper places. . . .
>
> In order to lay a due foundation for that separate and distinct exercise of the different powers of the government, which to a certain extent is admitted on all hands to be essential to the preservation of liberty, it is evident that each department should have a will of its own. . . .
>
> But the great security against a gradual concentration of the several powers in the same department consists in giving to those who administer each department the necessary constitutional means and personal motives to resist the encroachments of the others. . . . Ambition must be made to counteract ambition. The interests of the man must be connected with the constitutional rights of the place.[25]

The pattern of presidential-congressional relations has not been static. Some analysts point to a cyclical pattern of power aggrandizement by Congress or the presidency and a resurgence by the other that has operated from the Republic's beginning.[26] In the nineteenth century, the institutional surges and declines oscillated evenly within well-defined boundaries, but U.S. economic, social, and technological transformations and emergence from international isolation during the twentieth century created conditions that more frequently called for executive, rather than legislative, leadership. The president can act more quickly, more decisively, and more consistently than Congress, which has difficulty ascertaining its institutional will and coherently pursuing its goals. Therefore, it can be argued that in the twentieth century, presidential surges have resulted in permanent expansions of executive power and presidential aggrandizements, such as Johnson's use of the war powers to involve the United States in the Vietnam War (see chapter 10), Nixon's sweeping claims of executive privilege and his frequent impoundments of appropriated funds (see chapter 6), and George W. Bush's broad claims of prerogative grounded in the president's role as commander in chief. Along these lines, Republicans complained bitterly about Obama's unilateral decisions to delay mandates in the Affordable Care Act, to stop deporting young illegal immigrants, to halt prosecution of low-level drug offenders, to support same-sex marriage, and to make recess appointments (see chapter 6). Republicans' complaints about Obama's actions echoed what Democrats had said about Nixon forty years earlier, an "'overreach by the administration to unilaterally decide which laws to enforce and which laws to ignore.'"[27]

During the 1970s, Congress reasserted its constitutional authority in several areas and launched internal reforms, which continued throughout the 1980s and 1990s, that enhanced its legislative power.[28] Yet the nation found it needed presidential leadership to deal with difficult problems such as severe inflation, persistent budget deficits, economic interdependence, and international terrorism. Divided government prevailed throughout most of this period, giving congressional leaders the opportunity to challenge the policies of presidents from the other party. For example, Republicans followed their victory in the 1994 midterm elections with a new collective assertiveness that threatened to undermine Clinton's leadership. Under Newt Gingrich, the aggressive, ideologically conservative Speaker, House Republicans took action within the first one hundred days of the new Congress on the ten priorities outlined in the Contract with America, an election manifesto most Republican candidates for the House had endorsed. Yet Gingrich could not restore congressional ascendancy, as Senate Republicans pursued more moderate priorities and Clinton developed effective defensive tactics.[29]

The conflict between Congress and the presidency is not driven by partisan divisions alone. Even with a Congress controlled by his own party, George W. Bush self-consciously sought to recover some of the ground his predecessors lost to assertive Congresses in the years following Watergate. Bush issued an executive order restricting access to past presidents' records. Vice President Cheney refused to submit information to the Congress' Government Accountability Office when it sought documents on the energy task force he chaired in 2001.[30] The administration limited testimony by White House staffers on various occasions, even on key matters like the administration's antiterrorism strategy or the investigation by the National Commission on Terrorist Attacks Upon the United States, usually called the 9–11 Commission. And the administration invoked **executive privilege**—denying information to Congress on the grounds that confidentiality is necessary to preserve the quality of advice the president receives—when it refused a House committee's request for documents related to a terminated Justice Department investigation.[31] Critics were so concerned about decisions to delay declassifying documents from past administrations and making it easier to classify current information that they concluded, "[T]his White House is obsessed with secrecy."[32] And despite early promises that "my Administration is committed to creating an unprecedented level of openness in Government," few observers felt Obama's White House had been particularly transparent either.[33]

Conflicts Based on Constituency and Electoral Differences

In addition to institutional competition born of the separation of powers, conflict stems from the difference in the constituencies of the members of Congress and the president. The 535 congressional members represent constituencies that vary in geographic area, population, economic structure, and social composition. Every member depends for reelection on distinctive, constituency-based political forces, making all members necessarily narrow-minded on at least some policy choices. Their perspective on the national interest is shaped by their constituency's interests and their own needs to work for reelection.

Congressional parties have the potential to overcome constituency-based fragmentation, but creating party unity is a struggle. Party leaders cannot command their members' votes. The Senate majority leader remains especially dependent on a stubbornly independent membership and the minority party's ability to use the filibuster to stall legislative action.[34] The national interest emerges in Congress through bargaining among members and blocs of members responsive to particular interests.

In contrast, presidents claim the entire nation as their constituency and can say they speak on behalf of the national interest or act for various inarticulate and unorganized interests not adequately represented in Congress. Presidents can resist the demands of well-organized particular interests by posing as champions of the national interest, even though there may be times when they, too, respond to such pressures.

From 1946 to 1972, presidents took advantage of intraparty divisions to forge temporary majority coalitions to pass specific measures with bipartisan support. Congressional policymaking was deliberate, often incremental or piecemeal, and largely reactive to presidential leadership. Congress could not maintain consistency in its actions in different policy areas or cohesiveness within those areas. Speed, efficiency, consistency, and cohesiveness usually were lacking, except in a crisis.

After Vietnam and Watergate, however, presidents had less success in playing the national interest card, and party cohesion in Congress rose dramatically with a majority of one party confronting a majority of the other.[35] In part, this change was a reflection of the realignment of the South into a heavily Republican region so that the *conservative coalition,* the traditional alliance of Republicans with conservative southern Democrats, declined.[36] Congressional moderates had also disappeared—"liberal Republicans" and "conservative Democrats" had vanished. In short, the parties became more internally homogeneous and more distinct, and distant, from each other. Today's party leaders thus define a policy agenda with a more distinctive ideological cast and are constantly gauging how votes are likely to affect the next round of congressional elections, seeking to protect their more exposed members from potential campaign attacks. Rather than reaching out to build bipartisan majorities, they rely on a "majority of the majority" to push legislation forward.

Changes in electoral politics have widened the gap between presidents and Congress. Members of Congress are political entrepreneurs who routinely seek reelection through constituency-based electoral coalitions largely independent of party labels. Incumbents have been remarkably successful: from 1964 to 2016, across twenty-seven elections, an average of 93 percent of the House incumbents and 82 percent of the Senate incumbents were reelected.[37] The supposed "change" election of 2016 returned to office 97 percent of House members and 87 percent of senators seeking reelection. Members are nominated in direct primaries, their campaigns are financed heavily from nonparty sources, and they sustain electoral support through activities unrelated to party, such as providing service to constituents. Unlike parliamentary executives whose electoral success is directly linked to their party colleagues, presidents gain election on their own and seem to have less and less impact on the success of their copartisans in Congress. Presidential coattails—congressional seats won by candidates of the president's party because of strong public support—have nearly disappeared, and there are fewer seats in which the presidential victor's margin of victory exceeds that of the congressional candidates.[38] In 2016 close to 90% of House Republicans ran ahead of Trump in their districts.[39] Indeed, Trump, like Clinton and Bush before him, entered office with *negative coattails:* their parties lost seats in Congress in the 1992, 2000, and 2016 elections respectively. By contrast, when Obama took office, Democrats had added twenty-one seats in the House and eight in the Senate (though Democratic gains were much smaller in 2012.).

At most, the presidential vote has exerted only a small influence on the congressional vote in recent elections, certainly less than partisanship or incumbency.[40] This separation of presidential and congressional electoral coalitions means presidents can exert little leverage on members of their own parties by appealing to their shared electoral fates, and the potential to influence members of the opposition party has declined as well.

Divided Party Control of Government

Recent presidents have confronted a major strategic dilemma. Under the best of conditions, when a president's party controls both houses of Congress, party loyalty is a weak link. Even this connection is not available to a president faced with a Congress controlled wholly or in part by the opposition party. Since 1933, Democratic presidents have had to deal with an opposition Congress in 1947–1948, 1995–2000, and 2011–2016, and Republican presidents even more often: in all years except 1953–1954, 1981–1986, 2001, 2003–2006, and 2017–18 (see Table 5-1).

TABLE 5-1 Partisan Control of the Presidency and Congress, 1933–2018

Dates	*Presidency*	*Congress*
1933–1946	Democratic	Democratic
1947–1948	Democratic	Republican
1949–1952	Democratic	Democratic
1953–1954	Republican	Republican
1955–1960	Republican	Democratic
1961–1968	Democratic	Democratic
1969–1976	Republican	Democratic
1977–1980	Democratic	Democratic
1981–1986	Republican	Republican (Senate) Democratic (House)
1987–1992	Republican	Democratic
1993–1994	Democratic	Democratic
1995–2000	Democratic	Republican
2001 (through 6/6)	Republican	Republican
2001 (after 6/6)[a]	Republican	Democratic (Senate) Republican (House)
2003–2006	Republican	Republican
2007–2008	Republican	Democratic
2009–2010	Democratic	Democratic
2011–2014	Democratic	Democratic (Senate) Republican (House)
2015–2016	Democratic	Republican
2017–2018	Republican	Republican

[a] One Republican senator officially changed his affiliation to Independent and caucused with the Democrats.

Analysts differ sharply in their assessments of the consequences of divided partisan control shown in Table 5-1. The critics of divided government argue that it renders unworkable the Constitution's already cumbersome and inefficient separation-of-powers structure.[41] Critics blame the large federal budget deficits of the late 1980s and 1990s on divided government that gave each branch a stake in the failure of the other.[42] These critics also charge that divided government undermines electoral accountability because it is impossible for voters to hold either party responsible for policies adopted and results achieved since the last election.

Other researchers draw different conclusions.[43] After a systematic empirical analysis of significant legislation and congressional investigations since World War II, David Mayhew concluded that it does not make "much difference whether party control of the American government happens to be unified or divided."[44] Morris Fiorina, acknowledging that divided government results in more "conflictual" presidential-congressional relations, suggests that its consequences are not "necessarily bad."[45] Divided government may limit the potential for social gain through public policy, but it also limits potential loss through government mistakes, and divided government is the American electorate's way of establishing the type of coalition governments common in multiparty systems.[46] Moreover, a growing number of citizens are concerned about an activist government, preferring instead one whose powers will recede, along the lines of Alexander Hamilton's argument in *Federalist* No. 73: "I consider every institution calculated to restrain the excess of lawmaking, and to keep things in the same state in which they happen to be at any given period, as much more likely to do good than harm."

Divided government is more of a problem when the parties' policy preferences are polarized and there is little prospect for bipartisan cooperation, though action is possible even under these circumstances if the party controlling Congress wields a supermajority that can override presidential vetoes.[47] In any case it is clear that divided government dominated presidential-congressional relations for most of the last quarter of the twentieth century and reemerged in the twenty-first century.

Despite efforts to overcome internal fragmentation and fashion more coherent policy, Congress finds it difficult to compete with the relative decisiveness, cohesion, and consistency of the presidency as a national policymaking institution. Congress's oft-mentioned weaknesses—loosely structured congressional parties, party leaders with limited power, the absence of party discipline in congressional voting, the competition among strong committees and subcommittees, and the ambitions of individual members to enhance their reelection chances and to advance to higher office—are fundamental to its institutional design.[48] The short-lived experiment with Congress-centered party government under Gingrich in 1995 is a case in point: Many party members, worried about reelection, defied party leadership and moved to the center in 1996. The majority-Republican Congresses of 2015–2018 were likewise unified mostly in name.

Even an internally fragmented Congress can be assertive, but its thrust is to negate or restrain, not direct, presidential action. At present, Congress values the function of "representation" over that of "lawmaking,"[49] which means it is responsive primarily to constituency interests and well-organized interest groups. It also means Congress is more comfortable with distributive policies and programs, which provide widespread benefits, than with redistributive policies, which change society's allocation of wealth and power. Ironically, presidents have assumed responsibility for exercising the lawmaking function that translates electoral mandates into policies with broad societal impact. But their rationalizing proposals are rarely welcome when viewed through legislators' more myopic lenses.

Patterns of Presidential-Congressional Policymaking

To make national policy, the president and Congress must resolve conflicts. Some analysts have identified patterns in this relationship, which vary according to issues, presidential leadership styles, and political context. Presidents tend to prevail in foreign and military policy—for example, Bush's success on Iraq—and on those issues to which they attach high priority, such as Johnson's Great Society program.[50] Congress usually dominates on domestic policy, as it did in the 1970s, when it passed major legislation on the environment, consumer protection, and occupational safety; it also dominates on public works. Stalemate, in which differences prevent policy from moving forward, characterized much of the energy legislation proposed by presidents in the 1970s (and 2000s), as well as proposals for reducing the federal budget deficit in the 1980s and again in the 2010s and reforming Social Security from the mid-1990s to the present day. As noted, the last six years of the Obama administration were marked by near-total stalemate on the legislative front.

Occasionally, a proposal may be stalemated for years and then move rapidly to passage as conditions change or a new president takes office. Proposals for national health insurance had languished in Congress since first advanced by President Truman in 1946. The political climate turned favorable for liberal social legislation in 1964 and 1965, after President Kennedy was assassinated. Responding to Johnson's forceful leadership, Congress enacted legislation authorizing national health insurance for the elderly (Medicare) and the poor (Medicaid). But renewed efforts to establish national health care under the leadership of Bill and Hillary Clinton collapsed in 1993–1994, leading to a series of more limited proposals over the next decade that extended care to children and, under Bush, added to Medicare a prescription drug benefit for senior citizens. Obama made health care the centerpiece of his first two years in office, taking advantage of a temporary sixty-vote Democratic Senate majority to win passage of legislation that promised to establish near-universal health care coverage for 95 percent of the U.S. population, up from 83 percent, and reduce the rate of growth in health care spending. No Republicans voted for the law, requiring last-minute concessions by the president to secure the critical votes of antiabortion Democrats. [51]

Presidential ambition and leadership style can be important causes of conflict. An activist president committed to an extensive legislative program, such as FDR or Lyndon Johnson, typically tries to dominate Congress, whereas a less activist president, such as Eisenhower, Gerald R. Ford, or George H. W. Bush may be more inclined to cooperate with Congress or accept considerable congressional initiative in program development. The competitive setting affects how forceful a president will be. Presidents in the final two decades of the twentieth century and the first two of the twenty-first confronted a significantly different strategic environment, one that curtailed their ambitions. Frequently facing divided government, they selectively facilitated pursuing items where crossover agreement was possible rather than pushing a large-scale agenda of their own. Reagan, Bush, and Clinton were also forced to use veto threats more frequently than their predecessors to trigger negotiations.[52]

Clinton, a moderate with an ambitious reform agenda, initially attempted to dominate Congress through the Democratic majority and its more liberal leaders.[53] After Republicans gained congressional majorities in 1995, Clinton positioned himself as the moderate force between liberal Democrats and conservative Republicans (the so-called "triangulation" strategy), which enabled him to make alliances with any legislative group. For example, Clinton and congressional Republicans fashioned a major reform of national welfare policies in 1996 that angered many Democrats. Yet the latter rallied to his defense during the impeachment controversy.

George W. Bush entered office with a more ambitious legislative agenda than expected, given his narrow electoral victory. On some matters, most notably education reform, he sought common ground with Democrats, but on most issues (developing a national energy strategy and environmental policies, cutting taxes, repositioning national defense), he relied on support from conservative Republicans and a few conservative to moderate Democrats.[54] Bush consistently depended on the cohesive House Republicans to deliver a conservative version of his legislation that would prevail in negotiations with the more moderate Senate.[55] Iraq proved to be a major weight on Bush's second term; continued American battlefield deaths and the apparent lack of progress lowered the president's public approval ratings and generated early discussions about his **lame-duck** status. Neither Social Security reform nor tax code simplification nor immigration reform, the major domestic legislative goals of the second term, gained support in Congress, and the Democratic majorities elected in November 2006 quickly asserted their own priorities.

Although Barack Obama initially made efforts to find common ground with Republicans, he soon learned that the only votes he could count on would come from Democrats. As a result, congressional Democrats' policy preferences were critical to the administration's considerable legislative successes in 2009–2010. After the Democrats suffered heavy midterm election losses in 2010, Republicans aligned with the Tea Party movement rejected all compromises with the president. Obama launched a "charm offensive" early in his second term hoping that personal meetings with a broader range of Republicans, not just the leaders, would reduce ideological conflict. But all of Washington knew that Obama, too, would soon enough become a lame duck—a fate confirmed in the midterm elections of 2014 when Democrats lost their Senate majority in what was widely perceived as a public rebuke of the president's performance. Suddenly the president lost the administration's principal tactical support on Capitol Hill. His hope that Republicans would now be forced to find common ground on critical matters like the budget was borne out during a lame-duck session of Congress in late 2014 when a budget deal funded almost all the federal government through September 2015. Little else passed, though, in that session of Congress or the next. Important exceptions were an extension of the National Security Agency's surveillance authorities under the 2001 PATRIOT Act, imposing some limits on its activities, and a renewal of presidential trade negotiation authority, both passed in June 2015.

Donald Trump's victory, along with continued (if diminished) Republican majorities on Capitol Hill, seemed likely to energize the GOP policy agenda. Trump was hardly a Washington insider, but as he said of the House Speaker and Senate majority leader, "Paul Ryan right now loves me, Mitch McConnell loves me, it's amazing how winning can change things."[56] Still, the nonideological Trump did not have a comprehensive agenda ready to present to Congress during his first "100 days." As we have seen, his adoption of Ryan's proposal to "repeal and replace" the Affordable Care Act was repudiated not just by Democrats but by divergent Republican factions in Congress as well.

Presidents have two sets of tools, used simultaneously, to accomplish legislative goals: (1) formal powers vested in the presidency by the Constitution and by statute, and (2) informal resources inherent in the office. In the next two sections, each is examined separately.

The President's Formal Legislative Powers

Article 2, section 3, of the Constitution authorizes the president to call Congress into special session; it also requires that he "from time to time give to the Congress information of the state of the Union, and recommend to their consideration such measures as he shall judge necessary and expedient." Article 1, section 7, makes presidents direct participants in the legislative process by providing that the president approve or disapprove (through the veto) "every bill" and "every order, resolution, or vote to which the concurrence of the Senate and House of Representatives may be necessary." These formal legislative powers are augmented by statutory delegations of authority to the president and to administrative agencies.

Messages to Congress and Agenda Setting

Although contemporary presidents have not gained much leverage by calling special congressional sessions, they have derived substantial power from their constitutional duty to report on the state of the nation and to recommend legislation. Since passage of the Budget and Accounting Act of 1921 and the Employment Act of 1946, Congress has required that presidents annually submit messages explaining and justifying their budgets and reporting on the economy's condition. The State of the Union address and these fiscal messages enable presidents to set the congressional agenda by assessing the nation's problems and laying before Congress a comprehensive legislative program reflecting the president's goals and priorities. The messages are also efforts to enlist public opinion behind those priorities. Now delivered during a prime-time, televised speech to both houses of Congress and members of the cabinet, the Supreme Court, and the Joint Chiefs of Staff as well as ambassadors from around the world, the modern State of the Union address is a far cry from the tedious reading of a lengthy written message by a congressional clerk, as occurred as late as Teddy Roosevelt's administration. Donald Trump's first address to Congress on February 28, 2017, attracted some 48 million television viewers while millions of others streamed the event online.

Individual members of Congress still introduce a multitude of bills independently of the president, but the chief executive is in a position to substantially influence, if not dominate, the congressional agenda. In a comprehensive review of how presidents helped set the congressional agenda from 1953 to 1996, George

C. Edwards and Andrew Barrett concluded that the president generates about one-third of "the total number of significant bills on the congressional agenda," ranging from a high of 68.6 percent under Kennedy in 1961–1963 to a low of 0 percent under Clinton in 1995–1996, and that "presidential initiatives are more likely than congressional initiatives to become law." Presidents' success rates were nearly twice as high under unified, rather than divided, government.[57] Additional research has demonstrated that presidents fashion their agendas to fit the constraints of party support in Congress and the budget, and that they respond to public concerns within the context of election cycles.[58]

Only infrequently does Congress seek to seize the agenda-setting power. During the George H. W. Bush administration, the Democratic majority advanced proposals in areas the president did not address, such as civil rights and immigration—sometimes hoping to force a veto that would serve as a campaign issue later. Even more dramatically, Speaker Gingrich did much the same for Republicans following their 1994 victory, when Clinton's 1995 State of the Union address provided few specific legislative proposals.[59] But these efforts to replace presidential leadership with an agenda generated by Congress proved difficult to sustain. Clinton reemerged to steer legislative action in 1996 by taking advantage of the unpopularity of Republican tactics that closed the government and by co-opting much of the Republicans' agenda as his own.[60] Thus, both recent efforts to wrest the agenda-making power from the president were short-lived. In fact, a study of policy agendas in four major issue areas over the period 1956–2005 confirmed that the president, not Congress, is the nation's principal agenda setter and that "the president's agenda is more likely to influence public priorities than to reflect them."[61] Presidents have a reserved slot in the news cycle, with the ability to focus the nation's—and thus Congress's—attention on the issues they choose to highlight.

The Veto Power

The Constitution establishes a major legislative role for presidents by requiring their approval of measures passed by Congress (Article 1, section 7, paragraph 2). Within ten days (Sundays excepted) after a bill or joint resolution is presented to the White House, the president must (1) sign it into law; (2) disapprove or veto it and return it to the house of Congress in which it originated along with a message explaining this action; or (3) take no action on it, in which case it becomes law without the president's signature at the end of ten days. If Congress adjourns within that ten-day period and the president does not sign a measure awaiting action, then it does not become law and the president has exercised a **pocket veto**.

The president's action is final because adjournment prevents a measure from being returned to Congress for reconsideration and a possible override.

The veto is the president's ultimate legislative weapon; it carries the weight of two-thirds of the members of each house because that is what is required to overturn a veto. In his classic treatise *Congressional Government,* Woodrow Wilson noted the importance of the veto even when Congress dominated the national government: "For in the exercise of his power of veto, which is, of course, beyond all comparison, his most formidable prerogative, the President acts not as the executive but as a third branch of the legislature."[62] Andrew Jackson adopted a broad interpretation of the veto power, one giving him the right to reject legislation on the basis of its wisdom, merit, or equity as well as on constitutional grounds.[63] Most presidents since have espoused this view of the veto and have used it often.

The data in Table 5-2 demonstrate a more extensive use of the veto by Roosevelt, Truman, and Eisenhower than by their successors. The data also show that from 1961 through 1994 Democratic presidents vetoed fewer bills than did the Republicans, mostly because Democrats controlled Congress throughout much of that time—the Senate from 1961 through 1980 and 1987 through 1994, and the House from 1961 through 1994. President Clinton exercised no vetoes during the 103rd Congress, controlled by his own party, "the first time since the 32nd Congress (1851–1852) and the administration of Millard Fillmore that an entire Congress served without prompting a presidential rejection."[64] George W. Bush accomplished the same feat when he served for five and a half years before casting his first veto in September 2006 against an embryonic stem cell research bill. His second veto was exercised on Iraq appropriations, as described at the beginning of this chapter, and others occurred as Democrats' priorities clashed with the president's.

The veto power affects policy negatively and positively. It is negative by nature; once used, it signifies an impasse between the president and Congress, and prior policy is unchanged. Sometimes presidents find the veto the best means of emphatically communicating their intentions to Congress even when it goes against the wishes of a large legislative majority. Many of Ford's and Reagan's vetoes, for example, were intended to signal their view that the liberal Democratic Congress was engaging in wasteful overspending. [65] The positive aspect of the veto lies in its use as a bargaining tool to "shape, alter, or deter legislation."[66] By threatening to exercise the veto, presidents can define the limits of their willingness to compromise. They can state in advance what they will and will not accept, hoping to coax concessions from Congress and thereby reduce the likelihood of a showdown over a bill or to

TABLE 5-2 Presidential Vetoes of Bills, 1933–2017

President	*Regular Vetoes*	*Pocket Vetoes*	*Total*	*Number of Vetoes Overridden*	*Percentage of Vetoes Overridden*
FDR (1933–1945)	372	263	635	9	1.4
Truman (1945–1953)	180	70	250	12	4.8
Eisenhower (1953–1961)	73	108	181	2	1.1
Kennedy (1961–1963)	12	9	21	0	0.0
Johnson (1963–1969)	16	14	30	0	0.0
Nixon (1969–1974)	26	17	43	7	16.3
Ford (1974–1977)	48	18	66	12	18.2
Carter (1977–1981)	13	18	31	2	6.5
Reagan (1981–1989)	39	39	78	9	11.5
G. H. W. Bush (1989–1993)[a]	29	15	44	1	2.3
Clinton (1993–2001)	36	1	37	2	5.3
G. W. Bush (2001–2009)	12	0	12	4	33.0
Obama (2009–2017)[a]	12	0	12	1	8.3
Trump (2017–)[b]	0	0	0	0	—

SOURCE: Office of the Clerk, U.S. House of Representatives—http://artandhistory.house.gov/house_history/vetoes.aspx.

[a] George H. W. Bush attempted to pocket veto two bills during intrasession recess periods. Congress considered the two bills enacted into law because of the president's failure to return the legislation. The bills are not counted as pocket vetoes in this table. Obama described five of his vetoes as pocket vetoes but returned the bills to Congress; they are counted as regular vetoes here.

[b] As of April 18, 2017.

"stimulate serious bargaining."[67] Long before he had issued a single veto, George W. Bush said that "the best tool I have besides persuasion is to veto"—that is, to use the veto as a bargaining tool.[68] Indeed, veto threats have become a major means for presidents to force opposition majorities to make policy concessions in the "high-intensity partisan environment" that has characterized Washington since the Reagan administration.[69] In 2011, Obama issued two veto threats during the intense battles with House Republicans over the budget and national debt ceiling, among many others issued during his administration.[70] The Statements of Administration Policy (SAPs) issued by OMB even calibrate the level of threat—from noting that "senior advisers would recommend" a veto to the flat statement that "if the President were presented with [this bill], he would veto it."[71]

Republican congressional leaders worked hard to avoid presenting George W. Bush with objectionable legislation that he might veto; and as noted earlier, even with one chamber in opposition hands, the Democratic Senate did the same for Obama through 2014.[72] But another explanation for the strikingly small number of vetoes issued in recent years is the expanded use of **presidential signing statements**, "pronouncements issued by the president at the time a congressional enactment is signed that . . . identify provisions of the legislation with which the president has concerns," stating the president's alternative constitutional interpretation, and often directing the administration on how it should implement (or not implement) the law.[73] The Constitution stipulates that vetoes must be accompanied by a statement of the president's objections, but there is no comparable requirement that he make a statement when he signs a bill into law. This practice began under James Monroe in the early nineteenth century but became more prominent after Reagan began using statements to articulate disagreements with Congress that could become part of the legislative history of a law should it come before a judge. Scholars have emphasized the **constitutional signing statements** that challenge legislative decisions and declare the president's intent not to enforce them. Signing statements might also be issued to resolve policy disagreements with Congress, essentially having the last word in an argument the president had lost during the legislative process. Thus, signing statements seek to "nullify, ignore or otherwise work around legal restrictions Congress places into a bill."[74] A case can be made that **rhetorical signing statements**, almost always oral rather than written, thanking legislative sponsors or highlighting policy gains, are also significant in helping presidents build support in Congress and reward allies.[75]

Bush greatly expanded the use of constitutional signing statements. He issued 161 such statements challenging nearly 1,200 provisions of law, a major assertion of presidential prerogative.[76] Some were particularly controversial—such as the claim that the administration would enforce a legislative rider barring the use of torture in the war with terror only "in a manner consistent with the constitutional authority of the president to supervise the unitary executive branch and as commander in chief."[77]

Some legal scholars alleged that this practice was tantamount to a **line item veto**, the power that some governors can exercise to strike down portions of a law with which they disagree rather than veto the entire bill.[78] (Presidents had this power only briefly, in 1997; in *Clinton v. City of New York* (1998), however, the Supreme Court struck down the federal statute that had provided presidents with a line item veto.) Others have argued, however, that Bush's statements were largely rhetorical, intended for public relations purposes, and were designed to change understandings of presidential power rather than negate particular legal provisions.[79] At the request of Congress, the Government Accountability Office conducted a close study of nineteen signing statements issued by Bush in 2006 and determined that nearly a third involved instances of the administration not carrying out provisions according to law. "In all those instances, presidential signing statements had asserted that congressional demands were encroaching on Bush's prerogatives to control executive branch employees as he sees fit and to receive effective services from his employees."[80]

Though he criticized the scope of Bush's practice during the 2008 campaign, Obama never disavowed the use of signing statements himself. He issued some forty-one such statements during his eight years in office.[81] While that was far fewer than Bush, those statements could be quite sweeping: Obama issued thirty constitutional challenges on just five bills during his first year in office, tying George H. W. Bush for the most first-year challenges issued by a president.[82] Over time, too, the administration began to rely more heavily on alternative avenues to register constitutional objections, opinions from internal lawyers within the Departments of Justice or State or via the Statements of Administration Policy noted earlier.[83] Further, one scholar charged the administration with seeking to "conceal and deceive" its use of signing statements, making it extraordinarily difficult for the public to learn about the president's actions. Although scholars disagree on just how dangerous presidential signing statements may be, most agree that the practice is a strategy used by modern presidents to assert their preferences in the ongoing struggle with Congress.

The President's Informal Legislative Influence

In 1960, Richard Neustadt startled students of the presidency when, in his much celebrated treatise *Presidential Power,* he asserted that the formal powers of the president amounted to little more than a clerkship. The Constitution, Neustadt argued, placed the president in a position of mostly providing services to other participants in national politics. "Presidential power," Neustadt declared, "is the power to persuade."[84] Yet Neustadt recognized that the office's formal powers gave presidents key leverage in exercising that persuasion, in converting clerkship into leadership. Recent scholarship has built on that point, demonstrating how presidents since Nixon, confronting increasingly obdurate congressional majorities, have found new ways to derive advantages from formal and implied constitutional authorities. Nonetheless, informal influence remains at the center of presidential relations with Congress. It is not enough for presidents to present a legislative program to Congress; they also must persuade congressional majorities to enact its components. This is true even if their efforts can be effective only "at the margins."[85]

To do so, they employ mostly informal methods of influence. These tools can be used to exert indirect and direct pressure. Presidents may engage in bargaining, arm-twisting, and confrontation as general modes of working with Congress.

Indirect Influence

Presidents attempt to influence Congress indirectly through appeals to the public and by enlisting interest group support—a bank shot, of sorts. A careful appeal, usually launched with a major public address, can generate pressure that encourages Congress to act. George Edwards's research has made it clear that, although the president and political observers may believe such efforts make success more likely, presidents can seldom unilaterally create the conditions for success on Capitol Hill. They are more likely to be facilitators than directors of change.[86] Presidents are more likely to use popular appeals successfully in a crisis that appears to require congressional action and where conditions favor presidential leadership. Success is less likely when public opinion is divided and substantial opposition to the president's position exists. In any case, presidents use such appeals selectively. Congress may object to the president's "going over its head" to the people too frequently because in doing so the president attacks, directly or by implication, the members' wisdom and motives.

George W. Bush used his first televised address to a joint session of Congress on February 27, 2001, to launch an aggressive, campaign-style strategy to win support for his major legislative proposals. The administration had already displayed impressive organization by focusing in successive weeks on education, religious faith-based charities, and tax cuts—critical elements of the Bush program. Moreover, it developed talking points for Republican members of Congress so that the party message would be in harmony.[87] Bush followed up by visiting states where he had run well in 2000 and where influential Democratic legislators were located—Arkansas, Florida, Georgia, Iowa, Louisiana, Nebraska, North Dakota, Pennsylvania, and South Dakota. The president clearly wanted supporters attending the rallies to contact their Washington representatives. As Bush's spokesman explained, "Every day, in every way, whether it's at the White House or it's in travel, the president looks at how to get his plan across to the voters so voters can get their message to the Senators and congressmen."[88] The result of this carefully choreographed effort was a major tax-cut victory. But when Bush tried to repeat this formula for success in 2005 with a much larger campaign to reform Social Security, the effort failed. After launching the campaign in his State of the Union address, Bush visited twenty-nine states in an effort to convince the public that Social Security faced a crisis and that his proposal for individual retirement accounts was the best solution.[89] Polls showed that the public believed a problem existed but not that the president's solution was best.[90] In fact, at the end of the sixty-day period, approval for how Bush was handling the issue had dropped from 41 percent to 29 percent.[91] Instead of agreeing to negotiate on details, the Democrats refused to discuss the issue—nor were Republicans much more enthusiastic about taking on this contentious issue—and by the end of 2005 it was gone from the White House agenda.[92]

Direct Influence

In their direct efforts to persuade Congress, presidents use two informal tools. They may grant or withhold services and amenities at their disposal as rewards for support or sanctions for lack of it, and they may become personally involved in the legislative process. Presidents vary greatly in their skills at exploiting these resources.

Favors. Bestowing or denying favors to members of Congress gives presidents a measure of leverage. Such favors may be given to an individual member or to important people in his or her constituency, or the favor may be of benefit to the constituency itself.[93] Favors given as rewards to congressional members include appointments with the president and other high-ranking officials; letters or telephone calls from the president expressing thanks for support; campaign assistance in the form of cash from the party's national committee, a presidential visit to the constituency, or a presidential endorsement; the opportunity to announce the award of federal grants to recipients in the constituency; invitations to be present at bill-signing ceremonies, to attend White House social functions, and to accompany the president on trips; and White House memorabilia such as pens and photographs. Favors for influential congressional constituents include appointments, appearances by administration officials at organization meetings, invitations to social functions, mailings on important occasions such as anniversaries, memorabilia, and VIP treatment such as White House mess privileges. To some extent, all members of Congress share in such benefits, but the president's supporters have readier access to them and feel more comfortable asking for them than do others.

The most important constituency-related rewards are jobs and projects. Congressional recommendations by members of the president's party greatly influence the selection of U.S. district court judges, U.S. attorneys, U.S. marshals, customs collectors for ports of entry, and a variety of lesser positions. Projects often regarded as rewards include military installations; research and administrative facilities; public works such as buildings, dams, and navigational improvements to rivers and harbors; government contracts with local firms; grants to local governments and educational institutions; and the deposit of federal funds in banks. Presidents cannot direct projects exclusively to their supporters, but they have a fair bit of discretion over what has been termed "presidential pork."[94] As some federal activities are reduced in size, eliminated, or turned over to state governments, their potential for use as bargaining chips declines. But enticing individual legislators to break with one's own party and support the opposite party's president has become far more difficult in recent decades. Parties have become more homogeneous, and forces outside Congress enforce ideological purity by monitoring loyalty, threatening to support a challenger in the next election cycle. As Bert Rockman notes, "deal cutting is effective only when ideological absolutes are less robust than they have become."[95]

Involvement in the Legislative Process. Presidents can help themselves by becoming personally involved in the legislative process, but doing so requires knowledge and skill that are products of their political background, experience, and leadership style. To turn participation in the process to an advantage, a president should have knowledge of Congress and the Washington community, a sense of timing, command of a bill's substantive details, a willingness to consult with congressional leaders and to give them notice in advance of major actions, sensitivity to the institutional prerogatives of Congress and to the personal and political needs of its members, and a balance between firmness and flexibility in resolving differences with Congress.

No president has ever possessed all of these skills. By most accounts, however, Lyndon Johnson exhibited more than any other modern president and made the most effective use of his involvement in the legislative process. He believed that constant, intense attention by presidents and their administrations was necessary to move their legislative programs through Congress.[96] His success in persuading Congress to enact the unfinished agenda of President Kennedy's New Frontier program and his own Great Society bills makes his approach to Congress a good example for study. It should be noted, however, that Johnson's legislative triumphs were aided in no small measure by contextual factors ripe for success. In the aftermath of the Kennedy assassination, public support for the New Frontier measures was high, and Johnson's landslide victory in the 1964 election also brought him large, liberal Democratic majorities in the House and the Senate.

Still, Johnson grounded his legislative strategy in intimate knowledge of Congress as an institution and of its most influential members.[97] He knew whom to approach on specific issues and how to do so. Johnson also placed considerable emphasis on proper timing, waiting to send bills to Congress until the moment seemed right for the maximum support and least opposition. He sent bills singly, rather than in a package, so that opposition would not develop automatically around several measures at once. "Congress," he told a key aide, "is a whiskey drinker. You can put an awful lot of whiskey into a man if you just let him sip it."[98]

In addition, Johnson took care to consult with important senators and representatives in formulating legislation. Before sending a bill to Congress, the president and his top aides would hold a briefing for congressional leaders to explain its features. Cabinet secretaries were made responsible for the success of legislation in their areas, and the White House coordinated their efforts. Finally, when crucial votes were approaching on Capitol Hill, Johnson made intense personal appeals to the members whose votes served as cues for others and to members who were identified as uncommitted or wavering. Johnson sought to build congressional coalitions in support of his proposals. Through an analysis of head counts, used by Johnson's congressional liaison office to track House members' positions on bills over time, Terry Sullivan found that the Johnson administration built coalitions not just by mobilizing friends, but even by "converting hard core opponents."[99] Other research has shown, however, how difficult it is for presidents to convert opponents on high-visibility votes to override a presidential veto. (Even Ford, facing huge Democratic majorities, was overridden on barely one of four vetoes.)[100]

When the Vietnam War changed the political context, Johnson's approach to congressional relations proved less effective. The president became increasingly involved in foreign policy matters, and the momentum of the Great Society gave way to the unpopularity of the war. The loss of forty-eight Democratic seats in the House in the 1966 midterm elections dramatically changed Johnson's tactical conditions and adversely affected his ability to push bills through Congress. Despite changes in the political environment, today's presidents might still benefit from emulating Johnson's approach: gain detailed knowledge of Congress, respect its constitutional prerogatives, remain sensitive to its members' personal and constituency needs, and create the organizational and political capacity to build coalitions.

Although President Clinton lacked Washington experience, he had a close and cooperative relationship with the Democratic leadership during the 103rd Congress.[101] His legislative achievements were substantial: his economic program, which included a major deficit reduction, family and medical leave legislation, reauthorization and revision of the Elementary and Secondary Education Act (ESEA), expansion of Head Start, "motor voter" legislation, national service legislation, the Brady gun control bill, a comprehensive anticrime bill, the North American Free Trade Agreement (NAFTA), and legislation extending and expanding the General Agreement on Tariffs and Trade (GATT). Much of this list consists of Democratic initiatives that had been blocked during twelve consecutive years of Republican presidents.[102] Clinton failed, however, to secure passage of bills to reform health care and welfare, largely his own, rather than broadly shared, initiatives. And his legislative productivity earned him no political benefit from the voters in 1994.[103] With Republicans in the majority of both chambers of Congress for the first time since 1953, Clinton's rate of success on floor votes went from above 85 percent in 1993 to a record low of 36.2 percent in 1995.[104] Clinton tacked back to the middle, "triangulating" against both Democrats and Republicans in Congress, eventually signing compromise legislation on welfare reform, tax reduction, and a balanced budget (which was achieved ahead of schedule in fiscal year 1998). But congenial relations with Congress were a distant memory by 1998 when, as discussed later, the House voted to impeach him. His overall experience demonstrates that presidential congeniality cannot compensate for philosophical differences, partisan divisions, and an assertive opposition. In fact, individual efforts, no matter how skillful, cannot overcome an unreceptive environment.

Bush and Congress. George W. Bush, a Washington outsider without legislative experience, campaigned on a clear, limited agenda led by his promise to cut taxes and reform education, the issues most emphasized during his first year in office. Despite its controversial size and specific provisions, Bush secured passage of a $1.3 trillion, multiyear tax cut in May 2001, having relied on unified Republican support in the House and a few moderate Democrats in the narrowly divided (50–50) Senate. After a longer but more bipartisan process, the bulk of Bush's education reforms also became law, in the form of the No Child Left Behind statute. By then, though, the atmospherics in Congress had changed yet again. The terrorist attacks of 9/11 ushered in a nearly unprecedented era of "hyper-bipartisanship," characterized by warm relations and regular meetings among all four party leaders and the president as well as near-unanimous votes on using force in Afghanistan, providing law enforcement officials with additional powers to combat terrorism (the USA PATRIOT Act of 2001), rebuilding New York City, and enhancing airport security.[105]

That degree of cooperation did not last long. Early in 2002, Bush and the Democrats locked horns over trade promotion authority allowing the president to negotiate trade agreements that will be moved through Congress quickly and without amendments. Bush ultimately won a dramatic 215–214 vote in the House.[106] The bigger battle, however, was over creation of a Department of Homeland Security (DHS), originally a Democratic proposal advanced in 2000 but embraced by the

Bush administration in the summer of 2002 (see chapter 6). The parties stalemated over a set of worker and union protections rejected by House Republicans and the president. Bush made this the signature issue for the fall campaign, when he launched an unprecedented effort on behalf of Republican candidates, contributing to victories that doubled the Republican advantage in the House to twelve votes and regained a Republican majority in the Senate. In the election aftermath, a lame-duck session of Congress approved the Bush version of a DHS.

Moving toward reelection in 2004, Bush's public approval rose, and the Republican Congress remained supportive, if sometimes restive.[107] Even the situation in Iraq looked brighter when the first democratic elections were held in January 2005. But then things seemed to fall apart for the administration. Buoyed by a successful reelection in which he secured a narrow but clear victory, Bush set forth to shape his legacy by modernizing Social Security—but as noted above, he was unable to sway even Republicans to debate the issue. Then Hurricane Katrina struck New Orleans and the Gulf coast, shifting public attention, triggering an enormous but unknown financial commitment for the federal government, and highlighting the administrative failures of FEMA (the Federal Emergency Management Agency).

Chip Somodevilla/Getty Images

President Trump—pictured here with (from left) his budget director, Mick Mulvaney, House majority leader Kevin McCarthy (R-CA), Senate majority leader Mitch McConnell (R-KY), and Speaker of the House Paul Ryan (R-WI)—was part of the first unified Republican government since 2006. But even so, the president was frequently frustrated with the pace and substance of congressional action.

Compounding the political damage, conservative Republicans forced the administration to withdraw the nomination of White House counsel Harriet Miers for a vacancy on the Supreme Court, and Lewis Libby, the vice president's chief of staff, was indicted on perjury charges stemming from the investigation into the leak of a CIA operative's name to the press.[108] The news from Iraq again turned gloomy, and the press revealed the operation of a warrantless eavesdropping program conducted by the National Security Agency, which was gathering data on Americans' phone conversations. The Republican-controlled Congress flexed its muscles, enhancing its oversight of the war on terror: Sen. John McCain, R-AZ, led a crusade to establish an antitorture policy toward enemy captives as a way to protect American military personnel who might also be captured, but the administration asserted the right to determine when the limits would be observed. Congress accomplished little for the rest of the year, and the arrival of Democratic majorities in 2007 created an even more assertive Congress.

Obama and Congress. Barack Obama was only the third senator to move directly from Capitol Hill to the White House, but his legislative experience was limited: four years in Washington (two of which were spent campaigning to become president) and eight years in Springfield, Illinois, as a rank-and-file member of the state Senate. Nonetheless, Obama entered the White House surrounded by aides with Capitol Hill experience—led by ex-Rep. Rahm Emanuel, his chief of staff—and made it a point during the transition to solicit input from his future allies in the House and the Senate.[109] Jointly, the Democratic Party's congressional leaders and the White House established a legislative strategy for the upcoming 111th Congress, prioritizing the proposals that would be set forth, and they worked together to implement those strategies. Rapid action was taken on a number of issues that had been vetoed by George W. Bush and on passage of a $787 billion economic stimulus package. It is fair to argue that, throughout Obama's first two years in office, his strongest legislative resources were the experienced teams of Democratic Party leaders in both the House and the Senate.[110]

Because Republicans spurned his repeated efforts to win their support, Obama ended up relying on Democrats to pass his proposals. His overall agenda was ambitious. The number of legislative proposals put forth by Obama rivaled the total number proposed by Lyndon Johnson in 1965 and 1966; similarly, Obama's success rate on these major proposals during his first two years in office was second only to Johnson's among postwar presidents.[111] His most significant accomplishments were health care reform, reform of the financial regulatory system (known as

Dodd-Frank after the committee chairs who squired the reform), the Strategic Arms Reduction Treaty (START), and the economic stimulus package passed during his first month in office. His principal disappointments were on legislation to address climate change by creating a "cap-and-trade" system and immigration reform.[112]

The administration's consistent strategy was to establish the basic features of legislation that the president hoped to see Congress adopt and then let the majority party fill in the details, not unlike George W. Bush's strategy from 2001 to 2006. When necessary, the administration would step in to assert its priorities or provide a boost through presidential rhetoric or personal bargaining.

During the 111th Congress, the House, tightly disciplined by Speaker Nancy Pelosi, D-CA, consistently produced the successful outcomes needed by the administration. But the Senate became the graveyard for several administration proposals. While for a time the Democrats controlled sixty votes, the total required to invoke cloture and secure a vote on their proposals, they lost one vote on January 20, 2010, when a by-election in Massachusetts to fill the seat vacated by Ted Kennedy's death returned a Republican and altered the strategic calculus.

Whatever bargaining occurred was aimed to corral wayward Democrats. Republicans were almost uniformly opposed to the president's proposals, and the Senate rules allowed them to frustrate majority-party action time and again. Despite early efforts to build bipartisan support for the president's initiatives, the Republicans were unwilling to play ball. As Edwards concludes after an exhaustive review of partisan support patterns, "rather than surmounting partisanship, Barack Obama was engulfed in it."[113] Edwards links this failure to multiple factors: Partisan polarization in Congress had reached a high point in the final two years of the Bush presidency, only to be surpassed during the first two years of Obama's; relatively few Republican legislators came from districts or states that had supported the president in the 2012 election, and thus faced little pressure to do so now; and the partisan Republican media was determined from the outset that Obama should fail and that any Republican guilty of helping him succeed should be punished.

Obama's strategy and tactics began to change in December 2010. In the just-concluded midterm elections, Republicans had gained sixty-three seats in the House, regaining the majority they lost in 2006; Democrats lost six seats in the Senate but still controlled fifty-three, retaining enough votes to block proposals coming from the House but not sixty, the total needed to take action on their own. In the changed landscape, Obama successfully negotiated a tax deal with Republicans and secured approval during the lame duck session of not just START but a repeal of the "Don't Ask, Don't Tell" policy governing military service and sexual orientation.

With Boehner as Speaker and Sen. Mitch McConnell, R-KY, wielding greater influence, Obama found himself negotiating with an assertive House Republican majority while reassuring liberal Democrats that he was not abandoning them. But in 2011, the failure to reach a "grand bargain" with Boehner on the budget left both sides feeling betrayed. Obama turned away from negotiation and began to argue that "we can't wait" for Congress to act on a range of issues, pledging unilateral action instead wherever feasible in the run-up to his 2012 reelection.

Any hopes the Obama administration might have had of accomplishing its goals through a legislative strategy during its remaining years in office were dashed by the congressional election results of 2012 and 2014. Democratic gains in 2012 were insufficient to win a filibuster-proof majority in the Senate or a House majority. In 2014, Democrats lost the Senate majority, too, when the Republicans picked up a net of seven seats, giving them fifty-four; at the same time, Republicans expanded their House majority considerably, winning 247 of the chamber's 435 seats. In the wake of these election results, Washington became consumed by the ongoing budget battles waged between, on one side, dedicated advocates of spending cuts and balanced budgets, and on the other, defenders of social safety net programs who called for all Americans, including the wealthy, to pay their fair share of the costs of government. In his 2014 State of the Union address, Obama reiterated his commitment to acting without Congress, and he pushed a wide range of initiatives through regulatory interpretation or executive action. In 2015, these actions faced opposition both in the courts and on Capitol Hill. Republican lawmakers voted repeatedly to roll back administration proposals ranging from an increased minimum wage to environmental regulations and inserted themselves into diplomatic initiatives in Iran and Cuba. But division between the chambers, and within the majority party, made concerted action difficult—and made it impossible to overcome a series of threatened presidential vetoes.

In June 2015, Washington politics reversed polarity. In seeking to regain the **trade promotion authority** Bush had won in 2002, Obama worked closely with House Republicans, usually implacable opponents, to seek passage of trade legislation, while liberal Democrats, the president's loyal allies for more than six years, adamantly opposed his efforts.[114] Obama sought to regain "fast track" authority to advance trade as a necessary step to gaining approval for the Trans-Pacific Partnership, a massive trade agreement between the United States and eleven Pacific trade partners, part of the administration's effort to counter China's growing influence in the region. ("Fast track" is so-called since it allows the president to negotiate trade agreements that Congress could consider only in an up-or-down vote without amendments or filibusters.) On the eve of critical votes, only 21 of 188 House

Democrats had declared support for the president's initiative. Organized labor, environmentalists, and progressive groups within the Democratic Party believed that the agreements would encourage businesses to export more U.S. jobs overseas and damage the environment. Despite dramatic efforts to win support delivered in person by the president first at Nationals Park in Washington, D.C., and then the next morning on Capitol Hill, Democrats voted overwhelmingly (302–126) against a key provision that would provide assistance to workers displaced by trade agreements. On a second proposal, actual renewal of the trade authority, the president won the vote narrowly (219–211) with twenty-four Democrats supporting him, but he needed to win on both proposals. In the aftermath, the Republican leadership worked with the White House to devise a new legislative strategy that would provide enough Democratic votes to ensure success for the two critical bills in each house. In a rare example of Republican support for the president, a centerpiece of Obama's second-term legacy gained passage with the support of only twenty-eight Democrats in the House and thirteen in the Senate.[115]

If that partisan crossover was barely repeated during the rest of the 114th Congress—the 2016 campaign was marked by attacks on the Trans-Pacific Partnership and free trade generally—Donald Trump would soon discover that unified government had its own perils. While Speaker Ryan had hoped to unify Republicans around his "Better Way" agenda, its focus on cutting entitlement spending clashed with Trump's promises on the campaign trail to preserve the Social Security and Medicare programs. Trump's expensive plans to build infrastructure and build a border wall likewise conflicted with traditional GOP deficit reduction ideals. All factions of the majority argued in favor of replacing Obamacare and reworking the tax code, but had very different and often contradictory ideas of how to go about reforming these complicated statutes.

Modes of Presidential-Congressional Relations

In their relations with Congress, presidents follow certain modes or patterns of behavior: bargaining, arm-twisting, and confrontation. Bargaining is the predominant mode, and occasionally the president bargains directly with members whose support is deemed essential to a bill's passage. In May 1981, for example, the Reagan administration agreed to revive a costly program to support the price of sugar in exchange for the votes of four Democratic representatives from Louisiana (where sugar is a major crop) on a comprehensive budget reduction bill.[116]

Presidents usually try to avoid such explicit bargains because they have limited resources for trading, and the desire among members for these resources is keen.

Moreover, Congress is so large and its power so decentralized that presidents cannot bargain extensively over most bills. In some instances, the president may be unable or unwilling to bargain. Fortunately, rather than a quid pro quo exchange of favors for votes, much presidential-congressional bargaining is implicit, generalized trading in which tacit exchanges of support and favors occur.

If bargaining does not result in the approval of their proposals, presidents may resort to stronger methods, such as arm-twisting, which involves intense, even extraordinary, pressure and threats. In one sense, it is an intensified extension of bargaining, but it entails something more—a direct threat of punishment if the member's opposition continues. Donald Trump's White House, for example, threatened to run primary election opponents against Republicans reluctant to support the 2017 health care bill. Among modern presidents, Lyndon Johnson was perhaps the most frequent practitioner of arm-twisting. When gentler efforts failed, or when a once-supportive member opposed him on an important issue, Johnson resorted to tactics such as deliberate embarrassment, threats, and reprisals. In contrast, Eisenhower was most reluctant to pressure Congress. Arm-twisting is understandably an unpopular tactic and, if used, often creates resentment and hostility. Still, judicious demonstration that sustained opposition or desertion by normal supporters will exact costs strengthens a president's bargaining position.

Presidents unable to gain support through bargaining and arm-twisting may adopt a confrontational strategy. Confrontation might consist of appeals to the public, direct challenges to congressional authority, assertion of presidential prerogative, or similar tactics. Nixon confronted Congress often and more sharply than any other modern president. Disdaining the role of legislative coalition builder, he saw himself as deserving congressional support by virtue of his election mandate and his constitutional position as chief executive. The most visible confrontation occurred between 1971 and 1973, when he challenged congressional spending decisions at variance with his budget proposals by impounding more than $30 billion that Congress had appropriated. Nixon also claimed Congress could not question thousands of executive branch officials or have access to routine documentary information.

A strategy of confrontation is unlikely to result in sustained congressional responsiveness to presidential initiatives. Congress has constitutional prerogatives and constituency bases of support that enable it to resist presidential domination. The imperatives for cooperation between the two branches are so great that most presidents try to avoid such confrontations, entering them only when the presidency's constitutional integrity is at issue.

To oversee this system of bargaining, negotiation, and occasional confrontation, Eisenhower established the White House Office of Legislative Affairs, staffed by knowledgeable specialists who lobbied legislators in behalf of the administration's program. Every administration since has maintained such a unit. Although some administrations have made subtle changes in assignments and techniques, the activities have become largely institutionalized, reflecting a clear set of expectations about how staffers will conduct the job. With such a staff in place, there is continuity in legislative-executive relations and a reduction in the variation resulting from presidents' individual abilities and skills.[117]

Explaining Presidents' Legislative Success

If all presidents approach Congress with the same formal powers and informal tools of influence and use well-established staff arrangements to oversee day-to-day relations, what accounts for their legislative successes or failures? Studies have identified at least six factors that affect presidents' ability to achieve their legislative goals: (1) partisan and ideological support in Congress, (2) popular support, (3) style in dealing with Congress, (4) the contexts in which they must operate, (5) cyclical trends in presidential-congressional relations, and (6) the content of their domestic program. It is not possible to assess the relative importance of each factor thoroughly, but all have come into play since 1933, when FDR inaugurated the modern legislative presidency. The first five factors are examined here; the sixth, in chapter 8.

Congressional Support

Support in Congress depends heavily on the size and cohesiveness of a president's party strength there: This is the "gold standard" of presidents' legislative success.[118] Over time, Democratic and Republican presidents alike have consistently received strong support on roll call votes from their own parties' congressional members, and that support has only grown in recent years. From 1953 through 1980, presidents received support 66 percent of the time from fellow partisans in the House and the Senate, but that level rose to 75 percent from 1981 through 1996.[119]

More recent statistics are perhaps even more striking. The average level of support of House Republicans for George W. Bush was close to 90 percent until tailing off late in his term, but the parallel score for House Democrats hovered around 30 percent through 2006 and then plunged below 10 percent in 2007 and 20 percent in 2008. Yet in 2009, the two trend lines reversed themselves—Democratic support for the president went to 90 percent, and Republican support to 30 percent or less, moving below 10 percent by 2016. What caused the dramatic switch, of course, was one simple factor: the change in the party of the president.[120] Keep in mind, though, that support may vary by issue. Historically, Republican presidents have received stronger support overall on foreign policy legislation than on domestic policy issues, primarily because of increased backing from liberal Democrats on foreign issues.[121] Higher overall Senate support reflects some—though hardly complete—deference to the president on confirmation votes for executive branch nominees.

Partisan support for presidents in Congress apparently owes little to the storied effect of presidential coattails. The ability of presidents to transfer their electoral appeal to congressional candidates of their parties declined steadily from 1948 to 1988.[122] Even in 1984, when Reagan won a landslide victory, the measurable coattail effect was weak, albeit stronger than in 1980 and 1988.[123] Edwards attributes the decline to increased split-ticket voting, the reduced competitiveness of House seats, and the electoral success of incumbents since 1952.

FIGURE 5-1 Legislative Support Scores for the President: Average by Party and Chamber, 2001–2016

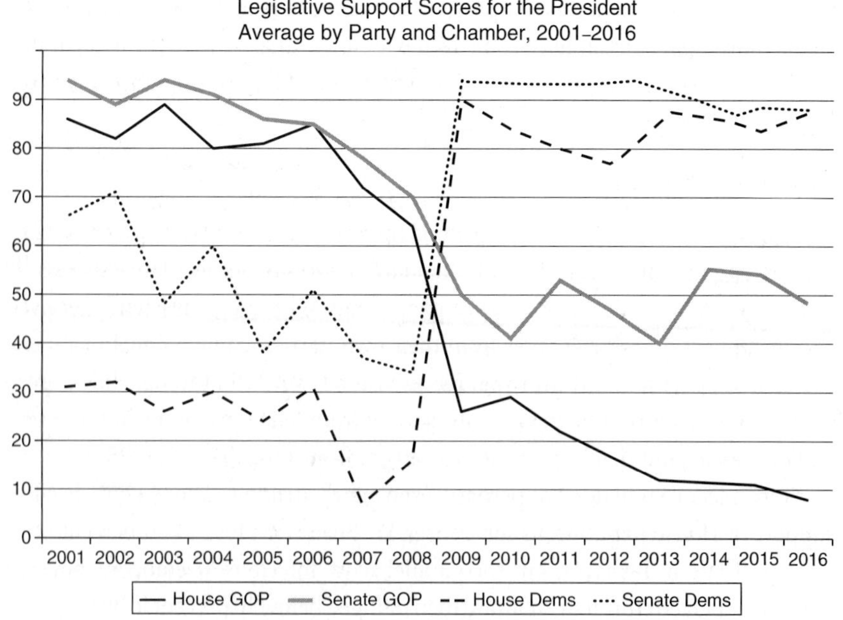

SOURCE: Calculated by Andrew Rudalevige from data in CQ almanacs.

Despite the shorter coattails in presidential election years, some presidents have sought to improve their chances of success by campaigning for candidates from their own party during midterm elections. Such efforts are usually unsuccessful, but as noted above, in 2002 George W. Bush demonstrated that it can be done. Bush sought to transfer his own relatively high public approval to Republican candidates by personalizing the election. By doing so, he could claim partial credit for bucking the historical trend in which members of the president's party lose seats in the midterm election, a trend violated over the past century only in 1934 and 1998.[124] The same was not true in 2006. Bush's approval rating had plunged, and Republican candidates were more anxious to distance themselves from the president than to receive an endorsement. Despite their efforts, they lost seats and control of Congress—as did Democrats in 2010 and 2014, seeking to escape blame for the Obama agenda. Matthew Dickinson argues that in recent years House elections have become more national in nature, but with the effect of reinforcing divided government in midterm years.[125]

Despite polarizing trends, presidents can rarely rely on full support from their own party members; thus, they must build coalitions by obtaining support from some opposition members.[126] Coalition building is of course especially important when the opposition controls one or both chambers of Congress—the situation for most presidents since 1969. Several factors other than party membership influence congressional voting decisions, including constituency pressures, state and regional loyalty, ideological orientations, and interest group influence.[127] On many occasions, presidents have received crucial support from the opposition. Eisenhower successfully sought Democratic votes on foreign policy matters; Republicans contributed sizable pluralities to the enactment of civil rights legislation in the 1960s; conservative Democrats, mainly from the South, often supported the domestic policy proposals of Nixon and Ford; conservative Democrats in the House were essential to Reagan's 1981 legislative victories; Clinton depended on Republican support for the passage of NAFTA and GATT; and George W. Bush received critical support from Democrats on his tax reduction and education reform proposals. Obama's economic stimulus package passed the Senate only after he made concessions to three Republican members, which secured their votes. Despite continuing instances when presidents assemble bipartisan coalitions to achieve legislative goals, evidence indicates that the opportunity to build bipartisan coalitions has declined sharply as polarization has risen since the mid-1990s. That heightened unity among partisans in Congress, along with internal congressional reforms, have made the president's task of winning in Congress much more difficult.[128]

In summary, congressional support for the president is built primarily on fellow partisans, but party affiliation by itself is seldom a sufficient basis for the enactment of the president's program. When constituency, regional, and ideological pressures reduce the number of partisan backers, the president must try to attract support from opposition members by appealing to these same pressures. A president's legislative success is, therefore, "mainly a function of the partisan and ideological makeup of Congress."[129]

Popular Support

The prestige, or popular support, of presidents also affects congressional responses to their policies. It has been widely observed that a popular president enjoys substantial leeway in dealing with Congress, and a president whose popularity is low or falling is likely to encounter considerable resistance. Bond and Fleisher argue, however, that popular support is related only marginally to presidential success on congressional floor votes.[130] Similarly, Edwards finds that public approval is a background resource that provides presidents with leverage but not control over Congress.[131]

Although popularity is clearly, if marginally, related to congressional support for the president's legislative program and can be used as a tool of influence, it cannot be easily manipulated. There are factors, such as the erosion of popular support over time and the economy's condition, over which the president has no control.[132] Presidents can take advantage of their popularity when it is high to influence congressional opinion, as Johnson did in 1964 and 1965 and Reagan did in 1981 and, to a lesser extent, in 1985 and 1986 to drive tax reform forward (his popularity then plummeted because of the Iran-contra affair). George W. Bush sought to draw upon his strong approval ratings in this way in 2003 but with mixed success: He had to retreat on the size and content of his tax-cut proposals and lost on the issue of oil drilling in Alaska's Arctic National Wildlife Refuge. Obama called upon the public to communicate their frustration to Congress during the 2011 showdown over the debt ceiling, but it was not clear that the appeal made any difference. Trump entered office with historically low approval ratings and found it difficult to attract those not already in his base to pressure legislators on behalf of his agenda.

Presidential Style and Legislative Skills

The president's style in dealing with Congress has long been considered an important determinant of legislative success. Style encompasses the degree to which presidents are accessible to members; their interactions with, and sensitivity to, the members; and the extent of their involvement in the legislative process.[133]

Modern presidents have varied greatly in their accessibility. Johnson and Ford were usually available to members and leaders, whereas Nixon was remote most of the time. Kennedy and Reagan frequently sought contact through telephone calls. George H. W. Bush maintained a wide range of congressional friends and acquaintances but was criticized for not consulting enough with influential party and committee leaders. During his first two years in office, Clinton was so accessible and made such efforts to cultivate personal relationships that his effectiveness may have been impaired.[134] That accessibility lessened when he was working with an assertive Republican majority and with Democrats who distanced themselves from a president they regarded as a political liability. George W. Bush met with a broad cross section of representatives and senators during his first months in office—more than ninety members in his first week, including many Democrats.[135] In those early days, Bush tried to set a nonconfrontational tone in the nation's capital, and his relations with Democratic leaders improved markedly for several months after 9/11. Obama began his presidency by consulting broadly with Democrats and Republicans in fashioning his economic proposals, going so far as to meet with the House Republican membership on Capitol Hill just one week after his swearing in. Over time, though, especially after the budget and debt ceiling negotiations of 2011 and 2013, he grew less interested in personal outreach to members of Congress. Although accessibility on demand is not feasible because of the pressures on a president's time, it enhances congressional support if members know they can reach the president on matters of great importance to them. Accessibility to congressional leaders of both parties is particularly important if the president is to work effectively with Congress.

It is not clear how much interpersonal relations influence congressional support, but they are a distinctive part of a chief executive's style and affect the disposition of leaders and members toward the president. If nothing else, popularity with members of Congress can improve relations even when there are sharp differences over issues. If the president has strained personal relations, sustained congressional support will be difficult to achieve even when the president's party has a majority and many members share his goals.

Similarly, presidential involvement in the legislative process varies. Kennedy, Johnson, Ford, and Reagan maintained close interest in the course of legislation, and Johnson actively directed its progress on occasion. At least on health care, Trump sought to close the deal with personal calls and meetings with recalcitrant legislators. In contrast, Eisenhower, Nixon, and Carter were more detached. George H. W. Bush displayed a varied pattern of interest in the progress of legislation, ranging from detachment to active engagement, as during the 1991 budget negotiations. Clinton developed a reputation for making concessions so early in negotiations that he drew criticism for making it "too easy" for his opponents.[136] George W. Bush delegated most of these decisions to the experts in his administration, relying more heavily on his vice president's advice and assistance than did most of his predecessors. Unlike most vice presidents, Dick Cheney had an office on both the Senate and the House sides of the Capitol building. Cheney attended weekly Republican policy meetings in the House and the Senate and regularly made himself available to listen to congressional concerns. Vice President Joe Biden was the Obama administration's point person on congressional negotiations until they reached the final stage of discussion.

Obama's own bargaining skills became an issue in late 2010 and 2011. The president engaged in a series of face-to-face budget negotiations with Republican leaders beginning in December 2010 and extending through spring and summer 2011, resulting in three major budget deals. Fellow Democrats feared that Obama would follow Clinton's lead from 1995 and 1996 and seek middle ground between conservative and liberal positions on policy issues.[137] In their view, Obama—hoping to serve as conciliator—gave up too much ground too soon in the discussions, agreeing to search for spending cuts in prized social programs. As Sen. Bernie Sanders, I-VT, was quoted as saying, "One side is enormously aggressive in pushing an agenda, and the other is saying, 'Let's all get along.'"[138] Vice President Biden convened many of the initial budget meetings, and Reid, the Senate majority leader, played an important role in finding common ground with his Republican counterpart, but only the president could seal the deal with Boehner and McConnell, his Republican opponents. Obama did not want to shut down the government, as Clinton had done. Thus, he avoided pushing the Republicans to take that action in April 2011, despite pressure to do so from liberal Democrats. Nor did he want to see the nation default on its obligations in August 2011. He sought to consistently be the "adult" in exchanges that sometimes became childishly shrill, a role more likely to win support from conflict-weary Independent voters and to reassure nervous investors around the world. This approach held true in October 2013, too, when the government did shut down over a Republican effort to defund the Affordable Care Act, to poor public reviews. But overall Obama was not seen as enormously engaged in relations with Congress, perhaps because he felt it would not do much to promote his legislative agenda.

Indeed, while conventional wisdom holds that presidents' legislative skills are major determinants of congressional support for their programs, empirical analyses provide little support for that argument. According to Edwards and others, presidential legislative skills are effective at the margins of congressional coalition building, not at the core.[139] Presenting a somewhat different argument, Mark Peterson states that presidents have some, but not unlimited, control over the timing, priorities, and size of their programs. By clearly establishing their priorities and adjusting their "ambitions to fit the opportunities of the day," he concludes, presidents can be perceived as successful leaders of Congress.[140] Some observers believed that Obama overestimated his ability to win congressional support for his ambitious first-year proposals. But by 2012, he told *Time* magazine

> [T]he truth is, actually, when it comes to Congress, the issue is not personal relationships. . . . In terms of Congress, the reason we're not getting enough done right now is because you've got a Congress that is deeply ideological. . . . John Boehner and I get along fine. We had a great time playing golf together. That's not the issue. The problem was that no matter how much golf we played or no matter how much we yukked it up, he had trouble getting his caucus to go along.[141]

Contextual Factors

Most students of presidential-congressional relations agree that contextual factors over which the president has virtually no control—such as the structure of political institutions and processes, public opinion, the alignment of political and social forces, economic and social conditions, and long-term trends in the political system—are more important than individual legislative skills as determinants of congressional decisions. For example, the cultural context of American politics is a source of frustration for presidents attempting to influence Congress. Edwards posits that phenomena such as extremely high and often contradictory public expectations of presidential performance, individualism, and skepticism of authority are powerful constraints on presidential leadership.[142] Bond and Fleisher argue that Congress-centered variables, such as the partisan and ideological predispositions of members and leaders, determined by the outcome of the last election, are of greater importance than presidency-centered variables in explaining presidential influence in Congress.[143]

Taking a middle position, Peterson provides the most comprehensive and extensive analysis of contextual factors affecting presidential success in Congress. He identifies four contexts that shape congressional action on presidential programs: (1) the "pure context," which includes the "institutional properties" of Congress, political parties, and interest groups and over which the president has little influence and no control; (2) the "malleable context," which consists of "dynamic" political conditions resulting from electoral cycles and economic conditions and over which the president has "greater but unpredictable influence" and no control; (3) the "policy context"—a context the president can influence and to some extent control by making "strategic choices" in developing an agenda—which includes the consequence of various proposals for the political system, the relative importance of proposals for presidential policy goals, and the controversy associated with those proposals; and (4) the "individual context," which includes personal attributes, such as style and skills, and the choices the president makes concerning the organization of the presidency for the exercise of influence that distinguish the president and the administration.[144]

However one defines and classifies the contexts that affect the president's influence or success in Congress, it is important to recognize that they function to provide both constraints upon and opportunities for the exercise of presidential leadership. To a considerable extent, the president can do little to alter most of these contexts. What a president can do is take maximum advantage of the opportunities they present. In doing so, the chief executive can act as a facilitator who encourages change but not as a director who determines it.

Cyclical Trends

Long-term cyclical fluctuations in presidential and congressional power also appear to affect the fate of specific presidential programs. In 1933, FDR initiated a period of presidential ascendancy that lasted until Nixon and the Watergate scandal. During that time, Congress made extensive delegations of power to the president and to executive branch agencies, presidents assumed responsibility for legislative leadership, Congress acquiesced in presidential domination of foreign and military policy, and the public looked to the presidency more than to Congress to solve the nation's problems.[145] The president and Congress clashed often during that period, but the dominant trend was one of presidential aggrandizement. When conflict occurred, Congress usually took defensive stands against presidential assertiveness.[146]

Angered over the conduct of the war in Southeast Asia and President Nixon's claims of budget impoundment powers and executive privilege, starting in 1973 Congress moved to reassert its constitutional prerogatives. Seizing the opportunity afforded by Nixon's preoccupation with Watergate and the plunge in public support, Congress enacted the War Powers Resolution of 1973, the Budget and Impoundment Control Act of 1974, the National Emergencies Act of 1976, and the Ethics in Government Act of 1978, major elements in a resurgence designed to restrain presidential power.[147] In July 1974, the House Judiciary Committee approved three impeachment charges against Nixon, who resigned on August 9 before the House could act on them. His two immediate successors, Ford and Carter, had to deal with a Congress intent on curbing presidential power and retaining the constitutional parity with the president it had at least partially regained. This period of congressional resurgence was marked by increased skepticism of claims for presidential prerogatives, careful scrutiny of presidential proposals and oversight of policy implementation, demands for more extensive White House consultation with congressional leaders, and more exacting senatorial confirmation hearings on presidential appointments.

With Reagan, Congress was more willing to accept presidential policy leadership and less assertive in insisting on its institutional prerogatives. The presidential-congressional relationship did not, however, return to the one that prevailed under the "imperial presidency."[148] (See chapter 1.) Reagan's relationship with Congress bent but did not break in 1987, following Democratic successes in the 1986 congressional elections and public disenchantment with his detached leadership, which the Iran-contra affair revealed as overly reliant on the delegation of presidential authority.

Presidents George H. W. Bush and Clinton had stormy relationships with Congress over the budget. In fall 1990, Bush became embroiled in a battle with members from both parties over the deficit in the 1991 budget. In October, a coalition of very liberal Democratic and very conservative Republican House members rejected a bipartisan plan negotiated by the administration and congressional leaders. Amid bitter exchanges within both parties, a compromise was reached. But even as that battle ended, a new one began, as Bush argued with Congress over whether legislative approval was needed to initiate military action against Iraq in the wake of its invasion of Kuwait. Although the administration never admitted it needed authorization, it did—successfully—request one.

Clinton's struggle was far more bitter and protracted. His battle with Congress over the 1996 budget escalated to new extremes with two government shutdowns that kept hundreds of thousands of government workers at home for several weeks. The remainder of 1996 proved to be a temporary, election-year truce that provided new grist for postelection congressional investigations of Clinton-Gore fund-raising abuses.

Conflict between the Congress and President Clinton escalated to new heights in 1998 and 1999 with the impeachment effort—one of only two times in history that the full House sought to remove a president from office. On December 19, 1998, the

House approved two articles of impeachment against Bill Clinton. By a 228–206 vote, the House accused the president of lying under oath while giving testimony to a grand jury in August 1999 and, by a 221–212 vote, accused him of obstructing justice by hiding his improper relationship with a White House intern. These votes came at the end of a lengthy investigation by independent counsel Kenneth Starr.[149] In a court deposition responding to a civil suit brought by a former Arkansas state employee that alleged sexual harassment, Clinton had denied having a relationship with former White House intern Monica Lewinsky. Clinton subsequently misrepresented that relationship to the public as well as a grand jury, setting the ground for a constitutional confrontation.

Starr subpoenaed Clinton, who on August 17, 1998, became the first sitting president to testify before a grand jury. In September, the independent counsel filed a report with Congress (which released it, replete with salacious details, to the public) that formed the basis for the House Judiciary Committee's recommendation, in a straight party vote, that the House conduct an impeachment inquiry. Throughout this saga, the meaning of "high crimes and misdemeanors," the constitutional grounds for removing a president, remained a central question. Advocates of removal believed that Clinton had undermined the "rule of law" enforced by the courts; defenders of the president believed that personal misconduct did not constitute a threat to the Republic.[150] As political scientist Peri Arnold noted, "Clinton turned the struggle into a question of whether a president who was performing well should be removed for actions unconnected to his official duties."[151]

The Senate began the impeachment trial on January 7, 1999. Although the members of the House deputed to manage the trial were distressed that Republicans in the Senate seemed less committed to removal than they were, Majority Leader Trent Lott, R-MS, realized how difficult it would be to generate the two-thirds majority needed for removal when the Democrats held forty-five seats. Test votes showed nowhere near enough support for conviction. When the House managers wanted a long list of witnesses to publicly testify to the president's immoral behavior, the Senate instead approved a short list of witnesses who were deposed in private, and their videotaped testimony was available only to Senate members.[152] In the end, neither article of impeachment received a majority vote on February 12, when the Senate concluded its consideration. The president survived, though impeachment will always help define his place in history.

Early in his presidency, George W. Bush's principal problem was with his own party's moderates. After announcing his intention to pursue an inclusive approach to working with Congress, one that would rest on cooperation with Democrats, Bush increasingly relied on a strong conservative base in the House to achieve his goals, and Republican moderates felt excluded. Many members of Congress came to believe that Bush was seeking to assert executive prerogatives at the expense of congressional powers. The administration's repeated refusals to share information even with the Republican-controlled Congress, to allow White House staff to testify before Congress, or to accept congressional limits in the conduct of the war on terror became a concern to Capitol Hill Democrats and Republicans alike. In fact, three Republican senators—John McCain of Arizona, Lindsey Graham of South Carolina, and John Warner of Virginia—challenged the administration over its use of torture in dealing with detainees. During a hearing of the Personnel Subcommittee of the Senate Armed Services Committee conducted in 2005, a Defense Department lawyer was unable to respond to questions about Congress's power to legislate regarding combatants during time of war. As Jack Rakove points out, "It defies belief, not to say political common sense, to send a senior lawyer to a serious congressional hearing, to confess that the only part of the Constitution with which he is familiar is Article 2," the one that deals with presidential power.[153] But the error was symbolic: The executive was unconcerned with Congress's authority and intent on asserting its own. For many observers of Washington politics, Bush represented a new incarnation of the imperial presidency that had been so closely associated with Presidents Johnson and Nixon.[154]

Obama aspired to bring a new spirit of bipartisanship to Washington, encouraging some to describe his goal as becoming a "post-partisan" president. But he was unable to overcome the polarization that had already set in between the parties. By the time Obama assumed office in 2009, both parties had become more ideologically uniform—another way of saying that there were fewer moderates in either party likely to cross party lines and support the proposals of the other. Consequently, party unity votes became more frequent—a majority of one party's members opposing a majority of the other party's members. Moreover, the expectations on Capitol Hill had changed. Whereas it had been accepted for most of the half-century from 1950 onward that members of Congress could vote their conscience and follow their constituency's interests, pressures had grown for the out-party (the one not controlling the White House) to oppose the program of the in-party. Thus, John E. Owens notes that Obama had to contend with both "ideological polarization" and "the contemporary confrontational ethos."[155] The result was disappointment of his many early efforts to win bipartisan support for initiatives. No Republicans in either chamber voted for the final version of health care reform, nor for financial regulatory reform, and only a handful for the stimulus package. As early as the evening of Obama's inauguration in 2009, Republican party leaders and campaign strategists calculated that their party's candidates would benefit most from putting the full burden of authorship on the Democrats, and the Democrats' congressional party leaders spent most of their time negotiating with members of their own party to ensure that the necessary votes would be there when needed.[156]

The "shellacking," as Obama called it, that Democrats received in the midterm elections of 2010 seemed to support that calculation. While Obama himself remained personally popular through the end of his term, that popularity did not translate to other Democrats, who lost significant ground after 2009 not only in Congress but also in state legislatures and governorships. In 2016, Donald Trump's surprise victory rested on major departures from Republican policy orthodoxy—on spending, trade, foreign policy, and social programs—complicating efforts to present a united legislative front. At least early on, most communications aimed across the aisle were in the form of insulting tweets (Trump, for instance, called Senate Minority Leader Chuck Schumer, D-NY, a "clown" who shed "fake tears.") Democrats, for their part, argued that the lesson of the Obama years was that partisan obstructionism was an effective method of achieving electoral success. It was a lesson their angry base voters fervently urged them to apply.

Conclusion: Legislating Together

The experiences of recent presidents in their relations with Congress provide a few lessons. These presidents found success far from automatic. Success requires consultation before and during legislative consideration and a willingness to negotiate and bargain with Congress. Legislative proposals must be coordinated between the White House and the executive departments and agencies. More important, cooperation between the president and congressional leaders and between the institutional presidency and Congress is essential. The framers of the Constitution created separate branches that could not function separately; rather, they must exercise their shared powers jointly.[157]

Yet if the constitutional separation of powers requires cooperation, it ensures conflict. The framers sought to prevent tyranny by establishing a balance between executive and legislative power. But this relationship is continually in flux. First one branch has expanded its authority; then the other branch has reasserted its prerogatives, recaptured lost powers, and acquired new ones. The cycle of institutional aggrandizement, decline, and resurgence reflects certain strengths and weaknesses in the presidency and Congress and the respective abilities of the branches to respond to social forces, economic conditions, and political change.

The need for presidential-congressional cooperation is clear, but there are few ways of obtaining it other than through consultation involving persuasion and bargaining. Presidents cannot command congressional approval of their proposals any more than Congress can direct presidents in the exercise of their own constitutional powers. The threat of government stalemate is always present, and more often than not policy is an unsatisfactory compromise of presidential and various congressional viewpoints.

Suggested Readings

Bond, Jon R., and Richard Fleisher., eds. *Polarized Politics: Congress and the President in a Partisan Era.* Washington, DC: CQ Press, 2000.

Cameron, Charles. *Veto Bargaining.* New York: Cambridge University Press, 2000.

Conley, Richard S. *The Presidency, Congress, and Divided Government.* College Station: Texas A&M University, 2003.

Dickinson, Matthew J. "President and Congress," in Michael Nelson, ed., *The Presidency and the Political System,* 10th ed. Washington, DC: Sage/CQ Press, 2013.

Edwards, George C., III. *On Deaf Ears: The Limits of the Bully Pulpit.* New Haven, CT: Yale University Press, 2006.

———. *Predicting the Presidency: The Potential of Persuasive Leadership.* Princeton, NJ: Princeton University Press, 2016.

Fiorina, Morris. *Divided Government,* 2nd ed. Boston: Allyn and Bacon, 1996.

Fisher, Louis. *Constitutional Conflicts between Congress and the President,* 6th ed. Lawrence: University Press of Kansas, 2014.

Jacobson, Gary C. *A Divider, Not a Uniter: George W. Bush and the American People.* New York: Longman, 2006.

Jones, Charles O. *Separate but Equal Branches: Congress and the Presidency,* 2nd ed. Chatham, NJ: Chatham House, 2000.

———. *The Presidency in a Separated System,* 2nd ed. Washington, DC: Brookings Institution Press, 2005.

Mayhew, David R. *Divided We Govern: Party Control, Lawmaking, and Investigations, 1946–2002,* 2nd ed. New Haven, CT: Yale University Press, 2005.

Mycoff, Jason, D., and Joseph A. Pika. *Confrontation and Compromise: Presidential and Congressional Leadership, 2001–2006.* Lanham, MD: Rowman and Littlefield, 2007.

Peterson, Mark A. *Legislating Together: The White House and Capitol Hill from Eisenhower to Reagan.* Cambridge, MA: Harvard University Press, 1990.

Rudalevige, Andrew. "The Executive Branch and the Legislative Process," in Joel Aberbach and Mark A. Peterson, eds., *The Executive Branch.* New York: Oxford University Press, 2005.

———. *The New Imperial Presidency: Renewing Presidential Power after Watergate.* Ann Arbor: University of Michigan Press, 2006.

Shull, Steven A., ed. *The Two Presidencies: A Quarter-Century Assessment.* Chicago: Nelson-Hall, 1991.

Spitzer, Robert J. *President and Congress: Executive Harmony at the Crossroads of American Government.* New York: McGraw-Hill, 1993.

Sundquist, James L. *The Decline and Resurgence of Congress.* Washington, DC: Brookings, 1981.

Thurber, James A. and Jordan Tama, eds. *Rivals for Power: Presidential-Congressional Relations,* 6th ed. Lanham, MD: Rowman and Littlefield, 2017.

Wayne, Stephen J. *The Legislative Presidency.* New York: Harper and Row, 1978.

Notes

1. David Nather, "Waging War on the Surge," *CQ Weekly Online,* January 15, 2007, 170–177, http://library.cqpress.com/cqweekly/weeklyreport110-000002428775.

2. Liriel Higa, "A Withdrawal-Free Supplemental," *CQ Weekly Online,* May 28, 2007, 1598–1600, http://library.cqpress.com/cqweekly/weeklyreport110-000002520622; Richard Cohen, "Congressional Chronicle—The Fog of War," *National Journal,* June 2, 2007; and Brian Friel, "Congress-Temperatures Rising on Iraq," *National Journal,* June 9, 2007.

3. Quoted in David Herszenhorn, "Reid's Chilly Relationship with Bush Enters Deep Freeze," *New York Times,* December 19, 2007.

4. Naftali Bendavid and Carol E. Lee, "Leaders Agree on Debt Deal," *Wall Street Journal,* August 1, 2011.

5. Fred Barbash and Richard E. Cohen, "Summer of Strife," *CQ Weekly,* August 8, 2011, 1736–1739.

6. *The Economist,* "No Thanks to Anyone," August 6, 2011.

7. Robert Costa and Amy Goldstein, "Trump Vows 'Insurance for Everybody' in Obamacare Replacement Plan," *Washington Post* (January 15, 2017), https://www.washingtonpost.com/politics/trump-vows-insurance-for-everybody-in-obamacare-replacement-plan/2017/01/15/5f2b1e18-db5d-11e6-ad42-f3375f271c9c_story.html?utm_term=.a95d2b476c98.

8. See the Trump quotes on Obamacare collected at the "On the Issues" website: http://www.ontheissues.org/2016/Donald_Trump_Health_Care.htm, as well as a collection of 68 Trump promises to repeal the law at https://thinkprogress.org/trump-promised-to-repeal-obamacare-many-times-ab9500dad31e.

9. Costa and Goldstein, "Trump Vows 'Insurance for Everybody' in Obamacare Replacement Plan."

10. Quoted in Thomas Pear, Thomas Kaplan, and Maggie Haberman, "In Major Defeat for Trump, Push to Repeal Health Law Fails," *New York Times* (March 24, 2017), https://www.nytimes.com/2017/03/24/us/politics/health-care-affordable-care-act.html?_r=0.

11. Josh Dawsey, "Republicans Really Don't Like the Health Care Bill They Just Passed," *Politico,* May 4, 2017, http://www.politico.com/story/2017/05/04/obamacare-repeal-bill-republicans-do-not-like-237982 ; Rachael Bade and Josh Dawsey, "'The White House Just Couldn't Let This Go': The Inside Story of How Trump and the Republicans Got Obamacare Repeal through the House," *Politico,* May 5, 2017, http://www.politico.com/story/2017/05/05/donald-trump-obamacare-repeal-timeline-238016.

12. Philip Bump, "It's True Trump Didn't Pledge Obamacare Repeal in 64 Days. He Pledged It in One." *Washington Post,* March 24, 2017, https://www.washingtonpost.com/news/politics/wp/2017/

03/24/its-true-trump-didnt-pledge-obamacare-repeal-in-64-days-he-pledged-it-in-one/?utm_term=.4d262a2e1bb0; Madeline Conway, "Trump: 'Nobody Knew That Health Care Could Be So Complicated,'" *Politico,* February 27, 2017, http://www.politico.com/story/2017/02/trump-nobody-knew-that-health-care-could-be-so-complicated-235436

13. Stephen J. Wayne, *The Legislative Presidency* (New York: Harper and Row, 1978), 8–12.

14. Theodore Roosevelt, *Autobiography* (New York: Macmillan, 1913), 292.

15. Woodrow Wilson, *Constitutional Government in the United States* (1908; repr., New York: Columbia University Press, 1961).

16. Richard E. Neustadt, "The Presidency and Legislation: The Growth of Central Clearance," *American Political Science Review* (September 1954): 641–670.

17. Richard E. Neustadt, "The Presidency and Legislation: Planning the President's Program," *American Political Science Review* (December 1955): 980–1018; Wayne, *The Legislative Presidency;* Larry Berman, *The Office of Management and Budget and the Presidency* (Princeton, NJ: Princeton University Press, 1979); and Paul Light, *The President's Agenda,* 3rd ed. (Baltimore, MD: Johns Hopkins University Press, 1998).

18. Samuel P. Huntington, "Congressional Responses to the Twentieth Century," in *The Congress and America's Future,* ed. David B. Truman (Englewood Cliffs, NJ: Prentice Hall, 1965), 23.

19. Ronald C. Moe and Steven C. Teel, "Congress as Policy-Maker: A Necessary Reappraisal," *Political Science Quarterly* (Fall 1970): 443–470; John R. Johannes, *Policy Innovation in Congress* (Morristown, NJ: General Learning Press, 1972); and Gary Orfield, *Congressional Power: Congress and Social Change* (New York: Harcourt Brace Jovanovich, 1975).

20. In the Senate, the Republicans had a 53–47 majority. In the House, the 192 Republicans, who voted together on the major elements of Reagan's economic legislation in a remarkable display of cohesion, were joined by a sizable bloc of conservative southern Democrats called the "Boll Weevils." In both chambers, Republicans and conservative Democrats maintained voting cohesion that enabled the majorities to enact the Reagan program.

21. For example, Clinton's budget proposals in 1993 passed by a single vote in both the House and the Senate without any support from Republicans. Barbara Sinclair, "Trying to Govern Positively in a Negative Era," in *The Clinton Presidency: First Appraisals,* ed. Colin Campbell and Bert A. Rockman (Chatham, NJ: Chatham House, 1996), 121. Also see Barbara Sinclair, "The President as Legislative Leader," in *The Clinton Legacy,* ed. Colin Campbell and Bert A. Rockman (Chatham, NJ: Chatham House, 2000), 72–83.

22. On Bush's relations with Congress, see Jason D. Mycoff and Joseph A. Pika, *Confrontation and Compromise: Presidential and Congressional Leadership, 2001–2006* (Lanham, MD: Rowman and Littlefield, 2007).

23. Emily Ethridge, "2013 Vote Studies: Presidential Support," *CQ Weekly,* February 3, 2014, 170–176, http://library.cqpress.com/cqweekly/weeklyreport113–000004417431. On the polarizing power of presidential proposals more broadly, see Frances Lee, *Beyond Ideology: Politics, Principles, and Partisanship in the U.S. Senate* (Chicago: University of Chicago Press, 2009).

24. Charles O. Jones, *The Presidency in a Separated System* (Washington, DC: Brookings, 1994), 16.

25. Alexander Hamilton, John Jay, and James Madison, *The Federalist Papers* (New York: Modern Library, 1938), 335–337.

26. Lawrence C. Dodd, "Congress and the Quest for Power," in *Congress Reconsidered,* ed. Lawrence C. Dodd and Bruce I. Oppenheimer (New York: Praeger, 1977), 298–302.

27. Sen. Charles Grassley, R-IA, as quoted in John Gramlich, "Precedence and a President," *CQ Weekly,* November 18, 2013, 1938–1944, http://library.cqpress.com/cqweekly/weeklyreport113-000004379565.

28. James L. Sundquist, *The Decline and Resurgence of Congress* (Washington, DC: Brookings, 1981); and Richard S. Conley, *The Presidency, Congress, and Divided Government: A Postwar Assessment* (College Station: Texas A&M University Press, 2003), 20, 24–26.

29. David S. Cloud, "Republicans Pushing the Envelope with Confrontational Approach," *Congressional Quarterly Weekly Report,* August 5, 1995, 2331–2334.

30. In December 2002, a federal district court decision denied that the GAO had standing to force release of the disputed documents, but a district judge ruled in favor of releasing information sought by the Sierra Club and Judicial Watch, a public interest group. When the Bush administration refused to comply, the Supreme Court reviewed the case and returned it to the federal appeals court. That court ruled on May 10, 2005, that the federal open meetings law did not apply to the activities of nongovernment participants in policymaking discussions unless they were voting members of an advisory committee or in position to veto committee recommendations. In short, the administration's position was upheld. News Release, *Judicial Watch,* May 10, 2005, www.judicialwatch.org/5309.shtml. See the appeals court decision at http://caselaw.lp.findlaw.com/data2/circs/dc/025354b.pdf.

31. Joel D. Aberbach, "The State of the Contemporary American Presidency: Or, Is Bush II Actually Ronald Reagan's Heir?" in *The George W. Bush Presidency: First Appraisals,* ed. Colin Campbell and Bert A. Rockman (Chatham, NJ: Chatham House, 2003), chap. 11.

32. "Secrecy: The Bush Byword," editorial, *New York Times,* March 28, 2003, www.nytimes.com/2003/03/28/opinion/secrecy-the-bush-byword.html?scp=4&sq=March+28%2C+2003+editorial& st=nyt.

33. Barack Obama, "Memorandum for the Heads of Executive Departments and Agencies, RE: Transparency and Open Government" (January 2009), https://www.whitehouse.gov/the-press-office/transparency-and-open-government.

34. However, frustration with the rampant use of the filibuster resulted in the (Democratic) Senate majority eliminating its use for most nominations in 2013, and the (Republican) majority eliminating it for Supreme Court nominations in 2017.

35. Conley, *The Presidency, Congress, and Divided Government,* 22.

36. In 2014, the last Senate Democrats serving in the Deep South were defeated: Kay Hagan (NC), Mary Landrieu (LA), and Mark Pryor (AR). After the election, no Democratic senator or governor remained from the Carolinas to Texas.

37. Calculated by authors based on data from Center for Responsive Politics, https://www.opensecrets.org/bigpicture/reelect.php. See also Paul R. Abramson, John H. Aldrich, Brad T. Gomez, and David W. Rohde, *Change and Continuity in the 2012 Elections* (Washington, DC: CQ Press, 2015), 241–245.

38. Conley, *The Presidency, Congress, and Divided Government,* 14–19.

39. Trump ran ahead of 12.6% (27 of 216) Republican incumbents seeking reelection. He ran behind about 2/3 of Republican congressional candidates overall, including those facing Democratic incumbents. See Philip Bump, "If the Kansas Shift Happened Nationally," *Washington Post* (April 12, 2017), https://www.washingtonpost.com/news/politics/wp/2017/04/12/if-the-kansas-shift-happened-nationally-democrats-would-have-a-stranglehold-on-the-house/?tid=sm_fb&utm_term=.fa6bef6b1085

40. Abramson, Aldrich, and Rohde, *Change and Continuity,* 263.

41. Among the classic criticisms of divided government, see James L. Sundquist, "Needed: A Political Theory for the New Era of Coalition Government in the United States," *Political Science Quarterly* (Winter 1988–1989): 613–635; Lloyd N. Cutler, "To Form a Government," *Foreign Affairs* 59 (Fall 1980): 126–143; Cutler, "Now Is the Time for All Good Men," *William and Mary Law Review* 30 (Fall 1989): 387–402; and Michael L. Mezey, *Congress, the President, and Public Policy* (Boulder, CO: Westview, 1989).

42. Gary W. Cox and Samuel Kernell, "Conclusion," in *The Politics of Divided Government,* ed. Gary W. Cox and Samuel Kernell (Boulder, CO: Westview, 1991), 242–243. Also see Mathew D. McCubbins,

"Government on Lay-Away: Federal Spending and Deficits under Divided Party Control," in Cox and Kernell, *The Politics of Divided Government,* 113–153.

43. For a good review of the findings and the theoretical roots of this debate, see John J. Coleman, "Unified Government, Divided Government, and Party Responsiveness," *American Political Science Review* 93 (December 1999): 821–835.

44. David R. Mayhew, *Divided We Govern: Party Control, Lawmaking, and Investigations, 1946–1990* (New Haven, CT: Yale University Press, 1991), 198. The 2005 edition covers 1946–2002.

45. Morris Fiorina, *Divided Government,* 2nd ed. (Boston: Allyn and Bacon, 1996), 107, 108.

46. Ibid., 110; chap 7.

47. David R. Jones, "Party Polarization and Legislative Gridlock," *Political Research Quarterly* 54 (March 2001): 125–141.

48. For a systematic analysis of the institutional roots of congressional parochialism, see William Howell and Terry Moe, *Relic* (New York: Basic Books, 2016).

49. Roger H. Davidson, Walter J. Oleszek, and Francis E. Lee, *Congress and Its Members,* 11th ed. (Washington, DC: CQ Press, 2007), chap. 1.

50. The main components of the Great Society were the Economic Opportunity Act of 1964, which launched a "war on poverty"; the Civil Rights Act of 1964; the Voting Rights Act of 1965; the Elementary and Secondary Education Act of 1965 (ESEA); and the Social Security Act Amendments of 1965, which created Medicare and Medicaid.

51. Karen Tumulty, "Making History: House Passes Health Care Reform," *Time,* March 23, 2010.

52. Conley, *The Presidency, Congress, and Divided Government,* 44–45.

53. This discussion follows Sinclair, "Trying to Govern Positively," 91–119.

54. Juliet Eilperin, "Bush to Woo Democratic Rank-and-File," *Washington Post,* January 22, 2001, A1; and Barbara Sinclair, "Bipartisan Governing: Possible, Yes; Likely, No," *PS: Political Science and Politics* 34 (March 2001): 81–83.

55. Barbara Sinclair, "Living (and Dying?) by the Sword: George W. Bush as Legislative Leader," in *The George W. Bush Legacy,* ed. Colin Campbell, Bert A. Rockman, and Andrew Rudalevige (Washington, DC: CQ Press, 2008), 164–187.

56. "Donald Trump's *New York Times* Interview: Full Transcript," *New York Times,* November 23, 2016, http://www.nytimes.com/2016/11/23/us/politics/trump-new-york-times-interview-transcript.html

57. George C. Edwards III and Andrew Barrett, "Presidential Agenda Setting in Congress," in *Polarized Politics: Congress and the President in a Partisan Era,* ed. Jon R. Bond and Richard Fleisher (Washington, DC: CQ Press, 2000), 120, 122, 127.

58. Matthew Eshbaugh-Soha, "The Politics of Presidential Agendas," *Political Research Quarterly* 58 (June 2005): 257–268; and Jeff Yates and Andrew Whitford, "Institutional Foundations of the President's Issue Agenda," *Political Research Quarterly* 58 (December 2005): 577–585.

59. David S. Cloud, "Lack of New Proposals Reflects New Dynamic on the Hill," *Congressional Quarterly Weekly Report,* January 28, 1995, 259–260; and Donna Cassata, "Swift Progress of 'Contract' Inspires Awe and Concern," *Congressional Quarterly Weekly Report,* April 1, 1995, 909–912.

60. Carroll J. Doherty, "Clinton's Big Comeback Shown in Vote Score," *Congressional Quarterly Weekly Report,* December 21, 1996, 3427–3428.

61. Heather A. Larsen-Price and Paul Rutledge, "Follow the Leader: Issue-Dependent Representation in American Political Institutions," *Congress & the Presidency* 40:1 (2013): 20.

62. Woodrow Wilson, *Congressional Government* (1885; repr., New York: Meridian, 1956), 53.

63. Joseph E. Kallenbach, *The American Chief Executive* (New York: Harper and Row, 1966), 354.

64. Mark A. Peterson, "The President and Congress," in *The Presidency and the Political System,* 6th ed., ed. Michael Nelson (Washington, DC: CQ Press, 2000), 476.

65. Richard S. Conley and Amie Kreppel, "Toward a New Typology of Vetoes and Overrides," *Political Research Quarterly* 54 (December 2001): 845.

66. Robert J. Spitzer, *The Presidential Veto: Touchstone of the American Presidency* (Albany: State University of New York Press, 1988), 100–103.

67. Janet Hook, "Avalanche of Veto Threats Divides Bush, Congress," *Congressional Quarterly Weekly Report,* September 22, 1990, 2991. Hook cites an OMB spokeswoman as stating that the Bush administration had issued 120 veto threats since January 1989.

68. Quoted in Rudalevige, "Executive Branch and Legislative Process," 441.

69. Barbara Sinclair, "Hostile Partners: The President, Congress, and Lawmaking in the Partisan 1990s," in Bond and Fleisher, *Polarized Politics,* 144. For a rational-choice analysis of these interactions, see Charles M. Cameron, *Veto Bargaining: Presidents and the Politics of Negative Power* (New York: Cambridge University Press, 2000).

70. John McCormack, "Two Obama Veto 'Threats': Compare and Contrast," *The Weekly Standard,* July 26, 2011.

71. SAPs from the current administration are available at https://www.whitehouse.gov/omb/legislative_sap_default.

72. Sinclair, "Living (and Dying?) by the Sword," 180.

73. Phillip J. Cooper, "George W. Bush, Edgar Allan Poe, and the Use and Abuse of Presidential Signing Statements," *Presidential Studies Quarterly* 35 (September 2005): 516–517.

74. Jeffrey Crouch, Mark J. Rozell, Michael A. Sollenberger, "The Law: President Obama's Signing Statements and the Expansion of Executive Power," *Presidential Studies Quarterly* 43:4 (December 2013): 889.

75. Christopher S. Kelley, Brian W. Marshall, and Deanna J. Watts, "Assessing the Rhetorical Side of Presidential Signing Statements," *Presidential Studies Quarterly* 43:2 (June 2013): 274–298.

76. T. J. Halstead, "Presidential Signing Statements: Constitutional and Institutional Implications," Congressional Research Service, September 20, 2006, updated April 13, 2007, www.coherentbabble.com/signingstatements/CRS/CRS-RL33667-4-07.pdf. Halstead's count is somewhat different from that of Christopher Kelley, who has catalogued the statements and the challenged provisions at www.coherentbabble.com/signingstatements/FAQs.htm#1.%20%20What%20are%20presidential%20signing%20statements. Halstead counted 161 and Kelley 172.

77. Elisabeth Bumiller, "For President, Final Say on a Bill Sometimes Comes after the Signing," *New York Times,* January 16, 2006.

78. Ibid. Popular concern about the practice grew after an article was published in the *Boston Globe.* Charlie Savage, "Bush Challenges Hundreds of Laws; President Cites Powers of His Office," *Boston Globe,* April 30, 2006, www.boston.com/news/nation/articles/2006/04/30/bush_challenges_hundreds_of_laws.

79. Curtis A. Bradley and Eric A. Posner, "Presidential Signing Statements and Executive Power," *Constitutional Commentary* 23 (Winter 2006): 307–358.

80. The GAO identified 160 provisions that had been challenged in signing statements. Of these, they focused on nineteen. Jonathan Weisman, "'Signing Statements' Study Finds Administration Has Ignored Laws," *Washington Post,* June 19, 2007, A4.

81. See the up-to-date list at the American Presidency Project, http://www.presidency.ucsb.edu/signingstatements.php?year=2016&Submit=DISPLAY#q1.

82. Christopher S. Kelley, "Rhetoric and Reality? Unilateralism and the Obama Administration," *Social Science Quarterly* 93:5 (December 2012): 1154.

83. Crouch, Rozell, and Sollenberger, "President Obama's Signing Statements," 890ff.

84. Richard E. Neustadt, *Presidential Power: The Politics of Leadership* (New York: Wiley, 1960), 10.

85. George C. Edwards III, *At the Margins: Presidential Leadership of Congress* (New Haven CT: Yale University Press, 1989).

86. Ibid. For a recent restatement of this argument applied to the Obama experience, see George C. Edwards, "Creating Opportunities? Bipartisanship in the Early Obama Administration," *Social Science Quarterly* 93:5 (December 2012).

87. Dave Boyer, "White House, GOP on Hill in Harmony," *Washington Times*, February 14, 2001, A1. On the speech, see Dan Balz, "President Begins His Toughest Sell," *Washington Post*, February 28, 2001, A1.

88. Ari Fleischer as quoted by Scott Shepard, Cox News Service, March 4, 2001. Also see Mike Allen, "It's Campaign 2001: President Hits the Trail to Pitch Tax, Education Plans," *Washington Post*, March 2, 2001, A6.

89. The campaign was well documented on the White House website, including a map and videos of the president's appearances. President Bush made three appearances in Florida, two in Kentucky, and two in Pennsylvania.

90. Adriel Bettelheim, "Bush's Rough Choice on Social Security: Backtrack or Take Flak," *CQ Weekly*, March 7, 2005, 550.

91. Matthew Esbaugh-Soha and Jeffrey S. Peake, "The Contemporary Presidency: 'Going Local' to Reform Social Security," *Presidential Studies Quarterly* 36 (December 2006): 689–705.

92. Mycoff and Pika, *Confrontation and Compromise*, chap. 7.

93. Joseph A. Pika, "White House Office of Congressional Relations: A Longitudinal Analysis" (paper presented at the annual meeting of the Midwest Political Science Association, Chicago, April 20–22, 1978). See also the discussion in Kenneth E. Collier, *Between the Branches: The White House Office of Legislative Affairs* (Pittsburgh, PA: University of Pittsburgh Press, 1997), 16–22.

94. John Hudak, *Presidential Pork* (Washington, DC: Brookings Institution Press, 2014). See also Douglas Kriner and Andrew Reeves, *The Particularistic President* (New York: Cambrige University Press, 2015).

95. Bert Rockman, "The Obama Presidency: Hope, Change, and Reality," *Social Science Quarterly* 93:5 (December 2012).

96. Lyndon B. Johnson, *Vantage Point* (New York: Holt, Rinehart and Winston, 1971), 448; and Doris Kearns Goodwin, *Lyndon Johnson and the American Dream* (New York: Harper and Row, 1976), 226.

97. George C. Edwards III, *Presidential Influence in Congress* (San Francisco: Freeman, 1980), 117–120. For the origins of Johnson's knowledge of the Senate, see Robert A. Caro, *The Years of Lyndon Johnson: Master of the Senate* (New York: Knopf, 2002). Caro's subsequent volume, *The Passage of Power* (New York: Knopf, 2012), discusses Johnson's efforts to pass Kennedy's (and his own) legislative agenda immediately after the JFK assassination.

98. He went on, "But if you try to force the whole bottle down his throat at one time, he'll just throw it up." See Joseph A. Califano, Jr., *The Triumph and Tragedy of Lyndon Johnson* (New York: Simon and Schuster, 1991), 142.

99. Terry Sullivan, "Headcounts, Expectations, and Presidential Coalitions in Congress," *American Journal of Political Science* (August 1988): 567. Elsewhere, Sullivan demonstrates that head counts are a valuable presidential tool for signaling congressional supporters and for obtaining information from them; Terry Sullivan, "Explaining Why Presidents Count: Signaling and Information," *Journal of Politics* (August 1990): 939–962.

100. Keith Krehbiel, *Pivotal Politics: A Theory of U.S. Lawmaking* (Chicago: University of Chicago Press, 1998); Rudalevige, "Executive Branch and the Legislative Process," Table 1, 431.

101. Sinclair, "Trying to Govern Positively," 96–100.

102. Conley, *The Presidency, Congress and Divided Government*, chap. 7.

103. Sinclair, "Trying to Govern Positively," 121.

104. Jon Healey, "Clinton Success Rate Declined to a Record Low in 1995," *Congressional Quarterly Weekly Report,* January 27, 1996, 193.

105. John C. Fortier and Norman J. Ornstein, "Congress and the Bush Presidency" (paper presented at the conference on "The Bush Presidency: An Early Assessment," Woodrow Wilson School, Princeton University, NJ, April 25–26, 2003), 24, 26.

106. Ibid., 34.

107. For example, House Republican conservatives refused to acquiesce in the Bush administration's compromise on intelligence reform. See Mycoff and Pika, *Confrontation and Compromise,* chap. 3.

108. Andrew Rudalevige, "The Contemporary Presidency: The Decline and Resurgence and Decline (and Resurgence?) of Congress: Charting a New Imperial Presidency," *Presidential Studies Quarterly* 36 (September 2006): 518–519.

109. For an extensive listing of aides with congressional experience, see John E. Owens, "A Post-Partisan President in a Partisan Context," in *Obama in Office,* ed. James A. Thurber (Boulder, CO: Paradigm Publishers, 2011), 111.

110. Barbara Sinclair, "Congressional Leadership in Obama's First Two Years"; and Owens, "A Post-Partisan President," 89–106.

111. Owens, "A Post-Partisan President," Table 7-2, 116.

112. Ibid., 115 ff.

113. Edwards, "Creating Opportunities," 1096.

114. Ian F. Ferguson, "Trade Promotion Authority (TPA) and the Role of Congress in Trade Policy," *Congressional Research Service* Report RL33743 (May 28, 2015), Appendix A, https://fas.org/sgp/crs/misc/RL33743.pdf.

115. Peter Baker and Jennifer Steinhauer, "Washington Dysfunction, with a Twist: Democrats Desert Their President," *New York Times,* June 12, 2015, http://www.nytimes.com/2015/06/13/us/politics/democrats-revolt-on-trade-bill-obama.html?smid=nytnow-share&smprod=nytnow&_r=0; Stephen Dinan, "Democrats Kill Obama's Trade Push," *Washington Times,* June 12, 2015, http://www.washingtontimes.com/news/2015/jun/12/democrats-kill-obamas-trade-push/?page=all#pagebreak; Susan Davis, "Congress Renews 'Fast-Track' Trade Authority," *USA Today,* June 24, 2015, http://www.usatoday.com/story/news/politics/2015/06/24/congress-renews-fast-track/29226629/; and Alexander Bolton, "Senate Approves Fast-Track, Sending Trade Bill to White House," *The Hill,* June 24, 2015, http://thehill.com/homenews/senate/246035-senate-approves-fast-track-sending-trade-bill-to-white-house.

116. Laurence L. Barrett, *Gambling with History* (Garden City, NY: Doubleday, 1983), 334.

117. The most thorough study of this staff unit is by Kenneth Collier, *Between the Branches: The White House Office of Legislative Affairs* (Pittsburgh, PA: University of Pittsburgh Press, 1997). Also see the discussion in John H. Kessel, *Presidents, the Presidency, and the Political Environment* (Washington, DC: CQ Press, 2001), 30–52.

118. Light, *The President's Agenda,* 281.

119. For data covering 1961 to 1986, see George C. Edwards III, *At the Margins: Presidential Leadership of Congress* (New Haven, CT: Yale University Press, 1989), chap. 3.

120. Data from Andrew Rudalevige, "'A Majority Is the Best Repartee': Barack Obama and Congress, 2009–2012," *Social Science Quarterly* 93 (December 2012), Figure 2, updated by author.

121. Edwards, *At the Margins,* 68–69; Jon R. Bond and Richard Fleisher, *The President in the Legislative Arena* (Chicago: University of Chicago Press, 1990), 171–175.

122. Gary C. Jacobson, *The Electoral Origins of Divided Government* (Boulder, CO: Westview, 1990), 80–81.

123. Gary C. Jacobson, *The Politics of Congressional Elections,* 3rd ed. (New York: HarperCollins, 1992), 161–162.

124. Fortier and Ornstein, "Congress and the Bush Presidency," 39–40. On midterm losses, see Abramson, Aldrich, and Rohde, *Change and Continuity,* 228.

125. Matthew J. Dickinson, "The President and Congress," in Michael Nelson, ed., *The Presidency and the Political System,* 10th ed. (Washington, DC: CQ Press, 2014), 426–433.

126. Sullivan, "Headcounts, Expectations, and Presidential Coalitions in Congress," 573–582.

127. John W. Kingdon, *Congressmen's Voting Decisions* (New York: Harper and Row, 1981); and Aage R. Clausen, *How Congressmen Decide* (New York: St. Martin's Press, 1973)

128. Conley, *The Presidency, Congress, and Divided Government,* 3–83.

129. Bond and Fleisher, *The President in the Legislative Arena,* 221.

130. Ibid., 182.

131. Edwards, *At the Margins,* 124–125.

132. John E. Mueller, *War, Presidents, and Public Opinion* (New York: Wiley, 1973).

133. Wayne, *The Legislative Presidency,* 166.

134. Elizabeth Drew, *On the Edge* (New York: Simon and Schuster, 1994), 54, 266.

135. Mark Lacey, "Bush to Attend Democratic Caucuses," *New York Times,* January 27, 2001, A11.

136. Drew, *On the Edge,* 266. For a more positive review of Clinton's personal effectiveness, see James Pfiffner, *The Strategic Presidency,* rev. 2nd ed. (Lawrence: University Press of Kansas, 180.

137. Susan Davis, "On Their Own," *National Journal,* April 16, 2011, 42.

138. Peter Wallsten, "Obama's Role in Debt Talks Scrutinized," *Washington Post,* August 5, 2011.

139. Edwards, *At the Margins,* 211. Also see Bond and Fleisher, *The President in the Legislative Arena,* 219; and Bert A. Rockman, *The Leadership Question: The Presidency and the American Political System* (New York: Praeger, 1984), 214.

140. Mark A. Peterson, *Legislating Together: The White House and Capitol Hill from Eisenhower to Reagan* (Cambridge, MA: Harvard University Press, 1990), 267.

141. Fareed Zakaria, "Inside Obama's World," *Time,* January 19, 2012, http://swampland.time.com/2012/01/19/inside-obamas-world-the-president-talks-to-time-about-the-changing-nature-of-american-power/. See, more broadly, George C. Edwards III, *Overreach: Leadership in the Obama Presidency* (Princeton, NJ: Princeton University Press, 2012).

142. Edwards, *At the Margins,* 8–15.

143. Bond and Fleisher, *The President in the Legislative Arena,* 220–234.

144. Peterson, *Legislating Together,* 92–94, chaps. 4–5.

145. Arthur M. Schlesinger Jr., *The Imperial Presidency* (Boston: Houghton Mifflin, 1973).

146. For an alternative view stressing legislative rather than executive dominance, see Keith E. Whittington and Daniel P. Carpenter, "Executive Power in American Institutional Development," *Perspectives on Politics* 1 (September 2003): 495–513.

147. Sundquist, *The Decline and Resurgence of Congress.*

148. In the second edition of *The Imperial Presidency* (Boston: Houghton Mifflin, 1989), Schlesinger maintains that Reagan moved two-thirds of the way toward restoring the imperial presidency. He met two of Schlesinger's "tests"—extensive presidential war making and heavy reliance on secrecy—but Reagan did not direct his powers against administration critics (451, 457).

149. Starr had expanded his investigation of Clinton's involvement in Whitewater, a failed land development project in Arkansas, to include other subjects of alleged wrongdoing, including the firing of White House employees in the travel office ("Travelgate"), the potential abuse of FBI files by the Clinton White House ("Filegate"), and the suicide of White House counsel Vincent J. Foster. See Andrew Rudalevige, "The Broken Places: The Clinton Impeachment and American Politics," in *42,* ed. Michael Nelson and Russell Riley (Ithaca, NY: Cornell University Press, 2016).

150. "Mr. Ruff for the Defense," editorial, *New York Times,* January 20, 1999, A30.

151. Arnold, "Bill Clinton and the Institutionalized Presidency," 31.

152. Evan Thomas, "Acquittal: The Inside Story," *Newsweek,* February 22, 1999, 24–31; and Kirk Victor and Carl M. Cannon, "Promise and Peril," *National Journal,* January 23, 1999, 170–175.

153. Jack N. Rakove, "Taking Prerogative out of the Presidency: An Originalist Perspective," *Presidential Studies Quarterly* 37 (March 2007): 85.

154. Rudalevige, "The Contemporary Presidency."

155. Owens, "A Post-Partisan President," 110.

156. Sinclair, "Congressional Leadership in Obama's First Two Years"; Robert Draper, *Do Not Ask What Good We Do: Inside the House of Representatives* (New York: Free Press, 2012), xv–xviii.

157. This is the central theme of Peterson's *Legislating Together,* in which he advocates a "tandem institutions" perspective on presidential-congressional relations.

CHAPTER 6

Executive Politics

Pete Marovich - Pool/Getty Images

President Trump displays a newly signed executive order in an early 2017 Oval Office ceremony. Trump issued more than thirty such orders during his first one hundred days in office.

Americans commonly think of the president as the "chief executive" of the federal government, held responsible for its many activities and responsibilities. As the federal government assumed more powers in the twentieth century, popular expectations rose and presidents became the focal point for citizens' blame or credit for bad or good times. Activist executives in the twentieth century—Theodore Roosevelt, Franklin D. Roosevelt, and Lyndon B. Johnson in the forefront—heightened this image of strong presidential leadership by launching major policy initiatives. Citizens imagine the president directing the activities of millions of federal officials. But presidents do not fully control the executive branch. Even following the terrorist attacks on New York City and Washington, D.C., in 2001, when the nation seemed most unified, President George W. Bush struggled to be master of his own house.

In the wake of 9/11, President Bush and his administration took responsibility for preventing another terrorist attack and for minimizing the consequences if one should occur. To accomplish this goal, Bush signed legislation in November 2002 creating the Department of Homeland Security (DHS). As he declared, "We're taking historic action to defend the United States and protect our citizens from the dangers of a new era."[1] The mammoth new department consolidated twenty-two agencies and units from other departments into a single entity with about 170,000 workers, making it the federal government's third biggest department. This move was the largest single government reorganization since the creation of the Department of Defense (DOD) in 1947.

Bush also proposed a new pay system for DHS that would replace the one created in 1949. In Bush's view and that of many other reformers, the old system rewarded employees' seniority rather than their performance on the job. Critics argued that the system rewarded mediocrity and caution rather than performance and initiative. The administration hoped to use the creation of DHS as the occasion to introduce a new pay scheme to the rest of the federal government, as well. As the president argued, in confronting the terrorist threat, "The new department must be able to get the right people in the right place at the right time with the right pay."[2] That was a shorthand call for a restructuring of the federal civil service.

Creating a huge federal bureaucracy was not the president's original solution at all. A month after the terrorist attacks, Bush chose Gov. Tom Ridge, R-PA, to serve as director of the Office of Homeland Security, a 100-person White House staff unit, and to oversee the Homeland Security Council, an interdepartmental coordinating committee designed to function much like the long-established National Security Council (NSC). Government officials resisted when Ridge sought to coordinate agency efforts in combating terrorism, and he was drawn into protracted legal battles with Congress over its right to oversee his activities.[3] Congressional Democrats generated a bipartisan, bicameral proposal to create a new department instead. To everyone's surprise, Bush suddenly endorsed the proposal as a way to regain the initiative on this highly visible issue.

Although the turf battles over which units would join the new department proved long and bitter, Bush ultimately got most of what he wanted, with numerous offices moving into the new structure. Among the agencies that moved were the Coast Guard (from Transportation), the Secret Service (from Treasury),[4] the Customs Service (from Treasury),[5] the Border Patrol (from Justice), the recently created Transportation Security Administration (from Transportation),[6] FEMA (the Federal Emergency Management Agency, an independent agency),[7] the Office of Domestic Preparedness (from Justice), the National Domestic Preparedness Office (from the FBI), the Computer Security Division (from Commerce), and the National

Communications System (from Defense). A tiny team of White House aides led by Bush chief of staff Andrew Card made the organization choices and avoided pressure by meeting secretly in a bunker under the East Wing.[8]

Secretary Ridge faced an enormous challenge: assembling a management team on short notice and pulling all the pieces into a coherent whole. Congress posed a major problem. According to the White House, "88 congressional committees and subcommittees have jurisdiction over issues related to homeland security, and . . . that gives the Homeland Security Department a lot of congressional bosses to work with—and answer to—in its drive to make America safer."[9] This legislative cross section included every single senator and 95 percent of the House members in the 107th Congress. In addition, the newly assembled pieces of the department brought with them established relationships with organized interests that hoped to protect the access and services they enjoyed under the old arrangements and a few newly organized interests as well.[10]

Congressional Democrats—urged on by public workers unions—opposed Bush's proposal to give DHS greater flexibility in hiring, paying, promoting, and disciplining its employees. Congress approved the changes at DHS only after they became a major campaign issue in the 2002 midterm elections and contributed to Democrats suffering major defeats.[11] DHS reduced the number of pay grades from fifteen to five and established a fast track for high-performing workers to earn earlier promotions and faster pay raises than under the old system. Unions representing government workers resisted further changes requested by Bush, and won cases in federal district and appeals courts, forcing the Bush administration to scrap the DHS system in 2008. Barack Obama's administration revoked all the civil service reforms in 2010.

Like Bush with his struggles to organize homeland security, most modern presidents have encountered difficulties in their efforts to direct the executive branch, whether it involved working with existing entities or creating new ones. John F. Kennedy lamented the inertia of the State Department, and Ronald Reagan made his campaign attack on an overgrown federal bureaucracy one of his presidency's enduring themes. Donald Trump likewise promised to slash regulations, restructure government agencies, and "drain the swamp"—even (in one staffer's phrase) to achieve the "deconstruction of the administrative state."[12]

Presidents proposing to harness the potential of government to deliver much-needed services must overcome the cynical belief that bureaucracy is the problem, not the solution. Bill Clinton's proposal to solve the nation's health care problems fell victim to the charge that it would create a bloated federal bureaucracy.

And when problems plagued Healthcare.gov, the website for citizens to enroll in federal health insurance exchanges under Obama's controversial reforms, it was taken as another example of administrative ineptitude. A frequently seen website message summarized critics' view of the administration's poor performance: "The system is down at the moment. We are experiencing technical difficulties and hope to have them resolved soon."[13]

Richard Rose, who studied the president as a manager, remarked that the "president's title of chief executive is a misnomer; he can more accurately be described as a nonexecutive chief."[14] The essence of Rose's argument is that, even within the executive branch, presidential powers of command are limited and that a president's success as an administrator depends greatly on the ability to win the trust of others. Presidents therefore confront a continuing challenge. The public expects them to produce results but is unsure of government's role, not wanting it to become too intrusive and doubting its effectiveness. Given this gap between expectations and powers, it should not be surprising that presidents gravitate toward instruments of unilateral power that provide them with greater leverage over the government. But, as noted in chapter 1, recent presidents' exercise of these unilateral powers created controversy. And even then, presidential command does not always lead to its immediate implementation.

In this chapter, we examine the president's responsibilities as chief executive and the factors that affect administrative performance. The chapter opens with a discussion of the president's executive role—its constitutional, legal, and administrative foundations. We then explore the president's relationships with the executive branch and the cabinet. After establishing that the president's powers of command over the units of the executive branch are limited, we analyze the formal powers and managerial tools that modern presidents have available for discharging administrative duties.

The President as Executive

The president's executive role is grounded in ambiguous language in Article 2 of the Constitution, which says "the executive Power" is vested in the president, who is directed to "take Care that the Laws be faithfully executed." The president may also "require the Opinion, in writing, of the principal Officer in each of the executive Departments" and "grant Reprieves and Pardons." Modern presidents have tended to interpret these provisions broadly and have derived substantial additional powers from them. In addition to these constitutionally based powers, presidents have received extensive delegations of statutory authority from Congress.

Yet presidents confront a paradox. Although they enjoy considerable formal legal powers and head a vast, complex military and civilian bureaucracy, their ability to direct that bureaucracy toward the achievement of the administration's policy objectives and program goals is frequently limited. To understand that paradox, we must examine the constitutional relationship of the presidency to the legislative and judicial branches as well as the nature of the federal bureaucracy and the president's relationship to it.

In administration as in so many other areas, presidents require the cooperation of Congress because only Congress can authorize government programs, establish agencies to implement the programs, and appropriate funds to finance them.[15] Presidents have strong preferences about governmental structure but find that congressional cooperation is often difficult to obtain in this area because, regardless of party loyalties, presidents and members of Congress have different constituency and institutional perspectives. There are also occasions when the exercise of presidential power must be acceptable to the judiciary (note, for instance, President Obama's struggle with the courts over his second-term immigration initiatives or President Trump's first, short-lived "travel ban" order.) In short, presidential power is not self-executing, and it is subject to restraint.

The federal bureaucracy—which today consists of fifteen cabinet departments and between forty and fifty special agencies, with a total workforce of more than 2 million civilian and 1.4 million active duty military personnel—is called the executive branch, but it is really the creation of the legislative branch. As noted earlier, the Constitution references "executive departments" but doesn't say what those departments should be, or what they should do. That is left to Congress and the lawmaking process. When Congress establishes federal departments and agencies, its members are responding not only to presidential needs and requests, but also to demands and pressures from various constituency forces, interest groups, and the general public. As a result, the structure of the federal bureaucracy tends to reflect the political fragmentation and committee jurisdictions of Congress, which often leads, as with homeland security, to multiple committees overseeing the activities of the same department. Presidents do not look down upon subordinate administrative units from a position at the apex of a pyramid of authority; instead, they confront a complex and confusing array of departments and agencies with varying degrees of independence.

In addition, presidents deal with career civil servants who staff bureaucratic units and constitute a permanent federal government. These civil servants respond to demands from interest groups and to direction from congressional committees as well as to presidential leadership. Most modern presidents have entered office believing—or they soon become convinced—that they cannot take the support and loyalty of the bureaucracy for granted but must constantly strive to earn both.[16]

The president's task as the nation's chief executive, therefore, is much more than issuing commands or finding ways to bring a large complex bureaucracy under operational control. The president must secure congressional cooperation while suppressing the executive branch's natural tendencies toward conflict with the legislative branch and must give direction to the bureaucracy so that it will help accomplish the administration's goals. As the functions of the federal government expanded from the New Deal onward, the task of defining objectives and coordinating their achievement has become more difficult for presidents.

The President and the Executive Branch

Presidents need help in discharging their ill-defined executive power, but the Constitution provided them with few sources of assistance. Presidents discover quickly that the reality of their relations with the federal bureaucracy bears little resemblance to the idealized vision that many hold of presidents issuing orders and bureaucrats scurrying to carry them out. Presidential appointees to posts in the government, collectively known as **political executives**, are expected to assist the president. Department secretaries and agency administrators appointed by the president are charged with directing the work of the career employees, coordinating the operations of their component bureaus, and developing and maintaining links with other federal departments and agencies as well as with state and local governments. The vice president, exercising his constitutional responsibility to preside over the Senate, was originally more an officer of Congress than a source of help to the president, but, as discussed below, that position changed dramatically in the second half of the twentieth century. Today, the president's greatest assistance in managing the federal bureaucracy comes from the staff housed in the White House Office and FDR's creation, the **Executive Office of the President** (EOP). Roosevelt convinced Congress to authorize the EOP to help him define objectives; convert them into operating programs; allocate resources to the agencies administering the programs; and coordinate the implementation of programs within the federal government and among federal, state, and local governments.

Tension among the president, presidential agents, and the bureaucracy has been present in every modern administration. It exists, at least in part, because of what Hugh Heclo has identified as the distinction between "political leadership in the bureaucracy" and "bureaucratic power."[17] The direction and effectiveness of the political leadership that presidents provide depend on their personalities, leadership style, and values as well as on external events and conditions. In contrast, bureaucratic power is relatively permanent, not dependent on personalities and transitory factors. That power belongs to the career civil servants who make up the permanent government—sometimes termed, whether respectfully or resentfully, the "deep state."

At least five general factors contribute to bureaucratic power and shape presidential-bureaucratic relations: (1) the size, complexity, and dispersion of the executive branch; (2) bureaucratic inertia and momentum; (3) executive branch personnel; (4) the legal position of the executive branch; and (5) the susceptibility of executive branch units to external political influence. Major consequences of the interaction of these factors are presidential frustration and a pattern of policymaking often sharply at odds with the norm of democratic accountability; it is a system that obscures those responsible for a policy and a decision.

Size, Complexity, and Dispersion of the Executive Branch

The scope of federal government activities has exploded since 1933, tremendously increasing the number of agencies and the range of programs they administer. Federal spending for 2016 was $3.85 trillion, and federal civilian employees and active duty military personnel numbered more than 3.4 million. Federal employees oversee domestic programs that reach into every community in the nation and touch the lives of individuals from birth to death. Many of those programs are delivered by nonfederal employees: One estimate sets the total number of jobs associated with federal government programs in 2005 at almost fifteen million when contract employees, grant recipients, and state and local employees working on government funding are included, and that total has probably grown.[18] Further, strategies designed to ensure national security extend U.S. military and foreign policy activities around the world. Providing leadership and direction to such a far-flung bureaucracy is difficult. It would be so even if the president could command prompt and unquestioning obedience.

The multiplicity of agencies and programs creates an additional obstacle to effective leadership. Overlapping jurisdictions lead in some cases to duplication of efforts and in others to contradictory efforts; one even finds competition among government agencies. Presidents must be coordinators. When they define goals for a policy area, they most often deal not with single administrative units but with many. Even after twenty-two administrative units were consolidated into the DHS, the military services, the FBI, and the CIA remained outside units whose cooperation and coordination are critical to success. A rigorous review of intelligence failures that preceded the 9/11 attacks identified competition within the intelligence community as a major problem, but the changes were modest—a new position to coordinate the intelligence community's efforts and yet another additional intelligence agency, making a total of sixteen.[19]

The tremendous size of the federal bureaucracy means its activities are widely dispersed. Presidents, their aides, and their principal political appointees are at the center of government. The people who operate programs, deliver services to individuals, and regulate the conduct of businesses and other organizations are at the periphery. These people, most of them civil servants, are there when a new president and staff take office and will be there after the political executives depart.

Bureaucratic Inertia and Momentum

Bureaucratic inertia means it is hard to get a new government activity started, and once it is under way, it is even more difficult to stop it or even significantly redirect it. In short, "bureaucracies at rest tend to stay at rest and bureaucracies in motion tend to stay in motion."[20] Much of this inflexibility arises because of organizational routines—prescribed operating procedures that have worked successfully in the past—or interest group efforts to preserve established programs.

The momentum of ongoing programs especially frustrates presidents. Government commitments are reflected in public laws, the amount of money allocated for those activities in annual appropriations, and the number of civil service and military employees who carry out the activities. In 2016, mandatory expenditures constituted nearly 70 percent of the government's budget.[21] The principal mandatory items included interest on the national debt; entitlement programs such as Social Security, Medicare, Medicaid, and farm subsidies; federal retirement and veterans' benefits; and unemployment compensation. Even the remaining, discretionary portion of the budget is highly resistant to cuts because of support from groups benefiting from those expenditures. Presidents can influence the shape of the federal budget, but major changes usually require years to be implemented. From one year to the next, presidents tend to be limited to incremental changes.

Given their fixed terms of office and the usual scope of their objectives, presidents find the incremental adjustments possible through annual budgeting inadequate.

For members of the permanent government, the time perspective is much different; they can afford to be patient. In the budget process, they fight to maintain their "base," which is their current appropriation, and to add as large an increment to it as possible.[22] Over time, small annual increases are transformed into large permanent gains. Bureaucratic momentum therefore works to the advantage of the permanent government and acts as a constraint on presidents who attempt to counter it. President Reagan and his successors tried to overcome the effects of incremental budgeting by means of a top-down process that restricted total government spending and forced agencies and their supporters to accept cuts or limited growth.[23] The Republican Congresses after 2010 adopted another budgetary tactic of the 1980s, the "sequester": automatic budget cuts that reduce the size and reach of government, though the cuts come only from discretionary spending.

The large number of career federal employees pressures the president to maintain ongoing programs. Major reductions in personnel or redirection of their activities are economically and politically costly. People will oppose actions that threaten to deprive them of their jobs or that require them to move, undergo additional training, or reduce their sense of security and importance. Most presidents can make only modest adjustments in the size and mission of the federal workforce. Bill Clinton was somewhat more successful in this regard than other modern presidents, eventually eliminating more than 300,000 jobs at the end of seven years as part of the "reinventing government" effort led by Vice President Al Gore.[24]

Bureaucratic Personnel

Presidents must depend on both political appointees and career officials to operate the federal bureaucracy. Until 1883, when the Pendleton Act created the federal civil service, no distinction existed between the two groups. Presidents could theoretically appoint all members of the federal bureaucracy, a **spoils system** of tangible rewards for party members who had supported the election winner. With the creation and steady expansion of the **civil service system**, which opened government jobs to all citizens based on their qualifications, presidential control of government personnel declined, and the characteristics and roles of appointed and career officials became more distinctive, often hindering presidential direction of programs. As the civil service became more professionalized and protected from political pressure, its members became more resistant to presidential pressure.

The political executives—those appointed by the president and charged with directing the careerists—are a weak substitute for the old patronage-based system and constitute what Hugh Heclo has called a "government of strangers."[25] Aside from cabinet officers, a few important subcabinet appointees, and the heads of major independent agencies, these political executives are largely unknown to the president and one another. Only loosely do they constitute a presidential team able to provide direction to the bureaucracy. "Although party is still the glue that seems to hold administrations together, this glue's consistency is much thinner than ever before and its holding power is greatly reduced."[26]

Cabinet selection involves the president directly in an attempt to build support for the administration, normally by including representatives of various constituencies in the party and the country.[27] Presidents sometimes appoint personal friends to especially important cabinet departments because of the close counseling relationship involved.[28] But selection of other political executives is affected by multiple and often conflicting pressures: loyalty to the president; party membership; technical competence; the wishes of the cabinet member under whom the appointee will serve; a demographic balancing act incorporating region, race, and gender; and the demands of congressional members, interest groups, and state and local party leaders. Moreover, anyone subject to Senate confirmation must be acceptable to the relevant committee members; usually this has meant having a sparkling clean financial and personal background.

When done with care and planning, recruiting people to serve in an administration has the potential to be an instrument of control over policy; a tool of administrative management; and an important component of presidential relations with Congress, interest groups, and political parties. Consequently, the process is highly political. The burden placed on a newly elected president to get a "team" in place is enormous and starts practically from scratch. As Joel Aberbach and Bert Rockman point out, "When a new president settles in, there is a need to recreate the executive personnel system in a far more extensive way than is typically the case in other developed democracies."[29] Presidents since Dwight D. Eisenhower have used personnel staffs located in the White House to run the appointment process, a group now more formally identified as the Office of Presidential Personnel.[30] The personnel process is always chaotic at the start of a new administration because of the many positions to be filled, pressures for jobs from campaign workers and party members, and uncertainty about how to proceed. The number of inquiries from job seekers can be crushing, reaching as many as 1,500 a day.[31] Eventually the search becomes more systematic,[32] and the office typically will coordinate the filling of about 7,500 positions during a presidential term, with many having to be filled multiple times because of turnover.[33]

Over time, centralization of appointment decisions in the Office of Presidential Personnel has increased presidential control and bureaucratic responsiveness, but the consequences have been costly. As Thomas Weko documented, centralization permits job seekers, interest groups, members of Congress, and campaign contributors to press their claims directly on the White House staff, transferring into the White House conflicts once waged outside it, diminishing the importance of substantive programmatic considerations, and provoking conflict between the appointments staff and the executive departments and agencies.[34] Indeed, the early days of the Trump administration were marked by sharp arguments between White House staff and multiple Cabinet secretaries over who those secretaries' subordinates would be.[35] The process also depends on an active president who provides sustained support for the selection of appointees. President Reagan excelled in this regard. The Reagan White House exercised tight control over recruitment, filling sensitive positions with loyal individuals committed to the president's ideology. Cabinet members could not conduct independent searches for subcabinet officials. Prospective appointees were screened for policy views, political and personal backgrounds, and, if considered necessary, expertise. The result was tighter control over the executive branch and greater cohesion within it than other modern presidents have achieved.[36]

Bill Clinton's experience illustrates the difficulty presidents encounter. The Clinton personnel operation had almost three hundred employees during the transition and more than one hundred in the Presidential Personnel Office in March 1993. The operation's objective was to create a competent staff that also responded to the claims and demands of campaign workers and contributors and represented the diverse blocs, movements, and constituencies that had brought electoral victory. The operation's political success was reflected in the diversity of the appointees, recruited to reflect "ethnicity, gender and geography" in a cabinet that "looked like America."[37] The preoccupation with diversity, ethical concerns, and a series of botched nominations, however, resulted in a slowed appointment pace that brought criticism from Congress, Democratic constituency groups, and the media.[38]

Because the outcome of the 2000 election long remained in question, George W. Bush's search for personnel got off to a late start. Even so, the administration was only a week behind Clinton's record in selecting the cabinet and was actually faster in naming the White House staff.[39] But there were other sources of delay. At the one-hundred-day mark, Bush was well behind Reagan and Clinton in getting appointees in place. With 488 top appointments to make, Bush had announced 177 candidates, but only 60 names had been submitted to the Senate, and of those, only 29 had been confirmed.

Obama's transition staff began to identify possible appointees before the election, and the president-elect began reviewing dossiers on top prospects soon after the election.[40] After Thanksgiving, senior members of the White House staff were announced first, and Obama then named "teams" of advisers for economic and national security policy with other domestic appointments following. The administration established very strict rules against former lobbyists working in agencies they had previously lobbied and precluded appointees from lobbying the administration after they left government for the duration of the Obama administration, perhaps discouraging some job seekers. Nonetheless, they provided waivers from these rules for some appointees.

Scrutiny of nominees' records was especially close.[41] Candidates were required to fill out a sixty-three-item questionnaire that asked, along with their employment history, whether they had ever written an embarrassing e-mail. The materials were then inspected (*vetted* is the Washington term) by the White House, the FBI, the Internal Revenue Service (IRS), the Office of Government Ethics, and the Senate committees that hold hearings on each candidate requiring confirmation.

An unusually large number of Obama's initial cabinet nominees encountered problems being confirmed. Three withdrew and another survived a scare, as described later. In the wake of these problems, the White House moved even more slowly on subcabinet appointments. By the end of March—two months into an administration confronting an historic economic challenge—only one of the top seventeen posts in the Treasury Department had been filled, the secretary, prompting a Brookings Institution publication to describe Secretary Geithner as "Home Alone."[42] The pace picked up, but by August, fewer than half of the administration's top five hundred jobs had been filled.[43] One cabinet position remained vacant for six months, and eighteen months after the administration had started, 25 percent of its top positions were vacant, partly because once-filled positions were reopening.

The Trump administration, however, made the Bush and Obama experiences seem rapid-fire. The Presidential Transitions Improvements Act of 2015 had provided candidates with additional resources to prepare well ahead of election day. However, the work done by the Trump transition team during the fall—identifying some 300 candidates for various government positions—was discarded when the president-elect removed its chair, Gov. Chris Christie (R-NJ), immediately after the election. Christie was replaced with vice president-elect Mike Pence, who began more or less anew.[44] The resulting process was carried out less systematically and largely in public, with prospective nominees for cabinet positions summoned to Trump Tower in New York for interviews. With no personnel chief in place until late January, consideration of subcabinet candidates languished.[45] By early May, of 556 key positions identified by the Partnership for Public Service, no one had been named to 464; only 41 people had been formally nominated. A parallel study found just 45 nominees for the 920 jobs it tracked, meaning the administration was running about a month behind its predecessors in that regard.[46]

Further, with each new administration, the confirmation process has grown longer. Some problems are self-inflicted. Tom Daschle, nominated by Obama to be secretary of the Health and Human Services Department and slated to play the leading role in health care reform, withdrew after reports that he had failed to pay taxes on a limousine service provided by a client. Treasury Secretary Timothy Geithner's confirmation was slowed because he had failed to pay taxes on some of his previous income, an especially unfortunate problem because Geithner would oversee the IRS in his new job. Eight years later, prospective Labor Secretary Andrew Puzder withdrew from consideration after criticisms were levelled at his business practices and personal behavior. To move faster, early Trump appointees were largely announced before internal vetting had been completed or ethics forms submitted; in some cases this led to revelations during Senate consideration that complicated their confirmations. At least four subcabinet members withdrew their nominations, often because separating themselves from their business interests to avoid conflicts of interest proved too arduous.[47]

The political executives who successfully navigate this gauntlet are often amateurs in the vicious world of Washington politics, lacking the political knowledge and substantive skills needed to provide effective leadership. They quickly discover their dependence on top-level career executives and lower-ranking civil servants for information and advice. That support is obtained only by paying a price, however, in the form of loyalty to the agency and support for its programs within the administration, before Congress, and with the public. Members of the president's team suddenly find themselves striking a balance between the often-conflicting claims of the White House and the agencies they lead. In general, it takes twelve to eighteen months for political executives to master their jobs. Their average tenure, however, is only two years. The high turnover rates make it difficult to develop teamwork within departments and agencies. Cabinet secretaries are continually adapting to new assistants, and people on the same administrative level barely get to know one another. One result is that expectations and roles are in flux, and coordination and control are problematic.

Political executives, who look upward to the president for support and direction and downward to the permanent government for support and services, are imperfect instruments for presidential control of the bureaucracy. They can best serve the president by winning the trust of the careerists, but to do so means establishing a considerable degree of independence from the White House.

Conflicts between the White House and the career executives arise for understandable reasons. The relatively secure tenure of upper-level civil servants (as opposed to the expendability and shorter tenure of political executives) allows them to take a more gradual approach to resolving problems and to pursue their objectives obliquely and by indirection, generating less opposition. In contrast, political executives, urged on by the White House, tend to pursue their goals quite directly and to see virtue in conflict. In addition, civil servants must remain politically neutral to remain civil servants; they are therefore cautious about becoming identified with a political party or appointee. Presidential appointees, many of whom are unfamiliar with bureaucratic ways, often mistake such caution for opposition or disloyalty. This viewpoint is reinforced by the high value career executives place on maintaining their relationships with clientele group representatives, congressional members and staff, and individuals outside the Washington community who are involved in, or knowledgeable about, their agencies' programs.

To correct perceived deficiencies in the career service and to increase presidential control over the higher ranks of the civil service, Jimmy Carter's administration engineered the passage of the Civil Service Reform Act of 1978 (CSRA). The CSRA established the Senior Executive Service (SES), a professional managerial corps of career civil servants whose members are eligible for financial performance bonuses. It also increased the ability of political executives to transfer career officials within and between agencies and to raise the number of noncareerists in the SES and lower positions.[48] Another provision of the CSRA replaced the three-person bipartisan Civil Service Commission with the single-headed Office of Personnel Management (OPM), which gave the president more control over the career service. Reagan's first director of the OPM, Donald J. Devine, aggressively implemented a partisan vision of leadership.[49] Neither of Reagan's immediate successors, George H. W. Bush and Bill Clinton, used politicization of the career service as extensively as Reagan did to direct the executive branch.

These Carter-era reforms have come under administration and congressional scrutiny.[50] George W. Bush's administration originally challenged civil service practices in security-related departments (DHS and DOD) and then proposed a "management agenda" that stressed evaluating agency performance in achieving five government-wide initiatives and broadcasting the results publicly on a web-based scorecard.[51] The most controversial feature of the agenda was requiring that outside companies be invited to compete for contracts to provide "commercial activities" performed by government workers, a process similar to "contracting out" or "outsourcing." Red flags went up on Capitol Hill and in government agencies when it seemed the Bush administration was aiming to open nearly 900,000 government positions to competitive bidding. Although the final effort was significantly smaller than originally feared, many observers remained concerned about the motives behind the Bush effort.[52]

The Obama administration made it known even before assuming office that it would reverse the Bush administration's efforts to contract out government programs. Initially the administration reduced pressures on the civil service; later, it streamlined the hiring process and considered more far-reaching reforms such as reducing the number of civil service levels and introducing bonus pay. The administration also faced the problem of widespread worker stress triggered by reductions in the federal budget—federal wages were frozen for several years after 2009—and attacks by congressional opponents of "big government."

President Trump, more sympathetic to that line of argument, imposed an immediate hiring freeze upon taking office. When that was lifted, in April 2017, Trump's budget director ordered agencies to submit plans that would implement both short- and long-term workforce reductions and "maximize employee performance."[53]

Legal Arrangements

The ambiguous legal position of the executive branch is the fourth factor that affects a president's control over the bureaucracy. Although the Constitution charges presidents with responsibility for executing the laws, their legal position as chief executive is somewhat unclear because Congress has—with presidential approval—delegated authority to, and imposed duties directly on, other administrative officials. In some cases, such as independent regulatory commissions and the Federal Reserve Board (see chapter 9), presidents have no formal power to direct agency actions or set agency policy, nor to remove appointees with fixed terms from office. Presidential influence is thus based on budgetary and appointment powers and persuasive abilities. For cabinet members, heads of independent agencies, and other political executives with operating authority to whom Congress has directly delegated power, the situation is ambiguous. As chief executive, the president, by virtue of the Constitution's "take care" clause and the ability to fire recalcitrant appointees who "serve at the pleasure of the president" (see below), can command the decisions of subordinates. In doing so, however, the president risks confrontation with Congress and with the clientele groups and individuals affected by the administrative units involved. In addition, the Supreme Court long ago ruled that the president must not interfere with the performance of a "purely ministerial" duty that does not involve the exercise of discretion or judgment.[54] Nor may the president prevent the execution of the law by subordinates.

Congress has provided administrative officials with broad delegations of discretionary authority because legislation can seldom be drafted in sufficient detail to cover all contingencies. Legislators also have made vague and general grants of power because it is politically advantageous to shift difficult and potentially unpopular decisions to the bureaucracy. The Supreme Court has approved such delegations with the proviso that they be accompanied by clear statutory guidelines.[55] The Court's insistence on specific statutory standards has, however, seldom been followed by Congress or by the lower courts.[56] The standards the Court uses have tended to be vague and unspecific, such as "just and reasonable rates," "excess profits," and "the public interest, convenience, and necessity." In spite of judicial review of the fairness of administrative procedures and judicial reference to the legislative history of statutes as found in congressional committee hearings, reports, and floor debates, administrative officials retain substantial discretionary authority that complicates the president's task of controlling the bureaucracy.

Susceptibility to External Influence

Although presidents try to impose control on the federal bureaucracy, the effort frequently falls short. The reach of appointees chosen on the basis of personal or party loyalty is limited. As a result, the federal bureaucracy is susceptible to other outside forces and depends upon them for political support. For some agencies, outside support is essential when a president fundamentally challenges their programs or ranks them low on the administration's priority list, which may threaten their funding. In addition, executive branch units confronted with external criticism and political pressure may find little support within an administration concerned with negative publicity and political fallout. If presidential support is lacking, the agency must look elsewhere for help in maintaining its authority, funding, and personnel. It turns to the public, especially to the individuals and groups affected by its programs, and it turns to Congress, particularly the committees or subcommittees with jurisdiction over its legislative authorizations and appropriations.

The regulations that agencies promulgate and enforce, or the benefits and services they deliver, provide the basis for the development of enduring ties between them and their clientele groups. An agency without a well-organized clientele is in a precarious position. Clientele groups can publicize an agency's accomplishments and defend it against attack. In exchange, the agency administers its programs with a manifest concern for the clientele's interests. The agency consults with clientele group officials and with individual notables attentive to its activities. Such outsiders often participate in agency decision making through informal personal contacts and advisory councils and panels. Agencies seldom draft guidelines and regulations or award grants without extensive external participation and consultation. There is also a two-way flow of personnel between agencies and clientele organizations. These mutually beneficial relations are characteristic of most domestic policy areas in the federal government.

For example, the National Education Association (NEA) and several other education interest groups provide support and protection to the Department of Education in exchange for access and information. The NEA led the congressional effort to elevate the former U.S. Office of Education to departmental status in 1979 and the battle to prevent the abolition of the fledgling department during the Reagan administration. Department of Education political executives have found employment with the NEA and other education interest groups; on occasion, those lobbies have helped to recruit or have provided agency staffers.

Agencies also find it easy and convenient to develop strong ties to the congressional committees or subcommittees that oversee them. Congressional requests for consideration on appointments and localized grants, suggestions concerning program administration, and inquiries on behalf of constituents are quickly acknowledged. Congressional influence with the agencies strengthens the committee members in their constituencies.[57] Bureaucrats use their connections with committee members to effect changes in their statutory authority and gain favorable treatment during budget negotiations. Agencies may use their committee ties to obtain more funds than the president has recommended or to modify their activities in a way not fully in accord with presidential preferences.

All of these factors we have reviewed provide centrifugal forces pulling agencies away from White House attempts to centralize control. Agencies are not, however, totally resistant to presidential directives; agencies and the president need each other to accomplish their goals. If the true test of presidential power is the power to persuade, one of the best measures of an agency's strength is the degree to which a president must "bargain with it in order to secure its cooperation."[58]

The President and the Cabinet

Most modern presidents have come to office announcing their intention to make more extensive use of the cabinet as a collective decision-making body than the previous incumbent did, pledges generally applauded by the media and academics. Yet, with the partial exception of Eisenhower, presidents have not used their cabinets as vehicles of collective leadership. As MaryAnne Borrelli summarizes, "Cabinet government is a promise made by candidates, an ideal endorsed by presidents-elect, and a practice abandoned by presidents."[59]

This gap between expectation and experience suggests the public and most political leaders lack understanding of the cabinet. In point of fact, the Constitution places executive authority, ultimately, in the president alone. The notion of **collective leadership** or **collegial leadership**—typically found among cabinet members in parliamentary systems, who share leadership responsibility as a group—is incompatible with constitutional reality and inconsistent with American practice. The president is not first among equals; rather, he (or she) is the person in charge. Cabinet members are presidential appointees, serving at the president's pleasure. The president is not obliged to consult them as a group or to act according to their preferences. As Abraham Lincoln reportedly said when announcing the result of a show of hands in his cabinet, "Seven nays and one aye. The ayes have it." The aye, of course, was Lincoln's.[60] Colin Powell, George W. Bush's first secretary of state, was reputed to have lost many battles over policy to administration hard-liners. He explained, "In the end, the president decides and we execute."[61]

The cabinet has no formal constitutional or legal standing. It exists by custom, and presidents may use it as little or as much as they see fit. Clinton met with his entire cabinet only twice from the beginning of 1998 to May 1999.[62] According to White House chief of staff Andrew Card, George W. Bush's cabinet met about once every two to three months during the first term.[63] The Bush system, however, was designed to implement White House directives, not to facilitate consultation, which became clear when the White House staff unit responsible for coordinating cabinet input was "effectively eliminated" in the second term.[64] During his two terms in office, Obama held only 29 cabinet meetings.

After two years in office, Obama's cabinet secretaries complained bitterly about being unable to influence administration policy or reach the president. Obama's new White House chief of staff, Bill Daley, made a number of changes on the heels of those already introduced by Pete Rouse, acting chief of staff.[65] To Washington observers, the complaints were familiar. White House aides dominated policy discussions, a tendency strengthened by the cohort of so-called policy czars (see below) who were charged with coordinating action on specific areas of administration concern. White House aides, in turn, complained about the poor performance of many cabinet secretaries who strayed from the official administration message or failed to follow through on assignments. So, too, were the solutions familiar: more face time with the president and a White House staff to coordinate communication with the cabinet. Briefly, cabinet secretaries had cause for optimism: Daley, a former secretary of commerce, was likely to understand the problem from both sides. But Daley left his White House job after only one year and the problems continued into the second term. Former defense secretary Robert Gates was not alone in complaining that "It's in the increasing desire of the White House to control and manage every aspect" of what he saw as his departmental business.[66]

Yet the cabinet does have political significance. Members are often the principal spokespersons for administration policy. They are also the top political executives expected to provide direction for those federal commitments deemed so important as to warrant cabinet-level status. Management tasks may be growing more important to cabinet members as their service in the job has become longer. Whereas the average tenure of cabinet members in Richard Nixon's shortened administration was 1.73 years, the like figure for Clinton's cabinet members was 4.08 years, 3.59 years for George W. Bush's, and 4.72 years for Obama's.[67] Finally, cabinet composition has great symbolic value as a means of representing major social, economic, and political constituencies in the administration's highest councils.[68] Newly elected presidents generally try to select cabinet members whose presence will unify those constituencies behind the new administration.

Political experience, group identification, and technical expertise are important criteria for selecting cabinet members. Appointees to head certain departments, such as agriculture, generally must be acceptable to clientele groups. In choosing the secretaries of defense and the Treasury, presidents may give special weight to the candidates' expertise and experience. Generalist administrators, however, often are named to head the Departments of Commerce, Health and Human Services, Housing and Urban Development, and Transportation. A study covering eight administrations found that on average, two-thirds of presidents' initial cabinet appointees since FDR have been "Washington outsiders" less familiar with their departments' program responsibilities and that presidents tend to appoint more experienced managers ("insiders") as replacements for their first picks. Similarly, one finds the emphasis on group relations and "liaison" backgrounds early in administrations with the percentage of "generalists" increasing as the term progresses.[69] While Donald Trump's initial appointees included high-profile businessmen with no previous experience in government—most notably Rex Tillerson at State, Steven Mnuchin at Treasury, and Wilbur Ross at Commerce—it also included former governors, members of Congress, and senior military officers, as described below. Most modern presidents develop close ties with the appointees Thomas Cronin refers to as the **inner cabinet**—the heads of the Departments of State, Defense, Treasury, Justice, and now Homeland Security. The activities and responsibilities of these departments are of the highest priority—foreign relations, civil rights, national security, the condition of the economy, and the administration of justice. Moreover, they cut across the concerns of the public and all members of Congress. These are the matters that dominate the president's time and attention.[70] The heads of the other departments usually constitute the **outer cabinet**.[71] Their departments have more sharply focused activities, and their leaders find themselves acting as advocates for clientele and congressional interests within the administration.[72] Frequently, those pressures conflict with the president's broader priorities.

President Obama depended heavily on government insiders to staff his initial cabinet, people with previous elective or appointed experience. All five secretaries heading inner cabinet departments had extensive experience in government service, and two were elected officials. One, Secretary of Defense Gates, was a holdover from the Bush administration and one of two Republicans included in the new cabinet; the other was Ray LaHood, and a third had been invited to join. The remainder of the cabinet included three governors, two House members, and one senator. Appointees without previous elected experience were notable for their technical expertise—a Nobel laureate in physics, chief executive of one of the nation's largest public school systems, a retired general, and an expert in urban housing—and three of these had also worked for government in the past. Obama continued the trend established under Clinton and George W. Bush of appointing more women to the cabinet, four of the initial fifteen members, and these nominees arguably brought even stronger qualifications to their positions.[73] Donald Trump's initial cabinet paid less heed to gender and ethnic diversity concerns; he named just two women, one of whom was Asian-American, along with one African-American man. No Latinos were named originally, but Alexander Acosta was chosen to replace Labor secretary-designate Puzder after he withdrew. His inner cabinet mixed businessmen (at State and

TABLE 6-1 Backgrounds of the Trump Cabinet through April 2017

Appointee	*Former Public Position*
Inner Cabinet	
Secretary of Defense	
James N. Mattis (1/20/17–)	Retired general, U.S. Marine Corps
Attorney General	
Jefferson B. Sessions (2/8/17–)	U.S. senator from Alabama
Secretary of State	
Rex W. Tillerson (2/1/17–)	CEO, Exxon-Mobil
Secretary of the Treasury	
Steven T. Mnuchin (2/13/17–)	Hedge fund investor, banker
Secretary of Homeland Security	
John F. Kelly (1/20/17–)	Retired general, U.S. Marine Corps
Outer Cabinet	
Secretary of Agriculture	
George E. ("Sonny") Perdue III (4/24/17–)	former Governor of Georgia
Secretary of Commerce	
Wilbur L. Ross Jr. (2/27/17–)	Private equity investor
Secretary of Education	
Elisabeth ("Betsy") DeVos (2/7/17–)	Education activist and philanthropist
Secretary of Energy	
Rick Perry (3/2/17–)	former Governor of Texas
Secretary of Health and Human Services	
Thomas E. Price (2/10/17–)	U.S. representative from Georgia
Secretary of Housing and Urban Development	
Benjamin S. Carson (3/2/17–)	retired surgeon, author
Secretary of the Interior	
Ryan K. Zinke (3/1/17–)	U.S. representative from Montana
Secretary of Labor	
R. Alexander Acosta (4/27/17–)	Law school dean; former member, National Labor Relations Board
Secretary of Transportation	
Elaine L. Chao (1/31/17–)	former U.S. Secretary of Labor; former deputy U.S. secretary of Transportation
Secretary of Veterans Affairs	
David Shulkin (2/13/17–)	Undersecretary of Veterans Affairs

(Continued)

TABLE 6-1 (Continued)

Appointee	*Former Public Position*
Nondepartment Cabinet-Level Positions	
Vice President	
Michael R. Pence	Governor of Indiana, former U.S. rep.
Ambassador to the United Nations	
Nimrata ("Nikki") Haley (1/24/17–)	Governor of South Carolina
EPA Administrator	
E. Scott Pruitt (2/17/17–)	Attorney General, Oklahoma
Office of Management and Budget (OMB) Director	
John Michael ("Mick") Mulvaney (2/16/17–)	U.S. representative from South Carolina
U.S. Trade Representative	
Robert E. Lighthizer (5/11/17–)	Attorney; deputy U.S. trade rep., Reagan administration
White House Chief of Staff	
Reinhold ("Reince") Preibus (1/20/17–)	Chairman, Republican National Committee

SOURCE: Compiled by authors using public sources.

Treasury) with retired generals (at Defense and Homeland Security), with one elected official—Attorney General Jeff Sessions, a senator and early endorser of Trump's candidacy. The remainder of the roster ranged from former governors (Rick Perry, Sonny Perdue) and members of Congress (Tom Price, Ryan Zinke) to newcomers (Ben Carson, Betsy DeVos). Only one new secretary had extensive executive branch experience outside the military: new transportation secretary Elaine Chao, who had served as George W. Bush's secretary of labor and as his father's deputy secretary of transportation.

Presidents tend to have considerable turnover in their cabinet membership over time. Harry S. Truman had thirty-five different department secretaries during his nearly eight years in office at a time when there were only eleven departments. George W. Bush also had thirty-five during his two terms, serving in fifteen departments. Obama's total was thirty-two, the last change coming in the Department of Education in March 2016.[74]

Presidents often try to use the cabinet as a decision-making body early in their administrations, but most eventually abandon the effort and rely on the White House staff instead.[75] They find that most cabinet members are concerned primarily with issues affecting their departments and that competition for the president's attention often occurs between cabinet members. Individual cabinet members feel loyal to the president and to the permanent governments within their departments. These conflicting loyalties inhibit the development of an informal sense of unity and purpose, without which the cabinet cannot realize its potential as a formal advisory body and policymaking mechanism.[76] Thus, cabinet meetings are unsatisfactory devices for focused, analytical discussion of major issues. At best they can serve as forums for informal discussion of issues and problems and for the exchange of information. Presidents and their aides in the EOP are the only source of cohesion and policy coordination. In most administrations, one or two cabinet members tend to stand out and to develop close ties with the president. During Reagan's second term, Attorney General Edwin Meese III and Secretary of the Treasury James A. Baker III enjoyed considerable leeway in pursuing their own agendas without aggressive interference from the White House staff, provided they did not conflict with the president's ideological precepts.[77] Treasury secretaries Lloyd Bentsen and Robert Rubin enjoyed independent stature in the Clinton administration because of their political and business experience, respectively.[78]

At the start of George W. Bush's administration, observers noted the influence of Vice President Dick Cheney, whose broad responsibilities and access apparently gave him more clout than any of the cabinet members, especially after Bush publicly contradicted positions taken by Secretary of State Colin Powell and EPA administrator Christine Todd Whitman (one of the first members of the original group to leave) during his first one hundred days. After 9/11, Bush became a wartime president, a development that narrowed his circle of cabinet interactions.[79] The "war cabinet"—Cheney, Card, Powell, national security adviser Condoleezza Rice, Secretary of Defense Donald Rumsfeld, Secretary of the Treasury Paul O'Neill, and CIA director George Tenet—met daily with the president to manage the immediate aftermath of the disaster and prepare the nation for a war on terrorism.[80]

Presidents generally look beyond the cabinet for policy advice. Since its creation in 1947, the NSC and its staff have been used extensively by presidents for foreign and military policy matters (see chapter 10). In economic policy areas, presidents work closely with the chair of the Council of Economic Advisers, the Office of Management and Budget (OMB) director, the secretary of the Treasury, and the chair of the Federal Reserve Board (see chapter 9). In domestic policy areas, which involve primarily the outer cabinet departments, domestic policy staffs and OMB have provided assistance to the president in policy formulation (see chapter 8), and cabinet committees, interagency committees, and policy councils have been employed to coordinate policymaking and implementation.

Cabinet committees, usually appointed on an ad hoc basis to handle specific problems, can focus quickly on them. Interagency committees, which operate mostly at the agency and subcabinet levels, may achieve a measure of coordination, but their work is often hampered by competition between agencies and by a lack of status and visibility.

Policy councils help presidents highlight particular problems. Nixon introduced a Domestic Council designed as an analogue to the NSC, and Gerald R. Ford created the Economic Policy Board (EPB). Both units have appeared under various names in successor administrations. Reagan established seven cabinet councils in addition to the NSC to help move issues upward to the cabinet and then the president. That group was later reduced to two: the Economic Policy Council and the Domestic Policy Council (DPC). George H. W. Bush continued to utilize the Economic Policy Council and the DPC but with apparently limited effectiveness due to squabbling and rivalries among his advisers.[81] Clinton replaced the EPC with a higher level domestic policy unit, the National Economic Council (NEC), though he also relied on high-level advisers such as Ira Magaziner, George Stephanopoulos, and First Lady Hillary Rodham Clinton. The fragmentation of advice that this structure produced reflected Clinton's desire to be at the center of an informal, collegial policymaking process, which he ran like a continuous seminar. With respect to selling and implementing his policy choices, however, Clinton preferred a more formal structure.[82] A reorganization eighteen months into his term (described later in this chapter) sought to rein in Clinton's freewheeling style more generally.

Obama, like his predecessor George W. Bush, retained the DPC and the NEC as White House coordinating units and staffed each, at the outset, with trusted campaign advisers. Consistent with all other presidents since Truman, he also utilized the NSC structure to help coordinate national security policy. Obama's principal—though not unprecedented—innovation was heavy reliance on "policy czars." These were White House aides given broad responsibility to coordinate major policy initiatives that straddled federal agencies, build cooperation with state and local governments, and create partnerships with the private sector.[83] Positions were carved out for energy and climate change, health care reform, economic policy, technology promotion, urban affairs, auto industry restructuring ("car czar"), financial bailouts, terrorism, drug control, and Native American policy.[84] In essence, the president was expanding a strategy dating to Woodrow Wilson: to assign a White House aide the responsibility to coordinate government action across departments and agencies. In some areas, the aide would enjoy staff support and prestige associated with a long-standing council, such as the Council of Economic Advisers, but in other areas the effort would be new. Much depended on the personalities of the assistants and how cooperative the cabinet secretaries would prove to be. (Also see chapter 8.) Advisers left the White House as tasks were completed, but Obama kept returning to the strategy. For example, in 2014, amid growing criticisms over an apparently incoherent response to the mounting Ebola crisis, Obama named another "czar" responsible for crafting a coherent government-wide response.[85] The early days of the Trump White House kept the various policy councils in place. NEC director Gary Cohn, a former Goldman Sachs executive, quickly established himself as a trusted adviser. Michael Flynn, Trump's first pick as national security adviser, was tarred by scandal and replaced after less than a month by a well-respected active-service general, H. R. McMaster. In general the early days of the administration were marked by the maneuvering of various factions seeking influence and the president's ear. These included the "establishment" wing of the White House, led by chief of staff and former Republican National Committee chair Reince Preibus; the "nationalist" wing, led by chief strategist Stephen Bannon; and, most notably, the "family" wing. Both Trump's daughter Ivanka and her husband, Jared Kushner, were given formal White House staff positions. Kushner was assigned an immense substantive portfolio that included government reorganization, the domestic opioid crisis, Mexican and Chinese relations with the United States, and the wider problem of Middle East peace.

The Vice President

George W. Bush's most controversial management innovation was the power delegated to Vice President Cheney, whose unprecedented influence could ultimately have negative consequences for an office that emerged from the shadows during the Carter administration. Historically, vice presidents were given little to do either by the Constitution or the presidents with whom they served. The position's constitutional powers are limited: to preside over the Senate, casting a vote only when there is a tie, and to succeed the president in the event of removal by "Death, Resignation, or Inability to discharge the Powers and Duties of the said Office."[86] Tie-breaking votes have been rare: only 258 in history. Cheney cast eight of those votes, six coming during the 2001–2003 period when the Senate's partisan balance was almost even. Biden cast none. But Mike Pence's vote was needed three times before he was in office three months, most notably to confirm Betsy DeVos as education secretary by a 51–50 tally.[87]

Nine vice presidents have succeeded to the presidency, constituting nearly a quarter of the nation's forty-four presidents. The Constitution's guidelines on succession are not very clear. In the event of the predecessor's death, would the new president be the "president" or the "acting president"? John Tyler asserted the former and in 1841 established the precedent that has been followed since. What happens in the event of a vacancy in the vice presidency? That question was not answered until 1967 with adoption of the Twenty-Fifth Amendment. In addition, over the years Congress has provided three different succession scenarios if neither the president nor vice president is able to serve. For the nation's first ninety-four years, the successor was the Senate's president pro tempore, followed by the Speaker of the House. For the next six decades, it was members of the cabinet in order of their office's creation. The most recent succession act, adopted in 1947, calls for the Speaker of the House, followed by the president pro tempore, followed by the cabinet secretaries in the order of their office's creation, which means the Secretary of Homeland Security comes last.[88]

What do vice presidents do? For many years, they were largely forgotten by presidents and public alike, dispatched around the world to attend ceremonial events and funeral services, and given the job of launching highly partisan attacks (considered beneath the dignity of the president) during political campaigns. Jimmy Carter and Walter Mondale are credited with modernizing the job to be an integral part of the president's support staff.[89] Mondale met regularly with the president, attended senior staff meetings, had a staff of his own, was given important assignments, and was treated with respect rather than derision. His successors—George H. W. Bush, Dan Quayle, and Al Gore—sought to build on that foundation, although Gore seemed to be Cheney's most influential predecessor.

At the outset of the Bush administration, Cheney was by far the most experienced person on the White House team. He had served seven years in the Nixon-Ford White House, including fifteen months as Ford's chief of staff. He then had ten years in the House of Representatives and rose through the ranks to become minority whip. Cheney next served as secretary of defense for nearly four years, heading the department during the Persian Gulf War. After George H. W. Bush's loss in 1992, Cheney became a multimillionaire as the chairman and CEO of Halliburton Company, an international oil services firm, his position when George W. Bush asked him to oversee the committee to select the Republican vice presidential candidate. Cheney himself was Bush's surprise choice.

All of this experience meant that Cheney was far more familiar with the ways of Washington than was his boss, and there is ample evidence that he used this knowledge to its fullest advantage to influence critical policy decisions of the Bush administration. After an extensive review of Cheney's record, the *Washington Post* concluded that he had "shaped his times as no vice president has done before."[90] He proved to be a masterful bureaucratic operator. Most important, Cheney enjoyed his boss's confidence, advising him in private and standing by his side in public. Much of Cheney's influence was behind the scenes: "The president is 'the decider,' as Bush puts it, but the vice president often serves up his menu of choices."[91] Cheney's fingerprints (seldom obvious) are alleged to have been on many of the most controversial actions of the Bush administration: establishing an eavesdropping program on international phone conversations of Americans outside of judicial control; using military commissions to process foreign terrorism suspects; authorizing use of interrogation techniques on terrorism suspects that fall outside the Geneva Conventions (in other words, using torture to extract information); pushing consistently for higher tax cuts for the wealthiest segment of the public; and leaking to the media the identity of Valerie Plame, a CIA operative and the wife of an outspoken critic of the Bush administration's Iraq policy. The leak ultimately led to the conviction of I. Lewis "Scooter" Libby, Cheney's chief of staff, for perjury and obstruction of justice.

Before he assumed office, Vice President Biden openly criticized Cheney's expansive notions of executive power and questionable policy positions on using torture as a means to protect the homeland from further terrorist attacks.[92] Biden returned to the Mondale model of the vice presidency—serving as an influential general adviser, assuming responsibilities as assigned by the president, and operating within more conventional definitions of the job.[93] At the outset of the Obama administration, he was asked to head the task force charged with improving the condition of the middle class, oversee implementation of the economic stimulus package, lead the administration's charge on controlling gun violence, and deliver important foreign policy messages to audiences overseas.[94] Biden assumed growing responsibility for liaison and negotiations with Congress as he got to know the president better, some of Obama's closest advisers left the administration, and Republicans gained control of the House in 2011 and the Senate in 2015. He led the discussions in April 2011 to avoid a government shutdown, again in July 2011 to avoid a government default, and yet again in 2012 to sidestep the "fiscal cliff." As a three-and-a-half decade veteran of Congress, the gregarious Biden had become a well-known and well-liked legislator, trusted by fellow Democrats and credible as a bargaining partner to Republicans, especially Senate minority leader Mitch McConnell, who had dealt with him many times over the years.[95] He played an ongoing role in helping to guide political developments in Iraq and Ukraine and tried to steer the Israel-Palestinian talks onto a more fruitful path. In short, Biden was heavily involved in the major decisions of the Obama presidency, and Obama asked him to take the lead on selected issues.

Early in his vice presidential service, Biden seemed to have no interest in eventually running for president, though he had mounted campaigns in 1988 and 2008. Following the successful 2012 campaign, his responses to media questions about his future plans were coy, and he later made it known that he was considering a run for the presidency in 2016. In the end, he opted not to run, in part because of the untimely death of his eldest son and in part because of efforts by Democratic luminaries to clear the field for Hillary Clinton. As noted in chapter 2, the vice presidency is a good position for seeking the presidential nomination, but vice presidents have seldom (only twice in history) been elected directly to the presidency, perhaps a reflection of the public's desire to have "that new car smell," as Obama put it.[96]

Biden was the third consecutive vice president to serve two full terms in office, the first time that had happened in American history. Gore, Cheney, and Biden all played major roles in their administrations, each had a different relationship with the president and a distinctive definition of the job, but each also drew on important precedents established since Nelson Rockefeller (Ford's vice president). Mike Pence seemed likely to continue that trend, directing the transition, serving early as a liaison to the Hill, and then undertaking a delicate diplomatic mission to east Asia. Continuing examples of vice presidential influence are likely to make both official Washington and the public more comfortable with vice presidents playing an important role in presidential administrations.

The First Lady

FDR needed Eleanor Roosevelt to travel the country in his stead, serving as his eyes, ears, and legs. She reported her observations back to him and was a vocal advocate for her causes, including civil rights, miner safety, women's rights, aid for the unemployed, and war relief. Like her husband did for the presidency, Eleanor Roosevelt is credited with transforming the position of first lady, using the strength of her public persona to exercise policy and political influence rather than simply serving as Washington's leading social hostess. The East Wing of the White House became her base of operations for a weekly newspaper column and regular radio appearances. She had carved out an independent political role from her husband well before he entered the White House and continued her activism after his death, serving as Truman's representative on the United Nations Commission on Human Rights.

Subsequent first ladies built upon Eleanor's experience, though not all were public activists. Bess Truman, Mamie Eisenhower, and Pat Nixon preferred to avoid the limelight and played a more traditional role as behind-the-scenes partners. (For example, Mamie entered the Oval Office only four times during Ike's eight years and was invited to do so each time.)[97] The celebrity status that surrounded Jackie Kennedy made her an important public relations asset to her husband, but her advocacy was limited to promoting the arts. Lady Bird Johnson was the next first lady to become a vocal policy advocate, for conservation and beautification projects. More in Roosevelt's vein, Rosalynn Carter and especially Hillary Clinton pursued active policy agendas, emphasizing expansion of programs to treat mental disabilities and to advance health care, respectively. Other first ladies emphasized volunteerism (Pat Nixon), drug awareness (Nancy Reagan), literacy (Barbara Bush), and childhood literacy (Laura Bush). Even though first ladies have largely chosen to emphasize noncontroversial, charitable causes, the first lady's many other political activities mean that over time "she has gone from being primarily a hostess to being an important spokesperson for her husband's political agenda."[98]

Similar to the changes that have transformed the vice presidency, modern first ladies now play an important role in the White House, to complement the informal influence they long played in advising their spouses privately. Modern administrations have seen first ladies add a chief of staff to help coordinate other specialists for scheduling, press relations, social events (a traditional area of responsibility), and various special projects. Moreover, the first lady's staff has been incorporated into the overall White House staff system rather than being treated as a separate, subordinate operation. Senior members of the first lady's staff commonly hold appointments as presidential advisers. This growth and professionalization has occurred as the first lady's job and her visibility have grown.[99]

Even more than the vice president, the first lady lacks "any clearly defined formal role" and receives no pay for her efforts, though the first lady's staff began to receive public support in the 1980s.[100] Vice presidents at least get a modest mention in the Constitution, officially stand for election (a major step beyond "two for the price of one," as the Clintons proclaimed during the 1992 election), and receive half the salary set for the president. But in many ways, the first lady's job is much tougher—she is "evaluated as a domestic partner at the same time that she is judged as a public figure"[101] and is subject to the public's contradictory expectations of women (support for independence and equality but even more support for preserving home and family), at least until "a woman is elected president and talk will not be of first ladies but of first spouses."[102]

Michelle Obama was a visible and highly popular part of the Obama presidency; her approval ratings were consistently in the 60 percent range even when her husband's settled in the low 40s. She embraced several major initiatives, including support for military families (Joining Forces), helping children lead healthier lives and fight childhood obesity (Let's Move), and encouraging U.S. youth to complete their education past high school (Reach Higher). She became an effective public speaker and public ambassador for the administration's programs, making well-received appearances on talk shows and late night television, and ultimately during the 2012 and 2016 campaigns. Her early emphasis was primarily on noncontroversial, family-oriented subjects centered on children and health, but over time she began to speak more about issues of race and economic opportunity. Her 2016 Democratic National Convention speech took direct aim at the Trump campaign's slogan. "I wake up every morning in a house that was built by slaves. And I watch my daughters—two beautiful intelligent black young women—play with the dog on the White House lawn," Obama said. ". . . . Don't let anyone ever tell you that this country is not great."[103]

Melania Trump, whose early career was as a fashion model, was a far more reticent first lady, at least during the early days of her husband's presidency. She opted against living in the White House in early 2017, so that the Trumps' young son could finish out his school year in New York City. Her low visibility role won praise as a return to a "traditional" role but garnered its own criticism on the same grounds, as well as for the additional expense of providing security for the first family in two separate homes. As Michelle Cottle of *Politico* summarized, "The post of first lady is never easy, bringing with it all of the scrutiny but none of the power of the presidency."[104]

Presidential Control of the Bureaucracy

Although presidents face substantial obstacles in seeking to control policymaking and implementation, they do have resources for this effort. They have substantial powers granted by the Constitution, delegated by Congress, and derived from the nature of their office. The most important are the powers to appoint and remove subordinates, to issue executive orders and other directives, and to prepare the annual federal budget and regulate expenditures.

Appointment and Removal

The Constitution gives the president broad powers of appointment (Article 2, section 2, paragraph 2), but it makes high-ranking officials subject to confirmation, and Congress, itself, determines which appointments warrant confirmation and which ones can be delegated to the president, department heads, or the courts. The Senate can also narrow the president's discretion in making appointments by establishing detailed qualifications for various offices. Congress cannot, however, give itself the power to appoint executive officials.[105] Neither can it force the president to make an appointment to a vacant position.[106] The president's appointive powers also are constrained by political considerations and practices such as senatorial courtesy, whereby senators effectively have veto power over certain administrative and judicial appointments from their home states (see further discussion in chapter 7).

The Senate generally has given presidents considerable leeway in the appointment of top-level executives. But confirmation is not automatic, and the Senate uses rejections to express disapproval of specific individuals or practices or to delay a new administration from taking charge of the bureaucracy and introducing changes.[107] Since Watergate (1972–1974), the Senate has tended to be more careful and procedurally consistent in examining nominees' backgrounds, qualifications, and relevant policy views. Enhanced vigilance has made the confirmation process "more tedious, time-consuming, and intrusive for the nominees," a situation exacerbated by interparty conflict.[108] For example, during the Clinton administration, the Senate finally confirmed Richard C. Holbrooke as U.S. permanent representative to the United Nations after a fourteen-month odyssey that included two federal ethics investigations, four hearings conducted by the Senate Foreign Relations Committee, and "holds"—objections to a nominee that delay action—placed by several Republican senators in an effort to wrest concessions from the administration on unrelated matters. George W. Bush's administration never succeeded in securing Senate approval for John R. Bolton's appointment to the same position despite two sets of hearings held by the Senate Foreign Relations Committee and multiple efforts to end a Democratic filibuster on the floor of the Senate. It took 166 days for the Senate to confirm the nomination of Loretta Lynch as attorney general in 2015, a delay occasioned by battles over President Obama's use of executive action and Senate scheduling. Faced by the prospect of such a tortuous and contentious process, candidates sometime withdraw from consideration or decline invitations to serve.[109]

At the beginning of his first term, George W. Bush had about 1,200 full-time positions subject to Senate confirmation, out of approximately 4,000 to fill, not including judgeships or the many advisory committees scattered across the government.[110] Bush confronted unusual hurdles in doing so. Not only were the nominations delayed by the 2000 election controversy, but also the new Senate was initially bogged down in a 50–50 stalemate, then experienced a change in the majority party from Republican to Democratic in June 2001, and finally experienced confusion after 9/11. All of this slowed the Bush administration in selecting top appointees. During Bush's first year in office, it took an average of 181 days for nominees to be confirmed, up from Clinton's 174 days and Reagan's 142. Overall, as a later study found, a full quarter of Bush appointees were never confirmed.[111] But Obama's record in securing confirmations was even worse: 30% of his nominees never wound up in office, including a remarkable 72% of those nominated in 2016, his last year as president.[112] Even at the outset of his term, Obama's nominees confronted delays nearly three weeks longer than Bush's.[113] By mid-May 2009, 85 nominated candidates awaited confirmation and 111 had been approved for the 486 top positions subject to Senate confirmation.[114] After one year, 63 percent of Obama's nominees had been approved, compared to Bush's 73 percent at the same point in his first term. Such delays could have devastating consequences on effectiveness. For example, the Department of the Treasury, where Secretary Geithner faced unprecedented challenges to fix the financial crisis, had twenty-three such positions to fill. Ten weeks into the administration, only one person other than himself had been confirmed, and through the administration's first one hundred days the total stood at only four. Without a senior leadership team, the department was likely to flounder.

Republican efforts to block Obama appointments later triggered unprecedented changes in the Senate. In November 2013, Senate Democrats adapted the Senate's rules to prevent filibusters of all presidential nominations to executive and judicial positions except the Supreme Court. Nominations would now be decided by a simple majority vote rather than the supermajority of sixty votes required to invoke cloture and cut off Senate debate. At the time, sixty-one nominees to executive branch positions and seventeen nominees to the federal judiciary were awaiting floor confirmation votes.[115] In making his case, Senate majority leader Harry Reid, D-NV, noted that half of all nomination filibusters in Senate history had occurred during Obama's terms, and he justified his action by pointing to the

Republicans' refusal to consider three nominations to the D.C. Court of Appeals as well as several administrative positions, including a two-year delay in confirming a head of the Consumer Financial Protection Bureau.[116] For a short time, Obama no longer needed to choose nominees who could attract Republican votes.

Republicans warned that Democrats would regret the action when the Senate majority changed hands (as it did in 2015), and indeed, Obama nominees were largely blocked during 2015 and 2016. When a Republican president also came to office in 2017, though, delays continued. By the end of his first 100 days in office, two of President Trump's cabinet members had yet to be confirmed, and hundreds of subcabinet positions remained vacant.

Trump tweeted as early as February that "It is a disgrace that my full Cabinet is still not in place . . . Obstruction by Democrats!"[117] Democrats did indeed oppose many of the president's nominees. But they had little leverage for effective obstruction, given the elimination of the filibuster for that purpose and near-unity among Republicans on behalf of even controversial nominees such as Betsy DeVos at Education or Scott Pruitt at the Environmental Protection Agency. Delays were attributable instead to the ethics and financial reviews required of the numerous nominees with complicated corporate ties. One of the two cabinet secretaries not in place by the Easter recess in April was former Georgia governor Sonny Perdue (Agriculture), whose paperwork was not ready for Senate consideration until mid-March. (The other, Alexander Acosta, was not named until mid-February, when he became the second Labor nominee after the first was withdrawn.) As noted above, the White House was even slower to name candidates to fill the vast majority of subcabinet vacancies, as the perpetual battle to balance loyalty and competence played itself out across different White House factions, cabinet secretaries, and the president himself. *Politico* reported in April 2017 that President Trump "personally oversees the hiring process for agency staff, . . . combing through a binder full of names each week" and "sign[ing] off on each one."[118]

Delays in the Senate are occasioned most often when senators apply "holds" that prevent Senate votes "often for reasons that have nothing to do with their qualifications to serve."[119] Senators often seek to bargain with the administration over a contentious policy matter important to the home state—essentially, "I'll remove my hold if you give in on. . . ." Since the administration of Ronald Reagan, however, more and more presidential nominations (both judicial and executive) died from "malign neglect," delaying action on the nominations for so long that the nominee withdraws, the president gives up, or the session concludes.[120] Now gone is the historic presumption that presidential nominees will be approved;

even now, the president's partisan opponents in the Senate can still systematically use a variety of delaying tactics to kill a nomination. Both Senate Democrats and Republicans have used such tactics. The Constitution also empowers the president to make appointments when the Senate is in recess. This power ensured government continuity when transportation was difficult and Congress met only part of the year. Such **recess appointments** must be confirmed by the end of the Senate's next session, but the appointee serves in the interim. Senators often object to recess appointments to high-level positions because they feel inhibited from thoroughly examining people who have already begun their duties. Recent presidents made surprisingly frequent use of recess appointments: Reagan made 232 recess appointments, George H. W. Bush made 78, Bill Clinton 139, and George W. Bush 171.[121] Barack Obama made just 32. But, frustrated by what he viewed as outright Republican obstructionism, Obama made fifteen recess appointments in March 2010, largely to positions with economic responsibilities. As a White House press release pointed out, the administration then had 217 nominations pending before the Senate, 77 of which were waiting for floor votes. The fifteen recess appointees had been pending for an average of 214 days.[122]

Recess appointments enable presidents to get the person they want—at least temporarily—without making policy compromises. But the tactic came under challenge in the courts. In January 2013, a three-judge panel from the U.S. Court of Appeals for the District of Columbia ruled that three recess appointments made by President Obama in January 2012 to the National Labor Relations Board (NLRB) were invalid. The judges ruled that presidents can make recess appointments only to positions that became vacant during intersession recesses, that is between annual sessions of Congress. During January 2012, when the appointments were made, the Senate had maintained the semblance of being in session by going through the formality of having a senator bang the gavel every three days.[123] If upheld, this decision would have voided hundreds of appointments made since Ronald Reagan.[124]

The Supreme Court decision rendered in June 2014 handed the Obama administration a loss—the court agreed unanimously that the three NLRB recess appointments were illegal—but gave the presidency a victory when a narrow majority of justices confirmed the historic practice of presidents making appointments during Senate recesses of ten days or more. The majority also ruled that presidents may make recess appointments to vacancies that arise before the recess begins. But in the case of Obama's appointments, the three-day pro forma sessions held during an extended break were viewed as legitimate (since the Senate makes its own rules as to when it is in session), and three days was too short a time for the constitutional provision to apply.[125]

Complementing the appointment power—and fundamental to presidential control of the executive branch—is the **removal power**. Without the ability to remove subordinate officials on performance or policy grounds, presidents cannot be held fully responsible for their actions or for a department's or agency's failure to achieve presidential objectives. The Constitution is silent, however, concerning the removal of executive officials other than through impeachment, a cumbersome process limited to conviction for "Treason, Bribery, or other high Crimes and Misdemeanors."

Removing subordinates from office can spur controversy: only ten days after taking office in 2017, for instance, President Trump fired acting attorney general Sally Yates when she said the Justice Department would refuse to enforce the president's so-called "travel ban" order halting immigration from a number of nations.[126] Critics called his action the "Monday Night Massacre," referencing a (far more problematic) Watergate-era scandal springing from the dismissal of an independent prosecutor in 1973. More generally, presidents have long clashed with Congress over the removal power. The post–Civil War conflict between President Andrew Johnson and Congress over Reconstruction policy involved the removal power. In 1867, Congress brought impeachment proceedings against Johnson for violating the Tenure of Office Act, which it had passed over his veto. That statute authorized all persons appointed with the advice and consent of the Senate to continue to hold office until the president appointed—and the Senate confirmed—a successor. Johnson tried to remove Secretary of War Edwin Stanton without permission. Although Johnson survived the impeachment trial by one vote, the issue of the removal power remained unresolved. (Congress repealed the Tenure of Office Act in 1887.)

The Supreme Court dealt directly with the removal power in a decision involving a challenge to Woodrow Wilson's summary removal of a postmaster.[127] In *Myers v. U.S.*, the Court invalidated an 1876 law that required the Senate's consent for a postmaster's removal. It held that the Constitution gave the president the removal power and Congress could not place restrictions on its exercise. Nine years later, however, the Court upheld the provisions of the Federal Trade Commission Act that limited the grounds for removal of its members.[128] The Court ruled that the president's unqualified power of removal is limited to "purely executive offices" and that Congress may prescribe conditions for the removal of officials performing "quasi-legislative" and "quasi-judicial" functions. The Court has not, however, fully clarified the meaning of these terms. A dramatic instance of the removal power occurred in August 1981, when President Reagan fired 11,400 striking members of the Professional Air Traffic Controllers Organization. A U.S. court of appeals upheld the action, interpreting it as a discharge of the president's obligation to enforce a statute prohibiting strikes by federal employees.[129] In 2016, the D.C. Circuit Court of Appeals ruled that the structure of the Consumer Financial Protection Bureau was unconstitutional, because it had a single director who could only be removed for cause. Following *Myers,* the majority held the director must serve at the pleasure of the president.[130]

Members of Congress can ratchet up pressure on political executives (and their boss), even if they cannot directly remove them without impeachment proceedings. In 2007, for instance, Senate Democrats, joined reluctantly by several Republicans, sought to force President George W. Bush to remove Attorney General Alberto Gonzales when controversy about the firing of eight U.S. attorneys, allegedly on "political grounds," embroiled the attorney general in sustained controversy. After several ineffective appearances before the Senate Judiciary Committee and additional controversy about his role in the administration's warrantless surveillance program while working in the White House, Gonzales

Olivier Doulier - Pool/Getty Images

President Trump visited the Central Intelligence Agency a day after taking office, seeking to reassure its staff after Trump feuded with the intelligence community during the transition. But his politicized remarks in front of the CIA's memorial wall caused their own controversy.

submitted his resignation in August 2007. The president accepted, expressing appreciation for his longtime aide's hard work and bitterness at what he saw as mistreatment of Gonzales. A similar drama unfolded for Obama's secretary of health and human services, when the controversy surrounding the faulty rollout of the federal health care website in fall 2013 triggered calls for Kathleen Sebelius to resign, which she did in April 2014.

Executive Orders and Unilateral Action

Recent presidents have used various forms of unilateral action, including executive orders and presidential memoranda, to take dramatic steps during their initial hours and days in office. Moments after delivering his first inaugural address, Reagan used a presidential memorandum to freeze federal hiring to support his contention that big government was the problem, not the solution. Clinton issued an executive order on ethics while still on Capitol Hill after delivering his first inaugural address. George W. Bush issued three memoranda on his first inauguration day, followed by several more in the next week, to emphasize high-level policy priorities including the redefinition of relationships between faith-based programs and the government.[131] Obama's first executive actions rolled back a number of his predecessor's efforts linked to the war on terror (such as the use of torture in questioning suspected terrorists) and practices on government secrecy.[132] On January 20, 2017, Trump issued an executive order seeking to "minimize the . . . burdens" of the Affordable Care Act; a flurry of orders and memoranda soon followed, drawing attention to campaign priorities such as the rollback of environmental regulations and the aggressive enforcement of immigration laws. These examples illustrate a long-standing presidential practice: to accomplish goals by using a variety of unilateral instruments or direct administration, including executive orders, directives, memoranda, proclamations, policy instructions, and interpretations of congressional intent. Scholars have increasingly focused on these examples of **unilateral executive power** as recent presidents confronted deep partisan opposition to their policy goals.

Under a strict interpretation of separation of powers, presidents have no direct legislative authority. From the beginning, however, they have issued orders and directives on the basis of Article 2. Most modern presidents have followed Theodore Roosevelt's "stewardship" theory of executive power (see chapter 1), which holds that Article 2 confers on them inherent power to take whatever actions they deem necessary in the national interest unless prohibited by the Constitution or by law. Executive orders have been a primary means of exercising this broad presidential prerogative power and are summarized in Table 6-2 for the period since 1969. "They are presidential edicts, legal instruments that create or modify laws, procedures, and policy by fiat" and have helped push "the boundaries of presidential power by taking advantage of gaps in constitutional and statutory language that allow them to fill power vacuums and gain control of emerging capabilities."[133]

Reliance on such strategies is especially notable in crucial policy areas such as civil rights, economic stabilization, and national security,[134] or when conflict with Congress means action cannot be accomplished through legislation. In civil rights, Franklin Roosevelt established a Fair Employment Practices Commission in 1943 to prevent discriminatory hiring by government agencies and military suppliers. In 1948, Harry Truman ended segregation in the armed forces by executive order. In March 1961, John F. Kennedy issued a sweeping order creating the Equal Employment Opportunity Commission and giving it broad enforcement powers. Lyndon Johnson went further, requiring by executive order the preferential hiring of minorities by government contractors.

More recently, after Congress failed to take action on immigration legislation that had languished for a year, President Obama issued a politically explosive directive in November 2014. In a nationwide television address, he explained that *prosecutorial discretion*—the ability of the president to set priorities for executive branch officials in enforcement—and precedents set under both

TABLE 6-2 Executive Orders, 1969–April 20, 2017

President/Years in Office	*Total Executive Orders Issued by Administration*	*Executive Orders per Year*
Richard Nixon (1969–1974)	346	62.9
Gerald R. Ford (1974–1977)	169	67.6
Jimmy Carter (1977–1981)	320	80.0
Ronald Reagan (1981–1989)	381	47.6
George H. W. Bush (1989–1993)	166	41.5
Bill Clinton (1993–2001)	364	38.5
George W. Bush (2001–2009)	291	36.4
Barack Obama (2009–2017)	276	34.5
Donald J. Trump (2017–)	25	—

SOURCE: See "Executive Orders Disposition Tables Index," *Federal Register,* www.archives.gov/federal-register/executive-orders/disposition.html. Also see The American Presidency Project, www.presidency.ucsb.edu/index_docs.php.

Republican and Democratic presidents legitimized taking action that could allow as many as five million undocumented immigrants to work in the United States without fear of deportation.[135] Obama's action should have surprised no one: He announced a week prior to the 2014 State of the Union message that he would use his "pen and phone" to pursue his agenda, the pen to sign executive actions and the phone to assemble like-minded Americans to pursue policies blocked by Republican tactics.[136]

An economic crisis often triggers unilateral action. FDR established broad precedents for the use of executive orders to achieve economic stability, and a number of his successors have followed suit. During World War II, he issued executive orders to establish the Office of Price Administration (OPA) and the Office of Economic Stabilization and to give them extensive powers over prices, wages, and profits. The OPA also rationed scarce consumer goods such as meat, butter, shoes, tires, and gasoline. As a basis for his actions, Roosevelt cited his responsibility to respond to the "unlimited emergency" created by the war. The Emergency Price Control Act of 1942 provided retroactive statutory endorsement for the establishment of the emergency agencies and the measures they implemented. In 1970, in the face of persistent inflation, Congress passed the Economic Stabilization Act, which authorized the president to issue orders that would control wages and prices, but with few criteria to guide these actions—Nixon used that power on August 15, 1971, to issue an executive order imposing a ninety-day freeze on nonagricultural wages and prices. An October 15 order extended the controls and established additional machinery to aid in administering them.[137]

Presidents also have used executive orders and national security directives to guide foreign policy. In 1942, for example, FDR issued an executive order requiring the internment of all persons of Japanese ancestry living in the Pacific coastal states, seventy thousand of them U.S. citizens. The Supreme Court upheld this massive deprivation of civil liberties on the basis of the commander in chief clause.[138] George W. Bush responded to the 9/11 attacks with a series of executive actions enabling him to wield wartime powers, including an order setting up military commissions, in lieu of civilian courts, to try detainees.

Among the eight most recently completed administrations, Jimmy Carter made the heaviest use of executive orders, partly because of his interest in government reorganization; presidents since 1981 have used them less (see Table 6-2). In the three months following 9/11, President Bush issued more executive orders than he had in the previous eight months, and several of them proved especially controversial.[139]

There is some disagreement over whether presidents confronted by a Congress controlled by the opposition party will make heavier use of executive orders. For example, year-to-year totals show that Clinton's use of executive orders actually declined rather than increased when he confronted a hostile Republican Congress after 1995, although he may still have used executive orders as a way to make progress on major policy initiatives.[140] In his exhaustive study of executive orders, Kenneth Mayer traces the pattern of their use from 1936 through 1995 and concludes that the issuance of orders "rises and falls in response to significant events."[141] The onset of war, for example, triggers new administrative arrangements and regulations governing economic controls and wartime mobilization, just as peace requires their removal. The focus of executive orders has also changed over time. Orders dealing with executive branch administration, foreign affairs, and domestic policy increased from 1936 to 1999.[142] Finally, Democrats make more use of executive orders than Republicans; more orders are issued at the end of a term and when the president's public support is low than under the opposite conditions; and more orders are issued when the president's party is in the congressional majority, a counterintuitive finding stemming from the fact that many orders simply implement new legislative mandates.[143] Mayer estimates that about one of every seven executive orders is significant—that is, it attracts media, congressional, or scholarly notice; triggers litigation; or represents a meaningful policy departure.[144] Trump issued 24 executive orders in the first three months of his term, many with elaborate signing ceremonies, as a high-profile way to argue he was making progress on his substantive priorities.

Phillip J. Cooper argues that the focus should be on the content, rather than the quantity, of such actions and the reasons presidents use them. In particular, recent administrations use "presidential memoranda" alongside, and interchangeably with, executive orders; and Clinton is credited with issuing 536 presidential memoranda, many more than his predecessors.[145] Unlike executive orders, memoranda do not have to be published in the *Federal Register,* in which rules and orders appear, nor is there a procedure for developing them, making them simpler to issue. Recent research has shown that the number of memoranda has grown over the past half-century as the number of executive orders has declined, quite possibly because of the greater publicity that orders attract. Under Obama, the number of memoranda surged and they played a particularly important role in the "we can't wait" campaign launched in 2011—as the president put it, "We can't wait for Congress to do its job. So where they won't act, I will."[146] As Obama explained to a crowd in Denver, Colorado, "I've told my administration we're going to look every single day to figure out what we can do without Congress." Examples given by the president included giving states flexibility on No Child Left Behind, the federal education policy; processing payments more quickly for small businesses that are federal contractors; eliminating regulations to save on health care expenses for hospitals and individuals; hiring veterans for health care and community service jobs; helping families refinance their mortgages; and linking federal purchasing to vendors' policies on wages and equal rights.[147]

Ultimately, the question will be whether Congress and others will accept such assertions of presidential prerogative. Unilateral presidential action can be reversed. During the Korean War, the Supreme Court invalidated Truman's seizure of the steel industry on the grounds that he had not used the machinery established in the Taft-Hartley Act of 1947 to avert a strike.[148] More recently, we have the example of successor presidents reversing an action of their predecessors, as Clinton,[149] George W. Bush, Obama and Trump all did. In that sense executive action is fragile—its fate rests with the next executive.

Not only can executive orders be reversed—they might not be obeyed. As Obama left office, more than 40 prisoners were still held at Guantánamo Bay. If bureaucrats find excuses to drag their feet, presidents might need to win their cooperation through bargaining. There is strong evidence that presidents do just that—craft directives that both the chief executive and career officials can support. As Andrew Rudalevige concludes, "the issuance of executive orders seems to involve as much consultation as command."[150]

From 1932 until 1983, Congress exerted a measure of control over executive lawmaking with the **legislative veto**. Provisions added to certain statutes gave Congress the power to review and reject executive orders or administrative regulations authorized by the legislation. The legislative veto took various forms. It allowed disapproval of regulations by concurrent resolution or by simple resolution of either house or by action of a committee of either house. In its most common form, the legislative veto required that the proposed action lie before Congress for a specified period—usually sixty or ninety days—during which either chamber could disapprove it. The president's reorganization authority, which Congress first authorized in 1939, carried such a procedure. Other major statutes that had a form of legislative veto include the War Powers Resolution of 1973, the Budget and Impoundment Control Act of 1974, the Federal Elections Campaign Act of 1974, and the National Emergencies Act of 1976. More than 250 statutes provided for some type of legislative veto before the Supreme Court declared it unconstitutional in 1983.

In *Immigration and Naturalization Service v. Chadha,* the Court held that the one-house legislative veto provision of the Immigration and Nationality Act was an unconstitutional breach of the separation of powers.[151] The Court reasoned that the veto involved "the exercise of legislative power" without "bicameral passage followed by presentment to the President." In other words, such actions were not subject to presidential concurrence or veto. Initial reaction to the decision was that it was not a definitive ruling and that somehow Congress would find a way statutorily to control executive branch lawmaking.[152] Although the Court threw out past practices, Congress has required agencies to obtain approval from the appropriations committees before taking specified actions and used informal agreements with agencies to achieve the same goal.[153]

Presidents and Money

Presidents have substantial financial powers, delegated by Congress, that they use in their efforts to control the bureaucracy. The most important is the power to formulate the budget, which controls the amount of spending by federal departments and agencies. The budget establishes the president's spending priorities, sets the timing of program initiatives, and distributes rewards to, and imposes sanctions on, executive branch units.[154] By controlling the total amount of the budget, the president can try to influence the economy's performance (see chapter 9).

Presidential use of the executive budget developed in the twentieth century. The enormous increase in expenditures during World War I and the task of managing the sizable national debt that resulted convinced Congress of the need for an executive budget. The Budget and Accounting Act of 1921 made the president responsible for compiling department and agency estimates and for submitting them annually to Congress in the form of a budget. The statute established the Bureau of the Budget (BOB), in the Treasury Department, to assist the president in assembling and revising the estimates. The statute barred departments and agencies from submitting their funding requests directly to Congress as they had done previously.

The initial emphasis in the development of the federal budget process was on control of expenditures and prevention of administrative abuses.[155] During the 1930s, the emphasis shifted from control to management. The budget was seen as a means of evaluating and improving administrative performance. The transfer of the BOB in 1939 from the Treasury Department to the new EOP symbolized the management orientation. The BOB was to become the president's management arm. A decade later, the government adopted a performance budget organized by functions and activities rather than by line items representing objects of expenditure.

The most recent development in budgeting is its orientation toward planning. This emphasis attempts to link annual budgeting, geared to the appropriations process in Congress, to long-range planning of government objectives. The limited success of the planning orientation is reflected in the rapid arrival and departure of budgeting systems, such as the program planning budgeting system and zero-base budgeting.[156] The budgeting process, as it had developed by the early 1970s, embodied all three orientations—(1) control, (2) management, and (3) planning—but it was least effective as a planning device.

Because the annual budget process is inherently incremental and subject to restrictions and conditions imposed by Congress, the executive budget has only limited utility as an aid to presidential decision making. The budget cycle forces the president and Congress to act according to a timetable that stretches from twenty-two months before the start of the fiscal year (October 1) through the ensuing year. Congress and the bureaucracy are concerned primarily with how large an increase or decrease will be made in a department's or an agency's budget. From 1982 to 1997, huge federal deficits accompanied by strong public resistance to tax increases caused presidential and congressional budget decisions to be focused primarily on reducing spending. The emergence of a budget surplus in 1998 ushered in a debate between Republicans and Democrats over the need for tax cuts. Republicans won the struggle in 2001, when George W. Bush engineered a massive tax cut to be spread over eleven years, and then accelerated in the additional cuts of 2003. But when the threat of deficits reemerged in mid-2001, questions again arose about the government's capacity to plan effectively, and several Democrats seeking the presidency in 2004 proposed that the tax cuts be rolled back. Faced with a severe economic recession, Obama proposed dramatically increased federal spending, delayed taking action on his campaign promise to increase taxes on the wealthiest Americans, but also discussed the need to return to a more responsible budget plan in the future. (See chapter 9.) Trump said he would cut back on domestic spending while cutting taxes, boosting defense and protecting entitlement spending. As his budget director soon recognized, this combination meant an accompanying promise to eliminate the national debt was necessarily "hyperbole."[157]

Congress has the power of the purse and makes its own budget decisions. It limits total spending through resolutions proposed by the budget committees in each house. Although the congressional budget total is usually fairly close to the president's, the priorities in the two budgets often differ sharply. Deficit politics constrained Bill Clinton when he attempted to use his first budget as a vehicle for policy change.[158] Although Congress narrowly (with no Republican support) accepted most of his five-year plan (1994–1998) to reduce the deficit by almost $500 billion, it embarrassed Clinton by rejecting a $16 billion package to stimulate the economy.[159] In 1995, the first Republican-controlled Congress in forty years ignored the administration's budget, which did not contain proposals for eventually eliminating the deficit, and adopted a budget resolution that projected a balanced budget in fiscal year 2002. Nearly two years of budget battles were finally resolved in a 1997 agreement on how to balance the budget.[160] George W. Bush, in contrast, found a cooperative Congress controlled by his own party during the first half of 2001 and secured passage of his tax cut. Donald Trump found resistance even among his own co-partisans to the large cuts to domestic programs he proposed for fiscal 2018.

In addition to budgeting, presidents have certain discretionary spending powers that increase their leverage over the bureaucracy. Presidents also have some ability, for instance, to steer federal grant funding to politically or electorally beneficial states and localities.[161] They also have substantial nonstatutory authority, based on understandings with congressional appropriations committees, to transfer funds within an appropriation and from one program to another. The committees expect to be kept informed of such "reprogramming" actions.[162] Fund transfer authority is essential to sound financial management, but it can be abused to circumvent congressional decisions. In 1970, Nixon transferred funds to support an extensive unauthorized covert military operation in Cambodia. Nevertheless, Congress has given presidents and certain agencies the authority to spend substantial amounts of money on a confidential basis, the largest and most controversial being for intelligence activities.

Presidents have exercised a measure of expenditure control through the practice of impoundment—failing to spend appropriated funds. Beginning with George Washington, presidents routinely impounded funds to achieve savings when actual expenditures fell short of appropriations.[163] They withheld funds when authorized or directed to do so by Congress to establish contingency reserves or impose a ceiling on total expenditures. Presidents from FDR through Lyndon Johnson also impounded some of the funds Congress had added, over their objections, for various programs. Although such actions often drew congressional criticism, they did not lead to confrontation because they occurred infrequently and were generally focused on expenditures for specific programs or projects. Congress recognized that circumspect use of impoundments helped its members resist pressure for increased spending.[164]

Impoundment became a major constitutional issue during the Nixon administration. Sweeping impoundments in domestic program areas, especially agriculture, housing, and water pollution control, led to charges that the president arbitrarily and illegally had substituted his spending priorities for those of Congress. Nixon's impoundments involved larger amounts, violated explicit congressional instructions to spend the funds, and were designed to terminate entire programs rather than individual projects. In short, Nixon used impoundment as the primary weapon in a battle with Congress over domestic spending priorities. He did not bargain or negotiate but imposed his priorities by fiat. Congress struck back with the Budget and Impoundment Control Act of 1974, which established procedures for congressional review by requiring the president to report all impoundments to Congress. Proposals to rescind appropriated funds, that is, to return them to the Treasury, must be approved by both houses within forty-five days. The original power of either house to disapprove proposals to defer spending to the next fiscal year disappeared when the Supreme Court invalidated the legislative veto.

In 1996, Clinton was the beneficiary of the Republican Party's promise in its 1994 election manifesto, the Contract with America, to establish a line-item veto for the president's use in fighting the budget deficit, a power many governors enjoy. Clinton was the first—and probably the last—president to have this power. The Line-Item Veto Act authorized the president to cancel specific spending items or tax breaks rather than veto an entire appropriations bill if the budget was in deficit. Presidential decisions would stand unless overturned by a two-thirds vote in both houses of Congress. The Court invalidated this statute in 1998[165] but not before Clinton invoked the authority eighty-two times. In 2006 and 2007, George W. Bush requested expedited rescission powers comparable to a line-item veto but requiring affirmative majority votes in both houses of Congress, a design he hoped the Court would not strike down.[166] The Obama administration proposed in 2010 that Congress consider a list of targeted cuts within forty-five days before voting on large appropriations bills and promised to pay particular attention to earmarks. Expedited rules would require a simple majority vote in both houses with no amendments or filibusters. Congress was not convinced.[167]

Obama did make efforts to make government spending more accountable and transparent. In conjunction with the economic stimulus package, the Obama administration created a publicly accessible website to track spending, overseen by a Recovery Accountability and Transparency Board consisting of government employees and presidential appointees. Similarly, the president created an Oversight and Accountability Board to monitor progress on reducing government waste. Vice President Biden was given the job of convening monthly cabinet meetings to track progress on waste reduction.[168]

Presidential Management of the Bureaucracy

In addition to their formal powers, modern presidents have relied on managerial tools in their efforts to coordinate and direct executive branch operations. Three major tools—(1) staffing, (2) reorganizing, and (3) planning—have been employed with mixed results. This is not to argue that the public sector is inhospitable to modern management techniques but to suggest that political forces significantly affect their use.[169]

Staffing

As discussed in chapters 1 and 4, the institutionalized presidency has grown steadily as presidents have used staff to direct the executive branch and fulfill its many functions. From the vantage point of the Oval Office, it may sometimes seem that there are "people, people everywhere but none to do his will."[170] Although recent administrations have used presidential staffs and the cabinet in different ways, the long-term trend has been toward increasing reliance on a strong, sizable, centralized White House staff to protect the political interests of presidents, to act as their principal policy advisers, and to direct (as opposed to monitor and coordinate) the implementation of presidential priorities by the bureaucracy. Centralizing power in the White House may appear to have been a *linear* process, but centralization is *contingent* on the president's needs, the shifting environment, and estimates of the full range of available strategies for accomplishing presidential goals.[171]

Critics of this development argue that centralization has undercut the cabinet's advisory potential, narrowed the president's perspective on policy choices, and inhibited effective and responsive bureaucratic performance. Stephen Hess cautions that reliance on a centralized White House staff has been "self-defeating."[172] Experiences under Nixon and Reagan support this view. Yet both Ford and Carter tried a decentralized model of White House staffing and abandoned it in favor of hierarchical alternatives.

George H. W. Bush adopted the hierarchical model of organization. Former governor John Sununu, R-NH, served as White House chief of staff, functioning as the guardian of the president's political interests, serving as his link to conservatives, and often appearing to set the administration's course on domestic social policy issues. In these roles, Sununu was the target of considerable congressional and media criticism that ultimately made him a liability.[173]

The Clinton White House reflected the leadership of a highly intelligent, energetic, and enormously self-confident president who lacked self-discipline, assumed many personal responsibilities, had difficulty focusing his goals and managing his efforts, and was reluctant to delegate. Clinton staffed the White House largely with consultants from his campaign and friends and political associates from Arkansas.[174] The staff lacked the Washington experience and political stature that might have prevented damaging early missteps such as the botched nominations of Zoë Baird and Kimba Wood to be attorney general, the conflict with Congress over ending discrimination against gays in the military, and the defeat of the administration's economic stimulus bill.

Clinton's first chief of staff, Thomas F. McLarty III, was replaced in June 1994 by OMB director Leon Panetta, who brought much-needed order. Panetta and his successors, Erskine Bowles and John Podesta, established control over the flow of communications and personal access to the president.[175] A greater degree of centralization and formal organization proved a necessity to counteract Clinton's lack of discipline. Clinton also demonstrated the ability to recognize his failings and take corrective action. White House staff at the start of Clinton's second term were more pragmatic and less ideological and had more Washington experience than their first-term counterparts.[176]

George W. Bush followed a modified version of the "spokes-in-a-wheel" White House structure so successful during Reagan's first term. In this model, a limited number of aides have access to a president who freely delegates responsibilities. Like Reagan, Bush had three principal aides (though they were far less competitive with each other than Reagan's "troika.") Andrew Card was Bush's first chief of staff, a position that has become so prevalent across both Republican and Democratic administrations as to warrant being described as "institutionalized." He was joined by Karl Rove, the political strategist, and Karen Hughes, the press and public relations adviser. Card, who began his government service in the Reagan administration, had served as deputy chief of staff and secretary of transportation in the George H. W. Bush administration. Rove and Hughes were longtime aides to George W. Bush in Texas.[177] Hughes left after two years, and Card resigned in April 2006, having served longer than any chief of staff in nearly a half-century.[178] Until his resignation in August 2007, Rove remained an influential White House figure, broadly responsible for political affairs. Investigators probed Rove's role in the outing of Valerie Plame, the firing of U.S. attorneys, the establishment of a shadow e-mail system that staff could use for political purposes, and pressure on government employees to help Republican allies.[179]

Two other advisers played a special role in the Bush administration. Vice President Cheney was given some of the most challenging assignments in the administration, including relations with Congress, developing a national energy strategy, and being a full participant (some would say the major architect) of the administration's policies to counter terrorism and the proliferation of weapons of mass destruction. Condoleezza Rice, first as national security adviser and then as secretary of state, was a public spokesperson called upon to explain and justify policies. As the administration responded to 9/11, Rice spent considerable time brokering discussions between two of the most forceful members of the Bush cabinet, Secretary of State Colin Powell and Secretary of Defense Donald Rumsfeld. Finally, Alberto Gonzales and Harriet Miers, during their time as White House counsel, also had ready access to President Bush, as did Josh Bolten, Card's successor as chief of staff.

In striking contrast to Clinton, Bush, the first president with an MBA, emerged as a "disciplined delegator," who drew upon the services of his able aides from the outset.[180] Critics, however, raised the same question they had asked about Reagan and Eisenhower: When presidents delegate, who's really in charge? For critics, it seemed that Vice President Cheney was exercising more responsibility than his constitutional superior.[181]

Obama proved to be a hands-on president who solicited advice from multiple sources. His chiefs of staff, Rahm Emanuel, Bill Daley, Jack Lew, and Denis McDonough, played key roles in coordinating White House activities, serving as "traffic cop" for the many inputs to the president and as enforcer of presidential decisions.[182] In general, chiefs of staff keep the White House running as efficiently as possible (administrator role), advise the president on pressing issues while coordinating the advice of others (advisor role), protect the president's time and interests (guardian role), and sometimes bargain in the president's stead (proxy role).[183] A close examination of Obama's first two chiefs concludes that Emanuel was particularly focused on representing the president's interests on Capitol Hill and advising the president on policy, whereas Bill Daley imposed unpopular new limits on the range of advisers meeting with the president (administrator role) but lasted only a year in the job.[184] Obama also came to rely increasingly on

Vice President Biden, though there was never a suspicion in the Obama White House that he overshadowed the president, and on Valerie Jarrett, a Chicago businesswoman and longtime family friend. David Axelrod and then David Plouffe were Obama's principal political advisers, veterans of Obama's first election campaign. Obama also seemed to rely heavily on several cabinet secretaries—Clinton in State, Geithner in Treasury, Robert Gates (followed by Leon Panetta and later Ash Carter) in Defense, and Arne Duncan in Education. Nonetheless, there was little doubt that the White House dominated policymaking.

Since the Reagan administration, the presidency has become increasingly centralized and politicized. Terry Moe defends these developments as an inescapable consequence of the expectations that impinge upon the presidency.[185] A similar conclusion emerged from a 1986 symposium featuring eight former White House chiefs of staff (or their functional equivalents), who served presidents from Eisenhower through Carter. In their views, "the demands for activism and the requirements of self-reliance encourage presidents to look favorably upon the kinds of services provided by a rationalized White House run by a strong chief."[186] At its outset, the Obama administration appeared to be squarely in this pattern, sending every indication that a hard-charging chief of staff, aided by a number of policy czars, would seek to run the government from the White House. Although it is possible to argue that the twin crises of foreign wars and domestic recession created the need for centralized decision making, Moe's research suggests that the Obama administration was simply falling into line with recent practice. Justin S. Vaughn points out that the use of policy czars—an Obama strategy of choice—arises from the same need to centralize leadership in the White House relying heavily on agents responsible exclusively to the president.[187]

The Trump White House certainly centralized authority vis-à-vis the Cabinet—but without the strong chief of staff model that had become the norm. Trump chief of staff Preibus was billed as co-equal with "chief strategist" Bannon. Another pole of influence was represented by Vice President Mike Pence, a social conservative with far more government experience than his colleagues. Yet another—and probably the most important—was occupied by Trump family members, notably Jared Kushner and Ivanka Trump.[188] As noted in Chapter 4, the factional competition that resulted was consistent with Trump's style of decision-making during his business career. But such an approach is difficult to reconcile with the workload of the modern White House and the strain it places on the president to coordinate the different streams of information competing staffers produce. Franklin Roosevelt was arguably the last president to successfully make such a system work for any length of time.[189]

Reorganization

It is almost an article of faith among political leaders and public administration theorists that executive reorganization can increase presidential power over the bureaucracy. Between 1932 and 1984, more than one hundred presidential proposals were submitted to Congress under varying congressional guidelines.[190] Lyndon Johnson, Nixon, and Carter believed the performance of the executive branch could be improved and the bureaucracy brought to heel through such changes. Johnson's efforts were, however, inconsequential, and Nixon's were interrupted by his resignation. By most accounts, the results of Carter's reorganization project—by far the most extensive—were modest.[191]

Organizational structure and administrative arrangements are significant because they reflect values and priorities and affect access to decision makers. The location and status of an administrative unit—as a department, an independent agency, or a component of a department—symbolize the importance of its goals and the interests it serves. Administrative arrangements also can contribute to or frustrate the achievement of accountability to Congress and the public. Reorganizing, however, does not necessarily result in increased operational efficiency, greater program effectiveness, or enhanced public accountability. There is no ideal form for a government agency or a consistent set of prescriptions for organizing the executive branch. One set of standard prescriptions tends to centralize authority; another tends to disperse it. The most profound consequences of organizational change are not in the "engineered realm of efficiency, simplicity, size, and cost of government"; rather, they lie in the areas of "political influence, policy emphasis, and communication of governmental intentions."[192] For example, the placement of the Occupational Safety and Health Administration in the Department of Labor rather than in the Department of Health, Education, and Welfare led to an initial focus of regulations on mechanical, rather than biological, hazards in the workplace. Experience has shown that although the rationale for reorganization is couched in the rhetoric of economy and efficiency, the crucial factors in decisions to reorganize are power, policy, and symbolic significance.

In 1939, Congress authorized presidents to propose executive reorganization plans that take effect after sixty days unless disapproved by both houses. When extending that authority in 1949, Congress allowed either house to disapprove such plans. Congress continued to renew the reorganization authority with little change until 1973. In 1977, Carter requested and received renewal of the authority with provision for veto by either house. The Supreme Court decision striking down the legislative veto necessitated changes in the review process that made Congress a full partner in reorganizations, but the authority lapsed in 1984 and was not renewed.[193] George W. Bush wanted to use reorganization as a strategy and requested restoration of the president's permanent reorganization authority, as did Obama. But in the absence of congressional action, Bush had to follow the normal legislative process in creating the Department of Homeland Security. (The same process was used earlier to create the Departments of Energy, Education, and Veterans Affairs.)[194] Obama's efforts to consolidate various trade and commerce functions into a single agency were simply abandoned.

Carter's reorganization achievements exceeded those of his immediate predecessors and of his successors but fell far short of the thorough restructuring of the executive branch and reduction in the number of agencies he had promised. Congress passed legislation that established the Departments of Energy and of Education and allowed five reorganization plans to take effect. Carter and his staff were unprepared for the jurisdictional conflicts that accompanied congressional consideration of reorganization proposals.[195] The president also lacked a well-conceived, comprehensive, politically defensible strategy. The Carter experience indicates that reorganization has its uses, but they are more in the realm of policy and politics than in management improvement.

The Clinton administration downplayed reorganization in favor of extensive personnel reductions called for in Vice President Gore's *National Performance Review Report,* along with the report's recommendations to cut red tape, enhance customer satisfaction, empower employees, and eliminate unneeded functions. That report broke sharply with the administrative management paradigm that had dominated presidential efforts to manage the bureaucracy since the Brownlow Committee report of 1937. That philosophy, which the reports of the First Hoover Commission (1949) and the Ash Council (1971) also embodied, "emphasized the need for democratic accountability of departmental and agency officers to the President and his central management agencies and through these institutions to the Congress."[196] In its stead, the Gore report embraced the entrepreneurial management paradigm popularized by David Osborne and Ted Gaebler in *Reinventing Government.*[197] These writers call for a "cultural and behavioral shift in the management of government" from a bureaucratic to an entrepreneurial government. In their view, public agencies are entrepreneurial organizations competing in a market environment in which success is determined by customer satisfaction. Clinton's reinvention effort evolved over time and in two later phases shifted attention to reducing government's cost and then to attacking complex problems, such as finding ways to create and maintain "safe communities," a highly complex issue for government to tackle.[198] Clinton's departure from administrative orthodoxy sparked extensive discussion among academics,[199] but in the short run, few conclusions can be drawn about his novel strategy.

George W. Bush made the Clinton strategy his own by adding a few distinctive features. He sought to reduce government employment by ultimately making at least half of the federal jobs subject to competitive bidding from the private sector.[200] Small reorganizations were introduced in agencies throughout the government and justified as improving performance. The administration called for a new "pay for performance" system that would not provide annual pay increases for civil service employees. They introduced this system for members of the SES and proposed extending it more generally.[201]

Obama, as noted, did not rely on reorganization as a management strategy, except during the brief life of his business and trade consolidation proposal in 2011. Donald Trump, however, issued an executive order in March 2017 that promised a "comprehensive plan for reorganizing the executive branch." Department heads were directed to develop "agency reform plans" that would "create a lean, accountable, more efficient government" by removing duplicative functions and reducing the size of the federal workforce.[202] These were to become part of the fiscal 2019 budget process.

Planning

Aaron Wildavsky defined planning as "current action to secure future consequences."[203] Foresight in anticipating problems and developing solutions is the essence of effective planning. Long-range planning is a hallmark of successful corporate management, but the federal government cannot make that claim.

Presidents have engaged in long-range planning with only limited success. Early efforts to include a permanent planning agency within the EOP never came to fruition.[204] And as noted, attempts to combine annual budgeting with comprehensive planning through the program planning budgeting system and zero-base budgeting have not succeeded. Both approaches entailed comprehensive attempts to relate spending decisions to long-term consequences. Each required extensive amounts of information and analyses that were never integrated with budget decisions, and bureau and agency officials did not find it worthwhile to take either process seriously. Their fatal defect was neglect of the hard political choices involved in the budget process.

Nixon had introduced a similar technique that focused on goals, called management by objectives, to strengthen his oversight of the executive branch. He directed twenty-one departments and agencies to prepare rank-order lists of their principal objectives. These presidential objectives then became the standard for monitoring the units' performances. Management by objectives focused first on immediate objectives, then on intermediate objectives that could be achieved in a fiscal year, and finally on long-term goals.[205] Other than to continue multiyear budgeting introduced by Carter, Reagan demonstrated little interest in planning. George H. W. Bush, although neglecting domestic policy planning, was committed to, and actively involved in, foreign and defense policy planning. Generally, planning has been more successful in these areas than in domestic policy, and future presidents will always need to engage in national security planning. Clinton's proposals for reforming health care and the welfare system included planning that linked them to the five-year deficit reduction that was integral to the 1994 budget. But he exhibited little planning after the Republicans assumed control of Congress in 1995. Moving toward a balanced budget then became the overriding concern. In the Clinton administration's final years, creating a legacy was more important than planning.

With a heavy emphasis on pursuing legislative victories during its early months, the George W. Bush administration did not show much attention to planning, with the notable exception of developing a coherent energy policy. Just two weeks into the new administration, Bush named Cheney to head a task force that released its recommendations on May 17, 2001, after meeting largely in secret. The administration's proposals focused primarily on ways to increase the supply of energy rather than conserve its use—encouraging oil and natural gas exploration, building electric transmission infrastructure, encouraging the use of coal, and supporting nuclear power generation.[206] But questions arose about whether an "energy industry that put its financial backing solidly behind Bush's election has received a plan that offers support for every major form of energy production and distribution."[207] The symbolic core of the proposals was to open the Arctic National Wildlife Refuge to oil exploration. The Senate repeatedly rejected it in dramatic showdown votes over three separate Congresses.

One could also argue that Bush's failed effort to reform Social Security, launched amidst much fanfare in 2005, was an example of long-range planning. Unique among government programs, Social Security is required by law to plan on a seventy-five-year timeline, but that requirement reduces confidence in policymakers' ability to project so far ahead. Similarly, Obama's efforts to reach a "grand bargain" with House Speaker John Boehner, R-OH, that would trim $3 trillion from spending while increasing revenues by $1 trillion over a decade is a version of planning. Although the details of the plan were never fully announced, it would have needed to curtail spending in Medicare and find ways to restructure other entitlement programs, including Social Security. The slow economic recovery from the Great Recession of 2008–2009 (see chapter 9) similarly made planning difficult.

Conclusion: The Frustrating Search for Control

Can the president lead the executive branch? Many of the studies discussed in this chapter raise doubts.[208] Although presidents have substantial formal powers and managerial resources, they wrestle with the problem of controlling their own branch of government. Their capacity to direct its many departments and agencies in the implementation of administration policies is limited by bureaucratic complexity and fragmentation, conflict between the presidency and the bureaucracy, external pressure and influence on the bureaucracy, and the extreme difficulty of establishing an effective management system within the government.

Important milestones in this effort can be found throughout the twentieth century. Roosevelt created the EOP in 1939, providing his successors with a critical group of presidential loyalists and policy experts independent of bureaucratic pressures. Johnson's enthusiastic endorsement of the program planning budgeting system in 1966 started a series of experiments in using the budget as a planning instrument. Nixon's centralization of decisions in the White House is a strategy his successors have emulated. Carter established the potential as well as the limits of using reorganization as a management tool, and his sponsorship of the CSRA created a new cadre of presidential allies in the civil service.

Reagan came closest to assembling these instruments of control into a coherent administrative strategy, a consensus that prevails more than three decades after he assumed office.[209] Reagan's centralized control of appointments fashioned a relatively unified "team" by making ideological compatibility with his goals the principal criterion for selection. Reagan also used cabinet councils as a means to link the White House staff with cabinet officials in directing policy efforts. Most important, he used the budget to enforce his spending priorities on departments and agencies: He reversed the traditional pattern of budget preparation from the bottom up, in which agencies attempt to protect their bases, and instituted top-down budgeting, with presidential and OMB decisions being determinative.[210] Finally, Reagan attempted to accomplish policy change administratively by establishing procedures for OMB review of regulations, diminishing the intensity of regulatory enforcement, and reinterpreting agency functions and relations with clientele in accordance with the administration's ideology.[211]

Reagan's successors learned these lessons of "presidential administration" and did likewise.[212] Yet each president faces anew the challenges of asserting control. George W. Bush and his White House aides were attentive students and launched a comprehensive effort to establish presidential control, but its results were mixed. Barack Obama faced similar struggles. Donald Trump promised to run government like a business—but was likely to find that the lessons of private sector management had limited application to the administrative presidency.

Suggested Readings

Arnold, Peri E. *Making the Managerial Presidency: Comprehensive Reorganization Planning, 1905–1980.* Princeton, NJ: Princeton University Press, 1986.

Borrelli, MaryAnne. *The President's Cabinet: Gender, Power, and Representation.* Boulder, CO: Lynne Rienner, 2002.

Campbell, Colin. *Managing the Presidency: Carter, Reagan, and the Search for Executive Harmony.* Pittsburgh: University of Pittsburgh Press, 1986.

Cohen, Jeffrey E. *The Politics of the U.S. Cabinet: Representation in the Executive Branch, 1789–1984.* Pittsburgh: University of Pittsburgh Press, 1988.

Cooper, Phillip J. *By Order of the President: The Use and Abuse of Executive Direct Action,* 2nd rev. ed. Lawrence: University Press of Kansas, 2014.

Cronin, Thomas E. *The State of the Presidency,* 2nd ed. Boston: Little, Brown, 1980.

Fisher, Louis. *Constitutional Conflicts between Congress and the President,* 6th ed. Lawrence: University Press of Kansas, 2014.

Hart, John. *The Presidential Branch: From Washington to Clinton,* 2nd ed. Chatham, NJ: Chatham House, 1995.

Hess, Stephen. *Organizing the Presidency,* 3rd ed. Washington, DC: Brookings, 2002.

Kumar, Martha Joynt, and Terry Sullivan, eds. *White House World: Transitions, Organization, and Office Operations.* College Station: Texas A&M University Press, 2003.

Lewis, David E. *The Politics of Presidential Appointments: Political Control and Bureaucratic Performance.* Princeton, NJ: Princeton University Press, 2008.

Light, Paul C. *Thickening Government: Federal Hierarchy and the Diffusion of Accountability.* Washington, DC: Brookings, 1995.

Mayer, Kenneth R. *With the Stroke of a Pen: Executive Orders and Presidential Power.* Princeton, NJ: Princeton University Press, 2001.

Nathan, Richard P. *The Administrative Presidency.* New York: Wiley, 1983.

Pfiffner, James P. *The Managerial Presidency,* 2nd ed. College Station: Texas A&M University Press, 1999.

———. *The Strategic Presidency,* 2nd ed. Lawrence: University Press of Kansas, 1996.

Warshaw, Shirley Anne. *Powersharing: White House–Cabinet Relations in the Modern Presidency.* Albany: State University of New York Press, 1996.

Weko, Thomas J. *The Politicizing Presidency: The White House Personnel Office, 1948–1994.* Lawrence: University Press of Kansas, 1995.

Resources on the Web

The American Presidency Project, www.presidency.ucsb.edu/index_docs.php.
Archive of CRS Reports, digital.library.unt.edu/explore/collections/CRSR/.
Essays on White House staff offices, http://whitehousetransitionproject.org.
Executive Orders, www.archives.gov/federal-register/executive-orders/.
Office of Personnel Management, www.opm.gov.

Notes

1. John Mintz, "Homeland Agency Launched; Bush Signs Bill to Combine Federal Security Functions," *Washington Post,* November 26, 2002, A1.

2. Shawn Zeller, "Civil Service Narrowly Misses Merit-Pay System," *CQ Weekly,* October 27, 2008, 2864–2865.

3. Brookings Press Briefing, July 15, 2002, "Brookings Report Urges Congress to Revise President Bush's Homeland Security Proposal," www.brookings.edu/~/media/Files/events/2002/0715homeland%20security/20020715homeland.pdf. Also see David Gunter et al., *Protecting the American Homeland* (Washington, DC: Brookings Institution Press, 2002).

4. Spencer S. Hsu, "A Public Coup for the Secret Service: Agency May Gain Clout after a Move to Planned Homeland Security Department," *Washington Post,* August 14, 2002, A27.

5. Edward Walsh, "Changing Customs: Can Free Trade Flourish with Focus on Terrorism?" *Washington Post,* July 26, 2002, A31.

6. Sara Kehaulani Goo, "Fledgling TSA Offers Lessons: Lawmakers Urged Not to Ask Too Much of New Department," *Washington Post,* July 22, 2002, A13.

7. Walter Pincus, "FEMA's Influence May Be Cut under New Department," *Washington Post,* July 24, 2002, A17.

8. Only the staffs of Ridge, Card, and Office of Management and Budget director Mitch Daniels were involved. See Mariano-Florentino Cuellar, *Governing Security: The Hidden Origins of American Security Agencies* (Stanford, CA: Stanford Law Books, 2013), 138.

9. Richard E. Cohen, Siobhan Gorman, and Sydney J. Freedberg Jr., "The Ultimate Turf War," *National Journal,* January 3, 2003, nationaljournal.com/members/news/2003/01/0103nj1.htm.

10. Siobhan Gorman, Sydney J. Freedberg Jr., and Peter H. Stone, "New Department, New Special Interests," *National Journal,* December 6, 2002, www.nationaljournal.com/members/news/2002/12/1206nj7.htm.

11. Christopher Lee and Stephen Barr, "New Agency, New Rules—and a Cost: Bush Gets Management Freedom, and a Measure of Mistrust among Workers," *Washington Post,* November 14, 2002, A31.

12. Philip Rucker and Robert Costa, "Bannon Vows a Daily Fight for 'Deconstruction of the Administrative State,'" *Washington Post* (February 23, 2017), https://www.washingtonpost.com/

politics/top-wh-strategist-vows-a-daily-fight-for-deconstruction-of-the-administrative-state/2017/02/23/03f6b8da-f9ea-11e6-bf01-d47f8cf9b643_story.html?utm_term=.38ba2375ff90

13. Michael D. Shear, "Sibelius Resigns after Trouble over Health Site," *New York Times,* April 10, 2014, www.nytimes.com/2014/04/11/us/politics/sebelius-resigning-as-health-secretary.html?_r=0.

14. Richard Rose, "Government against Subgovernments: A European Perspective on Washington," in *Presidents and Prime Ministers,* ed. Richard Rose and Ezra N. Suleiman (Washington, DC: American Enterprise Institute, 1980), 339.

15. For a view that regards presidents as much more than passive participants in agency design, see David E. Lewis, *Presidents and the Politics of Agency Design* (Stanford, CA: Stanford University Press, 2003).

16. James P. Pfiffner challenges this viewpoint and maintains that presidents tend to overestimate the opposition they will get from the bureaucracy. See Pfiffner, "Political Appointees and Career Executives: The Democracy-Bureaucracy Nexus in the Third Century," *Public Administration Review* (January–February 1987): 57–65.

17. Hugh Heclo, *A Government of Strangers* (Washington, DC: Brookings, 1977), 7.

18. Paul C. Light, "The New True Size of Government," Research Brief Number 2, Organizational Performance Initiative, Wagner Graduate School of Public Service, New York University, August 2006, wagner.nyu.edu/performance/files/True_Size.pdf.

19. Jason D. Mycoff and Joseph A. Pika, *Confrontation and Compromise: Presidential and Congressional Leadership, 2001–2006* (Lanham, MD: Rowman and Littlefield, 2007), chap. 3.

20. Francis E. Rourke, *Bureaucracy, Politics, and Public Policy,* 3rd ed. (Boston: Little, Brown, 1984), 32.

21. See the Congressional Budget Office data on the fiscal 2016 budget at https://www.cbo.gov/publication/52408

22. Aaron Wildavsky, *The New Politics of the Budgetary Process,* 2nd ed. (New York: HarperCollins, 1992), 87–88.

23. David A. Stockman, *The Triumph of Politics: Why the Reagan Revolution Failed* (New York: Harper and Row, 1986).

24. Paul C. Light, *Thickening Government: Federal Hierarchy and the Diffusion of Accountability* (Washington, DC: Brookings, 1995), 32–33.

25. Heclo, *A Government of Strangers.*

26. G. Calvin MacKenzie, "Partisan Presidential Leadership: The President's Appointees," in *The Parties Respond: Changes in American Parties and Campaigns,* 4th ed., ed. L. Sandy Maisel (Boulder, CO: Westview, 2002), 267.

27. Jeffrey E. Cohen, *The Politics of the U.S. Cabinet: Representation in the Executive Branch, 1789–1984* (Pittsburgh: University of Pittsburgh Press, 1988), chaps. 3, 4.

28. Thomas E. Cronin, *The State of the Presidency,* 2nd ed. (Boston: Little, Brown, 1980), 282.

29. Joel D. Aberbach and Bert A. Rockman, "The Appointments Process and the Administrative Presidency," *Presidential Studies Quarterly* 39:1 (2009): 38–59.

30. Bradley H. Patterson and James P. Pfiffner, "The White House Office of Presidential Personnel," *Presidential Studies Quarterly* 31 (September 2001): 415–439; and David E. Lewis, *The Politics of Presidential Appointments* (Princeton, NJ: Princeton University Press, 2008).

31. James P. Pfiffner, *The Strategic Presidency,* 2nd ed. (Lawrence: University Press of Kansas, 1996), 57. See also Lisa Rein, "This Beltway Insider Is in Charge of Hiring for the Trump Administration. It's Taking a While," *Washington Post,* April 19, 2017, https://www.washingtonpost.com/politics/this-beltway-insider-is-in-charge-of-hiring-for-the-trump-administration-its-taking-awhile/2017/04/18/06febf20–1b08–11e7-bcc2–7d1a0973e7b2_story.html?utm_term=.6b0ceff1e65b

32. G. Calvin Mackenzie, *The Politics of Presidential Appointments* (New York: Free Press, 1981).

33. Patterson, Pfiffner, and Lewis, "The White House Office," 5.

34. Thomas J. Weko, *The Politicizing Presidency: The White House Personnel Office, 1948–1994* (Lawrence: University Press of Kansas, 1995), 149–151, 157.

35. Josh Dawsey and Andrew Restuccia, "Cabinet Picks Clash with White House over Hiring," *Politico,* February 22, 2017, http://www.politico.com/story/2017/02/trump-cabinet-hiring-clash-235250.

36. Thomas J. Weko, *The Politicizing Presidency: The White House Personnel Office, 1948–1994* (Lawrence: University Press of Kansas, 1995), 149–151, 157.

37. Joel D. Aberbach, "A Reinvented Government, or the Same Old Government?" in *The Clinton Legacy,* ed. Colin Campbell and Bert A. Rockman (New York: Chatham House, 2000), 120; and Gwen Ifill, "Three Women Are Said to Be Candidates for Cabinet Posts," *New York Times,* December 7, 1992, A1.

38. Weko, *The Politicizing Presidency,* 100–103.

39. John P. Burke, "The Bush Transition in Historical Context," *PS: Political Science & Politics* 35 (March 2002).

40. John Burke, "The Obama Presidential Transition: An Early Assessment," *Presidential Studies Quarterly* 39:3 (July 2009): 577.

41. Ibid., 591.

42. William A. Galston and E. J. Dionne Jr., "A Half-Empty Government Can't Govern: Why Everyone Wants to Fix the Appointments Process, Why It Never Happens, and How We Can Get It Done," *Governance Studies at Brookings,* December 14, 2010. Also see Burke, "The Obama Presidential Transition," 594.

43. Peter Baker, "Obama's Team Is Lacking Most of Its Top Players," *New York Times,* August 23, 2009.

44. Dan Balz, "'It Went Off the Rails Nearly Immediately': How Trump's Messy Transition Led to a Chaotic Presidency," *Washington Post,* April 4, 2017, https://www.washingtonpost.com/politics/it-went-off-the-rails-almost-immediately-how-trumps-messy-transition-led-to-a-chaotic-presidency/2017/04/03/170ec2e8–0a96–11e7-b77c-0047d15a24e0_story.html?utm_term=.822cfaa5fc42

45. Rein, "This Beltway Insider Is in Charge of Hiring."

46. See the Political Appointee Tracker compiled by the Partnership for Public Service, and the White House Transition Project, at https://ourpublicservice.org/issues/presidential-transition/political-appointee-tracker.php and http://www.whitehousetransitionproject.org/appointments/respectively.

47. Tom Ricketts had been nominated as deputy secretary of Commerce, Vincent Viola and then Mark Green as secretary of the Army, and Philip Bilden as secretary of the Navy.

48. Mark W. Huddleston and William W. Boyer, *The Higher Civil Service in the United States: Quest for Reform* (Pittsburgh: University of Pittsburgh Press, 1996); and Edie N. Goldenberg, "The Permanent Government in an Era of Retrenchment and Redirection," in *The Reagan Presidency and the Governing of America,* ed. Lester M. Salamon and Michael S. Lund (Washington, DC: Urban Institute Press, 1984), 381–404.

49. Chester A. Newland, "A Midterm Appraisal—The Reagan Presidency, Limited Government, and Political Administration," *Public Administration Review* (January–February 1983): 15–16.

50. Testimony of Paul C. Light before the Government Reform Committee, U.S. House of Representatives, May 3, 2003, 1, www.brookings.edu/testimony/2003/0505governance_light.aspx.

51. John Maggs, "Compete or Else," *National Journal,* July 11, 2003, nationaljournal.com/members/news/2003/07/0711nj1.htm. For the scorecard designed under Bush, see www.whitehouse.gov/omb/budintegration/scorecards/agency_scorecards.html.

52. Office of Management and Budget, "Competitive Sourcing: Conducting Public-Private Competition in a Reasoned and Responsible Manner," July 2003, www.whitehouse.gov/omb/procurement/comp_sourc_addendum.pdf. For commentary, see Jia Lynn Yang, "An Evolving Civil Service," *National Journal,* July 11, 2003, nationaljournal.com/members/news/2003/07/0711nj4.htm.

53. Mick Mulvaney, Director, Office of Management and Budget, to Heads of Executive Departments and Agencies, "Comprehensive Plan for Reforming the Federal Government and Reducing the Federal Civilian Workforce," OMB Memorandum M-17–22, April 17, 2017.

54. *Kendall v. United States,* 37 U.S. (12 Pet.) 524 (1838).

55. *Panama Refining Co. v. Ryan,* 293 U.S. 338 (1934); and *Schechter Poultry Co. v. United States,* 295 U.S. 495 (1935).

56. Louis Fisher, *Constitutional Conflicts between Congress and the President,* 3rd ed. (Lawrence: University Press of Kansas, 1991), 98; and Theodore J. Lowi, *The End of Liberalism,* 2nd ed. (New York: Norton, 1979), chap. 5.

57. Morris P. Fiorina, *Congress: Keystone of the Washington Establishment,* 2nd ed. (New Haven, CT: Yale University Press, 1989).

58. Rourke, *Bureaucracy, Politics, and Public Policy,* 74.

59. MaryAnne Borrelli, *The President's Cabinet: Gender, Power, and Representation* (Boulder, CO: Lynne Rienner, 2002), 15.

60. Quoted in James Pfiffner, *The Modern Presidency,* 4th ed. (Belmont, CA.: Thomson-Wadsworth, 2005), 119.

61. "Grading the Cabinet," *National Journal,* January 24, 2003, nationaljournal.com/members/news/2003/01/0124nj1.htm.

62. Carl M. Cannon, "The Old-Timers," *National Journal,* May 22, 1999, 1387.

63. "The Cabinet's Keeper," *National Journal,* January 24, 2003, nationaljournal.com/members/news/2003/01/0124nj2.htm.

64. Andrew Rudalevige, "'The Decider': Issue Management and the Bush White House," in *The George W. Bush Legacy,* ed. Colin Campbell, Bert A. Rockman, and Andrew Rudalevige (Washington, DC: CQ Press, 2007), 147.

65. Anne E. Kornblut, "White House Moving to Repair Troubled Relationship with Cabinet," *Washington Post,* March 9, 2011.

66. Peter Beinart, "Chuck Hagel's Rise and Fall Had Nothing to Do with Foreign Policy," *Atlantic,* September 24, 2014, www.theatlantic.com/politics/archive/2014/11/chuck-hagels-rise-and-fall-had-nothing-to-do-with-foreign-policy/383125/.

67. Cannon, "The Old-Timers," 1388; Philip Bump, "Eric Holder and a Brief History of Cabinet Tenures," The Fix, September 25, 2014, www.washingtonpost.com/news/the-fix/wp/2014/09/25/eric-holder-and-a-brief-history-of-cabinet-tenures/. For the past five administrations, Bump reports an average tenure of Cabinet members of 3.46 years for Reagan, 3.06 for George H. W. Bush, 4.08 for Clinton, and 3.59 for George W. Bush. Obama's average calculated by the authors; it is skewed upwards slightly by Tom Vilsack's eight-year service and Arne Duncan's seven years.

68. Cohen, *The Politics of the U.S. Cabinet,* 173–176.

69. Borrelli, *The President's Cabinet,* 46–52. This pattern held true for seven of the eight administrations included in the study, with George H. W. Bush being the exception. Because Bush had been elected as a sitting vice president after eight years of Republican control, Borrelli suggests that Bush drew on his extensive network of experienced acquaintances and that the pool of outsiders was depleted. Borrelli's research covered administrations from FDR through George W. Bush, except for Truman, Kennedy, and Johnson. Also see Nelson W. Polsby, "Presidential Cabinet-Making Lessons for the Political System," *Political Science Quarterly* (Spring 1978): 15–25.

70. Cronin, *The State of the Presidency,* 270–272.

71. Ibid., 282–285.

72. In *The Politics of the U.S. Cabinet,* Cohen finds a distinction between the older and the newer outer departments based on "the importance of interests in creating the department and on the complexity of

its interest group environment" (144). The older departments—Agriculture, Commerce, Labor, and Interior—were created in response to demands from single interests that continue to provide them with some protection from presidential control. The newer departments tend to operate in "more complex interest group environments" that may result in "intradepartmental conflict among advocates of the competing interests" (138, 139).

73. Maryanne Borrelli, "The Contemporary Presidency: Gender Desegregation and Gender Integration in the President's Cabinet, 1933–2010," *Presidential Studies Quarterly* 40:4 (2010): 734–749.

74. Daniel A. Medina, "U.S. Cabinet Shakeups through the Years, Charted," *Quartz,* November 25, 2014, qz.com/301812/us-cabinet-shakeups-through-the-years-charted/.

75. Pfiffner, *The Strategic Presidency,* 41–42, 65–66; Stephen Hess, *Organizing the Presidency,* 2nd ed. (Washington, DC: Brookings, 1988), 200; and Shirley Anne Warshaw, *Powersharing: White House–Cabinet Relations in the Modern Presidency* (Albany: State University of New York Press, 1996), 228–233.

76. Richard F. Fenno Jr., *The President's Cabinet* (New York: Vintage Books, 1959), 132.

77. Ronald Brownstein and Dick Kirschten, "Cabinet Power," *National Journal,* June 28, 1986, 1582–1589.

78. James A. Barnes, "Like His Home-State Razorbacks . . . Clinton's Cabinet Plays to Win," *National Journal,* April 9, 1994, 852–853. Also see Warshaw, *Powersharing,* 198–227.

79. For discussions of pre-9/11 management practices, see Lizette Alvarez and Eric Schmitt, "Cheney Ever More Powerful as Crucial Link to Congress," *New York Times,* May 13, 2001, A1. On the general operation of the administration, see John F. Harris and Dan Balz, "Conflicting Image of Bush Emerges," *Washington Post,* April 28, 2001, A1. Also see Alexis Simendinger, "Stepping into Power," *National Journal,* January 27, 2001, 246–248.

80. Karen M. Hult, "The Bush White House in Comparative Perspective" (paper delivered at the conference on "The George W. Bush Presidency: An Early Assessment," Woodrow Wilson School, Princeton University, April 25–26, 2003), 20. For a detailed account of Bush's decision making in the aftermath of 9/11, see Bob Woodward, *Bush at War* (New York: Simon and Schuster, 2002).

81. Andrew Rosenthal, "Sununu's Out and Skinner Is In, but White House Troubles Persist," *New York Times,* February 11, 1992, A1, A13. Also see Burt Solomon, "Bush's Renovated Inner Circle Has a Bit of a Reaganesque Look," *National Journal,* February 8, 1992, 346–347.

82. Andrew Rosenthal, "Sununu's Out and Skinner Is In, but White House Troubles Persist," *New York Times,* February 11, 1992, A1, A13. Also see Burt Solomon, "Bush's Renovated Inner Circle Has a Bit of a Reaganesque Look," *National Journal,* February 8, 1992, 346–347.

83. James P. Pfiffner, "Organizing the Obama White House," in *Obama in Office,* ed. James A. Thurber (Boulder, CO: Paradigm, 2011), 80.

84. Will Englund, "Czar Wars: Who's on Obama's Front Line," *National Journal Special Report,* nationaljournalspecialreport.com/NatJournal_CzarWars.pdf.

85. Jake Tapper, "Obama Will Name Ron Klain as Ebola Czar," October 17, 2014, www.cnn.com/2014/10/17/politics/ebola-czar-ron-klain/index.html.

86. U.S. Constitution, Article 2, section 1.

87. Senate Historical Office, "Tie Votes," www.senate.gov/pagelayout/reference/four_column_table/Tie_Votes.htm.

88. However, that was not true for the first four years of that position's history, when it was placed eighth.

89. Paul C. Light, *Vice-Presidential Power: Advice and Influence in the White House* (Baltimore, MD: Johns Hopkins University Press, 1983).

90. Barton Gellman and Jo Becker, "A Different Understanding with the President," *Washington Post,* June 24, 2007, A1.

91. Jo Becker and Barton Gellman, "A Strong Push from Backstage," *Washington Post,* June 26, 2007, A1.

92. For an especially thorough review of Biden's service as vice president, see Jody Baumgartner and Thomas F. Crumblin, *The American Vice Presidency: From the Shadow to the Spotlight* (Lanham, MD: Rowman and Littlefield, 2015), chap. 9. My thanks to Professor Baumgartner for allowing me to read an advance copy.

93. Joseph A. Pika, "Dick Cheney, Joe Biden, and the New Vice Presidency," in *The Presidency and the Political System,* 9th ed., ed. Michael Nelson (Washington, DC: CQ Press, 2009).

94. Will Englund, "What Kind of Vice President Will Biden Be?" *National Journal,* March 7, 2009, www.nationaljournal.com/njmagazine/nj_20090307_9943.php.

95. Helene Cooper, "As the Ground Shifts, Biden Plays a Bigger Role," *New York Times,* December 12, 2010, 1. One indication of this Republican trust: Biden was the only person asked to eulogize both Strom Thurmond and Jesse Helms at their funerals. Evan Osnos, "The Biden Agenda: Reckoning with Ukraine and Iraq, and Keeping an Eye on 2016," *New Yorker,* July 28, 2014.

96. Lucy McCalmont, "Obama: 2016 Voters Will Want That New Car Smell," *Politco,* November 23, 2014, www.politico.com/story/2014/11/obama-2016-voters-will-want-that-new-car-smell-113118.html.

97. Gil Troy, "Copresident or Codependent? The Rise and Rejection of Presidential Couples since World War II," in *The Presidential Companion: Readings on the First Ladies,* ed. Robert P. Watson and Anthony J. Eksterowicz (Columbia: University of South Carolina Press, 2003), 253.

98. Valerie A. Sulfaro, "Affective Evaluations of First Ladies: A Comparison of Hillary Clinton and Laura Bush," *Presidential Studies Quarterly* 37:3 (2007): 488.

99. Anthony J. Eksterowicz and Kristen Paynter, "The Evolution of the Role and Office of the First Lady," in Watson and Eksterowicz, *The Presidential Companion.*

100. Kay M. Knickrehm and Robin Teske, "First Ladies and Policy Making: Crossing the Public/ Private Divide," in Watson and Eksterowicz, *The Presidential Companion,* 248.

101. Ibid.

102. Ibid., 249.

103. "Transcript: Michelle Obama's DNC Speech," CNN.com, July 26, 2016, http://www.cnn.com/ 2016/07/26/politics/transcript-michelle-obama-speech-democratic-national-convention/.

104. Cottle, "Leaning Out."

105. *Buckley v. Valeo,* 421 U.S. 1 (1976).

106. In 1973, President Nixon named Howard J. Phillips acting director of the Office of Economic Opportunity (OEO), an agency Nixon planned to dismantle. Phillips began to phase out its programs and withhold funds from it. Sen. Harrison A. Williams, D-NJ, took legal action to force Nixon either to submit Phillips's name to the Senate for confirmation or to stop dismantling the OEO. A U.S. court of appeals ruled that Phillips was illegally holding office and enjoined him from further actions. See James P. Pfiffner, *The President, the Budget, and Congress: Impoundment and the 1974 Budget Act* (Boulder, CO: Westview, 1974), 116–117. The effort was thwarted, but the decision did not settle the issue.

107. Three notable examples are the Senate's rejection of former senator John Tower, R-TX, to be secretary of defense in 1989, its long delay in acting on the nomination of Henry Foster Jr. to be surgeon general of the United States, and its narrow support in 2001 for former senator John Ashcroft, R-MO, to become attorney general.

108. Christopher J. Deering, "Damned If You Do and Damned If You Don't: The Senate's Role in the Appointment Process," in *The In-and-Outers,* ed. G. Calvin McKenzie (Baltimore, MD: Johns Hopkins University Press, 1987), 119. Also see G. Calvin McKenzie, ed., *Innocent until Nominated* (Washington, DC: Brookings, 2001).

109. Anthony Lake withdrew from consideration as nominee to head the CIA in March 1997 after concluding that he would be subjected to endless delays and partisan criticism. Juliana Gruenwald,

"Tenet Appears Likely to Win Confirmation as CIA Chief," *Congressional Quarterly Weekly Report,* March 22, 1997, 712–714. On the Holbrooke nomination, see Philip Shenon, "Holbrooke Nomination Passes One Hurdle but Faces Another," *New York Times,* July 1, 1999, A6; Philip Shenon, "Let's Slow Down on Holbrooke's Case, Lott Says," *New York Times,* July 23, 1999, A9; Eric Schmitt, "When Nomination Turns to Wrangling to Impasse," *New York Times,* July 28, 1999, A16; and Miles A. Pomper, "Holbrooke Confirmed as U.N. Envoy," *CQ Weekly,* August 7, 1999, 1961–1962.

110. Senate Committee on Governmental Affairs, *Policy and Supporting Positions* (Washington, DC: U.S. Government Printing Office, 2000), also known as the "plum book." For a fuller discussion, see Bradley H. Patterson and James P. Pfiffner, "The White House Office of Presidential Personnel," *Presidential Studies Quarterly* 31 (September 2001): 420. Patterson and Pfiffner identify 1,125 full-time positions subject to confirmation, including 185 ambassadors, 94 U.S. attorneys, 94 U.S. marshals, 15 in international organizations, and 4 in the legislative branch.

111. Anne Joseph O'Connell, "Staffing Federal Agencies: Lessons from 1981–2016," Brookings Institution, April 17, 2017, https://www.brookings.edu/research/staffing-federal-agencies-lessons-from-1981–2016/

112. O'Connell, "Staffing Federal Agencies."

113. Robert Brodsky, "Momentum Is Building to End Secret Holds," *Government Executive,* June 23, 2010, www.govexec.com/story_page.cfm?filepath=/dailyfed/0610/062310rb1.htm&oref=search.

114. The *Washington Post* maintained a running tally of positions at "Head Count," projects.washingtonpost.com/2009/federal-appointments.

115. Humberto Sanchez, "A Landmark Change to Filibuster," *CQ Weekly,* December 2, 2013, 1992–1993, library.cqpress.com/cqweekly/weeklyreport113-000004387403; and Jeremy W. Peters, "In Landmark Vote, Senate Limits Use of the Filibuster," *New York Times,* November 21, 2013, www.nytimes.com/2013/11/22/us/politics/reid-sets-in-motion-steps-to-limit-use-of-filibuster.html?pagewanted=1.

116. Adriel Bettelheim, "Senate Goes Nuclear," *CQ Weekly,* December 2, 2013, 19841989, library.cqpress.com/cqweekly/weeklyreport113-000004387396.

117. https://twitter.com/realDonaldTrump/status/829133645055135750.

118. Nancy Cook, Josh Dawsey, and Andrew Restuccia, "Why the Trump Administration Has So Many Vacancies," *Politico,* April 11, 2017, http://www.politico.com/story/2017/04/donald-trump-white-house-staff-vacancies-237081

119. Rebecca Adams, "With Nominees Stalled, Agencies Wait for Change," *CQ Weekly,* February 22, 2010, 428–429.

120. Jon R. Bond, Richard Fleisher, and Glen S. Krutz, "Malign Neglect: Evidence That Delay Has Become the Primary Method of Defeating Presidential Appointments," *Congress & the Presidency* 36:3 (2009): 226–243.

121. Henry B. Hogue, Maeve P. Carey, Michael W. Greene, and Maureen Bearden, "The Noel Canning Decision and Recess Appointments Made from 1981–2013," Congressional Research Service Memorandum, February 4, 2013, 4, democrats.edworkforce.house.gov/sites/democrats.edworkforce.house.gov/files/documents/112/pdf/Recess%20Appointments%201981-2013.pdf. Also see Pamela C. Corley, "Avoiding Advice and Consent: Recess Appointments and Presidential Power," *Presidential Studies Quarterly* 36 (December 2006): 671.

122. The White House, Office of the Press Secretary, March 27, 2010, www.whitehouse.gov/the-press-office/president-obama-announces-recess-appointments-key-administration-positions.

123. House Republicans had refused to adjourn Congress and thereby necessitated the three-day mock sessions. Both houses must agree to adjourn.

124. Charlie Savage, "Recess Appointments Ruling to Be Appealed," *New York Times,* March 13, 2013, www.nytimes.com.proxy.nss.udel.edu/2013/03/13/us/politics/obama-to-appeal-ruling-curbing-recess-appointments.html.

125. Charlie Savage, "Between the Lines of the Recess Appointments Decision," *New York Times,* June 26, 2014, www.nytimes.com/interactive/2014/06/25/us/annotated-supreme-court-recess-decision.html.

126. Michael D. Shear et al., "Trump Fires Justice Chief Who Defied Him," *New York Times,* January 31, 2017, A1.

127. *Myers v. United States,* 272 U.S. 52 (1926).

128. *Humphrey's Executor v. United States,* 295 U.S. 602 (1935).

129. Fisher, *Constitutional Conflicts,* 79.

130. *PHH Corporation v. CFPB,* U.S. Court of Appeals for the District of Columbia (No. 15-1177), October 11, 2016. The case was appealed from a three-judge panel of the circuit court to the full court, with oral arguments in the appeal held in late May 2017.

131. Phillip J. Cooper, *By Order of the President: The Use and Abuse of Executive Direct Action,* 2nd rev ed. (Lawrence: University Press of Kansas, 2014), 15, 81–83. By April 4, 2001, Bush had revoked six of Clinton's executive orders. Hult, "The Bush White House in Comparative Perspective," 27, n. 77.

132. A comprehensive list of executive orders from January 1937 can be accessed at www.archives.gov/federal-register/executive-orders/. For actions taken by President Trump, see https://www.whitehouse.gov/briefing-room/presidential-actions.

133. Kenneth R. Mayer, *With the Stroke of a Pen: Executive Orders and Presidential Power* (Princeton, NJ: Princeton University Press, 2001), 4.

134. For excellent discussions of presidential use of executive orders in the areas of information secrecy and intelligence organization as well as in civil rights, see Mayer, *With the Stroke of a Pen,* chaps. 5, 6.

135. Julie Hirschfeld Davis, "Obama's Immigration Action Has Precedents, but May Set a New One," *New York Times,* November 20, 2014, www.nytimes.com/2014/11/21/us/politics/obamas-immigration-decision-has-precedents-but-may-set-a-new-one.html?_r=0.

136. "Obama: I Will Use My Pen and Phone to Take on Congress," CBS News, January 14, 2014, www.cbsnews.com/news/obama-i-will-use-my-pen-and-phone-to-take-on-congress/.

137. *Amalgamated Meat Cutters v. Connally,* 337 F. Supp. 737 (1971).

138. *Hirabayashi v. United States,* 320 U.S. 581 (1943); and *Korematsu v. United States,* 323 U.S. 214 (1944).

139. Hult, "The Bush White House in Comparative Perspective," 27.

140. For an interpretation that Clinton relied more heavily on such instruments after the Republicans controlled Congress, see Aberbach, "A Reinvented Government," 128; and Alexis Simendinger, "The Paper Wars," *National Journal,* July 25, 1998, 1732–1739. Some reports confuse distinctions among the different forms of unilateral presidential action rather than adhering to the definition of executive orders maintained by the National Archives and Records Administration.

141. Mayer, *With the Stroke of a Pen,* 70.

142. Ibid., Table 3.3, 82.

143. Ibid., 102.

144. Kenneth R. Mayer and Kevin Price, "Unilateral Presidential Powers: Significant Executive Orders, 1949–99," *Presidential Studies Quarterly* 32 (June 2002): 375.

145. Cooper, *By Order of the President,* 13, 90–91. For a useful firsthand description of his tactics, see Elena Kagan, "Presidential Administration," *Harvard Law Review* 114 (2001): 2245–2385.

146. As quoted in Kenneth S. Lowande, "The Contemporary Presidency: After the Orders: Presidential Memoranda and Unilateral Action," *Presidential Studies Quarterly* (December 2014): 732.

147. Barack Obama speech, "Full text October 26, 2011," historymusings.wordpress.com/2011/10/26/full-text-october-26–2011-president-barack-obama-unveils-speech-student-loan-debt-relief-plan/.

148. *Youngstown Sheet and Tube Co. v. Sawyer,* 343 U.S. 579 (1952).

149. Lawrence R. Jacobs and Robert Y. Shapiro, "Public Opinion in Clinton's First Year: Leadership and Responsiveness," in Renshon, *The Clinton Presidency,* 201.

150. Andrew Rudalevige, "The Contemporary Presidency: Executive Orders and Presidential Unilateralism," *Presidential Studies Quarterly* 42:1 (2012): 138–160.

151. *Immigration and Naturalization Service v. Chadha,* 462 U.S. 919 (1983).

152. Joseph Cooper, "Postscript on the Congressional Veto," *Political Science Quarterly* (Fall 1983): 427–430; Barbara Hinkson Craig, *The Legislative Veto: Congressional Control of Regulation* (Boulder, CO: Westview, 1983), 139–150; and Fisher, *Constitutional Conflicts,* 152.

153. Fisher, *Constitutional Conflicts,* 150–152.

154. Richard M. Pious, *The American Presidency* (New York: Basic Books, 1979), 256–257.

155. Allen Schick, "The Road to PPB: The States of Budget Reform," *Public Administration Review* (December 1966): 243–258.

156. Wildavsky, *The New Politics of the Budgetary Process,* 436–440.

157. Becca Stanek, "Budget Director Says President Trump's Promise to Pay Off the National Debt was 'Hyperbole,'" *The Week,* April 12, 2017, http://theweek.com/speedreads/691841/budget-director-says-president-trumps-promise-pay-national-debt-hyperbole.

158. Allen Schick, *The Federal Budget: Politics, Policy, Process* (Washington, DC: Brookings, 1995), 2–4.

159. Bob Woodward, *The Agenda: Inside the Clinton White House* (New York: Simon and Schuster, 1994).

160. Daniel J. Palazzolo, *Done Deal? The Politics of the 1997 Budget Agreement* (Chatham, NJ: Chatham House, 1999).

161. See, for example, John Hudak, *Presidential Pork: White House Influence over the Distribution of Federal Grants* (Washington, DC: Brookings Institution 2014); and Douglas L. Kriner and Andrew Reeves, "Presidential Particularism and Divide-the-Dollar Politics," *American Political Science Review* 109 (February 2015): 155–171.

162. Louis Fisher, *Presidential Spending Power* (Princeton, NJ: Princeton University Press, 1979), chap. 4.

163. Ibid., 148.

164. Vivian Vale, "The Obligation to Spend: Presidential Impoundment of Congressional Appropriations," *Political Studies* (1977): 508–532.

165. *Clinton v. City of New York,* 524 U.S. 417 (1998). The case can be found at supct.law.cornell.edu/supct/html/historics/USSC_CR_0524_0417_ZS.html.

166. Steven T. Dennis, "A Promise for a Line-Item Vote," *CQ Weekly Online,* January 22, 2007, 252–252, library.cqpress.com/cqweekly/weeklyreport110-000002433724.

167. Brian Friel, "Line-Item Veto Gets Hearing Wednesday," *National Journal,* May 24, 2010.

168. Charles S. Clark, "All Agencies Looped into Campaign to Cut Government Waste," *National Journal,* June 14, 2011.

169. Peri Arnold concludes his authoritative study of "the managerial presidency" by observing that "no modern president has fully managed the executive branch." He further argues that the "managerial conception of the presidency is untenable" because it "places impossible obligations on presidents" and creates unrealistic "public expectations of presidential performance." Peri E. Arnold, *Making the Managerial Presidency: Comprehensive Reorganization Planning, 1905–1980* (Princeton, NJ: Princeton University Press, 1986), 361–362.

170. Andrew Rudalevige, *Managing the President's Program: Presidential Leadership and Legislative Policy Formulation* (Princeton, NJ: Princeton University Press, 2002), 7.

171. Ibid.

172. Hess, *Organizing the Presidency,* 230–231.

173. Ibid.

174. Fred I. Greenstein, "Political and Political Leadership: The Case of Bill Clinton," in Renshon, *The Clinton Presidency,* 141, 142.

175. Burt Solomon, "Clinton's New Taskmaster Takes Charge," *National Journal,* August 6, 1994, 1872.

176. Todd S. Purdum, "The Ungreening of the White House Staff," *New York Times,* December 22, 1996, E10.

177. Karen Hughes returned to Texas in July 2002. For a discussion of the Bush staff system, see Hult, "The Bush White House in Comparative Perspective."

178. Mark Leibovich, "Pressure Cooker: Andrew Card Has the Recipe for Chief of Staff Down Pat," *Washington Post,* January 5, 2005, C1.

179. Tom Hamburger, "Inquiry of Rove Brings Unit out of Obscurity," *Seattle Times,* April 24, 2007, seattletimes.nwsource.com/html/politics/2003678550_investigate24.html.

180. Alexis Simendinger, "Stepping into Power," *National Journal,* January 27, 2001, 247.

181. See, e.g., Shirley Anne Warshaw, *The Co-Presidency of Bush and Cheney* (Stanford, CA: Stanford University Press, 2009).

182. James P. Pfiffner, "Organizing the Obama White House," in Thurber, *Obama in Office.*

183. David B. Cohen, Karen M. Hult, and Charles E. Walcott, "The Chicago Clan: The Chiefs of Staff in the Obama White House," *Social Science Quarterly* 93:5 (December 2012): 1101–1126.

184. Ibid.

185. Terry M. Moe, "The Politicized Presidency," in *The New Direction in American Politics,* ed. John E. Chubb and Paul E. Peterson (Washington, DC: Brookings, 1985), 235–271.

186. Samuel Kernell, "The Creed and Reality of Modern White House Management," in *Chief of Staff: Twenty-Five Years of Managing the Presidency,* ed. Samuel Kernell and Samuel L. Popkin (Berkeley: University of California Press, 1986), 228.

187. Justin S. Vaughn, "The Contemporary Presidency: Reconsidering Presidential Policy Czars," *Presidential Studies Quarterly* 44:3 (2014): 522–536.

188. See, e.g, Sarah Ellison, "Inside the Kushner-Bannon Civil War," *Vanity Fair,* April 14, 2017, http://www.vanityfair.com/news/2017/04/jared-kushner-steve-bannon-white-house-civil-war; Peter Baker, Glenn Thrush, and Maggie Haberman, "Jared Kushner and Ivanka Trump: Pillars of Family-Driven West Wing," *New York Times,* April 15, 2017, https://mobile.nytimes.com/2017/04/15/us/politics/jared-kushner-ivanka-trump-white-house.html

189. Andrew Rudalevige, "Rivals, or a Team?" in Bert Rockman, Andrew Rudalevige, and Colin Campbell, eds., *The Obama Presidency: Appraisals and Prospects* (Washington, DC: CQ Press, 2012).

190. Henry B. Hogue, "Presidential Reorganization Authority: History, Recent Initiatives, and Options for Congress," CRS Report R42852, December 12, 2012, fas.org/sgp/crs/misc/R42852.pdf.

191. John R. Dempsey, "Carter Reorganization: A Midterm Appraisal," *Public Administration Review* (January–February 1979): 74–78; and Arnold, *Making the Managerial Presidency,* chap. 10.

192. Herbert Kaufman, "Reflections on Administrative Reorganization," in *Setting National Priorities: The 1978 Budget,* ed. Joseph A. Pechman (Washington, DC: Brookings, 1977), 403.

193. Harold C. Relyea, "93026: Executive Branch Reorganization," *CRS Issue Brief,* December 6, 1996, www.fas.org/spp/civil/crs/93-026.htm.

194. Harold C. Relyea, "Executive Branch Reorganization and Management Initiatives," *CRS Issue Brief for Congress,* September 23, 2003, digital.library.unt.edu/govdocs/crs/permalink/meta-crs-4579:1.

195. Dempsey, "Carter Reorganization," 75.

196. Ronald C. Moe, "The 'Reinventing Government' Exercise: Misinterpreting the Problem, Misjudging the Consequences," *Public Administration Review* (March–April 1994): 112.

197. David Osborne and Ted Gaebler, *Reinventing Government: How the Entrepreneurial Spirit Is Transforming the Public Sector from Schoolhouse to State House, City Hall to Pentagon* (Reading, MA: Addison-Wesley, 1992), 111.

198. Donald F. Kettl, *Reinventing Government: A Fifth Year Report Card,* Center for Public Management Report 98–1 (Washington, DC: Brookings, September 1998).

199. In "The 'Reinventing Government' Exercise," Ronald Moe argues that Clinton's effort substitutes results for processes and amounts to abandonment of public law as the basis of political accountability (112). Political scientist James Q. Wilson doubts whether in the era of big government "political accountability can any longer be equated with presidential power." James Q. Wilson, "Reinventing Public Administration," *P.S.: Political Science and Politics* (December 1994): 671. Well-known management consultant Peter Drucker called for a new theory that "asks what the proper functions of government might be and could be . . . [and] what results government should be held accountable for." Peter Drucker, "Really Reinventing Government," *Atlantic Monthly,* February 1995, 61.

200. Edwin Chen, "Bush Aims to Privatize Many Federal Jobs," *Los Angeles Times,* November 15, 2002, http://articles.latimes.com/2002/nov/15/nation/na-compete15.

201. Paul Singer, "By the Horns," *National Journal,* March 25, 2005, nationaljournal.com/members/news/2005/03/0325nj1.htm.

202. See Executive Order 13781, March 13, 2017; Mulvaney, "Comprehensive Plan."

203. Aaron Wildavsky, *Speaking Truth to Power* (Boston: Little, Brown, 1979), 120.

204. Ibid.

205. Richard Rose, *Managing Presidential Objectives* (New York: Free Press, 1976), chap. 6.

206. Peter Behr, "Energy Plan to Fuel Long Fight; at Issue Is Environmental Cost of Plentiful, Cheaper Power," *Washington Post,* May 15, 2001, A9.

207. Peter Behr, "Bush Places His Bet on Energy Industry," *Washington Post,* May 18, 2001, E1.

208. See, for example, Arnold, *Making the Managerial Presidency;* Colin Campbell, *Managing the Presidency: Carter, Reagan, and the Search for Executive Harmony* (Pittsburgh: University of Pittsburgh Press, 1986); and Rose, *Managing Presidential Objectives.* Also see Walter Williams, *Mismanaging America: The Rise of the Anti-Analytic Presidency* (Lawrence: University Press of Kansas, 1990).

209. Nathan, *The Administrative Presidency.*

210. Allen Schick, "The Budget as an Instrument of Presidential Policy," in Salamon and Lund, *The Reagan Presidency and the Governing of America,* 113.

211. Lester M. Salamon and Alan J. Abramson, "Governance: The Politics of Retrenchment," in *The Reagan Record,* ed. John L. Palmer and Isabell V. Sawhill (Cambridge, MA: Ballinger, 1984), 97; and Joseph A. Pika and Norman C. Thomas, "The President as Institution Builder: The Reagan Case," *Governance* (October 1990): 444–447.

212. Elena Kagan, "Presidential Administration," *Harvard Law Review* 114 (2001): 2245–2385; Andrew Rudalevige, "The Obama Administrative Presidency: Some Late-Term Lessons," *Presidential Studies Quarterly* 46 (December 2016): 868–890.

CHAPTER 7

Judicial Politics

The Asahi Shimbun via Getty Images

Supreme Court Justice Anthony Kennedy swears in Neil Gorsuch as a new member of the Court while President Trump and Gorsuch's wife, Louise, look on.

Today politics lies squarely at the heart of the U.S. Supreme Court appointment process. That is nothing new, but partisan maneuvering in the Senate, which has the power to confirm or reject Supreme Court nominees put forward by the president, went to new extremes during the last year of the Obama administration and the opening months of the Trump administration. When Justice Antonin Scalia, one of the most reliably conservative voters on the Court, died unexpectedly on February 13, 2016, Senate majority leader Mitch McConnell (R-Kentucky) almost immediately declared that the Republican-controlled Senate would not even consider any nominee put forward by the Democratic president, Barack Obama. Claiming that the Senate had a constitutional duty to act on a nominee, Obama nonetheless nominated Merrick Garland, the centrist chief judge of the D.C. Circuit, on March 16, 2016. He did so with more than ten months left in his term. Despite a long tradition of presidents nominating and the Senate considering Supreme Court nominees in election years, Republicans followed McConnell's lead and blocked hearings on Garland's nomination, which expired on January 3, 2017, at the end of the 114th Congress.[1] This allowed President Donald J. Trump to nominate Scalia's replacement. His choice, Neil Gorsuch—a judge on the U.S. Court of Appeals for the Tenth Circuit—faced opposition from Senate Democrats, who believed that Republicans had stolen a seat from President Obama. They also claimed that Gorsuch, predicted by some to be even more conservative than Scalia, fell outside the mainstream.[2] But when Democrats launched a filibuster that Republicans did not have the votes to overcome, Republicans employed the "nuclear option"—changing the rules of the game to prohibit filibusters of Supreme Court nominees and allow them to be approved by a simple majority vote. Democrats had likewise employed the "nuclear option" to end filibusters of lower federal court judges in 2013 when they controlled the Senate.

It is not surprising that the Supreme Court appointment process has become a high-stakes political battle. The ability to shape the future direction of the U.S. Supreme Court through appointments is no small opportunity. The Supreme Court is the ultimate arbiter of such politically volatile issues as same-sex marriage, health care reform, affirmative action, voting rights, gun control, immigration laws, and abortion restrictions, to name just a few. The Court split 5–4 on many of these issues during the Obama administration, with Justice Anthony Kennedy (who took his seat on the Court in 1988 after being nominated by Republican president Ronald Reagan) often acting as the "swing voter"—sometimes siding with the more liberal bloc (Ruth Bader Ginsburg, Stephen Breyer, Sonia Sotomayor, and Elena Kagan) and sometimes siding with the more conservative bloc (Antonin Scalia, Clarence Thomas, John Roberts, and Samuel Alito).

Supreme Court justices have life tenure, so predicting precisely who will choose to leave the Court, and when, is not easy, but by the end of President Trump's first term, three justices will be in their eighties: Ginsburg will be eighty-six, Kennedy will be eighty-three, and Breyer will be eighty-one. The likelihood that at least one of these will leave the bench during his term is high. Replacing Ginsburg and Breyer, in particular, would give Trump the opportunity to move the Court in a decidedly more conservative direction. Obama did not have the same opportunity to shift the Court to the left. He did replace two justices in his first two years in office who had been appointed by Republican presidents: David Souter (appointed by George H.W. Bush) and John Paul Stevens (appointed by Gerald R. Ford), but both Souter and Stevens had solidly aligned themselves with the Court's liberal voting bloc. Thus, replacing them with Sonia Sotomayor and Elena Kagan did not fundamentally alter the ideological balance of the Court.

In this chapter, we examine the relationship between the president and the federal courts. In the first section, we analyze the most important influence the president exerts over these courts: the power to nominate their members. We then explore other means by which the chief executive affects the business of the courts and, finally, the reverse situation: how the federal courts, and the Supreme Court in particular, influence the actions of the president.

Presidential Appointment of Federal Judges

Perhaps the greatest impact the president can have on the courts is the selection of federal judges who share the administration's policy goals. These judges include not only the nine justices of the U.S. Supreme Court but also more than eight hundred judges who sit on lower federal courts. The Constitution established (and requires) one Supreme Court. It authorized (but did not require) Congress to create lower federal courts. Congress created lower courts almost immediately through the Judiciary Act of 1789, and that system has grown and evolved since then. These federal judges are nominated by the president, confirmed by the Senate, and serve "during good Behaviour." In other words, they have life tenure subject to impeachment or resignation.[3] Once they are on the bench, federal judges can influence judicial policymaking for years, usually many more than the president who appoints them.

One might think that impartial judges who objectively apply the law according to set standards of interpretation should all arrive at the same "correct" outcome in cases that come before them. In practice, judges hold very different views about how to interpret legal texts. Moreover, judges are human beings who are influenced, at least in part, by their backgrounds, personal beliefs, and judicial philosophies. As a result, different judges can—and do—reach different conclusions when confronted with the same case. Presidents, therefore, work hard to nominate judges with a judicial philosophy similar to theirs. Interest groups—well aware of the impact judges can have on policy—also take keen interest in these nominees. So, too, does the Senate, given its power to confirm or reject nominees.

Selection of Lower Federal Court Judges

There are two basic types of lower federal courts: (1) trial courts, which are called U.S. district courts, and (2) appellate courts, called U.S. courts of appeals, or "circuit" courts.[4] These courts are distinct from state courts. The United States has an overlapping system of state and federal courts, and each state structures its own court system. As a result, the country has fifty-one court systems—one at the federal level and one for each of the fifty states. State courts usually hear cases involving state law, and federal courts hear cases involving federal law. Sometimes a single action can provoke cases in both state and federal court. Timothy McVeigh violated federal law in 1995 when he blew up the Federal Building in Oklahoma City and was therefore tried in federal court. But he could also have been tried in state court for violating state law against murder. Moreover, a case involving state law that begins in state court can be appealed to federal court if it involves a *federal question.* A federal question exists if a state law is alleged to violate federal law, a U.S. treaty, or the U.S. Constitution. It can also exist if police or prosecutors are alleged to have violated the constitutional rights of a criminal defendant. A person convicted in state court because of evidence gathered from an unreasonable search and seizure or a coerced confession could appeal to federal court. If there is no federal question, however, the highest state court remains the court of last resort. The manner of selecting state court judges varies from state to state and is completely unrelated to federal judicial selection.

Federal criminal and civil cases originate in U.S. district courts, which try the cases. Each of these courts has jurisdiction over a geographic area called a district. Each district falls within the boundary of a single state, and, by tradition, judges who come from that state are appointed to a district's courts.[5] Every state has at least one district. Those with heavier caseloads have more than one, and Congress occasionally adds new districts to accommodate increased caseloads. Because district courts are the point of entry to the federal judicial system, they hear more cases than any other kind of federal court. Currently more than 650 judges staff ninety-four district courts.

The courts of appeals are intermediate appellate courts between the district courts and the Supreme Court. Each has jurisdiction over a geographic area called a circuit, made up of several districts. There are twelve regional circuits: one for the District of Columbia and eleven numbered circuits covering the rest of the country. In addition, the Federal Circuit has nationwide jurisdiction to hear appeals in certain specialized types of cases (such as those involving patents), as well as appeals from the Court of International Trade and the Court of Federal Claims. Unlike districts, the numbered circuits have jurisdiction over several states: The First Circuit, for example, covers Maine, Massachusetts, New Hampshire, and Rhode Island. The circuit courts hear appeals from the trial courts and decide whether the trial court made a legal error in trying the case. In other words, courts of appeals answer questions of *law* rather than questions of *fact.* Unlike in proceedings in the district courts, there are no witnesses, no testimony, and no jury. Judges on the courts of appeals base their rulings on written legal arguments called briefs and on oral arguments presented by lawyers representing each side of the case. A panel of three judges usually hears appeals. A majority vote of the panel is necessary to overturn a lower court ruling, and the court of appeals issues a written opinion explaining its ruling.

Only about one-sixth of the litigants from the district courts appeal, so the caseload for the courts of appeals is significantly less than the caseload for the district courts. Even though they hear fewer cases than the district courts, the courts of appeals are influential because of their power to set precedents that are binding on the lower courts in their circuits. Because the U.S. Supreme Court accepts such a minuscule number of cases from the courts of appeals for review, the courts of appeals are effectively the court of last resort in more than 99 percent of the cases that come before them.[6] Therefore, appointments to these courts are especially significant.

In theory, the appointment process for lower federal courts is the same as for the Supreme Court: The president nominates, and the Senate either confirms or rejects. In practice, presidents have traditionally had less control over the selection of lower federal court judges than over the selection of Supreme Court justices. This is especially true at the district court level because of a practice called **senatorial courtesy**. This informal rule has existed since the early days of George Washington's administration. It means that the Senate (out of courtesy) will generally refuse to confirm people to federal positions who do not have the support of the senators from the state where the vacancy exists.

Senatorial courtesy was institutionalized in the 1940s through the routinization of the so-called **blue slip** procedure.[7] Both senators, regardless of party affiliation, from the state where the vacancy occurs receive a letter from the chairman of the Senate Judiciary Committee asking for advice about the nominee. Enclosed is a form, printed on blue paper, for the senator to comment on the nominee. Although senators may put their support or opposition in writing and return the form, it is understood that failure to return the blue slip amounts to a veto that will prevent committee hearings on the nominee—a de facto invocation of senatorial courtesy that usually blocks the nomination.[8]

The blue slip procedure is not a formal Senate rule and therefore has not been applied consistently over the years. For example, there has been disagreement as to whether home-state senators *not* of the president's party should be able to block a nomination. During certain periods, the Judiciary Committee chair counted only blue slip vetoes from senators of the president's party.[9] At other times, the chair held that either home-state senator, regardless of party, could scuttle a nomination. At the outset of the Trump administration, some commentators even advocated abandoning the blue slip procedure to make it easier to confirm lower court judges.[10]

Shifting standards for how to use the blue slip often reflect partisan politics. During the last six years of Bill Clinton's administration, when a Democrat controlled the White House and Republicans controlled the Senate, Judiciary Committee chairman Orrin Hatch of Utah routinely allowed blue slips from home-state Republicans to prevent hearings on many Democratic nominees. In other words, he allowed home-state senators who were not of the same political party as President Clinton to block his nominees. Once George W. Bush became president in 2001, however, Hatch abruptly shifted gears and sought to weaken the power of the blue slip. With a Republican in the White House, Hatch wanted to discount the veto power of home-state Democrats, saying that support of a home-state Republican should overcome opposition of a home-state Democrat. The *New York Times* called Hatch's turnabout both ironic and audacious: Opposition Republicans had for six years "routinely obstructed" Clinton's judicial nominations and were now trying to remove the possibility that opposition Democrats could do the same to Bush.[11]

As a result of senatorial courtesy and the blue slip, presidents traditionally turn to home-state senators for advice about whom to nominate. Home-state senators of the president's party have the most influence, but some presidents—such as Obama—have also sought advice from home-state senators of the opposition party.[12] (Even when they do so, presidents rarely appoint judges of the opposing party.) In the early days of the Republic—when communication was slow and difficult and the president was more isolated and removed from the various states than today—seeking advice made sense. It assumed that home-state senators were better able to select qualified individuals than the president because they knew more about the existing pool of candidates. Over time, however, senators came to treat district court appointments as a form of patronage. Robert F. Kennedy, who served as attorney general in his brother's administration, went so far as to call it "senatorial appointment with the advice and consent of the Senate."[13]

G. Alan Tarr has pointed out that senatorial courtesy has influenced the type of individuals appointed to district courts. Because these appointments have long served as a form of political patronage for home-state senators of the president's political party, it is not surprising that roughly 95 percent of all district court judges appointed during the past hundred years have come from the same political party as the appointing president. Tarr also notes that "district court judges have usually 'earned' their positions by active party service in their state prior to appointment."[14]

In an attempt to ensure the quality of these judges, the American Bar Association (ABA) created its Standing Committee on the Federal Judiciary in 1946 to review the qualifications of all federal judicial nominees.[15] Republicans on the Senate

Judiciary Committee embraced the ABA's role—partly to block some of President Harry S. Truman's Democratic nominees. When Republican president Dwight D. Eisenhower entered office in 1953, he established a formal link between the White House and the ABA. The ABA would review the qualifications of all potential nominees before the president nominated anyone.

By the 1980s, however, Republicans had come to view the ABA with suspicion. Once a conservative organization, the ABA had become more liberal over time. Republicans were especially angry that in 1987 four of the fifteen members of the ABA's standing committee had rated Ronald Reagan's failed Supreme Court nominee Robert Bork "not qualified." In March 2001, President Bush severed the White House link with the ABA—something his father had threatened to do in 1991. In a letter to ABA president Martha W. Barnett, White House counsel Alberto Gonzales, who became Bush's second-term attorney general, wrote: "We will continue to welcome suggestions from all sources, including the ABA. The issue at hand, however, is quite different: whether the ABA alone—out of the literally dozens of groups and many individuals who have a strong interest in the composition of the federal courts—should receive advance notice of the identities of potential nominees in order to render prenomination opinions on their fitness for judicial service."[16]

When Democrats regained control of the Senate from June 2001 through the 2002 midterm elections, and again after the 2006 midterm elections, they reinstated a role for the ABA by promising not to hold hearings on Bush's judicial nominees until the Senate Judiciary Committee received their ABA ratings. Shortly after taking office, President Obama overturned Bush's decision to sever the relationship between the White House and the ABA. Democrats argued that the ABA ratings validate a nominee's professional qualifications and maintained that Bush's attempt to bypass the ABA was part of an effort to appoint more ideologically extreme judges to the bench. The Trump administration once again jettisoned the ABA's official role in the nomination process, although the ABA said that it would continue to provide its evaluations to the Senate Judiciary Committee.[17]

Since Jimmy Carter's administration, presidents have exerted greater control over the selection of lower federal court judges than they used to, especially at the level of the courts of appeals. Some observers view this control as an attempt by presidents to appoint more ideological judges. Ironically, President Carter initiated the reform in order to institute merit selection of federal judges. He created the Circuit Court Nominating Commission by executive order in 1977. The commission diminished the role of senators in the selection of courts of appeals judges by taking control of the screening process for nominees. Under the new system, the commission would submit a short list of qualified nominees to the president, who would then nominate someone from that list.[18] Carter also urged senators to create, voluntarily, nominating commissions to advise him on the selection of district court judges from their states. By 1979, senators from thirty-one states had created such commissions.[19] The changes were made to help ensure that the awarding of judgeships would be based on qualifications and not used as political patronage.

Despite Carter's emphasis on merit in judicial selection, his appointments were partisan: Over 90 percent of his district court appointments and just over 82 percent of his appeals court appointments were Democrats.[20] Carter also practiced affirmative action when selecting judges. He made a deliberate effort to place women, African Americans, and Hispanics on the federal judiciary—appointing more of each than had been placed on the bench by all previous presidents combined.[21]

Ronald Reagan transformed the selection process when he took office in 1981. He abolished Carter's commission system and seized control of the selection process as part of an effort to identify nominees who reflected his administration's ideology. He created the President's Committee on Federal Judicial Selection, staffed by representatives of the White House and the Justice Department, to conduct the screening—which included extensive interviews of all leading candidates. Sheldon Goldman called it "the most systematic judicial philosophical screening of candidates ever seen in the nation's history."[22] Reagan's attorney general, Edwin Meese III, bluntly said the appointments were meant to "institutionalize the Reagan revolution so it can't be set aside no matter what happens in future presidential elections."[23] By the time he left office, Reagan had set a new record for the number of lower federal judges appointed: 290 district court judges and 78 appeals court judges.[24] George H. W. Bush appointed almost two hundred additional federal judges during his four years as president. Presidents Carter, Reagan, and George H. W. Bush all benefited from legislation that significantly expanded the number of federal judges, but no president since 1990 has enjoyed a similar expansion. For example, during Clinton's eight years in office, Congress created only 9 additional seats—as compared with 85 under Bush, 85 under Reagan, and 152 under Carter.[25]

Recent presidents have also faced deliberate slowdowns of the confirmation process. This is largely a result of extended periods of divided government, as discussed in chapter 5. For example, Clinton faced a Senate controlled by opposition Republicans during his last six years in office. In 1997, Republican senators orchestrated a slowdown of the confirmation process to protest what they called Clinton's "activist" (liberal) nominees. Such charges may have reflected partisan hyperbole more than fact. Studies suggest that Clinton's nominees were actually quite moderate, even the nominees confirmed before Republicans took control of the Senate.[26] Clinton's appointees also had the highest ABA ratings of the past four presidents.[27]

As a result of the Republican slowdown, 10 percent of seats on the federal judiciary were vacant by the end of 1997. In the face of such results, even Chief Justice William Rehnquist, a conservative appointed by Reagan, criticized the Senate slowdown. In his annual State of the Judiciary report he wrote: "The Senate is surely under no obligation to confirm any particular nominee, but after the necessary time for inquiry, it should vote him up or vote him down."[28] In part because of Rehnquist's criticism, Senate Republicans backed away from their slowdown, and the backlog of vacancies eased in 1998. But the delaying tactics returned in 1999 and continued through the rest of the Clinton presidency. In 2000, the Senate confirmed only thirty-nine of eighty-one judicial nominees Clinton put forward, and two other nominees withdrew. Nominations of forty-two judicial candidates remained unconfirmed when Clinton left office in January 2001—thirty-eight of them had never received a Judiciary Committee hearing.[29]

Despite the slowdowns and the lack of new judicial seats to fill, Clinton appointed 366 judges to the district courts, courts of appeals, and Supreme Court during his eight years in office. By the end of Clinton's second term, the number of his appointees serving on the courts narrowly surpassed the number of Reagan-Bush appointees still serving, 42.7 percent to 40.7 percent.[30] Even more than Carter had done, Clinton diversified the bench through these appointments. He appointed 108 women and 61 African Americans: more of each than Ford, Carter, Reagan, and Bush combined had appointed in nineteen years.[31] (See Table 7-1.)

George W. Bush also faced slowdowns. He took office with the Senate evenly divided between Democrats and Republicans. At first Republicans held nominal control (with the tie-breaking vote of Vice President Dick Cheney), but in June 2001—less than six months after Bush took office—Senator Jim Jeffords of Vermont left the Republican Party, thereby throwing control of the Senate to the Democrats. By October 2001, Bush had submitted sixty judicial nominations, but the Senate had confirmed only eight. Now Republicans accused Democrats of slowing down the confirmation process. They also charged that judicial vacancies would hamper the post–September 11, 2001, war on terrorism and mounted a Senate filibuster against a foreign-aid spending bill as retaliation for the confirmation slowdown. Democrats denied that they had deliberately slowed down the confirmation process as Republicans had done under Clinton, pointing out that they had controlled the Senate for only four months and that the legislative agenda had been interrupted during that time by the terrorist attacks of 9/11 and the recent anthrax scare on Capitol Hill.[32] The charges and countercharges further polarized the two sides. Democrats charged Bush with nominating ideologically extreme judges and blocked his nominations of Charles Pickering and Priscilla Owen to the Fifth Circuit Court of Appeals. President Bush, emboldened by his skyrocketing public approval after 9/11, charged Democrats with obstructionism and turned the "vacancy crisis" on the federal bench into a campaign issue during the 2002 midterm elections.[33]

Republicans regained control of the Senate in the midterm elections, and it appeared that Bush's nominees would be approved. Bush quickly renominated Pickering and Owen. Although Senate Democrats showed a willingness to vote for moderate nominees—all nine Democrats on the Senate Judiciary Committee voted in favor of Edward Prado, a Bush nominee to the Fifth Circuit Court of Appeals—they continued their vow to block "ideological extremists." To do so, they resurrected a tool used by Republicans in 1968 to block Lyndon B. Johnson's nomination of Abe Fortas to be chief justice of the United States: the filibuster. Under Senate Rule 22, it takes a vote of three-fifths of the entire Senate, sixty votes, to end a filibuster. Because Republicans could not muster the necessary sixty votes, Democrats succeeded in blocking ten nominations—prompting a Republican threat to change Senate rules regarding filibusters, a strategy dubbed the "nuclear option," so that Democrats could no longer use them against judicial nominees. Seven moderate senators from each party, the so-called "Gang of 14," brokered a temporary compromise that allowed judicial filibusters only in "extraordinary circumstances." By the time he left office, Bush had appointed 261 judges to the district courts, 59 judges to the courts of appeals, and 2 justices to the Supreme Court.

Judicial vacancies were initially filled at a slow rate under President Obama. The Obama administration contributed to the problem by being slow to make judicial nominations, and Republican obstruction furthered the delay. For example, the time from hearings on judicial nominees to their final confirmation vote more than doubled from George W. Bush to Obama (from 54 days for district court nominees under Bush to 139 under Obama's first term, and from 63 days for courts of appeals nominees under Bush to 177 under Obama's first term).[34] By the end of Obama's first two years in office there was renewed talk of a "vacancy crisis." According to a report by the Alliance for Justice, judicial vacancies grew from fifty-five to ninety-seven during those two years. "Judicial emergencies"—that is, vacancies that occur where case filings per judge exceed six hundred cases in district courts and seven hundred cases in courts of appeals—rose from twenty to forty-six.[35]

Republicans also revived the filibuster. They used it in May 2011 to block Obama's nomination of Goodwin Liu to fill a vacancy on the Ninth Circuit Court of

Appeals.[36] They used it again at the beginning of Obama's second term against Caitlin Halligan, who had been nominated to fill a vacancy on the U.S. Court of Appeals for the District of Columbia. Halligan later asked the president to withdraw her nomination. The threat of filibusters meant that Democrats no longer needed just fifty-one votes to confirm a nominee; now they needed sixty.[37]

Then, in November 2013, the Democrat-controlled Senate executed the "nuclear option" that Republicans had earlier threatened when Bush was president. In so doing, it took away the filibuster as a tool that could be used to block executive branch and judicial nominees (Supreme Court nominees remained a significant exception until 2017).[38] The move dramatically increased the number of judicial confirmations, at least in the short run.[39] Then, during Obama's last two years in office, Republicans regained a Senate majority. This allowed them to delay and obstruct new lower federal court nominees. As a result, the Senate confirmed only 18 of Obama's District Court nominees and only two of his Court of Appeals nominees during the entire 114th Congress, while failing to act on 52 of his nominations. This stood in stark contrast to how judicial nominees fared in the last two years of other recent two-term presidencies. For example, during Ronald Reagan's last two years (the 100th Congress), the Senate confirmed 67 District Court nominees and 17 Court of Appeals nominees; during Bill Clinton's last two years (the 106th Congress), the Senate confirmed 58 District Court nominees and 15 Court of Appeals nominees; and during George W. Bush's last two years (the 110th Congress), the Senate confirmed 58 District Court nominees and 10 Court of Appeals nominees.[40]

Nonetheless, Obama managed to bring real change to the type of judges confirmed during his administration by making a concerted effort to appoint a more diverse set of judges. By the end of his first term, he had already nominated more women and minorities in four years than his predecessor had in eight (see Table 7-1). The White House website touted the Obama administration's "unprecedented commitment to expanding the racial, gender, and experiential diversity of the men and women who enforce our laws and deliver justice." It listed a string a "firsts" ranging from the first Latina appointed to the U.S. Supreme Court to the first openly gay man confirmed to a federal court (President Clinton appointed the first openly gay woman in 1994).[41] By the end of 2014, Obama had appointed more female, Hispanic, Asian American, and LGBT judges than any other president, and in 2016 he became the first president to nominate a Muslim American to be a federal judge, Abid Riaz Qureshi (the Senate, however, took no action on Qureshi's nomination, which expired at the end of the 114th Congress).[42]

TABLE 7-1 Race, Ethnicity, and Gender of Appointments to the U.S. District Courts and Courts of Appeals, by Administration, Nixon through Obama

President	*Total Appointments*	*Male*	*Female*	*White*	*African American*	*Hispanic*	*Asian*	*Native American*
Obama	316	184	132	202	60	34	19	1
(2009–2017)		(58.2%)	(41.7%)	(63.9%)	(18.9%)	(10.7%)	(6.0%)	(0.3%)
G. W. Bush	320	251	69	263	24	29	4	0
(2001–2009)		(78.4%)	(21.6%)	(82.2%)	(7.5%)	(9.1%)	(1.3%)	
Clinton	366	259	107	274	61	25	5	1
(1993–2001)		(70.8%)	(29.2%)	(74.9%)	(16.7%)	(6.8%)	(1.4%)	(0.3%)
G. H. W. Bush	185	148	37	165	12	8	0	0
(1989–1993)		(80.0%)	(20.0%)	(89.2%)	(6.5%)	(4.3%)		
Reagan	368	340	28	344	7	15	2	0
(1981–1989)		(92.4%)	(7.6%)	(93.5%)	(1.9%)	(4.1%)	(0.5%)	
Carter	258	218	40	202	37	16	2	1
(1977–1981)		(84.5%)	(15.5%)	(78.3%)	(14.3%)	(6.2%)	(0.8%)	(0.4%)
Ford	64	63	1	58	3	1	2	0
(1974–1977)		(98.4%)	(1.6%)	(90.6%)	(4.7%)	(1.6%)	(3.1%)	
Nixon	224	223	1	215	6	2	1	0
(1969–1974)		(99.6%)	(0.4%)	(96%)	(2.6%)	(0.9%)	(0.4%)	

SOURCE: Drawn from Tables 2 and 4 in Sheldon Goldman et al., “Picking Judges in a Time of Turmoil: W. Bush’s Judiciary during the 109th Congress,” *Judicature* 90 (May–June 2007), 277 and 282; and from Table 6.1 (for Ford and Nixon) from Sheldon Goldman, *Picking Federal Judges: Lower Court Selection from Roosevelt through Reagan* (New Haven, CT: Yale University Press, 1997), 227–229. Figures for George W. Bush courtesy of Sheldon Goldman. Figures for Barack Obama from Tables 6 and 7 in Elliot Slotnick, Sara Schiavone, and Sheldon Goldman, “Obama’s Judicial Legacy: The Final Chapter,” working paper.

Selection of Supreme Court Justices

The president clearly dominates the process of selecting members of the U.S. Supreme Court. Despite the constitutional admonition that the Senate offer "advice and consent" on presidents' nominees, the extent to which presidents seek advice from senators on whom to nominate is minimal. A rare exception came in 1874, when President Ulysses S. Grant formally sought the advice of Senate leaders before nominating Morrison Waite to be chief justice. Bill Clinton is said to have consulted influential Senate Republicans about Ruth Bader Ginsburg in 1993 and Stephen Breyer in 1994 before nominating them.[43] Both were easily confirmed.

Although presidents have only recently come to appreciate and take full advantage of their ability to influence judicial policymaking through *lower* federal court appointments, they have long recognized the importance of Supreme Court appointments. Through its power of judicial review, the Court has the authority—when a legitimate case or controversy is brought before it—to review actions of the other branches of government and the states and to strike down those that violate the Constitution.

First used by the Supreme Court to strike down legislation in *Marbury v. Madison* (1803), the power of judicial review is a critical part of the U.S. system of checks and balances.[44] Judicial review is a way to police the actions of other government actors and ensure that they act in accordance with the Constitution. It prevents temporary legislative majorities from invading the rights of minorities and keeps strong-willed presidents from thwarting the Constitution. It is, in other words, a protection against "tyranny of the majority" and other abuses of power by government officials.

But judicial review also entails a certain amount of risk. After all, it is up to a simple majority of the Court to determine what the Constitution means and whether a government action violates it. The task may seem easy, but it is not. Many provisions of the Constitution are notoriously vague and ambiguous. As a result, they are susceptible to different interpretations. As we saw in chapter 1, the ambiguity of Article 2 has led to considerable disagreement over the scope of presidential power. Such ambiguity extends to many other provisions of the Constitution. For example, what does "equal protection" mean? "Unreasonable searches and seizures"? "Cruel and unusual punishment"? The First Amendment says that Congress shall make no law abridging freedom of speech. But what is "speech"? Does it include libel? Campaign contributions? False advertising? Obscenity? Advocacy to overthrow the government? Flag burning? Nude dancing? All of these questions have come before the Court. Smart, reasonable people have disagreed about how to answer them.

The real danger of judicial review lies in the possibility that a majority of the Court might take advantage of the Constitution's ambiguities to impose its own will. Under the guise of upholding the Constitution, five unelected judges could choose to impose policies they support and nullify those they do not. Judges from both ends of the political spectrum are susceptible to that temptation. Some observers say that is what happened when a conservative majority on the Court struck down government attempts to regulate business in the early twentieth century, or when a liberal majority in the 1960s and 1970s used an unenumerated "right of privacy" to strike down state laws that banned abortion and the use of contraceptives.[45]

Even when the Court is doing its best to apply the Constitution fairly and accurately, answers to many constitutional questions remain a matter of judgment. It is precisely for that reason that Supreme Court appointments matter so much. The Court's decisions are of vital interest to the president because they affect presidential programs, the operation of the entire political system, and the functioning of U.S. society in general. Presidents seek to affect those decisions through their appointments to the Court, and they tend to approach these nominations with great care.

Nominee Qualifications. Generally speaking, presidents and their aides look at three broad categories of qualifications when screening nominees: (1) professional, (2) representational, and (3) doctrinal.[46] The Constitution offers no guidance, as it contains no specific qualifications for being a Supreme Court justice. This deficiency stands in stark contrast to the very specific constitutional qualifications for the president, senators, and representatives. Because federal law has not mandated specific qualifications either, it "is legally possible, though scarcely conceivable, that a non-citizen, a minor or a non-lawyer could be appointed to the Court."[47]

Despite the lack of legally mandated qualifications, presidents recognize the importance of a nominee's *professional* qualification. President Trump severed the official relationship between the White House and the ABA in 2017 (something that George W. Bush also did during his administration), but will likely rely on other measures of professional experience when vetting nominees. And since the ABA vowed to continue to provide its ratings to the Senate Judiciary Committee, senators and the public will still be able to use them to gauge the professional merits of a nominee. The ABA bases its ratings largely on the nominee's professional qualifications—so, too, do others who assess whether an individual is fit to serve on the Supreme Court, such as the more conservative Federalist Society. Every justice who has served on the Court has been a lawyer, and high professional standards have been a basic criterion when selecting and confirming nominees.[48]

Representational qualifications include the partisan affiliation of potential nominees; their geographic region; and factors such as race, gender, and ethnicity. With rare exceptions, presidents appoint justices from their own political party. Early in the nation's history, geographic balance was also a major consideration for presidents when deciding upon a nominee because Supreme Court justices had the onerous responsibility of "riding circuit"—traveling around the country to preside over appeals in lower federal courts of the particular circuit to which they were assigned. Prior to the Civil War, presidents tried to have at least one justice from each of the circuits. When Congress abolished the requirement of circuit riding in 1891, the main reason for geographic balance disappeared. Still, presidents make some effort to represent different parts of the country on the Court. Occasionally, a president tries to use a Court appointment to curry favor with a particular region of the country. Herbert Hoover and Richard Nixon tried to appoint southerners to the Court as a way to build electoral support in the South.[49]

Religion, race, gender, and ethnicity have joined geography as representational concerns. Although the Court has historically had a distinctly white, male, and, until recently, Protestant bias, a "Catholic seat" has existed by tradition since 1836, as has a "Jewish seat" since 1916 (except for 1969 to 1993). With Trump's appointment of Gorsuch in 2017, six Catholics, three Jews, and no Protestants sat on the Court. George W. Bush's appointments of John Roberts and Samuel Alito had secured a Catholic majority for the first time in the Court's history, and Obama extended that majority with the appointment of Sonia Sotomayor in 2009. His appointment of Elena Kagan to replace John Paul Stevens resulted in a Court that for the first time had no Protestant representation. Since 1967, an African American has been a member. Since 1981, there has also been at least one woman (under Obama the number of women serving on the Court at the same time reached a new high: three). Both George H. W. Bush and George W. Bush as well as Clinton gave serious consideration to appointing the first Hispanic to the Court. Such an appointment, it was thought, could help to build support for the president's party among the growing Hispanic population in pivotal electoral states such as California, Florida, and Texas. Obama, with the appointment of Sotomayor, became the first president to do so.

Doctrinal qualifications refer to the perception that a nominee shares the president's political philosophy and approach to public policy issues, a critical issue given the Court's power to interpret the Constitution and exercise judicial review. Some presidents, such as Ronald Reagan and George W. Bush, made doctrinal considerations a central part of their screening process. Although Reagan's appointment of Sandra Day O'Connor was driven largely by representational concerns, he was careful to select a woman who fit his doctrinal qualifications. His elevation of Rehnquist to chief justice, his appointments of Antonin Scalia and Anthony Kennedy, and his unsuccessful nominations of Robert Bork and Douglas Ginsburg were motivated largely by doctrinal considerations. Bush's appointments of Roberts and Alito were also motivated by doctrinal considerations and resulted in a new 5–4 majority that shifted the balance on the Court.

In contrast, Bill Clinton was somewhat less concerned with doctrinal representation. Although applauded for their representational impact, Ruth Bader Ginsburg and Stephen Breyer actually drew some criticism from liberal Democrats who were distressed that the first Democratic president since Lyndon Johnson with the opportunity to fill vacancies on the Court (Carter made no appointments) appeared to be picking candidates with moderate, mainstream—rather than activist, liberal—constitutional views. Both justices were Democrats who were more liberal than Reagan's nominees, but in the interest of avoiding a confirmation battle in the Senate, Clinton selected experienced, moderate federal appeals court judges rather than ideologues to fill the Court vacancies. Ginsburg and Breyer had strong support from both liberals and conservatives on the Senate Judiciary Committee, and the two won easy confirmation. By 2016, when Obama nominated Merrick Garland, winning support across the aisle had become more difficult. Garland, too, could be described as a moderate, mainstream choice—certainly for a Democratic president's nominee—but this time Republicans did not even allow a hearing. Whether or not a nominee is "in" or "out" of the mainstream, of course, is often in the eye of the beholder. Republicans considered Gorsuch to be in the mainstream, though Democrats did not.

Initial Screening and Selection. As David Yalof points out, different presidents go about screening and selecting potential Supreme Court nominees in different ways. Even within a single administration, Yalof identifies a number of factors that influence the president's selection process. These include (1) the timing of the vacancy, (2) the composition of the Senate, (3) the public approval of the president, (4) attributes of the outgoing justice, and (5) the realistic pool of candidates available to the president.[50] If the vacancy occurs early in their terms, presidents are usually in a stronger position politically than if the vacancy occurs closer to the end of their terms. If the vacancy occurs shortly before their reelection campaigns or toward the end of their second terms, presidents may be more limited in the type of nominee they can send to the Senate and may feel compelled to nominate a more moderate, consensus candidate. The same is true if the opposition party controls the Senate or if a president's approval ratings are low. Choice of a successor may also be more limited if the outgoing justice represents a particular religious or demographic group or if the president feels that a particular region of the country needs representation on the Court. And, obviously, presidents are limited by the available pool of candidates and may find it difficult to identify a nominee who fits the precise mix of professional, doctrinal, and representational concerns they would like.

Since 1853, the Justice Department has had formal responsibility for identifying and recommending potential nominees. Historically, the attorney general, the head of the Justice Department, played the primary role in this process. As Yalof notes, however, the growth and bureaucratization of both the White House and the Justice Department have led to the emergence of specialized staff units assigned to vet potential nominees.[51] The Office of White House Counsel, created as part of the president's personal staff during the Truman administration, now plays a primary role in vetting nominees, with help from the chief of staff and other White House officials. The FBI is responsible for conducting background checks.

In some administrations, overlapping responsibilities between the White House and the Justice Department have led to internal power struggles over what type of judges to nominate. When Justice Lewis Powell resigned from the Court in 1987, Attorney General Meese and other Justice Department officials pushed for a staunchly conservative nominee: Robert Bork. White House counsel Arthur B. Culvahouse and chief of staff Howard Baker wanted a moderate consensus nominee. The Justice Department won, but the Senate went on to defeat the Bork nomination in a highly contentious confirmation battle.[52]

Many people have a desire to influence the nomination decision, including other lawyers. The legal community includes professional organizations such as the ABA, whose ratings can affect how the public and the Senate perceive the nominees. Other legal groups, as well as individual lawyers, also participate in the selection process. They may suggest nominees to the president or announce their evaluations of the person the president nominated. Coalitions of lawyers sometimes sign letters of support for, or of opposition to, specific nominees. Even Supreme Court justices themselves occasionally participate in the process by recommending a potential nominee to the president or even lobbying publicly for a candidate. Chief Justice William Howard Taft (1921–1930) was particularly active in that regard, and Chief Justice Warren Burger suggested the nomination of Harry Blackmun in 1970 and O'Connor in 1981.[53] Interest groups also lobby for and against the initial selection of nominees, although these groups are usually more active during the confirmation process.

As early as the 1880s, interest groups recognized how directly the Supreme Court could affect them, and they began to take an active interest in the Senate confirmation of nominees.[54] They also began to lobby presidents before nominations were announced.[55] Today, they sometimes announce their views on nominations even before vacancies on the Supreme Court occur.

TABLE 7-2 Failed Supreme Court Nominees

Nominee and Date of Nomination	*President and Party*	*Composition of Senate*	*Action/Date*
John Rutledge, 12/10/1795[a]	Washington	16 PA, 14 AA	Rejected 10–14; 12/15/1795
Alexander Wolcott, 2/4/1811	Madison (DR)	27 DR, 7 F	Rejected 9–24; 2/13/1811
John J. Crittenden, 12/17/1828	J. Q. Adams (AJ)	27 J, 21 AJ	Postponed 23–17; 2/12/1829
Roger B. Taney, 1/15/1835	Jackson (J)	26 J, AJ, 2 other	Postponed 24–21; 3/3/1835
John C. Spencer, 1/9/1844 (re-nominated 6/17/1844)	Tyler (I)[b]	29 W, 23 D	Rejected 21–26; 1/31/1844 (renomination withdrawn 6/17/1844)
Reuben H. Walworth, 3/13/1844 (re-nominated 12/4/1844)	Tyler (I)	29 W, 23 D	Postponed 27–20; withdrawn; 6/17/1844 (renomination withdrawn 2/4/1845)
Edward King, 6/5/1844 (re-nominated 12/4/1844)	Tyler (I)	29 W, 23 D	Postponed 29–18; 6/15/1844 (renomination withdrawn 2/7/1845)
John M. Read, 2/7/1845	Tyler (I)	29 W, 23 D	No action
George W. Woodward, 12/23/1845	Polk (D)	34 D, 22 W	Rejected 20–29; 1/22/1846
Edward A. Bradford, 8/16/1852	Fillmore (W)	36 D, 23 W, 3 other	No action
George E. Badger, 1/3/1853	Fillmore (W)	36 D, 23 W, 3 other	Withdrawn; 2/14/1853
William C. Micou, 2/14/1853	Fillmore (W)	36 D, 23 W, 3 other	No action
Jeremiah S. Black, 2/5/1861	Buchanan (D)	38 D, 26 R, 2 other	Rejected 25–26; 2/21/1861
Henry Stanbery, 4/16/1866	A. Johnson (D)	39 R, 11 D, 4 other	No action[c]
Ebenezer R. Hoar, 12/14/1869	Grant (R)	62 R, 12 D	Rejected 24–33; 2/3/1870

Nominee and Date of Nomination	*President and Party*	*Composition of Senate*	*Action/Date*
George H. Williams, 12/1/1873	Grant (R)	47 R, 19 D, 7 other	Withdrawn; 1/8/1874
Caleb Cushing, 1/9/1874	Grant (R)	47 R, 19 D, 7 other	Withdrawn; 1/13/1874
Stanley Matthews, 1/26/1881	Hayes (R)	42 D, 33 R	No action
William Hornblower, 12/5/1893	Cleveland (D)	44 D, 40 R, 4 other	Rejected 24–30; 1/15/1894
Wheeler H. Peckham, 1/22/1894	Cleveland (D)	44 D, 40 R, 4 other	Rejected 32–41; 2/16/1894
John J. Parker, 3/21/1930	Hoover (R)	56 R, 39 D, 1 other	Rejected 39–41; 5/7/1930
Abe Fortas, 6/26/1968[d]	Johnson (D)	64 D, 36 R	Withdrawn; 10/4/1968
Clement Haynsworth Jr., 8/21/1969	Nixon (R)	57 D, 43 R	Rejected 45–55; 11/21/1969
G. Harrold Carswell, 1/19/1970	Nixon (R)	57 D, 43 R	Rejected 45–51; 4/8/1970
Robert H. Bork, 7/7/1987	Reagan (R)	55 D, 45 R	Rejected 42–58; 10/23/1987
Harriet Miers, 10/7/2005	G. W. Bush (R)	55 R, 44 D, 1 other	Withdrawn; 10/28/2005
Merrick Garland, 3/16/2016	Barack Obama (D)	54 R, 44 D, 2 other	No action

SOURCES: Party division based on https://www.senate.gov/history/partydiv.htm. Dates, action, and votes based on http://www.senate.gov/pagelayout/reference/nominations/Nominations.htm.

NOTES: AA = Anti-Administration, AJ = Anti-Jackson (which later became the National Republicans), D = Democrat, DR = Democratic-Republican, F = Federalist, I = independent, J = Jacksonian Democrat, PA = Pro-Administration, R = Republican, W = Whig. Tyler, Fillmore, and Andrew Johnson had been vice presidents who ascended to office when the president died, so they had not been elected president in their own right. Political parties did not formally exist in 1795. President Washington had no political affiliation. Sixteen members of the Senate at that time are typically identified as supporting Washington (Pro-Administration) and thirteen as opposing him (Anti-Administration).

[a] Rutledge had previously served as an associate justice. The Senate rejected his nomination to be chief justice.

[b] Tyler had been elected vice president as a Whig. When he assumed the presidency he effectively acted as an Independent. Thus, while Whigs controlled the Senate, the situation amounted to divided government.

[c] The Judicial Circuits Act of 1866, signed into law on July 23, 1866, reduced the size of the Supreme Court, thereby eliminating the vacancy.

[d] Fortas sat as an associate justice when Johnson nominated him to be chief justice.

Senate Confirmation. Once nominated by the president, a candidate to the Supreme Court must be confirmed by the Senate. Confirmation needs only a simple majority vote. If one excludes consecutive nominations of the same individual by the same president for the same seat on the Court and President

Reagan's 1987 nomination of Douglas Ginsburg, which was announced but never formally submitted to the Senate, 154 nominations were submitted to the Senate through Trump's 2017 nomination of Neil Gorsuch. Of these 154 nominations, 7 of the nominees declined, 1 died before taking office, and 1 expected vacancy failed to materialize. In addition, George W. Bush's nomination of Roberts to fill O'Connor's seat was withdrawn before Senate action and then submitted to fill the chief justice's seat instead. Of the 144 remaining nominations, 117 were confirmed by the Senate. The other twenty-seven may be classified as "failed" nominations because Senate opposition blocked them: The Senate rejected twelve by roll call vote, voted to postpone or table another five, and passively rejected six others by taking no action. Presidents withdrew the remaining four in the face of certain Senate defeat. The number of "failed" nominations rises to twenty-eight if Douglas Ginsburg is included.

As can be seen in Table 7-2, the most recent failed nominee was Merrick Garland, picked by Obama to replace Scalia in 2016. All told, the failure rate of Supreme Court nominees is higher than for any other appointive post requiring Senate confirmation.[56] Six nominations (seven if you include Douglas Ginsburg) have failed just since 1968, a clear reflection of the concern for the profound effect Supreme Court appointments can have on public policy, and confirmation votes have become closer and more partisan. Gorsuch was confirmed by a 54 to 45 vote (with only three Democrats voting to confirm). Sotomayor and Kagan were confirmed by votes of 68 to 51 and 63 to 37, respectively. Roberts and Alito were confirmed by votes of 79 to 22 and 58 to 42. In stark contrast, the earlier nominations of Antonin Scalia (1986) and John Paul Stevens (1975)—both of whom would surely provoke controversy if they had to face the confirmation process today—sailed through the Senate by votes of 98 to 0.

Confirmation is also a test of presidential strength. "Weak" presidents—those who are unelected, those who face a Senate controlled by the opposition, and those in their final year in office—are statistically less likely to secure confirmation of their Supreme Court nominees. An unusually long period of divided government (with the White House controlled by one party and the Senate by another) has added to the contentiousness of confirmation battles. From 1969 through 2016, the same party controlled the Senate and the White House for only twenty-two out of forty-eight years. Also contributing to intense confirmation battles are the ongoing public policy debates over controversial issues such as race, abortion, and same-sex marriage—something that journalist E. J. Dionne has called a "cultural civil war."[57]

Interest groups fan the flames through their efforts for and against nominees. In the twentieth century, interest groups led the opposition to almost all the nominees rejected by the Senate or forced to withdraw. John J. Parker, a southern court of appeals judge nominated by Herbert Hoover in 1930, fell victim to the combined opposition of the American Federation of Labor and the National Association for the Advancement of Colored People (NAACP), who viewed him as antilabor and racist. Labor and the NAACP again joined forces to defeat two Nixon nominees: Clement Haynsworth, a federal court of appeals judge from South Carolina, in 1969 and G. Harrold Carswell, a federal court of appeals judge from Florida, in 1970.[58] Conservative groups bitterly attacked Johnson's nomination of Abe Fortas to be chief justice in 1968 because of his liberal decisions in obscenity cases and suits concerning the rights of the accused in criminal proceedings.[59] A major effort by civil rights, women's, and other liberal groups contributed to Bork's defeat in 1987.[60] In contrast, Miers withdrew her name before many interest groups had taken a stand. Much of the opposition to her came from the conservative base of the Republican Party.

Other problems may arise. Some people considered Fortas's acceptance of a legal fee from a family foundation and his advising President Johnson on political matters to be unethical activities for a justice of the Supreme Court.[61] Haynsworth was criticized for ruling on cases in which he had a personal financial interest. Much of the opposition to Carswell from members of the bar, particularly law professors, stemmed from his perceived lack of professional qualifications. Sen. Roman Hruska, R-NE, Carswell's leading supporter in the Senate, made the situation worse when he tried to make the nominee's mediocrity a virtue by saying on national television that mediocre people needed representation on the Supreme Court. Suddenly, Carswell was a national joke. This, coupled with some shockingly racist statements Carswell had made when running for public office ("I believe the segregation of the races is proper and the only practical and correct way of life in our states," and "I yield to no man . . . in the firm, vigorous belief in the principles of white supremacy, and I shall always be so governed"), doomed Carswell's nomination.[62]

Regular, repeat involvement by interest groups in the Supreme Court confirmation process dates back only to the 1960s or so. Although organized interests attempted to block Senate confirmation of a nominee as early as 1881, their success in blocking three confirmations in three years (Fortas in 1968, Haynsworth in 1969, and Carswell in 1970) marked a turning point. Since then, interest groups have taken an active stand on virtually every Supreme Court nominee, although their involvement accelerated dramatically with Bork in 1987. Starting with that nomination, interest groups moved beyond testifying at confirmation hearings and mobilizing their members to lobby their senators to launching a full-fledged public relations offensive, including television, radio, and print ads; mass mailings; and phone banks to sway public opinion. They also attempted to influence reporters and editorial writers through the use of press briefings and fact sheets they aggressively distributed.

Interest group action corresponded with the increased visibility of Senate Judiciary Committee hearings and floor votes on nominees. Prior to the twentieth century, the confirmation process was shrouded in secrecy. The committee held hearings behind closed doors and rarely even kept records of its proceedings. As the *New York Times* wrote in 1881, the "Judiciary Committee of the Senate is the most mysterious committee in that body, and succeeds better than any other in maintaining secrecy as to its proceedings."[63]

At that time, the committee usually deliberated without hearing from any witnesses. Interest groups seldom participated in this phase of the process (none testified until 1930), and no nominee appeared before the committee until Harlan Fiske Stone in 1925. Nominees actually thought it improper to answer any questions and maintained almost complete public silence. When a reporter from the *New York Sun* asked Louis Brandeis about his nomination in 1916, Brandeis quickly replied, "I have nothing to say about anything, and that goes for all time and to all newspapers, including both the *Sun* and the moon."[64] Presidents, too, maintained almost complete public silence about their nominees. When the full Senate finally voted on a nominee, it almost always did so in closed session and often with no roll call vote. The secrecy effectively minimized the influence of interest groups and any others concerned about the outcome of a nomination—so, too, did the fact that senators then were not popularly elected but chosen by state legislators. The lack of public participation removed the potential threat of retaliation against senators that the electorate now enjoys and on which interest groups can capitalize.

The situation changed in the twentieth century. Ratification of the Seventeenth Amendment to the Constitution in 1913 provided for the direct election of senators, and Senate rules changes in 1929 opened floor debate on nominations. Public opinion now mattered in a very direct way to senators—they were dependent upon it for reelection. The Senate began to use public Judiciary Committee hearings as a way of both testing and influencing public opinion. Since 1981, Judiciary Committee hearings have been broadcast live on television for the entire world to see. The emergence of the modern "public presidency" (see chapter 3) also led to greater involvement by presidents in promoting their nominees. As specialized staff units developed in the White House, they, too, came to be used as a way to secure support for nominees and thereby increase the likelihood of Senate confirmation. The Office of Communications, the Office of Public Liaison (renamed the Office of Public Engagement under Obama), the Office of Political Affairs, and other staff units have all been used in this manner.[65]

At the end of the day, after opponents find fault with a nominee's qualifications or record and supporters claim the opposite, it all comes down to ideology. How will the nominee vote if confirmed? The president tries to predict how the nominee will perform, but judicial appointees may fail to vote the way the president had hoped. Reagan and George H. W. Bush appointed six justices to the Supreme Court with the avowed hope of overturning *Roe v. Wade* (1973), the controversial abortion rights decision.[66] Three of those appointees went on to uphold *Roe.*[67] Some Republicans criticized John Roberts (a George W. Bush nominee) for being the decisive fifth vote to uphold the constitutionality of the Affordable Care Act in 2012, and Dwight D. Eisenhower lamented his appointment of Earl Warren as chief justice because of Warren's liberal voting record on the bench, and Truman—never one to mince words—was furious when Tom Clark, who had been Truman's attorney general, did not vote on the Court as the president had hoped. "I don't know what got into me," Truman later fumed.

He was no damn good as Attorney General, and on the Supreme Court . . . it doesn't seem possible, but he's been even worse. He hasn't made one right decision that I can think of. . . . It's just that he's such a dumb son of a bitch.[68]

Despite White House chief of staff John Sununu's prediction to George H. W. Bush that David Souter would be a "home run" for conservatives, Souter turned out to be one of the most liberal members of the Court. The in-depth screening of judicial nominees tends to minimize such "mistakes," but no one can completely predict the behavior of individuals once they sit on the Court.

Other Presidential Influences on the Federal Courts

The appointment of federal judges is the primary method by which presidents affect the courts, but presidents have other ways to influence judicial activities. The first is through the solicitor general, whom Robert Scigliano calls "the lawyer for the executive branch."[69] The second is through legislation that affects the operation of the Supreme Court—a means Congress, too, has tried to use to its advantage and the president's disadvantage. The third is through the enforcement—or nonenforcement—of court decisions.

Role of the Solicitor General in the Appellate Courts

The **solicitor general**, appointed by the president with the advice and consent of the Senate, is a major player in setting the agenda of the federal appellate courts. First, the solicitor general determines which of the cases the government loses in the federal district courts will be taken to the courts of appeals. Second, of the cases the government loses in the lower courts, the solicitor general decides which to recommend that the Supreme Court hear. Unlike the courts of appeals, which must take cases properly appealed to them, the Supreme Court chooses the cases it hears.[70] The Court is more likely to take cases proposed by the solicitor general than by other parties.

Once the Court accepts a case involving the federal government, the solicitor general decides the position the government should take and argues the case before the Court. Thus "the Solicitor General not only determines whether the executive branch goes to the Supreme Court but what it will say there."[71] And what it says there usually advances the policy goals of the incumbent president.[72] Moreover, the solicitor general's influence is not restricted to cases in which the federal government itself is a party. He or she also decides whether the government will file an amicus curiae (friend of the court) brief supporting or opposing positions by other parties who have cases pending before the Court.

Amicus filings by the solicitor general increased dramatically in the twentieth century. Steven Puro, who analyzed the briefs filed from 1920 through 1973, found that 71 percent occurred in the last twenty years of that period.[73] He concluded that whether by its own initiative or as a result of an invitation from the Court, the federal

AP Photo/Dana Verkouteren

This courtroom sketch captures the emotional argument delivered by U.S. solicitor general Donald Verrilli on March 27, 2012, to the U.S. Supreme Court asking them not to overturn the historic health care reform act, officially known as the Affordable Care Act and more popularly as Obamacare.

government participated as amicus in almost every major domestic question before the Court since World War II. Particularly prominent is the government's entrance into the controversial issues of civil liberties, civil rights, and the jurisdiction and procedures of the courts.

When the federal government becomes involved in a case before the Supreme Court, it is usually successful. Scigliano's analysis of Court opinions chosen at ten-year intervals beginning in 1800 shows that the United States consistently won 62 percent or more of its litigation there. Its record as amicus is even more impressive. Puro found that in the political cases he examined, when the federal government participated, it supported the winning side almost 74 percent of the time. An analysis of race discrimination employment cases from 1970 to 1981 showed that the government won 70 percent of the cases in which it was a direct party and 81.6 percent of those in which it filed amicus briefs.[74]

Much has been written about why solicitors general are so successful in their appearances before the Supreme Court. Kevin T. McGuire argues that it really boils down to one thing: litigation experience.[75] They are the prototypical "repeat player." Solicitors general or members of their staff argue far more cases than any other party, including any law firm in the country. They therefore develop a great deal of expertise in dealing with the Court. This expertise translates into high-quality briefs and an intimate understanding of the workings of the Court. Solicitors general may also build up credit with the Court because they help the justices manage their caseload by holding down the number of government appeals. Christopher Zorn also notes that amicus filings by the solicitor general "are highest when both the administration and the Court share similar policy preferences, and drop off substantially when those preferences diverge." Zorn concludes that, like other litigants, "The solicitor general appears to explicitly take into account the probability that his position will be received favorably by the Court when formulating his litigation strategies."[76]

The Reagan administration used the solicitor general's office particularly aggressively to promote its conservative policy agenda.[77] In tandem with Reagan's appointments to the Supreme Court and lower federal courts, Solicitor General Rex Lee led this "other campaign" to persuade the Supreme Court to change previous rulings on matters such as abortion, prayer in the public schools, busing, affirmative action, the rights of the accused in criminal cases, and federal-state relations.[78] Lincoln Caplan argued that this activity marked a shift away from the solicitor general's traditional posture of restraint to a posture of aggressively pushing the Court to take cases that advanced the administration's social policy agenda. The result, according to Caplan, was a temporary loss of the justices' trust in the solicitor general's presentation of facts and interpretation of the law.[79] Succeeding presidents did not use the solicitor general's office this way. Richard L. Pacelle Jr. has noted the many constraints solicitors general now face:

> In trying to assist the Court as tenth justice or fifth Clerk, while fulfilling the president's agenda as "attorney general as policy maker" or pursuing the Justice Department's more neutral obligations as the "attorney general as law enforcement officer," the solicitor general has to balance a number of roles. In attempting to fulfill these roles, the solicitor general has several potentially competing constituencies to satisfy. When these factors move in the same direction, there are opportunities for the solicitor general, but that was rare in the last half-century, as divided government has been the rule.[80]

Legislation Affecting the Supreme Court

The president also can affect the actions of the Supreme Court through legislation. Presidential authority to propose bills to Congress and to work for their adoption, as well as the power to oppose measures favored by members of Congress and, if necessary, to veto them, means the president can influence legislation affecting the Court. At the same time, Congress can pass legislation concerning the Court that threatens the president's power.

In 1937, Franklin D. Roosevelt became actively involved in trying to get Congress to exercise its power to expand the size of the Supreme Court. The Constitution grants Congress the power to establish the number of justices, and Congress has changed it several times. Historically, however, Congress has done so without prompting from the president. Sometimes it has altered the size of the Court in an effort to thwart a particular president. In the latter days of the John Adams administration, the lame-duck Congress—still controlled by the Federalists—passed the Judiciary Act of 1801. That act reduced the number of justices from six to five in an attempt to prevent the incoming president, Democratic-Republican Thomas Jefferson, from appointing a replacement for ailing justice William Cushing. (Because justices have life tenure, the size of the Court would not actually decrease until a justice left the bench.) The Democratic-Republicans quickly repealed the 1801 law and restored the number of justices to six when they took control of Congress later that year. In 1807, the Democratic-Republican Congress increased the number of justices to seven to accommodate population growth in Kentucky, Tennessee, and Ohio. The Federalists' attempt to thwart President Jefferson failed, and he went on to name three justices. Ironically, Justice Cushing recovered and lived until 1810; his successor was named by James Madison, not Jefferson.

Congressional manipulation of the size of the Court so as to affect presidential appointments also occurred in the 1860s. The 1863 Judiciary Act expanding the

Court from nine to ten members enabled Abraham Lincoln to appoint Stephen J. Field, who subsequently supported the president on war issues. Shortly thereafter, the Radical Republicans, who controlled Congress, passed legislation reducing the number of justices to prevent Lincoln's successor, Andrew Johnson, from naming justices they feared would rule against the Reconstruction program. Soon after Ulysses S. Grant was inaugurated in March 1869, the size of the Court was again expanded; this expansion, plus a retirement, enabled Grant to appoint Justices William Strong and Joseph P. Bradley. Both voted to reconsider a previous Supreme Court decision, *Hepburn v. Griswold,* that had declared unconstitutional the substitution of paper money for gold as legal tender for the payment of contracts. The new decision validated the use of "greenbacks" as legal tender.[81] The three successive changes in the size of the Court within a six-year period brought the results Congress desired.

Roosevelt's "Court packing" proposal was different from these earlier examples because of his aggressive efforts to promote congressional action. Frustrated by the invalidation of much of the early New Deal legislation—between January 1935 and June 1936 the Court had struck down eight separate statutes—Roosevelt proposed legislation in early 1937 that would permit him to appoint one justice, up to six in number, for each sitting member of the Court who failed to retire voluntarily at age seventy. Buoyed by his landslide electoral victory in 1936 and confident that the Democrat-controlled Congress would follow his lead, Roosevelt announced the proposal at a press conference without consulting with members of Congress. Samuel Kernell points to it as an early, failed attempt at "going public."[82] Although FDR contended that the additions were necessary to handle the Court's caseload, it was patently clear that his real purpose was to liberalize the Court. The proposal stimulated outrage from members of the bar, the press, and many of Roosevelt's political supporters in Congress who were angered that they had not been consulted about it. At this point, Justice Owen J. Roberts, a centrist who had been aligned with four conservative colleagues in striking down New Deal legislation, began to vote with the other four justices to uphold the legislation and give FDR the new majority he had been seeking. The unpopularity of Roosevelt's proposal, Justice Roberts's mitigating action (which observers dubbed "the switch in time that saved nine"), and the sudden death of Majority Leader Joseph Robinson of Arkansas, who was leading the president's effort in the Senate, resulted in Congress's failure to adopt the Court-packing plan. Kernell calls it "FDR's most stunning legislative failure in his twelve years in office."[83] Yet Roosevelt won the legal battle anyway. Once Roberts switched his vote, conservative members—now in the minority—began to leave the Court. By the time he died, Roosevelt had managed to appoint all nine justices and secure a majority willing to uphold his policies.

In addition to its power to change the size of the Court, Congress can also pass legislation altering its appellate jurisdiction.[84] President George W. Bush proposed and the Republican-controlled Congress passed the Military Commissions Act of 2006, which stripped federal courts of jurisdiction to hear habeas corpus petitions from detainees at Guantánamo Bay. When he signed the act into law on October 17, 2006, Bush called it "one of the most important pieces of legislation in the war on terror."[85] A three-judge panel for a U.S. court of appeals voted 2–1 to uphold the law, but in 2008 the U.S. Supreme Court reversed it by a 5–4 vote in *Boumediene v. Bush.*[86] The 2008 Republican Party platform endorsed jurisdiction-stripping in other areas. Noting that "a Republican Congress enacted the Defense of Marriage Act, affirming the right of states not to recognize same-sex 'marriages' licensed in other states," the platform urged Congress to "use its Article III, section 2 power [to withdraw appellate jurisdiction] to prevent activist federal judges from imposing upon the rest of the nation the judicial activism in Massachusetts and California."[87] Courts in both states had ruled that laws banning same-sex marriage violated each state's constitution. Congress did not follow the advice of the platform. With its jurisdiction intact, the U.S. Supreme Court ruled state-level bans on same-sex marriage to be unconstitutional in *Obergefell v. Hodges* in June 2015. The vast majority of jurisdiction-stripping proposals have failed.

Presidents occasionally urge Congress to propose constitutional amendments to overturn Court rulings or lobby for the passage of legislation that might undermine existing rulings. Republican presidents Reagan and George H. W. Bush sought to overturn *Roe v. Wade* by pressuring Congress to propose a constitutional amendment outlawing abortion. Although unsuccessful in this effort, both presidents signed legislation that limited use of federal funds for abortions and made access to abortions more difficult. Bush also supported a constitutional amendment to overrule a controversial Supreme Court decision, *Texas v. Johnson* (1989), which permitted flag burning as a form of protected symbolic speech.[88] George W. Bush called for a constitutional amendment to define marriage as the legal union of one man and one woman, and Obama called for one to overturn the controversial 2010 *Citizens United* decision, which held that the First Amendment prohibits the government from regulating political contributions from corporations and unions.[89]

Enforcement of Court Decisions

The federal courts have the authority to hand down decisions on cases within their jurisdiction, but they have no independent power to enforce their decisions. Lacking both the power of the purse and of the sword, the Supreme Court depends upon the executive branch to enforce its rulings. President Eisenhower called out federal troops in 1957 to enforce court-ordered school desegregation in Little Rock, Arkansas. The order was an outgrowth of the Court's landmark *Brown v. Board of Education* (1954) ruling that overturned the "separate but equal" doctrine of *Plessy v. Ferguson* (1896).[90]

Sometimes less forceful action by the president helps to bring about compliance with Supreme Court rulings. President John F. Kennedy, in a June 1962 press conference, publicly supported the Court's controversial ruling in *Engel v. Vitale,* which banned state-sponsored prayer in public schools, and set an example for others to follow.[91] Presidents also set an example by complying with court orders aimed at them. Immediately after the Court held in 1952 that President Truman's seizure of the steel mills was unconstitutional, the president ordered the mills restored to private operation.[92] Likewise, President Nixon complied with the Court's 1974 ruling in *United States v. Nixon* that he turn over to a federal district court tapes of his conversations with executive aides.[93] That action produced evidence of the president's involvement in the Watergate affair, which led to the House Judiciary Committee's approving three articles of impeachment against him and ultimately to Nixon's resignation.

Some presidents have defied—or threatened to defy—the Court. The fear that President Jefferson's secretary of state, James Madison, would (with the president's blessing) defy a court order to deliver commissions that would seat some Federalist judges probably influenced John Marshall's opinion in *Marbury v. Madison.* Marshall gave the Jefferson administration what it wanted—it did not force delivery of the commissions—but it did so by creating the power of judicial review. More blatantly, President Lincoln once ignored a federal court ruling that declared his suspension of habeas corpus unconstitutional.[94] But Lincoln's response was an exception to the rule, for chief executives typically have enforced judicial decisions, even when they would have preferred not to do so. When the justices struck down the Gun Free School Zones Act in *United States v. Lopez* (1995), President Clinton strongly criticized the decision and ordered Attorney General Janet Reno to come up with other ways to keep guns out of schools, but he did not defy the ruling.[95]

As discussed in chapter 1, George W. Bush embraced a theory of presidential power known as the unitary executive. A core element of that approach is the idea of "coordinate construction"—that presidents have the power to interpret the Constitution just as courts do. Rather than veto the legislation or wait for courts to rule on their constitutionality, Bush quietly used "signing statements" to indicate that he would not enforce those provisions of laws he found problematic. By the time he left office, Bush had challenged more than 1,100 specific provisions of bills he signed.[96]

For example, he used signing statements to signal that he would not enforce the provision of the Patriot Act that required the president to report to Congress when the executive branch secretly searches homes or seizes private papers. Another signing statement said that he reserved the right to ignore the McCain amendment forbidding U.S. officials to use torture.[97] Sometimes the signing statements were so general that it was not clear what provisions the president might choose not to enforce. But when Congress passed a law requiring the attorney general to submit to Congress a detailed list of provisions of bills that were not being enforced by the administration, Bush used a signing statement to reiterate presidential authority to withhold information from Congress—including such a list—whenever he deemed it necessary.[98] The use of signing statements, the embrace of coordinate construction, and his strong criticism of "activist" judges, suggested Bush's willingness to substitute his judgment of how the Constitution should be interpreted for that of the federal courts.

Moreover, Bush's expansive view of presidential war power held that presidents have broad authority to act unilaterally to promote the nation's interests. Taken to its extreme, this meant that presidents, in some instances, could take actions contrary to the Constitution. If that were the case, it followed that presidents could claim the authority to disobey the courts in such instances (as Lincoln did with regard to habeas corpus). Bush strongly asserted the view that his subordinates in the executive branch should not report directly to Congress. As noted by the ABA's Task Force on Presidential Signing Statements, he did so repeatedly "even though there is Supreme Court precedent to the effect that Congress may authorize a subordinate official to act directly or to report directly to Congress."[99] When Congress passed a law requiring that government scientists report their findings directly to Congress so that they could not be censored by the administration, Bush used a signing statement to prevent enforcement of the law. President Obama also used signing statements, but less aggressively than Bush.[100] He also embraced a broad interpretation of prosecutorial discretion to avoid enforcing laws that would force the deportation of undocumented immigrants who entered the United States before their sixteenth birthday—an interpretation that President Trump reversed in early 2017 through executive order.[101]

Judicial Oversight of Presidential Action

Through its power of judicial review, the Supreme Court has the ability to invalidate presidential actions and those of other parts of the executive branch. This is a significant check on presidential power but has been used infrequently. The founders originally left open the question of who had the final power to interpret the

Constitution. If, as Jefferson contended, each branch has the authority to interpret the Constitution as far as its own duties are concerned, then the president would be the judge of the constitutionality of executive actions. As a result of *Marbury v. Madison,* however, the Supreme Court has the power to make the final judgment on such matters. Although *Marbury* was decided in 1803, the Court did not declare a presidential action unconstitutional until after the Civil War.

Only a handful of presidents have been the objects of major Court decisions invalidating their actions. Even when invalidating a specific presidential action, the Court has often endorsed a broad reading of presidential power. For example, the Court, as previously noted, invalidated President Truman's seizure of steel mills during the Korean War.[102] Truman argued that government seizure to keep open the steel mills, which were involved in a labor dispute that threatened to shut them down, was essential to the war effort. But in seizing the mills, Truman ignored provisions of the Taft-Hartley Act, which had passed over his veto. The law permitted the president to obtain an injunction postponing for eighty days a strike that threatened the national safety and welfare. Instead, he issued an executive order seizing the mills, based on his authority under the Constitution and U.S. law and as commander in chief. The steel companies protested the seizure as unconstitutional, and the case went to the Supreme Court.

By a 6–3 vote, the Court invalidated the president's move. Although six justices voted against the specific action in question, six justices (three in the majority plus the three dissenters) explicitly recognized that presidents have a range of "inherent" power to take actions not explicitly authorized by the Constitution. The dissenters said that power was broad enough to cover Truman's seizure of the mills. The other three who recognized some degree of inherent power stressed that such power is not absolute and that it was not broad enough to cover a situation such as this in which the president went against the will of Congress. Even though the case invalidated an action taken by a specific president, it set a precedent that actually *expanded* presidential power through the Court's recognition of inherent power.

Similarly, a unanimous Court in *United States v. Nixon* ruled against President Nixon's refusal to surrender subpoenaed White House tapes to Watergate special prosecutor Leon Jaworski.[103] In refusing to surrender the tapes, Nixon claimed the existence of an "executive privilege" relating to private conversations between chief executives and their advisers. Although the Court rejected Nixon's specific claim of privilege, it recognized for the first time that the principle of executive privilege did have constitutional underpinnings. As with *Youngstown Sheet and Tube Co.,* the Court ruled against a specific exercise of presidential power while at the same time expanding the general scope of presidential power.[104]

The Court has been especially deferential to presidential power in the realm of foreign affairs. In *United States v. Curtiss-Wright Export Corp.* (1936), the Court suggested that presidents might have a wider degree of discretion in foreign affairs than they do in domestic affairs.[105] Justice George Sutherland went so far as to call the president "the sole organ of the federal government in the field of international relations."[106] Similarly, the Court has recognized that presidents have broad power to respond to military emergencies and wage war even without a congressional declaration of war. In *The Prize Cases* (1863), the Court recognized President Lincoln's power to impose a military blockade on southern ports—an act of war—even though Congress had not yet spoken.[107] During World War II, the Court upheld broad executive power to impose the forced relocation of Japanese Americans and others of Japanese ancestry to federal detention centers.[108] In 1981, the Court upheld the power of the president to seize Iranian assets and use them as a bargaining chip to help free American hostages held in the 1970s.[109] But the Court limited efforts by the Bush administration to curtail the civil liberties of detainees at Guantánamo Bay. In *Hamdan v. Rumsfeld* (2006), the Court ruled 5–3 (Chief Justice Roberts did not participate) that the president did not have inherent power to require that the detainees be tried by military commission rather than in federal court.[110] Although the decision was a setback for his administration, President Bush introduced and the Republican-controlled Congress promptly passed legislation that authorized the use of such tribunals and curtailed the habeas corpus rights of detainees—an action that the Supreme Court then struck down in *Boumediene v. Bush.*[111]

Of course, the Court's power of judicial review can also be used to challenge domestic legislation spearheaded by a president. Thus, Obama found his signature achievement—the Affordable Care Act (ACA)—challenged in two major cases before the Supreme Court. The Court, in a 5–4 decision written by Chief Justice Roberts in 2012, upheld Congress's power to impose a financial penalty in order to enforce the individual mandate—the portion of the act that requires everyone to purchase insurance—saying that it was a valid exercise of Congress's power to tax.[112] The Court subsequently accepted another challenge to the law. That case, *King v. Burwell,* questioned whether the U.S government regulation that offers tax credits to individuals who purchase competitively priced health insurance through the federal insurance marketplace, Healthcare.gov, is constitutional. Challengers argued that the ACA allowed such credits to be given only to individuals who purchase insurance through state-run exchanges, while the law's supporters argued that the law intended to cover both. A win by the challengers would have severely undermined the ACA by taking away tax credits from as many as six million Americans, but the Supreme Court ultimately upheld the tax credits in a 6–3 ruling, again written by Roberts. Obama publicly chafed at this and other legal challenges to his policies, saying that the Supreme Court should not have accepted the challenge to the tax credits and expressing frustration at a federal district court ruling that at least temporarily blocked his use of executive orders to implement immigration reform.[113] It was not his first public rebuke of the judiciary. In his 2010 State of the Union address, President Obama criticized the Supreme Court's *Citizens United* ruling in front of a group of the justices, saying that it would "open the floodgates for special interests—including foreign corporations—to spend without limit in our elections." Justice Alito could be seen shaking his head and mouthing the words, "not true."[114] President Trump went even further. Although directed at a lower federal judge rather than a Supreme Court justice, President Trump in February 2017 questioned the "so-called judge" who temporarily blocked his executive order banning travel to the United States from seven Muslim-majority countries.[115] During the 2016 presidential campaign, Trump also questioned the legitimacy of federal judges, leading critics to charge that Trump did not respect the rule of law.

In addition to establishing general parameters of presidential power and reviewing presidential initiatives, Supreme Court decisions can have other significant repercussions on the fate of particular presidents. Two such decisions had a particular bearing on Bill Clinton. Had it not been for a 1988 ruling upholding (over the lone dissent of Antonin Scalia) the constitutionality of the independent counsel law and a unanimous 1997 ruling that allowed a sexual harassment lawsuit against the president by Paula Jones to proceed while he was still in office, Clinton might have been spared the independent counsel investigation by Kenneth Starr and the impeachment trial brought about as a result of the Monica Lewinsky scandal.[116]

Conclusion: A Balancing Act

The relationship between the presidency and the judiciary can be described as a balancing act. The judiciary has the power to hand down rulings that have a direct effect on presidents and their policies, but presidents can influence the federal courts through the power to nominate judges to serve on them. Both have long-term consequences. Supreme Court rulings are not easy to overturn. Those based on the Constitution can be overruled only by the Court itself or through the passage of a constitutional amendment. The president's power to appoint can also be far-reaching. Federal judges, unlike members of Congress and the political appointees of the executive branch, serve for life. That fact all but guarantees that judicial nominees will continue to be closely scrutinized and, in all likelihood, hotly contested.

Suggested Readings

Abraham, Henry. *Justices, Presidents, and Senators: A History of U.S. Supreme Court Appointments from Washington to Clinton,* 5th ed. Lanham, MD: Rowman and Littlefield, 2008.

Baum, Lawrence. *The Supreme Court,* 12th ed. Washington, DC: CQ Press, 2016.

Binder, Sarah A., and Forrest Maltzman. *Advice & Dissent: The Struggle to Shape the Federal Judiciary.* Washington, DC: Brookings, 2009.

Caldeira, Gregory, and John Wright. "Lobbying for Justice." *American Journal of Political Science* 42 (April 1998).

Caplan, Lincoln. *The Tenth Justice: The Solicitor General and the Rule of Law.* New York: Random House, 1987.

Comiskey, Michael. *Seeking Justices: The Judging of Supreme Court Nominees.* Lawrence: University Press of Kansas, 2004.

Epstein, Lee, and Thomas G. Walker. *Constitutional Law for a Changing America: Institutional Powers and Constraints,* 9th ed. Washington, DC: CQ Press, 2016.

Gerhardt, Michael J. *The Federal Appointments Process: A Constitutional and Historical Analysis.* Durham, NC: Duke University Press, 2000.

Goldman, Sheldon. *Picking Federal Judges: Lower Court Selection from Roosevelt through Reagan.* New Haven, CT: Yale University Press, 1997.

Goldman, Sheldon, Sara Schiavoni, and Elliot Slotnick. "W. Bush's Judicial Legacy: Mission Accomplished." *Judicature* 92 (May–June 2009).

Goldman, Sheldon, Elliot Slotnick, Gerard Gryski, and Gary Zuk. "Clinton's Judges: Summing Up the Legacy." *Judicature* 84 (March–April 2001).

Johnson, Timothy R., and Jason M. Roberts. "Presidential Capital and the Supreme Court Confirmation Process." *Journal of Politics* 66 (August 2004).

Maltese, John Anthony. *The Selling of Supreme Court Nominees.* Baltimore, MD: Johns Hopkins University Press, 1995.

O'Brien, David M. *Judicial Roulette.* New York: Priority Press, 1988.

Pacelle, Richard L., Jr. *Between Law and Politics: The Solicitor General and the Structuring of Race, Gender, and Reproductive Rights Litigation.* College Station: Texas A&M University Press, 2003.

Salokar, Rebecca Mae. *The Solicitor General: The Politics of Law.* Philadelphia: Temple University Press, 1992.

Wittes, Benjamin. *Confirmation Wars: Preserving Independent Courts in Angry Times.* Lanham, MD: Rowman and Littlefield, 2006.

Yalof, David Alistair. *Pursuit of Justices: Presidential Politics and the Selection of Supreme Court Nominees.* Chicago: University of Chicago Press, 1999.

Notes

1. For more on Supreme Court nominations during presidential election years, see: John Anthony Maltese, "Rivalry for Power in the Judicial Appointment Process," in *Rivals for Power: Presidential-Congressional Relations,* 6th ed., ed. James A. Thurber and Jordan Tama (Lanham, MD: Rowman & Littlefield, 2017).

2. See, for example: Alicia Parlapiano and Karen Yourish, "Where Neil Gorsuch Would Fit on the Supreme Court," *New York Times,* February 1, 2017, www.nytimes.com/interactive/2017/01/31/us/politics/trump-supreme-court-nominee.html?_r=0.

3. In addition to so-called Article III courts, whose judges have life tenure, Congress can also create so-called Article I courts, such as the U.S. Court of Military Appeals and U.S. Court of Veterans Appeals, whose judges have fixed terms of office. A wide range of administrative law judges also do not have life tenure. Article III courts consist of the U.S. Supreme Court, the federal courts of appeals and district courts, and the U.S. Court of International Trade.

4. In addition to the district courts and the courts of appeals, there are several specialized courts, including the U.S. Court of International Trade and the U.S. Court of Federal Claims.

5. The District of Columbia and U.S. territories, such as Guam, also have district courts.

6. G. Alan Tarr, *Judicial Process and Policymaking,* 2nd ed. (New York: West/Wadsworth, 1999), 40.

7. David M. O'Brien, *Judicial Roulette* (New York: Priority Press, 1988), 70.

8. Howard Ball, *Courts and Politics: The Federal Judicial System,* 2nd ed. (Englewood Cliffs, NJ: Prentice Hall, 1987), 199.

9. Ibid., 199–200.

10. For example: Hugh Hewitt, "The One Obstacle to an Originalism-Driven Judiciary," *Washington Post,* April 11, 2017, www.washingtonpost.com/opinions/the-one-obstacle-to-an-originalism-driven-judiciary/2017/04/11/57aa2ae2-1e4e-11e7-a0a7-8b2a45e3dc84_story.html?utm_term=.e29ea6c87b2c.

11. "Doing Business in the Senate," editorial, *New York Times,* June 19, 2001, A22.

12. Sheldon Goldman, Elliot Slotnick, and Sara Schiavoni, "Obama's Judiciary at Midterm," *Judicature* (May–June 2011): 266–267.

13. O'Brien, *Judicial Roulette,* 33.

14. Tarr, *Judicial Process,* 75.

15. Sheldon Goldman, *Picking Federal Judges: Lower Court Selection from Roosevelt through Reagan* (New Haven, CT: Yale University Press, 1997), 86; see also Joel B. Grossman, *Lawyers and Judges: The ABA and the Politics of Judicial Selection* (New York: Wiley, 1965), chap. 3.

16. Quoted in Neil A. Lewis, "White House Ends Bar Association's Role in Screening Federal Judges," *New York Times,* March 23, 2001, A13. For a scholarly assessment of the ABA's ratings, see Susan Brodie Haire, "Rating the Ratings of the American Bar Association Standing Committee on Federal Judiciary," *Justice System Journal* 22:1 (2001): 1–17.

17. Adam Liptak, "White House Ends Bar Association's Role in Vetting Judges," *New York Times,* March 31, 2017, www.nytimes.com/2017/03/31/us/politics/white-house-american-bar-association-judges.html.

18. Larry C. Berkson and Susan B. Carbon, *The United States Circuit Judge Nominating Commission: Its Members, Procedures, and Candidates* (Chicago: American Judicature Society, 1980).

19. Alan Neff, *The United States District Judge Nominating Commissions: Their Members, Procedures, and Candidates* (Chicago: American Judicature Society, 1981).

20. Harry P. Stumpf, *American Judicial Politics,* 2nd ed. (Upper Saddle River, NJ: Prentice Hall, 1998), Tables 6-2 and 6-3, 180–183.

21. Goldman, *Picking Federal Judges,* 282; Stumpf, *American Judicial Politics,* 183.

22. Sheldon Goldman, "Reagan's Judicial Legacy: Completing the Puzzle and Summing Up," *Judicature* 72 (April–May 1989): 319–320.

23. Quoted in O'Brien, *Judicial Roulette,* 61–62.

24. Goldman, *Picking Federal Judges,* Tables 9.1 and 9.2. The total number of federal judicial appointments with life tenure rises to 372 if Reagan's four Supreme Court appointments are included. It rises slightly higher if one includes his appointments of non–Article 3 judges who staff specialized courts and do not have life tenure.

25. Alliance for Justice Judicial Selection Project, "2000 Annual Report," 3, www.afj.org/jsp.

26. Ronald Stidham, Robert A. Carp, and Donald Songer, "The Voting Behavior of President Clinton's Judicial Appointees," *Judicature* 80 (July–August 1996): 16–20. See also Alliance for Justice Judicial Selection Project, "2000 Annual Report," 4–5; Sheldon Goldman and Elliot Slotnick, "Picking Judges under Fire,"

Judicature 82 (May–June 1999): 265–284; and Nancy Scherer, "Are Clinton's Judges 'Old' Democrats or 'New' Democrats?" *Judicature* 84 (November–December 2000): 151–154.

27. Goldman and Slotnick, "Picking Judges under Fire," 282.

28. John H. Cushman Jr., "Senate Imperils Judicial System, Rehnquist Says," *New York Times*, January 1, 1998, A1.

29. Alliance for Justice Judicial Selection Project, "2000 Annual Report," 5.

30. Ibid., 2.

31. Ibid., 1. See also Sheldon Goldman et al., "Clinton's Judges: Summing Up the Legacy," *Judicature* 84 (March–April 2001): 228–254.

32. Helen Dewar, "Foreign Aid Bill Held Up by GOP; Senators Demand Action on Nominees," *Washington Post*, October 13, 2001, A3.

33. See John Anthony Maltese, "Confirmation Gridlock: The Federal Judicial Appointments Process under Bill Clinton and George W. Bush," *Journal of Appellate Practice and Process* 5 (Spring 2003): 1–28.

34. Russell Wheeler, "Judicial Nominations and Confirmations in Obama's First Term," *Governance Studies at Brookings*, December 13, 2012, www.brookings.edu/~/media/research/files/papers/2012/12/13%20judicial%20nominations%20wheeler/13_obama_judicial_wheeler.

35. Jennifer Bendery, "White House Poised to Take on Judicial Vacancy 'Crisis,'" *Huffington Post*, June 13, 2011, www.huffingtonpost.com/2011/06/13/white-house-poised-to-take-on-judicial-crisis_n_876185.html.

36. Paul Kane, "Senate Republicans Block Judicial Nominee Goodwin Liu," *Washington Post*, May 19, 2011, www.washingtonpost.com/politics/judicial-nominee-goodwin-liu-faces-filibuster-showdown/2011/05/18/AF6ak76G_story.html.

37. Goldman, Slotnick, and Schiavoni, "Obama's Judiciary at Midterm," 292.

38. Paul Kane, "Reid, Democrats Trigger 'Nuclear' Option; Eliminate Most Filibusters on Nominees," *Washington Post*, November 21, 2013, www.washingtonpost.com/politics/senate-poised-to-limit-filibusters-in-party-line-vote-that-would-alter-centuries-of-precedent/2013/11/21/d065cfe8-52b6-11e3-9fe0-fd2ca728e67c_story.html.

39. Al Kamen and Paul Kane, "Did 'Nuclear Option' Boost Obama's Judicial Appointments?" *Washington Post*, December 17, 2014, www.washingtonpost.com/blogs/in-the-loop/wp/2014/12/17/did-nuclear-option-boost-obamas-judicial-appointments/.

40. Figures for the 100th and 106th Congresses drawn from Table 5 of Denis Steven Rutkus and Mitchel A. Sollenberger, "Judicial Nomination Statistics: U.S. District and Circuit Courts, 1977–2003," *CRS Report for Congress*, updated February 23, 2004. Figures for 110th Congress drawn from "List of federal judges appointed by George W. Bush," https://en.wikipedia.org/wiki/List_of_federal_judges_appointed_by_George_W._Bush. Figures for 114th Congress from: https://www.justice.gov/archives/olp/114th-congress-judicial-nominations-list.

41. White House, "Infographic: President Obama's Judicial Nominees," www.whitehouse.gov/infographics/judicial-nominees.

42. White House, "This Is the First Time Our Judicial Pool Has Been This Diverse," www.whitehouse.gov/share/judicial-nominations. "Obama Nominates First Muslim Federal Judge," *CNN.com*, September 7, 2016, http://www.cnn.com/2016/09/07/politics/obama-nominates-first-muslim-judge/.

43. Joan Biskupic, "The Next President Could Tip High Court," *USA Today*, March 30, 2004, 1A.

44. Drawn from Tables 2 and 4 in Sheldon Goldman et al., "Picking Judges in a Time of Turmoil: W. Bush's Judiciary during the 109th Congress," *Judicature* 90 (May–June 2007), 277 and 282; and from Table 6.1 (for Ford and Nixon) from Sheldon Goldman, *Picking Federal Judges: Lower Court Selection from Roosevelt through Reagan* (New Haven, CT: Yale University Press, 1997), 227–229. Figures for George W. Bush courtesy of Sheldon Goldman. Figures for Barack Obama from Tables 6 and 7 in Elliot

Slotnick, Sara Schiavone, and Sheldon Goldman, "Obama's Judicial Legacy: The Final Chapter," working paper.

45. *Lochner v. New York,* 198 U.S. 45 (1905); *Roe v. Wade,* 410 U.S. 113 (1973); and *Griswold v. Connecticut,* 381 U.S. 479 (1965). See Robert H. Bork, *The Tempting of America* (New York: Free Press, 1990), for a criticism of both lines of cases.

46. Robert Scigliano, *The Supreme Court and the Presidency* (New York: Free Press, 1971), chap. 4.

47. Joel B. Grossman and Stephen L. Wasby, "The Senate and Supreme Court Nominations: Some Reflections," *Duke Law Journal* (August 1972): 559, n. 8.

48. All Supreme Court justices have been lawyers, but not all have had law school degrees. Law schools as we know them did not exist in the early part of the nineteenth century, and a majority of the lawyers learned the profession through apprenticeship into the early part of the twentieth century. See David M. O'Brien, *Storm Center: The Supreme Court in American Politics,* 5th ed. (New York: Norton, 2000), 34.

49. See John Anthony Maltese, *The Selling of Supreme Court Nominees* (Baltimore, MD: Johns Hopkins University Press, 1995), chaps. 4, 5.

50. David Alistair Yalof, *Pursuit of Justices: Presidential Politics and the Selection of Supreme Court Nominees* (Chicago: University of Chicago Press, 1999), 4–5.

50. Ibid., 7, 12–13.

51. Ibid.

52. Ethan Bronner, *Battle for Justice: How the Bork Nomination Shook America* (New York: Norton, 1989), 29–36; and Mark Gitenstein, *Matters of Principle: An Insider's Account of America's Rejection of Robert Bork's Nomination to the Supreme Court* (New York: Simon and Schuster, 1992), 28–37.

53. Lawrence Baum, *The Supreme Court,* 9th ed. (Washington, DC: CQ Press, 2006), 31.

54. Scott H. Ainsworth and John Anthony Maltese, "National Grange Influence on the Supreme Court Confirmation of Stanley Matthews," *Social Science History* 20 (Spring 1996): 41–62.

55. For early examples of lobbying, see Maltese, *The Selling of Supreme Court Nominees,* 47–49, 53.

56. P. S. Ruckman Jr., "The Supreme Court, Critical Nominations, and the Senate Confirmation Process," *Journal of Politics* 55 (August 1993): 794. If the two nominations withdrawn on a technicality are included, the failure rate rises to 19.5 percent.

57. E. J. Dionne, "A Town Hall Meeting: A Process Run Amok—Can It Be Fixed?" *ABC News Nightline,* October 16, 1991.

58. For case studies of these three nominations, see Maltese, *The Selling of Supreme Court Nominees,* chaps. 1, 4, 5.

59. Liberal groups protested Associate Justice William Rehnquist's nomination for chief justice in 1986 because of his alleged insensitivity to the rights of minorities and women. He was ultimately confirmed, but the thirty-three votes against him were the most ever cast against a confirmed justice up to that point.

60. See Patrick B. McGuigan and Dawn M. Weyrich, *Ninth Justice: The Fight for Bork* (Washington, DC: Free Congress Foundation, 1990); and Michael Pertschuk and Wendy Schaetzel, *The People Rising: The Campaign against the Bork Nomination* (New York: Thunder's Mouth Press, 1989).

61. Robert Shogan, *A Question of Judgment: The Fortas Case and the Struggle for the Supreme Court* (New York: Bobbs-Merrill, 1972).

62. Maltese, *The Selling of Supreme Court Nominees,* 14, 16.

63. "The Electoral Count," *New York Times,* January 30, 1881.

64. Quoted in Alpheus Thomas Mason, *Brandeis: A Free Man's Life* (New York: Viking, 1946), 467.

65. See Maltese, *The Selling of Supreme Court Nominees,* for accounts of these developments.

66. *Roe v. Wade,* 410 U.S. 113 (1973).

67. O'Connor, Kennedy, and Souter, *Planned Parenthood of Southeastern Pennsylvania v. Casey,* 505 U.S. 833 (1992).

68. Quoted in David M. O'Brien, *Storm Center: The Supreme Court in American Politics,* 5th ed. (New York: Norton, 1993), 84.

69. Scigliano, *The Supreme Court and the Presidency,* chap. 6. See also Lincoln Caplan, *The Tenth Justice: The Solicitor General and the Rule of Law* (New York: Random House, 1987); and Rebecca Mae Salokar, *The Solicitor General: The Politics of Law* (Philadelphia: Temple University Press, 1992).

70. The Supreme Court's discretion has changed over time and since 1988 is almost absolute. Cases now come to the Court almost exclusively by way of a writ of certiorari. To grant "cert" (agree to hear a case), four of the nine justices must vote to accept review. See Craig R. Ducat, *Constitutional Interpretation,* 7th ed. (Belmont, CA: West, 2000), 31.

71. Scigliano, *The Supreme Court and the Presidency,* 172.

72. Christopher Zorn, "Information, Advocacy, and the Role of the Solicitor General as Amicus Curiae" (working paper, Emory University, 1999), 1.

73. Steven Puro, "The United States as Amicus Curiae," in *Courts, Law, and Judicial Processes,* ed. S. Sidney Ulmer (New York: Free Press, 1981), 220–230.

74. Scigliano, *The Supreme Court and the Presidency,* chap. 6; Puro, "The United States as Amicus Curiae"; and Karen O'Connor, "The Amicus Curiae Role of the U.S. Solicitor General in Supreme Court Litigation," *Judicature* 66 (December 1982–January 1983): 261.

75. Kevin T. McGuire, "Explaining Executive Success in the U.S. Supreme Court," *Political Research Quarterly* 51 (June 1998): 522.

76. This situation is to be contrasted with the paucity of experience attorneys general have before the Court: Traditionally, they argue only one case before their terms are over. For an interesting account of Robert Kennedy's first appearance before the Court two years after he became attorney general, see Victor Navasky, *Kennedy Justice* (New York: Athenaeum, 1980), chap. 6.

77. Caplan, *The Tenth Justice.*

78. Elder Witt, *A Different Justice* (Washington, DC: Congressional Quarterly, 1986), chaps. 6, 7.

79. Caplan, *The Tenth Justice,* 79–80, 255–256.

80. Richard L. Pacelle Jr., *Between Law and Politics: The Solicitor General and the Structuring of Race, Gender, and Reproductive Rights Litigation* (College Station: Texas A&M University Press, 2003), 265.

81. *Hepburn v. Griswold* (*First Legal Tender Case*), 75 U.S. (8 Wall.) 506 (1870); and *Knox v. Lee, Parker v. Davis* (*Second Legal Tender Case*), 79 U.S. (12 Wall.) 457 (1871).

82. Samuel Kernell, *Going Public,* 4th ed. (Washington, DC: CQ Press, 2007), 134.

83. Ibid.

84. For a useful review of this power, see Gerald Gunther, "Congressional Power to Curtail Federal Court Jurisdiction: An Opinionated Guide to the Ongoing Debate," *Stanford Law Review* 36 (1984): 895. The most famous Supreme Court case involving this issue is *Ex parte McCardle,* 74 U.S. 506 (1869).

85. "President Signs Military Commissions Act of 2006," text of remarks at signing ceremony, October 17, 2006, www.whitehouse.gov/news/releases/2006/10/20061017-1.html.

86. *Boumediene v. Bush,* 553 U.S. 723 (2008). See Michael C. Dorf, "A Federal Appeals Court Upholds the Jurisdiction-Stripping Provisions of the Military Commissions Act of 2006, but Overlooks the Possibility of an Evolving Conception of Habeas Corpus," *FindLaw,* February 28, 2007, writ.news.findlaw .com/dorf/20070228.html.

87. "2008 Republican Platform," 53, platform.gop.com/2008Platform.pdf.

88. *Texas v. Johnson,* 491 U.S. 397 (1989).

89. "Bush Calls for Ban on Same-Sex Marriages," *CNN.com,* February 25, 2004, www.cnn.com/2004/ALLPOLITICS/02/24/elec04.prez.bush.marriage/; *Citizens United v. FEC,* 558 U.S. 310 (2010); Fredreka Schouten, "President Obama Wants to Reverse *Citizens United,*" *USA Today,* February 9, 2015, onpolitics.usatoday.com/2015/02/09/president-obama-wants-to-reverse-citizens-united/.

90. *Brown v. Board of Education,* 347 U.S. 483 (1954); and *Plessy v. Ferguson,* 163 U.S. 537 (1896).

91. Stumpf, *American Judicial Politics,* 429; and *Engel v. Vitale,* 370 U.S. 421 (1962).

92. *Youngstown Sheet and Tube Co. v. Sawyer,* 343 U.S. 579 (1952).

93. *United States v. Nixon,* 418 U.S. 683 (1974).

94. *Ex parte Merryman,* 17 Fed. Cas. 144 (1861).

95. Stumpf, *American Judicial Politics,* 429; and *United States v. Lopez,* 514 U.S. 549 (1995).

96. For a list of signing statements by Presidents Bush and Obama, see www.coherentbabble.com/listGWBall.htm. In 2006, the American Bar Association Task Force on Presidential Signing Statements issued a report on President Bush's use of the practice. See "Report," August 2006, www.abanet.org/media/docs/signstatereport.pdf.

97. "Report," 16.

98. Ibid., 17.

99. Ibid., 16.

100. For a list of Obama's signing statements, see *The American Presidency Project,* a website maintained at the University of California, Santa Barbara: www.presidency.ucsb.edu/signingstatements.php.

101. Jerry Markon and Sandhya Somashekhar, "Obama's 2012 DACA Move Offers a Window into Pros and Cons of Executive Action," *Washington Post,* November 30, 2014, www.washingtonpost.com/politics/obamas-2012-daca-move-offers-a-window-into-pros-and-cons-of-executive-action/2014/11/30/88be7a36-7188-11e4-893f-86bd390a3340_story.html.

102. *Youngstown Sheet and Tube Co. v. Sawyer.* See Maeva Marcus, *Truman and the Steel Seizure Case: The Limits of Presidential Power* (Durham, NC: Duke University Press, 1994).

103. *United States v. Nixon.*

104. For accounts of executive privilege, see Raoul Berger, *Executive Privilege: A Constitutional Myth* (Cambridge, MA: Harvard University Press, 1974); and Mark J. Rozell, *Executive Privilege: The Dilemma of Secrecy and Democratic Accountability* (Baltimore, MD: Johns Hopkins University Press, 1994).

105. *United States v. Curtiss-Wright Export Corp.,* 299 U.S. 304 (1936).

106. See Lee Epstein and Thomas G. Walker, *Constitutional Law for a Changing America: Institutional Powers and Constraints,* 6th ed. (Washington, DC: CQ Press, 2007), 263–267. The Court's use of this phrase has been strongly criticized; see, e.g., Louis Fisher's "Erroneous Dicta in *Curtiss-Wright,*" an amicus brief to the Supreme Court in the 2014 Zivotofsky case, available at http://www.loufisher.org/pip.html

107. See Lee Epstein and Thomas G. Walker, *Constitutional Law for a Changing America: Institutional Powers and Constraints,* 6th ed. (Washington, DC: CQ Press, 2007), 263–267. The Court's use of this phrase has been strongly criticized; see, e.g., Louis Fisher's "Erroneous Dicta in *Curtiss-Wright,*" an amicus brief to the Supreme Court in the 2014 Zivotofsky case, available at http://www.loufisher.org/pip.html

108. *Korematsu v. United States,* 323 U.S. 214 (1944). See Peter Irons, *Justice at War: The Story of the Japanese-American Internment Cases* (New York: Oxford University Press, 1983).

109. *Dames & Moore v. Regan,* 453 U.S. 654 (1981).

110. *Hamdan v. Rumsfeld,* 126 S.Ct. 2749 (2006).

111. *Boumediene v. Bush.*

112. *National Federation of Independent Business v. Sebelius,* 132 S.Ct. 2566 (2012).

113. Ben Wolfgang, "Obama: Court Shouldn't Have Considered Health Law Challenge," *Washington Post,* June 8, 2015, www.washingtonpost.com/world/europe/obama-high-court-shouldnt-consider-health-care-challenge/2015/06/08/c1a48e22–0def-11e5-a0fe-dccfea4653ee_story.html; and Jonathan H. Adler, "President 'Frustrated' with Court Decision on Immigration Reforms," *Washington Post,* June 8, 2015, www.washingtonpost.com/news/volokh-conspiracy/wp/2015/06/08/president-frustrated-with-court-decision-on-immigration-reforms/.

114. Robert Barnes, "Reactions Split on Obama's Remark, Alito's Response at State of the Union," *Washington Post,* January 29, 2010, www.washingtonpost.com/wp-dyn/content/article/2010/01/28/AR2010012802893.html.

115. Amy B. Wang, "Trump Lashes Out at 'So-Called Judge' Who Temporarily Blocked Travel Ban," *Washington Post,* February 4, 2017, www.washingtonpost.com/news/the-fix/wp/2017/02/04/trump-lashes-out-at-federal-judge-who-temporarily-blocked-travel-ban/.

116. *Morrison v. Olson,* 487 U.S. 654 (1988); and *Clinton v. Jones,* 520 U.S. 681 (1997). For a discussion of the Lewinsky scandal, see Mark J. Rozell and Clyde Wilcox, eds., *The Clinton Scandal and the Future of American Government* (Washington, DC: Georgetown University Press, 2000).

CHAPTER 8

The Politics of Domestic Policy

KENA BETANCUR/AFP/Getty Images

Donald Trump promised to "Make America Great Again" and has already chosen the campaign slogan for 2020: "Keep America Great." His challenge in the interim is to create jobs, repeal and replace Obamacare, increase the pace of economic growth, deregulate business, reform taxes, reduce illegal immigration, and rebuild the nation's infrastructure.

Domestic issues, headed by the economy, dominated the national agenda in the presidential election years of 2008, 2012, and 2016. The Iraq War had dominated the 2006 midterms and remained an important part of the Democrats' nomination contest in 2008, with Barack Obama gaining an advantage over his opponents who had voted for the war. But as the economy quickly slid into recession in September and October 2008, foreign policy, terrorism, and homeland security took a backseat to domestic issues. In 2012 and 2016, Republicans highlighted the sluggish economic recovery and opposition to the Patient Protection and Affordable Care Act, quickly dubbed **Obamacare.** Democrats had pushed changes in national health care programs through Congress in 2010 with minimal Republican help. Energy, immigration, and environmental regulation were other areas of deep partisan disagreement. This was a return to pre–9/11 politics.

Some presidents have made domestic policy initiatives central to their administrations. Bill Clinton in 1992, the first election after the end of the Cold War, was the first president since Franklin D. Roosevelt to win election with a campaign focused almost exclusively on domestic problems. Clinton sharply criticized George H. W. Bush for neglecting serious social and economic conditions in the United States while concentrating on foreign policy. Domestic issues also dominated the 2000 election between Al Gore and George W. Bush. After winning, President Bush placed tax cuts and education reform at the top of his agenda until September 11 redirected the nation's attention. President Obama made economic recovery, financial regulation, and health care reform top administration priorities even though he had two wars to deal with. President Trump's quest to Make America Great Again stressed job creation, deregulation, and immigration.

During the twentieth century, as a result of two world wars and the transportation and communication changes that produced a more tightly connected society, the federal government vastly expanded the range of policies it enacted. Whether they campaign on them or not, presidents confront a vast array of domestic issues, demands for government action, and competition among complex and costly programs competing for limited funds. Many of these programs enjoy the support of powerful interest groups and members of Congress. Whatever the administration does (or fails to do) in response to public demands is likely to cost the president political support. How do we make sense of this congested policy landscape consisting of interrelated, overlapping, and layered issues?[1]

Political scientists have used many ways to bring order to this bewildering array, but the most widely used classification scheme, or typology, is Theodore Lowi's division of policies into three categories: (1) distributive, (2) regulatory, and (3) redistributive.[2] He based his categories on the identity of those affected by the policies—from individuals to society as a whole—and the likelihood that the government will have to exercise coercion to implement the policy.

Distributive policies have the most diffused impact. They affect specific groups of people and provide individualized benefits. They have low visibility, produce little conflict, and are not likely to require the application of coercion. Examples of distributive policies include agricultural price supports, public works projects, and research and development programs. **Regulatory policies** affect large segments of society and involve the application of coercion. Although regulatory issues tend to be highly technical, they often are quite visible and controversial. Examples include pollution control, antitrust violations, and occupational safety and health requirements. **Redistributive policies** have the broadest impact on society. They involve the transfer of resources (wealth and income) from certain groups to others. They require coercion, are highly visible, and usually are accompanied by social or class conflict. Examples of redistributive policies include Social Security, tax reform, and health care.

Lowi argued the flipside of the usual equation. Instead of politics making policy, he argued that policy makes politics: that is, the type of policy determines the focus and behavior of political actors. The politics of distributive policy involves limited presidential and extensive congressional participation and decision making that relies heavily on logrolling—the mutual exchange of support for legislation that ensures benefits go to many different constituencies. Regulatory policy politics creates moderate presidential and substantial congressional interest and involvement, with frequent conflict between the president and Congress. Conflict may increase as presidents turn away from the frustrations of lawmaking in a highly polarized Washington (see chapter 5) and toward seeking to implement their policy preferences using administrative strategies. Redistributive policy politics often is fraught with ideological disputes and presidential-congressional conflict. Presidents tend to be most involved with redistributive policy issues, and they are involved whether the government is seeking to expand or to limit the scope of its activities. The future of federal redistributive policies, particularly Social Security, Medicare, and the Obama health care reforms, were at the heart of the budget battles waged by Obama and congressional Republicans throughout his term in office.

Steven Shull has used Lowi's policy typology to examine presidential and congressional roles in domestic policy formation. He found "some differences in presidential and congressional behavior . . . along lines anticipated by the 'theory'" and that "modest empirical distinctions" existed among the three policy categories.[3] The principal problem with Lowi's typology is the difficulty in making it operational for purposes of measurement—an issue may change its designation over time, starting out, for example, as a redistributive issue and later becoming distributive. That is what happened to Title I of the Elementary and Secondary Education Act of 1965 (ESEA), a program of federal assistance to local school districts for economically disadvantaged children. As a new program, it sparked controversy because of its redistributive effects, but over time it became a routine distribution of federal funds that was part of the established structure of school finance. When ESEA was reauthorized in 2002 as the No Child Left Behind Act, it became more regulatory in nature as it compelled school districts across the nation to adhere to a new set of federal requirements. The reauthorization of ESEA in 2016 provided relief from much of that regulation. In other words, Lowi's categories are not fixed in time. Shull concluded that Lowi's typology is not as useful as substantive classification based on policy content.

John Kessel used policy content to classify domestic policy into areas involving social benefits, civil liberties, natural resources, and agriculture.[4] Each area entails a specific type of politics and its own temporal pattern, both of which have implications for presidential participation. The politics of social benefits, such as housing and the Social Security retirement program, involves the allocation of resources. In this way, it resembles Lowi's distributive and redistributive categories. Presidents use the distribution of social benefits to build public support. They tend to pay most attention to social benefits as they approach reelection; afterward, the winners are much less concerned with these benefits. Civil rights politics are regulatory and highly sensitive because of differing conceptions of fairness. Presidents are most likely to act on civil rights issues immediately after election because these issues are highly controversial and because campaign promises must be fulfilled. The politics of natural resources, which includes environmental protection, is primarily regulatory, and agriculture mostly involves allocation. Kessel argued that natural resource and agricultural policy politics are shaped by long-range developments, and presidential participation is limited.

Whether one approaches domestic policy using Lowi's analytic typology or Kessel's substantive classifications, it is clear that as a practical matter presidents can become fully involved with only a small number of problems and issues. The Lowi and Kessel approaches suggest that in domestic policy, presidents will focus on matters such as maintaining the financial integrity of the Social Security system, reforming welfare, and dealing with major civil rights proposals. They do not take up all major redistributive, social benefit, and civil rights issues and may consciously avoid those issues that could involve enormous financial or political costs. They are unlikely to become bogged down with established distributive policies or with the technicalities of economic and social regulation. Most presidents have been content to leave the distribution of "pork barrel" projects to Congress. Jimmy Carter harmed himself politically when he tangled with Congress over eighteen water projects he regarded as unnecessary. Although George W. Bush initially vowed to cut such pork in half, he backed off in the summer of 2001 to avoid such a fight with Congress. Bush later resumed his battle with a Democratic Congress over **earmarks**, spending directed to home-district or home-state projects by members of Congress that frequently have not been approved by formal votes in the normal legislative process. Barack Obama promised to roll earmarks back to 1994 levels—that is, before the Republicans regained control of Congress—but was forced to accept a large number of them in order to pass the final version of the fiscal year 2009 appropriations bill.[5] Most presidents decide not to invest time and energy in such frustrating efforts.

To work through the enormous congestion one finds in domestic policy, the nation needs **coordination**, and no one is better situated than the president to provide this essential function. Coordination has been complicated, however, by the interrelatedness of domestic, economic, and national security policy. If, on the one hand, presidents attempt to coordinate specific policies through simplification—say, by proposals to balance the budget or reorganize the bureaucracy—they encounter the opposition of powerful forces mobilized around the policy areas likely to be affected. Ronald Reagan's 1982 proposals to move toward a balanced budget by reducing Social Security cost-of-living allowances provide an excellent example. Opposition from the "gray lobby" (senior citizens) and most members of Congress quickly stymied the idea. If, on the other hand, presidents fail to maintain the initiative in coordinating complex policies effectively, they not only risk losing popular and congressional support but also have to deal with interest group opposition. This scenario played out early in Clinton's first term when he lost control of his health care proposal. Lack of coordination in selling the proposal to Congress and the public allowed opponents to pick apart the plan. As cracks appeared, opponents took control of the agenda, dooming the president's proposal.

Health care reform was second only to the economy on President Obama's domestic agenda (indeed, he saw the two areas as closely linked). Learning from Clinton's experience, he began the effort by convening a White House summit on health care that assembled members of Congress and representatives from all the major interests that would be affected by reform in an attempt to establish a common commitment to moving forward. Controlling health care costs, argued the administration, was linked to restoring the nation's economy, given that health care accounted for some 15 percent of the U.S. gross domestic product (GDP) at the time. As always, however, negotiating the details of change was the key to success, and Obama appointed a health care czar to serve as the point person for this effort, though White House chief of staff Rahm Emmanuel also played a key role. As head of the White House Office on Health Reform, Nancy-Ann DeParle coordinated legislative efforts with Secretary of Health and Human Services Kathleen Sebelius and a wide range of outside consultants.[6]

Obama's effort succeeded where Clinton's had failed. Obama started with "the highest first-term popular vote percentage of any Democrat since FDR" (Clinton had won only 43 percent), and a filibuster-proof Senate, at least until January 2010.[7] Groups representing hospital, drug, and health insurance companies won key concessions (sometimes described as "sweetheart deals"[8]) from the administration, which ensured they would support the reforms rather than oppose them as they had under Clinton. Democrats united around a set of technical fixes to specific problems instead of presenting contending solutions,[9] and the economic crisis made the problems in health care even more pressing than they had been fifteen years earlier. Unlike Clinton, the Obama administration did not draft an elaborate proposal that was then presented to Congress. Instead, it let legislators craft the reforms, negotiate with health care interests, and bargain with their colleagues. Administration representatives intervened when necessary to defend the president's preferences, negotiate deals with key groups, and build public support, typified by the president's address to a joint session of Congress on September 9, 2009, designed to answer mounting criticisms. Although the president was unable to secure support from Republicans—and the final vote was a nail biter after Republicans regained the ability to filibuster in a Massachusetts special election to fill the vacancy left after Ted Kennedy's death—this time the strategy worked.

But passage of the Affordable Care Act did not ensure victory. Implementing the new policy proved difficult. The administration was slow in issuing the rules insurers needed so that they knew what plans they could offer, and it paid scant attention to the technical difficulties of connecting millions of uninsured people to new coverage via brand new websites. In 2013, the new Healthcare.gov system crashed with embarrassing frequency.[10] It didn't help that Republicans, once again the House majority after 2010, repeatedly sought to repeal and defund Obamacare. Many Republican governors refused to expand Medicaid in order to cover large numbers of low-income persons without health care, and the Supreme Court agreed in 2013 that the federal government could not coerce the states to do so. But in the same 5–4 decision, the deeply divided Supreme Court declared constitutional the **individual mandate**, a key provision of the law that requires most Americans to have health insurance or pay a tax penalty.

In 2015, the Court agreed to hear a challenge to another critical feature of the system, tax credits that made health care affordable for lower income citizens. In this case, *King v. Burwell,* Chief Justice Roberts, writing for the 6–3 majority, wrote that while Congress was "inartful" in its use of language (four words seemed to provide tax subsidies only for citizens enrolled in state-based exchanges and not the many millions more in federal exchanges), Congress's clear intent was to improve the nation's health insurance system, a goal that would not be served if they did not uphold the tax credits. It had been estimated that at least six million Americans in thirty-four states would likely be unable to afford health insurance if the subsidies applied only to state exchanges.[11] President Obama and supporters of the law crowed that the decision should bring the series of judicial challenges to an end,[12] but additional challenges were inevitable.[13]

Reform, even with the president's full support, is not easy to achieve. In 2005, President George W. Bush tackled the long-term problem of keeping Social Security solvent—that is, ensuring that enough money will be available to meet commitments to retirees over the next seventy-five years. His central recommendation—that younger workers be allowed to create personal retirement accounts—generated intense opposition from the largest lobbying group in the United States, AARP, and unified resistance by congressional Democrats.[14] Attempts to reform immigration policy illustrate the interrelatedness of issues. Immigration affects Hispanics, an important and growing domestic constituency; has a direct bearing on labor needs in important industries; and is a critical issue to many nations around the world, as they absorb refugees displaced by conflicts. Congress, confronted with competing pressures, refused in 2007 and again in 2010 and 2013 to follow the president's lead and fashion bipartisan, comprehensive reform. At its outset, the Trump administration used executive orders to redirect national immigration policy and sought funding to build a wall along the border with Mexico.

The Domestic Policy Process

The domestic policy process consists of actions that culminate in the development and presentation of legislative proposals to Congress, the issuance of executive orders and regulations, and the preparation and submission of annual budgets. There is a cyclical regularity to much of the policy process because presidents use annual events such as the State of the Union, budget, and economic messages to define the broad outlines of their program.[15] (Although these events occur at approximately the same time each year, the full cycles last longer than a year. The budget for the fiscal year beginning on October 1, 2017, for example, had its origins in the budget review process begun in spring 2015.) Presidents also make policy proposals at other times during the year, sometimes in response to unexpected events.

Policy Streams

The process of setting the president's domestic policy agenda can be understood as the convergence in the White House of three tributary streams. The first identifies *problems and issues* requiring attention, the second produces *proposed solutions* to the problems, and the third carries the *political factors* that establish the context for policymaking. According to John Kingdon, these three streams operate largely, but not absolutely, independently of one another. Problems and solutions develop separately and may or may not be joined, and political factors may change regardless of whether policymakers have recognized a problem or whether a potential solution exists.[16]

The First Stream: Problems and Issues. Problems and issues move onto the president's domestic policy agenda either because their seriousness and high visibility make it impossible to avoid them or because of presidential initiative. Unavoidable problems that force the president to react include matters such as energy shortages, a failing economy, high rates of inflation or unemployment, climate change, the emergence of major threats to public health, problems resulting from increased drug abuse, the rising cost of health care, racial discrimination in law enforcement, and parental dissatisfaction with the quality of education. Other times, presidents act more proactively by adding items they believe are instrumental to the achievement of their goals.

Once enough influential people, inside and outside the government, think something should be done about a certain problem or issue, it is likely that the president will react by adding the item to the administration's domestic agenda.[17] This pressure may occur as a consequence of changes in economic and social indicators, such as rates of inflation, unemployment, energy costs, infant mortality, and students' scores on various standardized tests. Decision makers in the presidency, the bureaucracy, Congress, the private sector, and state and local governments routinely monitor changes in a large array of indicators. Whether these changes require a response from the federal government is a matter of interpretation based on the problem's symbolic significance, the personal experiences of the president and other decision makers, and how the subject relates to other problems and issues.

Sometimes a "focusing event," such as a disaster or a crisis, moves the president and other decision makers to recognize a condition as a compelling problem. The near meltdown of a reactor at the Three Mile Island power plant in western Pennsylvania in March 1979 thrust nuclear safety to the forefront of the domestic agenda; prior to this event, safety proponents had struggled for years with little success to call attention to the issue. The massive power outage that left eight states in the dark in August 2003 drew attention to the vulnerability of the nation's aging electrical grid and brought debate over a proposed energy bill to the forefront. The terrorist attacks of 9/11 forced the issue of domestic security onto the agenda and led to quick passage of the USA PATRIOT Act. The devastation wrought by Hurricane Katrina in August 2005 triggered a debate on governments' preparedness for responding to natural disasters; the consensus was that "disaster response policy [became] a significant political disaster for Bush."[18] The BP oil spill during 2010 that dumped nearly five million barrels of oil into the Gulf of Mexico triggered reviews of offshore drilling and U.S. energy policy. Sustained demonstrations in Ferguson, Missouri, after the shooting of Michael Brown forced the Justice Department to undertake investigations of alleged police discrimination in enforcing the laws. On occasion, presidents have no choice but to deal with a problem, even though they may prefer not to do so. Shootings at a Connecticut elementary school in December 2012 pushed gun control onto Obama's legislative program even though it had received no attention during the 2012 campaign.

Some problems and issues remain on the agenda through successive presidential administrations. Feasible solutions may not have been found, solutions may have been tried unsuccessfully, or the problem may have been "solved" only to reemerge in a different form. Health care exemplifies such an issue. Harry S. Truman proposed a comprehensive national health insurance program in 1945 as an additional Social Security benefit, an initiative left unfinished from the New Deal.[19] The American Medical Association and major business groups successfully fought the proposal by labeling it "socialized medicine" at a time when Americans' fear of communism was growing. Congressional committees, controlled by Republicans, refused to act on the proposal. Both John F. Kennedy and Lyndon B. Johnson advanced proposals for national health insurance, and in 1965 Congress crafted a partial response with Medicare, a health insurance plan for Social Security retirees age sixty-five and older, and Medicaid, a health care program for the poor. Even Republican presidents Richard Nixon and Gerald R. Ford sought ways to expand health coverage as did Democrat Jimmy Carter. Although Clinton made health care reform a central issue in his 1992 presidential campaign, his 1,342-page plan did not even get voted on in Congress. George W. Bush managed to add prescription drug coverage to Medicare in 2003, but by 2007, an estimated forty-five million Americans lacked any form of health insurance.[20] Had it been implemented fully, the Obama-sponsored reforms would have extended health care coverage to 95 percent of the population, up from the pre-reform 83 percent. After changes made by Congress and won by the states in the courts, 89 percent of the nonelderly population was expected to be covered.[21] But Republicans remained unconvinced that Obama's solutions were appropriate and sought to design a new health care framework under President Trump.

Sometimes presidents have broader discretion to determine which problems and issues to emphasize. In such cases, three goals affect the selection of problems and issues to address: (1) reelection (for a first-term president), (2) historical achievement (legacy), and (3) a desire to shape public policy.[22] Presidents vary in the emphasis they place on these goals. Nixon's willingness to propose innovative policies for environmental protection, welfare reform, and sharing federal revenue with state and local governments, even at the expense of alienating some of his conservative supporters, reflected his concern with historical achievement.[23] As he approached his reelection campaign, Carter shifted from making agenda decisions on the basis of his beliefs to making them on the basis of politics, a charge also leveled at Obama during his budget negotiations with Republicans in 2011. Second-term presidents, including George W. Bush and Barack Obama, are usually seen as focused on their historical legacy.

The Second Stream: Solutions. Once a problem or an issue has been recognized, the availability of a solution helps determine whether it rises to a high position on the president's agenda.[24] Solutions take several forms, ranging from *direct actions,* such as legislative proposals or administrative directives, to *symbolic actions,* such as appointment of a study commission or a task force, to *no action.* Problems can have several solutions, and a single solution can be applied to more than one problem. Some solutions come attached to a problem; others are consciously selected from among competing alternatives. Most solutions come from ideas generated outside the White House because of the time constraints facing executive advisers and the small size of the institution of the presidency in relation to the policymaking environment as a whole. Aside from the presidency, the principal sources of policy ideas are Congress, the bureaucracy, interest groups, universities, think tanks (research institutes), and state and local governments. Within the presidency, the incumbent's campaign promises are a source of policy proposals and a benchmark for evaluating externally generated ideas.[25] Obama's 2008 pledge to raise taxes only on those with incomes above $250,000 is an example. (That income limit later rose to $450,000 for couples.) The president's domestic policy staff and other units in the Executive Office of the President (EOP) might develop new ideas once the president is in office, but these aides often become bogged down in day-to-day problems.

Many of the ideas that emerge as proposed solutions to problems on the president's agenda have been circulating among members of **issue networks**. Issue networks are groups of individuals and organizations trying to shape certain policies. Such networks might consist of members of Congress and their legislative aides, bureaucrats, interest groups, the media, scholars and other experts in research organizations, and representatives of state and local government. Together they promote specific ideas and proposals, such as campaign finance reform, energy policy, and a patients' bill of rights. Issue networks are motivated by their participants' desire to advance personal and organizational interests and to influence public policy in accordance with the groups' values. Network participants study, analyze, and discuss problems and solutions among themselves, and they attempt to inform and influence the major decision makers in government, the most important of whom is the president.

The process by which policy ideas develop, advance, and either succeed or fail is often lengthy and generally diffuse. John Kingdon describes it as a "policy primeval soup" in which ideas are continually bumping into one another and surviving, dying, combining, or emerging into new forms.[26] The ideas that do manage to become incorporated into a president's specific policy proposal are evaluated according to three criteria: (1) economic, (2) political, and (3) technical feasibility.

The *economic feasibility,* or cost, of a potential solution is especially important, as demands for federal expenditures far outweigh the government's capacity to supply the necessary funds. Few proposals for major new spending programs survive in an era of resource constraints. Proposals that restrain or reduce spending are more attractive to a president struggling to control a budget deficit. A proposal's *political feasibility* is determined initially by its compatibility with the values and interests of other important decision makers, particularly those in Congress. Ultimately, a proposal must gain the acquiescence, if not the acceptance, of the public and the relevant interest groups. A proposal's *technical feasibility*—the question of its workability—does not receive as much attention as its economic and political costs. Some ideas—such as proposals for welfare reform that maintain reasonably high payments, reduce inequities between recipients in different states and between recipients and the working poor, and do not increase the cost to the government—are economically and politically attractive but unworkable in practice. Presidents Nixon and Carter made this discovery, much to their dismay, after the failure of their major efforts to achieve welfare reform.[27] Financial costs may rule out a proposal that is politically and technically feasible, such as rapid cleanup of toxic waste sites. Political costs may prevent acceptance of a workable proposal that is compatible with a tight budget, such as freezing Social Security cost-of-living increases. Eventually, a short list of presidential proposals emerges from a multitude of potential solutions.

The Third Stream: Political Factors. The last of Kingdon's three policymaking streams is the one carrying political factors.[28] Such factors affect the setting and implementation of the president's agenda, and they include the national mood, the balance of political forces, and events within the government.

The *national mood* is a somewhat amorphous term, difficult to define. It is not identical to public opinion, nor can it be measured through survey research. National mood is perhaps best described as the perception among decision makers that a consensus exists or is building among various attentive publics and political activists for specific government policies. Politicians sense this mood in suggestions, requests, and other communications from interest groups, state and local government officials, corporate executives, and politically active citizens; in news media coverage of events; in blog entries; and in editorial commentary. The national mood also reflects the influence of social movements such as civil rights, environmentalism, and family values. Without a favorable national mood, major new policies are unlikely to be adopted. In short, the national mood is a reflection of the politically relevant climate or temper of the times. Counting on a national mood that supports "change"—his campaign mantra—President Obama initially pushed several major reforms through the system and took bold steps to remedy the economic emergency, but the administration gradually embraced fiscal responsibility after the 2010 midterm elections. President Trump also entered office as a change agent but with a far different purpose, to bring the federal government under control.

Considerably more concrete than the national mood is the extent of consensus and conflict that determines the *balance of political forces.* The prospects for adoption of a proposed policy change depend on the balance of organized interests and other forces, but assessing the balance on any issue is largely a matter of informed guesswork. The complex pattern of pluralistic political forces and the fragmentation of government authority combine to provide a strong advantage to the *opponents* of policy change.

Often, heavy political costs are associated with just raising an issue for consideration, let alone obtaining adoption of a proposal. This problem arises when the administration attempts to change existing government programs, most of which have powerful clientele groups ready to defend them. Clientele interests, in triangular alliances with agencies that administer the programs and congressional subcommittees with jurisdiction, engage in bargaining and logrolling to maintain and enhance the programs. To overcome government's natural inertia, a strong constituency for political change must be mobilized; without it, a proposal will encounter great difficulty. The Carter administration's efforts to enact a national energy policy were unsuccessful despite widespread shortages of fuels until compromises made the proposal acceptable to the oil industry and consumer interests. Clinton's proposal for health care reform failed because strong opposition from a variety of special interests tipped the balance of political forces against the proposed change.

George W. Bush succeeded in convincing the public that Social Security was running out of money, but groups representing seniors worked strenuously against his preferred solution. Senators representing agricultural, mining, and manufacturing interests scuttled Obama's efforts to pass climate change legislation in 2010, fearful of the costs their constituents would bear in a "cap and trade" system. Obama turned instead to a regulatory strategy that utilized aggressive interpretations of the 1970 and 1990 Clean Air Acts to limit coal emissions. When opponents of Obama's proposed limits realized that they could not win critical votes in Congress to overturn the new regulations, they developed a strategy based on state challenges through the courts.[29] President Trump, in turn, used executive orders to begin the process of rescinding Obama-era regulations on coal, to change the way the government accounted for the costs of climate change when considering projects' environmental impact, and to reverse Obama's disapproval of building the Keystone XL oil pipeline. Trump also installed a well-known opponent of federal environmental controls, Scott Pruitt, as director of the Environmental Protection Agency.

Events within government are the third major political factor shaping the president's policy agenda. The principal event is a national election, which can produce fundamental changes in the agenda. The 1980 election brought Ronald Reagan to the presidency and gave the Republicans control of the Senate after a quarter-century in the minority and was certainly such an event. An ideologically defined, conservative agenda replaced the liberal agenda in effect since the New Deal. Similarly, the 1994 election, in which the Republicans captured control of both houses of Congress for the first time in forty years, profoundly reshaped President Clinton's domestic agenda. Much of the revised agenda consisted of defensive reactions to Republican proposals to curtail affirmative action and reverse regulatory policies affecting the environment, occupational health and safety, and business and financial practices. The 2006 midterm elections returned Democrats to the majority in the House and the Senate, triggering agenda clashes between the White House and Congress. This pattern was partially repeated after the 2010 midterms when Republicans regained control of the House. Divided government has also made implementing policy more difficult. From 1969 through 2018, the same political party controlled the White House and both houses of Congress for only thirteen out of forty-nine years.[30]

Two researchers looking at presidential action on crime issues over a fifty-year period concluded that the president's electoral cycle is the single strongest determinant of when such a discretionary policy issue becomes part of the president's agenda.[31] Matthew Eshbaugh-Soha argues that the political composition of Congress and the condition of the federal budget determine both the number and the significance of policies the president might propose; budget and political constraints lead presidents to emphasize unimportant or short-term policies.[32] Obama determined that higher government spending was needed to combat the recession and counted on the broad public support registered in the election to enable him to pass an ambitious reform agenda. But the sluggish economic recovery convinced much of the public that government stimulus plans were ineffective, contributing to the Democrats' 2010 midterm losses.

Jurisdictional matters are another intragovernmental factor that may affect agenda setting. Disputes over bureaucratic and committee turf often delay or prevent action, although jurisdictional competition occasionally accelerates consideration of a popular issue. In addition, a proposal may be structured so that it will be handled by a committee or an agency favorably disposed to it.

In sum, the most significant domestic policy actions are likely to occur when the national mood and election outcomes combine to overcome the normal inertia produced by the balance of political forces and the fragmentation of government authority among numerous bureaucratic and congressional fiefdoms. Once items begin to rise on the agenda, however, organized political forces attempt to shape policy proposals to their advantage or to defeat the proposals outright. Despite the tools at their disposal, presidents largely remain "prisoners of circumstance" in domestic policy. For George W. Bush, those circumstances were shaped largely by the events of 9/11 in New York City and Washington, D.C., as well as the hurricane winds of August 2005 in New Orleans.[33] For Obama, the nation's economic problems, bad as they were, briefly opened a window for significant policy initiatives such as health care reform and financial industry regulation. For Trump, it is still unclear what forces will shape his domestic policies.

Resources and Opportunities

Successful policy leadership results from advancing appropriate solutions to specific problems under favorable political circumstances. Relatively few policy proposals can receive presidential attention and consideration. Some are not compatible with an administration's overall objectives and ideology, but many otherwise acceptable proposals never become part of the president's agenda because limited resources cannot be devoted to them. Quite simply, presidents must establish priorities.[34] Presidents establish priorities through what political scientist Paul Light calls a "filtering process," which maintains an orderly flow of problems and solutions to the president and merges them to produce policy proposals. The objectives of the process are to control the flow so that important problems, issues, and alternatives receive attention without overloading the president and to ensure that policy proposals are formulated with due regard to relevant substantive and political factors. As they are melded into presidential decisions, problems and solutions pass through two filters: (1) resources and (2) opportunities.

Resources: Political Capital. One of the president's most important resources is **political capital**, the reservoir of popular and congressional support with which presidents begin their terms. As they make controversial decisions, presidents "spend" some of their capital, a resource they can seldom replenish. Presidents must decide which proposals merit the expenditure of political capital and in what amounts. Reagan, for example, was willing to spend his capital heavily on reducing activities of the federal government, cutting taxes, and reforming the income tax code but not on antiabortion or school prayer amendments to the Constitution. Material resources determine which proposals for new programs can be advanced and which existing programs should be emphasized.

SAUL LOEB/AFP/Getty Images

Surrounded by congressional leaders and an eleven-year-old boy, Marcelas Owens, President Obama signed the historic legislation reforming the nation's health care on March 23, 2010. Three years earlier, the boy's mother died without health insurance after losing her job. President Obama's mother had also struggled with health insurance providers before dying of cancer.

Clinton began his presidency lacking sufficient political capital to enact his ambitious agenda.[35] Although he won a clear Electoral College victory and had a 6 percent vote margin over incumbent president George H. W. Bush, he received only 43 percent of the popular vote because of Ross Perot's third-party candidacy. Immediately after the election, the Republican Senate leader, Bob Dole, pointedly claimed to speak for the 57 percent of the electorate who had opposed Clinton. Clinton's New Democrat philosophy was not shared by a majority of congressional Democrats, who were considerably more liberal. Finally, campaign allegations of sexual misconduct and avoiding military service in Vietnam reduced the public's trust and support of the president. These factors limited the capital Clinton had to spend on advocating potentially controversial domestic policies.

George W. Bush also entered office with limited political capital. In the 2000 presidential election, he lost the popular vote to Al Gore and took power only after a protracted dispute over which candidate had won Florida's electoral votes. In addition, he faced what at the time was the highest disapproval rating of any incoming president since polling began—25 percent, according to a Gallup poll.[36] In May 2001, he lost the marginal control of the Senate that Republicans had enjoyed since January after Sen. James Jeffords, R-VT, defected and became an Independent. The return to divided government lasted until the 2002 midterm elections and made passage of Bush's initiatives more difficult. But Bush proceeded confidently, as if he had a mandate for his conservative agenda. "I know the value of political capital," Bush said just before his inauguration, "how to earn it and how to spend it."[37] He swiftly advanced a few proposals that enjoyed broad support, such as tax cuts and education reform. After 9/11 Bush, suddenly had a free hand in foreign policy and sought—with mixed success—to parlay his high public approval ratings into support for his domestic policy initiatives.

Two days after he was reelected, Bush again spoke of his prospects during a press conference. "I earned capital in the campaign, political capital, and now I intend to spend it. . . . [Y]ou've heard the agenda: Social Security and tax reform, moving this economy forward, education, fighting and winning the war on terror."[38] But Bush's approval ratings began a downward slide caused by Iraq, a White House scandal, a botched Supreme Court nomination, and faulty relief efforts after Hurricane Katrina.[39] As a result, neither of his top two domestic priorities was realized, and the chance to regain capital in the 2006 midterm election disappeared.

Obama entered office with a solid electoral victory based on a charismatic but vague promise of change as well as public hopes that he was the right candidate to repair the economy. His campaign excited millions of first-time and young voters, and he seemed to embody a new beginning on many fronts—in race relations, bipartisan discussions of common problems, and international negotiations. Expectations were especially high as he entered the White House with a Democrat-controlled Congress, potentially setting him up for a backlash if results proved disappointing. Riding on the crest of electoral victory and widespread popularity, he advanced an ambitious agenda that ran the risk of overreaching. Carter and Clinton had swamped Congress with too many proposals during their first two years in office, but neither of them had enjoyed as much public support as Obama, who was counting on his ability to link his policy initiatives together as necessary to strengthen the economy in both the short and long term. Health care reform was the crowning achievement of his first two years, but public support declined. Critics charged that Obamacare would add to the growing national debt and was another example of big government intruding on private lives, particularly by mandating that everyone have health insurance. Obama's political capital evaporated on the night of the 2010 midterm elections, and though he rebuilt it in the 2012 campaign no one knew for how long. That election did not bring a Democratic majority back to the House, though, and any renewed capital drained away with the bungled rollout of Obamacare in the fall of 2013 and disappeared in the 2014 midterms when Republicans also won a Senate majority. In response, the president adopted more unilateral strategies to achieve his goals, as discussed in chapter 6.

Despite his claims to the contrary, Trump's election victory in 2016 gave him a less powerful mandate than Bush's in 2000 and Obama's in 2008. Democrats could argue that a majority of voters had not supported Trump for president, and although the president declared that millions of illegal votes had been cast for the Democrats and proclaimed that he had won an electoral college landslide, neither claim was true.[40] Republicans maintained control of both houses of Congress, but many members had held Trump at arm's length during the election. Unlike most presidents, Trump quickly lost public approval after his inauguration (discussed in chapter 3) rather than building his political capital during the honeymoon period. His initial strategy was to fulfill as many campaign promises as possible through executive orders. The administration pressured Congress to move quickly to repeal and replace Obamacare, but divisions among Republicans doomed at least the initial effort. Prospects were similarly grim for legislative action on tax reform, an especially complex issue. Slow progress in staffing the political and policy positions throughout government also suggested progress would be slow on other issues.

Opportunities. In addition to resources, Light argues, presidents need **opportunities** to formulate the agenda. These opportunities are often described metaphorically as windows: They open for a while and then close. They may be scheduled or unscheduled. Scheduled opportunities to shape the agenda occur in conjunction with the annual cycle of presidential messages to Congress (State of the Union, budget, and economic report), the congressional calendar, and action-forcing deadlines, such as renewals of program authorizations. An administration's greatest opportunity to set the agenda occurs during January and February, when Congress begins a new session and presidents deliver their messages, and in August and September, when Congress returns from recess and earlier proposals can be replaced or modified.[41] As the fiscal year comes to a close in late September, presidents can also often take advantage of their veto leverage given the need to pass a budget before the government shuts down.

Unscheduled opportunities come about as the result of focusing events or changes in political conditions. Both scheduled and unscheduled windows of opportunity eventually close, some sooner than others. An opportunity is more likely to be seized and an issue given a high place on the president's agenda when problems, solutions, and political factors come together.[42] Without a viable solution and in the absence of favorable political conditions, a problem has a limited chance of moving up on the agenda. For example, popular support for biomedical research is substantial, but the slow pace of development of treatments and cures for diseases such as cancer limits presidential attention to the issue.

Opportunities also fluctuate as a presidential term progresses. In a president's first year in office, Congress and the public have high expectations of policy change based on campaign promises and the election mandate. Opportunities tend to be at their peak during a new administration's so-called honeymoon period. In the second and fourth years of a president's term, concern begins to focus on the forthcoming election campaigns, and policy opportunities decline. The third year frequently is regarded as crucial, for the administration is by then experienced, mature, removed from immediate electoral pressures, and anxious to make its mark.[43] Opportunities are most likely to be exploited effectively then and in the first year of a president's second term—assuming there is one. Because (since the 1950s) a second term is also a final term, the president becomes a **lame duck**, which tends to restrict further policy opportunities. The effects of lame-duck status on presidential initiatives are especially notable following the midterm congressional election in a president's second term. In anticipation of losing control of Congress in the November 2006 elections, George W. Bush asked department secretaries for lists of "initiatives that could be accomplished without congressional approval."[44] Instead, he would employ regulations and other unilateral action powers. As Republican opposition stalled progress on Obama's legislative agenda in early 2010, his administration considered using executive authority as the best way to achieve its goals.[45] In a very specific instance, when Congress failed to reauthorize federal legislation on federal aid to schools (No Child Left Behind), the administration announced that it would allow states to apply for waivers from the guidelines set up by the 2002 law, saving them from the law's sanctions if they changed education policies to match the administration's preferences. This effectively made unilateral changes in the law.[46] Entering his second term, Obama knew that his window for legislative initiatives would be brief, but even as a lame duck he could pursue his goals through administrative action, as his pledge in the 2014 State of the Union address to utilize his "pen and phone" made clear.

The patterns in the progression of opportunities conflict as presidents move through their terms. On the one hand, as they acquire experience and expertise, presidents become more effective and therefore increase their policy opportunities. On the other hand, as their congressional and popular support declines through the term, they lose opportunities. Light describes these as **cycles of increasing effectiveness and declining influence**.[47] It is ironic that as presidents become more skilled at finding opportunities, they become less able to use them.

The Domestic Policy Environment

The most outstanding characteristic of the domestic policy environment is its complexity. Myriad actors—individuals, groups, and other government institutions and agencies—all pursue a seemingly incalculable range of objectives and protect countless interests. Although presidential power is limited, the president is better situated than anyone else to give direction and bring a degree of coordination to the federal government's domestic policies.

The fragmentation of political power and influence that is the hallmark of the U.S. political system is the product of a heterogeneous and pluralistic society and of constitutional arrangements designed to produce deliberate, rather than expeditious, government decision making. Nowhere is the fragmentation of power more apparent and more profound than in the domestic policy environment.

Interest Groups

Outside the government, thousands of interest groups constantly seek to influence policy. They range from organizations concerned with all of the government's activities, such as Americans for Democratic Action, to those focused on a single issue, such as the National Rifle Association (NRA). Interest groups are concerned not only with virtually every government program that distributes benefits to individuals and organizations and regulates their conduct but also with possibilities for new programs. Simply stated, the objectives of interest groups are to secure the adoption of policies beneficial to their members and to prevent the adoption of policies they view as harmful to them. Interest groups operate in all sectors of domestic policy. They include organizations that represent business; labor; the professions; consumers; state and local governments and their subdivisions; public officials; social groupings based on age, sex, race, religion, and shared attitudes and experiences; and groups presenting themselves as protectors of the unorganized public interest. In sum, interest groups represent every aspect of society and help convey our myriad concerns to policymakers.[48] Within the national government, interest groups attempt to exert influence directly on Congress, the bureaucracy, the courts, and the presidency. As we saw in chapter 3, presidents have responded to the growing influence of interest groups by assigning individual White House aides as liaisons to groups in policy areas such as civil rights, education, and health. Interest groups have also attempted to exert influence indirectly, principally by endorsing and making campaign contributions to presidential and congressional candidates and by urging their members to bring pressure to bear on the White House and on their representatives in Congress.

It is difficult to measure the effectiveness of interest group influence on public policy because of multiple points of access to government decision makers; numerous groups usually seek to influence a particular policy or set of related policies, and other powerful forces are also at work. Nevertheless, many observers believe that the growth in interest group activity since 1965 has contributed substantially to the rise in federal spending on domestic programs and the expansion of federal regulation into noneconomic areas, such as consumer protection, product safety, and occupational safety and health.[49] The demands of interest groups, often asserted as a matter of "right" and defended on grounds of fairness or improvement of quality of life, have strained the federal government's fiscal capacity and created societal conflicts.

Economist Mancur Olson has argued that societies with large numbers of powerful "distributional coalitions" (his term for interest groups) have experienced insupportably high public spending and little or no economic growth as a consequence of those groups' political influence. The groups press for public benefits for their members even though the result may be disadvantageous to the community as a whole. According to Olson, unless an interest group encompasses most of the population, there is "no constraint on the social cost such an organization will find it expedient to impose on the society in the cause of obtaining a larger share of the social output for itself."[50] To a substantial extent, domestic policy politics can become the pursuit of narrow group interests, even at the expense of the general public interest, which is usually unorganized, unarticulated, and difficult to identify or define. The president is better situated, in terms of political resources, than anyone else to define, enhance, and defend the public interest. That is the president's principal challenge in the domestic policy area. Harry Truman, echoing an argument heard since Theodore Roosevelt's presidency, was fond of saying his job was to act as a lobbyist for the American people, most of whom are unrepresented by lobbyists.

Separation of Powers and Federalism

The pattern of interest group activity traditionally has been described as **policy subgovernments**, mutually beneficial triangular relationships among interest groups, administrative agencies, and congressional subcommittees. Subgovernments, and the more open and amorphous issue networks that cut across and intersect with them, contribute to the fragmentation of power and influence in the domestic policy environment. That fragmentation is enhanced by constitutional arrangements dividing power among the government branches and between the national and state governments and by the internal structures of Congress and the federal bureaucracy. The constitutional design, which established a system of "separated institutions sharing powers," was created to prevent the abuse of power.[51]

The framers invented federalism as a means of resolving the seemingly intractable conflict between advocates of a consolidated system of government and the proponents of state sovereignty. Their ingenious compromise, which artfully avoided establishing a precise boundary between national and state powers, has been adapted to the needs of the times by successive generations of political leaders. The current system of federalism still leaves primary responsibility for most basic government services in the hands of the states and their local subdivisions. These services include public education; public health; public safety; and the construction and maintenance of streets, roads, and highways. The federal government has programs that help finance state and local activities in these and other areas, and it exerts a substantial degree of influence on them by virtue of its grant and regulatory programs. For example, even though the federal government provides only 8–9 percent of the funding spent nationally on kindergarten through twelfth grade public education, George W. Bush's administration and Congress imposed a common system of accountability on all states through the No Child Left Behind Act and gained compliance by threatening to withdraw federal funding from states that failed to meet federal regulations.[52] Still, most of the federal government's domestic policy activity does not entail direct federal administration.

Presidential leadership in domestic policy requires the president to work with Congress, federal administrators, and state and local officials. In these relationships, the president has limited power to command and must rely primarily on personal skills as a political leader—principally persuasion and bargaining—to achieve goals.

The structure of authority in Congress has varied over time, with a prevailing tendency toward fragmentation. The reforms of the early 1970s, while strengthening somewhat the majority party leadership in the House, provided individual members with extensive opportunities to influence policy.[53] Consequently, in the following decades Congress often found it difficult to give direction to public policy, and presidents encountered problems in their relations with Congress. Unlike their predecessors in the late 1950s and 1960s, presidents from the mid-1970s to the early 1990s could not easily negotiate agreements with top party leaders and with one or two influential chairs in each house and be confident those agreements would prevail in floor voting. Rather, the presidents had to deal separately, in each chamber, with several committee chairs, subcommittee chairs, and party leaders. Agreements reached at one stage in the legislative process often came undone later.

The congressional environment changed dramatically following the Republican takeover in 1994. In the House, the new majority leadership under Speaker Newt Gingrich, R-GA, imposed tight discipline on Republican members and committee chairs, all eager to implement a conservative policy revolution.[54] Party government, not seen since the first decade of the twentieth century, seemed to have returned, even though the new Senate predictably was less disciplined than the House. But Clinton repeatedly foiled plans for the conservative revolution, and even the election of George W. Bush in 2000 and the results of the 2002 midterm elections did not ensure a uniform Republican agenda. House Republicans, whipped by the heavy hand of Majority Leader Tom DeLay, remained generally supportive of the administration's goals, but the votes were sometimes costly.[55] Moreover, moderate Republicans in the Senate frequently clashed with the more ideologically unified House majority. The Democratic majority that took control of Congress in 2007 clashed repeatedly with President Bush, a prolonged conflict that kept the party relatively unified in both the House and the Senate. With substantial help from congressional party leaders Nancy Pelosi and Harry Reid, Obama's strategy kept congressional Democrats together during his first term, and they were essential to his success in getting Congress to support his initiatives. The administration allowed Congress to write the principal legislation pushed by the administration, giving them a hand in the final product and preventing the defections that dogged Presidents Carter and Clinton. But going into his second term, Obama could expect more Democrats to defect. Nor could Obama find an authoritative Republican bargaining partner. House Speaker Boehner lost control of his membership when a majority would not support his budget strategy in December 2012, and he later faced a coup organized by Tea Party Republicans who opposed his willingness to compromise. Similarly, twenty-five House Republicans voted for someone other than Boehner in January 2015 as they hoped to prevent the incumbent Speaker from winning a clear majority on the first ballot (the last time this happened was 1923) and force him to withdraw.[56] Paul Ryan (R-WI), Boehner's successor as Speaker, lost his first major legislative battle over health care in 2017 when moderate and conservative House Republicans could not find common ground. Ryan explained that this was evidence that the majority was still learning how to be a governing party rather than an opposition party.[57]

Congressional fragmentation has had mixed effects on the president's involvement in domestic policy. Congress has been unable to counterbalance the presidency by providing alternative policy leadership, but at the same time presidents have found it difficult to lead Congress. Congressional influence has been extensive, if only in a negative sense, because of its inertia and its ability to resist presidential direction. Yet that cuts both ways: When the president acts unilaterally, a divided Congress may find it hard to overturn that action.

Fragmentation of a different sort characterizes the federal bureaucracy. As noted in chapter 6, an independent power exists in the bureaucracy that is based in career civil servants, who constitute a permanent government. The members of the permanent government have professional and agency loyalties and close ties to the interest groups that constitute their clientele and to the congressional subcommittees with jurisdiction over their appropriations and the legislation that authorizes their programs. Subgovernments and issue networks comprise members of the permanent government and complicate presidential control of policy development and implementation in or by the bureaucracy. In addition, the fragmentation resulting from the size and complexity of the federal bureaucracy creates enormous problems of management and policy coordination for the president.

The Domestic Policy Apparatus

The need for presidential coordination in domestic policy has been recognized for some time. By developing a domestic policy staff apparatus in the EOP, it was hoped that presidents could provide the necessary level of coordination. The domestic policy staff evolved slowly, in conjunction with the development of the president's legislative role (see chapter 5). This evolutionary process relied initially on the Bureau of the Budget (BOB); eventually it saw the establishment of a separate staff to formulate and implement domestic policy.

BOB: Central Clearance and Legislative Program Planning

From the early nineteenth century until the creation of the BOB in 1921, the president's role in domestic policy formulation was ad hoc and unorganized.[58] In its first year of operation, the BOB established the requirement that all agency legislative proposals for the expenditure of federal funds had to be submitted to it before being sent to Congress. Any proposal the bureau determined not in accord with the president's financial program would not be sent forward to Congress. Moreover, agencies were to inform Congress if any pending legislation had been found not in accord. This procedure, known as central clearance, was expanded during Franklin Roosevelt's administration to cover the substantive content of proposed legislation and executive orders. Early on, **central clearance** was used to ensure that legislative proposals of various departments and agencies were compatible with the president's overall program goals.[59] Over time, it acquired additional functions, among them supervising and coordinating executive branch initiatives, providing a clear indication to congressional committees of the president's position on proposed legislation, and making various administrative units aware of one another's goals and activities.

Beginning in 1947, the BOB's domestic policy role expanded to include participation in the development of the president's annual legislative program.[60] The bureau's Legislative Reference Division worked directly with Truman's White House staff in reviewing agency recommendations and integrating them into a comprehensive legislative program. The additional responsibilities to formulate policy involved BOB personnel in the pursuit of the president's political goals. Dwight D. Eisenhower delegated even more power to the BOB. When he first took office in 1953, Ike was unprepared to send a legislative program to Congress. He was also less interested in domestic policy than Truman had been. He therefore relied heavily on the BOB to formulate a domestic program. The centralized clearance and planning processes lodged in the bureau were compatible with Eisenhower's penchant for systematic staff operations, so he continued to employ it as a clearinghouse for policy throughout his presidency. By 1960, annual submissions to the BOB of legislative proposals by departments and agencies were commonplace. The result was a highly routinized process nearly impervious to outside ideas. This system suited Eisenhower and his limited interest in domestic policy initiatives. It did not suit Kennedy or Johnson, both of whom placed a high priority on domestic policy. To overcome the rigidities and bureaucratic domination of the BOB-based program planning process, JFK and LBJ sought ideas and suggestions from nongovernment sources.[61]

Task Forces and Study Commissions

The mechanism used by Kennedy and Johnson for gathering policy advice was the task force, a group consisting of experts from inside and outside the government. Before his inauguration, Kennedy appointed several such groups to advise him on the major issues and problems the new administration would be facing. The reports of these task forces, and of a number of others appointed after he took office, provided the basis for much of Kennedy's New Frontier program.[62] Although Kennedy remained eager for new ideas and suggestions, he did not rely exclusively on outside sources of advice after the initial round of task forces. Instead he turned primarily to his cabinet for suggestions.

In spring 1964, President Johnson appointed task forces with the specific mission of developing a distinctive program for his administration. They were made up of outsiders and operated in secret. Johnson was so pleased with their reports, which furnished much of the form and substance of his Great Society program, that he made task forces a regular part of his program development process. The White House staff coordinated task force operations, and the BOB integrated the proposals into the annual legislative program. Johnson favored the task force process because it largely avoided the ordeal of bargaining with departments and agencies and because it was not adulterated by bureaucratic, congressional, and interest group pressures.[63]

The presidents who followed Johnson made little use of task forces. Instead, they developed larger White House policy staffs and relied on more formal advisory bodies, such as commissions and White House conferences, to study issues and problems and to gather outside recommendations. Presidential commissions are broadly representative bodies often appointed to defuse highly sensitive issues. In September 1981, for example, President Reagan appointed the National Commission on Social Security Reform to develop a solution to a Social Security funding crisis. Although the commission did not solve the problem, it provided "cover" under which the principals, Reagan and House Speaker Thomas P. O'Neill, D-MA, could work out a compromise.[64] As one of his first official actions, President Clinton appointed the Task Force on National Health Care Reform to develop the administration's proposed legislation within one hundred days.[65] Headed by the first lady, Hillary Rodham Clinton, and the senior adviser for policy development, Ira Magaziner, the task force consisted of five hundred experts from inside and outside government who divided themselves into thirty-four groups and operated secretly. The unprecedented size, the cumbersome secret process, and Hillary Clinton's role made the task force a target for criticism well before it had finished its work. The delay in developing the proposal postponed congressional consideration of it until 1994, when it got caught up in election-year politics. The proposal's "complexity, high cost, and obtrusive bureaucracy made it an easy target for Republicans" and contributed to the failure of Congress to enact it.[66]

Shortly after assuming office, President George W. Bush asked Vice President Cheney to chair the National Energy Policy Development Group, a task force charged with developing a new national energy policy. Learning from the Clinton example, the group was kept small and simple—a six-person staff that wrote a 170-page report, far shorter than Clinton's 1,350-page product.[67] Like the Clinton effort, however, the task force became controversial: Its recommendations were considered highly favorable to the energy industry, and the White House refused to release information on the commission's membership and its meetings with industry leaders and groups. Court decisions blocked the release of that information to environmental groups and Congress. Shortly after taking office, President Obama formed a task force on helping the middle class and announced new initiatives for cities, women and girls, and science and technology policy. All of these areas drew heavily for advice on sources outside the government.

Because their membership seeks broad representation and tries to obtain consensus, presidential commissions often issue reports that blur critical issues. Commissions may also make findings and suggestions that embarrass the president, as did the 1970 Scranton Commission report, which blamed campus unrest on President Nixon. Obama created the National Commission on Fiscal Responsibility and Reform to craft a bipartisan strategy to control the nation's long-run budget and debt problems. However, the commission's members were unable to agree on a final report in December 2010, previewing the partisan discord that plagued Washington leading up to the 2012 elections.

White House conferences bring together groups of experts and distinguished citizens for public forums held under presidential auspices. Their principal function is to build support among experts, political leaders, and relevant interests for presidential leadership to deal with the problems at issue. Neither White House conferences nor presidential commissions have served as the basis for major legislative proposals, but they have given legitimacy to certain presidential undertakings.

As the Clinton and Bush cases suggest, task forces, because they are more closed and focused on presidential priorities, are likely to produce controversy about their content and process.

Domestic Policy Staffs

Nixon, Ford, and Carter Administrations. Since Johnson, presidents have used domestic policy staffs in the EOP and a politicized Office of Management and Budget (OMB)—the new name for BOB—to develop legislative programs. Nixon established the Domestic Council in 1970 as part of a broader reorganization of the presidency that also revamped BOB into OMB. The Domestic Council comprised the president; the vice president; the attorney general; and the secretaries of agriculture, commerce, housing and urban development, interior, labor, transportation, Treasury, and health, education and welfare, as well as the director and deputy director of OMB. The council was to be a top-level forum for discussion, debate, and determination of policy analogous to the National Security Council (NSC). (See chapter 10.) Like the NSC, the Domestic Council had a staff of professionals and support personnel. Headed by John Ehrlichman, the presidential assistant for domestic policy, the staff dominated Nixon's domestic policymaking process during the last two years of his first term (1971–1972).[68]

The council's working groups prepared options papers for the president, evaluated departmental proposals for legislation, and participated in drafting presidential messages to Congress and preparing supportive materials for specific legislative proposals. In addition to assisting the president in formulating policy proposals, the Domestic Council advocated, monitored, and evaluated policy.[69] This arrangement, in effect, made Ehrlichman the president's general agent for domestic policy. Under him, the council centralized control over domestic policy in the White House. The president's interests, as defined and expressed by Ehrlichman, took precedence over the interests of departments and agencies, as conveyed by cabinet members and agency heads.

The council's domination of domestic policy did not survive Ehrlichman's departure from the White House in April 1973.[70] The influence of the staff was clearly a function of Ehrlichman's status with the president. Under Ehrlichman's successor, Kenneth Cole, the Domestic Council became more of a service unit, and OMB resumed many of the functions of planning legislative programs.

In addition to the development of a presidential staff for domestic policy, Nixon effected a major transformation in OMB by expanding its management staff and by adding a layer of political appointees above OMB's career staff. The OMB director became indistinguishable from other high-level presidential assistants. Nixon's politicization of OMB sparked considerable debate; though the agency had always been responsive to presidential needs, critics argued these developments reduced its ability to serve the institutional needs of the presidency as an impartial professional staff agency.[71]

President Ford used OMB to facilitate the unusual transfer of power from Nixon to himself after Nixon's resignation, and Ford then relied on it to help plan and coordinate programs in a more traditional and less partisan manner than Nixon had. Initially, Ford intended to give the Domestic Council a major planning role by making Vice President Nelson Rockefeller its chair, but Rockefeller never became Ford's general agent for domestic policy. The long delay in congressional confirmation of Rockefeller's appointment and his conflict with White House chief of staff Donald Rumsfeld appear to have prevented such a development.[72] Ford preferred advice from a wide range of sources and seldom used the Domestic Council for policy planning.[73] President Carter abolished the council shortly after taking office, but he retained a domestic policy staff headed by one of his top aides, Stuart Eizenstat. In some respects, Eizenstat and his staff acquired a policymaking role resembling that of Ehrlichman and the Domestic Council in the Nixon administration. But Eizenstat and his staff members did not dominate the domestic policy process, and they functioned more in the roles of "effective administrator and of contributing advisor."[74]

Reagan and George H. W. Bush Administrations. Ronald Reagan, who came to office with a set, ideologically defined policy agenda, created a new policy apparatus. The principal units were OMB, the Office of Policy Development (OPD), and seven cabinet councils. OMB's domestic policy involvement was especially crucial during Reagan's first year in office (1981), when the prime objective of drastically reducing the role of the federal government was linked to a budget reduction strategy implemented through use of the congressional budget process (see chapter 9). OMB director David Stockman was the principal architect of the first substantial rollback of the government's domestic programs since the New Deal.

The OPD, the Reagan administration's equivalent of Carter's domestic policy staff, worked through cabinet councils that had jurisdiction over economic affairs, commerce and trade, human resources, natural resources and environment, food and agriculture, legal policy, and management and administration.[75] The councils' members included appropriate cabinet and subcabinet officers and OMB personnel and the White House staff. Each council had a secretariat composed of department and agency representatives and used working groups to provide expertise and analyze issues. The cabinet council system did not, however, become the directing force for domestic policy. Other factors, particularly the president's long-range objectives and budget pressures, determined the agenda from the administration's beginning. Reagan's domestic policy apparatus worked out "details secondary to the president's fixed view of government,"[76] and its influence declined in his second term. Donald Regan, the newly appointed White House chief of staff, moved quickly to bring the three major policy areas—(1) economics, (2) national security, and (3) domestic policy—under his control. Because the two remaining cabinet councils were chaired by Edwin Meese and James Baker, former White House advisers to the president, they enjoyed substantial autonomy to pursue their own policy projects, such as the major tax reform passed in 1986. Mostly, the administration's orientation shifted from changing policies to defending them. Having accomplished most of his initial domestic agenda, principally curtailment of the growth of federal agencies and a reduction in spending on them, Reagan concentrated his energies on national security and economic policy objectives.

The same situation continued under George H. W. Bush.[77] The assistant to the president for economic and domestic affairs, Roger Porter, a once and future Harvard professor, directed the OPD. The OPD and the White House Office of Cabinet Affairs provided staff support for the Domestic Policy Council (DPC) and the Economic Policy Council. Major issues usually bypassed the cabinet council system and were resolved by White House chief of staff John Sununu or the budget director, Richard Darman. Sununu's self-defined role was to protect the conservative integrity of the administration against those who urged the president to pursue more politically pragmatic options, and Darman functioned as a nonideological guardian of the budget and advocate of economic growth. Both intervened frequently on low-level issues, and Darman had a key role in the 1990 budget summit with legislative leaders. Some cabinet members, such as Secretary of Housing and Urban Development Jack Kemp and Secretary of Transportation Samuel Skinner, however, took the lead in developing major domestic legislative proposals and pushing them in Congress.[78]

Clinton Administration. The domestic policy process during the first two years of the Clinton administration was frequently frenetic and uncoordinated.[79] The DPC did not meet regularly. Development of health care reform—the principal initiative—was the responsibility of the large task force headed by Hillary Clinton and Magaziner. Cabinet members, such as Health and Human Services secretary Donna Shalala, did not play major roles in developing initiatives.

Although formally lodged in a policy council chaired by a high-level presidential assistant, the policy process was operationally centered in the president himself. Clinton, with his deep interest in domestic policy, presided over numerous wide-ranging and intensive meetings with his advisers that shifted back and forth between various policy alternatives. No single individual, such as the chief of staff, or group comparable to Reagan's Legislative Strategy Group was responsible for resolving disputes, imparting coherence and practicality to the many proposals, and moving them to Congress in a timely manner. Clinton resisted delegating such authority, and despite his intellectual brilliance and energy, he was unable to "ringmaster" the domestic policy process effectively on his own.[80]

The situation changed dramatically after the Republicans won majorities in both congressional houses in the 1994 midterm elections. (Republicans had controlled the Senate as recently as 1986, but they had not led the House since 1954.) The new Republican majority largely controlled policymaking through most of 1995, and for a time the "Republican revolution" seemed to live up to its name.[81] Then came the notorious budget battle of 1995–1996, when Republicans pushed for sharp cuts in entitlement programs. President Clinton reasserted himself, exercised his first veto in response to the proposed cuts, and rallied opposition to the Republican plan. House Speaker Newt Gingrich refused to compromise, and the stalemate led to government shutdowns, which the public blamed on the Republicans. In the end, Clinton won the political battle.

Paul J. Quirk and William Cunion noted that the government shutdowns led to a new phase of Clinton's domestic presidency. It began in January 1996 and ran through the eruption of the Monica Lewinsky scandal in January 1998. It was marked by an unusual degree of cooperation between Clinton and the Republican majority in Congress, leading to a "notable amount of significant legislation," including a major overhaul of the welfare system.[82] With the help of political strategist Dick Morris, Clinton followed a centrist strategy of "triangulation" and finally seemed to master the art of domestic policymaking. But cooperation and policy output came to a halt in 1998 and 1999 with the Lewinsky scandal and Clinton's impeachment.

In contrast to Clinton's frenetic style, George W. Bush's domestic policy process was highly structured. Bush, unlike any of his predecessors, came to office with a master's degree in business administration (from Harvard Business School). He surrounded himself with high-level advisers with experience not only in government but also as chief executive officers of major businesses. The strength of this business model was its efficiency; Bush insisted on a highly disciplined staff. He was comfortable working with a strong team of advisers, and he proved willing to delegate decision making. Yet he was also willing to assert control.[83]

George W. Bush Administration. Domestic policy seemed to be secondary in the Bush administration. Bush's DPC attracted far less attention than the NSC, its foreign policy counterpart, where policies on terrorism and Iraq were hammered out. Indeed, the Domestic Policy Council's profile was so low that for a period it was unclear who the director of the council was.[84] John Bridgeland and Jay Lefkowitz were variously described in the media as the director, whereas other accounts identified Margaret L. Spellings (secretary of education in Bush's second term) as the director and the others as her deputies.[85] There is little doubt that Spellings, as director of the OPD, supervised the others.[86]

In the view of one insider, it made little difference who headed the council. Domestic policy was dominated by the dictates of domestic politics, and that was the preserve of Karl Rove, the president's principal political adviser and head of the White House Office of Strategic Initiatives.[87] Ron Suskind, quoting extensively from off-the-record interviews and a long exchange with the original director of the Office of Faith-Based and Community Initiatives, John DiIulio—which DiIulio later disavowed—described the Bush White House as evidencing little serious discussion of domestic policy matters. (In the second term, Rove was formally given responsibility for coordinating policy.) Karl Zinsmeister became the Domestic Policy Council's director in June 2006 after his predecessor, Claude A. Allen, was charged with "stealing more than $5,000 in a phony refund scheme" from retail stores.[88] Zinsmeister was best known for his outspoken defense of the administration's Iraq policy, further testimony to the short shrift the administration gave to domestic policy.

Obama Administration. Like its predecessors, the Obama administration established procedures to coordinate policymaking. Melody Barnes, the campaign's domestic policy adviser and a former staffer to Sen. Ted Kennedy, D-MA, was named to head the DPC. She had staff experience in both the House and the Senate and had worked at the Center for American Progress, a think tank for progressive Democrats, before joining the campaign. Her expertise centered on civil rights and voting rights, women's health, and religious liberties.[89] But there were many higher profile advisers located in the White House, especially Obama confidante Valerie Jarrett, who oversaw the Office of Public Engagement, and the series of staffers coordinating specific policy areas across departments and agencies, dubbed "policy czars" by the media. For example, there were czars for health care reform (Nancy-Ann DeParle), auto industry restructuring (Steven Rattner, Ron Bloom), energy (Carol Browner), urban affairs (Adolfo Carrion), executive pay (Ken Feinberg), drugs (Gil Kerlikowske), economic recovery (Paul Volcker), green jobs (Van Jones), and other areas. Both Democratic and Republican legislators charged that heavy reliance on aides outside the usual purview of congressional oversight was troubling or even unconstitutional.[90]

Indeed, Barnes was overshadowed during the first two years of the administration when the emphasis was on the economy and health care. Her staff included specialists on AIDS policy, disability policies, and social innovation, low-profile issues compared with the rest of the agenda. With virtually no hope of future legislative successes, the Obama administration shook up its organization and turned to other issues in 2011. Barnes and the DPC benefited from the changes. The Office of Health Reform was dissolved; its responsibilities absorbed by the DPC; and DeParle, its director, became a deputy chief of staff. Similarly, the staff of the Office of Energy and Climate Change Policy moved to the DPC when Carol Browner left the administration in spring 2011 after Congress failed to adopt cap-and-trade legislation.[91] The DPC played a greater role as the policy agenda shifted prior to the 2012 election. Education rose in importance, as did immigration, an area where legislation had stalled. Barnes left the administration early in 2012, succeeded by Cecilia Muñoz, the director of intergovernmental affairs and the lead adviser on immigration reform following a long career as an advocate for immigration rights. Muñoz, the daughter of immigrants from Bolivia, was at the center of the controversial presidential decision to delay deportation of perhaps as many as 5 million of the estimated 11 million undocumented immigrants in the nation who are parents of U.S. citizens or parents of lawful permanent residents. The Office of Legal Counsel in the Justice Department, working with the Department of Homeland Security, not the DPC, decided who would be eligible for this delayed action.[92] Nor was immigration the only controversial area of DPC action: The council was also tasked with developing a rating system for colleges to help potential students know "What am I getting for my dollars?" The system was supposed to compete with the widely used ratings provided by *U.S. News and World Report.*[93]

Trump Administration. The President named Andrew Bremberg, a former member of Mitch McConnell's senate staff and a veteran of HHS, as director of the Domestic Policy Council. He had served during the 2016 Republican convention as policy director for the party platform, making him a close co-worker of Reince Priebus, Trump's chief of staff, who had previously been chair of the Republican

National Committee. Within the White House organization, however, Bremberg officially would report to Stephen Miller, who held the title of Senior Advisor to the President for Policy. During the presidential campaign, Miller preceded Trump at major rallies, warming up the crowd for his boss. He joined the campaign after serving several years as director of communications for future attorney general Jeff Sessions's senate staff, best known for heading the effort to torpedo immigration reform.[94] Miller would work closely with Stephen K. Bannon, chief strategist and senior adviser in the Trump White House, who was widely viewed as the person responsible for keeping the administration focused on fulfilling Trump's campaign promises, commitments the "two Steves" had worked so hard to fashion. Bannon served as Trump's third campaign manager, taking a leave of absence as executive director of Breitbart News.[95] There is every reason to believe that Miller and Bannon, who crafted the administration's initial strategy centered on the use of executive orders, would be the real forces on Trump domestic policy, not Bremberg. There was one other White House contender to guide domestic policy, Jared Kushner. Trump's son-in-law was tasked with overhauling technology and workforce training for the federal government and with helping to fulfill Trump campaign pledges to reduce opioid addiction, improve veteran health care, and rebuild national infrastructure.[96] There could be too many cooks in this kitchen.

Conclusion: Providing Policy Leadership

Presidents approach the task of making domestic policy with varying political resources and differing policy opportunities. Their domestic policy leadership depends to a large extent on their effectiveness in using the available resources to exploit existing opportunities and create new ones. They are most apt to succeed when the three components of the policy stream—(1) problems, (2) solutions, and (3) politics—converge. A president's ability to bring these three tributary streams together is one indication of effective policy leadership.

Successful policy leadership requires presidents to spend their resources carefully and exploit opportunities skillfully. To do so they must pay particular attention to four strategic factors: (1) goals, (2) priorities, (3) timing, and (4) costs and benefits.

Modest, flexible *goals* usually are easier to achieve than those that are extensive and ideologically derived. So, too, are goals that enjoy substantial support among the public and policymaking elites. In establishing their goals, presidents take such considerations into account, along with their own values and beliefs. A primarily pragmatic set of objectives tends to be easier to accomplish than one ideologically derived. Such aims are less likely, however, to have an impact on society than more visionary and comprehensive objectives. In some circumstances, ideological goals may be highly appropriate. For example, Ronald Reagan initially struck a responsive note in Congress and the public with his unabashedly conservative domestic program. Presidents are free to be as pragmatic or as ideological as they wish in establishing their goals. However they decide, the mix they choose affects their policy leadership.

Closely related to goals, *priorities* also affect policy leadership. Presidents who clearly define their priorities generally have been more successful than those who have not done so because the policy process can handle only a few major issues at a time, even though many contend for attention. If a president does not indicate preferences, other participants will pursue their own objectives, possibly to the detriment of the president's. Nor is it realistic for presidents to expect that all of their goals will receive consideration to the exclusion of those of other participants. In this respect, a comparison between Carter and Reagan is instructive. Carter developed a lengthy domestic agenda and insisted that all of his goals were vitally important to the nation and deserving of enactment. Congress responded by taking its time in dealing with Carter's program and by pursuing many of its own objectives. Some of Carter's wishes, such as welfare reform and national health insurance, were never adopted; others, such as a national energy policy, were passed in greatly modified form after extensive delay and bargaining. Many congressional Democrats complained that Carter failed to provide them with direction and guidance for his domestic proposals. In contrast, Reagan made his priorities clear from the beginning and continued to do so. Congress had little doubt about which goals Reagan considered vital—and on which he would spend political capital—and which were less important to him. Cutting domestic spending, strengthening national defense, and reducing and reforming taxes took precedence over balancing the federal budget, ending legalized abortion, and restoring school prayer.

Timing, the third strategic consideration in successful policy leadership, is crucial to effective exploitation of opportunities. If opportunities are missed, they may be lost indefinitely. Good timing also involves taking advantage of the regular policy and electoral cycles. Proposals submitted at appropriate times in those cycles have greater likelihood of adoption. Proposals also can be withheld until conditions are ripe for their submission. A proposal with limited support can be moved to the top of the agenda and pushed successfully as the result of a focusing event such as a disaster or a crisis. Presidents able to time the presentation of proposals to coincide with favorable events and conditions are more likely to be effective policy leaders than those lacking such a sense of timing. Two presidents with effective timing of domestic proposals were Franklin Roosevelt, during the first one hundred days of the New Deal when the Great Depression provided the rationale for a comprehensive set of economic recovery and reform laws, and Lyndon Johnson, who in early 1964 used the shock of the Kennedy assassination to secure passage of the Civil Rights Act. In contrast, Bill Clinton's poor timing of his health care reform and initial welfare reform proposals contributed to their failure.

Finally, successful policy leadership requires presidents to be attentive to the *costs and benefits* of raising problems for consideration and posing solutions. As presidents decide which problems and issues to emphasize, they focus on political benefits. They select agenda items according to the prospective electoral, historical, and programmatic benefits of the times.[97] When presidents select solutions for problems they are addressing, their emphasis is on costs.[98] Political costs, assessed in terms of congressional, electoral, bureaucratic, and interest group support, enter presidential calculations at each stage of the process, and presidents and other actors have tended to view political costs in terms of avoiding blame and claiming credit for the outcomes, a pattern already visible in the 1980s and even more prominent in the decades that followed.[99]

Economic costs sharply limit the policy alternatives. Budget pressures force presidents to make hard choices, such as whether to support new programs and which existing programs to emphasize, maintain, or reduce. Technical costs and questions of workability also enter the selection of policy alternatives.

No prescription or formula can guarantee that a president will provide successful domestic policy leadership, in part because some problems are very difficult to solve, or solutions do not exist. Another reason for the absence of a workable formula is that conditions change constantly. Some problems may be solved only to reemerge in a new form; others may decline in importance. Solutions viable today may not be a few years hence, or solutions may have unanticipated consequences that become problems in their own right. Political conditions, such as the popular mood or control of Congress, are in flux, so strategies may have to be modified frequently. Because many of the requirements of successful policy leadership are not fixed, what worked well for one president may be only partially useful to those who come later.

Even presidents who take office committed to concentrating their energies on domestic policy encounter extensive frustrations. They may enjoy some initial successes—as did Reagan—but the difficulties of accomplishing additional objectives eventually increase, and the sharing of power with Congress, the bureaucracy, and organized interests becomes ever more burdensome. The natural tendency is for presidents to turn their attention to national security or economic policy. In these areas, the challenges are more immediately threatening to the general welfare; the constraints on a president's ability to act, although very real, are not as frustrating; and successful policy leadership appears less elusive. Presidential difficulties in achieving domestic policy progress have mounted so rapidly that Paul Light, a long time student of presidential policy making, wondered aloud at the end of the Clinton years "whether the presidency as an institution is properly configured for making domestic policy."[100] Taking a long-term look, he found that as the organizational capacity to make policy grew, the actual product—the number of proposals and their scope—declined.

Suggested Readings

Ainsworth, Scott H. *Analyzing Interest Groups: Group Influence on People and Policies.* New York: Norton, 2002.

Baumgartner, Frank R., and Byron D. Jones. *Agendas and Instability in American Politics.* Chicago: University of Chicago Press, 1993.

Kessel, John H. *Presidents, the Presidency, and the Political Environment.* Washington, DC: CQ Press, 2001.

Kingdon, John W. *Agendas, Alternatives, and Public Policies,* 2nd ed. New York: Longman, 2003.

Lammers, William W., and Michael A. Genovese. *The Presidency and Domestic Policy: Comparing Leadership Styles, FDR to Clinton.* Washington, DC: CQ Press, 2000.

Light, Paul C. *The President's Agenda: Domestic Policy Choice from Kennedy to Clinton,* 3rd ed. Baltimore: Johns Hopkins University Press, 1999.

Rudalevige, Andrew. *Managing the President's Program: Presidential Leadership and Legislative Policy Formulation.* Princeton, NJ: Princeton University Press, 2002.

Shull, Steven A. *American Civil Rights Policy from Truman to Clinton: The Role of Presidential Leadership.* Armonk, NY: M. E. Sharpe, 1999.

Warshaw, Shirley Anne. *The Domestic Presidency: Policy Making in the White House.* Boston: Allyn and Bacon, 1996.

Notes

1. The concept of "issue congestion" was developed by Hugh Heclo, "One Executive Branch or Many?" in *Both Ends of the Avenue,* ed. Anthony King (Washington, DC: American Enterprise Institute, 1983), 26–58.

2. Theodore J. Lowi, "American Business, Public Policy, Case Studies, and Political Theory," *World Politics* (July 1964): 677–715.

3. Steven A. Shull, *Domestic Policy Formation: Presidential-Congressional Partnership?* (Westport, CT: Greenwood Press, 1983), 155; and Steven A. Shull, "Change in Presidential Policy Initiatives," *Western Political Quarterly* (September 1983): 497.

4. John H. Kessel, *Presidential Parties* (Homewood, IL: Dorsey, 1984), 112–115.

5. Obama said that this was business carried over from the previous year and that henceforth he would reject them. His explanation opened him up to criticisms of having a double standard. J. Newton-Small and Michael Scherer, "Does Obama Have a Double-Standard on Earmarks?" *Time,* February 26, 2009, www.time.com/time/politics/article/0,8599,1881855,00.html.

6. See Steven Brill, *America's Bitter Pill: Money, Politics, Back-Room Deals, and the Fight to Fix Our Broken Health Care System* (New York: Random House, 2015).

7. Mark A. Peterson, "It Was a Different Time: Obama and the Unique Opportunity for Health Care Reform," *Journal of Health Politics, Policy and Law* 36:3 (2011): 435.

8. Jacob S. Hacker, "The Road to Somewhere: Why Health Reform Happened or Why Political Scientists Who Write about Public Policy Shouldn't Assume They Know How to Shape It," *Perspectives on Politics* 8:3 (September 2010): 865.

9. James A. Morone, "Big Ideas, Broken Institutions, and the Wrath at the Grass Roots," *Journal of Health Politics, Policy and Law* 36:3 (2011): 375–385.

10. Brill, *America's Bitter Pill.*

11. Jeffrey Toobin, "Obama's Game of Chicken with the Supreme Court," *New Yorker,* May 21, 2015, www.newyorker.com/news/daily-comment/obamas-game-of-chicken-with-the-supreme-court.

12. Adam Liptak, "Supreme Court Allows Nationwide Health Care Subsidies," *New York Times,* June 26, 2015, www.nytimes.com/2015/06/26/us/obamacare-supreme-court.html?emc=edit_th_20150626&nl=todaysheadlines&nlid=69310600&_r=0; Henry J. Aaron, "*King v. Burwell*: Chalk One Up for Common Sense," *Health 360 Brookings Blog,* June 26, 2015, www.brookings.edu/blogs/health360/posts/2015/06/25-king-v-burwell-decision-common-sense-aaron.

13. Elise Viebeck, "House GOP Can Pursue Part of Health Care Lawsuit, Judge Rules," *Washington Post,* September 10, 2015.

14. Jason D. Mycoff and Joseph A. Pika, *Confrontation and Compromise: Presidential and Congressional Leadership, 2001–2006* (Lanham, MD: Rowman and Littlefield, 2007), chap. 7.

15. Kessel, *Presidential Parties,* 68–69.

16. The policy-stream metaphor borrows from Paul Light, "The Presidential Policy Stream," in *The Presidency and the Political System,* ed. Michael Nelson (Washington, DC: CQ Press, 1984), 423–448; and John W. Kingdon, *Agendas, Alternatives, and Public Policies,* 2nd ed. (New York: HarperCollins, 1995), 85–86.

17. This discussion follows Kingdon, *Agendas,* chap. 5.

18. Christopher H. Foreman Jr., "The Braking of the President: Shifting Context and the Bush Domestic Agenda," in *The George W. Bush Legacy,* ed. Colin Campbell, Bert A. Rockman, and Andrew Rudalevige (Washington, DC: CQ Press, 2007), 267.

19. The discussion of the development of the health care issue follows B. Guy Peters, *American Public Policy: Promise and Performance,* 3rd ed. (Chatham, NJ: Chatham House, 1993), 230–235. Also see David Blumenthal and James Morone, *The Heart of Power: Health and Politics in the Oval Office* (Berkeley, CA: University of California Press, 2009).

20. Robin Toner, "2008 Candidates Vow to Overhaul U.S. Health Care," *New York Times,* July 6, 2007, www.nytimes.com/2007/07/06/us/politics/06health.html?ex=1186113600&en=2fafcafdf4fa57ca&ei=5070.

21. Congressional Budget Office, "Updated Estimates of the Effects of the Insurance Coverage Provisions of the Affordable Care Act, April 2014," cbo.gov/sites/default/files/cbofiles/attachments/45231-ACA_Estimates.pdf.

22. Paul Light, *The President's Agenda: Domestic Policy Choice from Kennedy to Reagan,* 3rd ed. (Baltimore, MD: Johns Hopkins University Press, 1991), chap. 3; and Light, "The Presidential Policy Stream," 427–428.

23. Ironically, Nixon's preoccupation with the judgment of history helped cut short his presidency. He consistently explained the installation of the secret taping system in the Oval Office as motivated by his desire to have a complete and accurate record for use by historians. That taped record provided the "smoking gun" that led the House Judiciary Committee to vote impeachment charges, which prompted his resignation in August 1974.

24. Kingdon, *Agendas,* 142–143.

25. Jeff Fishel, *Presidents and Promises: From Campaign Pledge to Presidential Performance* (Washington, DC: CQ Press, 1984).

26. Kingdon, *Agendas,* 131.

27. Vincent J. Burke and Vee Burke, *Nixon's Good Deed: Welfare Reform* (New York: Columbia University Press, 1974); and Laurence E. Lynn Jr. and David D. Whitman, *The President as Policymaker: Jimmy Carter and Welfare Reform* (Philadelphia: Temple University Press, 1981).

28. This discussion is based on Kingdon, *Agendas,* chap. 7.

29. Coral Davenport and Julie Hirschfield Davis, "Move to Fight Obama's Climate Plan Started Early," *New York Times,* August 3, 2015, www.nytimes.com/2015/08/04/us/obama-unveils-plan-to-sharply-limit-greenhouse-gas-emissions.html?_r=0.

30. Democrats maintained united government from 1977 through 1980, 1993 to 1994, and again from 2009 through 2010. Republicans maintained united government from the 2002 midterm elections through the 2006 elections.

31. Jeff Yates and Andrew Whitford, "Institutional Foundations of the President's Issue Agenda," *Political Research Quarterly* 58 (December 2005): 577–585.

32. Matthew Eshbaugh-Soha, "The Politics of Presidential Agendas," *Political Research Quarterly* 58 (June 2005): 257–268.

33. Foreman, "The Braking of the President," 282.

34. This discussion follows Light, "The Presidential Policy Stream," 440–446.

35. Paul J. Quirk and Joseph Hinchcliffe, "Domestic Policy: The Trials of a Centrist Democrat," in *The Clinton Presidency: First Appraisals,* ed. Colin Campbell and Bert A. Rockman (Chatham, NJ: Chatham House, 1996), 264–267.

36. David W. Moore, "Initial Job Approval for Bush at 57 Percent, but Highest Disapproval of Any President since Polling Began," Gallup Poll release, February 6, 2001, www.gallup.com.

37. Quoted in Ron Fournier, "Bush's Test: To Unite the Great Divide," *Pittsburgh Post-Gazette,* January 21, 2001, A9.

38. Transcript, Bush press conference, November 4, 2004, www.nytimes.com/2004/11/04/politics/04BUSHTRANS.html.

39. Gary C. Jacobson, *A Divider, Not a Uniter: George W. Bush and the American People* (New York: Longman, 2006).

40. Arnie Seipel, "Fact Check: Trump Falsely Claims a 'Massive Landslide Victory,'" *NPR* (December 11, 2016), http://www.npr.org/2016/12/11/505182622/fact-check-trump-claims-a-massive-landslide-victory-but-history-differs.

41. Light, "The Presidential Policy Stream," 444–445.

42. Kingdon, *Agendas,* 194–195.

43. Kessel, *Presidential Parties,* 60.

44. Rebecca Adams, "Lame Duck or Leap Frog?" *CQ Weekly,* February 12, 2007, 450.

45. Peter Baker, "Obama Making Plans to Use Executive Power," *New York Times,* February 12, 2010.

46. Department of Education press release, "Obama Administration Proceeds with Reform of No Child Left Behind Following Congressional Inaction," August 8, 2011, www.ed.gov/news/press-releases/obama-administration-proceeds-reform-no-child-left-behind-following-congressiona; and Rebecca Kaplan, "Education Department Moving Forward on NCLB Waivers for States," *National Journal,* August 8, 2011.

47. Light, *The President's Agenda,* 36–38.

48. For an excellent account of interest groups, see Scott H. Ainsworth, *Analyzing Interest Groups: Group Influence on People and Policies* (New York: Norton, 2002).

49. Harold Wolman and Fred Teitelbaum, "Interest Groups and the Reagan Presidency," in *The Reagan Presidency and the Governing of America,* ed. Lester M. Salamon and Michael S. Lund (Washington, DC: Urban Institute Press, 1985), 299–301.

50. Mancur Olson, *The Rise and Decline of Nations* (New Haven, CT: Yale University Press, 1982), 44.

51. Richard E. Neustadt, *Presidential Power and the Modern Presidents: The Politics of Leadership from Roosevelt to Reagan* (New York: Free Press, 1990), 29.

52. Mycoff and Pika, *Confrontation and Compromise,* chap. 2.

53. Leroy Rieselbach, *Congressional Reform: The Changing Modern Congress* (Washington, DC: CQ Press, 1994); and Roger H. Davidson, ed., *The Postreform Congress* (New York: St. Martin's Press, 1992).

54. Donna Cassata, "Republicans Bask in Success of Rousing Performance," *Congressional Quarterly Weekly Report,* April 8, 1995, 986, 988, 990; Jennifer Babson, "Armey Stood Guard over Contract," *Congressional Quarterly Weekly Report,* April 8, 1995, 987; and Adam Clymer, "House Party: With Political Discipline It Works Like Parliament," *New York Times,* August 6, 1995, E6.

55. The Republicans angered Democrats by holding open the vote on the Medicare prescription drug bill for nearly three hours rather than the usual fifteen minutes to secure the requisite number of votes.

56. Aaron Blake, "John Boehner Just Endured the Biggest Revolt against a House Speaker in More Than 150 Years," *Washington Post,* January 6, 2015, www.washingtonpost.com/blogs/the-fix/wp/2015/01/06/boehner-could-face-biggest-speaker-defection-since-1923/.

57. MJ Lee, "What's next for Paul Ryan?" *CNN* (March 24, 2017) http://www.cnn.com/2017/03/24/politics/paul-ryan-health-care/index.html

58. Lester M. Salamon, "The Presidency and Domestic Policy Formulation," in *The Illusion of Presidential Government,* ed. Hugh Heclo and Lester M. Salamon (Boulder, CO: Westview Press, 1981), 179.

59. Richard E. Neustadt, "The Presidency and Legislation: The Growth of Central Clearance," *American Political Science Review* (September 1954): 641–670; and Robert S. Gilmour, "Central Clearance: A Revised Perspective," *Public Administration Review* (March–April 1971): 150–158.

60. Richard E. Neustadt, "The Presidency and Legislation: Planning the President's Program," *American Political Science Review* (December 1955): 980–1018; Larry Berman, *The Office of Management and Budget and the Presidency* (Princeton, NJ: Princeton University Press, 1979), 42–43; and Stephen J. Wayne, *The Legislative Presidency* (New York: Harper and Row, 1978), 103–105.

61. Norman C. Thomas and Harold L. Wolman, "The Presidency and Policy Formation: The Task Force Device," *Public Administration Review* (September–October 1969): 459–471.

62. Text of the reports were published in *New Frontiers of the Kennedy Administration* (Washington, DC: Public Affairs Press, 1961).

63. Lyndon B. Johnson, *The Vantage Point* (New York: Holt, Rinehart and Winston, 1971), 326.

64. Paul Light, *Artful Work: The Politics of Social Security Reform* (New York: Random House, 1985), 232.

65. Quirk and Hinchcliffe, "Domestic Policy," 274–275.

66. Ibid., 275.

67. Michael Abramowitz and Steven Mufson, "Papers Detail Industry's Role in Cheney's Energy Report," *Washington Post,* July 18, 2007, A1.

68. Raymond J. Waldman, "The Domestic Council: Innovation in Presidential Government," *Public Administration Review* (May–June 1976): 260–268.

69. Margaret Jane Wyszomirski, "The Roles of a Presidential Office for Domestic Policy: Three Models and Four Cases," in *The Presidency and Policy Making,* ed. George C. Edwards III, Steven A. Shull, and Norman C. Thomas (Pittsburgh: University of Pittsburgh Press, 1985), 134.

70. John Helmer and Louis Maisel, "Analytical Problems in the Study of Presidential Advice: The Domestic Council Staff in Flux," *Presidential Studies Quarterly* (Winter 1978): 52–53.

71. A sharp debate raged over politicization of the Office of Management and Budget (OMB) and the institutionalized presidency generally. Berman, in *The Office of Management and Budget,* argued that politicization damaged, if not destroyed, the capacity of OMB to serve the institutional needs of the presidency in a professional manner. In contrast, Terry Moe, in a seminal essay, viewed politicization as a logical (indeed necessary) institutional development resulting from the extensive and steady growth of "expectations surrounding presidential performance." See Terry Moe, "The Politicized Presidency," in *The New Direction in American Politics,* ed. John E. Chubb and Paul E. Peterson (Washington, DC: Brookings, 1985), 269. Andrew Rudalevige and Matthew Dickinson argue that BOB had always been a responsive agency but that the kind of responsiveness presidents from Nixon onward wanted was different and more difficult to provide. See "Revisiting the Golden Age at the Bureau of the Budget," *Political Science Quarterly* 119 (Winter 2004): 633–654.

72. Wyszomirski, "The Roles of a Presidential Office," 136–137.

73. Wayne, *The Legislative Presidency,* 123.

74. Wyszomirski, "The Roles of a Presidential Office," 140.

75. For an extended description of the Office of Policy Development (OPD)–cabinet council system, see Chester A. Newland, "Executive Office Policy Apparatus: Enforcing the Reagan Agenda," in Salamon and Lund, *The Reagan Presidency,* 153–159. Martin Anderson, who was Reagan's first director of the OPD, provides a participant's perspective on the cabinet councils in *Revolution* (New York: Harcourt Brace Jovanovich, 1988), chap. 19.

76. Newland, "Executive Office Policy Apparatus," 160.

77. This discussion follows Colin Campbell, "The White House and the Presidency under the 'Let's Deal' President," in *The Bush Presidency: First Appraisals,* ed. Colin Campbell and Bert A. Rockman (Chatham, NJ: Chatham House, 1991), 210–212.

78. Julie Rovner, "On Policy Front, Home Is Not Where Bush's Heart Is," *Congressional Quarterly Weekly Report,* February 2, 1991, 292.

79. This discussion follows Colin Campbell, "Management in a Sandbox," in Campbell and Rockman, *The Clinton Presidency,* 77–80.

80. Ibid., 79.

81. Paul J. Quirk and William Cunion, "Clinton's Domestic Policy: The Lessons of a 'New Democrat,'" in *The Clinton Legacy,* ed. Colin Campbell and Bert A. Rockman (New York: Chatham House, 2000), 208.

82. Ibid., 210–211.

83. Bill Keller, "The Radical Presidency of George W. Bush," *New York Times Magazine,* January 26, 2003, 26.

84. For an account of this confusion, see Timothy Noah, "Who Is the Director of the Domestic Policy Council?" *Slate,* January 15, 2003, www.slate.com/id/2077046/.

85. Martha Joynt Kumar, "Recruiting and Organizing the White House Staff," *PS: Political Science and Politics* 35 (March 2002): 38

86. Andrew Rudalevige, "'The Decider': Issue Management and the Bush White House," in Campbell, Rockman, and Rudalevige, *The George W. Bush Legacy,* 144.

87. Ron Suskind, "Why Are These Men Laughing," *Esquire,* January 2003, www.ronsuskind.com/newsite/articles/archives/000032.html; and www.esquire.com/features/ESQ0103-JAN_ROVE_rev_2. DiIulio's original communication is also available at www.esquire.com/features/dilulio.

88. Michael A. Fletcher, "Editor at Conservative Magazine to Be Top Policy Adviser to Bush," *Washington Post,* May 25, 2006, A4. On Allen, see Ian Urbina and David D. Kirkpatrick, "For Ex-Aide to Bush, Quick Fall after Long Climb," *New York Times,* March 14, 2006, A1.

89. See Domestic Policy Council at www.whitehouse.gov/administration/eop/dpc/.

90. Randy James, "A Brief History of White House Czars," *Time,* September 23, 2009; Tom Hamburger and Christi Parsons, "President Obama's Czar System Concerns Some," *Los Angeles Times,* March 5, 2009; and Neil King Jr., "Role of White House Czars Sparks Battle," *Wall Street Journal,* September 11, 2009.

91. Matthew DoBias, "White House to Reshuffle Energy, Health Reform Offices," *National Journal,* March 1, 2011; and Amy Harder, "Browner's Successor Says the Agenda Hasn't Changed," *National Journal,* March 3, 2011.

92. Nora Caplan-Bricker, "Obama's Immigration Gurus," *National Journal,* January 23, 2015.

93. Ronald Brownstein, "How to Put Colleges on the Hook," *National Journal,* November 14, 2013.

94. Julia Ioffe, "The Believer: How Stephen Miller Went from Obscure Capitol Hill Staffer to Donald Trump's Warm-Up Act—and Resident Ideologue," *Politico Magazine* (June 27, 2016), http://www.politico.com/magazine/story/2016/06/stephen-miller-donald-trump-2016-policy-adviser-jeff-sessions-213992.

95. Joshua Green, "This Man Is the Most Dangerous Political Operative in America," *Bloomberg Businessweek* (October 8, 2015), https://www.bloomberg.com/politics/graphics/2015-steve-bannon/; and Josh Dawsey, Eliana Johnson and Annie Karni, "The Man Behind Trump? Still Steve Bannon," *Politico* (January 27, 2017), http://www.politico.com/story/2017/01/donald-trump-steve-bannon-234347.

96. Jason Linken, "White House Announces Jared Kushner Is Now Responsible for Everything," *Huffington Post* (March 28, 2017), http://www.huffingtonpost.com/entry/jared-kushner-everything-czar_us_58d95499e4b02a2eaab6664f.

97. Light, *The President's Agenda,* 71.

98. Ibid., 134–136.

99. R. Kent Weaver, *Automatic Government: The Politics of Indexation* (Washington, DC: Brookings Institution Press, 1988), ch. 2.

100. Paul C. Light, "Domestic Policy Making," *Presidential Studies Quarterly* 30 (March 2000): 111.

CHAPTER 9

The Politics of Economic Policy

National Archives

During the Great Depression, Franklin D. Roosevelt used radio broadcasts from the White House, known as fireside chats, to persuade the public to support his unprecedented economic policies.

Americans expect presidents to provide them with peace and prosperity. As Barack Obama left office, both dimensions were in flux. Many economic indicators—the stock market, the unemployment rate—looked quite rosy by the end of 2016. Yet growth in the gross domestic product was subpar (just 1.4% annually in the 2nd quarter), and those workers hit hard by declining industrial employment felt that the new jobs created were a poor substitute for those lost to new technology and a globalized economy. While the American combat mission in Iraq and Afghanistan had theoretically ended by 2016, U.S. troops remained in both countries and military activity against the so-called Islamic State terrorist group had ramped up across the Middle East.

The 2008 and 2012 election cycles had been dominated by concerns about the economy (see chapter 2). When President Obama took office in 2009, some economists feared that the recession had the potential to become a second Great Depression—the prolonged period of massive unemployment that gripped the United States and the world during the 1930s. By 2015, the nation had survived the worst but important questions remained: Had Obama's policies worked, particularly the stimulus program? Were the huge deficits caused by his policies jeopardizing the financial standing of the nation? Why was the recovery taking so long to help everyone? In the 2012 election, Republican presidential aspirants jointly denounced Obama's performance, arguing that the wrong policies threatened the nation with financial ruin and continued high unemployment. Voters, however, reelected Obama, placing the bulk of the blame for the original crisis on his predecessor.[1]

During the 2016 campaign, Republicans continued to attack Obama's record. Political science models based on economic performance suggested that either side could win the 2016 presidential election, with a slight edge to the incumbent party. But rather than highlighting the Democrats' performance on the economy, Hillary Rodham Clinton focused nearly all of her attention on attacking Donald Trump's character: only 9 percent of her television ads were about the economy.[2] Trump, too, engaged in personal attacks, but the single advertisement he aired most—"Two Americas: Economy"—contrasted a bleak big-government, high-tax future under Hillary Clinton ("where the middle class gets crushed") with a Trump utopia in which "small businesses thrive," there are "millions of new jobs," "wages go up," and "the American dream [is] achievable." Clinton's silence on this point allowed Trump's interpretation of "the worst so-called recovery since the Great Depression" in which "the hard times never seem to end" to take hold, at least among those most nervous about the economic and social effects of globalization and immigration.[3]

All of this showed the importance of economic policy to the presidency. The "Great Recession" had long-lasting political—not to mention tangible—impacts beginning late in the George W. Bush administration. In fall 2008, a late-summer crisis in the U.S. mortgage market triggered massive losses on stock markets around the globe and threatened to destroy the world's banking and financial system. The buildup to the crisis was gradual. Lenders in the United States had been too eager to make new loans during the mid-decade housing boom, and as unemployment and interest rates rose in the summer of 2007, large numbers of borrowers defaulted not only on their mortgages but also on other debts accumulated over the preceding decades. Several mortgage companies went bankrupt. Housing sales suddenly came to a screeching halt, prices dropped, and the construction industry began laying off workers, with ripple effects in related industries. Employment levels continued to slide through the next year and, to make matters worse, American consumers were hit with a dramatic rise in oil prices that resulted in increased prices for food and gas.[4] Banks were dangerously overcommitted to many bad loans. And the problem became global when the value of securities that rested on the U.S. mortgage market (a financial *derivative* developed over the decade) declined rapidly; panic ensued among individuals and institutions that owned the investments.

The Bush administration and the Federal Reserve Board (usually referred to as "the Fed") tried to respond. Their initial actions were piecemeal, aimed at propping up single banks and firms that came under financial pressure. The Wall Street investment bank Bear Stearns was kept out of bankruptcy with a $29 billion package from the Fed, but another firm, Lehman Brothers, was allowed to go bankrupt in September 2008 with near-catastrophic consequences. Freddie Mac and Fannie Mae, two government-backed companies central to the U.S. mortgage industry, were tottering. Congress authorized Treasury Secretary Henry Paulson to save the companies with a $200 billion bailout. Nevertheless, the nation's banks were experiencing a growing crisis in liquidity—the ability of consumers and businesses to borrow money to spend or invest—and investment in new plants and enterprises ground to a halt. Consumer purchases of cars and other items declined precipitously. Banks had used up their own reserves and were unable to make new loans. There was fear that depositors would soon start taking their money out of banks and force many of them to fail. The conditions likely to produce an economic depression were lining up like a row of dominoes ready to topple.

Dramatic action was needed. Treasury Secretary Paulson and Fed chairman Ben Bernanke frantically devised a plan to restore confidence in the banking industry by buying up distressed assets—those based on mortgages that were going into default. The Troubled Asset Relief Program (TARP) would allow the Treasury Department to spend up to $700 billion to stabilize U.S. banks. The cost of the plan, the absence of details (the proposal was originally only three pages long), the sweeping delegation of power to the executive branch, and the potential consequences for a free-market economy raised red flags on Capitol Hill. Despite predictions of dire consequences, the House of Representatives initially rejected the proposal; even President Bush's own partisans voted overwhelmingly against it. In response, the stock market suffered what was then the largest one-day sell-off in the history of the market, with the Dow-Jones industrial average plunging 778 points. The Senate stepped in two days later and approved a plan modified to appease the House. Two days after that, under pressure from party leaders and the president, the House reversed course, although a majority of Republicans still voted no. Congress had imposed conditions, insisting on oversight powers and a reduced initial outlay of $350 billion. (The Obama administration later asked for the remainder and extended aid to automakers GM and Chrysler, as well.) In fact, Treasury soon reconsidered the original plan and decided not to purchase bad loans; instead, it invested the money in the banks, expecting them to start lending to consumers. In essence, the taxpayers became investors in the banks—and then the auto companies—but had little control over how the funds would be used. To the outrage of many, banks did not simply turn around and pump new liquidity into the system. Some continued to conduct business as usual, holding staff retreats at expensive resorts and awarding large year-end bonuses to employees. As Obama entered office, then, he gave top priority to combating the recession—and his actions would be judged not just in 2012, but in 2016. Donald Trump, as we have seen, berated the slow pace of recovery. In turn he promised to slash taxes, cut regulations, renegotiate trade agreements, slow immigration, and spend perhaps $1 trillion to construct and reconstruct American infrastructure, all designed to create jobs.

Economic issues are often at the heart of national politics. They helped account for George H. W. Bush's loss in the 1992 election. The public blamed him for the 1991–1992 recession. Charging that Bush had indeed neglected the economy, Democratic candidate Bill Clinton focused his campaign on economic issues. (A sign stating "It's the Economy, Stupid" hung on the wall of his national campaign headquarters.[5]) That year's Independent candidate, Ross Perot, stressed the importance of ending the deficit and reducing the national debt. The electorate responded by choosing Clinton while giving Perot 19 percent of the vote. The deficit and economic issues dominated Clinton's first two years in office, but Clinton got only modest credit for presiding over a period of record economic growth with low inflation that coincided with a near-miraculous transformation in the annual budget from a $290 billion deficit in 1992 to a $69.2 billion surplus in 1998. Clinton enthusiasts hailed this turnaround as a great achievement, but many analysts saw it as the product of luck and the efforts of the long-serving Fed chairman, Alan Greenspan.[6]

Like Obama, George W. Bush also began his presidency with a slowing economy, but he largely escaped blame for rising unemployment, dramatically lower stock prices, a resurgence in budget deficits to record highs, and declining public confidence in corporate America.[7] The public blamed 9/11 for the nation's economic problems arising from damage to its financial infrastructure and an almost fatal blow to the nation's airlines. But the recession that started in 2007 and the worsening conditions in 2008 were laid at Bush's door and heavily influenced the fall elections.[8]

Modern presidents are highly attentive to economic conditions, but that has not always been the case. Some presidents who confronted serious economic adversity, such as Martin Van Buren in 1837, Ulysses S. Grant in 1873, Grover Cleveland in 1893, Theodore Roosevelt in 1907, and Warren G. Harding in 1921, did little more than ride out the storm. The electorate, however, reacted by denying reelection to Van Buren and by inflicting sizable losses on the president's party in the midterm congressional elections of 1838, 1874, and 1894. In fact, the existence of a relationship between business cycles and election results was known long before Edward Tufte's precise empirical analysis of the phenomenon.[9] Only since the 1930s, however, have presidents attempted to *control* business cycles through public policy, and the public has come to expect them to do so.

In this chapter, we examine the president's economic policy responsibilities and activities. We begin by distinguishing between actions designed to manage the entire economy (macroeconomic policy) and those meant to control specific aspects of the economy (microeconomic policy). The primary focus of the chapter is on macroeconomic policy. We review presidential efforts to manage the economy from 1933 to early 2017 and then describe the politics of macroeconomic policymaking. Next we analyze how the president makes economic policy and how presidents since Dwight D. Eisenhower have handled the problem of coordinating economic policy. The chapter concludes with an assessment of the congressional role in macroeconomic policymaking.

Macroeconomic Policy

Not since the Great Depression of the 1930s have Americans been so keenly aware of the ways that government can intervene to influence the economy, efforts known as **macroeconomic policy**. The government has two principal strategies at its disposal: (1) fiscal policy and (2) monetary policy. Using **fiscal policy**, the government tries to regulate the level of the nation's economic activity by varying taxes and public expenditures. A policy of higher spending and lower taxes—adopted by the Obama administration in 2009, and urged in the first Trump budget as well—aims to expand the economy; one of lower spending and higher taxes—potentially necessary to rein in inflation if the economic stimulus is too great—aims to contract it. The orthodox view is that a **budget deficit**, which occurs when spending exceeds tax revenues, stimulates economic activity, and a **budget surplus** (tax revenues exceed spending) slows the economy. The president and Congress jointly make fiscal policy. They determine expenditures through budgeting and appropriations, and they establish taxes through legislation. **Monetary policy** refers to a government's efforts, through its central bank (in the United States, the Federal Reserve System), to regulate economic activity by controlling the supply of money—currency and credit. An independent agency, the Board of Governors of the Federal Reserve System, makes monetary policy. Although fiscal policy and monetary policy constitute distinct realms of policymaking, decision makers usually seek to coordinate them.

Since the Depression, the goals of macroeconomic policy have remained constant: *to hold down the rate of inflation, to establish and maintain full employment,* and *to achieve a steady rate of economic growth.* Policymakers, however, have pursued these goals through alternative theories: classical conservative economics, Keynesianism, monetarism, and supply-side economics.

Conservative economic theory lost credibility during the Depression when the administrations of Herbert Hoover and Franklin Roosevelt (initially) stressed balancing the budget and failed to restore confidence in the economy and produce the desired upturn. FDR quickly discovered that emergency spending and loan programs provided relief and produced a measure of recovery. The ideas of **John Maynard Keynes**, a British economist Roosevelt met in 1934, offered an explanation for why fiscal stimulus is effective and eventually provided a rationale for deficit spending. Keynes argued that a drop in private demand for goods and services causes an economic decline. A government could stimulate demand by increasing its own expenditures or increasing those of consumers by reducing taxes. The temporary deficits created by fiscal stimulation would be financed by government borrowing and repaid during good economic periods. Eventually the economy recovered aided by expanded government spending during World War II. This experience provided most economists with empirical validation of Keynes's basic theories. Conservative economics, however, retained its hold on many political leaders, such as Eisenhower, who made balanced budgets the goal and regarded fiscal stimulation of lagging demand as an emergency measure. We saw evidence of these beliefs following 2009 when the startlingly large deficits arising from President Obama's stimulus spending and the ongoing wars triggered the Tea Party movement inside the Republican Party and resulted in grassroots pressures to cut spending and balance the federal budget.

While **Keynesianism** was establishing itself as the new orthodoxy, another theory emerged to challenge it. The monetarists, under the leadership of economist **Milton Friedman**, held that the key to maintaining economic stability lay not in stimulating demand but in limiting the growth rate of the money supply to no more than the growth rate of the economy. Inflation occurs, monetarists claim, when the money supply expands too rapidly. The only remedy for inflation is a painful contraction in the money supply, which can be brought about by raising interest rates. Monetarists hold that fiscal policy and the size of budget deficits are subordinate to monetary policy and the growth rate of the money supply, which for them constitute the basic means of managing the economy.

Monetarism gained adherents as the limitations of Keynesianism became apparent during the 1970s. Keynesian theory has an inflationary bias—its primary defect as a macroeconomic theory. Decisions on taxing and spending are made by the president and members of Congress—politicians concerned with reelection—and not by professional economists. Consequently, it has proved easier in practice to increase spending and cut taxes, the Keynesian prescription for expansion, than to cut spending and increase taxes, the theory's remedy for inflation. In the 1970s, when inflation became the nation's leading economic problem, political decision makers were unwilling to impose the Keynesian solution. Although the inflationary bias of Keynesianism is a political defect rather than a weakness in the theory itself, this bias nevertheless has made it less attractive as a guide to policy.

Monetarism, whatever its theoretical merits and limitations, offered a politically palatable way to control inflation through the autonomous **Federal Reserve Board**, which reduces inflation by contracting the money supply. Political officeholders can blame the consequences of monetary contractions—high interest rates and rising unemployment—on the Fed and its amorphous supporters: "Wall Street" investing interests and the banks. But monetarism also became politically unattractive—though substantively effective—when efforts to control inflation proved especially painful to consumers during the late 1970s. By the early 1980s, a new theoretical approach, **supply-side economics**, emerged and President Reagan embraced it.

Essentially, supply-side economics is an amalgam of Keynesianism and monetarism.[10] Supply-siders endorse strict monetary restraint as the means of controlling inflation, but they also believe, unlike pure monetarists, that fiscal policy can be used to achieve macroeconomic policy objectives. The supply-siders assert, however, that the Keynesians misdirect government efforts. Instead of stimulating demand through government spending and tax cuts for consumers, the supply-siders seek to stimulate supply through tax cuts for businesses and investors that provide incentives to encourage additional investments and enhanced productivity, which in turn increase the supply of goods and services. The additional jobs created ultimately fuel consumer buying, although the focus of the policy is producers, not consumers. Supply-siders are not disturbed by budget deficits resulting from tax-cut incentives. They believe an expanded economy will not be inflationary and eventually will generate enough revenues, even at lower rates of taxation, to balance the budget.

Supply-side economics draws sharp criticism from both liberals and conservatives who doubt the validity of assumptions on which the theory rests. Liberals charge that it is another version of the discredited "trickle-down" approach to economic policy, under which tax advantages for the affluent are justified on the grounds that they eventually lead to prosperity for all. Conservatives fear that supply-side tolerance of budget deficits leads to excessive rates of inflation and erodes confidence in the monetary system. Some critics would like supply-side policies to work but do not believe they can. Experience since 1981 with a massive cut in federal income taxes, phased in over several years and based on supply-side reasoning, supports their pessimism. The economy expanded steadily during the 1980s and 1990s, but a balanced budget was not achieved until 1998, when there was a modest surplus. The Democrats, whose willingness to raise taxes in 1990 and 1993 helped increase government revenues, claimed credit for this accomplishment. But when signs of an economic slowdown emerged in late 2000, tax cuts became a campaign issue. With a new administration in place, the Republican Congress passed three tax reductions at the urging of President George W. Bush. These cuts provided another opportunity to observe how the federal budget is affected by supply-side policies in the long run. In his memoir, Alan Greenspan harshly criticized this new round of supply-side tax cuts, which were taken with little consideration of how they would increase the deficit.[11] (Committed supply-siders, it should be pointed out, will disagree with this account. In their view, Reagan's tax cuts fueled the economic boom of the 1990s, not the Democrats' and George H.W. Bush's commitment to a balanced budget.)

The George W. Bush tax cuts again took center stage in 2010 and 2011 when they were scheduled to be phased out. Democrats wanted rates restored to the pre-Bush levels for the wealthiest Americans, but congressional Republicans were adamant that there be no tax increases, especially in the midst of economic weakness.

President Obama's 2010 agreement with the Republican majority in the House upset many of his own supporters: retaining the Bush-era tax cuts but extending unemployment benefits that Republicans had wanted to cut. The tax battles abated in December 2012 when the Bush tax cuts, scheduled to expire, were left in place for individuals earning less than $400,000 and couples earning less than $450,000. Tax rates rose for those earning more.

During the 1980s and 1990s, federal policymakers were forced to rely more heavily on monetary policy than on fiscal policy to manage the economy. Coping with large and persistent deficits, presidents had little room to increase spending or reduce taxes. Moreover, Republicans and Democrats disagreed vehemently over the level and purposes of government spending and the structure of taxes—who pays how much. In this intractable setting, monetary policy instruments became the only viable alternative for macroeconomic management, effectively the only game in town to shape economic policy.[12] The sudden appearance of budget surpluses seemed to breathe new life into fiscal policy, but this revival proved short lived. The Bush tax cuts adopted from 2001 to 2003 were so large that, combined with the post-9/11 economic slowdown, the federal government once again began to run a substantial deficit. The Obama budgets adopted to fight the recession set new peacetime deficit records.

Efforts to Stabilize the Economy, 2008–2017

The severe recession that began in 2007 once again highlighted the unique role played by the federal government in combating nationwide economic problems. Both fiscal and monetary policies sought to counteract the severe contraction in consumption, investment, and jobs experienced by the country. In effect, only the federal government could take action. State and local governments, which are required by law to balance their budgets, are forced to behave like Herbert Hoover did between 1929 and 1932. By contrast, the Fed has the authority to print currency, thereby expanding the money supply, and Congress and the president can adopt expansionary fiscal policies—that is, increase government spending and reduce taxes. Working together, the instruments of both monetary and fiscal policy were put into motion in 2008–2009.

By February 2009, the national unemployment rate stood at 8.1 percent, a figure that translated into 12.5 million unemployed Americans, a level well above what is considered acceptable in the United States. The economy was contracting, not growing, at a rate of 6.2 percent over the final three months of 2008, and both figures were moving in the wrong direction; unemployment increased from month to month as more workers received pink slips and economic activity declined. The Bush administration and Congress had tried to head off the recession a year earlier with a modest stimulus package: $168 billion in individual tax rebates and larger business deductions. The downside of these actions was that both the annual budget deficit and the national debt (total indebtedness) rose to unprecedented levels.[13]

The Fed aggressively used monetary policy to combat the worsening economy. It began to cut interest rates in September 2007 on the short-term loans it makes to banks and continued to reduce that rate until it reached virtually zero in December 2008 and remained there well into 2015 when economic growth continued to be sluggish. The Fed backed the bailouts of investment bank Bear Stearns and American International Group (AIG), the giant insurance company that has been blamed for many of the riskiest loan transactions that began to echo through the economy. Chairman Bernanke then invented new ways—collectively termed "quantitative easing"—that the Fed could build liquidity back into the system and get money flowing again. By February 2009, the Fed had injected an additional $1.9 trillion in credit throughout the financial system while working first with Secretary Paulson and then with Timothy Geithner, Obama's first Treasury secretary.[14] Bernanke, a professional economist with a research specialty in the Great Depression, made speeches and appeared frequently before Congress to explain these strategies.

When the economy continued in its tailspin, the Obama administration proposed an even larger stimulus package. The American Recovery and Reinvestment Act of 2009 (ARRA) was approved exactly a year after George W. Bush signed the earlier effort. It infused some $787 billion into the economy through a combination of tax cuts and new government spending. The goals of the legislation were twofold: (1) reduce taxes on middle class Americans who, it was hoped, would spend the additional money and (2) create jobs through targeted spending on public works, energy research, expanded social programs, and aid to state and local governments. This was a classic Keynesian formulation sold by President Obama as a way to improve the country and save jobs at the same time.

The Republicans were not buying. They complained that Democrats had added many of their pet projects onto this almost 1,100-page bill, not as a way to help the economy but as a way to expand government. In the House, not a single Republican voted for any version of the bill; three Senate Republican moderates won concessions from the Democrats, and later conference committee negotiations reduced the overall projected cost of the bill to $787 billion, with over $280 billion in tax cuts and more than $500 billion in additional spending.[15] The scope of the package, likened by many to Roosevelt's New Deal, was nevertheless challenged by some economists as too small, and in fact, the administration had underestimated how quickly unemployment would grow and the economy contract. Again, the package relied on borrowed money and increased the size of the deficit. Ultimately, the Obama administration spent about $840 billion on the ARRA with most of the spending concentrated during late 2009 into 2010.[16] Despite this effort, the economy seemed to drift toward a second recession in August 2011 when job growth fizzled to zero, evidence, liberals believed, that the stimulus should have been larger. Conservatives, by contrast, saw the effort as too large, driving up the size of the deficit. Nearly three-quarters of the public believed that most of the money had been wasted.[17]

Government's Four Strategies to Rescue the Economy

Traditional macroeconomic policy was only part of the government's effort. The Bush and Obama stimulus packages together totaled $914.9 billion, money essentially spent by *government as a consumer,* one of several roles identified by *CQ Weekly* as a way to describe the many emergency actions taken. This was the traditional countercyclical effort prescribed by Keynesian thinking. But the Obama administration also announced two other major initiatives to address the nation's economic problems. An additional financial rescue package would spend the second $350 billion appropriated for TARP and fund a new program titled TALF (Term Asset-Backed Loan Facility) intended to stimulate consumer borrowing. Treasury Secretary Geithner also announced an ill-defined public-private partnership to remove bad assets from banks with an unknown cost. The third leg of the administration's economic rescue strategy was designed to help homeowners renegotiate the terms of their mortgages in order to keep them in their homes, a program that lenders resisted and the Treasury Department never implemented effectively.[18]

Therefore, in addition to being a direct purchaser and stimulator of services, the government committed even more money to these other roles. At the forefront was *government as an investor* when the Treasury and the Federal Reserve put money into banks and the automotive industry (TARP), acquired bad mortgage assets, helped homeowners refinance their mortgages, and provided help to Fannie Mae and Freddie Mac. By February 2009, these commitments were estimated at $1.6 trillion. The Federal Reserve played the role of *government as lender,* pumping nearly $850 billion into banks and two major automakers on a short-term basis to help them remain in business. Finally, the *government served as guarantor* of loans on bad assets that would otherwise have forced some banks out of business. As *CQ Weekly* sought to make sense out of all these transactions and the overlapping categories, it estimated about $2 trillion had been made in loans and guarantees. The government's efforts to right the economy had already amounted to approximately $4.5 trillion and could double in the long run if all the guarantees had to be paid; even so, President Obama kept reminding Americans that this investment might not be enough.[19] The magnitude of the effort testified to the size of the problem.

Microeconomic Policy

Microeconomic policy is a term used to describe government regulation of specific economic activities; it also encompasses antitrust policy, which is designed to prevent business monopolies and stimulate competition. Microeconomic policies focus on specific industries or on economic practices in several industries. They are designed to affect directly the infrastructure of the economy and only indirectly its overall performance. Modern presidents generally have paid less attention to microeconomic than to macroeconomic policy, largely because the impact of the former is more narrowly focused. But in the wake of the financial crisis came a renewed awareness that unregulated economic activities and weak enforcement can have deleterious effects; there was a widespread demand that government establish new controls on the practices that brought the American economy to its knees. Much of the public debate from the late 1970s onward focused on the benefits of deregulating major sectors of the economy and the costs of environmental regulations. The Obama administration came to power in the midst of a broad rethinking of those policies—an understanding of why some economic practices must be regulated and a strong commitment to protecting the environment. Democrats began to reassert the need for regulation. Republicans pushed back, stressing roll-back of regulations central to shrinking a bloated government. More than a dozen congressional resolutions rescinding rules finalized late in the Obama administration were signed into law during President Trump's first one hundred days in office; his early executive actions likewise focused on encouraging deregulation. Thus, microeconomic policy is likely to be an important area of continued debate and activity.

Before the Great Depression, presidents were involved exclusively with microeconomic policy and did not regard overall management of the economy as a primary policy responsibility. To preserve competition in the market, Theodore Roosevelt and William Howard Taft vigorously enforced the Sherman Antitrust Act of 1890—Roosevelt with great fanfare and Taft with quiet effectiveness. Woodrow Wilson persuaded Congress to establish an independent regulatory agency, the Federal Trade Commission, with extensive authority to regulate anticompetitive and unfair business practices. Roosevelt, Taft, and Wilson believed the federal government should serve as an umpire and act to correct imperfections in the operations of the free market economy.

During the New Deal, Franklin Roosevelt endorsed legislation that established or strengthened independent regulatory agencies: the Securities and Exchange Commission, the Federal Power Commission, the Federal Communications Commission, the Civil Aeronautics Board, and the National Labor Relations Board. These agencies received broad grants of authority to regulate the interstate aspects of specific industries such as trade in stocks and bonds, electric power and natural gas, broadcasting and wire communications, and air transportation, as well as economy-wide activities such as labor-management relations. FDR experimented with government intervention, hoping to improve the operation of certain economic sectors or the overall health of the economy.

FDR's successors varied in their use of microeconomic policies. Presidents Harry S. Truman, Dwight D. Eisenhower, John F. Kennedy, and Lyndon B. Johnson accepted the legitimacy of government regulation of economic activity that had been established by 1940, including antitrust policy. They differed mainly in the intensity with which they enforced regulations and in their willingness to use certain microeconomic policy tools.

Beginning in the late 1960s and continuing into the 1970s, Congress expanded federal regulation of economic activity as a way to achieve noneconomic goals, such as a cleaner physical environment, safer automobiles and other consumer products, and a higher degree of safety and health in the workplace. Presidents Richard Nixon and Gerald R. Ford initially approved the new regulatory activities, but they raised questions when the economic costs of regulation became apparent. A deregulation movement gained support, endorsed by Ford, Jimmy Carter, and Ronald Reagan. Ford and Carter used the Office of Management and Budget (OMB) and Council of Economic Advisers (CEA) to analyze the impact of regulations on inflation and later to review new rules and regulations with significant economic costs. These actions did not materially reduce the volume of new regulations or the economic impact of regulation on industry.[20] Carter also supported legislation that deregulated the airline and trucking industries.

Reagan's 1980 campaign pointed to federal regulation as a primary cause of the decline of productivity in the economy. Vice President George H. W. Bush headed the Task Force on Regulatory Relief, which analyzed the economic effects of existing and proposed regulations. The task force also prepared the way for using the recently created Office of Information and Regulatory Affairs (OIRA) within OMB to review proposed agency regulations. Reagan mandated by executive order that all major regulations be subjected to analysis to ensure their benefits outweighed their costs. The administration enforced regulations less intensely and relied on cooperative, rather than confrontational, means to achieve compliance.[21] President George H. W. Bush maintained Reagan's regulatory review process and involved his own vice president, Dan Quayle, in an antiregulation effort, naming him chair of the Council on Competitiveness, which had broad authority to intervene in drafting federal regulations. Unlike Reagan, Bush did not oppose occupational safety and environmental protection, and he gave stronger support to economic regulatory policy while appointing moderates to regulatory positions, in sharp contrast to Reagan's practice of naming conservative appointees philosophically opposed to regulation.[22]

The Clinton administration abolished the Council on Competitiveness, enhanced public access to decision making, and shifted regulations' substantive emphasis. But to the dismay of some Democrats, Clinton continued to utilize regulatory review through the OIRA process. Whereas Reagan and Bush had required that the benefits of regulations outweigh costs, Clinton "required only that benefits justify costs,"[23] and sometimes used administrative memoranda to the departments to prompt new regulatory activity. Regulation became a political issue when Republicans, following their takeover of Congress in 1995, introduced legislation designed to provide businesses and individuals with relief from environmental regulation.[24] As the Clinton years came to a close, a fateful policy emerged: Congress approved the activities that would ultimately trigger the economic problems nine years later by allowing the sale of financial derivatives—securities marketed on the basis of pooled assets such as mortgages—by unregulated entities, including AIG, which later received nearly $170 billion in federal assistance to prevent its collapse.

During the early months of his administration, George W. Bush triggered fears among environmentalists, organized labor, and consumer advocacy groups that he would overturn regulations deemed harmful by business. The administration declared a sixty-day delay while it reviewed new rules approved by the departing president during his final days in office. These included rules to lower the level of arsenic in drinking water, ban road construction and limit logging in federal forests, require higher efficiency for air conditioners, reduce diesel exhaust in the air, and reduce repetitive-motion injuries in the workplace.[25] Some rules were reversed, grabbing the headlines and allowing critics to suggest Bush would favor business interests, but OMB ultimately acted with greater moderation and in a less probusiness manner than it had initially.[26] But there can be little doubt the administration pursued an agenda of reduced regulation. OMB annually solicited suggestions about federal regulations that should be revised or rescinded; in subsequent years, the administration established "a higher threshold for reaching scientific certainty in regulatory decisions, and create[d] new opportunities for outside experts to challenge the government's conclusions about the dangers that a rule is designed to mitigate."[27] OIRA also got involved with rulemaking at an earlier stage in the process, and a Bush executive order required that a political appointee be in charge of each agency's annual regulatory agenda. Obama rescinded that order but also maintained a high-profile OIRA regulatory review process. His first appointee, Harvard Law School professor Cass Sunstein, had long been committed to using cost-benefit analysis in various areas of public policy and in 2011 instituted a "regulatory lookback" to remove outdated or counterproductive regulations from the books.[28]

Trump, in turn, instituted his own regulatory freeze, and soon issued an executive order mandating that for every new regulation promulgated by an agency, it would have to recommend two existing regulations for elimination.[29] Given legal requirements for canceling rules, how that might be achieved was not clear—but there could be no doubt about the administration's attitude towards regulation generally. In other executive actions Trump directed his department heads to examine environmental, energy, financial, and health care rules with an eye towards rolling back what he termed "excessive regulation [that] is killing jobs" and "driving companies out of our country like never before."[30] Critics argued that the benefits as well as the costs of regulation needed to be considered in regulatory review.

Microeconomic policies have been secondary to macroeconomic policy in all administrations since FDR's. Following the economic collapse of 2008 and 2009, however, both Congress and the administration placed a high priority on reestablishing vigorous regulation of financial markets and effective enforcement. The Federal Deposit Insurance Corporation (FDIC), which regulates the operations of commercial banks, had no powers to regulate investment banks or nonbanking financial entities such as insurance companies and hedge funds. When those businesses engaged in especially risky transactions, there was no one to blow the whistle and few powers to intervene. The Obama administration, in conjunction with Bernanke, proposed reforms in March 2009 that would create a single regulator responsible for overseeing large companies with the potential to damage the economic system, reducing gaps between regulatory authorities, and improving international coordination.[31] The proposal triggered immediate criticism on Capitol Hill and an aggressive lobbying campaign by the financial industry, which opposed the reforms.

What emerged was the Wall Street Reform and Consumer Protection Act, known commonly as the Dodd-Frank Act, after Chris Dodd and Barney Frank, chairs of the Senate and House committees overseeing financial affairs. Passed in summer 2010, the legislation created a new Consumer Financial Protection Bureau and a Financial Stability Oversight Council, with the power to determine the systemic importance of financial institutions, that is, which banks are too big to fail.[32] The FDIC was granted authority to oversee the orderly liquidation of assets of any financial entity whose failure would constitute "significant risk to the financial stability of the United States."[33] Dodd-Frank also established new capital requirements for banks, restrictions on trading certain types of derivatives mentioned earlier, and clearer regulation of the credit rating agencies whose optimistic evaluations of investments had helped to fuel the excessive optimism of investors. Critics noted that the bill did not address Freddie Mac or Fannie Mae, the two mortgage giants that greatly contributed to the financial meltdown. Many specific reforms were left for the regulators to decide, which would delay their implementation and potentially enhance the ability of the affected interests to control the rulemaking process.[34]

Microeconomic policies cannot replace fiscal and monetary policies as the primary means by which presidents guide the nation's economy, but there is a renewed appreciation of their importance. Dodd-Frank was certainly not the last word on financial regulation, and the Trump administration was eager to work with the law's critics on Wall Street and in Congress to adjust its requirements and guidelines.

Presidents and the Economy: 1933–2017

The president's role as manager of the economy dates from FDR's New Deal, with its commitment to use the federal government's power to bring about recovery from the Great Depression. Keynesian economics and its prescription of increased government spending to compensate for inadequate private spending for investment and consumption provided a theoretical justification for government intervention. Ultimately, it was not the New Deal reforms or recovery programs that ended the Depression but the huge increase in government spending during World War II. All of the nation's unused productive capacity—capital facilities and human resources—were mobilized to achieve victory, and government borrowing financed much of that mobilization.

After World War II, Congress passed the **Employment Act of 1946**, committing the government to the maintenance of "maximum employment, production, and purchasing power." This act translated into law the widespread expectation, developed during the Roosevelt administration, that the government would take an active role in maintaining a prosperous economy. The forty-four-year record of administrations on inflation, unemployment, and budget balancing is shown in Table 9-1. It also made the president primarily responsible for providing economic policy leadership, although it failed to furnish the office with many new tools or powers for the task. The Employment Act created the CEA and an accompanying staff to provide professional analysis and advice, and it required the president to report annually to Congress on the condition of the economy and to offer proposals for maintaining or improving its health. Ultimate power over the president's economic proposals, however, remained with Congress.

TABLE 9-1 Inflation, Unemployment, and Federal Budget Deficits/Surpluses, 1970–2016

	Inflation[a]	*Unemployment*[b]	*Deficit/Surplus*[c]
1970	5.7%	4.9%	$–2.84
1971	4.4	5.9	–23.03
1972	3.2	5.6	–23.37
1973	6.2	4.9	–14.91
1974	11.0	5.6	–6.14
1975	9.1	8.5	–53.24
1976	5.6	7.7	–73.73
1977	6.5	7.0	–53.66
1978	7.6	6.6	–59.19
1979	11.3	5.8	–40.73
1980	13.5	7.1	–73.84
1981	10.3	7.6	–78.98
1982	6.2	9.7	–127.99
1983	3.2	9.6	–207.82

	Inflation[a]	*Unemployment*[b]	*Deficit/Surplus*[c]
1984	4.3	7.5	–185.39
1985	3.6	7.2	–212.33
1986	1.9	7.0	–221.25
1987	3.6	6.2	–149.77
1988	4.1	5.5	–155.19
1989	4.8	5.3	–152.48
1990	5.4	5.6	–221.23
1991	4.2	6.8	–269.36
1992	3.0	7.5	–290.40
1993	3.0	6.9	–255.11
1994	2.6	6.1	–203.28
1995	2.8	5.6	–164.01
1996	3.0	5.4	–107.51
1997	2.3	4.9	–21.99
1998	1.6	4.5	+69.19
1999	2.2	4.2	+125.6
2000	3.4	4.0	+236.4
2001	2.8	4.7	+128.2
2002	1.6	5.8	–157.8
2003	2.3	6.0	–377.6
2004	2.7	5.5	–412.7
2005	3.4	5.1	–318.3
2006	3.2	4.6	–248.2
2007	2.9	4.6	–160.7
2008	3.9	5.8	–458.6
2009	–0.4	9.3	–1,413.0
2010	1.6	9.6	–1,294.0
2011	3.2	8.9	–1,300.0
2012	2.1	8.1	–1,087.0
2013	1.5	7.4	–679.5
2014	1.6	6.2	–484.6
2015	0.1	5.3	–438.5
2016	1.3	4.9	–587.3

SOURCES: For data on inflation and unemployment, see Department of Labor, Bureau of Labor Statistics, Household Data, CPI Detailed Report "Table 24. Historical Consumer Price Index for All Urban Consumers (CPI-U)," https://www.bls.gov/cpi/cpid1703.pdf and www.bls.gov/web/empsit/cpseea01.htm. For budget deficits, see Congressional Budget Office Historical Budget Data, www.cbo.gov/publication/45249.

[a] Percentage increase in the consumer price index

[b] Percentage of the civilian noninstitutional population sixteen years of age or over

[c] In billions of dollars

From the end of World War II until the late 1960s, presidents and Congress fought over economic policy. Truman struggled unsuccessfully with Congress over its desire to reduce wartime taxes, but he was somewhat more effective in controlling the inflation that resulted from spending for the Korean War. Eisenhower's conservative policies prevailed over the plans of a Democratic Congress to increase domestic spending during recessions in 1954 and 1958, with economic expansion between them. The Kennedy-Johnson administration fully embraced Keynesian theory, and a 1964 income tax cut expanded the economy and increased revenues. It was thought that economic forecasting and management of the economy had developed to the point where it was possible to fine-tune unemployment and the inflation rate.[35]

The Vietnam War disrupted the economy: As expenditures rose rapidly, the deficit increased, and President Johnson shifted his focus from economic expansion to economic restraint. Congress resisted Johnson's requests for higher excise taxes, and at first he did not ask for income tax increases, fearing that Congress would raise embarrassing questions about the war and its cost on the eve of the 1966 midterm elections. Later, Johnson requested additional income taxes and Congress approved a temporary 10 percent income surtax, but the economy had already begun a prolonged inflationary period that drastically changed conditions that had been relatively stable since 1946. (The first twenty-five years of the post–World War II period were characterized by an inflation rate of approximately 3 percent a year, unemployment that varied between 4 percent and 8 percent, and sustained growth in the gross domestic product.)

Presidents since Johnson have had to contend with a changing and frequently intractable economy. Inflation rates crept upward into double digits in the late 1970s and early 1980s before declining, unemployment remained high by postwar standards into the mid-1990s, and the federal budget ran a deficit every year between 1970 and 1997 (see Table 9-1). Underlying these developments were systemic factors beyond the control of the government: the increased dependence of the economy on foreign sources of raw materials, especially oil; the growing interdependence of the U.S. economy with those of other industrial democracies; the declining productivity of the U.S. economy in relation to foreign competition; the growth and maturation of domestic social welfare programs based on statutory entitlements; and a commitment to improve the quality of the physical environment even at substantial cost to economic growth and productivity.

Richard Nixon responded to the changing economic environment by consistently pursuing the classical conservative course: reducing federal spending to balance the budget. In addition, he took the extraordinary step, for a conservative Republican, of freezing prices and wages in August 1971. Roosevelt and Truman had imposed wage and price controls during World War II and the Korean War, but Nixon was the only president to adopt them when the nation was not fully mobilized for war. He acted under authority Congress delegated to the president in the Economic Stabilization Act of 1970. The wage and price freeze experience from 1971 through 1973 suggests that peacetime wage and price controls are at best a temporary means of curbing inflation and that they can quickly become a political liability unless their impact is moderated—Nixon did not suffer the political consequences in 1972, but congressional Republicans did.

Upon taking office in August 1974, President Ford assumed that the principal economic problem confronting the United States was inflation, and he famously pushed to "Whip Inflation Now," in part by cutting federal spending. Instead, economic conditions changed, and Ford spent his last year as president combating a recession that contributed to his electoral defeat in 1976. Ford's successor, Jimmy Carter, fared little better. Carter initiated an antirecession program of increased federal spending and tax cuts to stimulate business investment. The economy responded almost too quickly, and he was confronted with surging inflation rates that reached double digits during his last two years in office.

Perhaps Carter's most important decision affecting the economy was to select Paul Volcker as chairman of the Federal Reserve Board in 1979. Volcker's appointment reflected Carter's frustration with Keynesian theory's inability to provide solutions to the problem of "stagflation," a combination of a stagnant economy and rising prices. Essentially a monetarist, Volcker moved quickly to curb inflation by restraining the growth of the money supply, the first time monetarism had a prominent role in macroeconomic policymaking.

The rate of inflation did not respond quickly to Volcker's efforts to tighten the money supply, but interest rates on consumer loans rose sharply, undoubtedly contributing to Carter's defeat by Reagan in the 1980 election. One of Reagan's campaign pledges had been to restore vitality to the economy through a revolutionary program of major reductions in taxes and spending. Congress supported Reagan's initiatives in 1981 by enacting the largest income tax cut in U.S. history to that point and by reducing domestic spending in nonentitlement programs. Congress also supported Reagan's proposals for a major defense buildup, projected over five years, from 1981 through 1986.

The results of the Reagan administration's macroeconomic policies were mixed. The Fed can claim credit for curtailing inflation, which fluctuated between annual rates of 1.9 percent and 4.3 percent from 1983 through 1988. The economy also began a sustained period of growth that lasted from 1983 through 1990. Before that growth spurt, however, the United States experienced what was then the most severe recession since World War II, with unemployment rising to 10.75 percent in the fourth quarter of 1982. In spite of the prosperity achieved after 1982, unemployment did not drop below 5 percent until fifteen years later.

On the negative side, the Reagan administration's macroeconomic policies produced massive federal budget deficits. The deficits grew rapidly through a conjunction of forces: The 1981–1982 recession caused revenues to fall and triggered automatic countercyclical spending (such as unemployment compensation); the tax cuts and increased defense spending authorized in 1981 reduced revenues and increased some expenditures. The result was a large structural, or permanent, deficit as the increases in federal revenues promised by supply-side advocates failed to materialize and Congress refused to provide sizable additional cuts in nondefense spending. Finally, interest payments rose quickly to pay for government borrowing needed to close the gap between spending and revenues. From $990 billion in 1980, the debt rose to $3.1 trillion ten years later.[36] Of course, that seems tiny compared to the nearly $20 trillion accrued by early 2017.

There was a political advantage to unprecedented deficit spending. It put money in the pockets of American consumers, creating additional demand that in turn stimulated the economy and served as the basis for the sustained recovery from the 1981–1982 recession. That recovery was crucial to Reagan's 1984 reelection victory, for voters concluded that his economic policies had worked quite well. (Vice President Dick Cheney would later conclude, "Reagan proved deficits don't matter."[37]) The deficits also provided Reagan with an effective argument for restraining the growth of nondefense spending.

George H. W. Bush's victory in the 1988 presidential election was an endorsement of the status quo. The country was prosperous and not at war. Bush pledged during the campaign to support "no new taxes," a promise he kept until October 1990, when he faced the prospect of a large deficit that would trigger automatic budget cuts. His administration negotiated a budget deal with Congress that would balance the budget by 1996, a goal suddenly overwhelmed by unanticipated expenditures for the Persian Gulf War and the costs of bailing out failed savings and loan institutions insured by the federal government.[38] The deficits for fiscal 1991 ($269.36 billion) and 1992 ($290.40 billion) were the highest to that point in U.S. history. As a result of the high deficit, Congress and the president could use neither spending cuts nor tax reductions to combat the recession that began in late 1990 and continued into 1992.

The 1992 election registered voter dissatisfaction with the condition of the economy, but it produced no broad agreement on economic policies. Bill Clinton won a tepid electoral mandate—only 43 percent of the vote—and he had failed to provide concrete proposals for deficit reduction out of fear of antagonizing the voters. During the campaign, Clinton promised an economic stimulus package and a middle-class tax cut; deficit reduction was a distant concern. This plan began to change on December 3, 1992, during his first meeting with Fed chair Alan Greenspan, who argued that the key to prosperity was convincing Wall Street that the new administration was committed to reducing the budget deficit.[39]

Clinton moved quickly to address economic problems with a three-part plan unveiled within a month of his swearing-in. The plan included deficit reduction; long-term investments in research, education and training, and physical infrastructure; and short-term spending to stimulate the economy. By a single vote in each chamber, Congress passed legislation that reduced the deficit by $496 billion over five years, mainly through tax increases on the wealthy. (Much of this package should sound familiar to anyone following Obama's proposals.) A Senate filibuster mounted by Republicans killed the stimulus package, but economic conditions improved quickly: Unemployment dropped, inflation was moderate, and the economy grew at a healthy annual rate.[40] As a result of the 1993 deficit reduction package and a stronger than anticipated economic performance, the budget deficit fell from nearly $300 billion in 1992 to just over $108 billion by 1996,[41] and it turned the corner with a modest surplus in 1998. This goal was reached in just one year, five years earlier than anticipated in the 1997 budget agreement between Clinton and congressional Republicans.[42]

The Republicans were in the majority by then, which helped shape Clinton's policy choices as well. In the 1994 congressional elections, regarded as a referendum on Clinton's overall performance, the Democratic Party suffered a stunning defeat as the Republicans gained control over Congress for the first time in forty years. No Republican legislator had voted for the economic package, and the Democrats were branded as the party of high taxes. During the 1996 election and by the end of Clinton's term, however, his contributions to national prosperity seemed to underlie his reelection and the strong public support he received even in the midst of the impeachment controversy (see chapter 5).

Ultimately, "Clinton's fiscal policy served as a laboratory for a change in economic thought." Rather than relying on government deficits to stimulate economic activity, Clinton sought "balanced budgets—or better yet, surpluses—[which] are believed to hold down interest rates, free capital for the private sector and reassure investors about long-term economic stability."[43] The conventional Keynesian strategy for pursuing an expansionary fiscal policy was turned on its head. Ironically, this challenge to traditional economic thinking may have laid the groundwork for George W. Bush's initial legislative victories on economic policy.

Approval of a massive tax cut at the start of the Bush administration reversed a major part of the Clinton legacy—budget surpluses large enough to pay off the accumulated national debt and maintain solvency for the big-ticket programs of Social Security and Medicare. Clinton had been almost too successful. When estimates of future surpluses grew to $5.6 trillion over ten years, Democrats' arguments against "giving the people their money back" (Bush's central position) were undermined.[44] This debate occurred before 9/11 and the new pressures to increase spending for defense and homeland security. When the economy lagged, government revenues fell even farther and the deficit mounted for the **fiscal year**, the government's financial year that begins on October 1 and is commonly abbreviated FY. From a surplus of $128 billion in fiscal year 2001 (FY 2001), the federal budget returned to deficits of $158 billion in FY 2002 and $413 billion in FY 2004 (then an all-time record) before tapering off somewhat. At midyear 2007, the Congressional Budget Office (CBO) projected a surplus in 2012. Instead, deficits grew dramatically, reflecting the slowing economy and tax cuts (which resulted in lower revenues) as well as stimulus efforts (higher spending). The FY 2008 deficit of $454.8 billion was immediately dwarfed by a new record deficit of $1.4 *trillion* for FY 2009. President Obama's budgets for 2010 and 2011 led to deficits of $1.3 trillion, nearly a 50 percent increase from what the administration had projected in 2009.[45] But the deficit shrank in 2012, 2013, and 2014 as the economy began a slow but steady rebound (see Table 9-1). The CBO's projected deficit for FY 2017 was $559 billion.[46]

Even before the mammoth effort to stave off another depression, the erosion in federal finances was significant. Democrats point to Bush's tax cuts as the culprit; but huge new expenditures for homeland security added to the deficit, as did the wars in Iraq and Afghanistan. Those concerned with the rising national debt point to the sudden reversal after Clinton. "It took the federal government 28 years (1970–98) to produce a surplus, but only 4 years to return to deficit."[47] According to Peter Peterson, "A policy of endlessly rising deficits . . . constitutes an explicit decision by today's adults to collectively shift the current cost of government from themselves to their children and grandchildren."[48] The national debt ceiling—the limit to which the Treasury is authorized to borrow—was quietly raised on the day after approval of the 2003 tax cuts to $7.384 trillion to accommodate deficit spending accumulating at the rate of more than $1.5 billion a day. By contrast, the battle to raise the debt ceiling in 2011 dominated headlines for months. By February 2009, the national debt stood at $11.12 trillion, an increase of more than $5 trillion during the Bush presidency.[49] By April 2017, it had reached $19.8 trillion.[50]

Congress had moved quickly in February 2009 to pass Obama's economic stimulus package designed to combat the Great Recession. But suddenly, the national debate shifted. Huge budget deficits in FY 2009 and FY 2010 pushed the national debt dramatically higher, spawning political pressure to balance the national budget. Nor was there immediate evidence that the administration's economic policies were working. Not enough new jobs were being created to reduce the backlog of unemployed workers, and there were growing fears of a "double-dip recession," a second economic decline on the heels of the earlier Great Recession.

Aware of growing concern about the rising national debt, Obama convened a White House summit early in his administration focused on restoring budget discipline, and created the bipartisan National Commission on Fiscal Responsibility and Reform in 2010 to lay out options for returning the nation to a balanced budget even in the face of soaring costs. Bush had tried and failed to solve the gathering crisis in Social Security and Medicare, programs projected to run enormous deficits as the baby boom generation retires and becomes eligible for full benefits with Medicare. As one study concluded, "[A] significant opportunity to pre-fund future retirement and health benefits was missed" when the Clinton surplus disappeared.[51]

In the midst of bad economic news came bad political news for the Democrats: large midterm losses and the change of party control in the House. The new House Republican majority, energized by eighty-seven freshman members, insisted on immediate spending cuts. As a result, Congress passed the FY 2011 budget in April 2011 (more than six months late) only after the president agreed to cut spending by $38 billion in the final six months of the fiscal year. Then Republicans refused to raise the nation's debt ceiling unless there were spending cuts of $2.4 trillion over a decade, some identified immediately and others by a bipartisan joint "supercommittee" before Thanksgiving 2011. While the National Commission on Fiscal Responsibility and Reform's proposals to reduce federal spending by $4 trillion established a context for this discussion, the partisan debate became increasingly heated. When the August 2011 jobs report showed that no new jobs had been created, the administration developed a new $447 billion jobs plan, Republican presidential candidates highlighted the administration's poor job record, and congressional Republicans proposed their own plan, a massive reduction in regulations and taxes.

Coming congressional and presidential elections made bipartisan agreement impossible to reach, and the supercommittee failed to meet its target. Instead, White House and congressional negotiators put in place such an unattractive agreement that they were sure the parties would reach a future compromise: tax increases (anathema to Republicans) when the decade-old Bush tax cuts expired, accompanied by mandatory spending cuts (the **sequester**) of $1.2 trillion over ten years split evenly between domestic spending (which Democrats would hate) and defense spending (which Republicans would hate). (Also see chapter 5.) The first mandatory cuts were scheduled for 2013. The deadline for action was December 31, 2012, termed the "fiscal cliff" by the media. Obama and House Speaker John Boehner negotiated, but House Republicans would not support any tax increases, even on millionaires. Instead, Senate minority leader Mitch McConnell reached an agreement with Vice President Joe Biden on less extensive tax hikes and modest spending reductions, which were approved late on New Year's Day 2013. After another two months of fruitless talks, the sequester was implemented: $85 billion in automatic spending cuts went into effect, frustrating most members of Congress, Democrats and Republicans alike. The cuts were taken almost exclusively from **discretionary spending**, about 30 percent of the annual federal budget but not including the big-ticket items that most observers believed were driving budget growth: Social Security and Medicare.

But the budget wars were not over. In fall 2013, conservative Republicans refused to fund the federal government in an effort to destroy Obamacare, the target of repeated efforts to repeal the law since its passage in 2010. Nonessential federal workers were furloughed for sixteen days in October 2013, and the Treasury Department warned that the United States was dangerously close to defaulting on paying its bills. Again, a resolution was worked out in the Senate, and the House, the focus of the repeal campaign, went along reluctantly even though most Republicans remained opposed to compromise.[52] A different but similar scenario unfolded in 2015 when conservative Republicans, emboldened by their seat gains in the House and Senate in 2014 midterm elections, launched a new budget attack on the immigration initiatives announced by Obama after the 2014 elections. House opponents sought to defund the Department of Homeland Security, responsible for immigration enforcement as well as antiterrorism programs, while keeping the rest of the government funded. Conservative Republicans in the House hoped that the threat of shutting down the department would force the president to rescind his order that delayed deportation for millions of uncredentialed immigrants.

Once again, Senate Republicans refused to go along with their more extreme co-partisans, partly the result of their desire to show how the party could govern responsibly. House Republicans fractured badly between those seeking a way forward and those preferring a continued confrontation with the president. Facing the risk of appearing irresponsible in combating terrorism, a minority of House Republicans voted with House Democrats to approve a Senate version of Homeland Security funding crafted by Senator McConnell.

In early 2017, President Trump presented a budget outline for FY 2018 that proposed boosting defense spending by about 10 percent (a hefty $54 billion) while slashing domestic discretionary spending—notably environmental, scientific, health, and arts programs—by about the same amount. But the Trump agenda was far from deficit-neutral. The president held to his campaign pledge not to reduce entitlement spending, which continued on a sharp upward trajectory as the U.S. population grew older. He also asked for an additional, immediate $30 billion for the Pentagon (along with a $1 billion down payment on a southern border wall), joined with a pledge to seek as much as $1 trillion in infrastructure investment and a tax plan he said would be "bigger I believe than any tax cut ever."[53]

Treasury secretary Steve Mnuchin argued, congruent with the tenets of supply-side economics reviewed earlier, that "the plan will pay for itself with growth." Budget director Mick Mulvaney dismissed the issue entirely. "I'm really not interested in how tax reform handles the deficit," he told CNBC, since in his view tax cuts led to the most efficient allocation of societal resources.[54]

The Politics of Macroeconomic Policymaking

Presidents do not make macroeconomic policy in a vacuum or solely according to economic theories. As we have just seen in the case of budget decisions during the period 2011–2015, their decisions in this crucial area are intensely political and are affected by consideration of other policy goals (including microeconomic policy), electoral politics, interest group politics, and bureaucratic politics among institutional participants in the policymaking process. In a very real sense, the United States has a *political* economy, the nation is an economic *polity,* and the president is the focal point of the relationships involved in both.

Policy Politics

The achievement of macroeconomic policy goals is affected by, and has an effect on, other policy goals. National security policy objectives, for example, have a profound impact on economic policy. In the 1980s, substantial increases in defense spending beginning in FY 1982 reflected the consensus that U.S. military strength had declined compared with that of the Soviet Union. These increases hindered efforts to balance the budget. The end of the Cold War between the United States and the Soviet Union in late 1991 precipitated a budget struggle over the disposition of the "peace dividend" that congressional Democrats believed should result from the reduction of tensions. By fiscal 2016, the United States had spent nearly $3.7 trillion on the war on terror, the war in Afghanistan, and the Iraq War, an important contribution to the growing deficits.[55] As of the end of 2016, the Pentagon estimated that $10.99 billion had been spent on efforts to combat the so-called Islamic State, via airstrikes and the use of special operations forces in Iraq and Syria.[56]

Since 1990, budget-balancing efforts in domestic programs conflicted with commitments made to Social Security beneficiaries, welfare recipients, retired federal employees, and numerous other groups served by federal programs. In addition, the macroeconomic goals of economic growth, increased productivity, and full employment often appeared to be at odds with regulatory policies designed to improve environmental quality, enhance occupational safety and health, increase the safety of automobiles and other consumer products, and protect consumers against a variety of unfair business practices. Fiscal policy frequently served as the arena for resolving trade-offs among these conflicting goals.

Electoral Politics

Macroeconomic policy has important implications for electoral politics. It has long been recognized that presidential administrations and congressional majorities manipulate fiscal policy to produce short-term improvements in economic conditions to enhance their party's election prospects. They may adjust the timing and location of benefits to achieve this end, making policies that amount to marginal adjustments rather than fundamental restructuring of the economic system.

Presidents do not automatically avoid hard political choices and cave in to election pressures from party and special constituencies.[57] Ronald Reagan remained firm throughout his presidency in his commitment to the 1981 income tax cut based on supply-side theory, even though it meant proposing and defending record peacetime budget deficits (of around $200 billion) that were anathema to his conservative supporters. (Reagan did sign a number of countervailing tax increases into law.) George H. W. Bush reluctantly agreed to larger tax increases of $146 billion as part of a five-year, $496 billion deficit reduction package. (Opponents attacked him in the 1992 election campaign for breaking his "no new taxes" pledge, and he expressed regret at having done so.) In response to congressional pressures from Republicans and conservative Democrats and advice from his economic advisers, Bill Clinton abandoned his campaign promise of a tax cut for the middle class and settled for half of the major investments in human resources and infrastructure that were major elements in his proposed 1993 economic program.[58] During his first two-and-a-half years in office, George W. Bush saw 2.5 million jobs disappear during a sluggish recovery. To counter charges that he had ignored problems at home to address those abroad, the president accepted a tax cut in 2003 that was less than half his original proposal and failed to include several important policy changes (such as eliminating double taxation of dividends), calculating that it was the best he could achieve.[59] Obama remained true to his campaign promises of helping the middle class weather the economic storm. He included proposals in both the stimulus package and his initial budget to cut taxes for those who made less than $200,000 per year, as he proposed to phase out the Bush tax cuts for upper-income earners. But, as noted earlier, following the Democrats' 2010 midterm losses, Obama negotiated an agreement with Republicans to extend the Bush tax cuts in exchange for continued unemployment benefits.

Interest Group Politics

In making economic policy, presidents and Congress are subjected to pressures from interest groups, including business, labor, agriculture, the financial community, state and local governments, and foreign governments. The effect of these interests on policy varies according to the issues and the current economic conditions at home and abroad.

Business and labor interests are the most organized and thoroughly entrenched. Businesses use umbrella organizations, such as the U.S. Chamber of Commerce and the National Association of Manufacturers, to exert influence, as well as industry-based trade associations, such as the Automobile Manufacturers Association and the American Gas Association. Individual companies, especially large corporations, also try to shape policy. Businesses usually concentrate their lobbying on microeconomic policies that specifically affect their operations but may also be concerned about areas of macroeconomic policy: inflation, tax burdens, and interest rates.

Organized labor encompasses the giant AFL-CIO (American Federation of Labor-Congress of Industrial Organizations) and a host of independent unions. Labor's position on macroeconomic policy issues usually contrasts sharply with that of business. Labor worries more about unemployment than inflation, stresses "fair" rather than "free" trade, supports fiscal stimulation of the economy in periods of recession, and opposes the use of monetary restraints to curb inflation. Like business, labor takes great interest in microeconomic policy directly affecting its interests, including regulation of labor-management relations and regulations to promote occupational safety and health.

Agricultural interest groups, though shrinking in membership, remain quite diverse. The American Farm Bureau Federation and the National Grange support conservative policies, while the National Farmers Union and the National Farmers Organization take more liberal stances. Regardless of their ideologies, farm organizations tend to oppose monetary policies that result in high interest rates because the use of credit is an essential part of farm management.

The financial community consists of two principal components, the securities exchanges—Wall Street—and banks and other financial institutions. (Wall Street and financial institutions buy and sell "paper"—government and private financial obligations—and bonds, the longer-term securities.) Wall Street registers its reactions to monetary and fiscal policies—investor confidence—through the prices of corporate stocks traded on the major stock exchanges. Bond prices move up or down inversely with interest rates and reflect monetary policy shifts; interest paid on short-term government and commercial paper also fluctuates as monetary policy changes. Administrations seek to have their policies favorably received by Wall Street and by major banks and other leading financial institutions. A vote of "no confidence" by the financial community in the government's economic policies makes the administration vulnerable to criticism by political opponents and weakens its popular support. As in the broader business world, members of the financial community tend to support conservative fiscal policies and monetary restraint to control inflation. They fear large deficits, whether due to high spending levels or sizable tax cuts. Similarly, some bankers considered the terms associated with the financial help they received in 2008 and 2009 as too intrusive, arguing that government was restricting their decisions. By contrast, Obama officials were roundly criticized for allowing banks to continue to pay extravagant salaries and conduct business as usual. Dodd-Frank was the target of intense lobbying as it was being drafted and moved through Congress—and afterwards, as it was being implemented.

With the advent of the Great Society domestic programs in the mid-1960s, state and local governments became vitally interested in macroeconomic policy. The federal government is a source of funding for a wide range of state and local programs in education, welfare and social services, housing and urban development, transportation, and health care. Consequently, many state and local governments, collectively—through national associations, such as the U.S. Conference of Mayors—and individually—through the efforts of members of Congress—have exerted pressure to maintain the flow of federal funds, even though this goal could be accomplished only at the expense of larger and potentially inflationary budget deficits.

Presidents Reagan and George H. W. Bush sought to reduce state and local dependence on federal funding. This effort failed to accomplish its most revolutionary goals, but it triggered a rethinking of federal aid and its implications for macroeconomic policy.[60] Conservatives demanded that financial responsibility for major redistributive programs be shifted to the states, and in 1995 the Republican majority in Congress proposed ending entitlement status for welfare (Aid to Families with Dependent Children) and Medicaid by converting federally funded programs—accompanied by extensive federal rules and regulations—to programs giving block grants to states. Clinton vetoed two Republican versions of these changes, but in 1996 he compromised with the Republicans. Welfare (but not Medicaid) lost its entitlement status and became a block grant program.[61] House Republicans, however, continued to press similar proposals for Medicaid, and included them in efforts to repeal the Affordable Care Act in 2017.

Presidents and their administrations are constrained to some degree by concerns about how their economic policy decisions will affect the economies of other nations. Friendly governments—the European Union, Japan, and Saudi Arabia—favor a dollar that is neither overvalued nor undervalued and a healthy U.S. economy with full employment and a low inflation rate. If the dollar is weak, the value of much of their international currency reserves declines, and their goods are less competitive in U.S. markets, a problem that arose during 2002 and 2003. If the dollar is too strong, foreign investment capital migrates to the United States, and the high competitiveness of foreign products in U.S. markets threatens to provoke trade restrictions. When unemployment in the United States rises, the demand for foreign products contracts. In 2011–2015, anomalous conditions arose: Unstable financial conditions abroad caused capital to flow into the United States even though U.S. interest rates were lower. Consequently, foreign governments usually press U.S. administrations to keep the exchange value of the dollar from fluctuating widely and to hold down interest rates. The unusually strong U.S. dollar in 2014–2015 (with a strong currency, one dollar buys more of a foreign currency) raised the price of U.S. products sold abroad but did the opposite for foreign suppliers of goods to U.S. consumers.

Presidents do not respond to all interest group constituencies, and the constituencies whose support they do seek vary in importance to them. In no case, however, do presidents make macroeconomic policy decisions without regard to some interest groups, which are major factors in the politics of economic policymaking.

The Economic Subpresidency

In discharging the role of economic manager, chief executives seek to meet popular and elite expectations that their actions will result in a prosperous economy. Presidents must develop and implement policies and build support for them in the public and in the Washington community. To accomplish these complex and demanding tasks, presidents need information, advice, and administrative assistance to focus energy on major issues, integrate the policies of their administrations, take account of all-important interests, and maintain the administration's cohesion. This advice and assistance is provided by a set of specialized organizations located in the White House and in the executive branch, organizations that have been called the "economic subpresidency." All those engaged in making, defining, communicating, and implementing economic policy decisions, "whether they act personally or as part of an institution," are part of this policymaking system.[62] How presidents use the economic subpresidency varies across administrations and with economic conditions, but the system is central to policymaking and presidential management of the economy. Staff members serve in one of four major administrative units—the CEA, OMB, the Treasury Department, or the Fed—or on various intragovernmental committees and councils. Leading members of these units since the early 1950s are listed in Tables 9-2 through 9-5.

Council of Economic Advisers

The CEA has three members, appointed by the president and subject to Senate confirmation, plus a small staff of twenty-five to thirty-five, divided between professional economists and support personnel. Traditionally, most CEA members and professional staffers have had extensive experience in business or government. The CEA's chair (see Table 9-2) is responsible for administering

TABLE 9-2 Chairs of the Council of Economic Advisers, 1953–2017

President	*Chair*	*Years*
Eisenhower	Arthur F. Burns	1953–1956
	Raymond T. Saulnier	1956–1961
Kennedy	Walter W. Heller	1961–1963
Johnson	Walter W. Heller	1963–1964
	Gardner H. Ackley	1964–1968
	Arthur M. Okun	1968–1969
Nixon	Paul W. McCracken	1969–1971
	Herbert Stein	1972–1974
Ford	Herbert Stein	1974
	Alan Greenspan	1974–1977
Carter	Charles L. Schultze	1977–1981
Reagan	Murray L. Weidenbaum	1981–1982
	Martin Feldstein	1982–1984
	Beryl Sprinkel	1985–1989
G. H. W. Bush	Michael J. Boskin	1989–1993
Clinton	Laura D. Tyson	1993–1994
	Joseph E. Stiglitz	1995–1997
	Janet L. Yellen	1997–1999
	Martin Baily	1999–2001
G. W. Bush	R. Glenn Hubbard	2001–2003
	N. Gregory Mankiw	2003–2005
	Harvey S. Rosen	2005
	Ben S. Bernanke	2005–2006
	Edward P. Lazear	2006–2009
Obama	Christina Romer	2009–2010
	Austan Goolsbee	2010–2011
	Alan Krueger	2011–2013
	Jason Furman	2013–2017
Trump	Kevin Hassett	Nominated 2017

SOURCE: Compiled by authors from https://obamawhitehouse.archives.gov/administration/eop/cea/about/former-chairs.

the council hiring staff, representing the CEA on other government councils and committees, and reporting to the president. He or she establishes the council's orientation according to the president's overall objectives. The chair's relationship with the president largely determines the CEA's influence in shaping economic policy.

The CEA has no operational responsibilities but serves entirely in a staff capacity as a sort of in-house think tank. It gathers information, makes economic

TABLE 9-3 Directors of the Budget Bureau/Office of Management and Budget, 1953–2017

President	*Director*	*Years*
Eisenhower (BOB)	Joseph M. Dodge	1953–1954
	Rowland R. Hughes	1954–1956
	Percival F. Brundage	1956–1958
	Maurice Stans	1958–1961
Kennedy	David E. Bell	1961–1962
	Kermit Gordon	1962–1963
Johnson	Kermit Gordon	1963–1965
	Charles E. Schultze	1965–1968
	Charles J. Zwick	1968–1969
Nixon (OMB)	Robert P. Mayo	1969–1970
	George P. Shultz	1971–1972
	Caspar Weinberger	1972–1973
	Roy L. Ash	1973–1974
Ford	Roy L. Ash	1974–1975
	James P. Lynn	1975–1977
Carter	Bert Lance	1977
	James T. McIntyre	1977–1981
Reagan	David Stockman	1981–1985
	James C. Miller III	1985–1988
	Joseph R. Wright Jr.	1988–1989
G. H. W. Bush	Richard G. Darman	1989–1993
Clinton	Leon E. Panetta	1993–1994
	Alice Rivlin	1994–1996
	Franklin D. Raines	1996–1998
	Jacob J. Lew	1998–2001
G. W. Bush	Mitchell E. Daniels Jr.	2001–2003
	Joshua B. Bolten	2003–2006
	Rob Portman	2006–2007
	Jim Nussle	2007–2009
Obama	Peter R. Orszag	2009–2010
	Jacob Lew	2010–2012
	Sylvia M. Burwell	2013–2014
	Shaun Donovan	2014–2017
Trump	John Michael "Mick" Mulvaney	2017–

SOURCE: Compiled by authors, https://obamawhitehouse.archives.gov/omb/organization_former_directors/.

forecasts, analyzes economic issues, and prepares the annual *Economic Report of the President,* presented to Congress. It provides the president with expert economic advice, and the members occasionally act as public spokespersons for

TABLE 9-4 Secretaries of the Treasury, 1953–2017

President	*Secretary*	*Years*
Eisenhower	George M. Humphrey	1953–1957
	Robert Anderson	1957–1961
Kennedy	C. Douglas Dillon	1961–1963
Johnson	C. Douglas Dillon	1964–1965
	Henry H. Fowler	1965–1968
	Joseph W. Barr	1968–1969
Nixon	David M. Kennedy	1969–1971
	John B. Connally	1971–1972
	George P. Shultz	1972–1974
	William E. Simon	1974
Ford	William E. Simon	1974–1977
Carter	W. Michael Blumenthal	1977–1979
	G. William Miller	1979–1981
Reagan	Donald T. Regan	1981–1985
	James A. Baker III	1985–1988
	Nicholas F. Brady	1988–1989
G. H. W. Bush	Nicholas F. Brady	1989–1993
Clinton	Lloyd M. Bentsen	1993–1994
	Robert E. Rubin	1995–1999
	Lawrence H. Summers	1999–2001
G. W. Bush	Paul H. O'Neill	2001–2002
	John W. Snow	2003–2006
	Henry M. Paulson	2006–2009
Obama	Timothy F. Geithner	2009–2013
	Jacob J. Lew	2013–2017
Trump	Steven T. Mnuchin	2017–

SOURCE: U.S. Department of the Treasury, "Secretaries of the Treasury," www.treasury.gov/about/history/Pages/edu_history_secretary_index.aspx.

the president. The council usually does not broker agreements among conflicting parties or coordinate policymaking within the administration, although its members tend to reflect the theories and policy views of the president. In general, Democratic presidents have had Keynesian CEA members, and Republicans have selected classical conservative and monetarist economists. Reagan, for example, appointed a conservative economist to chair the CEA at the start of his presidency and added a monetarist and a supply-sider. All three were committed to free trade, reduced government spending, a balanced federal budget, and limited federal intervention in the economy.

TABLE 9-5 Chairs of the Federal Reserve Board, 1951–2017

President	*Chair*	*Years*
Eisenhower	William McC. Martin	1951–1961
Kennedy	William McC. Martin	1961–1963
Johnson	William McC. Martin	1963–1969
Nixon	William McC. Martin	1969–1970
	Arthur F. Burns	1970–1974
Ford	Arthur F. Burns	1974–1977
Carter	Arthur F. Burns	1977–1978
	G. William Miller	1978–1979
	Paul A. Volcker	1979–1981
Reagan	Paul A. Volcker	1981–1987
	Alan Greenspan	1987–1989
G. H. W. Bush	Alan Greenspan	1989–1993
Clinton	Alan Greenspan	1993–2001
G. W. Bush	Alan Greenspan	2001–2005
	Ben S. Bernanke	2006–2009
Obama	Ben S. Bernanke	2009–2014
	Janet L. Yellen	2014–2017
Trump	Janet L. Yellen	2017–

SOURCE: Board of Governors of the Federal Reserve System, "Membership of the Board of Governors of the Federal Reserve System, 1914-Present," www.federalreserve.gov/aboutthefed/bios/board/boardmembership.htm.

If presidents believe they need economic expertise and share basic interests and values with CEA members, the council may significantly influence economic policymaking. The council's expertise enhances presidential policies, and its analyses and forecasts acquire political significance through association with the presidency. In the long run, however, the council can do only what the president asks and allows it to do.

The CEA played a more significant role with respect to the deficit in the George H. W. Bush administration than under Reagan. Its chair, monetarist economist Michael J. Boskin (1989–1993), enjoyed Bush's confidence and often acted as a spokesperson for the administration. Clinton appointed Laura D'Andrea Tyson (1993–1994) of University of California, Berkeley, who was an expert on trade policy and not a professional macroeconomist, to chair his CEA. When Tyson became chair of another White House coordinating unit—the National Economic Council (NEC)—in 1995, three others succeeded her as CEA chair in rapid succession. The turnover is one indicator that the CEA may not have influenced Clinton's policymaking.

The council's forecasts help set the boundaries of the president's legislative program and budget proposals. It is to the president's advantage for the council to approach its advisory task deductively, fitting program pieces together within the framework of the president's overall objectives. The council's contribution to policymaking is primarily conceptual and not in the realm of implementation or coordination. This is the reality that confronted George W. Bush's first CEA chair, R. Glenn Hubbard (2001–2003), a professor of economics and business at Columbia University, who had served in the Treasury Department under George H. W. Bush and was a major architect of the administration's 2003 tax-cut proposals.[63] He was succeeded by Harvard economist N. Gregory Mankiw and a series of others, including Ben S. Bernanke, who went on to become chairman of the Federal Reserve Board (see below).

Obama selected Christina Romer as his first CEA chair. Known for her research on the Great Depression, Romer taught at the University of California, Berkeley, and Princeton University and served as codirector of the Program in Monetary Economics at the National Bureau of Economic Research and vice president of the American Economic Association.[64] But Romer stayed only a little more than a year and complained after leaving that her advice had been excluded by other members of the Obama subpresidency.[65]

Jason Furman succeeded Austan Goolsbee and Alan Krueger, assuming the chair's role in August 2013. Furman was part of the administration from the outset after working on the 2008 campaign as a top Obama adviser on economic policy, a role he had also played for John Kerry during the 2004 campaign. He was heavily involved in economic policy during the design and implementation of the economic stimulus program in 2009–2010. Though he held a Ph.D. in economics, like all CEA chairs so far, unlike many of his predecessors Furman built his career by being a policy adviser rather than an academic economist.

Trump waited until early April 2017 before naming Kevin Hassett to chair his CEA. Hassett's career brought him from the Federal Reserve Board staff to Columbia University and, in 1997, to the American Enterprise Institute, a Washington think-tank. He was well-known in conservative economic circles and had more traditional views on trade (and trade wars, for instance with China) than others on Trump's economic team.

Office of Management and Budget

Presidents receive economic advice of a different sort from the five hundred or so employees in OMB. Whereas the CEA's primary concern is controlling the business cycle and achieving sustained economic growth, OMB's major focus is allocating resources to federal administrative agencies and their programs through the annual preparation of the president's budget. Its institutional bias is toward holding down spending and improving governmental efficiency. It is the principal instrument through which the president fashions the expenditure component of fiscal policy. In addition, OMB provides economic forecasts to the president and acts as a management consultant to the agencies as well as a "legislative and regulatory gatekeeper" that conducts detailed policy analysis of proposed bills and agency rules.[66]

OMB began life as the Bureau of the Budget (BOB) in the Treasury Department, and was moved into the president's inner orbit by Franklin Roosevelt in 1939. OMB is staffed by an elite group of government careerists devoted to serving the presidency, whoever the particular president might be. Since 1970, when Nixon reorganized it, OMB has been more actively involved in serving the president's political needs. But OMB directors (see Table 9-3) have long participated in developing presidential policies and building support for them. The budget has become as much a political weapon as a managerial tool or an instrument of fiscal policy.

The political use of the budget was never more apparent than during the Reagan administration and David Stockman's tenure as budget director (1981–1985). Stockman dominated federal budgeting in a manner previously unknown. He centralized the presidential advice about the executive budget process in OMB and involved himself extensively in the congressional budget proceedings through direct negotiations and bargaining with congressional committees.

Under Stockman's successor, economist James C. Miller III (1985–1988), OMB continued to serve Reagan's political interests but much less visibly. During the George H. W. Bush presidency, OMB was a major player in the economic subpresidency. Its director, Richard G. Darman (1989–1993), and the White House chief of staff, John Sununu, were the principal negotiators with Congress concerning fiscal policy. (Darman dealt primarily with spending and Sununu with taxes.) OMB also became the dominant agency for economic forecasting.

The budget remained the main instrument for achieving the president's policy goals during the Clinton administration. Clinton named Leon E. Panetta (1993–1994), chair of the House Budget Committee, as his first OMB director. (Panetta went on to be Clinton's White House chief of staff and later served Obama as director of the CIA and secretary of defense.) Panetta was a "deficit hawk" (a strong advocate for deficit reduction) and a Democratic loyalist who possessed parliamentary acumen and budgetary expertise.[67] He was influential in shaping Clinton's 1993 economic plan and selling it to Congress. When Panetta became Clinton's chief of staff in June 1994, economist Alice Rivlin (1994–1996) became OMB's director. Rivlin had served previously as director of the Congressional Budget Office and was even more hawkish on the deficit than Panetta. Their presence "ensured that deficit reduction would command considerable attention" as the administration shaped economic policy.[68] Rivlin was succeeded by Franklin D. Raines (1996–1998) and Raines by former congressional staffer Jacob J. Lew (1998–2001).

George W. Bush chose as OMB director Mitchell E. Daniels Jr. (2001–2003), a pharmaceutical executive with extensive political experience on Capitol Hill and in the Reagan White House but not in budget-related positions.[69] He named Joshua B. Bolten, a lawyer and investment banker who was serving as Bush's deputy chief of staff, as Daniels's successor in May 2003. When Chief of Staff Andrew Card resigned in 2006, Bush moved Bolten back to the White House and named Rob Portman to head OMB. Portman was the U.S. Trade Representative, but had served on the House Budget and Ways and Means Committees. After one year, Portman left, and former representative Jim Nussle of Iowa took the post. Nussle's credentials rested on his six years as chair of the House Budget Committee, where he established a reputation as a highly partisan defender of Republican priorities, a style he brought to the White House.

Peter Orszag became Obama's first OMB director after completing nearly two years as director of the Congressional Budget Office, serving on the Clinton administration's CEA staff, and spending an extended period at the Brookings Institution, a liberal Washington think tank.[70] When Orszag left in mid-2010, there was a temporary director until Jacob Lew was convinced to return to the position he formerly held under Clinton. When Lew became Obama's White House chief of staff in January 2012, Jeffrey Zients resumed the position of acting director, eventually succeeded by former OMB deputy director Sylvia M. Burwell. Burwell served for just a year before she became secretary of Health and Human Services, where she worked to solve the problems that arose in implementing the Affordable Care Act. Shaun Donovan, secretary of Housing and Urban Development since 2009, then became the OMB director until the end of Obama's term.

Trump selected Rep. Mick Mulvaney (R-S.C.) as his first budget director. Mulvaney was a member of the House Freedom Caucus and known for his confrontational stance on fiscal issues; he had actively supported the showdowns (and government shutdown) over the debt limit during the Obama administration.

His stance favoring cuts to entitlement programs seemingly put him in conflict with his new boss, but Trump soon entrusted him with assignments ranging from regulatory relief to negotiations over health care legislation.

Treasury Department

The third institutional participant in the economic subpresidency is the Treasury Department, which is responsible for collecting taxes, managing the national debt, controlling the currency, collecting customs, and handling international monetary affairs, including management of the balance of payments and the value of the dollar in relation to other currencies. With more than 100,000 employees, it is the primary government source of information on revenues, the tax system, and financial markets. It also takes the lead in developing tax bills and steering them through Congress.[71]

Traditionally, the Treasury Department has been concerned with the adequacy of revenues, the soundness of the dollar, and the cost of financing the debt. To finance the debt, the department has advocated either low interest rates or a balanced budget. Before the Reagan administration, a situation in which high interest rates accompanied a large deficit was anathema to the institutional interests of the Treasury. Its position altered substantially under President Reagan and Secretary of the Treasury Donald T. Regan (1981–1985) (see Table 9-4). An avowed believer in supply-side economics, Regan argued that temporary deficits resulting from tax-cut incentives would ultimately lead to economic growth, expanded revenues, and balanced budgets. He opposed efforts to reduce the deficit by raising taxes. He was more concerned with the supply of money in the domestic economy than with the exchange value of the dollar. Regan's successor as secretary, James A. Baker III (1985–1988), concentrated heavily on exchange rate problems.

Secretary of the Treasury Nicholas F. Brady played a marginal role in the economic subpresidency under President George H. W. Bush. One veteran White House observer and analyst suggests that the "patrician" Brady was no match for the "pit bull approach of his two economic policy colleagues," Darman and Sununu.[72]

President Clinton's first two secretaries of the Treasury, Lloyd M. Bentsen (1993–1994) and Robert E. Rubin (1995–1999), were central participants in the economic subpresidency. By appointing Bentsen, a moderate Democrat with business experience who chaired the Senate Finance Committee, Clinton sought to reassure the business community.[73] The appointment of Rubin, a Wall Street investment banker who had served as Clinton's chair of the NEC (see the discussion below), accomplished a similar purpose. Both men were deeply involved in shaping the 1993 economic program.[74] Lawrence H. Summers, a Rubin protégé as deputy secretary, served as secretary from 1999 to 2001.

George W. Bush selected Paul H. O'Neill (2001–2002) as Treasury secretary. O'Neill was a ten-year veteran of OMB who later worked for International Paper before becoming CEO of Alcoa Aluminum.[75] But O'Neill proved to be an outspoken cabinet secretary. He sometimes questioned the administration's tax-cutting policies (he was not a supply-sider), frequently irked influential members of Congress, and failed to calm investors in 2002 during the corporate scandals; in January 2003 he became the first member of the Bush cabinet to leave his position.[76] John W. Snow, CEO of a railroad freight company and chair of the Business Roundtable, an elite corporate lobbying group, took over until mid-2006. He was succeeded by Henry M. Paulson, former chair and CEO of Goldman Sachs, one of New York City's most successful investment banks. Timothy Geithner, Obama's choice to lead the Treasury Department, had worked there during three administrations. He also worked for the International Monetary Fund and was president and chief executive officer of the Federal Reserve Bank of New York before joining the administration.[77] When Geithner left government shortly after Obama was sworn in for a second term, the president moved his White House chief of staff and former director of OMB, Jacob Lew, into the Treasury job. Lew's White House role had no doubt provided him with the most critical qualifications that any adviser could hope for—the president's confidence. Lew helped lead the administration's negotiations during the 2013 debt limit and government shutdown talks, discussed earlier. Donald Trump's first choice to lead Treasury was Steven Mnuchin, whose career was entirely in the private sector; he had been a hedge fund investor and film financier after seventeen years at financial firm Goldman Sachs. Mnuchin was an early supporter of the Trump campaign and served as its national finance chair.

Organizationally, the Treasury Department is divided between large units with major line responsibilities, such as the Internal Revenue Service (IRS), and policy-related units, such as the office of the undersecretary for monetary affairs. The policy-related units, located in the office of the secretary, never have provided coordination of economic policy for an administration, although the potential exists for them to do so.[78] About 20 percent of the department's workforce, including the Secret Service; the Customs Service; and much of the Bureau of

Alcohol, Tobacco, Firearms and Explosives was shifted to the new Department of Homeland Security.

Federal Reserve Board

The Federal Reserve Board is an independent agency charged with responsibility for regulating the money supply and the banking system. Its seven members are appointed by the president to fourteen-year terms with the consent of the Senate—a period that ensures each member will outlast at least one presidential administration. Further, unlike most executive branch agencies, the Fed does not rely on annual congressional appropriations, which also aids its institutional independence.

The president designates one member of the board to act as its chair for a four-year term, but the chair, an important source of institutional influence, often serves beyond that limit, as shown in Table 9-5. The Fed has three traditional ways of controlling the money supply: (1) the discount rate; (2) reserve requirements; and (3) open-market operations, the buying and selling of government securities that set the federal funds rate. In an effort to combat the recession of 2008 and 2009, the Fed developed new strategies to stimulate the economy.

The discount rate is the interest rate charged commercial banks to borrow from the Federal Reserve. An increase in the discount rate tightens the availability of credit because it forces banks to charge more to their borrowers. Reserves are liquid assets banks hold to meet demands for ready cash from their depositors. The Federal Reserve requires commercial banks belonging to it to maintain a certain percentage (usually ranging from 10 percent to 20 percent) of their deposit liabilities in the form of cash in their vaults or on account with the regional reserve bank for this purpose. A reduction in the reserve requirement increases the amount of money banks may loan to their borrowers, and an increase in the reserve requirement decreases the availability of bank credit.

The Federal Open Market Committee (FOMC) approved thirteen consecutive reductions in the federal funds rate after Bush took office in January 2001. From a level of 6.5 percent, on January 1, 2001, the rate was progressively reduced to 1 percent, on June 25, 2003, producing the lowest consumer interest rates since 1958. These policy decisions were designed to encourage economic expansion. Unemployment had risen from an annual average of 4.0 percent in 2000 to 6.4 percent in June 2003. Thereafter, the funds rate was raised steadily over four years to 5.25 percent, as economic growth accelerated and the Fed sought to slow inflationary pressures. But with the advent of the global credit crisis, the Fed reversed course in September 2007, began sharply reducing the federal funds rate and the discount rate. By December 2008 that rate was effectively zero, where it stayed for seven years. The rate rose by 0.25 percent in December 2015 but with the economy still sluggish stayed there for a full year, finally rising twice in relatively quick succession in early 2017, though still at barely 1 percent.

In 1995, the FOMC began releasing explicit statements of its short-term policy objectives.[79] It now issues a statement after each of its meetings, not just those in which a rate change has been approved. Since March 2002, it has also reported the positions of its twelve voting members, the seven members of the Federal Reserve Board and five of the twelve Federal Reserve Bank presidents.

Although neither the president nor Congress can tell the Fed how to conduct monetary policy, the board traditionally has been the target of political pressures, especially during adverse economic conditions. Depending on circumstances, the inflation resulting from expansionary monetary policy or the stagnation and unemployment caused by restrictive policy can draw fire. During the Clinton administration, members of Congress and Wall Street frequently criticized the Fed for raising interest rates at the first sign of inflation and reducing them too slowly, but relations were generally cordial between Clinton and Greenspan, the Fed chair.[80] Clinton twice reappointed Greenspan (1996 and 2000) to the post he first assumed in 1987, and George W. Bush reappointed him when his term expired in 2004. After serving an unprecedented five terms as Fed chairman, Greenspan retired in January 2006. Expressing popular sentiment, Mankiw wrote, "No aspect of U.S. policy in the 1990s is more widely hailed as a success than monetary policy. Fed Chairman Alan Greenspan is often viewed as a miracle worker."[81] That reputation dimmed after the severe recession's onset, and Greenspan acknowledged having made policy errors.

Greenspan generally worked well with the Clinton administration and admired the president's commitment to fiscal responsibility. His relations with George W. Bush were sometimes rocky. Although he had endorsed Bush's 2001 tax cuts, in February and July 2003, he warned Congress about the impact of ballooning deficits projected to flow from another round of cuts. By stressing the need for budget discipline, he weakened the case for even larger proposed tax cuts, and his memoir expressed strong disagreement with the Bush administration's policies. Greenspan was replaced by Ben Bernanke, former chair of the CEA, who was expected to provide a smooth transition to a post-Greenspan era. An expert on the Great Depression, Bernanke worked closely with Paulson and Geithner to fashion effective strategies to prevent a financial collapse and avoid having the recession become a depression.

Many observers credited Bernanke with saving the world's financial system during the 2008–2009 financial crisis, though some critics questioned whether policymakers were merely bailing out the wealthy, irresponsible bankers who had caused the disaster. Criticism mounted as Bernanke changed his focus from rescuing the financial system to helping the economy recover. Liberal economists argued that the Fed should be pumping even more money into the economy in order to raise wages and generate more jobs, even if that might cause inflation (a rise in prices). Conservative economists feared inflation, believed that the Fed was doing too much, and preferred that markets be allowed to do their job even if that produced high unemployment, loan defaults, and business failures. Thus, Bernanke had to steer the Fed through a difficult balancing act. Even the members of the Fed's policymaking committees were divided on what to do and unsure about what policies might work, though minutes from their meetings show they agreed "it was worth trying everything."[82] Reducing short-term interest rates and keeping them near zero was the conventional policy to stimulate the economy, but Bernanke also employed other relatively novel actions designed to lower long-term interest rates. To critics from the right, particularly in the Tea Party, the Fed

Scott J. Ferrell/Congressional Quarterly/Getty Images

Treasury Secretary Timothy Geithner and Federal Reserve Chair Ben Bernanke testified before Congress in March 2009 on the government's financial support for the failed insurance company, American Insurance Group (AIG). The severity of the economic crisis produced close cooperation among policymakers during both the Bush and Obama administrations.

seemed to be printing money, distributing it widely, and running up the nation's debt, though in fact the Fed's actions were "loans," not deficit spending, and had no impact on the nation's debt.

When the economic recovery seemed to falter, both liberal and conservative critics became more outspoken: The Fed was not doing enough; the Fed was doing too much. President Obama nominated Bernanke (a Republican) in 2010 to a second term as chair, and the Senate voted 70–30 to approve the appointment, the smallest margin of victory for any Fed chair in history.[83] The public was understandably unhappy with the condition of the economy—the number of new jobs remained low, wages were not growing for most workers, and new loans were hard to get as banks imposed tougher criteria for approval. Public disapproval of Bernanke persisted despite the chairman's unprecedented efforts to explain the reasons behind his policies—holding press conferences and town hall meetings, appearing on talk shows, and participating in interviews. After leaving office in early 2014, when he was succeeded by Janet Yellen, Bernanke remained an influential commentator on economic policy.[84]

Presidents and Economic Policy Coordination

The independence of the Fed, the operational needs and organizational interests of the Treasury Department, and the institutional perspectives of other departments and agencies have led presidents to seek various ways to coordinate economic policy. For reasons explained in chapter 6, the cabinet has not been a satisfactory vehicle for collective leadership. Instead, presidents have developed a variety of intragovernmental councils and committees designed to provide a cohesive macroeconomic policy and integrate it with other policy objectives. Most of these entities failed to survive the administrations of their creators because subsequent presidents sought mechanisms more compatible with their own operating styles. A brief review of these undertakings, however, reveals common patterns in their approaches and indicates the essential requirements for a minimal amount of coordination. The most important institutional relationship has been with the Fed; it has been essential that administrations establish coordination through regular meetings as a means to share information and policy intentions so that the two sides can avoid pursuing contradictory policies.[85] This has not always happened; the Johnson, Nixon, Reagan, and George W. Bush administrations made less effort to consult with the Fed than to assert their own policy preferences.

Probably the most significant development for macroeconomic policymaking occurred under President Kennedy with the creation of the "troika," an informal committee consisting of the chair of the CEA, the secretary of the Treasury, and the budget director. The troika's original purpose was to coordinate economic forecasting, but it quickly became a mechanism for developing cooperation within the economic subpresidency in formulating fiscal policy. President Eisenhower's groups met often but were too numerous to bring about effective coordination. When joined by the chair of the Fed to coordinate monetary policy, the group has been known as the "quadriad." The participants have a "mutual interest in cooperation, not in their legal independence from each other. For an administration's economic policy to succeed, the Fed should pursue a parallel monetary policy" and vice versa.[86]

Working with staff support from the CEA, the Treasury Department, OMB, and occasionally the Fed, the troika/quadriad has helped many presidents formulate macroeconomic policy in a rapid, adaptive manner with some measure of protection from political and bureaucratic pressures. Not all presidents have made extensive use of the troika, but it is a natural institutional grouping that continues to operate, with the Treasury Department assuming responsibility for revenue estimates, OMB generating estimates of federal expenditures, the CEA forecasting economic trends, and the Fed (when involved) projecting money supply requirements.

Under President Lyndon B. Johnson, the troika emerged as the principal mechanism for the development of fiscal policy advice and alternatives.[87] President Nixon was uncomfortable with attempts to make policy by cabinet-level committees, and in early 1971 he designated Secretary of the Treasury John B. Connally (1971–1972) as his economic "czar," with responsibility for making major decisions. Connally dominated the troika, but his successor as Treasury secretary, George P. Shultz (1972–1974), operated in a more collegial manner. At the start of his second term, in January 1973, Nixon made Shultz assistant to the president for economic affairs and named him to chair a new cabinet-level coordinating body, the Council on Economic Policy. Shultz, working through interdepartmental committees, became the dominant figure in making and expounding economic policy for the Nixon administration.

Thus started a series of presidential experiments with coordinating councils or "troika plus" groups. Gerald Ford used the Economic Policy Board (EPB), which operated in a formal and structured way to coordinate domestic and foreign economic policies. The secretary of the Treasury chaired the EPB, which also included the secretaries of labor, commerce, and state; the chair of the CEA; the director of OMB; and the assistant to the president for economic affairs. The latter official also directed the small EPB staff, housed in the Executive Office of the President (EOP). Departments and agencies provided information, analysis, and expertise.[88] President Carter replaced the EPB with the Economic Policy Group (EPG), cochaired by the secretary of the Treasury and the chair of the CEA. This large, unwieldy body had no staff; its operations remained so unstructured that it was unable to coordinate even minor policy initiatives.[89]

President Reagan replaced the EPG with the Cabinet Council on Economic Affairs (CCEA). Like its predecessor in the Nixon administration, the CCEA was a forum for discussion of issues and alternatives. Roger Porter, veteran of the Ford EPB, was its secretary and informally coordinated its operations. In addition to the council, the troika met regularly to coordinate economic forecasting. But coordination efforts did not ensure that struggles for influence would disappear. The major participants in these battles were Regan, Stockman, Baker, and Meese. There were sharp disagreements over the means to accomplish the administration's macroeconomic policy goals: to reduce the role of the federal government in the U.S. economy, thus reducing taxes and spending, and to increase productivity, savings, and investment to ensure vigorous and sustained economic growth and full employment. The conflict reflected competition among classical conservative, monetarist, and supply-side theories and focused on the significance of federal budget deficits. The winners were Regan and Meese, the supply-side advocates, with Stockman unsuccessful in his efforts to promote far larger spending cuts.[90] In the second term, Baker (now at Treasury) spearheaded a major tax reform that aimed to be revenue-neutral—it lowered tax rates but reduced taxpayers' deductions.

President George H. W. Bush continued the advisory group, renaming it the Economic Policy Council. Porter once again managed its activities, with the help of his staff in the Office of Policy Development, and served as assistant to the president for economic and domestic affairs.[91] But the council met irregularly and did not establish an effective roundtable process for preparing issues for presidential decisions. Nor did the troika, which had fallen into disuse during Reagan's second term, regain its importance. No individual or group had responsibility for defining how policies were to be integrated.

Given the high priority President Bill Clinton placed on economic issues during the 1992 campaign, it is not surprising that he was deeply involved in making economic policy. One of his first acts was to establish the NEC to coordinate domestic and international economic policies in a way similar to the

National Security Council's coordination of foreign and military policymaking.[92] Operating with a professional staff of about twenty, the NEC's first chair, Robert Rubin, established an open, collegial, and nonhierarchical process that incorporated a wide and balanced range of economic considerations into the issue recommendations sent to the president.[93] The NEC was effective during the 1993 budget battles: Cabinet members worked through the budget and refrained from the infighting and leaks that had plagued previous administrations.[94] But all was not well: Clinton's economic advisers frequently clashed with his political advisers, who had managed his campaign, over the primary focus of the administration's economic program.[95] The economic advisers stressed the importance of deficit reduction and the impact of policy on financial markets. The political advisers wanted to emphasize the populist issues that had helped to elect Clinton.[96] Rubin emerged as the dominant economic adviser and continued in that role after becoming secretary of the Treasury. His successor at the NEC, Laura Tyson, was unable to parlay coordination into influence; Gene Sperling, the next director, proved more successful.[97]

Lawrence Lindsey, President George W. Bush's initial director of the NEC, brought an especially rich foundation of personal experience to the position. A former member of the Fed's Board of Governors, Lindsey served on the CEA's staff under Reagan and became a staunch defender of supply-side tax cuts; he also was a special White House assistant in the George H. W. Bush administration. As the younger Bush's economic adviser during the 2000 presidential election and the architect of his tax-cut plan, Lindsey entered the White House amid widespread expectations that he would enjoy the president's confidence, but he wound up resigning his post in December 2002 at the same time Treasury Secretary O'Neill quit, a major shakeup in the administration's economic team that attracted much media attention.[98] Lindsey was succeeded by Stephen Friedman, a longtime partner in the Wall Street investment firm of Goldman Sachs, with extensive experience in public service.[99] Allan Hubbard, a classmate of the president's in the Harvard MBA program, assumed the director's job in 2005.

Most observers expected Lawrence Summers, President Obama's new NEC chair, to play a pivotal role in fashioning the administration's economic policy. Summers, a former secretary of the Treasury and president of Harvard University, was a mentor to Secretary Geithner and comfortable playing a public role. When Geithner received negative marks in the media for his public announcements and appearances before Congress during the first months of the administration, Summers began to play a more visible role. Journalistic accounts of the Obama administration suggest that Summers's aggressive personality dominated policymaking; he did not define his White House role as being an "honest broker" who ensures that others' policy advice reached the president.[100] Gene Sperling replaced the notoriously temperamental Summers in 2011, thereby returning to the job he held in the Clinton White House. He played an important role negotiating with Congress over debt and tax issues. Jeffrey Zients, with experience running both OMB and the "tech surge" that rebuilt the Healthcare.gov website in late 2013, succeeded Sperling in 2014.

Trump's choice to chair NEC was Gary Cohn, president of Goldman Sachs (and reputedly a liberal Democrat) who quickly established himself as an influential moderating force among the factions seeking the president's ear.[101]

As in other areas of policy, the nation is heavily dependent on presidents' attitudes, values, and operating styles for economic leadership. Congressionally established advisory mechanisms, such as the CEA, are helpful, and presidents can take other measures to assist themselves in identifying issues and achieving policy coordination; however, advisory staffs and coordinating mechanisms provide no guarantee that the president will adopt effective policies or achieve his objectives. There is also an important check on presidential economic policymaking—Congress's power over taxing, spending, and the monetary system.

Congress's Role in Macroeconomic Policy

Most of the executive branch agencies and processes involving macroeconomic policy and the president's economic role were established by statute: the Federal Reserve Act of 1914, the Budget and Accounting Act of 1921, and the Employment Act of 1946. Traditionally, Congress dealt with economic policy through separate consideration of tax legislation and annual appropriations. Tax bills entailed redistributive issues—that is, questions of who bears the burdens and which special interests will secure favorable provisions, or "loopholes." The congressional tax-writing committees (House Ways and Means and Senate Finance) jealously guard their powers and are reluctant to propose new tax legislation that does not accommodate special interests. Appropriations decision making, centered in the House and Senate Appropriations Committees, traditionally focuses on incremental changes in department and agency budget requests. The politics of the budget process is a highly stylized game in which the institutional participants play specific roles. The primary consideration in Congress is the amount of increase or decrease in each agency's base, which is the previous year's appropriation. The total level of expenditures is the sum of the twelve major appropriations bills passed annually.[102]

Congress seldom attempts consciously to shape fiscal policy through its taxing or spending legislation. Rather, its money decisions are the product of its fragmented authority structure, as reflected in the multiplicity of powerful committees and subcommittees, the weakness of party organizations, and the strong constituency orientation of members because of their constant concern with reelection.

Congress required the president to prepare an annual budget and comprehensive plan for spending in the Budget and Accounting Act of 1921, an important change in the process that also provided the president with staff assistance in the Bureau of the Budget (BOB) originally located in the Treasury Department. The Employment Act of 1946 required an annual economic report projecting revenues and expenditures in light of economic forecasts, an overview to be completed by the newly created Council of Economic Advisers. But Congress imposed no such discipline on itself. Fiscal policy was whatever remained of the president's program after it emerged from "a piecemeal and haphazard legislative process."[103] The inability of Congress to participate rationally on an equal basis with the presidency in shaping fiscal policy led to conflict during the Nixon administration, when federal spending became a politically significant issue. Spending grew rapidly in response to previously enacted statutory **entitlements** that could not be disregarded without revising the original authorizing legislation. Entitlements include Social Security benefits, Medicare and Medicaid, federal civilian and military retirement, and unemployment benefits. Most entitlement payments to individuals increase automatically with the cost of living.[104]

Runaway budget deficits started in 1971 and continued for another fifteen years as spending on entitlements and other mandatory programs grew four times faster than did spending in discretionary areas.[105] Nixon challenged Congress to curb spending; when it did not do so, he frequently vetoed spending bills and made extensive use of impoundment. The primary response of Congress to this controversy with Nixon and to frustration over its inability to shape policy was the Budget and Impoundment Control Act of 1974, which created a procedure for handling proposed impoundments. More important, that statute established a congressional budget process, created House and Senate Budget Committees, and provided Congress with independent staff support for macroeconomic forecasting and budget analysis in the form of the **Congressional Budget Office**. On the first Monday in February, presidents are supposed to submit to Congress their annual proposals for the upcoming fiscal year. Presidents often miss the deadline, but

Congress often fails to complete its own work by the end of September when the new budget year begins. Fiscal years begin on October 1 and run through the next September 30. Thus, fiscal year 2017 (FY 2017 for short) begins October 1, 2016, and runs to September 30, 2017. When Congress fails to adopt the new budget on time, it frequently adopts a **continuing resolution** that usually keeps spending at last year's level until a new budget is adopted.

Central to the congressional budget process in its present form are the **budget resolution** and the **reconciliation legislation**.[106] The budget resolution must be approved by both the House and the Senate but does not require the president's signature. As such it does not have the force of law, but it serves as the vehicle for changes in budget policy, allocates available money to congressional appropriations committees, and may activate reconciliation legislation that requires authorizing committees to change law in order to meet budget priorities. Usually the budget resolution is merely the means by which Congress organizes its action, but it has also set in motion major changes in fiscal policy. Presidents Reagan (in 1981) and Clinton (in 1993), each with sharply different objectives, used the congressional budget process to change taxing and spending policy. In 1995, Republican congressional leaders used the budget process to impose far-reaching policy changes that Clinton strongly opposed. Congress adopted budget resolutions each year from 1976 to 1998 but in the next seventeen years adopted only eight resolutions. In the absence of a new resolution, the government operates according to the previous year's resolution.

Each budget resolution contains totals for revenues, expenditures, the deficit or surplus, and the national debt for the next fiscal year. Congress must adhere to these totals as it makes taxing and spending decisions. The budget resolution also contains target totals for the next four fiscal years and allocations of new budget authority for the next year to the major areas of federal spending, for example, defense, agriculture, and interest on the national debt.[107]

Reconciliation is the process Congress uses "to bring revenue and spending under existing law into conformity with the levels set in the budget resolution."[108] First, Congress incorporates in the budget resolution binding instructions to specific committees—those that have jurisdiction over revenues and mandatory spending programs—to recommend statutory changes that will achieve the spending and revenue levels set in the resolution. Next, the House and the Senate enact the committees' recommendations in a reconciliation bill. Reconciliation is an optional process that has tended to be used when either the president or Congress seeks a multiyear deficit reduction agreement. Reconciliation legislation became the major means of reducing the deficit but has also been used for other purposes. In 2010, Democrats used the reconciliation process to win final support from wavering House Democrats for the Senate version of the Affordable Care Act. Shortly after the bill passed Congress and the president signed it into law, the House used reconciliation to change financial terms contained in the Senate version of Obamacare. This strategy made it immune to a filibuster by Senate Republicans. In 2017, Republicans sought to turn the tables by utilizing reconciliation to repeal Obamacare, but faced early difficulties in drafting legislation that could bridge the various wings of the party.

The redesigned congressional budget process may be losing its potential to guide decisions. For a while, the increased centralization of budgetary decision making in Congress enhanced the legislative branch's ability to influence presidential budget policies while providing the president with greater leverage over congressional budget decisions. Congress and the president became, as Allen Schick put it, "more interdependent: each [was] more vulnerable than before to having its budget preferences blocked or modified by the other."[109] Budget resolutions, however, increasingly include unrealistic appropriations targets, and the budget committees have receded into the background.[110]

From 1981 onward, Congress was locked in protracted conflict with presidents Reagan, Bush, and Clinton over fiscal policy and the deficit. After a brief respite, the same held true for George W. Bush. Both he and Obama experienced the same pattern—cooperation followed by conflict. Congress invented a new set of mechanisms in the 1980s to rein in runaway spending. The Balanced Budget and Emergency Deficit Control Act of 1985 established a mechanism to trigger automatic spending cuts—a sequester—when budget limits had been exceeded. These mechanisms expired in 2002, but the Budget Control Act of 2011 reintroduced a variation. The new provisions apply to discretionary spending, both defense and nondefense, during fiscal years 2012–2021 (later extended to 2023).[111]

Clinton won congressional support for his five-year deficit reduction package in 1993 but then waged intense budget battles with a Republican-controlled Congress during his final six years in office. Although George W. Bush won congressional support for massive tax cuts during his first months in office, subsequent battles focused on the timed phase-in of those cuts and the administration's spending priorities. Cutting the budget deficit proved not to be a winning election issue in the 1990s, but cutting taxes and expanding the deficit proved successful for Bush's reelection. Obama, presiding over the largest deficits in history caused by spending increases at a time of reduced revenues, blazed new paths in this evolving relationship when the Republican Congress insisted on dramatic spending cuts and then prescribed further tax reductions and regulatory rollbacks while refusing to raise the debt limit. Trump seemed to have the early advantage of unified party government, but as noted at the start of the chapter, his program of tax cuts and spending increases seemed likely to increase the deficit further. Republicans in Congress who had argued against Obama's spending proposals and vehemently opposed raising the debt limit therefore found themselves in a difficult position, not least with their base voters.

Conclusion: Avoiding Economic Disorder

Can the president bring order and cohesion to macroeconomic policy? Can the presidency serve as the instrument for effective management of the economy?

Four major obstacles confront presidents in the performance of their economic policymaking roles: (1) Expectations are inordinately and unrealistically high, (2) presidents have only limited authority to meet those expectations, (3) the base of knowledge on which they act is often limited and unreliable, and (4) economic theory is not keeping pace with real-world experience. The problem of unrealistic expectations is not unique to macroeconomic policy. To be elected, modern presidents have tended to make sweeping promises, and the American people have developed a deep faith that a strong, capable president can provide solutions to their most pressing problems.

As presidents try to develop policies that meet popular expectations, they encounter all kinds of difficulties. George H. W. Bush discovered as the recession of 1991 dragged into 1992 that the public is impatient for tangible results and the pressure is great for actions that can provide a "quick fix." Clinton, George W. Bush, and Obama encountered the same impatience for immediate results, heightened by the election cycle. Nor is it easy to sort through conflicting goals. Curbing inflation, for example, may lead to unwelcome consequences, such as increased unemployment and higher interest rates. The popular bias against inaction runs deep, but sometimes inaction may be the most prudent course to follow. In short, exaggerated popular expectations that the president will manage the economy effectively may limit his capacity to do so.

Presidents quickly discover that their authority to act is limited. In macroeconomic policy, three factors restrict the ability to act: (1) congressional prerogatives, (2) the independence of the Federal Reserve Board, and (3) the limits of coordinating power within the executive branch. Presidents must collaborate with Congress in making fiscal policy. Their ability to increase or reduce taxes or spending depends on congressional responsiveness to their leadership, to their effectiveness as communicators and persuaders. In the face of the 2008–2009 crisis, Congress was persuaded to follow first President Bush and then President Obama in adopting a rescue plan for the financial sector and then a massive stimulus package. Without dire predictions, the debate would have been more protracted and more difficult, but when there was no rapid improvement of conditions, the public was ready to try a different set of policies.

Monetary policy is equally confining because of the Fed's independence. The only resources the president has available to influence the Fed are persuasion and the periodic opportunity to appoint new members to the board and to designate its chair. Although presidents have regularly tried to pressure the Fed, there is no assurance that monetary policy will be compatible with fiscal policy or that it will not impede the achievement of other policy objectives. As John Kessel concludes, "Presidents are in the position of having only partial control (shared power in fiscal policy, only power to persuade in monetary policy) over blunt instruments that only sometimes lead to the desired economic results."[112]

Economic forecasting is an inexact science subject to large margins of error. (Harry Truman supposedly joked that he wanted to hire a one-armed economist, since he was sick of his advisers qualifying their claims by saying "on the other hand. . . .") The validity of the projections provided by the CEA, OMB, the Treasury Department, and the Federal Reserve Board depends on the assumptions that underlie them and on the quality and quantity of information available. The assumptions vary with the institutional orientation of the agency making the forecast, the theories of the economists on the agency's staff, and political pressures affecting the agency. The Fed's assumptions, for example, reflect the influence of monetarism; OMB's, a traditional concern with budget balancing. Forecasters may feel pressured to resolve budget problems by adopting best-case scenarios of economic performance.[113] If the assumptions underlying a forecast prove wrong, then policies based on the forecast may lead to unanticipated outcomes. The record deficits incurred during his administration caught President Reagan by surprise because he enthusiastically accepted OMB's rosy scenario. As President Obama noted during his second prime-time press conference, a small difference in anticipated growth rates produced dramatically different projections of deficits for the coming decade. As he pointed out, however, many other decisions about the budget would be made during that time and would alter the picture.

The nation has moved from a conservative consensus on economic policy in the 1920s and early 1930s to a Keynesian consensus in the 1950s and 1960s to a lack of consensus from the 1980s to the present day. Policies have shifted from Nixon's imposition of wage and price controls to Reagan's embrace of supply-side theory, the older Bush's pragmatism, Clinton's emphasis on long-term growth and investment in human capital, the younger Bush's embrace of supply-side prescriptions for growth, to Obama's efforts at balancing long-term investments with responsible fiscal policy, to an odd mix of fiscal stimulus and supply-side tax reform under Trump. Keynesianism emerged in response to an unprecedented economic challenge; no similar breakthrough in economic thinking has occurred in response to the most recent crisis.[114] Despite all these changes, presidents still lack the capacity to control the economy even though rapidly changing economic conditions, in the United States and elsewhere, would seem to require the maximum amount of adaptiveness. The president's ability to respond to new situations, such as a sudden, large increase in the price of oil or the collapse of a major financial institution, is limited. The factors that appear to affect economic policymaking most substantially are a president's ideology and ability to persuade other influential decision makers.

Suggested Readings

Fisher, Louis. *Congressional Abdication on War and Spending.* College Station: Texas A&M Press, 2000.

Frankel, Jeffrey, and Peter Orszag. *American Economic Policy in the 1990s.* Cambridge, MA: MIT Press, 2002.

Greenspan, Alan. *The Age of Turbulence: An Adventure in a New World.* New York: Penguin Press, 2007.

Kessel, John H. *Presidents, the Presidency, and the Political Environment.* Washington, DC: CQ Press, 2001.

Kettl, Donald F. *Leadership at the Fed.* New Haven, CT: Yale University Press, 1986.

Mills, Gregory B., and John L. Palmer, eds. *Federal Budget Policy in the 1980s.* Washington, DC: Urban Institute Press, 1984.

Morgan, Iwan. *The Age of Deficits: Presidents and Unbalanced Budgets from Jimmy Carter to George W. Bush.* Lawrence: University Press of Kansas, 2009.

Niskanen, William A. *Reaganomics.* New York: Oxford University Press, 1988.

Palazzolo, Daniel J. *Done Deal? The Politics of the 1997 Budget Agreement.* Chatham, NJ: Chatham House, 1999.

Porter, Roger B. *Presidential Decision Making: The Economic Policy Board.* New York: Cambridge University Press, 1980.

Schick, Allen. *The Federal Budget: Politics, Policy, Process,* 3rd ed. Washington, DC: Brookings, 2007.

Stein, Herbert. *Presidential Economics: The Making of Economic Policy from Roosevelt to Reagan and Beyond,* rev. 3rd ed. Washington, DC: AEI Press, 1994.

Stockman, David A. *The Triumph of Politics: Why the Reagan Revolution Failed.* New York: Harper and Row, 1986.

Tatalovich, Raymond, Chris J. Dolan, and John Frendreis. *The Presidency and Economic Policy.* Lanham, MD: Rowman and Littlefield, 2008.

Tufte, Edward R. *Political Control of the Economy.* Princeton, NJ: Princeton University Press, 1980.

Wessel, David. *Red Tape: Inside the High-Stakes Politics of the Federal Budget.* New York: Crown Business, 2012.

Wildavsky, Aaron, and Naomi Caiden. *The New Politics of the Budgetary Process,* 5th ed. New York: Longman, 2003.

Resources on the Web

For a primer on how the federal budget is made, see Center on Budget and Policy Priorities, "Policy Basics: Introduction to the Federal Budget Process," www.cbpp.org/research/policy-basics-introduction-to-the-federal-budget-process?fa=view&id=155.

Notes

1. James Campbell, "The Miserable Presidential Election of 2012: A First Party-Term Incumbent Survives," *The Forum* 10 (2012): 20–28.

2. Lynn Vavreck, "Candidates Fed a Focus on Character over Policy," New York Times, November 25, 2016, A16.

3. Andrew Rudalevige, "The Meaning of the 2016 Election: The President as Minority Leader," in Michael Nelson, ed., *The Elections of 2016* (Washington, DC: Sage/CQ Press, 2017), 224–225.

4. Edmund L. Andrews, "Bad News Puts Political Glare on the Economy," *New York Times,* September 8, 2007, www.nytimes.com/2007/09/08/business/08policy.html?hp.

5. John P. Frendreis and Raymond Tatalovich, *The Modern Presidency and Economic Policy* (Itasca, IL: Peacock, 1994), 300.

6. "[T]he bounty of the 1990s resulted less from Clinton's personal stewardship of prosperity than from his willingness to follow the learned advice of others and, more fundamentally, from economic forces beyond his control." Raymond Tatalovich and John Frendreis, "Clinton, Class, and Economic Policy," in *The Postmodern Presidency: Bill Clinton's Legacy in U.S. Politics,* ed. Steven E. Schier (Pittsburgh: University of Pittsburgh Press, 2000), 41–42. Also see the review of Clinton's accomplishments by Paul J. Quirk and William Cunion, "Clinton's Domestic Policy: The Lessons of a 'New Democrat,'" in *The Clinton Legacy,* ed. Colin Campbell and Bert A. Rockman (Chatham, NJ: Chatham House, 2001), 214–216.

7. Technically, the National Bureau of Economic Research sets the recession's beginning at March 2001; it lasted until November 2001, www.nber.org/cycles.html.

8. On the economy and 2010, see M. Stephen Weatherford, "The Wages of Competence: Obama, the Economy, and the 2010 Midterm Elections," *Presidential Studies Quarterly* 42:1 (March 2012), 8–39.

9. Edward R. Tufte, *Political Control of the Economy* (Princeton, NJ: Princeton University Press, 1978).

10. James Reichley, "A Change in Direction," in *Setting National Priorities: The 1982 Budget,* ed. Joseph A. Pechman (Washington, DC: Brookings, 1981), 236–240.

11. Bob Woodward, "Greenspan Is Critical of Bush in Memoir," *Washington Post,* September 15, 2007, A1. As noted below, however, Greenspan endorsed the first and largest of the Bush tax-cut proposals at the time it was proposed.

12. John H. Kessel, *Presidents, the Presidency, and the Political Environment* (Washington, DC: CQ Press, 2001), 150–151. Ben Bernanke uses the "only game in town" argument in "Ben Bernanke's Blog, WSJ Editorial Page Watch: the Slow-Growth Fed," Brookings Institution, April 30, 2015, www.brookings.edu/blogs/ben-bernanke/posts/2015/04/30-wsj-editorial-slow-growth-fed.

13. David M. Herszenhorn, "Bush and House in Accord for $150 Billion Stimulus," *New York Times,* January 25, 2008, www.nytimes.com/2008/01/25/washington/25fiscal.html?sq=2008.

14. "Sorting Out the Bailouts," *CQ Weekly Online,* February 23, 2009, 394; "Federal Reserve: Opening the Flood Gates," *CQ Weekly Online,* February 23, 2009, 406–407, library.cqpress.com/cqweekly/weeklyreport111-000003058068.

15. Michael Fletcher, "Obama Leaves D.C. to Sign Stimulus Bill," *Washington Post,* February 18, 2009, A5. "Economic Stimulus," Times Topics, *New York Times,* March 25, 2009, topics.nytimes.com/topics/reference/timestopics/subjects/u/united_states_economy/economic_stimulus/index.html.

16. Recovery.gov, "The Recovery Act," http://recovery.defense.gov/.

17. Gary Burtless, "Crisis No More: The Success of Obama's Stimulus Program," Brookings Institution, August 17, 2010, https://www.brookings.edu/wp-content/uploads/2016/06/0817_stimulus_success_burtless.pdf.

18. Weatherford, "The Wages of Competence," 19.

19. "Sorting Out the Bailouts."

20. Alan Stone, *Regulation and Its Alternatives* (Washington, DC: CQ Press, 1982), 262.

21. Lester M. Salamon and Alan J. Abramson, "Governance: The Politics of Retrenchment," in *The Reagan Record,* ed. John L. Palmer and Isabel V. Sawhill (Washington, DC: Urban Institute Press, 1984), 47.

22. Marshall R. Goodman, "A Kinder and Gentler Regulatory Reform: The Bush Regulatory Strategy and Its Impact" (paper presented at the annual meeting of the Midwest Political Science Association, Chicago, April 1991).

23. Robert W. Hahn and Robert N. Stavins, "National Environmental Policy during the Clinton Years," in *American Economic Policy in the 1990s,* ed. Jeffrey Frankel and Peter Orszag (Cambridge, MA: MIT Press, 2002), 587.

24. David S. Cloud, "Industry, Politics Intertwined in Dole's Regulatory Bill," *Congressional Quarterly Weekly Report,* May 6, 1995, 1219–1224; and Bob Benenson, "GOP Sets the 104th Congress on New Regulatory Course," *Congressional Quarterly Weekly Report,* June 17, 1995, 1693–1697.

25. James A. Barnes, "Is Bush Poisoning His Well?" *National Journal,* April 14, 2001, 1120–1121; and Eric Pianin, "Administration Revisits Forest Lands Rules; Paper Industry, Western Governors Want Protective Regulation Scaled Back," *Washington Post,* July 7, 2001, A2.

26. Eric Pianin and Mike Allen, "Clinton Forest Rules to Stand," *Washington Post,* May 4, 2001, A1; Cindy Skrzycki, "OMB to Revisit Costs, Benefits of Rules," *Washington Post,* May 29, 2001, E1; Amy Goldstein, "'Last-Minute' Spin on Regulatory Rite: Bush Review of Clinton Initiatives Is Bid to Reshape Rules," *Washington Post,* June 9, 2001, A1; Marilyn Geewax, "Bush Proving to Be No Radical When It Comes to Regulation," Cox News Service, June 13, 2001; and Juliet Eilperin, "GOP Won't Try to Halt Last Rules by Clinton: Hill Power Shift Forces Retreat on Spring Plans," *Washington Post,* July 30, 2001, A1.

27. Paul Singer, "By the Horns," *National Journal,* March 25, 2005.

28. Cass R. Sunstein, *Simpler: The Future of Government* (New York: Simon and Schuster, 2013).

29. See Executive Order 13771, issued January 30, 2017.

30. Jacob Pramuk, "Trump Signs Another Executive Order in Push to Slash Regulations," CNBC.com, February 24, 2017, http://www.cnbc.com/2017/02/24/trump-signs-another-executive-order-in-push-to-slash-regulations.html.

31. Benton Ives and Phil Mattingly, "Geithner Outlines Regulatory Overhaul," *CQ Weekly Online,* March 30, 2009, 728–730, library.cqpress.com/cqweekly/weeklyreport111-000003087459.

32. Douglas Elliott, "Financial Reform: Now It's Up to the Regulators," *Huffington Post,* July 12, 2010, www.huffingtonpost.com/douglas-j-elliott/financial-reform-now-its_b_643457.html.

33. Weatherford, "The Wages of Competence," 27.

34. Douglas Elliott, "The Dodd-Frank Financial Reform Bill Is a Valuable Step Forward," Brookings Institution, June 25, 2010, https://www.brookings.edu/blog/up-front/2010/06/25/the-dodd-frank-financial-reform-bill-is-a-valuable-step-forward/.

35. Walter W. Heller, *New Dimensions in Political Economy* (New York: Norton, 1966).

36. Jackie Calmes, "The Voracious National Debt," *Congressional Quarterly Weekly Report,* March 24, 1990, 896.

37. Quoted in Ron Suskind, *The Price of Loyalty* (New York: Simon and Schuster, 2004), 291.

38. George Hager, "Deficit Shows No Gain from Pain of Spending Rules," *Congressional Quarterly Weekly Report,* July 20, 1991, 1963. Bush also encountered shortfalls in revenues arising from "technical reestimates" and higher projected spending for Medicaid.

39. Richard W. Stevenson, "The Wisdom to Let the Good Times Roll," *New York Times,* December 25, 2000, A1.

40. Clinton's term averages can be found in Tatalovich and Frendreis, "Clinton, Class, and Economic Policy," Table 1, 44. Unemployment data can be found in Harold W. Stanley and Richard G. Niemi, *Vital Statistics on American Politics 1999–2000* (Washington, DC: CQ Press, 2000), Table 11-10.

41. George Hager, "Time Is Ripe for Agreement but Gridlock Dies Hard," *Congressional Quarterly Weekly Report,* November 16, 1996, 3280–3281.

42. Daniel J. Palazzolo, *Done Deal? The Politics of the 1997 Budget Agreement* (Chatham, NJ: Chatham House, 1999). Palazzolo contends that the process of moving toward a balanced budget was fifteen years in the making, stretching back to 1982.

43. Stevenson, "The Wisdom to Let the Good Times Roll," A12.

44. Glenn Kessler, "Bush Tax Cut Pares Government's Role," *Washington Post,* May 21, 2001, A1.

45. Office of Management and Budget, *Fiscal Year 2012 Mid-Session Review,* September 1, 2011, https://obamawhitehouse.archives.gov/sites/default/files/omb/budget/fy2012/assets/12msr.pdf.

46. Congressional Budget Office, "The Budget and Economic Outlook, 2017–2027."

47. Allen Schick, "Bush's Budget Problem" (paper presented at the conference on "The George W. Bush Presidency: An Early Assessment," Princeton University, April 25–26, 2003), 4.

48. Testimony of Peter G. Peterson, president, the Concord Coalition, before the House Financial Services Committee, April 30, 2003, 3, http://archives.financialservices.house.gov/media/pdf/043003pp.pdf. At the time of his testimony, Peterson was chair of the Federal Reserve Bank of New York; he had served as secretary of commerce in the Nixon administration.

49. See U.S. National Debt Clock, http://www.usdebtclock.org/.

50. For accurate official figures, see TreasuryDirect.gov, "The Debt to the Penny and Who Holds It," https://treasurydirect.gov/NP/debt/search?startMonth=04&startDay=20&startYear=2017&endMonth=04&endDay=20&endYear=2017.

51. Douglas W. Elmendorf, Jeffrey B. Liebman, and David W. Wilcox, "Fiscal Policy and Social Security Policy during the 1990s," in Frankel and Orszag, *American Economic Policy in the 1990s,* 117.

52. Jonathan Weisman, Ashley Parker, "Republicans Back Down, Ending Crisis over Shutdown and Debt Limit," *New York Times,* October 16, 2013, www.nytimes.com/2013/10/17/us/congress-budget-debate.html?_r=0.

53. Julie Pace, "Trump Says He Will Release Tax Reform Package Next Week," AP News.com, April 21, 2017, https://apnews.com/17ded6ce025547e29615a0a0245fe80b.

54. Damien Paletta and Max Ehrenfreund, "Trump's Treasury Secretary: The Tax Cut Will 'Pay for Itself,'" *Washington Post,* April 20, 2017, https://www.washingtonpost.com/news/wonk/wp/2017/04/20/trumps-treasury-secretary-the-tax-cut-will-pay-for-itself/?utm_term=.e67b8528ee8d; John Harwood, "Trump's Budget Director on What's on, and off, the Table for Cuts," CNBC.com, April 12, 2017, http://www.cnbc.com/2017/04/11/trumps-budget-director-is-at-home-in-the-eye-of-the-storm.html.

55. Neta Crawford, *US Budgetary Costs of Wars through 2016,* Brown University Watson Institute of International and Public Affairs, September 2016. Table 1. See also Amy Belasco, "The Cost of Iraq, Afghanistan, and Other Global War on Terror Operations since 9/11," CRS Report for Congress RL33110, updated December 8, 2014, fas.org/sgp/crs/natsec/RL33110.pdf.

56. See https://www.statista.com/chart/7889/cost-of-war-against-isis-reaches-dollar11-billion/.

57. Paul E. Peterson and Mark Rom argue that presidents have little incentive to "manipulate the economy for either electoral or partisan reasons." In Peterson and Rom's view, presidents can best achieve their diverse objectives through economic policies that maintain a balance between inflation and steady economic growth with minimal rates of unemployment. See Peterson and Rom, "Macroeconomic Policymaking: Who Is in Control?" in *Can the Government Govern?* ed. John E. Chubb and Paul E. Peterson (Washington, DC: Brookings, 1989), 149.

58. George Hager and David S. Cloud, "Democrats Tie Their Fate to Clinton's Budget Bill," *Congressional Quarterly Weekly Report,* August 7, 1993, 2122–2129.

59. Richard W. Stevenson, "Bush Signs Tax Cut Bill, Dismissing All Criticism," *New York Times,* May 29, 2003, www.nytimes.com/2003/05/29/politics/29TAX.html.

60. David R. Beam, "New Federalism, Old Realities: The Reagan Administration and Intergovernmental Reform," in *The Reagan Presidency and the Governing of America,* ed. Lester M. Salamon and Michael S. Lund (Washington, DC: Urban Institute, 1984), 440; and Paul E. Peterson, *The Price of Federation* (Washington, DC: Brookings, 1995), 69.

61. Peri Arnold, "Clinton and the Institutionalized Presidency," in Schier, *The Postmodern Presidency,* 26–28.

62. James E. Anderson and Jared E. Hazleton, *Managing Macroeconomic Policy: The Johnson Presidency* (Austin: University of Texas Press, 1986), 14.

63. For a brief profile, see "The Decision Makers," *National Journal,* June 23, 2001, 1896.

64. Council of Economic Advisors, "Members of the Council of Economic Advisors," https://obamawhitehouse.archives.gov/administration/eop/cea/about/members.

65. Thomas M. Frank, "Key Economic Aides Undermined Obama during U.S. Financial Crisis, Says New Ron Suskind Book," *New York Daily News,* September 17, 2011.

66. Joseph A. Davis, "Policy and Regulatory Review: Growth in Legislative Role Sparks Concern in Congress," *Congressional Quarterly Weekly Report,* September 14, 1985, 1809.

67. M. Stephen Weatherford and Lorraine M. McDonnell, "Clinton and the Economy: The Paradox of Policy Success and Political Mishap" (paper presented at the annual meeting of the American Political Science Association, Chicago, August 31–September 3, 1995), 21.

68. Ibid., 28.

69. For a brief profile, see "The Decision Makers," 1905.

70. See Office of Management and Budget, "OMB Leadership," https://obamawhitehouse.archives.gov/omb/organization_office/.

71. Anderson and Hazleton, *Managing Macroeconomic Policy,* 27.

72. Colin Campbell, "The White House and the Cabinet under the 'Let's Deal' President," in *The Bush Presidency: First Appraisals,* ed. Colin Campbell and Bert A. Rockman (Chatham, NJ: Chatham House, 1991), 211.

73. Frendreis and Tatalovich, *The Modern Presidency,* 56.

74. Weatherford and McDonnell, "Clinton and the Economy," 20–21.

75. For a brief profile, see "The Decision Makers," 1987.

76. "Treasury: Blunt? Yes. Politically Savvy? No," *National Journal,* January 24, 2003, nationaljournal.com/members/news/2003/01/0124nj_oneill.htm.

77. See U.S. Treasury, "Timothy F. Geithner," www.treasury.gov/about/history/Pages/tgeithner.aspx.

78. Colin Campbell, *Managing the Presidency: Carter, Reagan, and the Search for Executive Harmony* (Pittsburgh: University of Pittsburgh Press, 1986), 123–135. Also see Kessel, *Presidents, the Presidency, and the Political Environment,* 127–129.

79. Cheryl L. Edwards, "Open Market Operations in the 1990s," *Federal Reserve Bulletin,* November 1997, 862, www.federalreserve.gov/pubs/bulletin/1997/199711lead.pdf.

80. For a brief biography of Greenspan, see www.biography.com/articles/alan-greenspan-9319769.

81. N. Gregory Mankiw, "U.S. Monetary Policy during the 1990s," in Frankel and Orszag, *American Economic Policy in the 1990s,* 19.

82. Benyamin Appelbaum, "In the Eye of Economic Storm, the Fed Blinked," *New York Times,* March 4, 2015, www.nytimes.com/2015/03/05/business/economy/fed-2009-transcripts-quantitative-easing.html?emc=eta1.

83. Roger Lowenstein, "The Villain," *The Atlantic* (April 2012), www.theatlantic.com/magazine/archive/2012/04/the-villain/308901/.

84. In responding to a *Wall Street Journal* editorial calling for an end to the low interest rate policies put into place at the height of the Great Recession, Bernanke acknowledged that monetary policy is not a panacea but went on to argue, "We shouldn't be giving up on monetary policy, which for the past few years has been pretty much the only game in town as far as economic policy goes," and supported expanded federal investments in infrastructure as a way to boost the economy. Ben S. Bernanke, "Ben Bernanke's Blog: WSJ Editorial Page Watch: The Slow-Growth Fed?" Brookings Institution, April 30, 2015, www.brookings.edu/blogs/ben-bernanke/posts/2015/04/30-wsj-editorial-slow-growth-fed.

85. See the insightful review of this history by M. Stephen Weatherford, "The President, the Fed and the Financial Crisis," *Presidential Studies Quarterly* 43:2 (2013): 299–327.

86. Kessel, *Presidents, the Presidency, and the Political Environment,* 138.

87. Anderson and Hazleton, *Managing Macroeconomic Policy,* 83.

88. Roger B. Porter, *Presidential Decision Making: The Economic Policy Board* (New York: Cambridge University Press, 1980).

89. Campbell, *Managing the Presidency,* 138.

90. David A. Stockman, *The Triumph of Politics: Why the Reagan Revolution Failed* (New York: Harper and Row), 1986.

91. Campbell, "The White House and the Cabinet," 210.

92. Frendreis and Tatalovich, *The Modern Presidency,* 70.

93. Paul Starobin, "The Broker," *National Journal,* April 16, 1994, 878–883.

94. Weatherford and McDonnell, "Clinton and the Economy," 21.

95. Bob Woodward, *The Agenda: Inside the Clinton White House* (New York: Simon and Schuster, 1994).

96. Ibid.

97. Kessel, *Presidents, the Presidency, and the Political Environment,* 143; Tatalovich and Frendreis, "Clinton, Class, and Economic Policy," 47; and Stevenson, "The Wisdom to Let the Good Times Roll," A13. For an overall evaluation of the Clinton economic policymaking system, see Jonathan M. Orszag, Peter R. Orszag, and Laura D. Tyson, "The Process of Economic Policy-Making during the Clinton Administration," in Frankel and Orszag, *American Economic Policy in the 1990s,* 983–1027.

98. For a brief profile, see "The Decision Makers," 1894–1895. Still another major figure, Harvey Pitt, chairman of the Securities and Exchange Commission, had resigned a month earlier amid controversy over his role in selecting members to serve on a corporate accounting watchdog board.

99. See the White House press release from 2002 at https://georgewbush-whitehouse.archives.gov/news/releases/2002/12/20021212-8.html.

100. Ron Suskind, *Confidence Men: Wall Street, Washington, and the Education of a President* (New York: Harper, 2011); George E. Condon Jr., "Summers Announces Departure," *National Journal*, September 21, 2010.

101. Damian Paletta, "Within Trump's Inner Circle, a Moderate Voice Captures the President's Ear," *Washington Post*, April 13, 2017, https://www.washingtonpost.com/business/economy/within-trumps-inner-circle-a-moderate-voice-captures-the-presidents-ear/2017/04/13/7a7f87b0-1fa7-11e7-be2a-3a1fb24d4671_story.html?utm_term=.7b5eeaced7bf.

102. The annual appropriations do not include entitlement programs, such as Social Security, Medicare, and Medicaid, or interest on the national debt.

103. James L. Sundquist, *The Decline and Resurgence of Congress* (Washington, DC: Brookings, 1981), 199.

104. R. Kent Weaver, *Automatic Government: The Politics of Indexation* (Washington, DC: Brookings, 1988).

105. Ibid.

106. This discussion follows Allen Schick, *The Federal Budget: Politics, Policy, Process* (Washington, DC: Brookings, 1995), chap. 5.

107. Schick defines budget authority as "legislation that enables an agency to incur obligations. Obligations occur when agencies take any action . . . that commits the government to the payment of funds." Ibid., 19.

108. Ibid., 82.

109. Allen Schick, "The Evolution of Congressional Budgeting," in *Crisis in the Budget Process: Exercising Political Choice*, ed. Allen Schick (Washington, DC: American Enterprise Institute, 1986), 15.

110. Stan Collender, "Happy New Year?" *National Journal*, July 1, 2003, www.nationaljournal.com/members/buzz/2003/budget/070103.htm.

111. James V. Saturno, "The Congressional Budget Process: A Brief Overview," Congressional Research Service RS20095, August 22, 2011, fas.org/sgp/crs/misc/RS20095.pdf. Also see Center on Budget and Policy Priorities, "Policy Basics: Introduction to the Federal Budget Process," April 20, 2015, www.cbpp.org/research/policy-basics-introduction-to-the-federal-budget-process?fa=view&id=155.

112. Kessel, *Presidents, the Presidency, and the Political Environment*, 151.

113. Stockman, *The Triumph of Politics*, 97–98, 329–332.

114. Jim Tankersley and Michael Hirsh, "Neo-Voodoo Economics," *National Journal*, May 20, 2011.

CHAPTER 10

The Politics of National Security Policy

REUTERS/Win McNamee

George W. Bush delivered extemporaneous remarks to relief workers during a September 14, 2001, visit to "Ground Zero" at the site of New York's World Trade Center, noting that their courageous efforts had served as an example for the entire nation.

National security policy ideally responds to long-term geopolitical conditions in the world. Examples are the long-standing alliance of the United States with the United Kingdom; the forty-five-year conflict between the United States and the Soviet Union following World War II; the intractability of religious and cultural differences in the Balkans, the Middle East, and Northern Ireland; and the vital role played by oil-producing states in the global economy. Seldom do single events serve as dramatic turning points that reshape the nation's security policies, but millions of citizens were convinced that their lives and U.S. foreign policy were permanently altered by the events of September 11, 2001, when terrorist attacks fully or partially destroyed two symbols of American power in the world: the twin towers of the World Trade Center in New York City and the Pentagon, headquarters of the U.S. military, just across the Potomac River from Washington, D.C.

In a coordinated attack, three airliners carrying large fuel supplies were hijacked by small groups of men, who then sacrificed their own lives and those of the passengers by flying the planes directly into the targets. A fourth aircraft, presumably headed for Washington, D.C., crashed in Pennsylvania, the attack foiled by passengers aboard the plane. Millions witnessed the second attack on the World Trade Center on live television. The fireball and crumbling towers became horrific images in their collective memory. For days the nation's normal life seemed suspended as attention focused on stories of emergency evacuations, reports of heroic rescue efforts, the search for missing loved ones, and the expanding investigation. Approximately three thousand people had been killed. In the aftermath, the economy was seriously disrupted: The stock exchanges closed for four days and the nation's air transportation system first shut down, and then resumed operation at severely reduced levels. The airlines entered a prolonged financial tailspin.

Only the surprise Japanese attack on Pearl Harbor, on December 7, 1941, which led to U.S. involvement in World War II, had a similar galvanizing effect on the nation. Before the week was over, President George W. Bush had secured congressional approval of an emergency appropriation of $40 billion for disaster relief and increased preparedness. Congress also approved, by near unanimous votes (98–0 in the Senate; 420–1 in the House), a resolution authorizing the president to use "all necessary and appropriate force against those nations, organizations, or persons he determines planned, authorized, committed or aided the terrorist attacks . . . or harbored such organizations or persons."[1] National unity and patriotic fervor prevailed on Capitol Hill, where partisan conflict and recrimination had been building in the expected battle over budget priorities. In a vast outpouring of solidarity, people throughout the nation attended religious services and nondenominational ceremonies, gave blood, donated money, and flew the American flag in remembrance of and support for those who had died or suffered losses. As the government prepared a response, Americans seemed almost reluctant to return to their daily routines, an unspoken acknowledgment, perhaps, that life in the United States had been irrevocably changed.

In fact, 9/11 decisively shaped U.S. foreign policy for the next decade and beyond. The Bush administration assembled a multinational intervention in Afghanistan, blessed by the United Nations, to pursue al-Qaida, the terrorist organization that claimed credit for the 9/11 attacks, and to displace the Taliban regime that had sheltered the terrorists. Although initially successful militarily, the coalition made little headway in creating a new democracy in Afghanistan, especially after the Taliban began to reestablish control over large sections of the country, returning from their sanctuaries in Pakistan. Although by the end of his term Obama had ended active military engagement, thousands of U.S. troops remained to assist Afghan forces.

The effort in Afghanistan was slowed by a second war, the U.S. invasion of Iraq. When President George W. Bush pushed for invading Iraq in March 2003, international opposition was widespread. France, Germany, Turkey, Russia, and China objected in the United Nations, but the administration persisted, supported by a "coalition of the willing" comprised of Great Britain, Spain, Australia, and a collection of smaller nations. Again, initial military success was followed by problems as Iraqi resistance grew and a civil war ignited. Invading Iraq also had political reverberations at home, costing the Republicans control of Congress in 2006 and influencing the elections of 2008. Barack Obama fulfilled his campaign pledge to wind down the U.S. role in Iraq and emphasize Afghanistan and Pakistan instead, the region he saw as far more critical for the country's long-run interests. And Osama bin Laden, after being hunted for nearly a decade, was assassinated in Pakistan by a team of Navy SEALs in late April 2011. Despite the sense of national satisfaction occasioned by bin Laden's death, casualties continued and public support waned, even as new terrorist threats arose in Iraq and Syria and U.S. forces began to return to the region.

The war on terrorism was a far cry from the national security challenges that had prevailed during the last half of the twentieth century, which centered on the global rivalry between the United States and the Soviet Union. As the dominant countries in world affairs following World War II, they led two armed camps of nations—one including the world's principal democracies, the other directed by Communist dictatorships. The industrial democracies and the Communist bloc coexisted in an uneasy peace, maintained in part by the threat of mutual nuclear annihilation. At the same time, each super power actively courted the support of the "uncommitted" developing countries. These countries, most facing enormous economic and social problems, varied in their orientations toward Washington and Moscow. Superimposed on the basic pattern of U.S.–Soviet competition was the twentieth-century technological revolution in communications, transportation, and weaponry, which had the effect of shrinking the world and making the risks of military confrontation greater than ever. In addition, the United States grew more economically interdependent with other countries, especially suppliers of basic raw materials, such as oil.

From administration to administration, specific challenges might change, but two essentials of the international environment remained the same: military engagement and economic interdependence. Donald Trump came into office apparently intent on disrupting this enduring U.S. role. But Trump quickly learned another truth: No chief executive can focus primarily and indefinitely on domestic policy. Modern presidents from Franklin D. Roosevelt to Trump were drawn almost irresistibly to concentrate on national security policy (foreign affairs and military policy). This predictable emphasis across administrations arose from at least two reasons: first, the crucial importance of the United States in the international community and, second, the political advantages presidents normally derive from devoting much of their energy to national security.[2]

Ronald Reagan came into office in 1981 committed to bringing about a conservative revolution in domestic and economic policy but found himself drawn toward national security issues. His successor, George H. W. Bush, was preoccupied with foreign and military policy from the start of his administration and only reluctantly turned his attention homeward when the economy faltered and his reelection campaign approached. In that campaign, Bill Clinton successfully attacked Bush for neglecting the health of the economy and other serious domestic problems and promised that, if elected, he would concentrate on them. Much to his dismay, Clinton discovered upon taking office that the end of the Cold War brought new conflicts and still greater uncertainty to international affairs. Clinton eventually involved himself extensively with foreign policy; in the last few months of his presidency, he seemed to be consumed by the desire to produce a long-evasive Middle East peace settlement. (It evaded him, too.)

During his first half-year in office, George W. Bush dealt primarily with domestic policy except for one incident when a U.S. plane collided with a Chinese jet fighter, a reminder that foreign policy can intrude unexpectedly on the national agenda. The attacks of September 2001 changed the administration's focus. The war on terrorism and the overthrow of Saddam Hussein's regime in Iraq became the defining features of Bush's presidency.

Barack Obama confronted an especially challenging set of problems when he entered the White House, as Thomas Ricks of the *Washington Post* explained: "President Obama has my sympathy. He has inherited the worst foreign policy situation that any new president has taken on. And what's really scary about that statement is, it's not even his number one problem."[3] With wars raging in Iraq and Afghanistan, instability in Pakistan, nuclear threats in Iran and North Korea, and anti-Americanism widespread even in NATO nations, Obama faced a daunting set of international issues that were still overshadowed by the economic problems at home. In short, the president did not have the luxury of choosing among problems; instead, he had to move forward on multiple fronts simultaneously. And with the recession spreading globally, the two sets of problems intersected.

Trump promised to put "America First"[4] by creating jobs, ending illegal immigration, renegotiating or withdrawing from one-sided trade deals, denouncing China's unfair trade practices, forcing NATO allies to pay their fair share of alliance costs, halting the entry of radical Islamic jihadists into the country, and building a wall along the southern border paid for by Mexico. Like a bull in a china shop, Trump initially declared NATO obsolete, rhetorically cozied up to Russian president Vladimir Putin, and insulted some of America's closest postwar allies including Australia, Germany, the United Kingdom and Mexico. And Trump proudly proclaimed that he was "President of the United States," not "President of the world," signalling a withdrawal from the leadership role the nation had played in the international system since World War II. Yet, even early in his term, Trump backed away from some of those statements and assumed a more activist stance, approving a SEALs raid in Yemen and launching missile strikes on a Syrian airfield in retaliation for Syria's use of chemical weapons on its citizens. The missile attack was especially significant, representing the first time American force was used directly against Syria in the years-long civil war. Ardent advocates of the "America first" policy denounced Trump's wavering on Syria[5] even though the strike was supported by a majority of the public and Congress.[6] The administration's warnings to Iran and North Korea, as well as the call for a major rebuilding of the American military, suggested that additional flexing of American muscle might be expected in the future.

In this chapter, we examine the president's role in making and directing national security policy. We first review the major concepts and issues that have dominated that policy area since World War II. We then define the essential paradox in national security policymaking as one in which the president is both the solution and the problem. Finally, the discussion turns to the relationship between the president and Congress with respect to national security and the problem of organizing an effective policymaking system for national security.

Issues in National Security Policy: Search for a New Consensus

For more than two decades, from the end of World War II until March 1968, America's principal national interest was clear-cut: military containment of communism. But when public reaction to the North Vietnamese Tet offensive precipitated Lyndon B. Johnson's decision to end the escalation of American involvement in the Vietnam War, the broad consensus undergirding U.S. national security policy began to disintegrate, a process that continued until Communist power collapsed in Eastern Europe in 1991. Until Tet, a succession of presidents from both political parties had consistently pursued the doctrine of **containment**. Bipartisan support for the consensus in Congress gave presidents a virtually free hand in formulating and implementing foreign and military policies. The only effective constraints imposed on presidential actions were the boundaries of the consensus, which began to break up in 1968, when it became apparent that containment could be preserved only through an indefinite, limited war in Vietnam or greatly expanded U.S. involvement that carried risks of conflict with the Soviet Union.

Even after the United States failed to "contain" communism in Vietnam, presidents continued to employ single, overarching concepts to build domestic political support for their national security policies. They found that "selling programs to Congress and the American people in the postwar era was always made easier if they could be clothed in one garment."[7] Détente, human rights, the "evil empire," a "new world order," engagement, and enlargement emerged as successors to containment, but none proved to be the core of an enduring national consensus. The George W. Bush administration's response to the threats of terrorism, tyrants, and weapons of mass destruction failed to provide the sustained political support missing for so long. A 2003 study from the Council on Foreign Relations eloquently made the case for the importance of having such a consensus:

> From the fall of the Berlin Wall in 1989 to the fall of the Twin Towers in 2001, and even now after the Iraq War of 2003, the United States has not had a consistent national security strategy that enjoyed the support of the American people and our allies. This situation is markedly different from the Cold War era, when our nation had a clear, coherent, widely supported strategy that focused on containing and deterring Soviet Communist expansion. The tragic events of September 11, the increase in terrorism, and threats from countries such as North Korea and, until recently, Iraq create an imperative once again to fashion and implement a coherent national security strategy that will safeguard our national interests.[8]

Obama proved to be no more successful than his immediate predecessors in fashioning a national consensus, and Trump's willingness to challenge U.S. commitments suggested that the foreign policy debate would become even more heated.

Efforts to Rebuild Consensus, Nixon through Clinton

In 1972 and 1973, President Nixon told the American people that a policy of **détente** would ease, if not end, the U.S.–Soviet tensions of the Cold War. The government would implement détente through actions such as cultural exchanges, increased trade between the two countries, and negotiations to limit strategic nuclear weapons. Established attitudes and behavior patterns are not easy to change, however, and Nixon and his successor, Gerald R. Ford, found it convenient to seek support for their policies by citing threatening Soviet actions in various parts of the world, such as Africa, Latin America, and the Middle East.

Jimmy Carter effectively campaigned on the pledge, which he reaffirmed at the outset of his administration, that morality, manifested in universal commitment to the defense of **human rights**, would be the cornerstone of U.S. foreign policy. But the United States found it easier to protest and threaten to take action against human rights violations in countries of non-allies, such as the Soviet Union and the Eastern Bloc, than in those of allies, such as South Korea and South Africa. The United States did not have the capacity to enforce the doctrine against powerful violators.

Reagan took office proclaiming stridently that his administration's framework for national security policy was continued opposition to, and competition with, the Soviet Union, which he once called "the evil empire."[9] Before becoming president, he assured an advisor that "I do have a strategy: 'We win–they lose!'"[10] In practice, however, his anti-Soviet stance was less than doctrinaire—strong rhetoric was combined with restrained conduct. For example, Reagan achieved the first arms reduction agreement of the Cold War, the Intermediate Range Nuclear Forces Treaty. It was a singular accomplishment, and it was realized not through belligerent opposition but through painstaking, lengthy give-and-take negotiations.

Reagan's ability to construct a new consensus with a strategic vision based on superpower conflict was undercut by the **Iran-contra affair**.[11] Journalists and political critics questioned whether the president set American foreign policy, or rather his aides in the State Department, the Central Intelligence Agency (CIA), and the National Security Council (NSC). These doubts seemed fully justified when the administration acknowledged in November 1986 that it had sent a small number of obsolete weapons to Iran as a means of contacting and encouraging moderate political elements. Hostages were also released. Reagan vigorously denied that there had been any explicit exchange of arms for hostages, even though each hostage's release had been preceded by an arms shipment. In late November 1986, the president acknowledged that profits from the arms sales, between $10 million and $30 million, had been diverted to the Nicaraguan contras through a numbered Swiss bank account. This was a direct violation of the Boland amendment, adopted by Congress in 1984, which prohibited use of government funds to support covert operations against the government of Nicaragua. Reagan claimed he had not been fully informed about the matter. Rather than establishing a new consensus, Reagan's methods provided lessons in how not to manage foreign policy. His detached administrative style, which entailed extensive delegation and a disdain for factual details, allowed him to address "the big picture" but left the NSC staff to play an independent role.

In contrast to Reagan, George H. W. Bush was a hands-on president deeply engaged in the formulation and implementation of national security policy. He concerned himself with its details and participated actively in negotiations with foreign leaders, approaching foreign policy with a pragmatic, rather than ideological, orientation. Critics complained, however, that his administration's foreign policy was purely tactical and lacked a strategic design.[12] Because of its unclear meaning, the "new world order" Bush announced following the collapse of communism in Russia and throughout Eastern Europe proved unable to sustain a national consensus. Bush continued the policies of the late Reagan years but with greater flexibility and adaptiveness,[13] "a kind of competent Reaganism" highlighted by his skillful guidance of an international coalition against Saddam Hussein in the 1991 Persian Gulf War. From the start, the Clinton administration embraced numerous high-minded goals: expand democracy and human rights; alleviate disease, hunger, and poverty; encourage free markets within states and the growth of free trade between them; and control weapons of mass destruction.[14] Frequently, however, the administration found it difficult to translate these goals into workable policies in specific instances: nation building failed in Somalia, half-hearted intervention failed to restore democracy in Haiti, indecision plagued Bosnia policy, and genocide was tolerated in Rwanda. Nor did the administration ever clearly resolve the question of when military power could appropriately be employed, despite using force in Bosnia, Haiti, Somalia, Iraq, Afghanistan, Sudan, and Kosovo. Clinton's administration also vacillated between multilateralism and unilateralism as means to achieve its ends, sometimes acting alone and at other times refusing to act unless allies joined in the effort.

The Clinton administration won congressional support for the North American Free Trade Agreement (NAFTA) and expanding the General Agreement on Tariffs and Trade (GATT), justified as means to improve the American economy. By 1998, emphasis shifted to defending the nation from terrorism, drug trafficking, and crime, as well as from weapons of mass destruction. Managing international financial markets was another critical task, an appropriate goal given the global impacts of financial crises in Mexico and Asia.[15] The nation still lacked a unifying statement of purpose.

George W. Bush's National Security Strategy

On September 17, 2002, the Bush administration released a long-awaited statement on national security strategy, the first since 1999. Although Congress mandates that such a report should be issued within a president's first five months in office and annually thereafter, the Clinton administration skipped its final report, and Bush's first report was twenty months late. The year-long review, interrupted by the

9/11 attacks, was a reformulation of American strategy praised by some observers as the boldest, most sweeping statement of grand strategy since the Marshall Plan was introduced in 1947.[16] Others reviled it as an attempt to create an "arrogant empire."[17]

Even before 9/11, the Bush administration had withdrawn from five international treaties; discontinued major peace initiatives launched by the Clinton administration toward North Korea and the Middle East; and adopted an assertive tone that suggested a unilateral, rather than multilateral, mode of action. The terrorist attacks heightened these trends, focusing American power on a smaller range of its own problems while treating allies less respectfully.[18]

In his State of the Union message of January 2002, President Bush called Iraq, Iran, and North Korea an "axis of evil" and warned them to halt their pursuit of weapons of mass destruction and their sponsorship of terrorism.[19] In confronting the dangers posed by terrorist and rogue states, Pakistan was pressured to support American efforts in Afghanistan and Turkey to support the invasion of Iraq. Pakistan complied, but Turkey resisted. France, Germany, and Russia defied American pressure in the United Nations and opposed action against Iraq, signaling a political division that threatened the foundations of NATO, the cornerstone of American foreign policy for a half-century.

How should the United States wield its dominant power in the world? The Bush administration focused on three threats: (1) terrorists, who use "premeditated, politically motivated violence" against innocents;[20] (2) rogue states led by tyrants who sometimes support terrorists and aggressively seek weapons of mass destruction to further their own goals; and (3) failing states, "countries in which the central government does not exert effective control over . . . significant parts of its own territory" and that are therefore susceptible to terrorist intimidation or become sources of regional instability.[21] Notably, Russia and China, great power competitors of the past and future, were portrayed as sharing values with the United States and engaging in peaceful competition.

The new strategy provoked enormous controversy.[22] Promoting democracy, free markets, and free trade throughout the world, particularly in Muslim nations, could be a means to enhance self-determination and human rights or a means to extend America's global control. Was the administration sincere in endorsing multinational institutions such as the United Nations, the World Trade Organization, and NATO, or did it prefer "coalitions of the willing"—temporary assemblages of supportive allies? How would the administration resolve the contradiction between promoting democracy and using undemocratic regimes to combat terrorism? Two controversial military strategies provoked the most discussion: "preemption—striking an enemy as it prepares an attack, [and] prevention—striking an enemy even in the absence of specific evidence of a coming attack."[23] After 9/11, the administration argued that action must be taken before the United States suffered another catastrophic attack. The United States and its allies therefore must use intelligence to discover capabilities and then act appropriately even if an attack may not be imminent. This logic underlay the U.S. action against Iraq, whose leader, Saddam Hussein, resisted international inspection of his chemical, biological, and nuclear weapons programs, thereby providing a justification for preventive action.

Consensus remained elusive. Neoconservatives, liberals, and moderates offered contending perspectives on the new global realities, with military dominance, diplomatic and economic cooperation, and alliances lying at the center of their thinking, respectively.[24] The Bush administration delivered the opening salvo on a major foreign policy debate that continued throughout Bush's time in office and was exacerbated by the frustrating experience in Iraq.

President Bush's second inaugural address delivered an even clearer message: "The survival of liberty in our land increasingly depends on the success of liberty in other lands. The best hope for peace in our world is the expansion of freedom in all the world."[25] In this spirit, America would oppose tyrants and encourage democratic movements. Although this message harkened back to a traditional American mission of spreading democracy, it did not provide the foundation for a new consensus on foreign policy. Instead, the administration stubbornly proceeded to pursue its own policy. The president spurned a bipartisan strategy on Iraq formulated by the Iraq Study Group, cochaired by former secretary of state James Baker (a Republican) and Lee Hamilton (a Democrat), former representative and deputy chair of the 9–11 Commission. Instead of embracing regional diplomacy and rapid withdrawal of U.S. forces, the president proposed **the surge**, an increase of 30,000 American troops in Iraq pursuing a strategy designed by the new commander, Gen. David Petraeus. The president had clearly decided to "go it alone" in this major military crisis, rejecting the 2006 election judgment, the results of national polls, and a Capitol Hill majority. Iraq was "Bush's war."

During his final months in office, Bush saw the surge strategy succeed militarily, and negotiated a new agreement with Iraq that American troops would fully withdraw by December 2011. But Iraqi politicians failed to take advantage of the opportunity the surge provided to build a stronger, united government, and sectarian divisions continued to undermine Iraq's stability. Bush's final visit to

Iraq in December 2008 was marred by an Iraqi journalist hurling his shoes at the president during a press conference, an insult in Arab culture.

The Obama Era

When he issued his administration's initial *National Security Strategy* in May 2010, President Obama clearly framed his global strategy as the rhetorical and pragmatic opposite of the Bush-Cheney strategy. Whereas Bush had often moved forward alone, Obama's strategy emphasized a renewed commitment to multilateralism as essential to fortifying America's leadership.[26] During the campaign, he had promised to withdraw U.S. combat troops in sixteen months, a deadline that he lengthened to nineteen months at the request of the U.S. commander in Iraq. In an August 31, 2010, address to the nation, the president proclaimed, "the American combat mission in Iraq has ended. Operation Iraqi Freedom is over, and the Iraqi people now have lead responsibility for the security of their country."[27]

Nevertheless, governance in Iraq was fragile and the political process stalled even after the seven-and-a-half-year war was officially over. Parliamentary elections held in early March 2010 produced no clear winner until October when a coalition government emerged.[28] And the world was later reminded just how insecure Iraq's situation was as the forces of a new terrorist group, the Islamic State (IS and also known as ISIS or ISIL) seized large areas of Iraq and even threatened Baghdad in early 2015.

Obama's new strategy for Afghanistan concentrated on the challenges posed by extremism in both Afghanistan and Pakistan to achieve American political and military objectives. After an extensive internal debate, the administration dispatched additional combat troops to Afghanistan, totaling 100,000, to secure civilian populations, "to disrupt, dismantle, and defeat al Qaeda in Pakistan and Afghanistan, and to prevent their return to either country in the future."[29] Missiles launched from unmanned aerial vehicles (drones) and raids by Special Operations Forces attacked extremist groups in Pakistan.

During the prolonged process of settling on a new strategy, military and political advisers disagreed about the necessary force levels—the generals wanted higher levels and a coalition of Vice President Biden and White House aides pushed for lower levels.[30] Tension surfaced again in summer 2010, when Gen. Stanley McChrystal, commander of the International Security Assistance Force in Afghanistan, made disparaging remarks about the vice president that were published in a *Rolling Stone* article. President Obama immediately recalled General McChrystal to Washington and accepted his resignation.[31] Obama then turned to General Petraeus, hero of the Iraqi troop surge, to implement a new counterinsurgency strategy in Afghanistan.

Petraeus later served as director of the CIA but resigned in disgrace after the press revealed an extramarital affair during which he compromised classified materials.[32]

On other fronts, the administration sought to repair its ties with Russia, describing the need to "reset or reboot the relationship," a phrase used in various ways by the president, the vice president, and Secretary of State Hillary Clinton. The clear implication was that things had gotten so bad during the Bush years that it was time for the two nations to start over. [33] The Obama administration engaged Russia in negotiations over a new nuclear arms reduction treaty, the New START, a step likely to reduce mutual fears and help achieve Obama's stated goal of realizing a world without nuclear weapons.[34] A lame-duck session of the Senate ratified the New START in December 2010, which would reduce deployed nuclear warheads to no more than 1,550 and create a new inspections system.[35] Progress toward nuclear disarmament was a cornerstone of Obama's foreign policy and was one of the most important considerations in his being awarded the Nobel Peace Prize in 2009, long before his international efforts could produce results.[36]

There were other diplomatic successes: President Obama's 2009 speech in Cairo, where he sought to engage the Muslim world and repair America's image; the Palestinians and Israelis resumed negotiations in September 2010; Obama's late charge in Copenhagen to secure an international climate agreement, albeit imperfect; and the administration's imposition of tougher sanctions unilaterally against Iran in June 2010, a month after additional UN sanctions were imposed on the intransigent state.[37] Perhaps the administration's greatest first-term test was the so-called Arab Spring, which altered the geopolitical landscape of the Middle East and North Africa.

In spring 2011, mass uprisings took place across North Africa and the Middle East, spreading from Tunisia to Egypt, Libya, Yemen, Syria, and Bahrain. These uprisings were largely orchestrated by young, educated Arabs who adroitly used social media to voice their dissatisfaction with the corrupt and ossified regimes of the Arab world and call for increased liberalization. The success of these protests varied. In Tunisia and Egypt, peaceful demonstrators forced presidents Ben Ali and Mubarak, respectively, to step down; similar demonstrations in Syria, Bahrain, and Yemen were met with brutal repression.

How far could the Obama administration go in responding to such a dramatic reorientation of the sociopolitical landscape of the Arab world? Initially, the administration sought to assure the embattled Mubarak and other Arab leaders that they remained strategic allies of the United States, while also publicly calling for an "orderly transition" to democracy in Egypt.[38] However, as the masses in Cairo's Tahrir Square swelled and calls for regime change grew louder, Mubarak lost all claim to legitimacy, and Obama adopted a different tone, announcing that "the universal rights of the Egyptian people must be respected, and their aspirations must be met"[39] and "nothing less than genuine democracy will carry the day."[40]

Libya presented a different challenge, degenerating quickly into a bloody civil war between rebel forces and those loyal to Libyan dictator Muammar al-Qadhafi. As the conflict progressed, Obama endorsed the rebel movement and condemned the brutality of Qadhafi's forces.[41] Ultimately the Obama administration acted to freeze a record $30 billion in Qadhafi's assets[42] and implemented a UN-sanctioned no-fly zone over Libya as well as an arms embargo to protect civilians. American forces, in concert with NATO allies, struck at loyalist supply lines and air defenses.[43] After two weeks, the United States relinquished command of the mission to NATO but pledged to continue providing logistical, intelligence, and technical support.[44] Once the rebels gained control, Secretary of State Hillary Clinton visited Libya to offer support, but the United States reassessed after a September 2012 attack on the U.S. consulate in Benghazi killed four Americans. This incident triggered multiple congressional inquiries into the security of U.S. missions abroad and whether the administration's public statements about the attack had intentionally misled the public at the height of a presidential election. As Hillary Clinton launched a campaign for president in 2015, the Republican leaders of the House renewed their investigations into the Benghazi incident.

Defenders claim that the administration's handling of the Arab Spring showed that U.S. responses dealt differently with diverse situations, reflecting the reality that the United States could not aggressively promote democracy in every case. Pressure on Mubarak to leave Egypt and a firm push in Libya but caution in Yemen: The Obama administration had been assertive at times but generally patient as events unfolded.[45] Syria was a bigger problem. Public demonstrations against the regime began in 2011 and escalated quickly to an all-out civil war with a death toll of 80,000 (UN estimate) by early 2013. With help from Russia, Bashar al-Assad, the Syrian dictator, held on to power while holding chemical weapons in reserve. Obama refused to become enmeshed in the conflict, although the CIA began to share intelligence and provide limited training to non-Islamist rebels while coordinating policy with key allies in the region, including Turkey, Israel, and Jordan.[46] Leaders in Congress pressured the administration to do more to quell the blood bath and intervene on rebels' behalf.

How different was Obama's pragmatism from that of George H. W. Bush, which had been criticized so roundly as lacking a clear direction? Some observers sought to identify a broader "Obama Doctrine" that used humanitarian interests to justify limited military intervention (without ground forces), employed only after circumspect deliberation and through alliances that distribute the burden and costs of intervention. But was this any more than pursuing limited interests with limited means, a necessity when fighting multiple wars? Early in his second term, Obama himself tried to sum up his approach with an off-color quip: "Don't do stupid [stuff]."[47]

Thus, President Obama navigated numerous national security issues during his first term in office. From nurturing a fragile stability in Iraq to recommitting American resources and attention to Afghanistan to intervening in Libya's burgeoning civil war while side-stepping Syria's, the president showed he was not afraid to employ America's military strength to secure its interests and values abroad. In navigating the turbulent Arab Spring, reviving relations with Russia, securing tougher sanctions on Iran, trying to curtail North Korea's nuclear aspirations, and "pivoting" American foreign policy toward Asia, Obama demonstrated a capacity for nimble diplomacy as well as a commitment to international engagement. If the president's goal, like Bush's, was to renew America's leadership in the world, his means were far different. Obama faced an increasingly war-weary public and inevitable reverberations that the Arab Spring would create throughout the Middle East.[48]

The second term proved far more challenging. Promising democratic changes in Egypt, Libya, and Tunisia soured completely or limped along. The military seized power in Egypt and ousted the elected president. Libya returned to civil war, and in Tunisia, where the Arab Spring began, the government held on for dear life against a growing terrorist threat. Syria remained immersed in a bitter civil war, with its government even using chemical weapons against rebel-held territory. The regime's atrocities finally forced the Obama administration to provide greater help to train and arm moderate rebels, a move that advocates of more forceful intervention regarded as too little and too late. Of even greater concern was the emergence of the Islamic State, an extremist Islamic group that used mass killings and videotaped beheadings to terrorize populations and fill the authority vacuum in vast stretches of territory across Syria and Iraq. By mid-2015, IS had captured such major cities as Palmyra, Mosul, and Ramadi. When IS threatened Baghdad, the administration increased military aid and air strikes to assist Iraqi, Kurd, and Iranian-supported Shiite militia forces in retaking cities and reducing IS military effectiveness. In June 2015, Obama authorized additional military advisers and special forces personnel in Iraq and new U.S. training bases.[49] Resetting relations with Russia worked out no better. Faced with the prospect of ever-closer ties between neighboring Ukraine and Western Europe, Russian president Vladimir Putin seized Ukrainian territory and encouraged a pro-Russian separatist movement in eastern Ukraine. Russia annexed Crimea in March 2014 by facing down a hopelessly outgunned Ukrainian military and daring NATO to respond. Civil war expanded steadily in areas of Ukraine along the Russian border, and Russian military assistance, barely camouflaged though publicly denied, buttressed the separatists. NATO's response was predictably slow and uncertain as Western European leaders sought to avoid military confrontation with an important trade partner that provided critical supplies of natural gas.

Probably the most controversial of the administration's second-term initiatives were the multinational negotiations (in lieu of military action) to limit Iran's development of nuclear weapons. Economic sanctions that the United States and allied nations had imposed during Obama's first term now became leverage: If Iran promised verifiable limits on its nuclear program, sanctions could be lifted. Just as negotiators were reportedly narrowing differences after months of tortuous work, forty-seven of the fifty-four Senate Republicans sent an open letter to Iran's leaders warning them to proceed carefully in concluding any agreement. The Senate, they said, would have to review any treaty concluded with the Obama administration, and the next president (possibly a Republican) could revoke any executive agreement. Predictably, the administration saw this as an effort "to undercut a sitting President in the midst of sensitive international negotiations."[50] But many Democrats were also wary of continuing presidential unilateralism and joined Republicans in a bipartisan coalition to pass a law (by veto-proof margins) that required any Iranian nuclear agreement to be reported to Congress, giving legislators time to review the deal and preventing the president from lifting sanctions until that review had been completed.[51] In September 2015, Senate Democrats blocked a congressional resolution condemning the agreement, ensuring that the agreement would take effect.

This sequence followed on the heels of a second dramatic challenge to the president. On March 3, 2015, House Republicans invited Israeli prime minister Benjamin Netanyahu to address a joint session of Congress to explain his concerns about the emerging Iranian nuclear deal. The Obama administration had been at odds with the hawkish Netanyahu on a number of issues, and he was perhaps the most vocal opponent of a negotiated agreement. Not only was this invitation extended without consulting the administration—which refused to attend the speech or meet with the prime minister—but it also came just a few weeks before the date of a hotly contested Israeli election, making it clear that Netanyahu's trip was likely to have an electoral effect. Thus, opponents to the nuclear deal with Iran had sown important doubts even before the negotiating parties released a framework agreement in early April 2015.

Five years after issuing its first *National Security Strategy,* the Obama administration released its second and last (the sixteenth since 1987), taking the opportunity to assess its own record and the challenges confronting the nation. The United States still faced dangerous threats including cyberattacks, Russian military aggression, attacks from religious extremists and an evolving terrorist community, climate change, and outbreaks of infectious diseases. Though military capability is important, the administration stressed that the economic recovery, a growing national workforce, the world's leading higher education system, and the nation's undiminished entrepreneurial spirit are the true foundations of America's security in the world.[52] U.S. force levels in Afghanistan and Iraq stood at 15,000 in February 2015, in sharp contrast to the 180,000 when Obama took office six years earlier. And the administration reviewed its self-proclaimed successes in leading international coalitions to combat IS in the Middle East, the Ebola virus in West Africa, and Russian aggression in Ukraine. Moreover, it was leading international efforts to reduce global warming, control the spread of nuclear weapons, and establish shared guidelines for cybersecurity. It further pointed to initiatives in relations with China, a deepening relationship with India, and the reestablishment of diplomatic relations with Cuba as critical to the future.

But what held all these pieces together? Was there an overarching coherence? While acknowledging that the "bipartisan center" had disappeared, Obama argued that "what unites us is the national consensus that American global leadership remains indispensable."[53] Obama added, "As powerful as we are and will remain, our resources and influence are not infinite. . . . [W]e have to make hard choices among many competing priorities."[54] Obama's approach to the world rested on patience, multilateralism, and the determination not to rely reflexively on military force.[55] As he told West Point graduates in 2014, "Just because we have the best hammer does not mean that every problem is a nail."[56] But U.S. officials in the executive branch and in Congress would disagree over the priority to be assigned to different problems and the appropriate response. It is hard to imagine a more forceful statement of pragmatism.

The Trump Era

Initially, Trump sought to distinguish his foreign policy from Obama's. Far from embracing Obama's identified consensus that "American global leadership remains indispensable," Trump questioned the costs of that leadership, campaigning on a message of **economic nationalism** that rejected international economic agreements (specifically denouncing NAFTA and the Trans-Pacific Partnership) and portrayed the United States as the victim of other nations' predatory trading practices, especially China's. Moreover, he threatened to rip up the Iran nuclear agreement which he denounced as one of the worst international deals in history and adopted a more assertive stance toward North Korea. Where Obama's relations with Russian president Putin and Israeli prime minister Netanyahu had reached new lows in personal chilliness, Trump warmly greeted the Israeli leader in the White House and refused to acknowledge that Russia had sought to influence the 2016 election. The president went out of his way to create disputes with NATO and the leaders of major western democracies like Germany, the United Kingdom, Australia, Canada, and Mexico.

The administration's foreign policy differed from Obama's in process as well as substance. Policymaking was unusually chaotic even for a new administration. Michael Flynn, Trump's first national security adviser, was forced to resign less than a month into the administration after the public revelation that he had lied to Vice President Pence about a conversation held with Russian ambassador Sergei Kislyak during the transition. Flynn told the vice president that he and Kislyak had not discussed U.S. sanctions leveled against Russia, but intelligence intercepts made it clear that they had. Although Acting Attorney General Sally Yates had warned Trump that Flynn's false statements could make him subject to Russian blackmail, the administration took no action until leaks revealed the truth.[57] In fact, Trump and the intelligence community had engaged in a running feud during the election, the transition, and his first weeks in office. Trump challenged the veracity of two reports released by the intelligence community about Russia's role in the 2016 election, and the president blamed intelligence officials for other damaging leaks. Relations became so heated that on his first day in office, President Trump traveled to CIA headquarters to meet with the agency's staff and blamed the purported feud on the media.[58]

Traditional sources of foreign policy advice were not visibly influential during Trump's first few months in office. Secretary of State Rex Tillerson was often out of the country, and the Department of State seemed to be under a media blackout—the department discontinued daily media briefings which had been standard practice since the 1950s, and the secretary traveled without the usual phalanx of reporters covering his meetings with foreign officials. As a result, the White House became the principal source of news on foreign policy, an arrangement that favoured the messages crafted by the president's political aides. In a break with past practice, Trump initially made Stephen K. Bannon, the president's principal political adviser, a member of the National Security Council while the director of National Intelligence (DNI) and chairman of the Joint Chiefs of Staff (JCS) only participated in the group as needed. After Flynn left the White House, his successor, Lt. General H.R. McMaster, exercised greater control over the foreign policy structure; Bannon lost his NSC membership and the DNI and JCS chair regained theirs.[59] Secretary of Defense James Mattis and Secretary of Homeland Security John Kelly, both former generals, remained influential throughout.

Approaching the end of Trump's initial one hundred days in office, there were signs that the president's initial impulse to shake up U.S. foreign policy had abated. Being unpredictable and impulsive had been Trump's route to success in business, but the same style, when followed in foreign policy, made allies and opponents alike wary of dangerously erratic behavior. Trump seemed to gain surer footing during a week in which he met with the leaders of Egypt and Jordan and ordered the launch of missiles at a Syrian government airbase while meeting with China's president from whom he sought help in dealing with North Korea.[60] Moreover, the Syria strike was followed by an unexpectedly assertive meeting between the globe-trotting Secretary of State Tillerson and Russian leaders, including President Putin, even as NATO relations seemed to reach a better footing.[61] Washington's foreign policy establishment and the nation's allies hoped that Trump was learning on the job but feared lest the president slip back into his tweet-from-the-hip mode of operations.

Michael Reynolds/Pool via Bloomberg

President Trump meets with Secretary of State Rex Tillerson (left) and Secretary of Defense Jim Mattis. National security adviser H. R. McMaster is behind Mattis; behind Tillerson is Trump's son-in-law, Jared Kushner, a White House staffer.

A Frustrating Search

Perhaps we should not be surprised that successive administrations have found it difficult to develop broad public support for a strategic consensus. Articulating a new foreign policy requires taking positions on scores, if not hundreds, of difficult issues, something politicians are reluctant to do.[62] Moreover, from an American perspective, the international environment is full of contradictory pressures and has become more and more unmanageable. With the disappearance in 1991 of the Soviet Union as one of the world's two superpowers, the number of regional and communal (ethnic, religious, tribal) conflicts proliferated. China aspires to become a global power, and other nations, such as Iran, hope to become regional powers. Numerous history-laden animosities have come to the surface, for example, between India and Pakistan, between Turks and Kurds, in the Balkans—where the United States and its NATO allies intervened in Bosnia and Kosovo—and most recently in Arab states.

"Security" has also taken on new meanings, with threats arising from uncontrolled immigration, international drug dealers, cyberattacks, and most dramatically, international terrorists. George W. Bush's administration believed that these threats from nonstate actors are as pressing as those from ambitious nation-states. In marked contrast to the Cold War era, the new international agenda is heavily—some argue predominantly—economic, raising issues that intermingle with domestic social and macroeconomic policy matters and triggering lobbying efforts by a new range of interest groups. The Bush strategy, weighed down by Iraq, was unable to win sustained public support, and only Obama's most ardent supporters thought he had articulated a broad message in foreign policy. Trump's efforts to disrupt the status quo and put "America First" did not represent a new, coherent strategy.

The Problem with National Security Policymaking

Exercising effective international leadership is difficult for the United States; the government structure established in the Constitution—separate institutions sharing powers—creates continuing tension between the president and Congress over the control of national security policy. Edward S. Corwin observed that the Constitution "is an invitation to struggle" between the two branches "for the privilege of directing American foreign policy."[63] Although the struggle continues and power over foreign policy is divided, the president has played the dominant role in shaping national security policy through most of the country's history. Presidential advantages of unity, secrecy, and dispatch (as Alexander Hamilton observed back in *Federalist* No. 70) are especially compelling during periods of crisis and potential conflict.

Dependence on presidential leadership carries risks, however. The idiosyncrasies of individual presidents' operating styles and personalities (see chapter 4) can be sources of uncertainty and unpredictability in policy and can exacerbate the institutional tensions between the legislature and the executive. The United States needs in its national security policy "institutions that provide continuity" and "structures and processes that promote coherence."[64] The problem is that if institutions, structures, and procedures respond to the short-term needs and whims of individual presidents, discontinuity in policy is likely to multiply. National security policymaking presents the United States with a circular and seemingly inescapable problem: The country depends on the president for central policy leadership, born of constitutional arrangements and operational imperatives, but as the system moves from one president to the next, the nation runs the risk of jarring changes in policy and a noncohesive policymaking system, both arising precisely because of the president's domination. Trump's early months in office illustrate the dilemma. The remainder of this chapter explores this paradox.

The President, Congress, and National Security

The powers of the federal government in international affairs are "inherent, plenary, and exclusive."[65] They are not granted expressly by the Constitution; rather, they derive from the nation's existence as a sovereign entity in the international community and cannot be exercised by the states or anyone else. The Constitution, however, is ambiguous in its assignment of the power to control foreign relations. Both the president and Congress have formal constitutional powers in this area, indicating that the founders intended control to be shared. In a 1793 debate with James Madison in the *Gazette of the United States,* Alexander Hamilton argued that direction of the nation's foreign policy is inherently an executive function.[66] Madison's position—that because the power to declare war is vested in Congress, presidential powers in this regard are merely instrumental—has not been borne out by subsequent events. Long-standing practice and necessity have combined to make the president the United States' dominant player in the conduct of its external affairs. Presidents have monopolized negotiations and communications with other governments from the early years of the Republic. This has been such a settled practice that even the 2015 Republican challenges to Obama's negotiations with Iran seemed peripheral—an open letter to Iran's leadership and an invited speaker to a joint session of Congress.

Congress, however, has retained the ability to influence the substantive content of the foreign and defense policies the president implements. It was a bipartisan majority that insisted on legislative review of any agreement with Iran in 2015. Major policies developed by the president cannot remain viable for long without congressional support in the form of implementing legislation and appropriations. Presidents may see themselves as the "sole organ" of foreign relations,[67] but Congress can choose the tune that organ will play. Nevertheless, throughout most of U.S. history the president has been, and is today, the "most important single factor in the determination of American foreign policy."[68]

Powers of the President

In addition to the inherent powers derived from the country's involvement in the international community, the president has formal and delegated powers over national security. These stem, respectively, from specific constitutional provisions and Congress. The constitutional foundation is relatively modest: the power to receive ambassadors and ministers, the power to negotiate treaties, designation as commander in chief of the armed forces, the general grant of executive power, and the clause enjoining the president to "take care that the laws be faithfully executed." Operationally, these provisions result in four major areas of presidential authority—(1) recognition and nonrecognition of other governments; (2) making, implementing, and terminating international agreements; (3) the appointment of personnel to conduct foreign and military policy; and (4) the use of overt and covert military force as a means of achieving policy goals.

Recognition and Nonrecognition of Foreign Governments. Article 2, section 3, of the Constitution grants the president power to "receive Ambassadors and other public Ministers"—in essence, authority to recognize foreign governments. Because foreign diplomats are accredited to the president, the decision about whether to receive them and, in doing so, recognize their governments is exclusively the president's. By implication, the chief executive can also refuse to grant recognition or withdraw it.

Traditionally, under international law, governments grant recognition to other governments provided the latter are stable, have effectively established their authority, and are meeting their international obligations. Recognition allows the American government to express its approval or disapproval of foreign regimes, an effective weapon when exercised by a nation as powerful and influential as the United States. Other nations may alter their conduct at the prospect of U.S.

recognition or the threat of its withdrawal. Once recognition is granted or relations are broken, this leverage is lost.

There are some well-known instances in American diplomatic history concerning the use of this power. After the Russian Revolution in 1917 and 1918, the United States refused to recognize the Communist government of the Soviet Union on the grounds that it had obtained power illegally, expropriated foreign-owned property without compensation, and oppressed its citizens. Yet in 1933 FDR established diplomatic relations with the Soviet Union when practical considerations made recognition advantageous to the United States. President Harry S. Truman overruled strong opposition in the State Department when he granted recognition to the new state of Israel in 1948, making the United States the first nation to do so. U.S. support has been vital to the survival of Israel ever since.

When a Communist regime took power in China in 1949 after a revolutionary struggle, the United States refused to recognize it, instead regarding the Nationalist government on the island of Taiwan as the legitimate government of China. Not until 1979 did the United States establish diplomatic relations with the People's Republic of China (PRC) and withdraw recognition from Taiwan. At the same time, however, the United States did not recognize PRC sovereignty over Taiwan. Clinton's decision to reestablish normal relations with Vietnam in July 1995 was controversial, but the administration argued that both countries would gain economically and the action would end the internal debate that had divided America for thirty years.

In a recent case, the Obama administration recognized the Transitional National Council as the legitimate government of Libya in July 2011, well before that revolutionary group had established effective control over all Libyan territory. This action surprised some international lawyers since it threw into question just who had responsibility for upholding Libya's international obligations. Great Britain, by contrast, refused to go as far as the U.S. government.[69]

Presidents are legally free to exercise the recognition power on their own. Indeed, in June 2015 the Supreme Court held that this power was so robust that it could not be infringed upon by legislative action.[70] Even so, political prudence dictates that presidents take congressional views and public opinion into consideration, effectively limiting the range of their discretion.

International Agreements. The Constitution also provides the president with authority to conduct negotiations with other nations that result in treaties or binding executive agreements. The constitutional basis for the treaty-making power is found in Article 2, section 2, which declares that the president "shall have power, by and with the Advice and Consent of the Senate, to make Treaties, provided two thirds of the Senators present concur." The Senate's own members limited its role in the treaty-making process in 1789, when they set a precedent by refusing to advise George Washington on provisions of a treaty under negotiation. The Senate may, however, amend or attach reservations to treaties submitted for its approval. Amendments change the content of a treaty and therefore require additional negotiations with the foreign nation, while reservations merely clarify the Senate's understanding of the treaty's provisions. The requirement of a two-thirds vote for approval gives the Senate substantial leverage over the executive in the treaty-making process, something presidents can sidestep by using executive agreements instead.[71]

Treaties require Senate approval, but executive agreements do not. The authority to make executive agreements is not mentioned explicitly, but its constitutionality is "universally conceded,"[72] perceived as arising from the president's role as the nation's official channel for the conduct of foreign relations and as a means for exercising powers in the commander in chief and "take care" clauses of the Constitution.[73] Congress authorizes most executive agreements either before or after they are concluded, or they are based on preexisting treaties. The most controversial are **sole executive agreements** made without congressional authorization, which constitute perhaps 10 percent of the total.[74]

Table 10-1 illustrates the dramatic change in the relative importance of executive agreements and treaties. By the late nineteenth century, agreements concluded in the previous fifty years slightly outnumbered treaties. That ratio widened over the next fifty-year period (1889–1939) and then exploded during the period 1939–1989, when 11,698 new executive agreements were concluded, as opposed to 702 treaties. The disparity narrowed only slightly from 1989 to 1999. A 2015 publication from the Congressional Research Service summarized that "over 18,500 executive agreements have been concluded by the United States since 1789 (more than 17,300 of which were concluded since 1939), compared to roughly 1,100 treaties that have been ratified by the United States."[75]

Congress repeatedly has expressed its disapproval of the use of executive agreements in lieu of treaties, but the only limitation it has imposed, in the Case-Zablocki Act of 1972, is to require that the legislature be notified of all such agreements. Although Congress is free to take action against executive agreements to which it objects, it has been unable to impose effective limits on the president's power to make them.[76] As Table 10-2 shows, the ratio of executive agreements to treaties

TABLE 10-1 Treaties and Executive Agreements Concluded by the United States, 1789–1999

Period	*Treaties*	*Executive Agreements*
1789–1839	60	27
1839–1889	215	238
1889–1939	524	917
1939–1989	702	11,698
1990–1999	249	2,857
Total	1,750	15,737

SOURCE: *Treaties and Other International Agreements: The Role of the U.S. Senate, Congressional Research Service,* Library of Congress, January 2001, Table II-1. Report submitted to the Committee on Foreign Relations, U.S. Senate, 106:2, Senate print 106–71.

TABLE 10-2 International Agreements, 1969–2015

President/Term	*Executive Agreements*	*Treaties*	*Ratio*
Nixon (1969–1974)	1,116	180	14.2:1
Ford (1974–1977)	677	99	25.6:1
Carter (1977–1981)	1,169	148	17.9:1
Reagan (1981–1989)	2,840	125	22.7:1
G. H. W. Bush (1989–1993)	1,350	67	20.2:1
Clinton (1993–2001)	2,058	209	9.9:1
G. W. Bush (2001–2009)	1,876	131	14.3:1
Obama (2009–04/30/2015)	531	23*	23:1

SOURCES: *Treaties and Other International Agreements: The Role of the U.S. Senate,* Congressional Research Service, Library of Congress, January 2001. Data from Table II-2. Report submitted to the Committee on Foreign Relations, U.S. Senate, 106:2, Senate print 106–71. U.S. Department of State, Treaty Affairs, Reporting to Congress under Case Act, www.state.gov/s/l/treaty/caseact/index.htm. Subsequent data from U.S Department of State, Treaty Actions, www.state.gov/s/l/treaty/c3428.htm, and U.S. Congress, "Treaty Documents," www.congress.gov/treaties?q=%7B"treaty-status"%3A" ReceivedReferred"%7D&pageSort=numberDesc.

*Treaties submitted to Senate through April 30, 2015. Beyond official agreements, there are also gentlemen's agreements among nations and between heads of state. These understandings are impossible to enumerate and are not legally binding but may involve significant commitments by a current president to a foreign leader.

changed markedly under Clinton compared with his immediate predecessors, mainly because of the unusually large number of trade treaties concluded during his administration. The agreement-to-treaty ratio under George W. Bush moved closer to the historical pattern but revealed a striking decline in overall activity during the administration's first two years, probably reflecting both the emphasis on counterterrorism and the shift away from multilateralism.

Why use treaties at all? Presidents are compelled by domestic political considerations to submit international agreements for Senate approval as treaties. Approval by the Senate gives an international agreement a degree of legitimacy that it would otherwise lack. And unlike treaties, executive agreements cannot override prior statute.[77] Carter submitted the agreement providing for gradual termination of U.S. control of the Panama Canal to the Senate as a treaty. He apparently calculated that such action would be difficult to defend publicly in any case and avoiding Senate approval could impose unacceptable political costs on his administration. For similar reasons, Carter submitted the second Strategic Arms Limitation Talks (SALT II) agreement to the Senate as a treaty even though approval was unlikely.

On several occasions, however, modern presidents have taken important action through executive agreements, knowing that Congress was unlikely to support a treaty or to bless an agreement. In 1940, Franklin Roosevelt exchanged fifty "surplus" destroyers for ninety-nine-year leases on bases in British possessions in the Western Hemisphere; in 1973, the United States and North Vietnam ended hostilities and exchanged prisoners of war through an executive agreement; and in 1981, the United States and Israel negotiated an agreement for strategic cooperation in the Middle East. As noted earlier the 2015 deal limiting Iran's nuclear program was consummated as an executive agreement rather than a treaty, as were 2016 thaws in the U.S. relationship with Cuba.

The decision to designate an international agreement as a treaty is the president's, based on political, rather than legal, grounds.[78] But few agreements are self-executing, forcing presidents to take note of congressional views because the administration will require legislation or an appropriation for implementation. During the Clinton administration, two important trade agreements, NAFTA and GATT, required legislation to become effective, allowing Congress to conduct an extensive debate over the merits and demerits of the agreements. Clinton needed the support of congressional Republicans because a majority of Democrats—fearing negative consequences for U.S. jobs—opposed both bills.

Although the president's power to negotiate international agreements is subject to political and constitutional limitations, the power to terminate such agreements is not. In 1979, a Circuit Court ruled that the president could unilaterally abrogate a defense treaty with Taiwan that was part of the agreements establishing diplomatic relations between the United States and the PRC; the Supreme Court refused to get involved in the substance of the case at all, upholding Carter's action.[79] The Bush administration likewise pulled out of the Anti-Ballistic Missile treaty with Russia in late 2001.

Appointments. As noted in chapter 6, the power to appoint subordinates is an important part of presidential control over policy, but it is a power shared with the Senate. The most important appointments affecting national security are the positions of secretary of state, secretary of defense, director of national intelligence, the head of the CIA, and the president's assistant for national security affairs. With these appointments, presidents indicate the direction and orientation of the foreign and military policy of their administrations.

The choice of a well-known figure with definite policy views to serve as secretary of state—such as the selection of Gen. George C. Marshall by Truman, John Foster Dulles by Dwight D. Eisenhower, and Gen. Alexander Haig by Reagan—reflects the intention to rely heavily on the secretary for advice and guidance. If presidents choose a relatively unknown individual—John F. Kennedy's designation of Dean Rusk, Richard Nixon's of William P. Rogers, and Donald Trump's of Rex Tillerson—it indicates that the executive intends to play the dominant role in foreign policy formulation and to relegate to the secretary management of the foreign affairs bureaucracy. Clinton signaled the intention to rely more heavily on the Department of State at the beginning of his second term when he named Madeleine K. Albright, known for her strong policy views, to replace Warren M. Christopher, a soft-spoken negotiator. George W. Bush's selection of Gen. Colin L. Powell communicated the president's intention to assemble an experienced and respected group of foreign policy advisers. Condoleezza Rice replaced Powell in the second term, moving from the White House to Foggy Bottom, and was generally viewed as Bush's most trusted adviser on foreign policy. Hillary Clinton was an especially high-profile choice as secretary of state under Obama, interpreted as evidence of his own self-confidence but also recognition that his former opponent for the presidential nomination would project to the world the kind of image he sought for the United States. John Kerry, a former colleague of Obama's on the Senate Foreign Relations Committee, moved to State at the outset of the second term after Clinton returned temporarily to private life. Rex Tillerson moved from his job as chairman and CEO of ExxonMobil, a global oil company, to the State Department. Tillerson had extensive personal experience in the Middle East and in Russia where he negotiated a major deal for drilling rights in the Arctic and developed a personal relationship with Russian president Putin.

Similarly, the choice for the secretary of defense indicates the president's plans for that department. Kennedy's choice, Robert S. McNamara, president of Ford Motor Company, signified the president's determination to make the armed forces more efficient through application of modern management techniques. In 2001, Bush's selection of Donald Rumsfeld, a senior Republican with extensive Washington experience and a reputation as a hard-driving manager, made it clear that Bush would assemble a star-studded team of national security advisors. Only after Iraq had severely tarnished Rumsfeld's luster did the president accept the secretary's resignation and replace him with Robert Gates, a former director of the CIA. Obama reassured many observers of his commitment to continuity as well as change when he retained Gates in the new cabinet. Gates stayed until mid-2011, when he was replaced by Leon Panetta, already a member of the foreign policy team as director of the CIA, a move that again signaled policy continuity. Former senator Chuck Hagel, a moderate Republican, moved to Defense in 2013 after a bruising confirmation battle but stayed less than two years. Hagel left amidst reports that conflicts with national security advisor Susan Rice and his inarticulate defense of administration policies led to his departure.[80] Ashton Carter assumed office in February 2015, winning strong support from the Senate after accumulating extensive experience in the department as the second- and third-ranking official. On the same day as Trump's inauguration, the Senate approved James Mattis by a vote of 98–1 to become Trump's secretary. This unusual degree of bipartisan agreement reflected the fact that Mattis had embraced mainstream U.S. foreign policies during his confirmation hearing in contrast to the president's more daring pronouncements.[81] To ensure Mattis's eligibility, Congress approved a one-time waiver from the requirement that military personnel must have been retired for at least seven years before serving as secretary. Mattis had been retired from the Marine Corps only three years.

The position of director of central intelligence involves managing the CIA; further, until 2004, the director was charged with coordinating the activities of the entire intelligence community.[82] This position became politically controversial after Congress revealed in the 1970s that the CIA and other intelligence agencies had sought to assassinate foreign political leaders and overthrow foreign governments. Periodically, critics also charge the CIA with ineffective intelligence work: the failure to anticipate the Iranian revolution of 1978 and 1979, Iraq's invasion of Kuwait in 1990, the collapse of the Soviet Union in 1991, and the terrorist attacks of 2001. In 2014, a lengthy report by the Senate Intelligence Committee charged the CIA's use of "enhanced interrogation techniques" (or torture) in response to those attacks had also been excessive and ineffective.[83]

CIA directors have been either intelligence professionals, such as William Colby and Gates, or experienced politicians, such as George H. W. Bush and William Casey, Reagan's first CIA director. George W. Bush retained Clinton's final CIA director, George J. Tenet, a move designed to enhance continuity, much as Kennedy had retained Allen Dulles[84] as CIA director and Nixon had kept Richard Helms. Tenet was succeeded by former congressman Porter Goss and then Air Force general Michael Hayden. Pursuant to recommendations of the 9–11 Commission, which pointed out many intelligence failings, a new position, director of national intelligence, was created to coordinate intelligence gathering and analysis for the entire government. Longtime diplomat John Negroponte first held this position, from 2005 to 2007, and was replaced by retired vice admiral John Michael McConnell.

Under Obama, Leon Panetta was a surprise choice as director of the CIA, but his previous experience in the House and as White House chief of staff probably helped guide the agency through the political minefield of criticism and investigation expected to follow the Bush years. When Panetta moved to Defense in 2011, he was replaced by David Petraeus, chief architect of the military strategies in Iraq and Afghanistan. When Petraeus resigned in the face of a personal scandal just after the 2012 election, John Brennan, Obama's White House advisor on homeland security and terrorism and former deputy director of the CIA under Tenet, took over the job. Retired admiral Dennis Blair was initially named director of national intelligence but clashed with Panetta and was replaced in August 2010 by James Clapper, a retired Air Force general and veteran of multiple intelligence positions in the Department of Defense. Mike Pompeo, a West Point and Harvard Law School graduate, had served three terms in the House of Representatives from Kansas before becoming Trump's director of the CIA. His intelligence experience arose from service on the House Permanent Select Committee on Intelligence.

One of the most important national security appointments, that of assistant to the president for national security affairs, is not subject to Senate approval, even though these appointees often dominate foreign policy decision making. Recognizable names—McGeorge Bundy, Henry Kissinger, Zbigniew Brzezinski, Colin Powell, and Condoleezza Rice—have held this post. Obama chose retired general James Jones, a skilled diplomat and advocate of the AfPak strategy, to fill this position. Thomas Donilon, a deputy of Jones and veteran of the Clinton State Department, took the job in October 2010. Susan Rice moved to the White House job from her position as ambassador to the United Nations to succeed Donilon in July 2013. Rice had served on the Clinton White House's national security staff, had advised both Kerry and Obama during their presidential campaigns, and was prominently mentioned as a possible successor to Hillary Clinton as secretary of state, a move opposed by Republicans. Michael T. Flynn served in the role less than a month, and he was followed by Lt. General H.R. McMaster, a highly decorated Army veteran who had served in Iraq and Afghanistan as well as writing extensively about Vietnam.

The appointment power helps presidents control both the conduct and the content of foreign and defense policy. Presidents enjoy wide latitude in exercising the power, but they must be sensitive to the limits imposed by international and domestic politics reflected in the Senate. They must realize, too, that the national security bureaucracy is large and unwieldy, and past policy choices have an inertia that cannot always be reversed even by high-profile appointments.[85]

The Use of Military Force. The Constitution states, "The President shall be Commander in Chief of the Army and Navy of the United States" and of the state militia when it is called into federal service (Article 2, section 2). It does not, however, define the nature of the president's powers and duties as commander in chief. In fact, extensive powers pertaining to the use of military force are found in Article 1, the legislative article. Most important, Congress is empowered to declare war.

Constitutionally, then, the power to use military force is shared between Congress and the president. Historical practice, however, has resulted in a vast expansion of presidential authority to use force at the expense of the powers of Congress. The dominance of the president in this regard has been almost total in wartime; in times of peace, Congress has only partially reclaimed the ground it lost. The result has been the continual aggrandizement of presidential power, the rise of an "imperial presidency," as it was dubbed by Arthur M. Schlesinger Jr.[86]

Presidents have sweeping war powers based on the Constitution, statutory delegations of authority by Congress, and judicial interpretations. The constitutional foundation of the president's war powers was established early in the Civil War when Abraham Lincoln linked the commander in chief clause to the take care clause.[87] As discussed in chapter 1, Lincoln used the resulting war powers to justify a wide range of actions to suppress the rebellion: activation of state militias, expenditure of appropriated funds for unauthorized purposes, suspension of the writ of habeas corpus in militarily insecure areas, and the imposition of a naval blockade of Confederate ports. The Supreme Court upheld the legality of the blockade in the *Prize Cases,* in which it declared that the president had a duty to defend the nation by appropriate means, including military action.[88] The refusal of the Court to overturn any of Lincoln's actions until after the war set a precedent of judicial deference during wartime.

Lincoln's actions demonstrated that the president's war powers extend far beyond mere military command. Under FDR, the president's powers as commander in chief expanded exponentially during World War II. Among other things, Roosevelt ordered the internment of all persons of Japanese ancestry, including naturalized and native-born U.S. citizens, who were residing in the Pacific Coast states. The Supreme Court acquiesced in this deprivation of basic civil liberties.[89] Roosevelt created emergency agencies with sweeping regulatory powers and demanded that Congress enhance his powers by repealing certain constraining sections of the Emergency Price Control Act.

Delegations by statute have further contributed to the development of the president's war powers. As discussed in chapter 1, during World War I, Congress enacted laws that authorized the president to regulate, requisition, and purchase a wide range of materials and products, to prohibit exports, to license trade, to censor international communications, to regulate enemy aliens in the United States, and to seize and operate the railroads. These powers were expanded during World War II, and many delegations of power were open-ended and neither revised nor withdrawn until long after the conclusion of the war with passage of the National Emergencies Act of 1976.

In short, once war is declared, presidential powers are vast. To ensure national survival, presidential directives are followed without regard to constitutional considerations and with the acquiescence, if not full approval, of the Supreme Court and Congress. Attorneys in the George W. Bush administration argued, "in order to respect the President's inherent constitutional authority to manage a military campaign," laws limiting that authority "must be construed as inapplicable. . . ."[90] Some leading constitutional scholars have charged that the Constitution is suspended in wartime and the president becomes a de facto dictator.[91]

The president's power to use military force in peacetime, or even in periods of undeclared war, is less clear-cut. The Court has been reluctant to resolve questions in this area, but Congress at times attempts to assert its prerogatives. The president still has substantial responsibilities and concomitant powers to protect American lives and property abroad, discharge international obligations, and preserve national security. Constitutional language is vague, and statutory enactments are an incomplete guide to the exercise of this authority.

After World War II, Congress and the president were united in the effort to contain communism, but the authority of the president to commit U.S. troops to fight abroad remained a sensitive issue. On several occasions between 1945 and 1965, presidents sent U.S. forces into combat or placed them in situations that could easily lead to combat.[92] These included the Korean War, the dispatch of four divisions to Western Europe as a permanent commitment to NATO, Eisenhower's responses to Chinese pressures on Taiwan and to increased tensions in the Middle East, the 1965 intervention in the Dominican Republic, and the Vietnam War.

TABLE 10-3 Duration of U.S. Wars since 1900

War	*Date War Began*	*Length*
World War I	April 6, 1917	1 year, 7 months, 5 days
World War II	Dec. 8, 1941	3 years, 8 months, 6 days
Korea	June 27, 1950	3 years, 1 month
Vietnam	Feb. 14, 1962	10 years, 11 months, 13 days
Persian Gulf	Jan. 17, 1991	1 month, 10 days
Kosovo	March 24, 1999	2 months, 27 days
Afghanistan	Oct. 7, 2001	15 years, 6 months
Iraq	March 19, 2003	7 years, 5 months, 12 days

SOURCE: *USA Today*, March 26, 2003. Reported on History News Network, www.hnn.us/articles/1689.html; updated April 2017.

Vietnam produced the most extensive and controversial instances of presidential war making in the post–World War II era, partly because it was America's longest conflict of the twentieth century (see Table 10-3). Beginning with Truman, presidents had made commitments of military aid and provided military advisers to the government of South Vietnam. By the end of 1963, more than 16,000 military advisers were in Vietnam, many of them actively participating in combat although not formally authorized to do so. In August 1964, the Johnson administration reported a confrontation between a North Vietnamese gunboat and a U.S. destroyer in the Gulf of Tonkin. At Johnson's request, Congress passed the Gulf of Tonkin Resolution, which authorized the president to "take all necessary steps including use of armed force" to assist nations belonging to the Southeast Asia Treaty Organization (to which the United States was a signatory) in defense of their freedom. On the authority of the Constitution, the Southeast Asia Treaty, and the Gulf of Tonkin Resolution, Johnson ordered a vast increase in the strength of U.S. forces in Vietnam, which by late 1967 exceeded half a million. He also authorized military commanders to conduct air raids against military targets in North Vietnam.[93] President Nixon extended the scope of military operations even while trying to negotiate an end to U.S. involvement in the war. In 1970, he ordered a covert invasion of Cambodia and the bombing of Laos to destroy enemy supply and staging areas, and in December 1972, he authorized the bombing of the North Vietnamese capital city of Hanoi and the major port city of Haiphong. These actions were taken without consulting Congress.

Initially, Congress backed administration efforts to contain communism in Southeast Asia through the use of military force; in July 1965, Johnson's request for $700 million in supplemental appropriations to expand the war won near-unanimous votes in both chambers. As the war dragged on, however, popular support began to wane, a widespread domestic protest movement took shape, and opposition to U.S. policy rose abroad from the country's allies and from developing nations. Many members of Congress questioned the wisdom and the legality of placing the decision to use military force entirely in the president's hands. As long as presidential use of force appeared to be successful, congressional opposition was minimal. When the use of force appeared to be failing, or the risks increased and the costs in popular support became too great, Congress reasserted its constitutional authority to participate as an equal partner with the president in determining where and under what conditions the United States would wage war.

Although Americans remain sensitive to the experience with war powers during the Vietnam years, events can overtake caution. Congress overwhelmingly endorsed President Bush's request for authority to wage war on terrorism in September 2001, passing a broad Authorization for the Use of Military Force (AUMF) that some critics called a "blank check" to take whatever action he deemed necessary.[94] In October 2002, some caution reemerged. Congress did not approve the original administration version of a resolution for the use of force in Iraq that was described as "the broadest request for military authority by any White House since President Lyndon B. Johnson won approval of the Gulf of Tonkin resolution in 1964."[95] Instead, Congress approved a version negotiated by the House International Relations Committee that placed modest restrictions on the president's actions.[96] Nevertheless, Presidents Bush and Obama stretched the 2001 AUMF over the next 14 years to justify a wide array of actions typical of wartime, "including indefinite detention, military tribunals, and National Security Agency (NSA) domestic surveillance without a warrant" as well as "target(ing) emergent terrorist organizations" with little or no relationship to al-Qaida and far from the Middle East.[97]

As American casualties rose and the end of conflict was nowhere in sight, public and congressional opposition to the Iraq War grew stronger. The 2006 congressional elections that produced Democratic majorities in the House and the Senate were viewed widely as a repudiation of the administration's policy in Iraq. Democrats thus attempted to impose a timetable for withdrawing American troops, withdraw the 2002 authorization to use force, cut off funding for the war, and redefine the role of American forces. By the end of 2007, none of these efforts had succeeded. The president remained committed to success in Iraq and implemented the "surge" in force levels that triggered new tactics. Democrats lacked the sixty votes in the Senate that were needed to prevent a filibuster. After reporting on the string of unsuccessful votes, *CQ Weekly* concluded the following: "In effect, the votes reaffirmed that the president, not Congress, is in charge of the war. Unless there is a significant shift on the battlefield in Iraq or in the dynamics on Capitol Hill, that's not expected to change."[98] As with Vietnam, Congress once again confronted a president relying on his own discretion in using military force.[99] And Schlesinger, among others, saw a return to the imperial presidency of the 1960s.[100] Obama brought the American combat role in Iraq to a conclusion, though up to 50,000 U.S. training and support forces remained in the country until most left in December 2011, only to see a limited return in 2015. As noted earlier, the success of IS in taking over not just Syrian but Iraqi territory led to renewed discussions about returning troops to the region.

Most U.S. troops left Afghanistan by December 2014, when the United States and its remaining allies transitioned to military operations led by Afghan forces.[101] A residual force of just under 15,000 allied troops included approximately 11,000 U.S. soldiers, and in October 2015 Obama announced that U.S. forces would remain through 2016, a deadline that has been extended indefinitely. The U.S. military dropped the largest conventional bomb in the American arsenal on an IS tunnel complex in Afghanistan in April 2017, exercising more flexibility from political oversight than it enjoyed under Obama.[102]

Covert operations provide another arena for presidents to use force. The Dulles brothers, Secretary of State John Foster and Director of Central Intelligence Allen, coordinated violent attacks against leaders around the world who were regarded as dangerous influences by the Eisenhower administration during the early years of the Cold War, and subsequent presidents have found more sophisticated ways to act secretly.[103] Actions may involve the military's special forces, such as SEAL Team 6,[104] or CIA operatives.[105] Prominent examples—some considered successful at least at the time, some far less so—include the toppling of Iranian prime minister Mossadegh in 1953, the 1961 Bay of Pigs invasion, the 1973 military coup in Chile, the failed attempt to rescue American hostages from Tehran in 1979, the Iran-contra operations on the mid-1980s, the opening salvos of the Afghan war in 2001–2002, and the 2011 assassination of Osama bin Laden detailed later in this chapter. Intelligence and surveillance operations in general may fall within this category as well. After the 9/11 attacks, for example, President Bush ordered the National Security Agency (NSA) to greatly increase its monitoring of U.S.-based communications with foreign nationals, without the court oversight required by the Foreign Intelligence Surveillance Act (FISA) of 1978. With the rise of Internet technology, much of it moving through American-based servers, the NSA and other intelligence agencies found themselves able to collect data from an immense amount of electronic and cellular communications as well as older land-line calls.

By definition, such operations are conducted out of the public eye, giving less traction for congressional consultation or oversight. As discussed below, as with military action generally, Congress has tried to require presidents to provide more information about such activities, even as it has generally approved the use of additional presidential powers aimed to keep up with new technologies and new threats. The PATRIOT Act of 2001 and the FISA Amendments Act of 2008, for example, legalized most aspects of the Bush surveillance plan, and while the USA FREEDOM Act of 2015 was praised by civil libertarians for halting some activities, it had little impact on the vast majority of ongoing intelligence programs.

Still, presidents have often been unhappy with their inability to maintain secrecy within their administrations. The 1971 publication by the *New York Times* and the *Washington Post* of the *Pentagon Papers,* dealing with the history of the Vietnam War, infuriated the Nixon administration and led to illegal wiretaps of NSC staff members; later, a CIA report detailing many of the agency's covert actions since the 1940s (its "family jewels") was leaked to a reporter in late 1974. The Internet age has further undermined efforts at confidentiality. During the Bush and Obama administrations, thousands of military, diplomatic, and intelligence documents were published online. Two major contributors were the "Wikileaks" website, starting in 2006, and former NSA contractor Edward Snowden, starting in 2013.[106] Both presidents warned that such actions threatened national security and could endanger individuals specifically mentioned in the documents; the unrepentant whistleblowers claimed that excessive secrecy made it impossible to hold those presidents accountable for their policy choices. The Obama administration aggressively pursued leakers under the 1917 Espionage Act, prosecuting six government employees and two contractors; only three such prosecutions had been mounted by all other presidents.[107]

Powers of Congress

Congress has substantial constitutional powers enabling it to claim parity with the president in shaping national security policy: the Senate's role in the appointment confirmation process and treaty approval, authorizations and appropriations needed to implement presidential decisions that are not self-executing, a variety of authorities regarding military regulations and "rules concerning capture on land and water," and of course the power to declare war. Congress, however, confronts steep hurdles in exercising those powers. During the Cold War, a bipartisan foreign policy consensus produced presidential domination, with many arguing that executive control was required by operational realities: Congress could never match the president's superior capacity to guide national security coherently.

The failure of the Vietnam War—labeled by critics as a "presidential war"—ended, at least temporarily, Congress's deference to White House domination of national security policy. During the 1970s, Congress limited presidents' ability to wage undeclared war, reduced unrestrained use of executive agreements, restored the treaty as the principal means of making international agreements, reassessed its sweeping delegations of authority to presidents in past wars and emergencies, and curbed secrecy and covert activities in the conduct of foreign and military affairs. Permanent committees on intelligence were created in both chambers of Congress, for instance. The subsequent Intelligence Oversight Act was designed to require that presidents produce written findings justifying the need for covert action, that such action stay within the bounds of federal law, and that the intelligence committees be "fully and currently" informed of ongoing and anticipated covert activities.[108]

The most important congressional attempt to reclaim powers lost or given to the executive was the War Powers Resolution (WPR) of 1973. Passed over Nixon's veto, the WPR provided that the president might commit the armed forces to combat only in the event of a declaration of war, specific statutory authorization, or a national emergency created by an attack on the United States or its armed forces. The resolution urged the president to consult with Congress in "every possible instance" before committing forces to combat abroad, and it required consultation after such commitment. Specifically, it required a written report to Congress within forty-eight hours of a commitment and required ending the commitment within sixty days unless authorized by Congress. The commitment could be extended for thirty additional days if the president certified to Congress that military conditions required continued use of the forces to ensure their safety. Finally, it stated that, through use of a concurrent resolution that would not be subject to presidential veto, Congress might order U.S. forces to disengage before the end of the first sixty days. (A Supreme Court decision in an unrelated case would likely force Congress to substitute a joint resolution for the concurrent one, but joint resolutions are subject to a presidential veto.[109])

The War Powers Resolution now appears even less effective than before as a congressional means to control military actions initiated by presidents. Although presidents grudgingly continue to meet the procedural requirements of the act and file the required reports (see Table 10-4), most of these involve routine updates of ongoing force commitments.[110] In only one instance since the act's adoption—the rescue of the *Mayaguez,* a merchant ship seized by Cambodian gunboats in 1975—did the president trigger the sixty-day clock. Every president subject to the War Powers Resolution has regarded it as an unconstitutional encroachment on presidential power and issued reports that carefully avoided any acknowledgment of its constitutionality: They note they are reporting "consistent with" the WPR rather than "in accordance with" its provisions, for example. In addition, these presidents have circumvented the intent of the resolution by not activating the sixty-day clock and by stating that merely informing Congress meets the resolution's requirement of consultation. Congress has never challenged any president by starting the sixty-day clock on its own.[111] Individual members of Congress have complained, and even sued, but the branch as a whole has been unable to formulate a corresponding "unitary position or statement of institutional interest"[112] and courts have never found grounds to intervene.

President George H. W. Bush's actions during the Persian Gulf War of 1990 and 1991 are typical of how presidents deal with the War Powers Resolution.[113] Before sending U.S. armed forces to the gulf in response to Iraq's August 2, 1990, invasion of Kuwait, Bush on August 8 notified congressional leaders of the planned deployment. The next day, he sent the Speaker of the House and the president pro tempore of the Senate a letter stating that the report was "consistent with" the WPR. During the next six months, a massive buildup of U.S. forces took place in the Persian Gulf area, the

TABLE 10-4 Presidential Use of Force Reported, Consistent with the War Powers Resolution, 1969–2017

President/Term	*Reports under the War Powers Resolution*
Nixon (1969–1974)	0
Ford (1974–1977)	4
Carter (1977–1981)	1
Reagan (1981–1989)	14
G. H. W. Bush (1989–1993)	7
Clinton (1993–2001)	60
G. W. Bush (2001–2009)	39
Obama (2009–2017)	42
Trump (January 2017–March 2017)	1

SOURCES: Richard F. Grimmet, "War Powers Resolution: Presidential Compliance," original release March 2001 and updated versions February 2, 2009, April 12, 2011, September 25, 2012. CRS Issue Brief for Congress, Congressional Research Service, Library of Congress, March 21, 2001, February 2, 2009, April 12, 2011, September 25, 2012. Matthew C. Weed, "The War Powers Resolution: Concepts and Practice," April 3, 2015, CRS Report R42699. Also see CRS Report RL31185, "The War Powers Resolution: After Twenty-Eight Years." CRS Report R42699, "The War Powers Resolution: Concepts and Practice," March 28, 2017.

United States and Iraq exchanged bellicose threats, and the United Nations adopted a resolution imposing a deadline for Iraq to withdraw from Kuwait. At no point did either the president or Congress begin the sixty-day countdown. As he had from the beginning, the president continued to argue that he had the authority to force Iraq to leave Kuwait without congressional approval. Nevertheless, on January 8, 1991, one week before the UN deadline, Bush asked Congress to approve a joint resolution authorizing the use of force. Congress did so four days later by votes of 52 to 47 in the Senate and 250 to 183 in the House.[114] When Bush signed the resolution, he reasserted his position that the WPR was unconstitutional. The resolution approved on January 12, 1991, has been recognized as the functional equivalent of a declaration of war. Whether Bush weakened his position—that he already had the authority to initiate hostilities—is an unanswered question.

President Obama's relationship with the WPR has been instructive. He declined to ask Congress for authorization to join NATO in intervening in Libya in 2011; as the conflict continued, he argued that its limits did not apply anyway because the Libyan operation did not count as "hostilities" under the terms of the WPR. Later, when committing U.S. troops to the fight against IS, Obama held that the 2001 AUMF gave him authority to do so even though IS did not exist in 2001. Presidents have justified the unilateral use of force in the post-WPR era as a matter of self-defense, however indirect, or as an extension of existing authority obtained either from Congress or from treaty obligations (for example, to NATO or the United Nations).

When President Trump authorized missile strikes on Syria in retaliation for the use of chemical weapons against its own citizens, debate raged whether he had the authority to do so. In 2013, when Syria's use of chemical weapons against civilians crossed a "red line" the Obama administration had publicly announced, the president chose not to retaliate militarily without congressional authorization. Russia defused the crisis by negotiating an agreement to remove the Syrian government's chemical weapons, but obviously some survived. With that case of congressional inaction in mind, Trump did not seek legislative authorization in 2017. The administration argued the attack was designed to dissuade the Syrian government from further use or proliferation of chemical weapons, thereby promoting regional stability, the same argument Obama had considered (and that Trump, at the time, had opposed).[115] Some members of Congress insisted that President Trump should have requested authorization (thereby losing the element of surprise) while others said the president acted within his power.[116]

At best, the WPR provided Congress with a symbolic victory in the ongoing struggle between the president and Congress in making decisions about war and peace. It seemed to serve notice that sustained military commitments outside the country could no longer be made by presidential fiat but required congressional approval and, by implication, popular support. Presidents, however, have neither consulted Congress in "any meaningful manner" nor have they sought to make the law work by invoking its provisions.[117] Instead, they have sought to circumvent it. Ultimately, any expectation that the resolution's "procedures would actually lead to collective legislative-executive judgment in the war-making process was mistaken."[118] Presidential evasion, congressional acquiescence, and judicial deference have combined to bring about this result.[119]

Despite its failings, the resolution—and the Intelligence Oversight Act, which has suffered from similar lack of enforcement—persists because it suits congressional purposes. It "allows Congress the luxury of being politically comfortable with its decisions regarding a military action while providing a convenient forum for criticizing the President."[120] Congress can use the WPR to force the president to end an unpopular military operation, or it can criticize presidential failure to comply with the procedural requirements of the resolution when public opinion is supportive or divided. Either way, Congress cannot lose.[121] The resolution reminds presidents that under the Constitution, they share with Congress the crucial decision to lead the nation into war. Thus far, presidents have been no more willing than Congress to ask the Supreme Court to resolve the lingering ambiguities—an unwillingness that may stem on both sides from uncertainty about the outcome.[122]

Congress has not assumed added responsibility despite a desire and enhanced capacity to do so.[123] Even the traditional "power of the purse" that rests on congressional appropriation of funds has been eroded, with presidents supporting international projects by spending money from lump sum accounts and reprogramming funds from one purpose to another, effectively exercising "presidential spending power in national security."[124] Because of its internal fragmentation, Congress has difficulty asserting its prerogatives. Reforms during the 1970s, especially in the House, fragmented power even further with the addition of more subcommittees, making it still more difficult for Congress to speak authoritatively. These developments, along with additional pressures from interest groups and other domestic constituencies, made interbranch consensus more elusive. Although Republican majorities moved to consolidate legislative power in the 1990s (see chapter 5), the structural problems remain. Legislative leaders seldom exercise control. One result in Iraq was that a costly American effort was sustained despite widespread public disapproval, electoral repudiation, and active congressional opposition. In 2015, the new Republican majority demanded that Obama produce a draft authorization to use force against IS, but then failed to act on it when some members thought it gave the president too much power and others too little.

The constitutional "invitation to struggle" is still present. Four paths are possible for Congress:

- Acquiesce to presidential domination, the pattern that prevailed from World War II until 1973
- Direct policy on its own because the public opposes the president's policies
- Collaborate with a sense of constitutional and political responsibility to be constructively critical
- Engage in all-out conflict

This last possibility nearly erupted during the Clinton impeachment and again under Obama. On the eve of the scheduled House vote on articles of impeachment, Clinton ordered an air attack on Iraq for its failure to cooperate with UN weapons inspectors responsible for overseeing Iraq's disarmament after the Persian Gulf War. The impeachment debate was delayed for only one day. Congressional members questioned the president's motives in launching an attack that had been delayed numerous times in the past, including a month earlier. Republican leaders publicly spoke out against the action and expressed doubts about the president's credibility. Editorials wondered whether he was "risking lives to cling to power."[125] The impeachment imposed enormous strains on the delicate institutional relationships essential for effective foreign policy.

Obama faced criticism of his foreign policy on nearly all fronts in 2014 and 2015. Many members of Congress, both Republican and Democrat, believed he was too cautious in responding to Russia's virtual invasion of Ukraine and the rise of IS in Syria and Iraq.[126] Other observers viewed some Obama actions as overly assertive; opponents described moves to normalize relations with Cuba and defer deportation of some illegal immigrants through executive discretion as unconstitutional assertions of presidential power.[127] Obama's critics found many ways to challenge his actions. Funding for the entire Department of Homeland Security was held hostage in an unsuccessful attempt to get the immigration policy changed (see chapter 9), and opponents of Cuba normalization vowed to deny funds to the State Department to open an embassy and to Treasury and the Commerce Department to restore business and trade relations. Moreover, only Congress could fully remove the long-standing trade embargo with Cuba established by law, although the same law allows the president to loosen parts of the embargo.[128]

Organizing and Managing National Security

Beyond dealing with the constitutional issues and political considerations involved in national security policy, the president also confronts a formidable administrative task: organizing the presidency and the executive branch to formulate and implement these policies. To do so may require establishing and changing structures and processes to enhance decision making and interagency coordination. As the Iran-contra investigation revealed, a lax approach to these tasks can be costly, but it is also possible to overemphasize them. One has to remember that "good organization does not insure successful policy, nor does poor organization preclude it."[129] Designing an effective system accomplishes three primary functions: (1) it "creates capabilities" for performing tasks beyond the reach of individuals, (2) it "vests and weighs particular interests and perspectives" by increasing or reducing the probability of their inclusion in decision making, and (3) it "legitimates decisions" by ensuring that relevant parties are consulted and that decisions are made by proper authorities.[130]

Although national security organization does not have to conform to a specific model, whatever policymaking system is established must be capable of adapting to changing events and conditions, and it must be able to accommodate the operating style of the presidents, whose constitutional roles make them the focal point of the policymaking process. Congress has enacted legislation—the National Security Act of 1947 was the most far reaching—establishing organizational units to aid presidents in the conduct of national security policy. The principal units are the NSC and its staff; the Departments of State and Defense; the Joint Chiefs of Staff; and until 2005 the CIA, now superseded by the National Intelligence Council headed by the director of national intelligence. Congress established these staffing units, but it cannot prescribe how presidents employ them. How presidents choose to work through staff, cabinet, and independent agencies is a matter totally at their discretion.

Presidential Management Styles

The NSC is the basic structure for the management of national security affairs. Since the council's creation in 1947, presidents have used it in various ways. Congress established the NSC in response to the pressures of the Cold War and in reaction, at least in part, to the administrative confusion that often characterized Franklin Roosevelt's freewheeling approach to management. Chief executives, upon taking office, must define their roles in the national security policymaking system before they can design and manage the roles and relationships of other major participants in it.[131] According to conventional wisdom, the basic choice every president must make is whether to manage the system through the secretary of state and the State Department, as Truman did, or to centralize it in the White House, as Nixon did, with the national security advisor playing the major role. Failure to decide on a consistent approach is likely to result in confusion over policy goals and lack of cohesion in policy implementation, as was the case with Clinton.[132] Neither Clinton's assistants for national security and the NSC staff, which nearly doubled in size to an all-time high of one hundred professionals,[133] nor Clinton's secretary of state and the State Department were clearly in charge. The result was a series of ad hoc reactions to crises, problems, and domestic pressures.

Within this range of possibilities, who exercises responsibility for foreign policymaking and implementation? One useful typology identifies four presidential management styles—department-centered, formalized, collegial, and palace guard—and features an accompanying role for the national security advisor—administrator, coordinator, counselor, and agent (see Figure 10-1).[134] Presidents with limited interest in the formation and implementation of foreign policy—Truman was one—deputize the secretary of state to act and speak for them and rely primarily on the State Department for analysis and implementation. In this *department-centered* style, the national security assistant (Truman's was Adm. Sidney Souers) plays the corresponding role of administrator and acts primarily as a high-level staff aide who supervises the advisory process and facilitates the presentation of views to the president but does not act independently or function as a primary policy adviser.

Eisenhower exemplified the *formalized* management style. He relied on the Departments of State and Defense as well as the intelligence community to develop a range of proposals and present them for his review and decision. His national security advisor, Robert Cutler, coordinated the flow of ideas and information to the president and secretary of state whose joint decisions were final. Reagan and George W. Bush came the closest to following Eisenhower's management example, but scholars disagree over its desirability.[135]

In the *collegial* management style, typified by Kennedy and Johnson, the president deals with ad hoc working groups in an informal national security process. Decision making is centralized in the White House, with the NSC staff performing independent analysis and policy review functions. Assistants for national security serve as counselors, providing advice designed to safeguard the president's interests, a role exemplified by McGeorge Bundy under Kennedy and Walt Rostow in the Johnson administration. Brent Scowcroft played such a role in George H. W. Bush's administration,[136] and Clinton's management of national security policy evolved to

FIGURE 10-1 Presidential Management Styles and the National Security Advisor's Roles

		Implementation Responsibility	
		Low	High
Policymaking Responsibility	Low	Department-centered administrator	Formalized coordinator
	High	Collegial counselor	Palace guard agent

SOURCE: Cecil V. Crabb Jr. and Kevin V. Mulcahy, *American National Security: A Presidential Perspective* (Pacific Grove, CA: Brooks/Cole, 1991), 189.

approximate the collegial style, with Sandy Berger serving as a counselor.[137] George W. Bush made similar use of Condoleezza Rice and Stephen Hadley, blending features of the formalized and collegial styles.[138] The *palace guard* management style, associated with Nixon, centralizes policymaking in the White House and maintains a tight rein on implementation.[139] Nixon's national security advisor, Henry Kissinger, acted as the president's agent, directing the policymaking process, serving as the president's closest policy adviser, and on occasion actively implementing policy by conducting negotiations with foreign governments. Early in his administration, Trump leaned toward this style.

Experience since 1947 suggests the administrator role is likely to be ineffective unless the president and the secretary of state are capable, hands-on decision makers. The agent role carries the risk that national security aides may go into business for themselves, acting without presidential knowledge or approval, as Reagan's defenders claimed was the case with Adm. John Poindexter and his assistant, Lt. Col. Oliver North, in the Iran-contra affair. Whether presidents choose the coordinator or counselor role for a national security advisor should be determined by their management style. In either case, the national security advisor's personality must be compatible with the designated role.[140] Carter's system suffered because Zbigniew Brzezinski was an ambitious, assertive individual more suited to the role of agent than administrator, which Carter apparently wished him to play.

Not all presidents create a clearly articulated policymaking system. Reagan, who had six different national security advisors, failed to create a consistent approach. This instability became most evident during Reagan's second term, when turmoil prevailed in the relationship between Secretary of State George Shultz and the NSC staff. One national security advisor, Robert McFarlane, acted as a policy advocate rather than as an honest broker and carried out special missions for the president.[141]

Obama's system most closely resembled the *collegial* style, aided by a White House coordinator but with a highly engaged president at the center.[142] Retired general James Jones played a relatively self-effacing role and Thomas Donilon, his successor, was cut from the same cloth. Some observers argue that John Brennan, who served as Obama's advisor on terrorism before moving to become CIA director in 2013, was the most influential national security staffer in the White House.[143] True collegiality appeared to be in short supply under Susan Rice, who has been described as "needlessly combative," triggering conflicts with White House staff, cabinet secretaries, and international leaders.[144]

National Security Organization and Management under George W. Bush

President George W. Bush's first-term challenge was to harmonize many powerful voices. With high visibility, assertive personalities in cabinet positions, and a highly experienced vice president, observers wondered what kind of role Condoleezza Rice, the national security advisor, would assume at NSC. The president gave Rice a vote of confidence at the outset of the administration by designating her rather than Cheney to chair, in the absence of the president, meetings of the **principals committee**, "the senior interagency forum for consideration of policy issues affecting national security."[145] Rice was a steadying force during the period following 9/11, when the administration fashioned a response to terrorism and launched the military action in Afghanistan. Clashes between Secretaries Rumsfeld and Powell, veterans of many bureaucratic battles, were just as bitter as observers had predicted. Rice helped to manage the policymaking system and ensure that the president's options were preserved.[146] She also emerged as a forceful defender of the administration's policies on television talk shows and through newspaper interviews. Rice, a veteran of the NSC system operated by Scowcroft, seemed to fill a counselor's role.[147]

Rice and Bush created a policymaking structure that was a variation of Eisenhower's formalized system, which accommodates strong cabinet secretaries within a White House–centered staff system, reserving final judgment for the president. But a good structure cannot guarantee effective decision making.

The Bush team functioned smoothly during its first real test, the terrorist attacks on the World Trade Center and the Pentagon. President Bush and Secretary of State Powell were out of town at the time of the attack, but they returned to Washington to become central figures in fashioning the national response. Vice President Cheney and national security advisor Rice coordinated initial responses from the Presidential

Emergency Operations Center, a nuclear attack shelter in the basement of the White House. The president remained in contact with the White House team throughout the crisis by secure telephone and even convened a teleconference meeting of the NSC. Upon his return to Washington, the president met regularly with the NSC and coordinated action with the FBI and the Transportation Department as well. In short, the system worked smoothly, producing several critical decisions about both tactics and strategy and projecting an image of calm determination after a jittery first day.[148]

Far more controversial was the administration's performance prior to and following the March 2003 invasion of Iraq. A powerful alliance of Vice President Cheney, Secretary Rumsfeld, and his principal deputy, Paul Wolfowitz, pressed aggressively for action against the regime of Saddam Hussein, suspected of actively developing weapons of mass destruction. Advisers debated whether the United States should take unilateral action against this "outlaw regime" or work through the United Nations. Initially, Secretary Powell won the internal policy battle. The president challenged the United Nations during a September 12, 2002, speech to enforce its sixteen previous resolutions on Iraq and agreed to delay action until UN inspectors were once again dispatched to Iraq. When Hussein's regime refused to disclose and destroy its weapons, the United States prepared for military action, warned Hussein of the intent to act, and sought to build both national and international support. Although both traditional (France, Germany) and new (China, Russia) allies on the UN Security Council opposed military action, Britain, Spain, Italy, Poland, Australia, Japan, and forty-four smaller nations joined the truncated "coalition of the willing." (Many of the original allies later withdrew their forces as the conflict dragged on and political pressures at home forced a change in policy.)

Launched on March 19, 2003, the military action in Iraq proved remarkably successful. With the help of "embedded journalists" traveling with the American and British ground forces, audiences around the world watched the rapid advance of troops following a massive air assault. Iraqi forces used neither biological nor chemical weapons against the invaders; in fact, coalition forces were unable to find evidence that such weapons existed, the prime justification for the war. After President Bush announced the end of combat operations in a triumphal speech aboard the USS *Abraham Lincoln* on May 1, criticism mounted in both Britain and the United States that the respective administrations had used misleading intelligence to sell the military action to skeptical publics. American media particularly focused on the following sentence from the 2003 State of the Union message: "The British government has learned that Saddam Hussein recently sought significant quantities of uranium from Africa."[149]

As the State of the Union speech approached, several administration spokespersons had claimed that Iraq was reestablishing a nuclear weapons program, but each time, the claim was rebutted either within the government or by UN specialists, and Powell did not repeat it in his February 2003 presentation at the United Nations.[150] Nevertheless, the president used the nuclear threat as part of his justification for war. Without evidence of an imminent threat—a questionable nuclear argument and no evidence of chemical and biological weapons—the president's motivation, war rationale, and credibility were called into question.[151] Nation building in Iraq, led by the Christian, Western, pro-Israeli United States, proved enormously difficult in a confused political setting with warring religious and ethnic factions. U.S. public support eroded as isolated but steady attacks on American forces produced continued casualties, and the cost of maintaining American military forces in Iraq rose to about $4 billion a month.[152] As the 2004 elections loomed, Democrats made faulty intelligence about weapons of mass destruction into a campaign issue.[153]

John P. Burke analyzed the defects of Bush's policymaking on Iraq.[154] The prewar decision making was "ineffective in vetting information, exploring a full range of analysis, and considering competing views."[155] Dissenting views in the intelligence community were not debated in the NSC's principals committee, nor were the views of those less optimistic about the chances for establishing democracy in postwar Iraq. Instead of encouraging dissenting views, some of the president's advisers suppressed them—in some cases by creating alternate institutions that would provide the desired advice—and chose to maintain a disciplined administration message rather than reach high-quality decisions. Rice was unable to control the secretary of defense and vice president, who ran roughshod over her efforts to coordinate policy. Powell consistently lost policy arguments, and Rumsfeld's and Cheney's staffs dominated postwar planning. Jon Western, however, argued that the administration had one overriding success: convincing the American public that the threat from Iraq was real and that the United States "could effectively do something about it." In Western's account, Bush, like other presidents before him, "deliberately and selectively used its [the presidency's] executive advantages of intelligence collection and analysis to frame a particular version of the threat in order to influence public opinion."[156] The Bush administration was wildly successful in maintaining a unified front.

Barack Obama's National Security System

The best accounts of the Obama decision-making system stress White House control and the president's personal involvement in the process rather than reliance on a key adviser (an honest broker) to coordinate the process.[157] As James Pfiffner summarizes, in national security decisions as in other areas of policy Obama "did not . . . appoint honest brokers but chose to control the details of policy making himself."[158] James Jones, the retired Marine Corps general originally named as national security advisor, faced a task very different from Condoleezza Rice's. From all accounts, Secretaries Gates and Clinton liked and respected each other; moreover, Gates appreciated the value of pursuing political solutions to problems and Clinton realized the necessity of military muscle, leading them to agree, for example, on the buildup of U.S. forces in Afghanistan. In short, the traditional, heated clashes that NSC advisers have often had to mediate between advocates of conflicting policy options were muted.

Jones sought to follow many of the celebrated features of the Scowcroft advising system and tried to play the role of honest broker[159] during policy debates, but Jones lacked the clout with either the president or the president's inner circle to exercise much control. He had not established a strong relationship with the president during the 2008 campaign, was not fond of the nitty-gritty of bureaucratic coordination that the NSC adviser's job necessarily entails, was frequently out of Washington, and was determined to go home each night at a decent hour rather than stay at the White House well into the night. Coordination fell to Donilon, Jones's deputy and successor. Influence shifted to others—Donilon, Brennan, White House chief of staff Rahm Emmanuel, NSC director of communications and chief of staff Denis McDonough, who was involved in virtually all the major first-term foreign policy decisions.[160]

Above all else, however, was Obama's personal involvement. Rather than delegating the task of chairing principals meetings to others (as George W. Bush had done), Obama chaired the vast majority of these meetings on his own, especially during the first year. As one account puts it, "Mr. Obama has built a machine in which all roads lead to and from him."[161] Such a structure makes the policymaking system enormously dependent on the president's skills. In this regard, most anonymous sources praised the president as a quick learner but also as having relatively little prior experience in foreign affairs. As the administration deliberated for eight weeks over the new strategy in Afghanistan, criticism mounted. Former vice president Cheney called him "dithering."[162] But he could be a decisive, calculated risk-taker. A good example was the decision to launch the raid that killed Osama bin Laden.

The U.S. intelligence community had been hunting bin Laden since his 2001 escape from the battle at Tora Bora, a remote, mountainous area of northeastern Afghanistan near the border with Pakistan. Interrogators of detainees at Guantánamo Bay learned the name of an al-Qaida operative who served as a courier for "Crankshaft," the code name given bin Laden. Research constructed a list of the courier's associates, all of whom were put under electronic surveillance by the National Security Agency. Years passed before a July 2010 phone intercept traced the courier to a location in Pakistan. From there, he was shadowed by the CIA to a suspicious compound in Abbottabad, Pakistan, that was placed under surveillance by a spy satellite and later from a nearby house. As intelligence accumulated, the CIA and military began planning possible actions in early 2011.

On March 14, 2011, CIA director Panetta briefed President Obama and his advisers on three possible courses of action.[163] First, intelligence officials could continue surveillance on the compound that lay about 120 miles into Pakistan and hope that bin Laden would be positively identified. This, however, opened the possibility that the surveillance would be detected and the target would flee. Second, the United States could bomb the compound with B-2 stealth bombers able to escape detection by Pakistani radar, but to be confident of killing bin Laden if he had a bomb shelter, they would need to use thirty-two 2,000-pound bombs that would cause extensive destruction in the area. Such a massive attack would also make it impossible to identify the body and leave open the question of whether he survived. Third, they could deploy an elite Navy SEAL team by helicopter, though the complex action would have many opportunities for breakdowns.[164] There were vivid memories of the Carter administration's failed attempt to extract the Americans held hostage in Tehran and Clinton's debacle in Somalia that gave rise to *Black Hawk Down.*[165] Complicating the decision, the CIA was only 50 to 80 percent confident that bin Laden was there. During this meeting, the president ruled out cooperating with Pakistan.[166]

During a series of national security meetings in April 2011, Obama ordered a full review of the intelligence collected on the compound and instructed his team to plan for all contingencies, including performing a proper Islamic burial for bin Laden, and prohibited the release of any images of the dead terrorist leader in the immediate aftermath of the operation in order to avoid enflaming Muslim opinion.[167] A final precaution was to provide backup to the commandos in case their mission should go awry; an additional helicopter was added to the mission, and additional U.S. forces were pre-positioned in Pakistan and on the border with Afghanistan to come to the aid of the SEALs if they had to fight their way out.

Despite its high risk of failure, the raid was ordered on April 28. It did not go flawlessly (the backup helicopter was indeed needed), but it was successful. Nine years, seven months, and twenty days after the attacks on 9/11, bin Laden was dead.

Early accounts of the decision process praised Obama as circumspect yet decisive, willing to undertake a daring raid into a sovereign nation only after a judicious consideration of all the intelligence and its implications. Speaking on *60 Minutes,* Defense Secretary Gates lauded Obama's leadership during the raid, stating, "I worked for a lot of these guys [presidents] and this is one of the most courageous calls—decisions—that I think I've ever seen a president make."[168] As Gates confirms in his memoirs, he had opposed launching the commando mission for fear that the Pakistanis would respond by disrupting supply lines to U.S. forces in Afghanistan.[169] Supporters praised the nuance and care of Obama's decision, in contrast to what they portrayed as Bush's less patient and less subtle style.

The downside of close presidential control and involvement is that presidential weaknesses can also be magnified. David Rothkopf, a vocal critic of Obama's cautious policies on Ukraine and the Middle East during 2014, points to Obama's lack of foreign policy experience prior to entering the White House as the problem. This presidential weakness created a steep learning curve, made him more tactical than strategic in his approach (that is, responding to crises as they arose), gave him little trust in his team of expert advisers, and made him highly risk averse. While "the [NSC] system does have the capability of offsetting the weaknesses of a president, if he is surrounded by strong advisors to whom he listens and who he empowers to do their jobs, it can also reinforce and exacerbate those weaknesses—as it is doing now."[170] But no system can guarantee results. Recent research makes it clear that if President Kennedy had relied on his advisers during the Cuban missile crisis in 1962, a nuclear war would almost certainly have ensued. As the preeminent historian on the crisis concludes, "the president was *not* in fact guided by the cumulative wisdom and counsel of the ExComm [his advisers]; on the contrary, he goaded and channeled the discussions toward a negotiated solution which most of his advisers resisted or opposed."[171] For better or for worse, American national security remains highly dependent on the quality of the decision maker residing at 1600 Pennsylvania Avenue.

It is far too early to know how the Trump policymaking system will function. Questions particularly center on how deeply the president will become involved and how heavily he will rely on advisers with far greater substantive knowledge than himself. Early reads are that Trump respects the triumvirate of military advisers in key positions (Mattis, McMaster, Kelly) whose career backgrounds within staff systems make them familiar with coordinating advice. Tillerson could be the odd man out unless he forms a close alliance with Mattis. A wild card in this mix is the president's son-in-law, Jared Kushner, who could figure prominently in sensitive issues including the Middle East and relations with China and Mexico.

Conclusion: Limiting the Exercise of Power

National security is the president's most important policy responsibility, presenting complex problems of leadership and management. For the nation, preserving and protecting its sovereignty and independence is of paramount concern. National interests do not change dramatically simply because presidential terms do; thus, there is more continuity in foreign and security policy than in other arenas. To a great extent, though, success in protecting those interests depends on every president's personal performance.

Presidents must interpret and exercise their powers within constitutional and statutory limits. To succeed, they must have congressional cooperation, which requires consultation. Yet operational realities require that presidents be accorded ample latitude to act independently and often secretly. Tensions inevitably arise between Congress and the president over national security policy.[172] But the tasks involved are primarily executive in nature, and executive control of foreign and military policy persists in spite of Congress's major constitutional role.[173] As Alexander Hamilton wrote in 1793, the president is the first mover: "the Executive in the exercise of its constitutional powers, may establish an antecedent state of things" creating a new set of circumstances that constrain legislative options.[174] Congress often finds itself reacting rather than coming to proactive consensus about the proper "state of things."

Yet the Constitution and political prudence require "shared power and balanced institutional participation" as norms in national security decision making.[175] Perhaps the most important lesson in this regard is that since 1945 most of the nation's successful foreign policies—the Truman Doctrine, the Marshall Plan, NATO, the Panama Canal treaty, arms control, and the Persian Gulf War—were "adopted by Congress and the people after meaningful debate."[176] For the most part, the major failures—FDR's Yalta agreements with Stalin, the Bay of Pigs invasion, the Vietnam War, and the Iran-contra affair—were initiated and implemented unilaterally by presidents. In the case of the Iraq War, Congress approved action but gave the president a free hand in its execution: It seems likely that Bush's legacy will be a controversial if not a failed adventure.

In the ever-changing international system, the United States remains the world's dominant power militarily, though its economic clout has declined. Military dominance does not mean America can always assert its will unilaterally, a reality painfully rediscovered in Iraq and Afghanistan. Strategically, Obama's administration sought to refocus American efforts on Asia while rekindling traditional alliances in Europe and Latin America. Could the United States afford any longer to be a superpower? Confronting a seemingly out-of-control budget deficit, pressures mounted at home to reduce global military commitments. Did this mean withdrawing U.S. ground forces from overseas bases in Europe and Asia and instead relying on local powers to deal with regional problems? Or would a new strategy merely reduce those forward-based U.S. forces and find new ways to partner with allies around the world?[177] Finding the means to exercise power responsibly and at a tolerable price remains both the nation's and the president's major challenge.

Suggested Readings

Allen, Michael. *Blinking Red: Crisis and Confidence in American Intelligence after 9/11.* Washington, DC: Potomac Books, 2013.

Berman, Larry. *Planning a Tragedy: The Americanization of the War in Vietnam.* New York: Norton, 1983.

Burke, John P. *Honest Broker? The National Security Advisor and Presidential Decision Making.* College Station: Texas A&M University Press, 2009.

Burke, John P., and Fred I. Greenstein. *How Presidents Test Reality: Decisions on Vietnam, 1954 and 1965.* New York: Russell Sage Foundation, 1991.

Draper, Theodore. *A Very Thin Line: The Iran-Contra Affairs.* New York: Hill and Wang, 1991.

Fisher, Louis. *Presidential War Power.* Lawrence: University Press of Kansas, 1995.

———. *Congressional Abdication on War and Spending.* College Station: Texas A&M University Press, 2000.

Fowler, Linda L. *Watchdogs on the Hill: The Decline of Congressional Oversight of U.S. Foreign Relations.* Princeton, NJ: Princeton University Press, 2015.

George, Alexander L. *Presidential Decisionmaking in Foreign Policy: The Effective Use of Information and Advice.* Boulder, CO: Westview, 1980.

Glennon, Michael J. *National Security and Double Government.* New York: Oxford University Press, 2015.

Henderson, Philip G. *Managing the Presidency: The Eisenhower Legacy—From Kennedy to Reagan.* Boulder, CO: Westview, 1988.

Henkin, Louis. *Constitutionalism, Democracy, and Foreign Affairs.* New York: Columbia University Press, 1992.

———. *Foreign Affairs and the United States Constitution,* 2nd ed. Oxford: Oxford University Press, 1997.

Hinckley, Barbara. *Less Than Meets the Eye: Foreign Policymaking and the Myth of the Assertive Congress.* Chicago: University of Chicago Press, 1994.

Johnson, Loch K. *Bombs, Bugs, Drugs, and Thugs: Intelligence and America's Quest for Security.* New York: New York University Press, 2000.

Koh, Harold Hongju. *The National Security Constitution: Sharing Power after the Iran-Contra Affair.* New Haven, CT: Yale University Press, 1990.

Korb, Lawrence J. *A New National Security Strategy in an Age of Terrorists, Tyrants, and Weapons of Mass Destruction.* New York: Council on Foreign Relations, 2003.

Mann, Thomas E., ed. *A Question of Balance: The President, the Congress, and Foreign Policy.* Washington, DC: Brookings, 1990.

Peterson, Paul E., ed. *The President, the Congress, and the Making of Foreign Policy.* Norman: University of Oklahoma Press, 1994.

Pious, Richard M. *Why Presidents Fail: White House Decision Making from Eisenhower to Bush II.* Lanham, MD: Rowman and Littlefield, 2008.

President's Special Review Board (Tower Commission). *Report of the President's Special Review Board.* Washington, DC: Government Printing Office, 1987.

Savage, Charlie. *Takeover: The Return of the Imperial Presidency and the Subversion of American Democracy.* New York: Little, Brown, 2007.

Schlesinger, Arthur M., Jr. *The Imperial Presidency,* rev. ed. Boston: Houghton Mifflin, 1989.

———. *War and the American Presidency.* New York: Norton, 2005.

Western, Jon. *Selling Intervention and War: The Presidency, the Media, and the American Public.* Baltimore, MD: Johns Hopkins University Press, 2005.

Woodward, Bob. *Bush at War.* New York: Simon and Schuster, 2002.

———. *Obama's Wars.* New York: Simon and Schuster, 2010.

———. *State of Denial.* New York: Simon and Schuster, 2006.

Notes

1. "Authorization for Use of Military Force," Public Law 107–40, adopted September 14, 2001. Text in *Washington Post,* September 15, 2001, A4.

2. The "two presidencies" thesis holds that presidents enjoy relatively greater success with Congress in foreign policy than in domestic policy. According to Terry Sullivan, modern Republican and Democratic presidents have had approximately equal success with foreign policy proposals, but Democratic administrations have done better with domestic policy because of their party's longtime domination of Congress. See Sullivan, "A Matter of Fact: The 'Two Presidencies' Thesis Revitalized," in *The Two Presidencies: A Quarter Century Assessment,* ed. Steven A. Shull (Chicago: Nelson Hall, 1991), 143–157. On the rise of partisan and ideological bickering over foreign policy issues in Congress during the 1990s, see James M. McCormick, Eugene R. Wittkopf, and David M. Dana, "Politics and Bipartisanship at the Water's Edge: A Note on Bush and Clinton," *Polity* 30 (Fall 1997): 133–149.

3. Interview with Tom Ricks broadcast on National Public Radio's *Morning Edition,* March 4, 2009, www.npr.org/templates/story/story.php?storyId=101395478.

4. Mythili Sampathkumar, "Donald Trump Puts 'America First' Stating He Is Not President of the World," *The Independent,* April 5, 2017, http://www.independent.co.uk/news/world/americas/us-politics/donald-trump-america-first-not-us-president-world-nato-ntabu-trade-unions-workers-infrastructure-a7668576.html. Note that "America First" is a slogan that dates back to isolationists, notably Charles Lindbergh, who opposed American involvement in the Second World War. Critics of Trump's use of the phrase stressed its earlier usage and the de facto support of the then-rising Nazi regime in Germany it implied.

5. Ann Coulter, "We Want the 'President of America' Back, Not the 'President of the World,'" *VDARE.com,* April 12, 2017, http://www.vdare.com/articles/ann-coulter-we-want-the-president-of-america-back-not-the-president-of-the-world.

6. Pew Research Center, "Public Supports Syria Missile Strikes, but Few See a 'Clear Plan' for Addressing Situation," April 12, 2017, http://www.people-press.org/2017/04/12/public-supports-syria-missile-strikes-but-few-see-a-clear-plan-for-addressing-situation/.

7. James Chace, "Is a Foreign Policy Consensus Possible?" *Foreign Affairs* 57 (Fall 1978): 30.

8. Lawrence J. Korb, *A New National Security Strategy in an Age of Terrorists, Tyrants, and Weapons of Mass Destruction* (New York: Council on Foreign Relations, 2003), 1.

9. Strobe Talbott, *The Russians and Reagan* (New York: Vintage Books, 1984).

10. Richard Reeves, *President Reagan* (New York: Simon and Schuster, 2005), 6.

11. The most comprehensive and informative account of the Iran-contra affair is by Theodore Draper, *A Very Thin Line: The Iran-Contra Affairs* (New York: Hill and Wang, 1991). For the perspective of two participants in the congressional hearings, see William S. Cohen and George J. Mitchell, *Men of Zeal* (New York: Viking, 1988). The role of the CIA and Director William Casey receives careful attention from Bob Woodward in *Veil: The Secret Wars of the CIA, 1981–1987* (New York: Simon and Schuster, 1987). Also essential to a full understanding of Iran-contra is the report of the Tower Commission (John Tower, Edmund Muskie, and Brent Scowcroft): President's Special Review Board, *Report of the President's Special Review Board* (Washington, DC: U.S. Government Printing Office, 1987).

12. Terry L. Deibel, "Bush's Foreign Policy: Mastery and Inaction," *Foreign Policy* 84 (Fall 1991): 20–22; and Steven V. Roberts, "The Second Sin of George Bush," *New Leader*, March 11–15, 1991, 3.

13. Daniel P. Franklin and Robert Shepard, "Analyzing the Bush Foreign Policy" (paper presented at the annual meeting of the American Political Science Association, Washington, DC, August 29–September 1, 1991), 2–3.

14. David C. Hendrickson, "The Recovery of Internationalism," *Foreign Affairs* 73 (September–October 1994): 26–43. For similar criticisms, see Richard N. Haas, "Paradigm Lost," *Foreign Affairs* 74 (January–February 1995): 43–58; and Larry Berman and Emily O. Goldman, "Clinton's Foreign Policy at Midterm," in *The Clinton Presidency: First Appraisals*, ed. Colin Campbell and Bert A. Rockman (Chatham, NJ: Chatham House, 1995), 290–324.

15. William J. Clinton, *A National Security Strategy for a New Century* (Washington, DC: The White House, October 1998). For commentary, see Emily O. Goldman and Larry Berman, "Engaging the World: First Impressions of the Clinton Foreign Policy Legacy," in *The Clinton Legacy*, ed. Colin Campbell and Bert A. Rockman (New York: Chatham House, 2000); and James M. McCormick, "Clinton and Foreign Policy: Some Legacies for a New Century," in *The Postmodern Presidency: Bill Clinton's Legacy in U.S. Politics*, ed. Steven E. Schier (Pittsburgh: University of Pittsburgh Press, 2000).

16. John Lewis Gaddis, "A Grand Strategy of Transformation," *Foreign Policy* (November–December 2002): 50–57, doi:10.2307/3183557.

17. Fareed Zakaria, "The Arrogant Empire," *Newsweek*, March 24, 2003, 18ff.

18. Ibid.

19. George W. Bush, State of the Union, January 29, 2002, http://dev-www.cfr.org/publication/12473/.

20. Korb, *A New National Security Strategy*, Appendix B, 107.

21. Susan E. Rice, "The New National Security Strategy: Focus on Failed States," Brookings Policy Brief #116–2003, February 2003, 1, www.brookings.edu/research/papers/2003/02/terrorism-rice.

22. See, for example, three Brookings Institution policy briefs: Ivo Daalder, James M. Lindsay, and James B. Steinberg, "The Bush National Security Strategy: An Evaluation," Policy Brief #109–2002, https://www.brookings.edu/research/the-bush-national-security-strategy-an-evaluation/; Michael E. O'Hanlon, Susan E. Rice, and James B. Steinberg, "The New National Security Strategy and Preemption," Policy Brief #113–2003, https://www.brookings.edu/research/the-new-national-security-strategy-and-preemption/; and Rice, "The New National Security Strategy."

23. O'Hanlon, Rice, and Steinberg, "The New National Security Strategy and Preemption."

24. These three options are discussed in depth and presented as alternative drafts of presidential speeches in Korb, *A New National Security Strategy*, 1–96.

25. George W. Bush, Second Inaugural Address, www.vlib.us/amdocs/texts/bush012005.html.

26. Barack Obama, *National Security Strategy,* May 2010, https://obamawhitehouse.archives.gov/sites/default/files/rss_viewer/national_security_strategy.pdf.

27. Barack Obama, "Obama's Address on the End of the Combat Mission in Iraq, August 2010," Council on Foreign Relations, August 31, 2010, http://dev-www.cfr.org/iraq/obamas-address-end-combat-mission-iraq-august-2010/p22868.

28. "Iraqi Elections," *New York Times,* December 21, 2010, topics.nytimes.com/top/news/international/countriesandterritories/iraq/elections/index.html.

29. "Obama's Surge Strategy in Afghanistan," *New York Times,* November 30, 2009, roomfordebate.blogs.nytimes.com/2009/11/30/obamas-surge-strategy-in-afghanistan/; and Barack Obama, National Security Strategy, May 2010.

30. Helene Cooper and Eric Schmitt, "White House Debate Led to Plan to Widen Afghan Effort," *New York Times,* March 27, 2009, www.nytimes.com/2009/03/28/us/politics/28prexy.html?_r=1.

31. Max Boot, "Obama Shone in McChrystal Affair," Council on Foreign Relations, June 28, 2010, www.cfr.org/afghanistan/obama-shone-mcchrystal-affair/p22560.

32. Ibid. In April 2015, Petraeus was sentenced to two years' probation and fined $100,000 for leaking sensitive documents to his biographer and lover.

33. New START Treaty," *New York Times,* December 2010, topics.nytimes.com/top/reference/timestopics/subjects/s/strategic_arms_reduction_treaty/index.html.

34. Office of the Press Secretary, "Remarks by President Barack Obama," April 5, 2009, https://obamawhitehouse.archives.gov/the-press-office/remarks-president-barack-obama-prague-delivered.

35. "New START Treaty."

36. Lawrence J. Korb and Alexander H. Rothman, "Reclaiming and Rebuilding American Power," in *Obama in Office,* ed. James A. Thurber (Boulder, CO: Paradigm Publishers, 2011), 269–280.

37. Peter Baker, "Obama Signs into Law Tighter Sanctions on Iran," *New York Times,* July 1, 2010, www.nytimes.com/2010/07/02/world/middleeast/02sanctions.html.

38. Deborah Jerome, "Egypt's Diplomatic Challenge for the United States," Council on Foreign Relations, January 31, 2011, http://dev-www.cfr.org/egypt/egypts-diplomatic-challenge-united-states/p23941.

39. Office of the Press Secretary, "Statement of President Barack Obama on Egypt," February 10, 2011, www.whitehouse.gov/the-press-office/2011/02/10/statement-president-barack-obama-egypt.

40. David Sanger, "Obama Presses Egypt's Military on Democracy," *New York Times,* February 11, 2011, www.nytimes.com/2011/02/12/world/middleeast/12diplomacy.html.

41. Barack Obama, "Transcript of Obama's Remarks on Libya," *Wall Street Journal,* February 26, 2011, blogs.wsj.com/washwire/2011/02/23/transcript-of-obamas-remarks-on-libya/.

42. Helen Cooper, "U.S. Freezes a Record $30 Billion in Libyan Assets," *New York Times,* February 28, 2011, www.nytimes.com/2011/03/01/world/africa/01assets.html?scp=20&sq=action+in+libya&st=nyt.

43. Devin Dwyer and Luis Martinez, "U.S. Tomahawk Cruise Missiles Hit Targets in Libya," *ABC News/International,* March 19, 2011, abcnews.go.com/International/libya-international-military-coalition-launch-assault-gadhafi-forces/story?id=13174246.

44. Office of the Press Secretary, "Remarks by the President in Address to the Nation on Libya," White House, March 28, 2011, https://obamawhitehouse.archives.gov/the-press-office/2011/03/28/remarks-president-address-nation-libya.

45. Larry Diamond, "Democracy Promotion and the Obama Doctrine," Council on Foreign Relations, April 8, 2011, www.cfr.org/us-strategy-and-politics/democracy-promotion-obama-doctrine/p24621.

46. Adam Entous, Siobahn Gorman, and Nour Malas, "CIA Expands Role in Syria Fight," *Wall Street Journal,* March 22, 2013, www.wsj.com/articles/SB10001424127887324373204578376591874909434.

47. See, for example, Mike Allen, "Don't Do Stupid (Stuff)," *Politico,* June 1, 2014, tinyurl.com/n5mqurd.

48. Special thanks to Mitchell Freddura for assisting with this section of the chapter.

49. Michael Gordon, "U.S. Embracing a New Approach to Battling ISIS in Iraq," *New York Times,* June 9, 2015.

50. Joseph R. Biden, Jr., "Statement by the Vice President on the March 9 Letter from Republican Senators to the Islamic Republic of Iran," March 9, 2015, http://dev-www.cfr.org/congresses-parliaments-national-legislatures/statement-vice-president-march-9-letter-republican-senators-islamic-republic-iran/p36263.

51. The Iran Nuclear Agreement Review Act of 2015, Public Law 114–17.

52. Ibid.

53. Ibid., preface.

54. Ibid.

55. Janine Davidson, "Obama's Last National Security Strategy," *Foreign Affairs,* March 2, 2015, www.foreignaffairs.com/articles/143207/janine-davidson/obamas-last-national-security-strategy.

56. Office of the Press Secretary, "Barack Obama Speech at the U.S. Military Academy-West Point," May 28, 2014, www.whitehouse.gov/the-press-office/2014/05/28/remarks-president-united-states-military-academy-commencement-ceremony.

57. Maggie Haberman, Matthew Rosenberg, Matt Apuzo, and Glenn Thrush, "Michael Flynn Resigns as National Security Adviser," *New York Times,* February 13, 2017, https://www.nytimes.com/2017/02/13/us/politics/donald-trump-national-security-adviser-michael-flynn.html?_r=0.

58. Eugene Kiely, "Trump and the Intelligence Community," FactCheck.org, January 23, 2017, http://www.factcheck.org/2017/01/trump-and-intelligence-community/.

59. Brian Bennett, Noah Bierman, and Michael A. Memoli, "Trump Removes Stephen Bannon from National Security Council in Staff Shake-up," *Los Angeles Times,* April 5, 2017, http://www.latimes.com/politics/la-na-pol-trump-bannon-20170405-story.html.

60. David Ignatius, "Trump Got Syria and China Right," *Washington Post,* April 11, 2017, https://www.washingtonpost.com/opinions/global-opinions/trumps-week-of-good-decisions-could-rebalance-the-world-and-the-white-house/2017/04/11/9b3ebc6c-1eeb-11e7-be2a-3a1fb24d4671_story.html?utm_term=.7070f27aedfb.

61. David Ignatius, "Trump Gets a Taste of Success," *Washington Post,* April 13, 2017, https://www.washingtonpost.com/opinions/trump-gets-a-taste-of-success/2017/04/13/1aeb8f3a-2090-11e7-a0a7-8b2a45e3dc84_story.html?utm_term=.9a6a0c99a4f9.

62. See the comments of former representative Lee Hamilton, D-IN, as reported by Charlie Cook, "China Crisis Halts Slide of Bush's Poll Ratings," *National Journal,* April 21, 2001, 1186.

63. Edward S. Corwin, *The President: Office and Powers,* 4th ed. (New York: New York University Press, 1957), 171.

64. Ibid.

65. Joseph E. Kallenbach, *The American Chief Executive* (New York: Harper and Row, 1966), 485.

66. Corwin, *The President,* 179.

67. The term "sole organ" comes (in this context) from the 1936 Supreme Court decision *Curtiss-Wright Export Co. v. United States,* 299 U.S. 304; but see Louis Fisher, "Presidential Inherent Power: The 'Sole Organ' Doctrine," *Presidential Studies Quarterly* 37 (March 2007): 139–152.

68. Corwin, *The President,* 185.

69. Jason Ukman, "U.S. Recognition of New Libyan Government Raises Tough Legal Questions," *Washington Post,* July 19, 2011, www.washingtonpost.com/blogs/checkpoint-washington/post/us-recognition-of-new-libyan-government-raises-tough-legal-questions/2011/07/19/gIQAb9BdNI_blog.html.

70. See *Zivotofsky v. Kerry,* docket number 13–628, decided June 8, 2015.

71. The treaty-making process entails three distinct stages: (1) negotiation, (2) Senate approval, and (3) ratification by the president. Contrary to popular understanding, the Senate does not ratify a treaty—it *approves* the treaty negotiated by the president. The president may refuse to sign—that is, to ratify—a treaty approved by the Senate, either because of amendments or reservations or because it was negotiated by a previous administration.

72. Ibid., 213.

73. Ibid.; Kallenbach, *The American Chief Executive,* 502.

74. See the estimates provided by Loch Johnson in *The Making of International Agreements: Congress Confronts the Executive* (New York: NYU Press, 1984) and Glen S. Krutz and Jeffrey S. Peake, *Treaty Politics and the Rise of Executive Agreements: International Commitments in a System of Shared Powers* (Ann Arbor: University of Michigan Press, 2011).

75. Michael John Garcia, "International Law and Agreements: Their Effect upon U.S. Law," CRS Report RL32528, February 18, 2015, fas.org/sgp/crs/misc/RL32528.pdf.

76. Cecil V. Crabb Jr. and Pat M. Holt, *Invitation to Struggle: Congress, the President, and Foreign Policy,* 4th ed. (Washington, DC: CQ Press, 1992), 6.

77. Louis Fisher, *The Law of the Executive Branch* (New York: Oxford University Press, 2014), 290.

78. Harold Hongju Koh argues, however, that Congress should create by statute its own procedures for determining when international agreements should be submitted to the Senate for approval. See Koh, *The National Security Constitution: Sharing Power after the Iran-Contra Affair* (New Haven, CT: Yale University Press, 1990), 195.

79. *Goldwater v. Carter,* 444 U.S. 996 (1979). The Supreme Court, in the *Goldwater* case, held that since Congress had not acted as a body to stop the president, there was no conflict the Court could resolve. Although the circuit court based its decision on the recognition of foreign governments, the case has been interpreted as authorizing unilateral presidential breaking of treaties in accordance with their terms, as Bush did in 2001.

80. Helene Cooper, "Hagel Resigns under Pressure as Global Crises Test Pentagon," *New York Times,* November 24, 2014, www.nytimes.com/2014/11/25/us/hagel-said-to-be-stepping-down-as-defense-chief-under-pressure.html.

81. Rebecca Shabad, "Mattis Confirmed as Defense Secretary by Senate," *CBS News* (January 20, 2017), http://www.cbsnews.com/news/james-mattis-confirmed-defense-secretary-confirmation-vote/.

82. The intelligence community throughout most of the post–World War II period consisted of the Central Intelligence Agency (CIA); the National Security Agency; the Bureau of Intelligence and Research in the Department of State; the Defense Intelligence Agency; the intelligence offices of the U.S. Army, U.S. Navy, U.S. Air Force, and Marine Corps; the FBI; and the intelligence offices in the Departments of Energy and Treasury. Over time, the community grew to include units in the Coast Guard, the Department of Homeland Security, the Drug Enforcement Administration, and two specialized units in Defense, the National Geospatial Intelligence Agency, and the National Reconnaissance Office.

83. Carl Hulse, "For Dianne Feinstein, Torture Report's Release is a Signal Moment," *New York Times,* December 10, 2014.

84. Brother of John Foster Dulles, Eisenhower's secretary of state.

85. See, for example, Michael J. Glennon, *National Security and Double Government* (New York: Oxford University Press, 2015).

86. Corwin, *The President,* chap. 6; Arthur M. Schlesinger Jr., *The Imperial Presidency* (Boston: Houghton Mifflin, 1989), chaps. 1–7.

87. Corwin, *The President,* 229.

88. *Prize Cases,* 67 U.S. (2 Black) 635 (1863).

89. *Korematsu v. United States,* 323 U.S. 214 (1944).

90. U.S. Department of Defense, *Working Group Report on Detainee Interrogations in the Global War on Terrorism: Assessment of Legal, Historical, Policy, and Operational Considerations,* April 4, 2003, 21; more generally, see Andrew Rudalevige, "The Decline and Resurgence and Decline (and Resurgence?) of Congress," *Presidential Studies Quarterly* 36 (September 2006): 506–524.

91. Clinton Rossiter, *Constitutional Dictatorship: Crisis Government in Modern Democracies* (New York: Harcourt, Brace, 1963).

92. Such actions have numerous precedents, including Jefferson's dispatch of the Navy to stop the Barbary pirates from seizing U.S. merchant ships and holding their crews for ransom, and Theodore Roosevelt's contribution of U.S. Marines to the international expeditionary force that put down the Boxer Rebellion in China in 1904.

93. Larry Berman, *Planning a Tragedy: The Americanization of the War in Vietnam* (New York: Norton, 1982). For a comparative analysis of how Eisenhower and Johnson dealt with pressures to intervene militarily in Vietnam, see John P. Burke and Fred I. Greenstein, *How Presidents Test Reality: Decisions on Vietnam, 1954 and 1965* (New York: Russell Sage Foundation, 1989).

94. Ivo H. Daalder and James M. Lindsay, "The Bush Revolution: The Remaking of America's Foreign Policy" (paper delivered at the conference on "The George W. Bush Presidency: An Early Assessment," Woodrow Wilson School, Princeton University, April 25–26, 2003), 28.

95. Mike Allen and Charles Lane, "Resolution Likened to '64 Vietnam Measure," *Washington Post,* September 20, 2002, A20.

96. The House vote was 296–133, with all but six Republicans approving and Democrats dividing 81 yes and 126 no. The Senate vote was 77–23, with all but one Republican approving and twenty-one Democrats voting no; the independent also voted no.

97. Shoon Kathleen Murray, "The Contemporary Presidency: Stretching the 2001 AUMF: A History of Two Presidencies," *Presidential Studies Quarterly* 45 (March 2015): 175–198.

98. John M. Donnelly, "Hard-Line Anti-War Votes Fail," *CQ Weekly Online,* September 24, 2007, 2760–2762, library.cqpress.com/cqweekly/weeklyreport110-000002591148.

99. In his well-known concurring opinion in *Youngstown Sheet and Tube Co. v. Sawyer* (1952), Justice Robert H. Jackson identified three scenarios for presidential use of force: (1) presidents can act with the express or implied authority of Congress; (2) presidents can act in direct opposition to the will of Congress; or (3) presidents may act in the absence of express or denied authority, a "twilight zone." Louis Fisher, *Presidential War Power* (Lawrence: University Press of Kansas, 1995), 190.

100. Arthur M. Schlesinger Jr., *War and the American Presidency* (New York: Norton, 2005). Also see Charlie Savage, *Takeover: The Return of the Imperial Presidency and the Subversion of American Democracy* (New York: Little, Brown, 2007).

101. Lynne O'Donnell, AP, "U.S. and NATO Formally End War in Afghanistan," *New York Times,* December 28, 2014, www.nytimes.com/aponline/2014/12/28/world/asia/ap-as-afghanistan.html.

102. Helene Cooper, Mujib Mashal, "U.S. Drops 'Mother of All Bombs' on ISIS Caves in Afghanistan," *New York Times,* April 13, 2017, https://www.nytimes.com/2017/04/13/world/asia/moab-mother-of-all-bombs-afghanistan.html.

103. Stephen Kinzer, *The Brothers: John Foster Dulles, Allen Dulles, and Their Secret World War* (New York: Holt, 2013).

104. Mark Mazzetti et al., "The Secret History of SEAL Team 6," *New York Times,* June 7, 2015, A1.

105. See, for example, Mark Mazzetti, *The Way of the Knife: The CIA, a Secret Army, and a War at the Ends of the Earth* (New York: Penguin, 2013).

106. Raffi Khatchadourian, "No Secrets: Julian Assange's Mission for Total Transparency," *New Yorker,* June 7, 2010; Luke Harding, "How Edward Snowden Went from Loyal NSA Contractor to Whistleblower," *The Guardian,* February 1, 2014.

107. Karen McVeigh, "Obama's Efforts to Control Leaks 'Most Aggressive since Nixon,' Report Finds," *The Guardian,* October 10, 2013, www.theguardian.com/world/2013/oct/10/obama-leaks-aggressive-nixon-report-prosecution.

108. Eric Rosenbach and Aki J. Peritz, "Informing Congress of Intelligence Activities," in Rosenbach and Peritz, *Confrontation or Collaboration? Congress and the Intelligence Community* (Cambridge, MA: Harvard University Belfer Center for Science and International Affairs, 2009), 28–31.

109. The Supreme Court's decision in *Immigration and Naturalization Service v. Chadha,* 462 U.S. 919 (1983), which held that the legislative veto was unconstitutional, may have made this provision inoperative.

110. Richard F. Grimmett, "War Powers Resolution: Presidential Compliance," *CRS Issue Brief for Congress,* Congressional Research Service, Library of Congress, Washington, DC, March 21, 2001; updated June 9, 2003.

111. Congress considered triggering the clock in 1983, in legislation involving the multinational force in Lebanon, but ultimately authorized U.S. participation for eighteen months after reaching an agreement with the White House.

112. Robert A. Katzmann, "War Powers: Toward a New Accommodation," in *A Question of Balance: The President, Congress, and Foreign Policy,* ed. Thomas E. Mann (Washington, DC: Brookings, 1990), 55.

113. Joshua Lee Prober, "Congress, the War Powers Resolution, and the Secret Political Life of 'a Dead Letter,'" *Journal of Law and Politics* 7 (1990): 177–229.

114. Carroll J. Doherty, "Bush Is Given Authorization to Use Force against Iraq," *Congressional Quarterly Weekly Report,* January 12, 1991, 65–70.

115. John Bellinger, "President Trump's War Powers Report on the Syria Attacks," *Lawfare,* April 8, 2017, https://www.lawfareblog.com/president-trumps-war-powers-report-syria-attacks. Also see Jack Goldsmith and Matthew Waxman, "Obama, Not Bush, Is the Master of Unilateral War," *New Republic,* October 14, 2014, https://newrepublic.com/article/119827/obamas-war-powers-legacy-he-must-seek-congressional-authorization.

116. Charlie Savage, "Was Trump's Syria Strike Legal? Explaining Presidential War Powers," *New York Times,* April 7, 2017, https://www.nytimes.com/2017/04/07/us/politics/military-force-presidential-power.html

117. John M. Hillebrecht, "Ensuring Affirmative Congressional Control over the Use of Force: Two Proposals for Collective Decision Making," *Stanford Journal of International Law* 26 (1990): 511.

118. Michael J. Glennon, *Constitutional Diplomacy* (Princeton, NJ: Princeton University Press, 1990), 102–103.

119. Koh, *The National Security Constitution.*

120. Prober, "Congress, the War Powers Resolution," 229.

121. Ibid., 223–226, 229.

122. Citing as precedent the history of presidential war making, the Court could sustain the resolution. Or the Court might choose to overturn it, noting that because the resolution was forced on the presidency at a time of institutional weakness, it "undercuts the legitimacy of the executive branch." I. M. Destler, "The Constitution and Foreign Affairs," *News for Teachers of Political Science* (Spring 1985): 15.

123. James L. Sundquist, *The Decline and Resurgence of Congress* (Washington, DC: Brookings, 1981), 270.

124. William C. Banks and Jeffrey D. Straussman, "A New Imperial Presidency? Insights from U.S. Involvement in Bosnia," *Political Science Quarterly* 114 (Summer 1999): 200.

125. William Safire, "On Impeachment Eve," *New York Times,* December 17, 1998, A31. On the comments of Senate majority leader Trent Lott and House whip Tom DeLay, see R. W. Apple Jr., "No

Reservoir of Credibility," *New York Times,* December 17, 1998, A1, A15. On the air attacks more generally, see Francis X. Clines and Steven Lee Myers, "Biggest Attack since '91 War—Britain Gives Support," *New York Times,* December 17, 1998, A1, A15.

126. Josh Hicks, "Obama Foreign Policy Sparks Bipartisan Criticism," *Washington Post,* August 31, 2014, www.washingtonpost.com/blogs/post-politics/wp/2014/08/31/obama-foreign-policy-sparks-bipartisan-criticism/.

127. Christine Conetta, "House Republicans Call Obama's Actions on Immigration Unconstitutional," *Huffington Post,* December 3, 2014, www.huffingtonpost.com/2014/12/03/gop-obama-immigration_n_6259146.html; and Scott Bomboy, "Cuba as the Next Constitutional Fight between Congress, Obama," *Constitution Daily,* December 19, 2014, blog.constitutioncenter.org/2014/12/cuba-as-the-next-constitutional-fight-between-congress-obama/.

128. Kate Ackley and Tamar Hallerman, "As Door to Cuba Opens, Castro Foes Push Back," *CQ Weekly,* April 20, 2015, 32–34, library.cqpress.com/cqweekly/weeklyreport114-000004664311.

129. *Report of the U. S. Commission on the Organization of the Government for the Conduct of Foreign Policy* (Washington, DC: U.S. Government Printing Office, 1975), 1. Also see Burke and Greenstein, *How Presidents Test Reality,* esp. chap. 13.

130. Graham T. Allison and Peter Szanton, "Organizing for the Decade Ahead," in *Setting National Priorities: The Next Ten Years,* ed. Henry Owen and Charles Schultze (Washington, DC: Brookings, 1976), 232–233.

131. Alexander L. George, *Presidential Decisionmaking in Foreign Policy: The Effective Use of Information and Advice* (Boulder, CO: Westview, 1980), 146. For a history of the NSC, see David Rothkopf, *Running the World: The Inside Story of the National Security Council and the Architects of American Power* (New York: Public Affairs, 2005).

132. Burt Solomon, "When It Comes to Geopolitics . . . Who's Painting the Big Picture?" *National Journal,* March 5, 1995, 550–551.

133. Ivo H. Daalder and I. M. Destler, "A New NSC for a New Administration," Policy Brief #68–2000, Brookings Institution, November 2000, https://www.brookings.edu/research/a-new-nsc-for-a-new-administration/.

134. Cecil V. Crabb Jr. and Kevin V. Mulcahy, *American National Security: A Presidential Perspective* (Pacific Grove, CA: Brooks/Cole, 1991), chap. 9. The discussion relies on Crabb and Mulcahy. For a similar typology related to "control" and "coordination," see Margaret G. Hermann and Thomas Preston, "Presidents, Advisers, and Foreign Policy: The Effect of Leadership Style on Executive Arrangements," *Political Psychology* 15, no. 1 (1994): 75–96.

135. For opposing views, see Fred I. Greenstein and Richard H. Immerman, "Effective National Security Advising: Recovering the Eisenhower Legacy," *Political Science Quarterly* 115 (Fall 2000): 335–345; and Arthur Schlesinger Jr., "Effective National Security Advising: A Most Dubious Precedent," *Political Science Quarterly* 115 (Fall 2000): 335–351.

136. Larry Berman and Bruce W. Jentelson, "Bush and the Post–Cold War World: New Challenges for American Leadership," in *The Bush Presidency: First Appraisals,* ed. Colin Campbell and Bert A. Rockman (Chatham, NJ: Chatham House, 1991), 99–103. Also see Burt Solomon, "Making Foreign Policy in Secret May Be Easy, but It Carries Risks," *National Journal,* January 12, 1991, 90–91.

137. Anthony Lake, who held the position before Berger, is best thought of as a coordinator, according to a written communication from Kevin Mulcahy.

138. John P. Burke, "From Success to Failure? Iraq and the Organization of George W. Bush's Decision Making," in *The Polarized Presidency of George W. Bush,* ed. George C. Edwards and Desmond King (Oxford: Oxford University Press, 2007), 176.

139. Crabb and Mulcahy, *American National Security,* 189–190.

140. Ibid.

141. Kevin V. Mulcahy, "The Secretary of State: Foreign Policymaking in the Carter and Reagan Administrations," *Presidential Studies Quarterly* (Spring 1986): 296.

142. For an excellent summary of the evolution of the national security adviser's role and the choices facing the Obama administration at its outset, see John P. Burke, "The National Security Advisor and Staff," *Presidential Studies Quarterly* 39:2 (June 2009).

143. Connie Bruck, "The Inside War," *New Yorker*, June 22, 2015.

144. Transcript of interview of David Rothkopf conducted by Jeffrey Goldberg, "A Withering Critique of Obama's National Security Council," *The Atlantic*, November 12, 2014, www.theatlantic.com/-international/archive/2014/11/a-withering-critique-of-president-obamas-national-security-council/382477/.

145. To view the text of the National Security Presidential Directive that established the Bush system, see www.fas.org/irp/offdocs/nspd/nspd-1.htm. Jane Perlez, "Directive Says Rice, Bush Aide, Won't Be Upstaged by Cheney," *New York Times*, February 16, 2001, www.nytimes.com/2001/02/16/politics/16SECU.html. In the intelligence reforms adopted in 2004, the director of national intelligence replaced the director of the CIA.

146. For a fascinating account, see Woodward, *Bush at War* (New York: Simon and Schuster, 2002).

147. Written communication from Kevin Mulcahy.

148. David E. Sanger and Don Van Natta Jr., "In Four Days, a National Crisis Changes Bush's Presidency," *New York Times*, September 16, 2001, A1.

149. Full text of the speech is available at www.vlib.us/amdocs/texts/bush012003.html.

150. Walter Pincus, "Bush Faced Dwindling Data on Iraq Nuclear Bid," *Washington Post*, July 16, 2003, A1; Walter Pincus, "White House Backs Off Claim on Iraqi Buy," *Washington Post*, July 8, 2003, A1; and Walter Pincus, "CIA Asked Britain to Drop Iraq Claim; Advice on Alleged Uranium Buy Was Refused," *Washington Post*, July 11, 2003, A1.

151. Dana Milbank, "Bush Remarks Confirm Shift in Justifying War; Standard of Proof for Weapons Drops," *Washington Post*, June 1, 2003, A18. In early July 2003, the White House acknowledged that Bush's charge against Hussein rested on faulty intelligence, a report that CIA and State Department intelligence officials had questioned for months. A succession of administration figures then stepped up to shoulder the blame for the speech error: Tenet, Rice, Hadley, and Michael Gerson, director of presidential speechwriting.

152. Richard Morin and Claudia Deane, "Support for Bush Declines as Casualties Mount in Iraq," *Washington Post*, July 12, 2003, A1.

153. Jim VandeHei and Helen Dewar, "Democrats Sharpen Attack on Bush over Iraq," *Washington Post*, July 16, 2003, A17.

154. Burke, "From Success to Failure?"

155. Ibid., 178.

156. Jon Western, *Selling Intervention and War: The Presidency, the Media, and the American Public* (Baltimore, MD: Johns Hopkins University Press, 2005), 180, 217.

157. Edward Luce and Daniel Dombey, "U.S. Foreign Policy: Waiting on a Sun King," *Financial Times*, March 30, 2010; James P. Pfiffner, "Organizing the Obama White House," in *Obama in Office*, ed. by James A. Thurber, *Obama in Office*, 75–85. For an early read, see John P. Burke, "The Obama National Security System and Process: At the Six Month Mark," White House Transition Project, whitehousetransitionproject.org/.

158. James P. Pfiffner, "Decision Making in the Obama White House," *Presidential Studies Quarterly* 41:2 (June 2011): 244.

159. John P. Burke. *Honest Broker? The National Security Advisor and Presidential Decision Making* (College Station: Texas A& M University Press, 2009).

160. Mark Landler, "Obama Plans to Name Close Aide on National Security as Chief of Staff," *New York Times*, January 17, 2013, www.nytimes.com/2013/01/17/us/politics/obama-plans-to-name-national-security-deputy-as-chief-of-staff.html.

161. Luce and Dombey, "U.S. Foreign Policy."

162. Joel Achenbach, "Analysis: Obama Makes Decisions Slowly, and with Head, Not Gut," *Washington Post*, November 25, 2009.

163. Mark Mazzetti, Helene Cooper, and Peter Baker, "Behind the Hunt for Bin Laden," *New York Times*, May 2, 2011, www.nytimes.com/2011/05/03/world/asia/03intel.html?_r=1&hp.

164. For a riveting account of the raid see Nicholas Schmidle, "Getting Bin Laden," *New Yorker*, August 8, 2011.

165. David Von Drehle, "Killing bin Laden: How the U.S. Finally Got Its Man," *Time*, May 4, 2011, www.time.com/time/nation/article/0,8599,2069455,00.html.

166. Schmidle, "Getting Bin Laden."

167. Joe Klein, "Obama 1, Osama 0," *Time*, May 20, 2011, 32–35.

168. "Robert Gates Praises President Obama's Leadership on Bin Laden Raid," *Huffpost Politics*, May 15, 2011, www.huffingtonpost.com/2011/05/15/robert-gates-obama-bin-laden-dead_n_862207.html.

169. Robert M. Gates, *Duty: Memories of Secretary At War* (New York: Knopf, 2014), 538–546.

170. Transcript of interview with David Rothkopf in *The Atlantic*. See Goldberg, "A Withering Critique of Obama's National Security Council."

171. Sheldon M. Stern, *The Cuban Missile Crisis in American Memory: Myths versus Reality* (Stanford, CA: Stanford University Press, 2012), 157.

172. Barbara Hinckley suggests that the conflict between presidents and Congress is largely symbolic, staged to convince the public that both institutions are alert and active and that policymaking is democratic. Barbara Hinckley, *Less Than Meets the Eye: Foreign Policymaking and the Myth of the Assertive Congress* (Chicago: University of Chicago Press, 1994), 175, 193. See also Linda L. Fowler, *Watchdogs on the Hill: The Decline of Congressional Oversight of U.S. Foreign Relations* (Princeton, NJ: Princeton University Press, 2015).

173. Paul E. Peterson, "The International System and Foreign Policy," in *The President, the Congress, and the Making of Foreign Policy*, ed. Paul E. Peterson (Norman: University of Oklahoma Press, 1994), 12–14.

174. Hamilton, "*Pacificus*, No. 1," June 29, 1793, press-pubs.uchicago.edu/founders/documents/a2_2_2-3s14.html.

175. Koh, *The National Security Constitution*, 207.

176. Stephen E. Ambrose, "The Presidency and Foreign Policy," *Foreign Affairs* (Winter 1991/1992): 136.

177. Hans Bennindijk, "Rethinking U.S. Security Strategy," *New York Times*, March 24, 2013, www.nytimes.com/2013/03/25/opinion/global/rethinking-us-security-strategy.html.

CHAPTER 11

The Trump Transition and First One Hundred Days

Jabin Botsford/The Washington Post via Getty Images

President Barack Obama shakes hands with President-Elect Donald Trump in the Oval Office of the White House in Washington, November 10, 2016.

Donald J. Trump's election on November 8, 2016, has been described as "one of the most stunning upsets in American political history."[1] Although Trump and his rival, Hillary Rodham Clinton, both went into election day with historically high "unfavorable" ratings,[2] conventional wisdom held that Clinton would win. That is what projection models and most veteran observers predicted. Even the Republican National Committee's own internal model showed Trump coming up short of the 270 electoral votes needed to win.[3] On the day of the election, Nate Silver's widely reported election forecast gave Clinton a 71 percent chance of winning the White House, and exit polls showed Clinton winning four crucial swing states that ended up going to Trump.[4] Based on the polls, Trump later confessed that he went to his wife on election day and said, "Baby, I tell you what. We're not going to win tonight."[5]

But win he did, breaking through the Democrats' vaunted "blue wall" of the upper Midwest to carve out a majority in the Electoral College. And with the win came the monumental task of transitioning to power. On election night, the president-elect promised he would stress national unity after the hugely divisive campaign: "To all Republicans and Democrats and independents across this nation I say it is time for us to come together as one united people. It's time. I pledge to every citizen of our land that I will be president for all of Americans, and this is so important to me."[6]

Even under the best of circumstances, the presidential transition is a formidable challenge. Since 1936, when Inauguration Day moved from March to January, presidents have had just three months to pivot from full-time campaigning to full-time governing. As Stephen Hess once put it, this pivot involves a focus on the "three P's": personnel, process, and policy.[7]

The Transition

One of the first orders of business for a newly elected president is to select *personnel.* This step involves picking not only his most trusted advisers, including his White House staff, but also nominees to fill the top cabinet positions and a wide range of departmental slots. In addition to the fifteen cabinet secretaries and seven others often denoted as "Cabinet-level" (such as the budget director), there are more than five hundred other executive-branch positions that also require Senate confirmation. In all, some nine thousand jobs in the executive branch are listed and described in the so-called Plum Book, which the Government Printing Office publishes every four years to advertise jobs in the new administration.[8] Before filling these myriad positions, potential candidates must be systematically recruited and thoroughly vetted.

Selecting personnel gets a great deal of media attention, but *process* is just as important. Process refers to decisions about how the incoming president will organize his White House. Does he want a highly centralized staff structure with a chief of staff who acts as a gatekeeper or a more decentralized staff? Are there existing White House units he wants to abolish or new entities he wants to create? How will his staff relate to the cabinet? Such decisions may not get much publicity, but they can profoundly influence the effectiveness of the decision-making process in the new administration.[9]

Finally, the president-elect and his team must begin to craft a *policy* agenda for the new administration. Given the complexity of modern-day government and the magnitude of the issues it confronts, this task is very complicated. Moreover, establishing a policy agenda is only half of the puzzle. The transition team must also be thinking about how to implement it, which brings the discussion back to process. How will Congress, interest groups, and the public react to the policy proposals? In what order should they be introduced? How should they be promoted?

To deal with all of these issues, a transition team must be poised and ready to spring into action as soon as the election is over. Both Trump and Clinton put a transition team into place months before election day. Trump initially tapped New Jersey governor Chris Christie to lead this effort, but three days after the election Trump booted Christie and replaced him with Vice President-elect Mike Pence. Clay Johnson, who ran the White House Office of Presidential Personnel under President George W. Bush and advised the Trump transition team, said that the shift from Christie to Pence wiped out months of work and meant that the operation to select personnel started over from scratch after the election: "They started out at ground zero, without a playbook and no recommendations."[10]

Since passage of the Presidential Transition Act of 1963, the U.S. General Services Administration (GSA) has offered significant support to both the incoming and outgoing administrations. Upon request, it provides services and facilities to the president-elect and, prior to the election, to other eligible candidates.[11] The Trump transition team began taking advantage of that space in Washington, D.C., almost immediately after the election, but Trump opted to use his own properties—Trump Tower in Manhattan, which housed both his personal residence and the offices of the Trump Organization, Trump National Golf Club in Bedminster, New Jersey, and his Mar-a-Lago estate and golf club in Palm Beach, Florida—for most of the high-profile work of the transition. The locations proved convenient for Trump but led some critics to allege that he chose them to advertise his properties.[12] Providing security at these locations also proved to be expensive. New York City alone had to foot a bill of $25.7 million to protect Trump Tower between election day and the inauguration, a cost that federal taxpayers ultimately covered when Congress agreed to reimburse New York and other localities that protected Trump during the transition.[13]

In terms of personnel, Trump moved relatively quickly to identify his key advisers and Cabinet nominees. Just five days after the election, he named Republican National Committee chairman Reince Priebus as White House chief of staff and former Breitbart News executive Steve Bannon as White House chief strategist. He then announced his first Cabinet pick—Sen. Jeff Sessions (R-Ala.) as attorney general—just one week after election day. In contrast, Bill Clinton, who ran a notoriously bumpy transition in 1992, did not name his White House chief of staff until mid-December and did not announce his first Cabinet pick until over a month after the election.

However, Trump's relative speed in announcing senior nominees masked the fact that his transition team had done little and in some cases no advance vetting of those he selected.[14] In contrast, Barack Obama's 2008 transition team had begun vetting potential nominees before the election even took place, as did Hillary Clinton's transition team in 2016.[15] The Trump transition team's failure to do this meant that the time-consuming process of gathering documents for background checks and financial disclosure requirements delayed the confirmation process for some nominees, such as Andrew Puzder whom Trump nominated to be secretary of labor.[16] Puzder eventually withdrew from consideration after revelations about his business practices and personal life eroded support for his confirmation even among Republicans. Two days before Puzder withdrew, Michael Flynn resigned as Trump's national security advisor after less than a month on the job amid controversy over his contacts with the Russian government. Proper vetting earlier on might have avoided those embarrassments.[17]

The Trump transition team largely ignored another important aspect of personnel: sub-Cabinet appointments. In all, some 556 positions that the new president is expected to fill require Senate confirmation. By the end of his first hundred days in office, all fifteen of Trump's nominees to fill the Cabinet had been confirmed by the Senate (the last, Alex Acosta to be secretary of labor, on the ninety-ninth day), as had six of the seven other Cabinet-level appointments that require Senate confirmation (the last, the U.S. trade representative, was sworn in on May 15). But the president had not yet even nominated 465 of the 556 other executive-branch posts requiring Senate confirmation.[18] Hundreds of other key jobs also remained unfilled, stymieing the work of departments and agencies. Although Trump publicly claimed that he purposely left many of the posts unfilled because "they're unnecessary to have," evidence suggested that the vacancies had more to do with a chaotic selection process that, when Trump became president, appeared to be excessively micromanaged by warring factions within the White House.[19]

Those warring factions reflected Trump's preferred management style. In business, Trump liked to establish competing power centers with conflicting points of view, and he brought that style to the White House. Thus, during the transition, Trump embraced a "team of rivals" approach to staffing his inner circle of advisors, with Chief of Staff Priebus and Chief Strategist Bannon representing the competing camps. He appointed Kellyanne Conway, his third and final campaign manager, as another counselor to the president. But he also surrounded himself with family, naming his son-in-law Jared Kushner, a former real estate developer and newspaper owner with no experience in government, as senior advisor, and his daughter Ivanka (Kushner's wife), a former fashion model and Trump Organization executive, as assistant to the president. Rather than giving his chief of staff seniority over the other advisors, Trump initially gave equal access and authority to Priebus and Bannon, although many believed that Kushner, with his family connection, was—as

Kushner himself reportedly claimed—"first among equals."[20] Certainly he was in an advantageous position to sway the president.

Some presidents have used a "team of rivals" approach to great effect. Franklin Roosevelt, for example, used competition among his staff to extract the best possible range of policy options.[21] But for a president like Trump, with no government experience and an apparent lack of interest in the specifics of policy, the approach proved far less productive—at least in the early months of his administration. From his first day in office, the media focused on the power struggle among his senior advisors,[22] with political observers noting that Trump thrived on chaos.[23] Within a month, however, the chaos came to be described as a problem.[24] Although apparently intentional on Trump's part, the process he embraced arguably made enacting policy more difficult and led to a variety of self-inflicted wounds.

Policy remained the wild card during the Trump transition. Unlike Hillary Clinton, a policy wonk who surrounded herself with policy advisors and working groups, Trump's presidential campaign had avoided developing substantive white papers; his specific policy stances on many issues were still a mystery.[25] Observers looked at his appointments for clues, and while his attorney general and homeland security secretary backed away from enforcement of civil rights measures and ramped up enforcement of immigration law, as promised in the campaign, the "team of rivals" approach added little clarity in most areas. Even into the early weeks of his administration, Trump governed like he campaigned, with little interest in the specifics of his legislative proposals and a willingness to reverse course on his broad-brush pronouncements. He deemed NATO a "bulwark of international peace" after months of calling it "obsolete," authorized U.S. military intervention in Syria after years of opposing it, declared that China was not a currency manipulator after repeatedly railing against China for currency manipulation, expressed a willingness to renegotiate NAFTA after promising to withdraw from it on "Day One," and abruptly fired FBI director James Comey for (as the White House initially claimed) mishandling the investigation into Hillary Clinton's e-mail server after praising him for the way he handled the investigation during the campaign.[26] As Trump told reporters in April 2017, "I like to think of myself as a very flexible person. I don't have to have one specific way," adding that, particularly with regard to foreign policy, "I don't like to say where I'm going and what I'm doing."[27]

In short, in the early months of his administration, the Trump transition fell short on personnel-related issues, embraced an advising process that did not seem to help the president get the information he needed, and failed to articulate clear policy directions on many issues. Both of his predecessors came to office under much more difficult conditions: Bush after a contested election that was not decided until December, and Obama in the midst of the worst economic crisis since the Great Depression and while fighting two wars abroad. Nonetheless, the nonpartisan White House Transition Project concluded that the Trump vetting process lagged behind previous administrations, contributing to the slowest performance in overall nominations and confirmations of any president in the last fifty years.[28] The lack of support in the agencies, in turn, made it harder for the new administration to draw upon the wider executive branch for substantive advice or specific policy proposals.

The Inauguration

Almost none of the ceremony associated with modern-day inaugurations is formally required, but it has become an important ritual that helps to unite the nation behind its new leader. Planning this event is yet another challenge for any president-elect. The only constitutional requirement for the new president is to take the oath of office. Virtually everything else—taking the oath outdoors in front of a crowd, the use of a Bible during the swearing-in, giving an inaugural address, parades, balls—has emerged by way of tradition.

Modern-day inaugurations are elaborate affairs that require an enormous amount of planning. They are also very expensive. Private donations fund the inaugural balls, luncheons, and concerts. Trump raised a record $90 million to fund such events, but that is only part of the total cost.[29] Security alone can cost over $100 million. Preliminary estimates put the cost of the Trump inauguration at about $200 million—the most expensive in history, even though the Presidential Inaugural Committee cut back on the number of inaugural balls, trimmed the length of the inaugural parade, and provided fewer concerts (in the name of President Trump "get[ting] right to work").[30] Many accounts noted that those planning the inauguration had difficulty securing major performers to participate in inaugural events amid polls showing record-low support for the president-elect, but Trump boasted that "record numbers" would attend his inauguration.[31] When various metrics, including aerial photographs, indicated that the number of people attending Trump's inauguration fell far short of the estimated 1.8 million who attended Barack Obama's first inaugural, the president and his spokespeople pushed back. In his very first briefing, White House press secretary Sean Spicer accused the press of deliberately false reporting about the size of the crowd, saying, "This was the largest audience to ever witness an inauguration, period, both in person and around the globe." Spicer's claim was widely decried. When pushed by NBC reporter Chuck Todd to explain how the press secretary could make such a statement, Kellyanne Conway compounded the story by claiming that Spicer was merely offering "alternative facts."[32]

The president's continuing insistence that the "fake news" media lied about crowd size raised eyebrows, as did some of what he said in his inaugural address. Rather than using the speech as an opportunity for conciliation and unity—the themes he had highlighted on the night of his election—Trump continued to dwell on campaign tropes that stressed "us" versus "them." He excoriated the political establishment ("The establishment protected itself, but not the citizens of our country. Their victories have not been your victories"), painted a bleak picture of an America beset by the "carnage" of "the crime and the gangs and the drugs," promised that "From this day forward, it's going to be *only* America first," and reinforced fears of immigrants and terrorists ("We must protect our borders from the ravages of other countries. . . . We will bring back our borders . . . and reform the world against radical Islamic terrorism"). James Fallows, a former presidential speechwriter and journalist, contrasted Trump's tone with that of the fellow populist Trump often praised, Andrew Jackson. Jackson said in his first inaugural address in 1829:

> A diffidence, perhaps too just, in my own qualifications will teach me to look with reverence to the examples of public virtue left by my illustrious predecessors, and . . . induces me to hope for instruction and aid from the coordinate branches of the Government, and for the indulgence and support of my fellow-citizens generally.[33]

President Trump made no such plea for cooperation across the branches or for broad public support. Indeed, he went on to criticize the opinion of the "so-called judge" that struck down his immigration order, accused former President Obama of being a "bad (or sick) guy" and indeed a criminal (for supposedly wiretapping Trump Tower), derided congressional leaders (of both parties), and blamed the "archaic" rules of Congress (for better or worse, part of our system of checks and balances) for early setbacks on Capitol Hill.[34]

The First Hundred Days

In 1933, Franklin Roosevelt set a standard during his first hundred days in office that is hard to beat. When he was sworn in during the midst of the Great Depression on March 4, 1933, some wondered if American democracy would survive. The stock market had collapsed, banks had failed, unemployment had reached 25 percent, and the fear of public unrest was such that machine guns guarded government buildings.[35] Nonetheless, FDR embraced optimism, called for action, and rallied the spirit of a downtrodden people. Asserting that "the only thing we have to fear is fear itself," he called Congress into a special emergency session and promised to "recommend the measures that a stricken nation in the midst of a stricken world may require." That special session lasted three months, and people referred to it as the "Hundred Days."

The 1932 elections gave Roosevelt a powerful edge by sweeping into power an overwhelming majority of fellow Democrats in both the Senate (70 Democrats, 23 Republicans, and 2 others) and the House of Representatives (322 Democrats, 103 Republicans, and 10 others). Those hundred days produced 76 pieces of legislation, including 15 major bills that greatly expanded the size of the federal government through the creation of, among other things, the Federal Deposit Insurance Corporation to protect bank accounts, the Public Works Administration to provide jobs, and the National Industrial Recovery Act to regulate industry and stimulate the economy. Roosevelt touted the success of "the hundred days" in one of his Fireside Chats—thereby establishing a yardstick of success that has been used to measure the accomplishments of all subsequent presidents.[36]

As his own hundred days wound down, President Trump declared such a yardstick to be a "ridiculous standard."[37] Certainly it is an arbitrary one. Like any snapshot, it captures a particular period in time—one which, by definition, does not reflect a president's later successes or failures. The vast majority of presidents since FDR have not secured passage of landmark legislation during their first hundred days, even if the period is marked by a flurry of other legislative action.[38]

Still, an early assessment—whether at Day 87 or 106—is nonetheless appropriate. A president's patterns of decision making and his policy templates are set early—if not set in stone—and the first impressions of "Washingtonians," as well as the wider public, are hard to shake. Indeed, the focus on the first hundred days reflects a maxim that most presidential observers agree upon: it is important for new administrations to "hit the ground running." As political scientist James P. Pfiffner explains, presidents "want to take advantage of the 'mandate' from the voters and create a 'honeymoon' with Congress." Early victories in implementing their policy goals may provide momentum for additional victories. "This desire to move fast is driven by the awareness that power is fleeting."[39]

Donald Trump, as a candidate, himself set a specific marker for early accomplishment. In a signed "contract with the American voter" released in October 2016, Trump said that "on November 8, Americans will be voting for this 100-day plan" comprising administrative, legislative, and even constitutional change. Some of the actions, the "contract" said, would be pursued "on the first day of my term of office."[40] Once in office, Trump continued to tout his achievements in the context of a short temporal window. At a campaign-style rally in Nashville in mid-March 2017, he claimed that "we have done far more, I think maybe more than anybody's done in this office in 50 days. That I can tell you." A month later, in Wisconsin, he told a crowd that "no administration has accomplished more in the first 90 days." He offered a similar tribute relative to the standard landmark: "I truly believe that the first 100 days of my administration has been just about the most successful in our country's history."[41]

In light of these promises and claims it is worth reviewing the actions and achievements of the new administration in the various areas emphasized by earlier chapters of this book—tracking the legislative, administrative, and public presidencies.

Legislation

As noted by Pfiffner, presidents often seek to move quickly in the legislative sphere, hoping to take advantage of a honeymoon period in which members of Congress are deferential to the presumed mandate achieved by the president in the election just past. The Trump "contract" listed ten bills (as well as an additional constitutional amendment) to be introduced in the first hundred days of his administration. These included measures to repeal and replace the Affordable Care Act, raise tariffs, crack down on illegal immigration, lower taxes, and "clean up corruption."

Trump did have one clear legislative victory early on: the confirmation of Supreme Court justice Neil Gorsuch (see chapter 7). This fulfilled a campaign pledge that had been key to attracting social and religious conservatives to his electoral coalition. Of the ten promised contract bills, though, only the health care repeal-and-replace measure had even been introduced within a hundred days. It passed the House in early May (see chapter 5). The White House hastily unveiled a brief outline of tax reduction proposals on April 26 (Day 97), but without detailed legislative language. In the end, of the twenty-eight bills signed by Trump into law during this period, all originated in Congress rather than from the new administration. Nearly half of them were small-scale (though sometimes substantively important) resolutions rolling back Obama-era departmental regulations. The full presidential budget for fiscal year 2018 was not released until May 23. The plan proposed slashing domestic discretionary spending and other programs, prompting bipartisan criticism in Congress.

This slow start likely flowed in part from the slow pace of appointments noted earlier. Without a full slate of sub-Cabinet officials in place across the executive branch, the president was unable to take advantage of departmental expertise in drafting legislative proposals—expertise the government outsiders selected for top White House posts did not themselves possess.

Further, the Trump presidency came with neither a clear mandate nor much of a "honeymoon." That is not necessarily rare: political scientists John Sides and Lynn Vavreck caution against "assuming that [an election] constitutes a mandate for the winner's policy agenda," and a systematic study of congressional voting identifies only three elections over fifty years—1964, 1980, and 1994—with a clear causal effect on legislative behavior.[42] Despite the White House's spin ("Landslide. Blowout. Historic," Kellyanne Conway tweeted[43]), Trump's electoral victory did not add 2016 to that list. His winning margin in the electoral college, where he received 57 percent of the vote, ranked forty-sixth of fifty-eight U.S. presidential elections, while his popular vote share was forty-seventh of the forty-nine winning candidates since 1824. This gave Trump minimal leverage over members of Congress, who in most cases were more popular with their constituents than the president was. Lingering questions about links between the Trump campaign and the Russian government led to questions about the administration's credibility and, perhaps as crucially, to House and Senate investigations that further distracted congressional attention from substantive legislation. In short, Trump did little to heal the wounds of the campaign and he delivered a string of self-inflicted wounds that undermined his chances for legislative success.

Given the stark polarization between the parties and the divisions within the majority Republicans, building legislative majorities would have been difficult even for a president with extensive Washington experience, deep policy expertise, and longstanding relationships within his party. Trump, with none of that, allowed his frustrations to boil over in a string of tweets attacking the right-wing Freedom Caucus ("we must fight them, and Dems, in 2018!"), the congressional opposition ("Democrats jeopardizing the safety of our troops to bail out their donors"), and Senate rules allowing legislation to be delayed indefinitely unless sixty senators agreed to end a filibuster ("change the rules now to 51%").[44]

Administration

From the first week of his administration, President Trump embraced a unilateral exercise of executive power through the use of executive orders. After signing an executive order six days after taking office that directed the Department of Homeland Security to begin immediate construction of a 1,900-mile wall along the border with Mexico and to assign an additional 5,000 border protection agents to the area, Trump declared, "We do not need new laws."[45] But despite the power of some executive orders to achieve significant results, laws are, in fact, needed to accomplish many goals, such as appropriating funds to build a wall—which a Department of Homeland Security internal report said could cost $21.6 billion—or to hire additional border patrol forces.[46] Executive orders must also be able to survive legal challenges, as Trump discovered when courts struck down his early order to ban travel from a series of predominantly Muslim countries and his plan to punish "sanctuary cities" for not enforcing federal immigration laws.

By the end of his first hundred days, Trump had issued over thirty executive orders (plus numerous presidential memoranda), often utilizing elaborate public signing ceremonies. That amounted to a faster pace than any new president since 1945, when Harry Truman assumed the presidency after FDR's death and issued fifty-seven such orders. By comparison, in their first hundred days in office, Barack Obama issued nineteen executive orders; George W. Bush, eleven; and Bill Clinton, thirteen.

Presidents frequently use executive orders (EOs) to implement provisions of new laws. Since more laws are passed during periods when one party controls both the presidency and Congress, the number of EOs generally rises then as well. The Trump EOs, however, substituted for legislation rather than supplementing it—an approach far more common during periods of divided government, such as Obama's last six years in office, as opposed to periods of unified government, such as the one that prevailed in 2017. President Trump linked his executive actions to at least eight of the ten policy areas in which he had pledged to send bills to Congress. These orders served as placeholders on complicated questions of infrastructure and energy, community safety, national security, immigration, ethics, tariffs, education, and health care. Some of the directives had an immediate impact, such as urging far more aggressive deportations of individuals illegally resident in the United States; others had important but symbolic resonance, as in the formal removal of the U.S. from the Trans-Pacific Partnership trade pact (which, however, had not yet come into existence.)

Beyond Congress and the courts, Trump also needed executive branch cooperation to implement his orders, since many of them directed departments to review laws and regulations, with an eye toward proposing revisions to existing policy or agency organization. For example, his February 9 EO declared that "it shall be the policy of the executive branch to reduce crime in America" and demanded that the attorney general report at least once a year on ways to improve government efforts in that regard. An April 25 order replaced the Rural Council created in 2011 with a twenty-plus person task force with a 180-day deadline for recommendations aimed at "promoting agriculture and rural prosperity in America." Other orders setting similar deadlines—for identifying tax burdens, reviewing environmental rules, reorganizing government departments, setting "regulatory budgets," and so on—would come due throughout Trump's first year in office. Here too, though, the slow pace of sub-Cabinet appointments meant that fewer resources were available to conduct and monitor the many studies put in motion.

In short, Trump's first burst of executive orders, like those across presidential history, varied wildly in their significance. Thus, assessing the substantive content of Trump's executive orders is far more important a measure of impact than a simple count of how many he signed. Indeed, some suspected that Trump—who touted the sheer number of EOs as signifying success—purposely inflated the overall tally by using executive orders for departmental directions that could easily have been achieved through less formal communication with Cabinet heads. *Politico*'s Michael Grunwald, for instance, argued that the actions were "more about messaging than governing, proclaiming his priorities without really advancing his priorities."[47]

Even so, the Trump EOs succeeded in setting a clear tone for the new direction he wanted government to take: one that provided regulatory relief and prioritized economic development, that demanded more aggressive enforcement of some laws (notably, immigration and health care) and less attention to others (financial regulation or environmental protection, for example). Some of the processes set in motion by the Trump EOs were potentially important, notably in setting limits on how departments could promulgate new regulations. As of the hundred-day mark their impact remained far from certain. Below the radar, though, departments began to change how the Obama administration had interpreted the law—in areas ranging from minimum mandatory sentencing to student loan administration to Medicaid waivers—in ways more aligned with the new president's preferences (even where, as in the case of mandatory sentencing, these might be at odds with an emerging bipartisan consensus[48]).

These changes in statutory interpretation did not require new congressional action, nor did decisions removing the prior administration's tight rein on military tactics in Afghanistan and in the battle against IS and other terrorist groups. President Trump told *Time* magazine that "the lieutenants, the captains, their majors, their colonels, they're professionals. . . . They know every inch of the territory, right. I say why am I telling them? So I authorized the generals to do the fighting."[49] Trump also relied on executive authority to expand U.S. involvement in the Syrian civil war with missile attacks on a government airbase—an action that arguably did require congressional approval but that nonetheless faced little pushback from legislators (see chapter 10).

Communication

The public presidency relies on the president's standing as what Andrew Jackson called "the tribune of the people"—the only elected official chosen by the entire nation. President Trump fiercely resented critics who claimed his 2016 electoral victory was tainted by having received a minority of the national popular vote. Indeed, he claimed—falsely—"I won the popular vote if you deduct the millions of people who voted illegally."[50] Well into the spring of 2017 he even distributed maps of the Electoral College results to visitors to the Oval Office.[51]

Trump's efforts to claim the mantle of a wide public mandate, though, were made more difficult by the disjunction between his gracious call for national unity on election night and his subsequent policy proposals and communication strategy. The latter was especially divisive, driven by nearly one thousand tweets sent by Trump between the November elections and early May. Even before his inaugural, Trump had used social media to lash out at the intelligence community, Democrats (such as Senate "head clown Chuck Schumer"), civil rights icon John Lewis, an array of media outlets, and even the cast of the musical *Hamilton*.[52] The president's early-morning forays on Twitter, seemingly dictated by topics covered the night before on cable news outlets, often drove the administration's daily agenda.[53] As he had done with claims about voting fraud, the president repeatedly issued a litany of "false or misleading" statements—some 492 of them in the first hundred days of the administration, as tracked by media fact checkers.[54] Such scrutiny, in turn, prompted President Trump to decry what he termed "fake news" and to accuse the news media of being "the enemy of the American people."[55]

While this combative approach appealed greatly to Trump's most devoted supporters, it did nothing to expand his coalition past the 46 percent of the public who had originally voted for him. Nor did persistent complaints about the administration's ethics and transparency, driven partly by the president's decision not to divest from his holdings in the Trump Organization or release past tax returns. (He did give up his role in the daily operations of his business.) Questions regarding how economic motivations might drive White House behavior arose frequently, as when the Chinese government granted lucrative copyright protections to both the Trump Organization and Ivanka Trump's separate fashion line, the latter on the same day Ms. Trump dined with the Chinese premier. Charges of Russian meddling in the 2016 election and of improper Russian connections to Trump campaign personnel also dogged the new administration. President Trump exacerbated the appearance of impropriety when he abruptly fired the chief investigator of those charges, FBI director James Comey. "When I decided to just do it, I said to myself, I said 'you know, this Russia thing with Trump and Russia is a made-up story,'" Trump told an interviewer.[56] But only 29 percent of the public approved of Comey's removal. His firing helped prompt the appointment of former FBI director Robert Mueller as a special counsel with a broad charge to investigate Russia's involvement in the 2016 election as well as other matters that might arise, such as obstruction of justice.[57]

Partly as a result of Trump's divisive communications strategy, his approval ratings averaged only 41 percent during his first three months in office, the lowest of any president tracked by Gallup since regular polling began in the 1950s.[58] Bill Clinton, next lowest, had averaged 55 percent public approval at the start of 1993. It took Clinton more than 570 days to reach majority *dis*approval; it took Trump just 8. Of course, as Clinton himself showed, unpopular presidents can become popular again; Clinton left office in 2001 with the approval of two-thirds of the public. At least early on, though, the Trump administration did not enjoy the "public prestige" that can serve as a presidential resource in persuading others in Washington to follow his lead.[59]

President Trump: A Natural Experiment

The outcome of the 2016 election may be seen as the launch of what social scientists call a "natural experiment," one that asks: How will the 228-year-old Madisonian system of checks and balances respond when one of its three branches is suddenly thrown out of equilibrium? Donald J. Trump is the vehicle for that experiment, thrusting someone with no prior experience in government or public service into the position that is the lynchpin of modern government in the United States. He viewed the outcome of the election as a directive to disrupt a system founded on striking balances—between contending constituencies, between branches, between self-interest and the national interest. Disruption is a longstanding feature of Trump's personal style, developed over many years in business and now imported to the White House.

Trump's selection is only the most recent effort by voters fed up with Washington to secure change. Over a period of four decades, beginning with the election of 1976, American voters have repeatedly asked "outsiders" to change Washington. Governors Jimmy Carter, Ronald Reagan, Bill Clinton, and George W. Bush traveled from state capitals to the national capital based on promises to tell the truth, tame big government, restore hope, and restore personal integrity to the office of president. Barack Obama barely had time to learn the ways of Washington as a senator—just two years—before he launched his presidential campaign pursuing "change you can believe in."

As a result, with the exception of George H. W. Bush, the electorate has chosen a series of presidents with little or no experience in the national government. The rise of the Tea Party likewise reflected the disillusionment with government held by segments of the electorate. That movement served as a precursor to the broader populist tide that fueled the candidacies of Trump on the right and Bernie Sanders on the left in 2016, when those seeking change finally elected the ultimate outsider—a person with no prior government experience at any level to undertake the extensive repairs they demanded for a broken system. Trump tapped widespread economic despair and public distrust by denouncing everyone in Washington as the foolish catalysts of all the nation's problems and then by claiming that only he knew how to fix them.

Once in office, President Trump embraced disruption, chaos, and norm-breaking—precisely what his core base wanted and expected. With the exception of his national security team, many of Trump's chosen appointees were shrill critics of the bureaucracies they were chosen to lead. This was most striking in the Environmental Protection Agency, the Department of Education, and the Department of Health and Human Services where Trump charged appointees with dismantling programs built by past administrations of both parties. Trump also targeted the Department of State for extensive restructuring, suggesting the downgrading of diplomacy in favor of military might.

But instead of prompting the policy changes that Trump had promised, his chaotic and unpredictable style seemed to thwart them. The White House did a poor job coordinating action on several of the president's high-profile executive orders and often proved to be unable to provide clear explanations of the administration's policy positions or even how it reached policy decisions. Contradictory White House messages, often in the same week and sometimes on the same day, became the norm. This seemed to reflect the president's own capriciousness, which he often displayed in early morning tweets that reversed or challenged earlier administration positions.

Indeed, throughout the first hundred days, the White House seemed to operate largely at the president's whim. From the outset he ignored the modern norm of establishing a hierarchical White House system, usually centered on a powerful chief of staff. Nor did the president adhere to other norms that govern established ways of doing business. The president openly challenged other branches of government when they failed to do what he wanted; he mocked the judiciary, called for a loosening of our system of checks and balances to advance his preferred policy outcomes, and reportedly sought a pledge of loyalty from the FBI director he later fired even though presidents and legislators had worked for decades to depoliticize law enforcement. All of this renewed lingering concerns about Trump's commitment to the rule of law.

Trump was not the first president to operate ineffectively within the White House, using his system of advisers in ways that magnified rather than compensated for his personal weaknesses. Bill Clinton, for example, spent much of his first year in office conducting protracted debates over how to address various policy problems. Not until he brought in Leon Panetta as chief of staff did Clinton recognize the importance of having structured discussions that examined options systematically, reaching conclusions in a timely manner, and communicating clear guidelines to executives and legislators alike. With multiple competing centers of advice, Trump's clashing system of White House advisers made it all the more difficult to produce carefully developed results. And without strong staff discipline to structure his activities and utterances, the president followed his impulses. As head of a family business Trump had little experience with others challenging his preferences or structuring his activities, let alone with leading a complex structure like the executive branch. As his seventy-first birthday approached in June 2017, it was unclear whether he could learn new ways of doing things.

None of this should have been surprising. Trump's business career had been well documented, and his success often rested on tactics ill-suited to the constraints of government. That his unorthodox campaign culminated in his unexpected triumph in the 2016 campaign seemed to justify the continued use of such tactics in office. But, in government, adhering to accepted processes can be just as important as achieving a goal. Despite his vaunted ability to make deals, President Trump seemed highly frustrated when the rules of the game put him at a disadvantage. He had difficulty accepting that a checks-and-balances system distributes competitive advantages across the government and even outside government, with the media, for example, having a special role.

Throughout the twentieth and into the twenty-first century, America's system of government has depended heavily on a steady guiding hand provided by the president. Presidents both initiate action and provide cues to others about how to respond, whether favorably or unfavorably. What the nation witnessed in the early months of the Trump administration is how the system works when a president acts unpredictably and outside the range of normal practice. Will other institutions step up to fill the gap? Will Trump learn on the job what is needed to be effective? If he does not change, will Trump be able to trigger a change in rules and norms about how Washington goes about its business? These and other questions lie at the heart of the story that lies ahead for the administration of Donald J. Trump.

Notes

1. Eric Bradner, "5 surprising lessons from Trump's astonishing win," *CNN.com*, November 9, 2016, http://www.cnn.com/2016/11/09/politics/donald-trump-wins-biggest-surprises/.

2. Lydia Saad, "Trump and Clinton Finish with Historically Poor Images," *Gallup*, November 8, 2016, http://www.gallup.com/poll/197231/trump-clinton-finish-historically-poor-images.aspx.

3. Kenneth P. Vogel, "RNC Model Showed Trump Losing," *Politico*, November 9, 2016, http://www.politico.com/story/2016/11/rnc-model-showed-trump-losing-231074.

4. "Who Will Win the Presidency?" *FiveThirtyEight*, November 8, 2016, https://projects.fivethirtyeight.com/2016-election-forecast/; Caitlin Johnstone, "Exit Polls Predicted Hillary Clinton to Win Four of Donald Trump's Key Victories," *Inquisitr*, November 16, 2016, http://www.inquisitr.com/3719288/exit-polls-indicate-hillary-clinton-might-have-won/.

5. Jennifer Jacobs and Billy House, "Trump Says He Expected to Lose Election Because of Poll Results," *Bloomberg*, December 13, 2016, https://www.bloomberg.com/politics/articles/2016-12-14/trump-says-he-expected-to-lose-election-because-of-poll-results.

6. ABC News, "Full Text of Donald Trump's Election Night Remarks," http://abcnews.go.com/Politics/full-text-donald-trumps-2016-election-night-victory/story?id=43388317.

7. Stephen Hess, "A Checklist for New Presidents," *eJournal USA* 14, no. 1 (January 2009): 3.

8. Lisa Rein, "The Plum Book Is Here for Those Angling for Jobs in Trump's Washington," *Washington Post*, December 4, 2016, https://www.washingtonpost.com/news/powerpost/wp/2016/12/04/the-plum-book-is-here-for-those-angling-for-jobs-in-trumps-washington/.

9. Hess, "A Checklist for New Presidents," 5; John P. Burke, *Presidential Transitions: From Politics to Practice* (Boulder, CO: Lynne Rienner, 2000), 12.

10. Nancy Cook, Josh Dawsey, and Andrew Restuccia, "Why the Trump Administration Has So Many Vacancies," *Politico*, April 11, 2017, http://www.politico.com/story/2017/04/donald-trump-white-house-staff-vacancies-237081.

11. For more information, see "GSA's Role in Presidential Transitions," *Presidential Transition Directory*, https://presidentialtransition.usa.gov/gsas-role-in-presidential-transition/.

12. Drew Harwell and Lisa Rein, "Who's Helping Pay for President-elect Trump's Transition Effort? You Are," *Washington Post*, November 23, 2016, www.washingtonpost.com/news/powerpost/wp/2016/11/23/elizabeth-warren-wants-to-know-how-donald-trump-is-using-taxpayer-funds-for-his-transition/.

13. Laura Figueroa, "Trump Tower Security Costs to Be Paid by Feds in Budget Deal," *Newsday*, May 1, 2017, http://www.newsday.com/news/new-york/budget-deal-nyc-to-get-reimbursed-for-donald-trump-security-1.13548402.

14. Russell Berman, "A President without an Administration," *The Atlantic*, January 3, 2017, www.theatlantic.com/politics/archive/2017/01/trump-transition-cabinet-behind-schedule/511928/.

15. Nancy Cook and Andrew Restuccia, "Clinton Transition Team Taps Lawyers to Help Vet Nominees," *Politico*, October 27, 2016, http://www.politico.com/story/2016/10/hillary-clinton-transition-team-lawyers-vetting-230422.

16. Jonnelle Marte, "Labor Nominee Puzder's Confirmation Hearing Delayed a Fourth Time," *Washington Post*, January 31, 2017, https://www.washingtonpost.com/news/get-there/wp/2017/01/31/labor-nominee-puzders-confirmation-hearing-delayed-a-fourth-time/.

17. Frank Bruni, "Extreme Vetting? Not for Flynn, Puzder," *Seattle Times*, February 15, 2017, http://www.seattletimes.com/opinion/extreme-vetting-not-for-flynn/.

18. Rebecca Harrington, "Trump's First 110 Days: Here's How They Compare with Obama's, Bush's, and Clinton's," *Business Insider*, April 29, 2017, http://www.businessinsider.com/trump-first-100-days-how-compare-obama-bush-clinton-2017-4/#more-laws-fewer-words-1.

19. Nancy Cook and Andrew Restuccia, "Clinton Transition Team Taps Lawyers to Help Vet Nominees," *Politico*, October 27, 2016, http://www.politico.com/story/2016/10/hillary-clinton-transition-team-lawyers-vetting-230422.

20. Sarah Ellison, "The Inside Story of the Kushner-Bannon Civil War," *Vanity Fair*, May 2017, http://www.vanityfair.com/news/2017/04/jared-kushner-steve-bannon-white-house-civil-war.

21. See, e.g., Matthew J. Dickinson, *Bitter Harvest: FDR, Presidential Power, and the Growth of the Presidential Branch* (New York: Cambridge University Press, 1996).

22. Sara Murray, "The Power Struggle among Trump's Inner Circle," CNN.com, January 20, 2017, http://www.cnn.com/2017/01/19/politics/trump-priebus-bannon-conway-kushner/.

23. Chris Cillizza, "Donald Trump's White House Is in Chaos. And He Loves It," *Washington Post*, January 31, 2017, https://www.washingtonpost.com/news/the-fix/wp/2017/01/31/donald-trumps-white-house-is-in-chaos-and-he-loves-every-minute-of-it/.

24. Ashley Parker and Philip Rucker, "In Trump White House, Tumult Is Becoming the Norm," *Chicago Tribune*, May 8, 2017, http://www.chicagotribune.com/news/nationworld/politics/ct-trump-white-house-chaos-20170213-story.html; Ellison, "Inside the Kushner-Bannon Civil War."

25. Andrew Restuccia, Sarah Wheaton, and Nancy Cook, "Clinton's Transition Team Hits the Gas Pedal," *Politico*, October 21, 2106, http://www.politico.com/story/2016/10/hillary-clinton-transition-team-hiring-staff-230157.

26. Many observers suspected—and Trump himself seemed to confirm—that the real reason the president fired Comey was the FBI's aggressive investigation into the Trump campaign's possible connections with the Russian government. Zeke J. Miller, "The White House Keeps Changing Its Story about Why James Comey Was Fired," *Time*, May 11, 2017, http://time.com/4776388/james-comey-fired-trump-interview/. See also Gregory Krieg, "Trump Once Cheered Comey for the Same Reason He Just Fired Him," *CNN.com*, May 9, 2017, http://www.cnn.com/2017/05/09/politics/trump-democrats-change-position-on-comey/; David A. Graham, "All the President's Flip-Flops," *The Atlantic*, April 13, 2017, https://www.theatlantic.com/politics/archive/2017/04/the-flip-flop-president/522840/.

27. "Remarks by President Trump and His Majesty King Abdullah II of Jordan in Joint Press Conference," April 5, 2017, https://www.whitehouse.gov/the-press-office/2017/04/05/remarks-president-trump-and-his-majesty-king-abdullah-ii-jordan-joint.

28. http://www.whitehousetransitionproject.org/.

29. Roxanne Roberts, "With $90 Million Raised, Trump's Inaugural Team Is Ready to Party," *Washington Post*, January 13, 2017, https://www.washingtonpost.com/lifestyle/style/with-90-million-raised-trumps-inaugural-team-is-ready-to-party/2017/01/13/ddf5831e-d9be-11e6-b8b2-cb5164beba6b_story.html.

30. Nicholas Fandos, "How Much Will the Inauguration Cost, and Who's Paying?" *New York Times*, January 17, 2017, https://www.nytimes.com/2017/01/17/us/politics/trump-who-pays-for-inauguration-cost.html; Matthew Boyle, "Trump Inauguration to Have Less Pomp, Circumstance So He Can Get Right to Work," *Breitbart*, December 29, 2016, http://www.breitbart.com/big-government/2016/12/29/exclusive-behind-scenes-presidential-inaugural-committee-trump-inauguration-less-pomp-circumstance-can-get-right-work/.

31. Paul Schrodt, "9 Artists Who Reportedly Turned Down Performing at Trump's Inauguration," *Business Insider*, January 15, 2017, http://www.businessinsider.com/artists-who-turned-down-trump-inauguration-2017-1/#elton-john-1; Brett Edkins, "Trump Plans a Shorter, Media-Friendly Inauguration to Maximize Ratings and Interest," *Forbes*, January 18, 2017, https://www.forbes.com/sites/brettedkins/2017/01/18/trump-is-planning-a-shorter-media-friendly-inauguration-to-maximize-ratings-and-interest/#7be9fb2e2d42; Lydia Saad, "Trump Sets New Low Point for Inaugural Approval Rating," Gallup, January 20–22, 2017, http://www.gallup.com/poll/202811/trump-sets-new-low-point-inaugural-approval-rating.aspx.

32. Glenn Kessler, "Spicer Earns Four Pinocchios for False Claims on Inauguration Crowd Size," *Washington Post*, January 22, 2017; "Conway: Press Secretary Gave 'Alternative Facts,'" *Meet the Press*, January 22, 2017, http://www.nbcnews.com/meet-the-press/video/conway-press-secretary-gave-alternative-facts-860142147643.

33. James Fallows, "'American Carnage': The Trump Era Begins," *The Atlantic*, January 20, 2017, https://www.theatlantic.com/politics/archive/2017/01/american-carnage-the-trump-era-begins/513971/.

34. Michael Edison Hayden and Alexander Mallin, "Trump Slams 'So-Called Judge' Who Blocked Immigration Order," February 4, 2017, http://abcnews.go.com/Politics/trump-slams-called-judge-blocked-immigration-order/story?id=45266060; Daniella Diaz, "Trump Laments 'Archaic' Rules of Congress," CNN.com, May 1, 2017, http://www.cnn.com/2017/05/01/politics/archaic-system-congress-donald-trump/.

35. Anthony J. Badger, *FDR: The First Hundred Days* (New York: Hill and Wang, 2008), 169.

36. Franklin D. Roosevelt, Fireside Chat, July 24, 1933, text available at http://www.presidency.ucsb.edu/ws/?pid=14488.

37. Peter Baker, "Trump Wants It Known: Grading 100 Days Is 'Ridiculous' (But His Were the Best)," *New York Times*, April 24, 2017, https://www.nytimes.com/2017/04/24/us/politics/donald-trump-100-days.html?_r=0.

38. Only Lyndon Johnson (during the first hundred days of the term he won in own right in 1964) and Barack Obama met that standard according to one definition of "landmark legislation." David R. Jones, "This Is Why the First 100 Days Is a 'Ridiculous Standard' for Judging Presidents," *Washington Post*, April 25, 2017, https://www.washingtonpost.com/news/monkey-cage/wp/2017/04/25/this-is-why-the-first-100-days-is-a-ridiculous-standard-for-judging-presidents/?utm_term=.ef9f4e37bfd2. Overall though, neither Johnson (who signed ten bills into law during his first hundred days in 1965) or Obama (who signed eleven) saw passage of a particularly large number of bills—at least compared with FDR's seventy-six. If one measures only quantity of legislation passed, Trump (at twenty-eight) ranks high, but those bills contained relatively little of significance. Tamara Keith, "White House Touts 'Historic' 28 Laws Signed by Trump, but What Are They?" *NPR*, April 27, 2017, http://www.npr.org/2017/04/27/525753448/white-house-touts-historic-28-laws-signed-by-trump-but-what-are-they. For the number of bills signed by presidents since FDR during their first hundred days, see Julia Azari, "A President's First 100 Days Really Do Matter," *FiveThirtyEight*, January 17, 2017, https://fivethirtyeight.com/features/a-presidents-first-100-days-really-do-matter/.

39. James P. Pfiffner, *The Strategic Presidency: Hitting the Ground Running*, 2nd ed., rev. (Lawrence: University Press of Kansas, 1996), 6.

40. "Donald Trump's Contract with the American Voter," October 22, 2016, available at https://assets.donaldjtrump.com/_landings/contract/O-TRU-102316-Contractv02.pdf; see also "Trump's 100 Day Plan, Annotated," NPR.org, April 24, 2017, http://www.npr.org/2017/04/24/520159167/trumps-100-day-action-plan-annotated.

41. Remarks at a "Make America Great Again" Rally in Nashville, Tennessee," March 15, 2017, http://www.presidency.ucsb.edu/ws/index.php?pid=123554&st=&st1=; Remarks in Kenosha, Wisconsin, April 18, 2017, http://www.presidency.ucsb.edu/ws/index.php?pid=123817&st=&st1=; "The President's Weekly Address," April 28, 2017, http://www.presidency.ucsb.edu/ws/index.php?pid=123882&st=&st1=.

42. John Sides and Lynn Vavreck, *The Gamble: Choice and Chance in the 2012 Presidential Election* (Princeton, NJ: Princeton University Press, 2013), 227; Laurence Grossback, David Peterson, and James Stimson, *Mandate Politics* (New York: Cambridge University Press, 2006).

43. Glenn Kessler, "Fact Checker: Trump's Repeated Claim That He Won a 'Landslide' Victory," *Washington Post*, November 30, 2016, https://www.washingtonpost.com/news/fact-checker/wp/2016/11/30/trumps-repeated-claim-that-he-won-a-landslide-victory/.

44. On March 30, 2017; April 27, 2017; and May 2, 2017, respectively. See, e.g., http://www.cnbc.com/2017/04/27/trump-unleashes-tweet-storm-blasting-democrats-in-advance-of-shutdown-vote.html; http://www.cnn.com/2017/05/02/politics/donald-trump-shutdown-tweet/.

45. Lauren Said-Moorhouse, "What Trump Has Done So Far and What It All Means," CNN.com, February 10, 2017, http://www.cnn.com/2017/01/26/politics/executive-orders-presidents-actions-presidential-memoranda/.

46. "Trump's Border Wall Will Cost $21.6 Billion and Take 3.5 Years to Build, Report Says," *Fortune*, February 9, 2017, http://fortune.com/2017/02/09/trump-border-wall-mexico-cost/.

47. Michael Grunwald, "Trump's Executive Orders Are Mostly Theater," *Politico*, April 28, 2017, http://www.politico.com/magazine/story/2017/04/28/trumps-executive-orders-are-mostly-theater-215081; see also Andrew Rudalevige, "Trump May Have the 'Most Executive Orders' since Truman—But What Did They Accomplish?" *Washington Post*, April 28, 2017, https://www.washingtonpost.com/news/monkey-cage/wp/2017/04/28/trump-may-have-the-most-executive-orders-since-truman-but-what-did-they-accomplish/?utm_term=.2f88ce2f3d73.

48. Carl Hulse, "Unity Was Emerging on Sentencing. Then Came Jeff Sessions," *New York Times*, May 14, 2017, https://www.nytimes.com/2017/05/14/us/politics/jeff-sessions-criminal-sentencing.html.

49. Zeke J. Miller, "Donald Trump's Interview with *Time* on Being President," *Time*, May 11, 2017, http://time.com/4775040/donald-trump-time-interview-being-president/.

50. Glenn Kessler, "Recidivism Watch: Trump's Claim That Millions of People Voted Illegally," *Washington Post*, January 24, 2017, https://www.washingtonpost.com/news/fact-checker/wp/2017/01/24/recidivism-watch-trumps-claim-that-3-5-million-people-voted-illegally-in-the-election/?utm_term=.9d6daf54e99e.

51. Peter Baker and Maggie Haberman, "Months Later, Trump Still Craves Credit for Win," *New York Times*, May 14, 2017, A1, https://www.nytimes.com/2017/05/13/us/politics/election-is-over-but-trump-still-cant-seem-to-get-past-it.html?hp&action=click&pgtype=Homepage&clickSource=story-heading&module=first-column-region®ion=top-news&WT.nav=top-news&_r=0.

52. Tweets going back to the start of the Trump campaign are archived at http://www.trumptwitterarchive.com/archive.

53. Elaine Godfrey, "Trump's TV Obsession Is a First," *The Atlantic*, April 3, 2017, https://www.theatlantic.com/politics/archive/2017/04/donald-trump-americas-first-tv-president/521640/.

54. Glenn Kessler and Michelle Ye Hee Lee, "President Trump's First 100 Days: The Fact Check Tally," *Washington Post*, May 1, 2017, https://www.washingtonpost.com/news/fact-checker/wp/2017/05/01/president-trumps-first-100-days-the-fact-check-tally/?utm_term=.c0d89a963915.

55. Michael M. Grynbaum, "Trump Calls the News Media the 'Enemy of the American People,'" *New York Times*, February 17, 2017, https://www.nytimes.com/2017/02/17/business/trump-calls-the-news-media-the-enemy-of-the-people.html?_r=0.

56. James Griffiths, "Trump Says He Considered 'This Russia Thing' before Firing FBI Director Comey," *CNN.com*, May 12, 2017, http://www.cnn.com/2017/05/12/politics/trump-comey-russia-thing/.

57. Mark Murray, "NBC/WSJ Poll: Just 29 Percent Approve of Trump's Firing of James Comey," *NBC News*, May 14, 2017, http://www.nbcnews.com/politics/donald-trump/nbc-wsj-poll-just-29-percent-approve-trump-s-firing-n759196.

58. Jeffrey Jones, "Trump's Job Approval in First Quarter Lowest by 14 Points," *Gallup.com*, April 20, 2017, http://www.gallup.com/poll/208778/trump-job-approval-first-quarter-lowest-points.aspx. More generally see the Gallup "Presidential Job Approval Center" at http://www.gallup.com/interactives/185273/presidential-job-approval-center.aspx?g_source=WWWV7HP&g_medium=topic&g_campaign=tiles.

59. See Richard E. Neustadt, *Presidential Power and the Modern Presidents* (New York: Free Press, 1990), ch. 5.

APPENDIX A

Result of Presidential Contests, 1912–2016

Year	Republican Nominee (in italics) and Other Major Candidates	Democratic Nominee (in italics) and Other Major Candidates	Election Winner	Division of Popular Vote[a] (Percent)	Division of Electoral Vote[b]
1912	*William Howard Taft* (incumbent president)	*Woodrow Wilson* (governor of New Jersey)	Wilson (D)	42–23	435–8
	Theodore Roosevelt[c] (former president)	James Champ Clark (representative from Missouri and Speaker of the House)			
1916	*Charles Evans Hughes* (justice, U.S. Supreme Court)	*Woodrow Wilson* (incumbent president)	Wilson (D)	49–46	277–254
	Elihu Root (former secretary of state)	None			
1920	*Warren G. Harding* (senator from Ohio)	*James Cox* (governor of Ohio)	Harding (R)	60–34	404–127
	Leonard Wood (general)	William McAdoo (former secretary of the Treasury)			
	Frank Lowden (governor of Illinois)	A. Mitchell Palmer (attorney general)			
	Hiram Johnson (senator from California)				
1924	*Calvin Coolidge* (incumbent president)	*John W. Davis* (former solicitor general)	Coolidge (R)	54–29	382–136
	Hiram Johnson (senator from California)	Alfred Smith (governor of New York)			
		William McAdoo (former secretary of the Treasury)			
1928	*Herbert Hoover* (former secretary of commerce)	*Alfred Smith* (governor of New York)	Hoover (R)	58–41	444–87
	Frank Lowden (governor of Illinois)	James Reed (senator from Missouri)			
		Cordell Hull (representative from Tennessee)			
1932	*Herbert Hoover* (incumbent president)	*Franklin D. Roosevelt* (governor of New York)	Roosevelt (D)	57–40	472–59
	Joseph France (former senator from Maryland)	Alfred Smith (former governor of New York)			
		John Garner (representative from Texas and Speaker of the House)			

Result of Presidential Contests, 1912–2016 (Continued)

Year	*Republican Nominee (in italics) and Other Major Candidates*	*Democratic Nominee (in italics) and Other Major Candidates*	*Election Winner*	*Division of Popular Vote[a] (Percent)*	*Division of Electoral Vote[b]*
1936	*Alfred Landon* (governor of Kansas)	*Franklin D. Roosevelt* (incumbent president)	Roosevelt (D)	61–37	523–8
	William Borah (senator from Idaho)	None			
1940	*Wendell Willkie* (Indiana lawyer and public utility executive)	*Franklin D. Roosevelt* (incumbent president)	Roosevelt (D)	55–45	449–82
	Thomas E. Dewey (U.S. district attorney for New York)	None			
	Robert Taft (senator from Ohio)				
1944	*Thomas E. Dewey* (governor of New York)	*Franklin D. Roosevelt* (incumbent president)	Roosevelt (D)	53–46	432–99
	Wendell Willkie (previous Republican presidential nominee)	Harry Byrd (senator from Virginia)			
1948	*Thomas E. Dewey* (governor of New York)	*Harry S. Truman* (incumbent president)	Truman (D)	50–45	303–189
	Harold Stassen (former governor of Minnesota)	Richard Russell (senator from Georgia)			
	Robert Taft (senator from Ohio)				
1952	*Dwight D. Eisenhower* (general)	*Adlai Stevenson* (governor of Illinois)	Eisenhower (R)	55–44	442–89
	Robert Taft (senator from Ohio)	Estes Kefauver (senator from Tennessee)			
		Richard Russell (senator from Georgia)			
1956	*Dwight D. EIsenhower* (incumbent president)	*Adlai Stevenson* (previous Democratic presidential nominee)	Eisenhower (R)	57–42	457–73
	None	Averell Harriman (governor of New York)			
1960	*Richard Nixon* (vice president)	*John F. Kennedy* (senator from Massachusetts)	Kennedy (D)	49.7–49.5	303–219
	None	Hubert Humphrey (senator from Minnesota)			
		Lyndon B. Johnson (senator from Texas)			
1964	*Barry Goldwater* (senator from Arizona)	*Lyndon B. Johnson* (incumbent president)	Johnson (D)	61–39	586–52
	Nelson Rockefeller (governor of New York)	None			

Result of Presidential Contests, 1912–2016 (Continued)

Year	*Republican Nominee (in italics) and Other Major Candidates*	*Democratic Nominee (in italics) and Other Major Candidates*	*Election Winner*	*Division of Popular Vote[a] (Percent)*	*Division of Electoral Vote[b]*
1968	*Richard Nixon* (former Republican presidential nominee)	*Hubert Humphrey* (incumbent vice president)	Nixon (R)	43.4–42.7	301–191
	Ronald Reagan (governor of California)	Robert F. Kennedy (senator from New York)			
		Eugene McCarthy (senator from Minnesota)			
1972	*Richard Nixon* (incumbent president)	*George McGovern* (senator from South Dakota)	Nixon (R)	61–38	520–17
	None	Hubert Humphrey (senator from Minnesota)			
		George Wallace (governor of Alabama)			
1976	*Gerald R. Ford* (incumbent president)	*Jimmy Carter* (former governor of Georgia)	Carter (D)	50–48	297–240
	Ronald Reagan (former governor of California)	Edmund Brown Jr. (governor of California)			
		George Wallace (governor of Alabama)			
1980	*Ronald Reagan* (former governor of California)	*Jimmy Carter* (incumbent president)	Reagan (R)	51–41	489–49
	George H. W. Bush (former director of the Central Intelligence Agency [CIA])	Edward M. Kennedy (senator from Massachusetts)			
	John Anderson (representative from Illinois)				
1984	*Ronald Reagan* (incumbent president)	*Walter F. Mondale* (former vice president)	Reagan (R)	59–41	525–13
	None	Gary Hart (senator from Colorado)			
1988	*George H. W. Bush* (vice president)	*Michael Dukakis* (governor of Massachusetts)	Bush (R)	53–46	426–111[d]
	Robert Dole (senator from Kansas)	Jesse Jackson (civil rights activist)			
1992	*George H. W. Bush* (incumbent president)	*Bill Clinton* (governor of Arkansas)	Clinton (D)	43–37	370–168
	Patrick Buchanan (journalist)	Paul Tsongas (former senator)			
1996	*Robert Dole* (senator from Kansas)	*Bill Clinton* (incumbent president)	Clinton (D)	49–41	379–159
	Patrick Buchanan (journalist)	None			

Result of Presidential Contests, 1912–2016 (Continued)

Year	*Republican Nominee (in italics) and Other Major Candidates*	*Democratic Nominee (in italics) and Other Major Candidates*	*Election Winner*	*Division of Popular Vote[a] (Percent)*	*Division of Electoral Vote[b]*
2000	*George W. Bush* (governor of Texas)	*Al Gore* (incumbent vice president)	Bush (R)	47.9–48.4	271–266[e]
	John McCain (senator from Arizona)	Bill Bradley (former senator)			
2004	*George W. Bush* (incumbent president)	*John Kerry* (senator from Massachusetts)	Bush (R)	50.7–48.3	286–251[f]
	None	John Edwards (senator from North Carolina)			
2008	*John McCain* (senator from Arizona)	*Barack Obama* (senator from Illinois)	Obama (D)	52.9–45.6	365–173
	Mitt Romney (former governor from Massachusetts)	Hillary Clinton (senator from New York)			
2012	*Mitt Romney* (former governor from Massachusetts)	*Barack Obama* (incumbent president)	Obama (D)	51.02–47.16	332–206
	Rick Santorum (former senator from Pennsylvania)	None			
2016	*Donald J. Trump* (businessman and TV personality)	*Hillary Clinton* (former Secretary of State)	Trump (R)	46.1–48.2	304–227[g]
	Ted Cruz (senator, Texas)	Bernie Sanders (senator, Vermont)			

NOTE: The table begins with the year 1912 because presidential primaries were first held that year.

[a] Division of popular vote is between the Republican and Democratic nominees.

[b] Division of electoral vote is between the Republican and Democratic nominees.

[c] When the Republican convention failed to choose him as its nominee (selecting instead the incumbent president, William Howard Taft), former president Theodore Roosevelt withdrew from the party and created the Progressive Party. As the Progressive Party nominee, Roosevelt received 27 percent of the popular vote and eighty-eight electoral votes.

[d] One Democratic elector from West Virginia reversed the vote for president and vice president.

[e] One Democratic elector from the District of Columbia cast a blank ballot in protest.

[f] One Democratic elector from Minnesota cast ballots listing John Edwards for both president and vice president, presumably in error.

[g] One Democratic elector from Hawaii cast a ballot for Sanders. Four Washington state electors cast ballots for candidates other than Clinton, three for Colin Powell and one for Faith Spotted Eagle. Two Texas electors voted for someone other than Trump, one for Kasich and one for Ron Paul.

APPENDIX B

Personal Backgrounds of U.S. Presidents

	President	Age at First Political Office	First Political Office Last Political Office[a]	Age at Becoming President	State of Residence[b]	Father's Occupation	Higher Education[c]	Occupation
1	Washington (1789–1797)	17	County surveyor Commander in chief	57	VA	Farmer	None	Farmer, surveyor
2	Adams, J. (1797–1801)	39	Surveyor of highways Vice president	61	MA	Farmer	Harvard	Farmer, lawyer
3	Jefferson (1801–1809)	26	State legislator Vice president	58	VA	Farmer	William and Mary	Farmer, lawyer
4	Madison (1809–1817)	25	State legislator Secretary of state	58	VA	Farmer	Princeton	Farmer
5	Monroe (1817–1825)	24	State legislator Secretary of state	59	VA	Farmer	William and Mary	Lawyer, farmer
6	Adams, J. Q. (1825–1829)	27	Minister to Netherlands Secretary of state	58	MA	Farmer, lawyer	Harvard	Lawyer
7	Jackson (1829–1837)	21	Prosecuting attorney U.S. Senate	62	TN	Farmer	None	Lawyer
8	Van Buren (1837–1841)	30	Surrogate of county Vice president	55	NY	Tavern keeper	None	Lawyer
9	Harrison, W. H. (1841)	26	Territorial delegate to Congress Minister to Colombia	68	IN	Farmer	Hampden-Sydney	Military
10	Tyler (1841–1845)	21	State legislator Vice president	51	VA	Planter, lawyer	William and Mary	Lawyer
11	Polk (1845–1849)	28	State legislator Governor	50	TN	Surveyor	U. of North Carolina	Lawyer
12	Taylor (1849–1850)	–	None[a]	65	KY	Collector of internal revenue	None	Military
13	Fillmore (1850–1853)	28	State legislator Vice president	50	NY	Farmer	None	Lawyer
14	Pierce (1853–1857)	25	State legislator U.S. district attorney	48	NH	General	Bowdoin	Lawyer
15	Buchanan (1857–1861)	22	Assistant county prosecutor Minister to Great Britain	65	PA	Farmer	Dickinson	Lawyer
16	Lincoln (1861–1865)	25	State legislator U.S. House of Representatives	52	IL	Farmer, carpenter	None	Lawyer
17	Johnson, A. (1865–1869)	20	City alderman Vice president	57	TN	Janitor, porter	None	Tailor
18	Grant (1869–1877)	–	None[a]	47	OH	Tanner	West Point	Military
19	Hayes (1877–1881)	36	City solicitor Governor	55	OH	Farmer	Kenyon	Lawyer
20	Garfield (1881)	28	State legislator U.S. Senate	50	OH	Canal worker	Williams	Educator, lawyer
21	Arthur (1881–1885)	31	State engineer Vice president	51	NY	Minister	Union	Lawyer
22	Cleveland (1885–1889)	26	Assistant district attorney Governor	48	NY	Minister	None	Lawyer
23	Harrison, B. (1889–1893)	24	City attorney U.S. Senate	56	IN	Military	Miami of Ohio	Lawyer

Personal Backgrounds of U.S. Presidents (Continued)

	President	Age at First Political Office	First Political Office / Last Political Office[a]	Age at Becoming President	State of Residence[b]	Father's Occupation	Higher Education[c]	Occupation
24	Cleveland (1893–1897)							
25	McKinley (1897–1901)	26	Prosecuting attorney / Governor	54	OH	Ironmonger	Allegheny	Lawyer
26	Roosevelt, T. (1901–1909)	24	State legislator / Vice president	43	NY	Businessman	Harvard	Lawyer, author
27	Taft (1909–1913)	24	Assistant prosecuting attorney / Secretary of war	52	OH	Lawyer	Yale	Lawyer
28	Wilson (1913–1921)	54	Governor / Governor	56	NJ	Minister	Princeton	Educator
29	Harding (1921–1923)	35	State legislator / U.S. Senate	56	OH	Physician, editor	Ohio Central	Newspaper editor
30	Coolidge (1923–1929)	26	City councilman / Vice president	51	MA	Storekeeper	Amherst	Lawyer
31	Hoover (1929–1933)	43	Relief and food administrator / Secretary of commerce	55	CA	Blacksmith	Stanford	Mining engineer
32	Roosevelt, F. (1933–1945)	28	State legislator / Governor	49	NY	Businessman, landowner	Harvard	Lawyer
33	Truman (1945–1953)	38	County judge (commissioner) / Vice president	61	MO	Farmer, livestock	None	Clerk, store owner
34	Eisenhower (1953–1961)	–	None[a]	63	KS	Mechanic	West Point	Military
35	Kennedy (1961–1963)	29	U.S. House of Representatives / U.S. Senate	43	MA	Businessman	Harvard	Newspaper reporter
36	Johnson, L. (1963–1969)	28	U.S. House of Representatives / Vice president	55	TX	Farmer, real estate	Southwest Texas State Teacher's College	Educator
37	Nixon (1969–1974)	34	U.S. House of Representatives / Vice president	56	CA	Streetcar conductor	Whittier	Lawyer
38	Ford (1974–1977)	36	U.S. House of Representatives / Vice president	61	MI	Businessman	U. of Michigan	Lawyer
39	Carter (1977–1981)	38	County Board of Education / Governor	52	GA	Farmer, businessman	U.S. Naval Academy	Farmer, businessman
40	Reagan (1981–1989)	55	Governor / Governor	69	CA	Shoe salesman	Eureka	Entertainer
41	Bush, G. H. W. (1989–1993)	42	U.S. House of Representatives / Vice president	64	TX	Businessman, U.S. senator	Yale	Businessman
42	Clinton (1993–2001)	30	State attorney general / Governor	46	AR	Car dealer	Georgetown	Lawyer
43	Bush, G. W. (2001–2009)	48	Governor / Governor	54	TX	U.S. president	Yale	Businessman
44	Obama (2009–2017)	36	State legislator / U.S. senate	47	IL	Economist	Columbia	Lawyer
45	Trump (2017–)	–	None[a]	70	NY	Businessman	U. of Pennsylvania	Businessman, TV personality

[a] This category refers to the last civilian political office held before the presidency. Taylor, Grant, and Eisenhower had served as generals before becoming president; Trump was a businessman and TV personality.

[b] The state is where the president spent his important adult years, not necessarily where he was born.

[c] Refers to undergraduate education.

APPENDIX C

The Constitution of the Presidency

ARTICLE I

Section 3. The Vice President of the United States shall be President of the Senate, but shall have no Vote, unless they be equally divided.

The Senate shall chuse their other officers, and also a President pro tempore, in the Absence of the Vice President, or when he shall exercise the Office of President of the United States.

The Senate shall have the sole Power to try all Impeachments. When sitting for that Purpose, they shall be on Oath or Affirmation. When the President of the United States is tried the Chief Justice shall preside: And no Person shall be convicted without the Concurrence of two thirds of the Members present.

Judgment in Cases of Impeachment shall not extend further than to removal from Office, and disqualification to hold and enjoy any Office of honor, Trust or Profit under the United States: but the Party convicted shall nevertheless be liable and subject to Indictment, Trial, Judgment and Punishment, according to Law.

Section 7. ...Every Bill which shall have passed the House of Representatives and the Senate, shall, before it become a Law, be presented to the President of the United States; If he approve he shall sign it, but if not he shall return it, with his Objections to that House in which it shall have originated, who shall enter the Objections at large on their Journal, and proceed to reconsider it. If after such Reconsideration two thirds of that House shall agree to pass the Bill, it shall be sent, together with the Objections, to the other House, by which it shall likewise be reconsidered, and if approved by two thirds of that House, it shall become a Law. But in all such Cases the Votes of both Houses shall be determined by yeas and Nays, and the Names of the Persons voting for and against the Bill shall be entered on the Journal of each House respectively. If any Bill shall not be returned by the President within ten Days (Sundays excepted) after it shall have been presented to him, the Same shall be a Law, in like Manner as if he had signed it, unless the Congress by their Adjournment prevent its Return, in which Case it shall not be a Law.

Every Order, Resolution, or Vote to which the Concurrence of the Senate and House of Representatives may be necessary (except on a question of Adjournment) shall be presented to the President of the United States; and before the Same shall take Effect, shall be approved by him, or being disapproved by him, shall be repassed by two thirds of the Senate and House of Representatives, according to the Rules and Limitations prescribed in the Case of a Bill.

ARTICLE II

Section 1. The executive Power shall be vested in a President of the United States of America. He shall hold his Office during the Term of four Years, and, together with the Vice President, chosen for the same Term, be elected, as follows. Each State shall appoint, in such Manner as the Legislature thereof may direct, a Number of Electors, equal to the whole Number of Senators and Representatives to which the State may be entitled in the Congress: but no Senator or Representative, or Person holding an Office of Trust or Profit under the United States, shall be appointed an Elector.

[The Electors shall meet in their respective States, and vote by Ballot for two Persons, of whom one at least shall not be an Inhabitant of the same State with themselves. And they shall make a List of all the Persons voted for, and of the Number of Votes for each; which List they shall sign and certify, and transmit sealed to the Seat of the Government of the United States, directed to the President of the Senate. The President of the Senate shall, in the Presence of the Senate and House of Representatives, open all the Certificates, and the Votes shall then be counted. The Person having the greatest Number of Votes shall be the President, if such Number be a Majority of the whole Number of Electors appointed; and if there be more than one who have such Majority, and have an equal Number of Votes, then the House of Representatives shall immediately chuse by Ballot one of them for President; and if no Person have a Majority, then from the five highest on the list the said House shall in like Manner chuse the President. But in chusing the President, the Votes shall be taken by States, the Representation from each State having one Vote; a quorum for this Purpose shall consist of a Member or Members from two thirds of the States, and a Majority of all the States shall be necessary to a Choice. In every Case, after the Choice of the President, the Person having the greatest Number of Votes of the Electors shall be the Vice President. But if there should remain two or more who have equal Votes, the Senate shall chuse from them by Ballot the Vice President.][1]

The Congress may determine the Time of chusing the Electors, and the Day on which they shall give their Votes; which Day shall be the same throughout the United States.

No Person except a natural born Citizen, or a Citizen of the United States, at the time of the Adoption of this Constitution, shall be eligible to the Office of President; neither shall any Person be eligible to that Office who shall not have attained to the Age of thirty five Years, and been fourteen Years a Resident within the United States.

In Case of the Removal of the President from office, or of his Death, Resignation, or Inability to discharge the Powers and Duties of the said Office,[2] the Same shall devolve on the Vice President, and the Congress may by Law provide for the Case of Removal, Death, Resignation or Inability, both of the President and Vice President, declaring what officer shall then act as President, and such Officer shall act accordingly, until the Disability be removed, or a President shall be elected.

The President shall, at stated Times, receive for his Services, a Compensation, which shall neither be increased nor diminished during the Period for which he shall have been elected, and he shall not receive within that Period any other Emolument from the United States, or any of them.

Before he enter on the Execution of his Office, he shall take the following Oath or Affirmation: — "I do solemnly swear (or affirm) that I will faithfully execute the Office of President of the United States, and will to the best of my Ability, preserve, protect and defend the Constitution of the United States."

Section 2. The President shall be Commander in Chief of the Army and Navy of the United States, and of the Militia of the several States, when called into the actual Service of the United States; he may require the Opinion, in writing, of the principal Officer in each of the executive Departments, upon any Subject relating to the Duties of their respective Offices, and he shall have Power to grant Reprieves and Pardons for Offenses against the United States, except in Cases of Impeachment.

He shall have Power, by and with the Advice and Consent of the Senate, to make Treaties, provided two thirds of the Senators present concur; and he shall nominate, and by and with the Advice and Consent of the Senate, shall appoint Ambassadors, other public Ministers and Consuls, Judges of the supreme Court, and all other officers of the United States, whose Appointments are not herein otherwise provided for, and which shall be established by Law: but the Congress may by Law vest the Appointment of such inferior Officers, as they think proper, in the President alone, in the Courts of Law, or in the Heads of Departments.

The President shall have Power to fill up all Vacancies that may happen during the Recess of the Senate, by granting Commissions which shall expire at the End of their next Session.

Section 3. He shall from time to time give to the Congress Information of the State of the Union, and recommend to their Consideration such Measures as he shall judge necessary and expedient; he may, on extraordinary Occasions, convene both Houses, or either of them, and in Case of Disagreement between them, with Respect to the Time of Adjournment, he may adjourn them to such Time as he shall think proper; he shall receive Ambassadors and other public Ministers; he shall take Care that the Laws be faithfully executed, and shall Commission all the officers of the United States.

Section 4. The President, Vice President and all Civil Officers of the United States, shall be removed from office on Impeachment for, and Conviction of, Treason, Bribery, or other high Crimes and Misdemeanors.

ARTICLE VI

This Constitution, and the Laws of the United States which shall be made in Pursuance thereof, and all Treaties made, or which shall be made, under the Authority of the United States, shall be the supreme Law of the Land; and the Judges in every State shall be bound thereby, any Thing in the Constitution or Laws of any State to the Contrary notwithstanding.

The Senators and Representatives before mentioned, and the Members of the several State Legislatures, and all executive and judicial Officers, both of the United States and of the several States, shall be bound by Oath or Affirmation, to support this Constitution; but no religious Test shall ever be required as a Qualification to any Office or public Trust under the United States.

AMENDMENT XII *(Ratified June 15, 1804)*

The Electors shall meet in their respective states and vote by ballot for President and Vice-President, one of whom, at least, shall not be an inhabitant of the same state with themselves; they shall name in their ballots the person voted for as President, and in distinct ballots the person voted for as Vice-President, and they shall make distinct lists of all persons voted for as President, and of all persons voted for as Vice-President, and of the number of votes for each, which lists they shall sign and certify, and transmit sealed to the seat of the government of the United States, directed to the President of the Senate; — The President of the Senate shall, in the presence of the Senate and House of Representatives, open all the certificates and the votes shall then be counted; — The person having the greatest number of votes for President, shall be the President, if such number be a majority of the whole number of Electors appointed; and if no person have such majority, then from the persons having the highest numbers not exceeding three on the list of those voted for as President, the House of Representatives shall choose immediately, by ballot, the President. But in choosing the President, the votes shall be taken by states, the representation from each state having one vote; a quorum for this purpose shall consist of a member or members from two-thirds of the states, and a majority of all the states shall be necessary to a choice. [And if the House of Representatives shall not choose a President whenever the right of choice shall devolve upon them, before the fourth day of March next following, then the Vice-President shall act as President, as in the case of the death or other constitutional disability of the President—][3] The person having the greatest number of votes as Vice-President, shall be the Vice- President, if such number be a majority of the whole number of Electors appointed, and if no person have a majority, then from the two highest numbers on the list, the Senate shall choose the Vice-President; a quorum for the purpose shall consist of two-thirds of the whole number of Senators, and a majority of the whole number shall be necessary to a choice. But no person constitutionally ineligible to the office of President shall be eligible to that of Vice-President of the United States.

AMENDMENT XX *(Ratified Jan. 23, 1933)*

Section 1. The terms of the President and Vice President shall end at noon on the 20th day of January, and the terms of Senators and Representatives at noon on the 3d day of January, of the years in which such terms would have ended if this-article had not been ratified; and the terms of their successors shall then begin.

Section 2. The Congress shall assemble at least once in every year, and such meeting shall begin at noon on the 3d day of January, unless they shall by law appoint a different day.

Section 3.[4] If, at the time fixed for the beginning of the term of the President, the President elect shall have died, the Vice President elect shall become President. If a President shall not have been chosen before the time fixed for the beginning of his term, or if the President elect shall have failed to qualify, then the Vice President elect shall act as President until a President shall have qualified; and the Congress may by law provide for the case wherein neither a President elect nor a Vice

President elect shall have qualified, declaring who shall then act as President, or the manner in which one who is to act shall be selected, and such person shall act accordingly until a President or Vice President shall have qualified.

Section 4. The Congress may by law provide for the case of the death of any of the persons from whom the House of Representatives may choose a President whenever the right of choice shall have devolved upon them, and for the case of the death of any of the persons from whom the Senate may choose a Vice President whenever the right of choice shall have devolved upon them.

Section 5. Sections 1 and 2 shall take effect on the 15th day of October following the ratification of this article.

Section 6. This article shall be inoperative unless it shall have been ratified as an amendment to the Constitution by the legislatures of three-fourths of the several States within seven years from the date of its submission.

AMENDMENT XXII *(Ratified Feb. 27, 1951)*

Section 1. No person shall be elected to the office of the President more than twice, and no person who has held the office of President, or acted as President, for more than two years of a term to which some other person was elected President shall be elected to the office of the President more than once. But this Article shall not apply to any person holding the office of President when this Article was proposed by the Congress, and shall not prevent any person who may be holding the office of President, or acting as President, during the term within which this Article become operative from holding the office of President or acting as President during the remainder of such term.

Section 2. This Article shall be inoperative unless it shall have been ratified as an amendment to the Constitution by the legislatures of three-fourths of the several States within seven years from the date of its submission to the States by the Congress.

AMENDMENT XXIII *(Ratified March 29, 1961)*

Section 1. The District constituting the seat of Government of the United States shall appoint in such manner as the Congress may direct:

A number of electors of President and Vice President equal to the whole number of Senators and Representatives in Congress to which the District would be entitled if it were a State, but in no event more than the least populous State; they shall be in addition to those appointed by the States, but they shall be considered, for the purposes of the election of President and Vice President, to be electors appointed by a State; and they shall meet in the District and perform such duties as provided by the twelfth article of amendment.

Section 2. The Congress shall have power to enforce this article by appropriate legislation.

AMENDMENT XXV *(Ratified Feb. 10, 1967)*

Section 1. In case of the removal of the President from office or of his death or resignation, the Vice President shall become President.

Section 2. Whenever there is a vacancy in the office of the Vice President, the President shall nominate a Vice President who shall take office upon confirmation by a majority vote of both Houses of Congress.

Section 3. Whenever the President transmits to the President pro tempore of the Senate and the Speaker of the House of Representatives his written declaration that he is unable to discharge the powers and duties of his office, and until he transmits to them a written declaration to the contrary, such powers and duties shall be discharged by the Vice President as Acting President.

Section 4. Whenever the Vice President and a majority of either the principal officers of the executive departments or of such other body as Congress may by law provide, transmit to the President pro tempore of the Senate and the Speaker of the House of Representatives their written declaration that the President is unable to discharge the powers and duties of his office, the Vice President shall immediately assume the powers and duties of the office as Acting President.

Thereafter, when the President transmits to the President pro tempore of the Senate and the Speaker of the House of Representatives his written declaration that no inability exists, he shall resume the powers and duties of his office unless the Vice President and a majority of either the principal officers of the executive department or of such other body as Congress may by law provide, transmit within four days to the President pro tempore of the Senate and the Speaker of the House of Representatives their written declaration that the President is unable to discharge the powers and duties of his office. Thereupon Congress shall decide the issue, assembling within forty-eight hours for that purpose if not in session. If the Congress, within twenty-one days after receipt of the latter written declaration, or, if Congress is not in session, within twenty-one days after Congress is required to assemble, determines by two-thirds vote of both houses that the President is unable to discharge the powers and duties of his office, the Vice President shall continue to discharge the same as Acting President; otherwise, the President shall resume the powers and duties of his office.

Notes

1. The material in brackets has been superseded by the Twelfth Amendment.
2. This provision has been affected by the Twenty-Fifth Amendment.
3. The part in brackets has been superseded by Section 3 of the Twentieth Amendment.
4. See the Twenty-Fifth Amendment.

Index